international
AIR POWER
REVIEW

AIRtime Publishing
United States of America • United Kingdom

international
AIR POWER
REVIEW

Published quarterly by AIRtime Publishing Inc.
120 East Avenue, Norwalk, CT 06851, USA
*(Our UK office will be established shortly and
the address will appear in IAPR Vol. 2)*

© 2001 AIRtime Publishing Inc.
Breguet Br.1001-01 Taon cutaway copyright Mike Badrocke
Photos and other illustrations are the copyright
of their respective owners

ISSN 1473-9917 (Softbound Edition)
ISBN 1-880588-33-1 (Hardcover Deluxe Casebound Edition)

Publisher
Mel Williams

Editor
David Donald
e-mail: editor@airtimepublishing.com

Assistant Editor
Daniel J. March

Sub Editor
Karen Leverington

US Desk
Tom Kaminski

Russia/CIS Desk
Piotr Butowski, Zaur Eylanbekov
e-mail: zaur@airtimepublishing.com

Europe and Rest of World Desk
John Fricker, Jon Lake

Correspondents
Argentina: Jorge Felix Nuñez Padin
Australia: Nigel Pittaway
Belgium: Dirk Lamarque
Canada: Jeff Rankin-Lowe
France: Henri-Pierre Grolleau
Israel: Shlomo Aloni
Italy: Luigino Caliaro
Japan: Yoshitomo Aoki
Netherlands: Tieme Festner
Spain: Salvador Mafé Huertas
USA: Rick Burgess, Robert F. Dorr, Brad Elward, Peter Mersky,
Bill Sweetman

Artists
Piotr Butowski, Chris Davey, Keith Fretwell, Grant Race,
John Weal, Vasiliy Zolotov

Designer
Zaur Eylanbekov

Controller
Linda DeAngelis

Origination by Chroma Graphics, Singapore
Printed in Singapore by KHL Printing

International Air Power Review is published quarterly in two editions
(Softbound or Deluxe Casebound) and is available by subscription or as
single volumes. Please see details opposite.

Acknowledgments
We wish to thank the following for their kind help with the
preparation of this issue:

Gordon Bartley, BAE Systems
Paul E. Eden
Howard Gethin
Randy Harrison, Boeing Company
John Heathcott
Eric Hehs, LMTAS
Brenda Hogan, LMTAS
John Kent, LMTAS
Denny Lombard, Lockheed Martin Skunk Works
Peter R. March
Chick Ramey, Boeing Company
Nancy Tibeau, Boeing Company
Richard L. Ward
Simon Watson
David Willis

The editors welcome photographs for possible publication but can
accept no responsibility for loss or damage to unsolicited material.

Subscriptions & Back Volumes

**Readers in the USA, Canada, Central/South America and the rest
of the world (except UK and Europe) please write to:**

AIRtime Publishing, P.O. Box 5074,
Westport, CT 06881, USA
Tel (203) 838-7979 • Fax (203) 838-7344
Toll free 1 800 359-3003
e-mail: airpower@airtimepublishing.com

Readers in the UK & Europe please write to:

AIRtime Publishing, RAFBFE, P.O. Box 1940,
RAF Fairford, Gloucestershire GL7 4BR, England

**One-year subscription rates (4 quarterly volumes), via surface
delivery:**

Softbound Edition
USA $59.95, Canada Cdn $93, Mexico US $75,
South America US $79, Middle East & Africa US $85,
Asia and Australasia US $79, UK £48, Europe £55
Deluxe Casebound Edition
USA $79.95, Canada Cdn $122, Mexico US $95,
South America US $99, Middle East & Africa US $105,
Asia and Australasia US $99, UK £68, Europe £75

Single-volume/Back Volume Rates by Mail:

Softbound Edition
US $16, Cdn $25, UK £12 (plus ship. & hdlg for each)
Deluxe Casebound Edition
USA $20, Cdn $31, UK £17 (plus ship. & hdlg for each)

All prices are subject to change without notice. Canadian residents
please add GST. Connecticut residents please add sales tax. For
delivery rates by air please contact the publisher.

Volume One - Summer 2001

CONTENTS

MAJOR FEATURES PLANNED FOR VOLUME TWO
Focus Aircraft: Tu-160 'Blackjack', **Warplane Classic:** B-58 Hustler, **Air Power Analysis:** US Marine Corps
Technical Briefing: Eurofighter, **Variant File:** Puma, **Combat Colours:** USAAF Spitfires, **Air Combat:** Luftwaffe in Normandy

PROGRAMME UPDATE

Lockheed Martin F-22 Raptor

On 5 February 2001 Lockheed Martin announced the completion of the final two of the stated 11 Defense Acquisition Board (DAB) requirements clearing the way for the crucial F-22 low rate initial production (LRIP) decision. This had been scheduled for 3 January 2001, however, at that time the final three requirements had yet to be achieved, the delay being attributed to severe weather at the Marietta, Georgia test facility. It now seems unlikely that an LRIP decision will be reached before an overall Defense Department review by the new Bush administration is completed. The first indications as to a delay to the LRIP phase came from the Pentagon's director of Operational Test and Evaluation who recommended putting off initial production of the aircraft for at least nine months and possibly a year. The fiscal year 2001 Defense Bill includes US$2.1 billion for the first 10 LRIP F-22s and advanced funding for a second batch of 16.

By the end of 2000 the F-22 had achieved eight of the DAB requirements; critical design review for Block 3.1 avionics software, air vehicle final production readiness review, mating the fuselage, wing and empennage of aircraft 4008, first half engine qualification test, high angle-of attack flight with weapons bay doors open, missile separation for AIM-9 and

AIM-120 air-to-air missiles, initiating fatigue testing and completing static structural tests.

The fatigue testing element began in December 2000 when loads were applied to the rudders, leading-edge flaps and main weapons bay doors of Raptor 4000 (one of two non-flying airframes). Approximately 8,000 hours of fatigue testing are due to have been accomplished by November 2001 with an additional 24,000 hours by 2003.

The ninth requirement was achieved on 5 January 2001 when Boeing test pilot Randy Neville conducted the maiden flight of Raptor 4005, the first to be equipped with Block 3.0 avionics. Block 3.0 software controls the F-22's 'first look, first kill' capability, allowing multi-sensor fusion to acquire, track and engage

Raptor 4002 is seen during flight trials to fulfil the 'Initiate high AoA with weapons bay doors open' DAB requirement. This required the aircraft to fly with its centre weapons bay doors open and conduct extensive manoeuvres at a high angle-of-attack. Accomplished at 35,000 ft (10668 m), the tests included 360° rolls and full-rudder sideslips at various speeds, resulting in significant changes to the airflow pressure gradients generated on the weapons bay doors.

multiple targets. In addition, the software allows guidance of multiple weapon launches and can automatically initiate the F-22s countermeasures. F-22 System Program Director Brig. Gen. Jabour stated "Flying Raptor 4005 with Block 3.0 avionics represented the current programme's most technically demanding challenge".

PROJECT DEVELOPMENT

International

Boeing 737 AWACS advances

A Boeing-led team, that includes Northrop Grumman, Turkish Airlines and Turkish Aerospace Industries (TAI), has been selected to develop a new airborne early warning and control (AEW&C) system for Turkey. The programme includes six Boeing 737-700 AEW&C aircraft, ground support segments for mission crew training, mission support and system modification support. Turkey has also taken an option for a seventh

aircraft. The contract is believed to be valued at more than US$1 billion.

Turkey's selection of the Boeing team follows a similar decision by the Australian Ministry of Defence. On 19 December the contractor and Australia's Ministry of Defence signed a contract covering the development and acquisition of four 'Project Wedgetail' Boeing 737 AEW&C aircraft. The contract, believed to be worth US$1.1 billion, includes an option for three further aircraft. Delivery of the initial two aircraft, based on the 737-700, is scheduled for 2006.

Lockheed Martin teams with Korean Aerospace

Lockheed Martin and Korea Aerospace Industry have signed an agreement covering joint marketing of the Korean company's T-50 advanced jet trainer, previously known as the KTX-2. Under the agreement each company will market the aircraft within their respective home countries but marketing activity elsewhere will be conducted as a joint effort under the name 'T-50 International'. The T-50 is an advanced supersonic jet trainer and a derivative, known as the A-50, is a fighter lead-in trainer and light attack aircraft. Lockheed Martin currently serves as a subcontractor to KAI for development and production of the T-50, which is in full-scale development. The contractor is responsible for the wings, flight controls and avionics integration. The first test aircraft is scheduled to be rolled out on 28 September 2001 with first flight following in June 2002. The Republic of Korea Air Force (ROKAF) plans to replace its T-38, F-5 and A-37 fleets with the T-50/A-50 and expects to place an initial order for approximately 100 aircraft with first delivery in 2005.

China

Chengdu J-10 unveiled

First photographs on the internet of the Lavi-based Chengdu J-10 single-seat multi-role combat aircraft, which has been under development with Israeli assistance since the late 1980s, show a close similarity with the abandoned Israeli fighter. It is a similar tailless canard delta, although a higher degree of relaxed static stability is indicated by its foreplanes mounted considerably further forward, obstructively in line with the windscreen, and ahead of the curved rectangular ventral intake for its single AL-31FN turbofan. Developed by the Lyulka-Saturn design bureau for the J-10, the AL-31FN features a low-mounted rather than top-installed accessory gear-box, and its 27,558-lb (122.6-kN) take-off thrust is about 30 percent more than the Lavi's Pratt & Whitney PW1120 engine.

Unlike the Lavi, the J-10's wide-track mainwheels are under the wings, retracting inwards to the centre fuselage. Nosewheel retraction is aft, into the intake box. The J-10's CCV configuration includes full-span leading-edge flaps and

After a gap of some six years, NASA's X-31 concept demonstration aircraft made a return to the air at NAS Patuxent River on 24 February 2001. The aircraft has been returned to flying condition to participate in the joint US-European VECTOR test programme which is investigating the use of thrust vectoring to increase STOL capabilities.

Initiation of radar cross-section (RCS) testing, the penultimate DAB requirement, commenced in mid-January 2001 when ground measurements taken of an F-22 on an RCS turntable were compared to the dynamic measurements taken from an airborne example.

The DAB criteria were finally fulfilled on 5 February with the first flight of aircraft 4006. The 72-minute test mission was flown by Lockheed Martin test pilot Al Norman. After additional testing at Marietta, the aircraft will join the F-22 Combined Test Force (CTF) at Edwards AFB, California.

A further milestone was achieved on 15 November 2000 when Raptor 4004 completed a successful first flight equipped with the Northrop Grumman/Raytheon AN/APG-77 active electronically scanned array (AESA) radar. During the flight the radar successfully tracked multiple targets almost immediately after the aircraft lifted off from Marietta. Although the flight marked the first for the radar on the F-22A, it has been undergoing testing on Boeing's 757 Flying Test Bed (FTB) since early 1999. Subsequent tests will focus on particular capabilities and operational scenarios that cannot be duplicated using the FTB.

In order to continue scheduled programme development, the US Congress approved bridge funding while the LRIP descision is debated.

The USAF issued contracts to Lockheed Martin and United Technologies/Pratt & Whitney covering the advance procurement of materials associated with LRIP F-22A aircraft. Lockheed Martin received US$304 million while United Technologies was awarded US$46 million in advanced procurement for 20 F119 engines.

The USAF itself is confident that the F-22 programme will meet all performance requirements for the intended procurement of 339 aircraft within the Congressional funding cap, and are citing the additional bridge funding as a sign of Congress's faith in the aircraft. Subject to Defense Department review, the F-22 is slated to achieve IOC in late 2005.

A key DAB requirement accomplished in the second half of 2000 was demonstrating missile separation for the AIM-9 Sidewinder and AIM-120 AMRAAM missiles from the F-22's weapons bays. The trials were conducted at varying speeds and airframe attitudes including high angle-of-attack releases of the AIM-9 (below). Follow-on weapons trials by the F-22 CTF at Edwards AFB have continued through the first first quarter of 2001. This AIM-120 firing test (right) was conducted on 7 March.

dual elevon surfaces, operated by an active-control digital/analog fly-by-wire system, and it retains large twin rear ventral fins.

If the J-10 is similar in size to the Lavi, its extra power should allow substantial increases in performance and combat load capabilities, over the Israeli aircraft's maximum speed of Mach 1.8 and 16,000 lb (7257 kg) of external stores.

Although their existence has not so far been acknowledged by the Chinese government, at least four J-10 prototypes are believed to be undergoing flight development since the first initially became airborne on 24 March 1998. One reportedly crashed through fly-by-wire control problems in 1999, and doubts have been expressed concerning funding availability to continue J-10 development, in view of China's expanding Sukhoi Su-27/30 procurement and licensed production programmes.

Japan

New aircraft for Japan
Japan's Defense Agency has announced that it will invest about US$3 billion to develop an advanced anti-submarine patrol plane, tentatively called the PX, and plans to independently develop a range of advanced military aircraft over a 10-year period beginning in 2002.

Russia

Su-30MKI flight development
Sukhoi test pilots Vyacheslav Averyanov and Roman Konratyev started flight development of the first true Su-30MKI prototype, with definitive Saturn/Lyulka AL-31FP thrust-vectoring powerplant, canard foreplanes, standard Su-30 air refuelling capability and multi-national avionics, at Irkutsk on 26 November. The prototype Su-30MKI was then transferred to Moscow's Zhukovskiy LII flight-test institute in December 2000, to continue its flight development programme, before displaying at Aero India 2001, Bangalore in February.

The Su-30MKI's mission system equipment is configured to include Phazotron/NIIR's N010 Zhuk updated conventional radar, plus Thales MFD-55/66 multi-function colour cockpit displays, Totem INS/GPS and VEH 3000 holographic HUD. In addition to Vympel R-73E (AA-11 'Archer') high off-boresight close-combat AAMs, Vympel R-77E/RVV-AE (AA-12 'Adder') medium-range active radar-homing AAMs and a UOMZ Shch-3UM-1 helmet-mounted sight, IAF Su-30 weapons will now reportedly include Zvezda Kh-31A (AS-17 'Krypton' and Kh-35 (AS-20 'Kayak') AShMs.

Ukraine

An-70 prototype crash
Loss of power from two of its four ZMKB Progress/Zaporozhye D-27 propfans immediately after taking-off from Omsk in Siberia on 27 January, resulted in the prototype Antonov An-70 heavy-lift military transport making a wheels-up landing short of the airfield, after an attempted circuit. Four of its 33 occupants received minor injuries, but initial reports that the fuselage had broken in two were belied by an Antonov OKB spokesman. He reported slight damage to several lower fuselage skin panels and some sub-systems, and said that the An-70 required only field repairs, and a replacement port outer engine and APU, to be flown back to the Kiev factory for a full inspection and refurbishment.

The An-70 had been flown to eastern Russia to complete its cold-weather trials, for final certification later this year. Its take-off from Omsk for Yakutsk with 38 tonnes of fuel on board was made at ground temperatures of -60° C (-76° F). In that respect, its accident was similar to that of an An-124, which crashed fatally into an apartment block on take-off from IAPO's Irkutsk airfield in December 1997, while attempting to deliver two new Sukhoi Su-27UBs to Vietnam.

Its power loss was attributed to employing a mixture of summer and winter fuels.

A joint Ukrainian-Russian board is now investigating the An-70 accident, which Antonov maintains will not affect programme continuation. This involves planned procurement of up to 164 An-70s by the Russian air force and 65 for Ukraine's.

United Kingdom

FSTA contenders short-listed
Progress with UK MoD plans to replace the RAF's existing fleet of 20 BAe VC10 and nine Lockheed TriStar tanker/transports from around 2005-07, through its Future Strategic Tanker Aircraft (FSTA) project, was achieved in December 2000, when four industry consortia were short-listed for evaluation. Costing up to £9 billion over its 25-year life, the FSTA is the MoD's largest proposed Private Finance Initiative (PFI) programme to date.

PFI proposals for a complete air-to-air refuelling (AAR) service to the RAF will involve contractor ownership, management and maintenance of the aircraft, plus provision of training facilities and some personnel. The RAF would continue to retain key military responsibility for Britain's AAR capability, working closely with

Eurofighter Typhoon

By the end of 2000 some 94 per cent of the Initial Operating Capability (IOC) for the Eurofighter had been examined by the seven Development Aircraft (DA). These will be joined from August 2001 by the five Instrumented Production Aircraft (IPA), which will essentially represent the IOC of production aircraft.

The following table shows the status of each of the DA aircraft as of 22 February 2001.

DA2 formates with an RAF Tristar during air-to-air refuelling trials in the latter half of 2000. The aircraft has subsequently undergone fuel system modifications and resumed flight tests in mid-March 2001.

Aircraft	No. of flights	Flying hours	Status	Last flight
DA1	232	184 hrs 24 mins	Lay up (FCS installation)	11/09/00
DA2	345	303 hrs 3 mins	Lay up (Fuel mods)	18/12/00
DA3	246	191 hrs 51 mins	Lay up (Gun/ seat mods)	31/03/00
DA4	97	98 hrs 57 mins	Lay up (DASS ground trials)	13/04/00
DA5	176	136 hrs 17 mins	Flying	07/02/01
DA6	199	191 hrs 50 mins	Flying	16/02/01
DA7	177	94 hrs 21 mins	Flying	02/02/01

Boeing F/A-18E/F Super Hornet

The first of the five EMD (Engineering and Manufacturing Development) F/A-18Es completed its test flight programme in December 2000. In its five-year operational history, the aircraft was tasked with flight envelope expansion and various sub-system trials. Subsequently these trials were conducted carrying a wide range of potential ordnance intended for in-service examples.

Once the EMD phase had been completed in April 1999, the aircraft was modified for air-to-air refuelling trials fitted with an underfuselage refuelling store and four 480-US gal (1780-litre) additional fuel tanks on underwing hardpoints. Flight tests cleared the type to refuel the four carrier-based US Navy aircraft capable of air-to-air-refuelling – F-14 Tomcat, F/A-18 Hornet, EA-6B Prowler and S-3B Viking.

Shortly after this, on 4 December, the first VFA-122 student completed the compulsory 10-day and six-night arrested landings on the USS *Constellation,* becoming carrier qualified in the process. Upon completing transition training he will be assigned to VFA-115 which received its first F/A-18E, at its NAS Lemoore base, on 7 December 2000. VFA-115 is to be the first operational squadron for the Super Hornet, receiving its complement of flight crew and aircraft during the first eight months of 2001. VFA-115 will then make the type's maiden carrier deployment aboard the USS *Abraham Lincoln* in 2002.

---

industry. When not required for RAF use, the contractor could earn revenue by using spare aircraft to transport commercial loads, while maintaining the RAF's operational effectiveness.

In December, the four consortia

Matra BAe Dynamics (MBD) has successfully completed the first flight test of the Storm Shadow/SCALP EG air-to-surface missile. Fitted without a warhead, the test was carried out at the Centre d'Essais test range at Biscarosse, launched from a Mirage 2000N. The release height was 20,000 ft (6096 m) and the missile descended to low-level at Mach 0.8 for 250 km (155 miles) along its projected course before accurately striking its intended target.

bidders from six original contenders comprised Air Reach, led by Rolls-Royce; BAE Systems; Eurotanker, which included Cobham's FR Aviation and Thomson-Racal (now Thales Defence); and the Serco-led SSM group. Each had submitted outline proposals to the MoD in November 1999, followed by fully-costed submissions. In mid-January, however, Air Reach and Eurotanker joined forces with other major European companies as equal shareholders, to form the AirTanker group.

This now includes the European Aeronautic, Defence and Space Company (EADS), Rolls-Royce, Cobham, Brown & Root Services and Thales, reducing FSTA contenders to three groups. Several aircraft platforms are being considered as candidates for the tanker services, including Airbus-based and Boeing solutions.

Bidders' proposals will allow the MoD to decide whether PFI can provide the operational capability the RAF needs in a cost-effective way. Some difficulties are anticipated, however, in arranging worthwhile commercial transport contracts, while maintaining optimum force availability for priority military roles. A final decision on a PFI FSTA programme go-ahead is due in 2002.

United States

First flight for AH-1Z

Four years of development culminated on 7 December 2000 when aircraft Z1, the newest variant of the Cobra/Sea Cobra family, flew for the first time at Bell Helicopter's Flight Research Center in Arlington, Texas. Modified from an AH-1W, the aircraft (BuNo. 162549), the first of three AH-1Z prototypes, lifted off at 11:42 EST and carried out initial hover handling qualities and basic hover work before landing 15 minutes later. Equipped with a four-bladed, all composite, hingeless, bearing-less main rotor system and tail rotor, new avionics and structural modifications, the AH-1Z will be transferred to NAS Patuxent River, Maryland in March 2001.

Developed as part of the H-1 Upgrade Program, the AH-1Zs will be joined by two UH-1Y prototypes in a 30-month, 1,300-hour flight test programme carried out by an integrated test team consisting of contractor and government personnel. This programme will remanufacture 100 UH-1N transport helicopters and 180 AH-1W Super Cobra attack helicopters to an advanced configuration featuring common engines and flight dynamic components. First flight of the UH-1Y will take place in 2001

and deliveries to the US Marine Corps will commence in 2004.

JASSM development

During a flight test, held at White Sands Missile Range, New Mexico, a Joint Air-to-Surface Standoff Missile (JASSM) equipped with an imaging infra-red (IIR) seeker was launched from a 46th Test Wing F-16 flying at a speed of 500 mph (805 km/h) and an altitude of 15,000 ft (4572 m). After separating from the aircraft the weapon deployed its wings and tail section, and ignited its engine at the proper altitude and began a 70-mile (113-km) journey towards the target. Upon reaching the target, the JASSM performed a pitch-over manoeuvre and descended on the target at a 70° impact angle and, guided by the IIR seeker, impacted the target. The 2,250-lb (1021-kg) cruise missile is equipped with a 1,000-lb (305-kg) dual-purpose warhead capable of destroying soft and distributed surface targets or deeply buried, hardened structures. It has a range in excess of 200 nm (370 km) and can be deployed during the day or at night and in adverse weather. The USAF currently plans to order 2,400 JASSMs, and the missile will be carried on the F-16, B-1B, B-2A, and B-52H. A low-rate initial production decision is expected in

The two flying RAH-66 Comanche prototypes pose for the camera during a sortie over Florida. No. 1 (foreground) displays the new rotor hub and mock-up of the fire-control radar but does not feature the new tail surfaces. By mid-March 2001 the two aircraft had amassed some 350 flying hours between them, meeting programme goals in terms of speed, vertical rate of climb, manoeuvrability and infra-red signature.

Boeing Sikorsky RAH-66

Comanche Prototype No. 1 flew for the first time on 18 December 2000 from Sikorsky's Development Flight Center at West Palm Beach, Florida with a new empennage design. This tail unit consists of vertical and horizontal stabilisers with the latter incorporating vertical endplates. This reconfigurable arrangement permits adjustments of tail components to validate and optimise a final tail design for production aircraft.

The development process relied heavily on advanced 'Lean Initiative' engineering design software, allowing rapid fabrication and assembly of the unit in just a 10-month period. The initial flight lasted 1.4 hours with speeds of up to 165 kts (190 mph; 305 km/h) and banks of up to 45° recorded along with various controllability checks. The aircraft also incorporated a number of other recent modifications including lowered exhaust doors, a main rotor hub fairing, an aerodynamic representation of the Comanche fire control radar and an alternative main rotor pylon. The flight testing of these items, and the more powerful T-801 engine, are specific targets for the Interim Decision Review (IDR) scheduled for January 2003 .

Prototype No. 2 is scheduled to begin modification in May 2001 for Mission Equipment Package (MEP) flight test development as part of the Engineering and Manufacturing Development (EMD) phase, which commenced in June 2000. On returning to flight status (scheduled for December 2001) the aircraft will test the commercial displays and processors. This will be followed by Night Vision Pilotage System testing in the second quarter of 2002 and evaluation of the Target Acquisition System in late 2002. Following the allocation of additional funding, a total of 13 additional Comanches will be built as part of the EMD contract.

The RAH-66 programme has been boosted by significant support from the US Army leadership and is currently on schedule to achieve Initial Operational Capability (IOC) in 2006.

The new tail empennage, with its distinctive endplates, is clearly visible as prototype No. 1 departs West Palm Beach on its maiden flight with this arrangement. The tail unit will be refined during a number of test flights before validating the final production version.

late summer or early fall, with full-rate following in early 2003.

X-45A arrives at Edwards AFB

Boeing's Phantom Works has shipped the prototype X-45A unmanned combat air vehicle (UCAV) and supporting equipment from St. Louis, Missouri to NASA's Dryden Flight Test Center, at Edwards AFB, California. Initial flight tests of the UCAV were scheduled to begin in March 2001. Two X-45As will be used in mid-2002 to demonstrate simulated suppression of enemy defences (SEAD) missions.

The two demonstrators are primarily avionics test beds and are equipped with pallet-mounted avionics, however a third UCAV will have an updated stealth configuration and be built with newer materials and integrated avionics, freeing the weapons bay for weapons or additional electronics systems. Boeing is hoping to demonstrate that the X-45A can act as both an electronic warfare (EW) escort and as an in-target area weapons delivery vehicle. The UCAV advanced technology demonstration system is being developed under a US$131-million, 42-month programme jointly funded by the USAF, the Defense Advanced Projects Research Agency (DARPA) and Boeing.

Aero India 2001

Top: Following its first flight on 26 November 2000, the first pre-production standard Su-30MKI was demonstrated at Aero India from 7-11 February 2001. Three further pre-production examples built by the Irkutsk Aviation Production Association (IAPO) will join the flight test programme during 2001.

Centre: HAL's Do 228 demonstrator has been fitted with IAI's Airborne Observation System (AOS). Optimised for day and night surveillance/reconnaissance, the package offers real-time long-range observation, target image and co-ordinate information and full mission management.

Below: HAL, in conjunction with Ilyushin, has completed feasibility studies of a new twin-turbofan transport aircraft to meet the IAF's Tactical Transport Aircraft (TTA) requirement. Designated Il-214T, the aircraft will have a payload in the 20-ton class and will feature digital fly-by-wire controls, a glass cockpit and a full-width rear ramp door. The design and development period is estimated at 6-7 years with costs optimistically placed at US$350 million – shared equally between HAL and Ilyushin/IAPO/Aviaexport. It is hoped that the Il-214T will begin replacing the IAF's fleet of Antonov An-32s from 2007.

Above: Key to IAI's Peak 17 Mi-17 upgrade programme is a new NVG-compatible glass cockpit, combined with helmet-mounted sights, which gives the aircraft full day/night capability for transport and anti-armour/attack missions. Other modifications include an Elta Electronics-designed advanced EW suite and enhanced armament packages including Rafael NT-D Dandy and NT-S Spike short-range anti-armour missiles.

UPGRADES AND MODIFICATIONS

Brazil

F-5 upgrade approved

Financial terms were finally approved by the Brazilian Senate on 4 January for the US$250 million upgrade programme of its Northrop F-5E/F fighter-bomber force, for which Elbit Systems was selected as prime contractor in October 1998. EMBRAER is now expected to install new Israeli avionics and US structural components in some 48 Northrop F-5Es and nine F-5F two-seat combat trainers operated by three FAB squadrons, to extend their useful lives through 2012. Elbit's share of the funding, which includes replacement of the F-5Es' APQ-153/159 fire-control radar with the Alenia/FIAR Grifo F system, is over US$200 million and is due for completion by 2007.

Canada

CF-18 upgrade launched

Canada is planning to upgrade 80 of 122 CF-18A/B (CF-188) Hornet multi-role fighters with advanced avionics, to extend their operating lives to at least 2017. Elements of Boeing's Engineering Change Program (ECP) 583 to be incorporated in an eight-year rolling upgrade programme will include an enhanced General Dynamics Information Systems XN-8+ mission computer, Raytheon APG-65 radar upgrades to APG-73 standard, and new USN operational and EW software.

ECP 583 also includes a sixth multiplex bus, integrating new communications equipment, GPS, IFF with KIV-6/TSEC combined interrogator/transponder, and the AN/AYQ-9 stores management systems. Also involved will be structural reinforcements and a targeting pod, in an eventual $Can1.1 billion (US$733.5 million) programme.

Currently comprising four squadrons of 15 CF-18s, plus up to 27 in an OCU, the CAF's upgraded Hornet force will be only slightly reduced in numbers. Several options are being considered for the 42 surplus CF-18s. One was to keep them, and use their available flying hours to extend the lives of the rest of the fleet. Another was their immediate disposal as most have remaining fatigue lives which would allow operations until around 2010.

China

Chengdu F-7 proposals

Further F-7MG upgrades, which could possibly end prospects of planned joint Sino/Pakistani Klimov RD-93-powered Chengdu Super 7/FC-1 procurement, as the ultimate MiG-21 development, were revealed at Zhuhai by a model of the proposed F-7MF. In addition to cranked delta wings, the F-7MF has a relocated ventral rectangular engine inlet, leaving the nose clear for a larger diameter radome, and requiring an aft-located rearward-retracting nosewheel unit. It also features small fixed fuselage-mounted canards, and seven external stores pylons.

As another F-7MF development, a J-7FS prototype also shown at Zhuhai, has been flying since June 1998, with an interim chin intake and other changes. Having completed wind-tunnel testing, a prototype F-7MF is expected to fly by early 2002, with digital avionics and mission systems, including Russian, Israeli or other western equipment in the form of fire-control radar, and cockpit and head-up displays, for about a US$7-8 million price.

Egypt

CH-47 conversion contract

Boeing Defense and Space Group, Helicopter Division will upgrade six Egyptian CH-47C Chinooks to CH-47D configuration under a US$44.7 million contract.

The first ex-IDF/AF A-4N (N434FS), destined for service with BAE Flight Systems, underwent flight tests conducted by IAI in January 2001 prior to delivery.

France

Improved ESM for E-3 fleet

France's four Boeing E-3Fs have received upgraded electronic support measures (ESM). The passive surveillance system, which enables AWACS to detect, identify and track electronic transmissions from ground, airborne and maritime sources, was installed in the French aircraft by Air France Industries, at Le Bourget under subcontract to Boeing.

Germany

A310 MRT conversions

The Luftwaffe has placed a pair of A310s in service that have been modified as multi-role transports (MRT) by the A310 MRTT Air Force Consortium composed of EADS Airbus and LufthansaTechnik. Two additional aircraft will be modified and delivered to the Luftwaffe by the end of 2001. The conversion allows the Airbus to be used for aero-medical evacuation, as a troop transport or in a combination cargo and passenger aircraft. In the aeromedical role the A310 is equipped with six intensive-care stations and can accommodate 56 litter patients. When acting as a troop transport the aircraft can carry up to 214 soldiers and as many as 54 passengers when configured for a combination role. Between 2002 and 2004 all four of the MRT aircraft will be equipped with fuel tanks below the main cargo/passenger deck, refueling pods beneath both wings and an operator's station behind the cockpit for use as multi-role tanker transports, with the first to be delivered to the Luftwaffe in 2003.

Japan

Additional E-2C updates

Japan's Defense Agency has placed a US$60 million order with Northrop Grumman covering the upgrade of two additional E-2Cs to Hawkeye 2000 configuration. Japan had previously ordered one update kit and hopes to upgrade its entire fleet of 13 E-2Cs over the next five years. The first aircraft will be delivered by 2004. The upgrade includes the installation of a new mission computer, AN/APS-145 radar and advanced control indicator set (ACIS) displays, enhanced software, and a new vapour cycle cooling system. The kits will be manufactured by Northrop Grumman and installed by Kawasaki Heavy Industries at Gifu, Japan.

NATO

NATO AWACS programme

During January 2001 Boeing began flight-testing a NATO E-3A that has received a number of upgrades as part of the US$491 million Mid-Term Modernization Program. During the first flight operators aboard the E-3A evaluated the aircraft's radar, IFF electronics, navigation, computers/displays and mission systems. The upgrade provides the E-3A with 14 new work-station consoles with flat-panel situation displays, a new mission computing system, digital and satellite communications systems, new VHF radios and a new global positioning system. The flight test programme, including engineering

Belonging to 1° Esquadrão 'Pampa' of 14° Grupo, the first pair of FAB F-5s (one 'E' and one 'F') arrived at EMBRAER's São José dos Campos facility in late February to begin the F-5BR upgrade programme.

Nighthawks at Palmdale

Two unusually-painted F-117As (top) operated by the 410th Test Squadron conducted trials from Palmdale in late 2000. The two aircraft carried variations of a white finish with black trim. Also operating from Palmdale, 79-784 (above) has been modified to carry this red pod mounted outboard of the port undercarriage. This may be an inward-facing camera for recording weapons release.

test and evaluation and qualification testing, includes a total of 40 test flights. Retrofit of the entire fleet of 17 aircraft will be implemented under the terms of a follow-on contract.

Poland

Fighter update plans

Israel Aircraft Industries was expecting a Polish government contract early in 2001 to upgrade some of its 98 Sukhoi Su-22M4 'Fitter-K' single-seat ground attack fighters and Su-22UM3 'Fitter-G' two-seat combat trainers, with new digital mission system avionics for improved combat capabilities and NATO interoperability. Competing bids for this programme, which will also involve structural upgrades to extend Su-22 operating lives until 2015, were received from SAGEM, EADS and Elbit Systems.

As an IAI subsidiary, however, Elbit will probably be involved in any case in the Polish Su-22 upgrade, as supplier of multi-function and head-up cockpit displays, and other avionics, as will IAI's Elta Electronics division with its proposed EL/M-2032 fire-control radar. Funding limitations may restrict the initial Su-22 upgrade contract to 36 aircraft, within an approximate budget of US$80 million. Modernisation of all 98 Su-22s, probably undertaken by the Polish air force WZL-2 depot at Bydgoszcz, would cost around US$200 million.

Spain

IAI awarded F-5 contract

Israeli Aircraft Industries' Lahav Division has been selected to upgrade the Spanish air force's 22 remaining SF-5Bs (local designation AE.9) with a new avionics package. Used in the advanced training role by Ala 23, the SF-5 upgrade includes HUD installation, a new mission computer, LCD cockpit displays, electronic flight instruments system (EFIS), embedded INS using GPS and collision avoidance software. The total cost of the contract is some US$20 million.

United Kingdom

RAF Sentry upgrades

Boeing has installed Radar System Improvement Program (RSIP) kits and global positioning system/inertial navigation systems (GINS) in seven E-3D Sentry AEW.Mk 1s. The kits were installed at RAF Waddington by BAE Systems, under subcontract to Boeing. The RSIP improves the AWACS radar's counter-countermeasures capability and increases the sensitivity of the pulse Doppler mode, allowing it to detect and track smaller targets.

United States

F/A-18 structural upgrades

The US Navy and Boeing are developing a structural update programme that will add approximately 700 catapult launches and arrested landings to the life of the F/A-18C/D. Designated the Center Barrel Replacement plus (CBR+) Program, the update entails replacing the aircraft's centre section or barrel with a newly constructed module. Current planning calls for the update to be incorporated in 260 USN and 95 USMC aircraft. The Navy is also planning to conduct a service life assessment programme (SLAP) from 2001-03 that will determine which components are in need of repair/replacement. As part of this programme one F/A-18C will be tested to destruction. The results will be incorporated into a service life extension programme (SLEP) scheduled to begin in 2003.

New avionics for Hurons

Following a programme that updated the cockpits of 25 Army National Guard C-12Fs, the US Army plans to upgrade the cockpit avionics of its remaining 21 C-12Fs Hurons along with its 29 C-12Rs. The programme will provide the C-12F aircraft with digital displays, as part of the FMS-3000 flight management system (FMS), a traffic collision avoidance system (TCAS II), enhanced ground proximity warning system (EGPWS), cockpit voice recorder/flight data recorder (CVR/FDR), GPS, a new colour weather radar, radios and an updated transponder system. Once the modifications are incorporated the updated C-12F will be redesignated the C-12U and the modified aircraft will be delivered to the 204th Military Intelligence Battalion (MIB) at Fort Bliss, Texas. Although already equipped with digital displays, the C-12Rs will receive an enhanced FMS, TCAS II, EGPWS, CVR/FDR, enhanced GPS, and the updated transponder modes. The updated aircraft will become the C-12R1.

Turboprop-powered Predator

Powered by a Honeywell TPE-331-10T turboprop engine the Predator B UAV made its first flight at General Atomic's flight operations facility in El Mirage, California on 2 February 2001. Predator B serial 001 is capable of carrying a 750-lb (340-kg) payload to an altitude of 50,000 ft (15240 m) and flying at speeds of over 200 knots (370 km/h). Funded jointly by the manufacturer and NASA, 001 is the first of three air vehicles that will fly with varying configurations. Scheduled to fly in late 2001, Predator B 002 will be equipped with triple-redundant fault-tolerant avionics and a Williams FJ44-2A turbojet engine.

Talons re-winged

Northrop Grumman's Integrated Systems Sector has begun production of 55 replacement wings for the USAF's T-38 trainer as part of a programme to extend the service life of the aircraft by another four decades. The replacement wings will ensure that the aircraft remain serviceable while a new wing is designed. Deliveries are expected to begin in October 2001 and continue at a rate of one per month for the following 54 months. The manufacturer is already working on the improved design, which is scheduled to enter production in 2006 and will eventually be retrofitted to the entire T-38 fleet.

Dolphin modernisation

The US Coast Guard has undertaken an ambitious programme to update the avionics of its 96 HH-65As. The Dolphin entered service in 1984 and was expected to remain in service for only 15 years, however the service now plans to retain the helicopter through 2014. Much of the aircraft's instrumentation will be replaced by a Rockwell Collins integrated flight management avionics suite comprising a pair of CDU-900G control display units and four MFD-255 multifunction flat panel displays. In addition to providing the aircraft with a GPS capability it will also offer a significant increase in reliability and reduces the aircraft's empty weight by nearly 100 lb (45.4 kg). Upgraded aircraft will receive the designation HH-65B.

The USAF has concluded the first phase of flight tests demonstrating the ability of the General Atomics RQ-1A Predator UAV to deliver AGM-114 Hellfire anti-tank missiles. Modifications have been made to the Hellfire to allow it to be released from the RQ-1A's nomal operating altitude of 10,000 ft (3048 m) and above.

PROCUREMENT AND DELIVERIES

Algeria

More Su-24s from Russia

Having operated a dozen or so Sukhoi Su-24MK 'Fencer-Ds' and four Su-24MR 'Fencer-E' recce aircraft for several years from Laghouat air base, the Algerian air force is now receiving another 22 examples. Three other Su-24s were also delivered last year from a US$12 million contract placed by Algeria with Russia's Promexport surplus arms sales organisation, probably as attrition replacements. Before delivery, they were over-hauled by the Novosibirsk Aviation Production Association (NAPO), as original constructors, now undertaking the same work on the 22 Su-24s ordered from a reported US$120 million Promexport contract.

Australia

Project Wedgetail

Priority is currently being given to Australia's $A3 billion (US$1.64 billion) Project Wedgetail contract with Boeing, signed in December, for initial purchase of four 737 Airborne Early Warning & Control aircraft, with options on three more. Deliveries will start in 2006, and the first two aircraft will enter RAAF service with No. 2 Squadron at Williamtown, NSW, with a detachment at Tindal, NT, in 2007.

Armed helicopter requirement

Evaluations are being made of tenders invited in December for the army's $A1.2 billion Project Air 87 programme, for 20-24 armed reconnaissance helicopters. Contract signature is due within about a year.

Austria

Gripen on offer

Saab/BAE Systems responded to an Austrian request for information for a new fighter aircraft with a proposal offering 30 JAS39 Gripen fighters as part of an innovative finance package and offset programme. Russia's offer to provide 30 MiG-29s in exchange for partial relief from its US$2.84 million debt has been rejected by the Austrian government.

Brazil

Italian C-130s to Brazil

Beginning in May 2001 Brazil will take delivery of 10 C-130Hs formerly operated by the Aeronautica Militare Italiana. The aircraft, which had been sold back to Lockheed Martin as part of Italy's purchase of 22 new C-130Js and C-130J-30s will join five C-130Es, five C-130Hs and two KC-130H tankers already in service with the Força Aérea Brasileira (Brazilian Air Force). The initial six aircraft will be delivered beginning this May, with the remainder following by the end of November 2002.

Chile

New combat aircraft decision

Selection on 27 December of up to 12 new-build Lockheed Martin Block 50/52 F-16C/Ds to meet Chilean air force new combat aircraft requirements, followed extensive evaluations of most leading contenders. Apart from surplus US F-16A/Bs and MDC F/A-18A/Bs, finalists for replacement of the FACh's 30 or so Cessna A-37B Dragonflies, included the Dassault Mirage 2000-5 Mk 2 and SAAB/BAE JAS 39 Gripen. Negotiations were in hand with the US government in January for an estimated US$600 million FMS contract for Chilean F-16 procurement, now halved from its original requirement, for planned delivery from 2004. Chile's F-16 package will reportedly also include a surplus USAF KC-135 tanker, and new-technology weapons, although not initially the requested Raytheon AIM-120 AMRAAM advanced medium-range AAMs.

Colombia

US anti-drugs aid

Continuing US drug-interdiction aid of some US$1.3 billion to Colombia announced late last year for 2002-03, includes a further 16 Sikorsky UH-60L Black Hawks for the Colombian army, plus 30 more upgraded Bell UH-1 Huey IIs. Fifteen of 33 ex-Canadian CH-135 (UH-1Ns) acquired by the US were transferred to Colombia in January 2001, to complement 18 previously delivered, alongside 42 Huey IIs for police and army use. Planned US aid to Colombia also includes Northrop Grumman APG-66 air-to-air radars, FLIR and communications equipment for two FAC Swearingen C-26 Merlins, and conversion of an FAC C-47 to an AC-47, with FLIR, night-vision cockpit and fire-control system.

Czech Republic

RFP issued for new fighter

Despite a total military budget of only CKr45 billion (US$11.25 billion) for the coming year, the Czech government issued requests for proposals for 24-36 new combat aircraft in January. Industrial offsets of 150% are being sought for the estimated CKr100 billion contract, from contenders expected to include new or surplus Boeing F-15s, L-M F-16s, Dassault Mirage 2000-5s, SAAB-BAE Gripens, and Eurofighter Typhoons.

Denmark

New transport aircraft ordered

A DKr2.184 billion contract was signed at Air Materiel Command HQ, Vaerlose Air Base on 1 December for RDAF procurement of three Lockheed Martin C-130J-30 Hercules tactical transports. Due for delivery in late 2003, the RDAF C-130Js will incorporate enhanced cargo handling systems and integrated electronic warfare suites.

Radar selection

The Royal Danish Air Force has awarded a contract to Telephonics Corporation covering the delivery of a number of AN/APS-143B(V)3 OceanEye Sea Surveillance radar systems for installation on CL-604 Challengers. The RDAF has one CL-604 in service with two further examples awaiting delivery from Bombardier.

Egypt

K-8 contract progress

Long-rumoured EAF orders for 80 Hongdu K-8E basic jet-trainers costing some $345 million were finally confirmed at China's Zhuhai air show in November. The first 10 Chinese-built K-8Es are now being followed by another 15 as knocked-down kits, for assembly by a revived Arab Organisation for Industrialisation (AOI) in Cairo. The remainder will have increasing proportions of up to 90% Egyptian-produced components. All will be powered by Honeywell TFE731-2A-2A turbofans, from a recently received US$72 million contract for 100 more engines, following original deliveries of 58. With Egypt's

New Australian acquisitons displayed at Avalon

The Royal Australian Air Force formally placed the first 14 of 33 new Hawk Mk 127 lead-in fighter (LIF) trainers in service following a ceremony held at RAAF Base Williamtown, New South Wales. BAE Systems built the initial 11 aircraft in the UK and the remainder are being assembled locally in New South Wales. As a lead-in fighter, the Hawks will provide pilots chosen for fast-jet operations with an interim step between the RAAF's Pilatus PC-9A trainers and the front-line F/A-18 and F-111 fighters.

Left: The first of 17 upgraded AP-3C Orions has begun an extensive test and evaluation programme prior to the type's scheduled operational acceptance in autumn 2001. After delays of some three years, caused by software problems, prime contractor Raytheon forecast that the final upgraded aircraft will return to service in 2004.

Right: The Royal Australian navy has received the first of 11 SH-2G(A) Super Seasprites acquired for service aboard the RAN's eight ANZAC-class frigates. The aircraft will be armed with the AGM-119B Penguin missile (seen here), Mk 46 torpedoes or Mk 11 depth charges.

India is shortly expected to complete its planned order for navalised MiG-29Ks, for service aboard the ex-Russian aircraft-carrier Admiral Gorshkov which is currently undergoing refit. Indications are that between 40-60 will be acquired.

order, 116 K-8s have reportedly been sold to date, although China is now claiming 166. The extra 50 could represent initial AF/PLA procurement. This may include 30 K-8Js, with Motor Sich AI-25TLK turbofans, which were reportedly ordered by China in March 1997.

France

More VIP transports
Two Airbus A310s currently operated by ETEC 65, the French air force (AdlA) transport, training and calibration squadron, are to be supplemented in October 2001 and April 2002 by two Airbus A319CJs (Corporate Jets). With 50 luxurious seats, they will replace two venerable Dassault Mystère 20s and three Nord 262s operated from Villacoublay on presidential, government and senior military transport roles.

Cougar Mk 2 Plus delivered
The first of four Eurocopter EC725 Cougar Mk 2 Plus combat search-and-rescue (C-SAR) helicopters so far funded was delivered to AdA late last year, from up to 14 required. One EC725 was converted from a Cougar Mk II delivered to AdA in 2000, the others being newly constructed. All have provision for air refuelling, developed for Saudi Arabia's CSAR Cougars.

Greece

SAR Super Pumas
The Greek air force has placed an US$92.5 million order for AS332C Super Pumas for SAR and CSAR duties. The first two examples will be delivered within two years and will be equipped with a Bendix 1500B radar, Thomson-CSF Clio FLIR, a Spectrolab searchlight, hailers, a winch and life rafts.

India

Su-30 agreement signed
Despite delays in deliveries of some two years from earlier orders for 50 Sukhoi Su-30MKI multi-role thrust-vectored fighters, a US$3.3 billion government-to-government contract was signed on 28 December for licensed production of up to 140 similar aircraft. These will be built by HAL's Nasik division, initially from knocked-down kits from the Irkutsk Aviation Production Association factory in Siberia. Unlike China's parallel Su-27SK licensed production programme, however, India's will involve its Lyulka/Saturn AL-31FP turbofans and associated systems, and is scheduled for completion in 2017.

India is expecting the first of its 32 Su-30MKI deliveries between the end of this year and 2004. The 18 original ex-Russian/Indonesian air force Su-30K/KMs will also be upgraded to full Su-30MKI standards by 2004-5.

Mi-17-1V deliveries begin
Deliveries began on 1 December 2000 of the first eight of the IAF's 40 new and upgraded Mil Mi-17-1V transport helicopters. Ordered by the IAF in May 1999 from a US$170 million contract with Kazan, via Russia's Aviaexport and Promexport arms agencies, they will begin replacing the IAF's 75 Mi-8s, in two IAF squadrons in the Kargil and Siachen sectors by late 2001.

Hawk order delayed
Protracted delays by the Indian government in finalising planned large-scale procurement of BAE Systems Hawk advanced trainers were among the main factors in the group's recent forecasts of reduced profitability. The IAF has been urgently pressing the Delhi government for new advanced jet-trainers (AJTs) since its last two-seat Ajeet and Hawker Hunters were withdrawn from service in the early 1990s. The lack of an advanced trainer has contibuted to a poor safety record among the fast jet fleet. More than 60 IAF MiG-21s have crashed since 1996, about 40% through pilot error.

Last November it was announced that icensed production by HAL was planned in Bangalore of a further 42 similar aircraft, within an overall target programme cost of around Rs60 billion (US$1.28 billion). This would include training equipment, spares and technical support.

IAF Chief of Air Staff Air Chief Marshal A.Y. Tipnis said that more Hawks could be required for the AJT programme, for which contract signature was then expected by the year-end. It depends, however, on IAF requirements to eliminate all American components from its Hawks, mostly involving avionics, to avoid the threat of current or future US sanctions delaying spares supplies and procurement.

Israel

UH-60/AH-64 orders
Sikorsky has received a US$211.8 million Foreign Military Sales (FMS) order from the Israeli air force for 24 S-70A Blackhawks for delivery in 2002. Israel will also acquire nine AH-64D Longbow Apaches from Boeing through FMS. The programme is expected to be worth some US$500 million.

Piper Cub replacement
The IDF/AF issued a request for information (RFI) in January 2001 for replacement primary trainers, from a short-list of the Aermacchi/SIAI-Marchetti SF.260, ENAER's T-35 Pillán, and Pacific Aerospace Corporation's CT-4. The IDF/AF has operated up to 50 or more Cubs for many years, but is now seeking to buy flying hours, on the lowest cost basis, rather than ownership of the selected type, through a Private Finance Initiative.

Italy

AMI to acquire F-16s
Falcon Up structural upgrades, installation of uprated Pratt & Whitney F100-220E engines, and 45,000 flying hours are involved in a planned US$780 million Italian air force (AMI) lease package involving 30 surplus USAF F-16A air-defence fighters and four two-seat F-16B combat trainers, incorporating Block 15 Operational Capability Upgrades. The F-16s are urgently needed to replace the AMI's F-104S Starfighters and two squadrons of leased RAF Tornado ADVs, pending deliveries of 121 Eurofighters from 2003.

The Italian F-16 lease package also includes four stored USAF F-16A-15s for spares cannibalisation, plus four spare F100 powerplants, four AN/APG-66 fire-control radars, spares, support equipment and documentation. Raytheon AIM-120 AMRAAMs and AIM-9L Sidewinders are also specified in the AMI's initial five-year F-16 lease package, from which deliveries are planned from about 20 months of contract.

Pakistan

Chinese F-7PG deliveries
The Pakistan air force hopes to receive the first of about 60 uprated MiG-21-derived F-7PG variants later this year. With manoeuvring slats on the new outer wings, and combat flap settings, the increased wing area improves J-7E/F-7MG combat agility by 45%, plus gains in take-off, climb, ceiling and landing perfor-

The first of eight S-70B Seahawks for the Turkish navy has conducted its first flight at Sikorsky's Stratford, Connecticut facility. The aircraft is fitted with the Sikorsky glass cockpit, AN/APS-143 search radar, Helicopter Long-Range Active Sonar (HELRAS) and FLIR. Weapons options include Penguin and Hellfire missiles.

Boeing's McDonnell Douglas Corporation division has been awarded a US$225 million contract covering the procurement of an additional 14 T-45C Goshawks. The purchase is to be a constituent of the FY2001 budget.

mance. Contract completion has been delayed, however, pending choice of new radars for Pakistan's F-7MGs, between an upgraded GEC Marconi (now BAE Systems) Super Skyranger full-function pulse-Doppler lightweight unit, or a development of the Alenia/FIAR Grifo 7, produced under licence at Pakistan's Kamra aircraft factory. BAE Systems' proposed SSR installation also includes an air data computer, head-up display, hands-on-throttle-and-stick (HOTAS), and a Vinten video recording system.

Lebanese Mirages acquired
While still taking delivery of some 42 ex-French air force Mirage 5Fs and IIIBEs following their avionics upgrade by SAGEM and SOGERMA, the Pakistan air force is also reported to have purchased 10 Mirage IIIELs from the Lebanese government. Along with two Mirage IIIBL two-seat combat trainers, these were originally delivered to the Lebanese air force in 1967, but were withdrawn from service almost immediately, and have been in storage ever since. They are understood to have been acquired by Pakistan for purely nominal prices, but require complete refurbishment and upgrades before entering service.

Peru

Police K-Max orders
Five Kaman K-Max single-seat heavy-lift utility helicopters, funded through a US$30 million US aid programme, were scheduled for delivery to the Peruvian National Police in March and April 2001 for drug interdiction roles. Their sale increased overall K-Max orders to 36, with a current programme unit cost of US$4.2 million.

Spain

Seahawk strength doubled
A US$77.4 million contract was announced in late 2000 for Spanish naval aviation procurement of six new Sikorsky SH-60B (HS.23) Seahawk ASW helicopters. Six HS.23 Seahawks already in Armada service will also be modified to similar standards to the new aircraft from upgrade and armament kits. About 20% of this work will be undertaken at Rota air base, with completion scheduled for 2004.

VIP transport plans
Spanish air force (EdA) procurement is planned of two ex-airline Airbus A310s from a Pts28.6 billion (US$15.4 million) programme, by

CASA. These will replace three EdA Boeing 707s for royal family and government use.

Switzerland

CASA C-295M selected
After competitive evaluation against the Lockheed Martin/Alenia C-27J, two CASA C-295M twin-turboprop tactical transports have been selected by Switzerland, to meet the SAFAAC's tactical transport needs. Funding is being included in Switzerland's 2001 procurement bill for a SwFr120 million (US$69.2 million) contract, including full in-service support, for signature with the Military Transport Division of EADS in October. As the type's first export customer, SAFAAC will receive its C-295s in 2003. A Lockheed C-130H may reportedly be leased from Spain to cope with bigger loads.

Vietnam

Su-30s for Vietnam?
Russia's Sukhoi plans to offer a package to Vietnam that will include new Su-30MK fighters and an upgrade of the Su-22M4 strike aircraft. In addition, the company is considering constructing a maintenance facility in Vietnam. The facility would function as a service centre for Sukhoi aircraft deployed throughout Southeast Asia.

United States

C-37A deliveries
On 3 December 2000 the 89th Airlift Wing's 99th Airlift Squadron placed a new C-37A Gulfstream V in service. The aircraft will only operate from Andrews temporarily, however and will be transferred to the 86th Airlift Wing at Ramstein Air Base, Germany once it has received a 150-hour inspection from Gulfsteam Aerospace at its Savannah, Georgia facility.

UC-35 delivery dates
The first two UC-35B Citation Encores for the US Army are due to be delivered in late March 2001. It is

expected that three subsequent UC-35Bs will be delivered in July, October and November. Two Citation Encores ordered by the US Marine Corps in September 2000 will be delivered in August and September 2001 and will be designated UC-35D. Two further UC-35s were ordered in January 2001 under a US$14.7 million contract. Delivery is expected in February 2002 with one UC-35B going to the Army and the other to the USMC as a UC-35D,

USCG Gulfstream acquisition
The US Coast Guard has ordered a C-37A Gulfstream V for delivery in the second quarter of 2002. The aircraft will be used for domestic and international transport along with command and control duties.

Follow-on Clipper orders
A sixth Boeing C-40A has been ordered for the US Naval Reserve's Fleet Logistic Support Wing. Four C-40As are currently being modified to a 'combi' configuration with up to three cargo pallets and 70 passengers on the main deck. Additionally, the USAF has placed a US$59 million order for a single C-40B and taken options on an additional six aircraft. The USAF version, based on the 737-700 BBJ, is likely to serve as a CINC support aircraft.

Latest Hawkeyes
In late January 2001 the US Navy accepted the latest E-2C Group II Hawkeye from Northrop Grumman. The company will deliver the last Group II aircraft in mid-2001 with subsequent aircraft to be built to Hawkeye 2000 standard featuring a new mission computer, new workstations, cooperative engagement capability and other improvements. The first of 21 Hawkeye 2000s is due to be delivered in October 2001.

J-STARS received
The USAF has accepted a ninth E-8C J-STARS production aircraft from Northrop Grumman with delivery taking place on 19 December 2000 to the 93rd Air Control Wing based at Robins AFB, Georgia.

The first Lockheed Martin C-130J-30 was rolled out of the company's main production building on 25 January 2001. One of five extended-fuselage -30s currently under contract for the USAF, the aircraft will be delivered to Edwards AFB for flight testing.

AIR ARM REVIEW

Above: The Aviación Naval Argentina continues to operate this single Lockheed L-188 Electra WAVE specialised Sigint platform alongside its fleet of six P-3B Orions.

Left: The Royal Australian Air Force has announced plans to replace its fleet of five leased Falcon 900s with a type of longer range. Contenders include the Bombardier CL-604 Challenger and Dassault Falcon 900EX.

Australia

Helicopter school relocated

Australia's Minister for Defence recently announced that the Australian Defence Force (ADF) helicopter school is being decentralised and its basic training functions would be transferred from RAAFB Fairbairn to RANAS Nowra, New South Wales and the Army Air Corps facility at Oakey, Queensland. The Navy element of the ADF Helicopter School, comprising just three staff and 12 students per year, began transfering to Nowra in December 2000 and the Army element, composed of 43 staff and up to 44 students per year, will relocate to Oakey in December 2001. The MoD believes that this more focused approach to helicopter training will increase the effectiveness of training for each service and result in savings of up to US$382,000 per year.

Greece

Swedish Argus loan

One of the Swedish air force's six S 100B Argus (SAAB 340) AEW&C aircraft, from three held in reserve, is being leased to the HAF for training purposes with its Ericsson Erieye planar-array radar. This is part of a SKr4 billion (US$418 million) contract signed by Greece with Ericsson in early 1999 for four Erieye-equipped EMBRAER RJ145 twin-turbofan light transports for similar AEW&C roles, for planned delivery from 2002.

Nigeria

US aid for Nigerian air force

Funding of some US$4 million

No. 28 Squadron officially received the first four Merlin HC.Mk 3s at RAF Benson on 7 March 2001. The aircraft had received Release to Service (RTS) in January. A total of 22 HC.Mk 3s has been ordered by the RAF.

from US grant aid of US$10 million was allocated last year to overhaul, refurbish and return to service six Lockheed C-130Hs and a dozen Dassault/Dornier Alpha Jets of the Nigerian air force. Many NAF aircraft have been grounded for some years because of spares shortages through under-funding and UN arms embargoes. Recent deliveries have included two refurbished Mil Mi-24 attack helicopters from CIS surplus sources.

Taiwan

Taiwan's anti-submarine woes

The Republic of China's (Taiwan) Navy reports that only a small percentage of its Grumman S-2T anti-submarine aircraft have been operational recently, and although it would like to retire the aging Tracker fleet, it has nothing to replace them with. The Navy's chief of staff indicates that recently only six of the aircraft were capable of carrying out missions. The service, however, hoped to have 13 operational by early 2001. The S-2Ts, which are more than 40 years old, were updated by Grumman in the early 1990s but have become increasingly more difficult to maintain. Although the Navy would like to replace them with P-3Cs, it has been unable to fund the purchase of Orions.

United Kingdom

Eurofighter squadrons

From MoD sources come details of the first units to operate RAF Eurofighters. Initial production Eurofighters now taking shape on BAE's factory line will remain at

Warton to equip the RAF's Operational Evaluation Unit, also to be known as No. 17 Squadron, as a lodger unit from 2002. Two years later, the OEU will transfer to RAF Coningsby, in Lincolnshire, to join the Eurofighter Operational Conversion Unit, alias No. 29 Squadron, due to form at the same base in 2004. Seven RAF squadrons are initially due to be equipped with the Eurofighter.

Ukraine

'Blackjack' break-up

Ukraine reportedly broke up the last of its 19 Tupolev Tu-160 Blackjack strategic bombers at Pryluky Air Base on 2 February 2001. Under the terms of the 1991 Cooperative Threat Reduction Program, Ukraine was obligated to destroy the bombers along with 25 older Tu-95 Bear bombers inherited from the Soviet Union by the first quarter of 2002. Rather than destroying all of the aircraft, however, the Ukraine transferred eight Tu-160s, three Tu-95s and almost 700 cruise missiles to Russia in exchange for US$285 million worth of debt forgiveness. Although the two countries would like to have negotiated another deal for additional Tu-160s, objections from the United States, who subsidised the demolition of the bombers, ended those chances. Four remaining Tu-95s will be destroyed by May 2001.

United States

347th Wing loses units

The rundown of units within the 347th Wing continues at Moody AFB, Georgia. The unit was due to lose the 69th Fighter Squadron (FS) and the 68th FS in February 2001 and April 2001. Subsequently, on 1 May 2001 the wing and 347th Operations Group (OG) will be inactivated, and the 41st Rescue Wing and 41st OG will be activated in their place. The 41st Rescue Squadron (RQS) and 71st RQS will be transferred from the 347th to the 41st OG. The squadrons will be equipped with 10 HC-130Ps and 17 HH-60Gs.

EC-135E ARIA retired

The last EC-135E advanced range instrumentation aircraft (ARIA) assigned to the 452d Flight Test Squadron (FLTS) at Edwards AFB, California made its final flight on 2 November 2000. The aircraft (serial 60-0374) was retired at the conclusion of its four-hour cross-country flight from Edwards to Wright Patterson AFB, Ohio. Originally designated EC-135N, the aircraft were equipped with a seven-foot steerable dish antenna inside a 10-ft, elongated, bulbous nose and originally named Apollo Range Instrumentation Aircraft (ARIA). The aircraft, nicknamed 'Bird of Prey', will be put on display at the US Air Force Museum during May 2001.

Above: The USAF has selected Beale AFB, California as the preferred location for the first main operating base of the RQ-4A Global Hawk unmanned air vehicle (UAV). The basing decision will not be finalised until environmental assessments are completed in March 2001. Arrival of the first personnel associated with the RQ-4A and delivery of the first of 18 air vehicles is expected to occur sometime in 2002 and the UAV will achieve initial operational capability (IOC) in 2003.

The NF-16D VISTA (Variable-stability In-flight Simulator Test Aircraft) is being utilised by the USAF Test Pilot School to establish a syllabus for future electro-optical weapons training. Fitted with AGM-65 Maverick training missiles, the sorties allow student test pilots, test navigators and flight test engineers to observe the differences between visible and infra-red sensors for acquiring and attacking targets.

Last Seasprite squadrons

With its inactivation scheduled to take place on 31 March 2001, the 'Titans' of HSL-94 retired the last of their SH-2Gs on 13 December 2000. Several of the aircraft were transferred to the squadron's sister unit at NAS North Island, California, however the majority were sent to the Aerospace Maintenance And Regeneration Center (AMARC) at Davis Monthan AFB, Arizona for storage. The 'Thunderbolts' of HSL-84 at North Island are the last unit operating the Seasprite but its inactivation will follow on 30 June 2001. Replacing the two light anti-submarine warfare squadrons will be the 'Jaguars' of HSL-60 at Mayport, Florida. Activated on 1 April 2001, the squadron is equipped with SH-60Bs.

Service extension for Cobras

As part of the Army's Aviation Force Modernization Plan (AMP) AH-1F Cobra attack helicopters assigned to Army National Guard units in 15 states were to have been retired by 30 September 2000 without receiving replacements. The deadline was eventually pushed out to 16 December 2000, however, on 4 December it was again rescinded and a special task force was convened to take a closer look at the service's transformation plan. Among its other tasks, the task force will develop an aviation resourcing plan covering fiscal years 2002 through 2007 and a timeline for retirement of the AH-1F and the UH-1H. Adjutant Generals in the affected states are concerned about the readiness of their forces and would like to retain the Cobras until 2002. Under the Army's modernisation plan the Cobra units will convert to the AH-64 Apache and RAH-66 Comanche, however there are currently not enough Apaches available and the Comanche is still several years away from entering the active inventory. The Army plans call for delivery of OH-58 Kiowas to these units as an interim platform, although the Kiowa is also

scheduled to be retired in 2004. The plan also calls for the establishment of multi-function battalions with 20 attack/reconnaissance helicopters in each MFB and 12 in the cavalry units.

Squadron activation

The 310th Airlift Squadron (AS), last active at Howard AFB, Panama, was reactivated at MacDill AFB, Panama on 1 January 2001. The squadron will eventually operate three C-37A Gulfstream Vs in support of the Commander in Chiefs (CINC) of US Central Command (USCENTCOM) and US Southern Command (USSOUTHCOM).

B-2 production indicators

In the hope of building more B-2s, officials from Northrop Grumman briefed aides to President George W. Bush on the company's ability to restart production of the controversial aircraft. The company believes it could deliver a first demonstration aircraft in four years at a cost of US$3.8 billion and build 40 new B-2 bombers for about US$28 billion.

T-3A Firefly disposal

The USAF is looking at three options for disposing of 107 grounded T-3A Firefly trainers. The options include export, mothballing and selling the planes for parts. Purchased at a cost of US$32.4 million, the aircraft have not been flown by students since 1997 as a result of a three crashes that killed six aircrew. The USAF permanently grounded the aircraft in October 1999 following a lengthy flight test programme at Edwards AFB, California, that found 10 mechanical and engine problems. Attempts have been made to sell the aircraft back to the manufacturer, Slingsby Aviation in the UK.

Longest-serving F-16A retired

After serving the USAF for 22 years, F-16A serial number 75-0750 ended its career as an advanced technology test aircraft on 9 January 2001 when it landed at Wright Patterson AFB, Ohio. Built as part of the Full Scale Development programme, the sixth F-16A first flew on 19 April 1978 and was used for avionics systems and reliability and maintainability testing. It was later modified as an Advanced Fighter Technology Integration (AFTI) demonstrator and last served as a testbed for the Joint Strike Fighter programme. The aircraft will eventually be placed on display in the USAF Museum.

Joint use facilities

The US Federal Aviation Administration recently announced that it has selected Gray Army Airfield, Fort Hood, Texas, March Air Reserve Base in Riverside, California, and Mather Airport in Sacramento, California, for the Military Airport Program (MAP). The programme is designed to relieve stress on the nation's air traffic control system by allowing civilians to use airports previously reserved for the military. In a reversal of an earlier decision, the USAF has rejected a proposal to establish a civilian commercial airport at Homestead Air Force Station near Miami. Homestead was destroyed by a hurricane in 1993 and rebuilt as an Air Reserve Station. In 1994 the USAF announced it intended to turn the base into a civilian airport.

OPERATIONS AND DEPLOYMENTS

An IDF/AF C-130 is loaded at Lod Air Base on 29 January prior to departure to India following a severe earthquake in the Gujarat region. A total of four Lockheed C-130s and two Boeing 707s was used to transport a complete field hospital to the disaster area.

A total of 245,600 lb (111400 kg) of humanitarian aid was delivered to the earthquake region by the USAF, using a combination of three C-5As from Travis AFB and four C-17As from McChord AFB. The C-5As transported the cargo (including tents and blankets, forklifts, sleeping bags and lifting equipment) to Andersen AFB, Guam (right). Here, the cargo was loaded onto the C-17s for the 13-hour flight to Ahmadabad, utilising KC-135 refuelling assets from Kadena AFB, Japan. The C-17s delivered their load to Ahmadabad on 3 February (below).

UNAMSIL helicopter operations

The United Nations Assistance Mission in Sierra Leone (UNAMSIL) has increased the strength of its avaition detachment based at Lungi airport, in support of some 11,000 UN peacekeeping troops currently deployed to the region. With the rebel Revolutionary United Front (RUF) having been forced back into the diamond fields in the east of the country, airborne support and supply has become increasingly important. By February 2001 four Mil Mi-24 'Hind-F', six Mil Mi-8/-17 'Hip', three Mil Mi-26 'Halo' and two Sikorsky S-61N helicopters were on strength. The Russian element of the UN operation consists of 115 pilots and technicians together with the four Mi-24 'Hinds', and has been operating in Sierra Leone since August 2000.

Above: A total of four Russian army aviation Mi-24s are based at Lungi and are sanctioned for use in the attack role. A previous lack of spares and ammunition has recently been rectified and practice attacks, using B-8V20 80-mm rocket pods, have been conducted off the coast. More than 80 percent of the aircrew have had previous combat experience in Afghanistan and Chechnya.

Above: In addition to UNAMSIL's assets, the Sierra Leone Ministry of Defence charters this Mi-24V through one of two Sierra Leone-registered companies (Inter Air and Diamond Airlines). Seen here at its base at Cockerill Barracks, Freetown, the aircraft is used to supply the more remote areas in which the Sierra Leone army is deployed. It is currently flown by a South African crew.

Above: Two Sikorsky S-61Ns, leased to the UN by Bristow Helicopters of the UK and operated by civilian crews, are among the hardest-working aircraft in the theatre. Regular supply flights are made to UN Forces in rural areas.

Left: The six 'Hips' and three Mi-26s are mainly tasked with personnel and troop transport. This Mi-17 is one of a number flown by Russian civilian crews.

Joint US-UK strike on Iraq

On 16 February 2001 USAF, US Navy and RAF aircraft attacked Iraqi air defence installations north of the 33rd Parallel, marking a possible change in offensive policy. Four Tornado GR.Mk 1s, with crews believed to be from No. 12 Squadron, participated in the raid joining F/A-18 Hornets from USS *Harry S. Truman* and USAF F-16s. The raid struck four air-defence radar and command, control and communications sites close to the Iraqi capital Baghdad, in response to increasing threats to aircraft patrolling the southern no-fly zone.

The raid was not, however, a complete success. Most of the AGM-145A Joint Standoff Weapons (JSOWs) are believed to have missed their targets. Reports suggested that the launch profile did not provide adequate time for the weapon's software to calculate local wind conditions and as a result the majority of the weapons missed by a similar distance and bearing from the target.

Six days later on 22 February, USAF assets attacked an anti-aircraft artillery site in the northern no-fly zone which had been targeting aircraft on routine patrols.

The US Navy's aircraft carrier Harry S. Truman *launches an F/A-18 Hornet during the 16 February raids on Iraqi air defence systems. The carrier also provided F-14 Tomcats which mounted combat air patrols and EA-6B Prowlers which provided the electronic warfare element of the strike.*

Dutch Apaches to Djibouti

Four AH-64Ds of the Royal Netherlands Air Force were deployed to Djibouti at the end of 2000 in support of the UN peacekeeping operation between warring factions in Ethiopia and Eritrea. Tensions are such that the UN has considered withdrawing its ground forces from disputed areas. Additional Dutch assets in the region include four RNAF CH-47D Chinooks and two Royal Netherlands Navy SH-14D Lynxes.

Carrier Battle Group return

The USS *George Washington* Carrier Battle Group (CVBG) concluded a six-month Mediterranean Sea/Persian Gulf deployment in late December 2000. While in-theatre, the CVBG participated in Destined Glory, the largest NATO exercise of 2000. The *George Washington* covered more than 400,000 miles in the six-month period and its airborne assets made more than 9,000 sorties and arrested carrier landings, including 800 in support of Operation Southern Watch.

Mine warfare training

Personnel assigned to helicopter mine countermeasures squadron HM-15 based at NAS Corpus Christi, Texas and helicopter combat support squadron HC-6 from Naval Station Norfolk participated in Gulf of Mexico Exercise (GOMEX) in January 2001, as part of their preparation for a deployment aboard the mine warfare command ship USS *Inchon*. The squadrons are now qualified for integrated surface, air explosive ordnance disposal mine countermeasures operations.

CAF deployments

In late 2000 Russia deployed a number of Tu-95 'Bear' bombers to forward operating locations in northern Russia. In response the Canadian Armed Forces deployed CF-188 Hornets from 4 Wing, CFB Cold Lake, Alberta and a CC-130H tanker from 17 Wing at CFB Winnipeg, Manitoba to its forward operating location at Inuvik, Northwest Territories. US forces in Alaska also increased readiness as part of the NORAD response.

UK C-17 procurement

RAF receives new-build Block XIIs

Below: 'UK 1' nears completion at Boeing's Long Beach plant in January 2001. With deliveries some 150 days ahead of contract in 2000, the USAF has been reassured that its on-going deliveries will not be adversely affected by the four UK aircraft.

Above: The RAF's C-17s are finished in overall grey with No. 99 Squadron's puma badge on the tail. The aircraft carry their UK serial number on the rear fuselage and on the nose with the USAF serial also beneath the latter in smaller type. Standard RAF roundels and fin flashes are also carried.

On 17 May 2001 the RAF will receive the first of four Boeing C-17A Globemaster IIIs, leased from Boeing, almost exactly one year after the deal was announced. The aircraft have been acquired as a 'stop-gap' measure pending delivery of the Airbus A400M (currently due to enter service in 2008). Key to the C-17's acquisition was its ability to fulfil Staff Requirement (Air) 448, which called for an aircraft to 'deploy high readiness Joint Rapid Reaction Forces (JRRF), including outsize equipment such as attack helicopters (Apache AH.Mk 1), large military vehicles and some Royal Engineer heavy or outsize equipment'.

The C-17s are extended-range Block XII aircraft that incorporate an additional 10,000-US gal (37053-litre) fuel tank in the previously 'dry' bay in the wing centre-section, adding some 600 nm (690 miles; 1110 km) to the aircraft's range with a 90,000-lb (40823-kg) payload. This operational advantage is of particular importance to the RAF, as the aircraft retain the USAF-standard 'flying boom' air-to-air refuelling system, which is not compatible with the RAF tanker force's 'probe and drogue' system. Refuelling from USAF tankers remains a theoretical possibility, but there are no plans at present to incorporate this into the training syllabus. Other modifications to Block XII C-17s include new software allowing the aircraft to comply with future Global Air Traffic Management (GATM) requirements and redesigned cockpit multi-function displays (MFDs) born out of operational experience in USAF service.

The first Block XII was the 71st production example (P71) and made its maiden flight in December 2000 as the first of 50 destined for service with the USAF, completing the original order for 120 C-17As. The USAF is however, seeking funding for an additional 60 C-17As to be delivered by 2008.

The RAF's examples (P77, 78, 80 and 81) will receive the serial numbers ZZ171-ZZ174 and the initial handover on 17 May 2001 will be followed by delivery of the other three aircraft to be completed by late August 2001.

The C-17s will be operated by No. 99 Squadron, which re-formed in October 2000 at RAF Brize Norton, Oxfordshire and will be operated solely in the strategic transport role, which does not include any of the tactical roles employed by USAF C-17s such as airborne delivery, paratroop dropping or low-level flying. It is hoped that two of the aircraft will be operational with the squadron by the end of 2001 and it is likely that a pair of the C-17s may take part in the JRRF proving exercise Saif Sareea II to be held in Oman in October 2001.

The aircraft's UK Military Aircraft Release (MAR) date is set for 1 April 2000, with the C-17 becoming the RAF's first major aircraft acquisition since the end of World War II to enter squadron service without a flight test programme in the UK. DERA has worked closely with the USAF and Boeing in order to validate the USAF's 'qualification and certification' for RAF operations, achieving this in under 12 months. UK clearance for the carriage of passengers and aeromedical evacuation is likely to be incorporated at a later date.

The four aircraft remain under the ownership of Boeing and the two key elements of training and logistic support are fulfilled by a unique agreement between the USAF's Foreign Military Sales (FMS) and the UK's Defence Procurement Agency (DPA).

Under the FMS agreement the USAF Air Education and Training Command will provide training for the RAF's pilots and loadmasters at Altus AFB, Oklahoma. RAF personnel will be 'slotted' into the USAF's on-going courses conducted by the 58th Airlift Squadron, missing out the non-applicable 'tactical' elements of the training. Boeing will provide academic and 'ground school' elements of the course. Once RAF aircrew have completed the 10-week course at Altus they will undergo the 'seasoning' process at Charleston AFB, South Carolina. This 'OCU' phase of training involves acting as supernumerary crew members on a wide-range of missions as part of the 437th Airlift Wing. To assist follow-on courses in the UK, a USAF Mobile Training Team will be regularly deployed to Brize Norton on a consultative basis. Maintenance engineer training will also be conducted in Charleston at a purpose-built 'RAF school' before they too receive 'seasoning' training at the 437th AW's facilities.

For logistical support, the RAF's C-17 will effectively be placed into the USAF's Flexible Sustainment contract with Boeing, allowing logistical support to function as part of the USAF's 'virtual fleet'. This arrangement allows access to USAF-owned spares around the world as well as in-country field support, the supply and updating of technical orders and data, mission planning systems and electronic warfare support. At Brize Norton Boeing has established a field service team which will provide on-site technical support, 'off-wing' engine maintenance, asset management, stores control and other essential services. The RAF will be responsible for all on-aircraft maintenance including wheels, tyres and flight servicing.

In preparation for the C-17's arrival at Brize Norton, No. 99 Squadron's new headquarters and storage facilities are under construction, modifications have been made to the hangars to completely enclose the aircraft and a cargo bay mock-up is being assembled at the Joint Air Transport Evaluation Unit (JATEU) for the clearance of specific loads.

Daniel J. March

A key factor in the UK's decision to acquire the C-17 was the availability of the extended-range Block XII. The most obvious modification is the prominent additional fuel tank in the centre-section of the wing (above right). Other improvements to the Block XII are centred around the cockpit displays (below right) which have been improved in terms of performance and user-friendliness. The first production Block XII (below) is the 71st C-17 from Long Beach's production line and is seen in the unpainted condition in which it conducted a series of 'proving' flights in January 2001.

LCA development

LCA demonstrator begins flight tests

After one of the most protracted development periods in the history of aviation, India's indigenous Light Combat Aircraft (LCA) technology demonstrator finally took to the air for the first time on 4 January 2001.

The LCA project was launched by the Indian government in 1983 in response to an Indian Air Force (IAF) Air Staff Target issued in the late-1970s for a MiG-21 replacement. The aircraft was to be designed primarily for air defence, with a secondary close air support capability; it was also to be highly agile and incorporate state-of-the-art avionics and weapons systems.

Development of the aircraft was seen as the flagship constituent of a new indigenous aviation (and other military hardware) industry capable of supplying the Indian armed forces with modern, technologically advanced equipment and in the process eradicating India's reliance on Soviet or Western manufacturers and the prevailing politics of their governments.

India's experience in building post-war combat aircraft had been limited to the noticeably unsuccessful HAL HF-24 Marut of the 1960s and the industry was basically starting at 'ground-zero' with little in the way of design experience, technological expertise or construction facilities. After initial Indian research studies, four European aircraft manufacturers (BAe, Dassault, Dornier and MBB) were invited to submit feasibility studies for a low-cost fighter which could be developed and built indigenously but could

The first LCA technology demonstrator made its maiden 18-minute flight from HAL's Bangalore headquarters on 4 January 2001, piloted by Wing Commander Rajiv Kothiyal of ADA's National Flight Test Centre. Escorted by two IAF Mirage 2000Hs, the aircraft conducted a flypast at Aero India 2001, Yelahanka Air Base, during its fourth test flight five days later (above). A full-scale mock-up was exhibited at the show (top).

incorporate the technology envisaged for other 'fourth-generation' fighters. scheduled to enter service towards the end of the century.

MBB were awarded the consultancy contract in late 1983 for the LCA's project definition phase (PDP). Reports soon highlighted an almost complete lack of research and planning in aerospace technology and an unweildy and disparate industry lacking goals and central guidance.

In 1985, Dassault replaced MBB as the partner for detailed design work in conjunction with a new LCA project design team established at Bangalore under the leadership of Dr Kota Harinarayana (the influence of Dassault's Mirage 2000 is evident in the LCA's final configuration). The team would work under the umbrella of the newly formed Aeronautical Development Agency (ADA) – an autonomous branch of the government's Defence Research and Development Organisation (DR&DO). The first task undertaken by the ADA was a detailed survey of the available scientific talent and modern industrial capability throughout the country in

The ADA designed and built its own wind tunnel test facility for the LCA project. The tests were conducted by the National Aerospace Laboratories (NAL) and the results, along with aerodynamic computer simulations, played a major part in defining the LCA's configuration. Early designs with canards resembling those of the Saab Gripen were abandoned in favour of a single-wing, cranked-delta layout.

both private and public sectors. This initial work proved vital in the design and construction phases, with over 400 establishments eventually involved in the project.

By the mid-1980s the Indian Air Force had formalised its Air Staff Requirement (ASR) for the MiG-21 replacement with an in-service date of the mid-1990s. Many major obstacles needed to be overcome to meet such a demanding schedule, most notably in the development of a modern multi-mode radar, fly-by-wire controls systems, carbon composite construction techniques and a high-performance augmented turbofan engine.

With little Indian expertise in these areas the ADA was tasked with importing these technologies, from whatever source, and integrating the technology into the research and development institutions.

In June 1993, some 10 years after the project launch, ADA had progressed enough in terms of design work and forging alliances with foreign aerospace companies for the Indian government to formally sanction the LCA programme. A budget of Rs.2200 billion (US$630 million) was allocated for Phase I development, of which some 40 per cent was allocated to pay for essential foreign equipment and consultancy fees.

Construction of the first of two Full Scale Engineering Development (FSED) aircraft began within weeks. Non-representative of the produc-

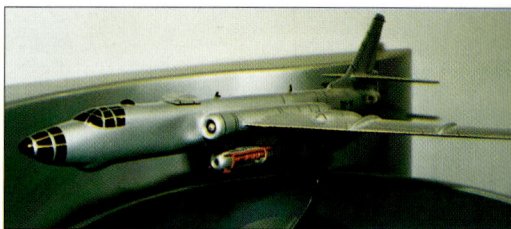

Above: The GTRE GTX-35VS engine is currently undergoing ground and flight tests at Russian facilities. Air tests are being conducted on a specially modified Tupolev Tu-16. Around 80 more hours of air testing, including high-altitude trials, are scheduled for 2001.

Left: The development of the LCA's multi-mode radar has been hit by numerous delays. Trials are conducted on this modified BAe 748, however, the final production version of the radar is unlikely to be available for several years.

tion version, the two technology demonstrators would, by necessity, incorporate many foreign components. International participation included Ericsson/Ferranti (multi-mode radar), Martin Marietta (flight controls), General Electric (F404-F2J3 turbofan), BAe (control law consultancy) and Alenia (CFC wing panels).

The first FSED aircraft (TD-1) was rolled out nine months behind schedule in November 1995, but already many of the essential components were subject to major delays and the planned first flight date of mid-1997 was viewed as optimistic in the extreme.

As the most experienced Indian aircraft manufacturer, Hindustan Aeronautics Ltd (HAL) is the principal partner responsible for the design and fabrication of the aircraft and the integration of the numerous components being developed by agencies around the country. Principal among these is the Aeronautical Development Establishment (ADE) – responsible for developing the flight control system, the cockpit displays and processors. Although running around three years behind schedule by 1997, the ADE had teamed-up with Lockheed Martin Control Systems and a joint development of an Engineering Test Station to test the Digital Flight Control Computer was underway. However, another major setback was to befall the LCA programme in mid-1998 with the imposition of US sanctions after India's Pokhran nuclear weapon tests. All US support for the LCA programme was withdrawn (a situation which remains today) causing not only the ADE to redesign the flight control system, but also major delays for most other major components which incorporated US technology to a greater or lesser degree.

Not least of these problems was the withdrawal of support by General Electric of its F404-F2J3 powerplant. Although never intended to power production versions of the LCA, 11 F404s were purchased for development aircraft and testing prior to the introduction of the indigenous GTX-35VS Kaveri engine.

The fate of the entire LCA project is inexorably linked to the successful development of the Kaveri. Initial design work on the GTX engine by the Gas Turbine Research Establishment (GTRE) actually commenced

Envisaged for service aboard India's new aircraft-carrier, the 'navalised' LCA prototype is scheduled to fly in 2003. ADA is confident that the development of trainer and naval versions will appeal to the export market helping drive down individual aircraft unit costs from US$17 million to US$15 million.

before the LCA project was officially sanctioned. In a mirror image of LCA itself, the Kaveri project team had to basically 're-invent the wheel' in gaining the experience, technology and construction techniques for producing a powerplant in this class. The F404 engine fitted to the TD aircraft represents the minimum standard required from the Kaveri in terms of thrust-to-weight ratio and fuel consumption. Current predictions by the GTRE predict the engine will be in the 80.45-kN (18,078-lb) thrust range – some 13 per cent more powerful than the F404.

Powerplant test programme

By February 2001 the first three prototype engines were undergoing tests in Russia including high-altitude trials, with the fourth and fifth engines joining the test programme by late 2001. A further 18 engines will be built for test purposes before the Kaveri is installed in the first of five Phase II aircraft (three single-seat fighters, one two-seat trainer and one aircraft carrier-compatible naval version). The flight test programme for the Kaveri is scheduled to be completed in mid-2002, with the first Kaveri-powered LCA scheduled to fly in 2003.

Surrounding the euphoria of TD-1's first flight, which Indian Minister of Defence George Fernandes called a "red letter day", adding "India has joined a club of seven to eight countries which have the capability of making a supersonic fighter aircraft", major debates concerning the 'indigenousness' of the aircraft continue. A report claiming that only 30 percent of the aircraft is of an indigenous nature was refuted by India's Scientific Adviser Dr V. K. Atre, who claimed that the aircraft had achieved 70 per cent localisation with "major efforts now being made to make that over 80 per cent". The IAF remains sceptical of the ADA's claims and unofficial reports intimate

that it has little enthusiasm for the project. A defence committee report published in January 2001 heavily criticised the Indian MoD for the protracted delays to the LCA programme stating "The long delay in developing the LCA has contributed enormously to the creation of a situation where the air force is facing an imminent depletion of strength". It also stated that doubts surrounding its future had forced the IAF to initiate expensive import (Su-27 and Su-30) and upgrade (MiG-21bis-UPG; see following page) projects. A previous Controller and Auditor General (CAG) report stated the programme was "beset with delays for almost every vital component of the aircraft". The flight control system, radar and Kaveri engine were behind schedule with "no amount of certainty about their date of of satisfactory development and final cost". Service officials briefed the Parliamentary Committee on Defence that the aircraft was unlikely to enter series production until 2015 – over 30 years after the project was initiated

What is certain is that many important features of the aircraft are yet to be integrated, including the radar, HUD (due to be tested on TD-2), some system avionics, the engine and the flight control laws. Radar development, conducted jointly by HAL and the Electronic Research and Development Establishment, hit further problems when in February 2001 a crucial deal for radars from the Swedish manufacturer Ericcsson fell through on price grounds. Although Ericsson have been retained on a consultancy basis it is inevitable that further delays in finalising a production standard multi-mode radar will ensue.

In contrast to scepticism, both within Indian and from foreign manufacturers, the ADA remains upbeat in the LCA's future. Dr Atre claims that the aircraft will be ready for series

The LCA is designed to carry 4000 kg (8,820 lb) of stores on seven weapon stations beneath the fuselage and wing. Projected ordnance includes close combat and beyond-visual-range missiles, air-to-surface missiles, anti-ship missiles, conventional bombs, EW pods and external fuel tanks. Some 2,000 hours of flight tests will be conducted before the aircraft receives operational clearance.

production in 2007. TD-2 is due to fly in mid-2001 with the first prototype to follow by the end of the year. The fourth aircraft will have the integrated weapons management system and the fifth will be complete in all respects. These will be followed in 2003 by the LCA trainer prototype and subsequently by the 'naval' LCA. Dr Atre has also stated that an intensive period of flight testing will be conducted with TD-1 over the following months with the first supersonic flight scheduled after some 40-50 flight envelope expansion sorties.

Ever growing concerns from within the IAF and government as to the viability and ever rising costs of the programme may well prompt a change of direction from independent indigenous development. In January 2001 Defence Minister Fernandes stated, "I know there will be several people who will be concerned about India's progress in aeronautics, and several of them who are jealous. We should ignore them all. There are several who want to join hands with us, and we will welcome them". This courting of risk-sharing partners has prompted an

immediate response with both BAE Systems and the Sukhoi design bureau expressing an interest in creating partnership agreements.

In spite of the major delays and cost overruns, the fact the LCA has now entered its flight test phase is rightly perceived as a major achievement by the Indian aerospace industry. Whether the project continues as a wholly indigenous or risk-sharing programme, the ADA is confident that the aircraft will form the backbone of India's fighter force for over 30 years.

Daniel J. March

IAF MiG-21 upgrade

MiG-21bis-UPGs return to India

The first MiG-21bis-UPG is seen at Nizhniy Novgorod during the handover ceremony to Indian officials. The MiG-21 upgrade programme was initiated due to delays in India's indigenous LCA project, which is unlikely to enter squadron service before 2010.

On completion of the flight test programme at the Russian air force's Akhtubinsk research centre, the first two upgraded MiG-21bis aircraft, C2777 (001) and C2769 (002), were handed over to Indian officials on 14 December 2000 at Nizhniy Novgorod, Russia. The upgrades were completed at the local Sokol factory and the aircraft have received the designation MiG-21bis-UPG, in place of the Russian designation MiG-21-93. Both examples returned to India on 25 December for official commissioning into the Indian Air Force.

The tests, during which both upgraded aircraft completed around 300 flights, concerned mainly the application of new types of armament, including close-air combat R-73 (AA-11 'Archer') missiles combined with helmet-mounted sight and medium-range RVV-AE (AA-12 'Adder') missiles, as well as KAB-500Kr guided bombs. The tests commenced in mid-May 1999, when a modernised MiG-21 shot down an La-17M target drone using an R-73 air-to-air missile. In August 1999, the medium-range RVV-AE missile was launched for the first time from one of the upgraded aircraft. The final tests, carried out in early October 2000, consisted of the simultaneous destruction of two La-17 targets by two RVV-AE missiles. Twelve missiles were launched

during the entire test programme, all of which were successful according to Russian sources.

The US$340 million contract, signed on 1 March 1996, provides for the modernisation of 125 MiG-21bis aircraft, with an option on a further 50. Following Indian air force evaluation, the subsequent 123 aircraft will be modernised by Hindustan Aeronautics Ltd. at Nasik, where a total of 180 MiG-21bises was manufactured between 1980 and 1987. Completion date for the entire upgrade programme was originally scheduled for 2000, but delays in finalising the exact specification for the aircraft's avionics and software have caused delays of some three years, with completion of the UPG programme now expected in 2003.

The first locally-upgraded MiG-21bis-UPG by HAL at Nasik is tabled to fly in the first half of 2001, with the completion of subsequent airframes depending largely on deliveries of the upgrade packages (with Kopyo radars) from Russia. In 2000 Russia delivered six upgrade packages, with the next nine packages being delivered in February 2001. Presently, 15 aircraft are being prepared for modernisation at Nasik, and HAL is optimistic that delivery of all 123 upgrade packages from Russia will be completed in 2002.

The upgrade package was designed and implemented by Sokol's Nizhniy Novgorod plant, the Russian Aircraft Corporation MiG and Phazotron-NIIR radar design bureau. Integration of the aircraft's systems was conducted by GosNIIAS State Scientific-Research Institute of Aviation. The principal feature of the upgrade is the inclusion of the Phazotron-NIIR Kopyo radar. In addition, India selected 10 systems of non-Russian manufacture, including the Sextant Avionique Totem 221G navigation system, Indian radio equipment (communications, radio altimeter, radio compass, transponder) and radar warning unit, Israeli-built flare dispensers, and a French video-recording system. The aircraft will also be equipped with Indian-designed EW equipment.

During the flight test programme in 2000, Russia offered to finish the aircraft with radiation absorbing paint as an additional supplement to the contract. In May 2000 a RAM-coated aircraft was demonstrated to Indian representatives at Nizhniy Novgorod. Flight test data revealed that the detection range of the aircraft with the absorbing coating was some 50 percent less by comparison with a standard aircraft. According to Russian theoretical calculation, the effective radar cross-section of a MiG-21 with the absorbing coating could be reduced to as low as 10 per cent compared to aircraft without the coating.

Piotr Butowski

Anatoliy Kanashtchenkov, director general of Phazotron-NIIR, expects follow-on orders for around 50-70 upgrade packages for the IAF's MiG-21 fleet. In addition, negotiations are underway for the licence production of the Kopyo radar in India, not only for the MiG-21, but also for predicted IAF MiG-29 upgrades and for the MiG-AT combat trainer, if selected.

Dassault Mirage F1

Armée de l'Air versions

Dassault's attractive Mirage F1 design may have been overshadowed in the fighter role by the fly-by-wire Mirage 2000, but the aircraft continues to play an important part in Armée de l'Air operations. Interceptors made redundant by the introduction of the Mirage 2000 have been reworked as fighter-bombers with considerable success, seeing action over Kosovo during Allied Force, while the Mirage F1CR retains its place as France's premier reconnaissance platform. The type will serve until sufficient numbers of Rafales become available some time in the next decade.

The two principal in-service variants are represented here by a Mirage F1CT of EC 2/30 'Normandie-Niémen' (right) and a quartet of F1CRs from ER 2/33 'Savoie' (below). Although they are primarily assigned to attack and reconnaissance, respectively, the CT retains full fighter capability (and some can undertake reconnaissance), while the CR is routinely used in its secondary bomber role.

Dassault has never built aircraft simply to meet Armée de l'Air requirements. The low cost and versatility required for export success have always been important design drivers for Dassault, although the Mirage F1 was actually designed to meet an Armée de l'Air specification which itself called for a dual-role aircraft. The French required a Mirage III replacement – a Mach 2.5-capable high altitude interceptor to replace the Mirage IIIC interceptor and a fighter-bomber to replace the Mirage IIIE. The new fighter was actually based on the fuselage of the Mirage IIIE, with the Atar 09K engine of the Mirage IV, married to a newly designed shoulder-mounted wing and a conventional horizontal tailplane, although it was originally designed around a larger fuselage and American TF30 engine.

The basic aircraft was offered in four basic sub-variants – the 'radar-less' day-attack Mirage F1A (exported to Libya and South Africa), the two-seat Mirage F1B and F1D trainers, the Cyrano IV-equipped Mirage F1C dedicated fighter, and the multi-role Mirage F1E. In the event, the French Armée de l'Air originally selected only the F1C fighter (and F1B trainer), using the type originally only as a Mirage IIIC replacement.

The Mirage F1's inherent versatility was exploited in a number of export versions (the first being South Africa's Mirage F1AZs and Ecuador's F1JAs) but France did not receive a multi-role F1 until 1983, with the delivery of the first F1CR reconnaissance aircraft.

Reconnaissance variant

The Mirage F1 was the natural choice when it came time to replace the Armée de l'Air's ageing Mirage IIIRs. In fact, a Jaguar recce version might have produced a better low-level tactical reconnaissance aircraft, but its half-British parentage and a shortage of available airframes counted against the SEPECAT aircraft, and the decision was taken to produce a recce version of the single-engined (but all-French) Mirage F1, despite the fact that (in French service at least) this had been designed and optimised as a fighter.

The Mirage F1CR was effectively a variant of the multi-role F1E, although the prototypes

were converted from F1C-200s taken from the Bordeaux production line. As such, the F1CR did have a stretched forward fuselage and fixed inflight refuelling probe, and the Cyrano IVM radar with expanded air-to-ground and mapping capabilities. These same modifications had already been applied to the basic F1C fighter to produce the Mirage F1C-200, which effectively became equivalent to the F1E, although the Armée de l'Air never exploited its latent multi-role capabilities. Previous French tactical recce aircraft had been fitted with dramatically re-designed nose sections housing the majority of their sensors. By contrast, the Mirage F1CR has a relatively limited internal mission fit, carrying most of its reconnaissance equipment in external pods.

Apart from its grey/green disruptive camouflage (ocassionally replaced in recent years by a sand/stone camouflage), the F1CR looked almost identical to the original F1C-200 fighter, externally. The new version did introduce a prominent undernose bulge with a lateral 'letterbox' aperture. This formed an access hatch over a new camera bay which could accommodate either a 75-mm focal length

Around 35 standard F1B two-seaters and F1C fighters remain in AdA service, primarily for conversion training (with EC 3/33 'Lorraine') although around eight of the F1Cs are allocated a front-line fighter role protecting the French outpost in Djibouti with EC 4/33 'Vexin'. The F1B cannot refuel inflight, but can mount a dummy probe to allow dry contacts to be made for training, as seen here.

The F1CR is expected to remain in service until around 2010-15, with Rafale eventually assuming the reconnaissance role. This trio is from ER 2/33, one of two sqaudrons which fly the type.

Thomson-TRT (Omera) 40 panoramic camera (recording onto 216-mm x 57-mm film) or a 150-mm focal length TRT 33 giving an image size of 114 x 114-mm. The starboard cannon was deleted and replaced by an SAT SCM2400

Super Cyclope IRLS, with a small (downward-looking) rectangular aperture immediately in front of the prominent underfuselage heat-exchanger intake. Data from Super Cyclope can theoretically be down-loaded in flight via an onboard datalink, though because this works by line of sight, range is very limited, except at high altitude. The normal cannon port and 'blast tube' remained visible below the

fuselage, albeit without the cannon muzzle projecting.

Under the skin, the Mirage F1CR has a multi-role avionics suite built around a Dassault Electronique central computer, SAGEM Uliss 47 INS and a new Thomson-CSF VE-120 CRT HUD, with refined cockpit displays and control panels. Even more interestingly, the F1CR has a zero-zero SEM/Martin Baker Mk 10 ejection seat

F1CR reconnaissance systems

Externally-carried recce equipment used by the Mirage F1CR includes a podded **RAPHAEL-TH** (RAdar de PHotographique Aérienne ELectrique á Transmission Hertzienne) SLAR (weighing in at 565-kg/1,246-lb) – sometimes referred to as SLAR-2000 – and the Thomson-CSF **ASTAC** (Analyseur de Signeaux TACtiques) Elint pod. The Cyclope IRLS pod used by the Mirage IIIR has been retired, replaced by the Mirage F1CR's internal fit, while the RP-35P (a modified fuel tank with an OMERA 60

A reconnaissance technician removes the film canister from the undernose TRT panoramic camera. Two cameras of different focal lengths are routinely used: the 75-mm TRT 40 and 150-mm TRT 33.

camera in the nose) originally used only by the F1Cs and F1C-200s deployed to Djibouti, has more recently been used by F1CTs over Kosovo and northern Iraq.

Various other recce pods have been cleared for use by the Mirage F1, but these are used only by export customers, and not by the F1CR. These include the Dassault HAROLD LOROP pod, containing a TRT 38 camera, the Dassault NORA pod, with real-time video sensors, and the similar Thomson-CSF TMV 018 Syrel pod. The Dassault COR-2 pod contains a mix of TRT-35 cameras, a panoramic TRT 70 and a Super Cyclope IRLS.

ER 33 has also received seven new Thomson-CSF Optronics **PRESTO** (Pod REconnaissance STand Off) reconnaissance pods. The PRESTO pod was delivered with a conventional 'wet film' MDS 610 LOROP camera with a 610-mm focal length f4 lens, though the pods are due to be upgraded to DÉSIRÉ (DÉmonstrateur SImplifé de Reconnaissance Électro-optique) standards with an EO version of the camera, using a 10,000-pixel CCD and a 240Mb per second high speed recorder instead of conventional film. The original DÉSIRÉ pod was evaluated in December 1997 during a Southern Watch mission, carried by a Mirage F1CR. The new camera will be linked to the aircraft's navigation and mission planning systems, allowing it to 'know' where to 'look' and to function autonomously, allowing the pilot to simply concentrate on flying his mission.

From 1984, each F1CR-equipped escadron received an air-transportable imagery exploitation facility, built up around eight processing, analysis and datalink caravans. This facility is known as **SARA** (Système d'Aérotransportable de Reconnaissance Aérienne).

The majority of the F1CR's mission equipment is carried in podded form under the belly. Shown above is the forward-looking infra-red pod used for low-level night flying, the fitment of which requires the removal of the remaining cannon. Below is an ASTAC pod, used for tactical Elint gathering.

rather than the zero-ninety F1RM4 seat (a seat requiring, at zero altitude, ninety knots forward speed) originally fitted to most F1s.

In Armée de l'Air service, the Mirage F1CR is very much a multi-role aircraft, with the ability to conduct armed reconnaissance missions, and with a real and frequently practised 'stand-alone' secondary ground attack commitment. The Mirage F1CR operated in the air-to-ground and recce roles in the Gulf War (known to the Armée de l'Air as Operation Daguet) sometimes using its air-to-ground radar modes to lead formations of Jaguars, and usually carrying a heavier load than the dedicated Anglo-French fighter bombers.

The Mirage F1CR's multi-role capability was enhanced by the upgrade of the radar to Cyrano IVMR standards, adding ground mapping, contour mapping, blind penetration and Doppler Beam Sharpening modes. From 1993, some Mirage F1CRs were fitted with a FLIR pod in place of the remaining (port) cannon, and they have begun to receive provision for Corail flare dispensers (like miniature underwing pylons) attached to the wing's lower surface between the root and the inboard hardpoint. More recently still, the Mirage F1CRs have had their RAPHAEL SLAR pods modified with a UHF real-time datalink, and synthetic aperture and MTI modes.

Illustrating the F1CR's secondary bombing role, this ER 2/33 aircraft is seen during a mission over Bosnia armed with a pair of GBU-12 Paveway II 500-lb (227-kg) bombs, as well as the standard wingtip self-defence armament of two R550 Magic IIs.

Remarkably, a small number of unmodified Mirage F1Cs remain in use in the air defence role (and for training) even within the French Armée de l'Air, though this has been limited to about eight aircraft based in Djibouti since the conversion of EC 5 (1988-1990) and EC 12 (1991-1995) to the Mirage 2000C, and the transfer of EC 30 to the air-to-ground role in 1993.

In December 1988, with the plentiful availability of the Mirage 2000C RDI, the Armée de l'Air began a programme to modify 41 surplus inflight refuelling-capable F1C-200 fighters for the fighter-bomber role as the Mirage F1CT, to replace the ageing Mirage 5F. Dassault had built

Carrying live Magic 2 missiles, an ER 1/33 F1CR flies over the Adriatic with a multi-sensor pod.

Below: Datalink equipment allows the F1CR to relay back real-time IR imagery to the SARA ground station.

Below: During the war in Bosnia, F1CRs often used the ASTAC pod, as carried by this aircraft about to refuel over the Adriatic. The pod allowed the location and analysis of air defence radars.

Mirage F1 defences

Right: This F1CT carries a Barax jamming pod on the outboard pylon, identified by the blade antennas projecting down from the pod. Between the inboard pylon and the fuselage is the Corail chaff/flare dispenser.

Left: A Mirage F1CT releases flares during a practice bomb run at Cazaux. The Corail dispenser usually houses flares, while chaff is released from a Phimat dispenser carried on the opposite pylon to the ECM pod.

Right: The second-generation Barracuda pod is replacing the Barax, and is identified by the two bulges at either end. This aircraft also carries an 18-round 68-mm rocket launcher, a weapon that is still employed on occasion by the F1CT.

some 103 standard F1Cs (four of which were converted to the later F1C-200 standard) plus 83 F1C-200s. The number of aircraft to be converted was subsequently raised to 55 in 1992, following the successful first flight of the prototype at the CEV at Istres on 3 May 1991. The two prototypes were converted by Dassault at Biarritz-Parme, while 'production conversions' were undertaken in the Atelier Industriel de l'Armée de l'Air at Clermont Ferrand/Aulnat.

The new fighter-bomber variant was in many respects similar to the recce F1CR, and introduced a Dassault Electronique M 182XR computer, a SAGEM Uliss 47R INS, a Thomson VE 120 HUD and a TMV 630A laser rangefinder in a new undernose fairing. The aircraft also received a new defensive aids system, with

During the F1CT conversion process, the fighter-bomber acquired the excellent navigation system proven in the F1CR. This led to a handful of aircraft being permanently detached to Africa, where precise autonomous navigation is required. Flying 'au radada' (as low-level is known in France) is an F1CT from the CEAM test centre's EC 5/330 'Côte d'Argent'.

Sherloc RHAWS. The latter equipment uses rectangular antenna fairings on the fin, providing an immediate recognition feature. The new avionics systems necessitated removal of the port cannon. Finally, the former air defence fighters were re-painted in a smart grey/green disruptive camouflage, similar to that applied to the Mirage F1CR, but extending, 'wraparound'-fashion, over the undersides.

Air defence role

The F1CT retained the type's ability to carry the BVR MATRA Super 530F AAM, and can be fitted with wingtip launch rails for R550 Magic II IR-homing AAMs for self defence. The aircraft retains the basic Cyrano IVM radar, with air-to-air modes, and front-line Mirage F1CTs have often flown air defence missions with full air-to-air armament. The aircraft has a centreline pylon 'fully plumbed' for the carriage of external fuel tanks, either of the standard 1200-litre (264-Imp gal) capacity or the grossly distended 2200-litre (484-Imp gal) 'Gros Bidon Irakien' (Big Iraqi Fuel Tank) used by F1C-200s and F1CRs during the Gulf War. Air-to-ground

weapons cleared for use by the Mirage F1CT include GBU-12 Paveway II or French 400-kg (882-lb) or 1000-kg (2,205-lb) LGBs, BAP 100 anti-runway weapons, BAT 120s, Belouga CBUs, and F4 rocket pods containing 18 68-mm rockets. The aircraft can also carry Phimat chaff dispenser pods, Corail flare dispensers, and Barracuda or Barax jammers.

The first Mirage F1CT unit was EC 1/13 'Artois' at Colmar, which officially received its first aircraft on 6 November 1992. The unit had in fact detached to Mont-de-Marsan to begin conversion in April, following the deployment of the first F1CT to the CEAM there on 13 February 1992.

EC 3/13 'Auvergne' at Colmar received its first Mirage F1CT on 23 April 1993. 'Artois' and 'Auvergne' were destined to have a short life with Mirage F1s. EC 1/13 'Artois' and EC 3/13 'Auvergne', respectively, became EC 1/13 'Normandie-Niémen' and EC 3/13 'Alsace' on 1 August 1993. Conversion of EC 13's last squadron (EC 2/13 'Alpes') was cancelled when it was decided to move to a two-escadron-per-escadre unit structure. The two squadrons were

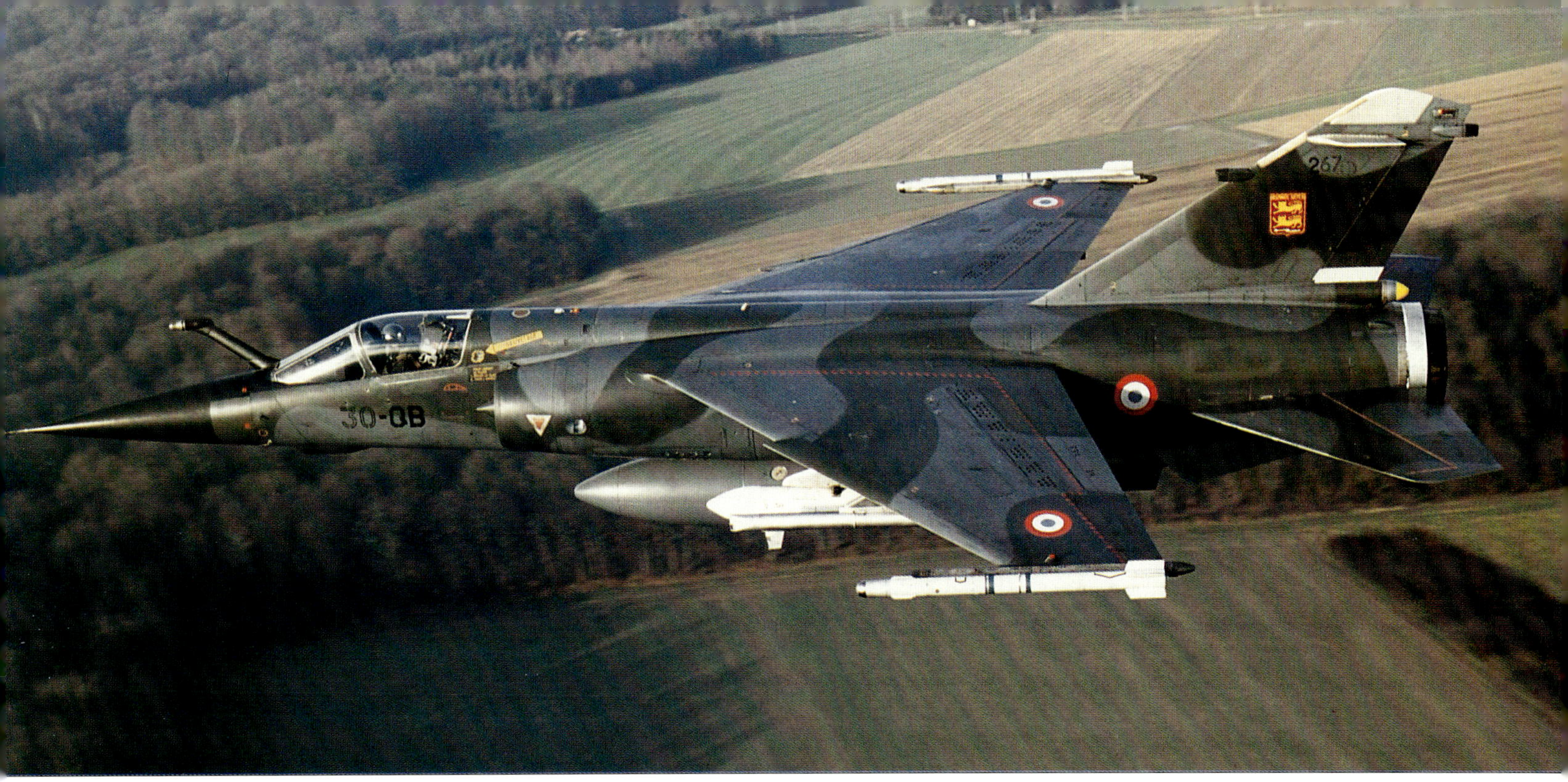

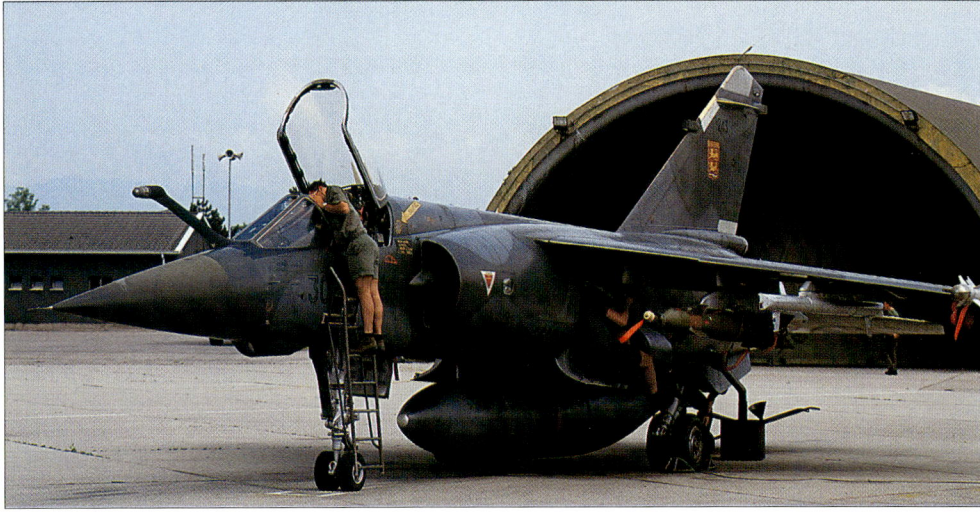

The F1CT programme has provided the AdA with two squadrons of highly versatile multi-role aircraft, able to undertake fighter, bomber or reconnaissance missions. They are consequently regularly called upon for out-of-area operations, and were highly successful during the Kosovo conflict. Above is an aircraft from EC 2/30 on a peacetime training mission, while at right is another aircraft from the squadron, armed with GBU-12s, caught between Allied Force missions at Istrana.

re-designated again on 1 July 1995, becoming EC 2/30 'Normandie-Niémen' and EC 1/30 'Alsace', respectively. Since the end of Desert Storm, the Mirage F1 force has continued to be extremely busy, participating in Operations over Bosnia, Kosovo and Serbia, and participating in the ongoing operations over Iraq. The Mirage F1CT offers a useful deployable asset; cheaper, more reliable and more robust than the over-tasked Mirage 2000D, and able to carry a larger warload than the Jaguar, which in any case has tended to specialise in delivery of (and designation for) PGMs and anti-radar missiles. Thus EC 3/7 'Languedoc' has tended to specialise in the delivery of LGBs and the AS30L missile, while EC 1/7 'Provence' uses the AS37 Martel missile. An British reader might be surprised by the apparent primacy of the Mirage F1 over the Jaguar, but should remember that the French Jaguars are very different animals to the much-modernised and upgraded Jaguars used by the RAF. The French aircraft never had even the original NAVWASS fitted to the first RAF Jaguars, and still have an extremely austere cockpit and avionics fit, while the aircraft are still powered by the original, rather inadequate 100-series Adour engine.

Most recently, the Mirage F1CT and F1CR

Mirage F1CT optics

Added to the F1CT for accurate bombing is the TMV 630A laser rangefinder. The later TMV 632 is being fitted across the fleet.

A number of F1CTs have been fitted with a small reconnaissance camera in the lower fuselage side, angled outwards and downwards.

A key feature of the F1CT is its rapid deployability to airfields with little or no ground infrastructure to support it. Here an F1CT refuels on the ground from a Transall C.160R of ET 1/64 in a scenario that could just as easily be played out at a remote strip in Africa.

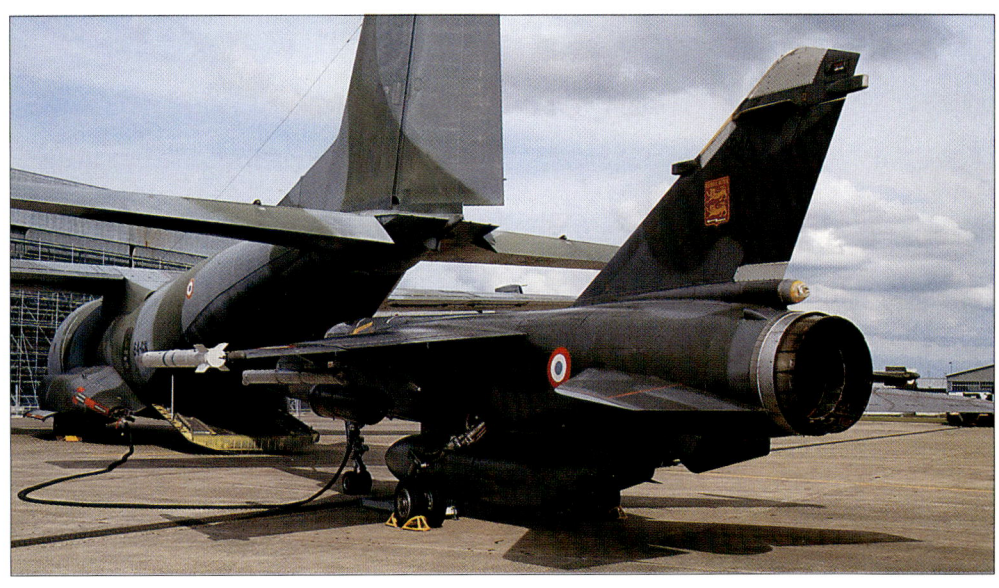

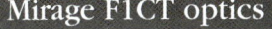

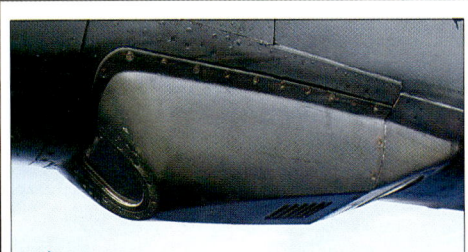

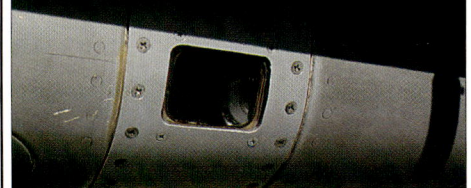

Above: An F1CT trails an F1C-200 (the suffix denoting the addition of a refuelling probe) during a flight from Mont-de-Marsan, home of the CEAM to which both aircraft belong. A few F1Cs retain the slate grey scheme worn when the type entered service as a pure fighter.

Left: The majority of surviving F1Cs wear the two-tone sand/brown camouflage adopted for operations in Djibouti. Escadron de Chasse 3/33 at Reims is the training unit, but also parents the operational fighter unit (EC 4/33) in Africa.

With around 90 front-line F1C/F1CR/F1CT aircraft still operational in 2001, and a figure of 55 projected for 2010, a sizeable training effort continues with EC 3/33. This trio of Mirage F1Bs carries MATRA Super 530F missiles for a missile practice camp at Solenzara on Corsica.

were heavily committed to Operation Allied Force over Kosovo. Ten F1CTs (229, 234, 237, 243, 244, 254, 256, 260, 278, and 280) drawn mainly from EC 1/30 were deployed to Istrana between 16 May and 25 June 1999, for Operation Trident (the French part of Allied Force). Eighteen pilots (four from 'Alsace') flew a total of 70 sorties, totalling 300 flying hours, and delivered 77 GBU-12 LGBs on a diverse range of targets. The aircraft each wore a small Varga-style nose art on their intakes, and had outline GBU-12s applied for each mission flown. The aircraft acted as pure 'LGB trucks', with ATLIS-equipped French Jaguars providing laser designation. Six F1CRs were deployed to Solenzara, Corsica, and 10 more (from ER 2/33) to Istrana, and these operated with the ASTAC

Elint pod, RAPHAEL SLAR, and with RP-35P, and PRESTO (and possibly DÉSIRÉ) pods.

The Mirage F1CT is presently expected to remain in service until replaced by the Rafale. The first Rafales are now expected to enter service in 2005, and the Mirage F1CT is expected to stay in the French front line for another 10 years, although a recently announced Jaguar upgrade may change the order in which EC 7 and EC 30 convert to the new aircraft. ER 33 seems likely to outlive both wings, although the F1CTs may yet take over the recce task, leaving Jaguars in the air-to-ground role, and allowing the retirement of the older and hard-worked F1CRs. The F1CTs are currently being upgraded with new EWS-A RWRs and upgraded Barax EW jamming pods, and a contract has been signed for the supply of 30 new TMV 632 laser rangefinders for the surviving F1CTs from 2000 onwards.

Jon Lake

Armée de l'Air Mirage F1 units

Expectations that the Armée de l'Air would concentrate all of its front-line Mirage F1s within a single 'Super Wing' at Colmar have failed to be realised, and the force remains at Colmar-Meyenheim (F1CT) and Reims-Champagne (F1CR and training), with an additional unit in Djibouti. Since the disbandment of all AdA escadres (wings), the F1 force is now operated by two escadrons (squadrons) with F1CTs, two with F1CRs, one flying F1B/Cs in the training role and one with F1Cs for the air defence of Djibouti. Each escadron has three constituent escadrilles (flights). The escadrons are theoretically independent, although they continue to operate on a loose 'wing' arrangement due to their co-location.

In 2001 the Armée de l'Air has no more than 129 F1s in service (comprising 12 F1Bs, 16 F1Cs, 11 F1C-200s, 43 F1CTs and 47 F1CRs) with 41 more in storage (these consisting of five F1Bs, 21 F1Cs, two F1C-200s, ten F1CTs and three F1CRs). This in-service total includes an F1B, two F1Cs, three F1CTs and three F1CRs with CEAM (the Centre d'Expérimentations Aériennes Militaires) at Mont-de-Marsan, and single examples of the F1C and F1CR with the CEV (Centre d'Essais en Vol) at Istres. This leaves 118 aircraft with the front-line/training units compared with a theoretical establishment (declared in late 1998) of 115 aircraft.

The F1CT conversion programme is now complete (though more could be produced from the 23 F1C/C-200s remaining in storage and the 27 still in service). The F1CTs retained their previous serials after conversion, and are (in serial order): 219-221, 223, 225-239, 241-249, 251-262, 264-265, 267-268, 271-275, and 278-283.

EC 1/30 'Alsace'

As 'Valois', EC 1/30 (with escadrilles commemorating and maintaining the traditions of SPA84 and SPA93) had operated Mirage F1C fighters from Tours until 1 June 1994, when it disbanded. The 'Alsace' identity re-appeared in August 1993, when EC 3/13 'Auvergne' at Colmar became EC 3/13 'Alsace'. The unit's F1CTs wore the same red shield (with six gold crowns) on each side of the tailfin, replacing the escadrille badges associated with 'Auvergne', which had been a pale blue shield with a thumb-down orange hand superimposed on a shield (GC II/9 2e 'Morietur') to starboard and a jester holding a trident (SPA85) to port. At least one aircraft (the CO's) wore a black chevron on the tailfin, in addition to the 'Auvergne' escadrille badges.

EC 3/13 'Alsace' was re-designated as EC 1/30 'Alsace' on 1 July 1995, retaining the same unit insignia, which is unusually worn on both sides of the fin, with no application of individual ('Strasbourg', 'Mulhouse' and 'Colmar') escadrille insignia. The 'Alsace' insignia consists of a gold-edged red shield with a diagonal gold band, with three gold crowns in each half of the divided shield. The squadron continues to operate 20 Mirage F1CTs from BA132 Colmar-Meyenheim, wearing codes starting with 30-SA, and using callsigns from F-UHSA.

All EC 1/30 aircraft wear the arms of Alsace on both sides of the fin.

EC 2/30 'Normandie-Niémen'

When the Mirage F1C-equipped EC 2/30 at Reims disbanded on 1 August 1993, the unit's name, traditions and insignia were immediately passed on to the second Mirage F1CT squadron, until then operating as EC 1/13 'Artois'. The latter unit had received its first F1CT (the third conversion, No. 278) by 14 June 1992, though training at CEAM did not begin until 1 September. It had returned to Colmar in early November, and had been declared operational in April 1993.

The unit became EC 1/13 'Normandie-Niémen' on 1 August 1993, when the black dragon on red disc badge of SPA85 (to starboard) and the SPA100 Hirondelle insignia (to port) gave way to the red shield with two gold lions of Normandie-Niémen, and the individual escadrille ('Caen' and 'Cherbourg') insignia were not applied. This historic badge was applied on both sides of the tailfin. EC 1/13 became EC 2/30 'Normandie-Niémen' on 1 July 1995, at Colmar-Meyenheim. Its 20 aircraft (all F1CTs) continue to use codes starting with 30-QA, and callsigns from F-UHQA.

ER 1/33 'Belfort'

The squadron's Mirage F1CRs wore the battleaxe insignia of SAL 33 on both sides of the fin until 1984, when a representation of St Exupéry's 'Petit Prince' was applied to port. The famous author had been killed while flying with EC 33 during World War II. Since then, some aircraft have received the red leopard badge of the unit's third escadrille, BR244.

ER 33's wing HQ disbanded on 1 August 1993, after which the surviving escadrons became autonomous, remaining at Strasbourg/Entzheim but with the intention of eventually joining a 'super-wing' with the Mirage F1CT units at Colmar. ER 1/33 moved to BA122 Reims-Champagne on 24 May 1994. Its 23 Mirage F1CRs still wear codes starting with 33-CA, and use callsigns from F-UICA. Its three escadrilles maintain the traditions of SAL33, EALA 9/72 and BR244.

The battleaxe insignia is worn by some ER 1/33 aircraft, while others wear a red leopard or the 'Petit Prince'. This F1CR is armed with BAP-100 anti-runway bombs.

ER 2/33 'Savoie'

The Mirage F1CRs of ER 2/33 initially wore the seagull insignia of SAL6 on both sides of the tailfin. ER 2/33 moved to Reims-Champagne on 24 April 1994, following the disbandment of the escadre HQ on 1 August 1993. Its 20 Mirage F1CRs wear codes starting with 33-NA, and use callsigns from F-UINA. Its three escadrilles maintain the traditions of SAL6, BR11 and C53, and each aircraft wears a different escadrille badge on each side of the tailfin, with the unit having taken over the red Cocotte once associated with ER 3/33 and the pennant of the third escadrille, C53.

EC 3/33 'Lorraine'

EC 3/30 'Lorraine' was for many years the Mirage F1 OCU, and was re-designated as EC 3/33 on 1 September 1994, retaining its conversion training role and supporting the Mirage F1C detachment in Djibouti. Its aircraft wore a badge consisting of three white alerions on a red stripe, superimposed on a yellow shield. On the conversion of EC 30 to the Mirage F1CT, the training commitment (and EC 3/30) passed to ER 33.

The original Mirage F1CR-equipped ER 3/33 'Moselle' had disbanded at Strasbourg on 31 July 1993, as part of the overall Armée de l'Air trend towards two-escadron wings. During this period, EC 3/33's Mirage F1CRs wore the Cocotte (an origami bird) badge on both sides of the tailfin. While operating from Incirlik during monitoring operations over northern Iraq, some of the squadron's aircraft wore prominent sharkmouths on their noses.

Today, EC 3/33 'Lorraine' operates 14 single-seat aircraft (drawn from a mix of eleven Mirage F1Cs and four F1C-200s) and 10 of 11 F1Bs from Reims-Champagne. Its aircraft wear codes starting with 33-FA, and use callsigns from F-UHFA. Its escadrilles ('Metz', 'Nancy' and 'Thionville') do not have individual insignia. Since 1994 the squadron has provided a two-ship aerobatic team, known as 'Voltige Victor'. As well the two display F1Cs, the team usually travels with a two-seat F1B as a spare aircraft.

A standard, non-probed F1C from EC 3/33 taxis for a training sortie at Reims.

EC 4/33 'Vexin'

The Djibouti-based Armée de l'Air fighter unit has carried on the traditions of 'Vexin' since it was formed on 1 September 1979, although it was known as EC 3/10 until 1 April 1985, and then as EC 4/30.

EC 4/33 'Vexin' now operates about eight Mirage F1Cs and F1C-200s in Djibouti, wearing codes starting 33-LA, and using callsigns from F-UILA. These seem to be drawn from a pool of four F1Cs and six F1C-200s. The unit's two escadrilles maintain the traditions of ERC 3/561 and ERC 4/561 and wear a musketeer badge in different colours on each side of the fin. Sharkmouths have been applied to some of the centreline fuel tanks of the 'Vexin' Mirage F1s.

Fuerza Aérea Boliviana

Photographed by Marnix Sap

Following refit (including 'glass' cockpit) by Kelowna Flightcraft in Canada, the Bolivian Lockheed 'T-birds' are now known as T-33-2000s. This was the first aircraft to be returned to Bolivia, arriving with two others at El Alto air base on 8 August 2000. It served as the test airframe for the upgrade, and underwent extensive ground and air testing before its redelivery.

Right: *Eighteen T-33s are to be updated to T-33-2000 standard, although the final unit assignment is not yet known. The first aircraft are expected to form the equipment of the new Escuela de Caza at El Trompillo, while others will go to the Grupo Aéreo de Caza 31, which presently parents the FAB's T-33 force.*

Below: *Bolivia received its first T-33s in August 1973, in the form of Canadair Silver Star Mk IIIs. Further deliveries included a batch of ex-French T-33SFs (illustrated). More may be acquired from Ecuador. The 18 aircraft due for T-33-2000 modernisation were dismantled for shipment by sea to Canada via the port of Arica. While Grupo Aéreo de Caza 31 at El Alto, La Paz oversees T-33 operations, there are detachments to GAC 32 (Santa Cruz), GAC 33 (Tarija) and GAC 34 (Cochabamba). The T-33's principal roles are counter-insurgency and reconnaissance.*

Above: *The first batch of 10 Pilatus PC-7s arrived in 1979, followed by 14 more in 1981. In 1986 they were concentrated in Grupo Aéreo de Caza 34 at Cochabamba for advanced/ weapons training, although between 1992 and 1996 six were assigned to the Peace Eagle programme. This was an anti-narcotics effort, and the PC-7s were used for intercepting drug-smuggling light aircraft, a role in which they were highly successful. In 1,527 operational sorties 337 intercepts were achieved.*

Right: Grupo Aéreo de Transporte 71 flies from El Alto, La Paz, on a variety of transport duties. These include airline-style operations serving remote communities under the title Transporte Aéreo Militar. The group has two squadrons: Escuadrón 711 operates the Lockheed C-130B/H, while Escuadrón 712 has a variety of airliner types. Among these are three immaculate Convair CV-580s, the first of which entered service in December 1974. The trio works hard on TAM operations into the interior.

Above and above right: The sturdy structure, reliability and economic operations of the Fokker F27-400M are appreciated by the FAB, which has three assigned to Escuadrón 712 of GAT 71. The aircraft are mostly operated on TAM services, which often involves flying to hot-and-high destinations.

Right: Grupo Aéreo de Transporte 72 flies this CASA 212-200 Aviocar from its base at Trinidad. Its main role is to connect outlying villages in the Beni region with the main town under the TAM umbrella. An IAI Arava used by the unit was lost in October 1999.

Below: The Servicio Nacional de Aerofotogrametria (national aerial photo-survey service) – also known as Grupo Aéreo de Exploración y Reconocimiento 81 – operates on a commercial basis from El Alto. The most important aircraft in the fleet are two Learjets: this Learjet 25A and a Learjet 25D. Both were purchased in the 1970s and continue to provide excellent service in the mapping role, equipped with various Wild cameras or a Zeiss RMK unit. As well this primary role, the pair is also used, when required, for fast VIP transport of the air force commander and other high-ranking staff.

Aviacíon del Ejército Boliviano

The Bolivian army maintains a small aviation component although it mostly relies on the FAB for its aerial transport requirements. The immaculate Beech King Air E90 (left) is based at Base Aérea General Jorge Jordan Mercado, El Alto, La Paz, for transport of the Bolivian army Commander-in-Chief, serving with Compañía Aéreo del Ejército 291. The independent Compañía Aéreo del Ejército Santa Cruz, which flies from El Trompillo, operates this Cessna 210 (above) on liaison duties, and also hopes to get its Cessna 152 and EMBRAER EMB-810 (licence-built Piper PA-34 Seneca) back into the air in the near future.

Above: As well as operating T-33s, Grupo Aéreo de Caza 31 at BA General Jorge Jordan Mercado, El Alto, also operates aircraft for VIP/staff transport. Pride of the fleet is this Rockwell Sabreliner 60, used for presidential transport. It was due to be replaced by a 'gift' Fokker F28 from Argentina, but the transfer was halted during 1999. GAC 31 also operates single examples of the Beech Baron, King Air 200 and Cessna 210.

Left: Taxying at Santa Cruz, this Beech King Air E90 formerly served with GAC 31 on staff transport duties. Following conversion by ENAER in Chile, it now flies on photo-survey duties with the SNA.

Right: Many of the FAB's light aircraft fleet was confiscated from drug smugglers. This Piper PA-32 Saratoga was such an aircraft, and is now assigned to the headquarters of the IIIª Brigada Aérea at El Trompillo. As well as liaison work, the aircraft is used against its former masters on anti-drug production surveillance missions.

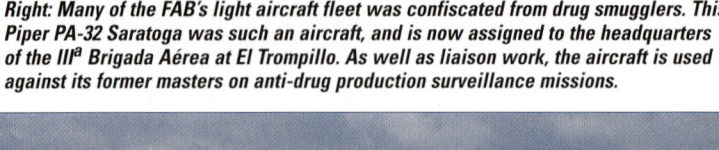

Fuerza de Tarea Aérea

The FTA – better known as the 'Diablos Rojos' (red devils) – is a special FAB unit dedicated to the eradication of drug production and trafficking within Bolivia, working closely with US organisations such as the Drug Enforcement Agency. The FTA's principal vehicle is the Bell UH-1H Huey (right), of which 18 are in service, most with door gun armament. Two Hueys serve as VIP transports in a smart quasi-civil scheme and 'Department of State Air Wing' titles. A Beech Baron and several Cessna 210s (above) are used for spotting and surveillance of the many illegal airstrips in Bolivia. Formed in 1982, the Fuerza de Tarea Aérea is due to disband in the next two years, in part a victim of its own success. Drug production has fallen sharply within Bolivia, while the funds and US personnel are now required more urgently in other areas of South America.

Above: Grupo Aéreo de Entrenamiento 21 at El Trompillo is the FAB's principal training unit. Much needed new equipment arrived in 2000 in the form of 11 ex-Uruguayan Beech T-34A/B Mentors, although one was soon written off. The 10 survivors provide basic training, students then progressing to the Pilatus PC-7s of GAC 34 at Cochabamba for advanced instruction.

Right: Maintained in airworthy condition by GAE 21 at El Trompillo is this Boeing PT-17 Stearman, one of 25 which were delivered under Lend-Lease in February 1945. Its colour scheme gave rise to its nickname of 'Barón Rojo' (red baron).

Below right: The Cessna 206 is the most numerous FAB aircraft, with most units having at least one assigned. This example flies with the Grupo Aéreo de Entrenamiento 22 at Puerto Suarez.

Below: For primary training 36 Aerotec T-23 Uiraparus were delivered from 1974 to the Colegio Militar de Aviación at El Trompillo. In 1984 the college's flying unit was reorganised as GAE 21, which continues to operate the six remaining Uiraparus.

JSF *X-32 and X-35: Joint Strike Fighter*

Although its future is far from assured, the Joint Strike Fighter programme is undoubtedly the most important new military aircraft project in the world. Whether it proceeds or not, it has redefined the 'state of the art' in terms of avionics, construction techniques, commonality and affordability.

In the spring of 2001 the two competing JSF industrial teams, led by Boeing and Lockheed Martin, were preparing to enter the most technologically challenging of the concept demonstration requirements – the display of controlled and reliable vertical flight. The teams have adopted very different approaches to reach the same JSF goals: Lockheed Martin's X-35 (this page) draws heavily on proven F-22 design while using a lift fan design for the STOVL portion of the requirement. Boeing's X-32 (opposite page), on the other hand, uses a radically novel design quite unlike any aircraft to have preceded it, and a direct-lift STOVL approach. The eventual decision (or 'downselect' in US parlance) on which team will proceed to the EMD phase will be based just as much on cost, commonality and maintainability factors as it will on 'traditional' values such as performance, systems and weapons capability.

From this angle the Lockheed Martin JSF design clearly shows F-22 parentage. However, the JSF is another generation beyond in terms of manufacturing, avionics and data fusion/ presentation. Although neither project is assured of going ahead, the USAF is planning to operate F-22 and JSF in close co-operation, viewing the types as entirely complementary. Despite its spectacular air-to-air capabilities, the JSF is tailored towards the attack mission.

One engineer has compared the Pentagon's Joint Strike Fighter programme to the development of the intercontinental ballistic missile (ICBM) in the 1950s, in its size, scope, ambition and potential impact. If JSF proceeds as planned, it will be the largest single defence project in history, with a potential market for 5,000-8,000 aircraft, and it will reverse the trend towards higher unit costs in military aircraft.

The JSF will also be a breakthrough combat aircraft, not on account of its speed or agility but because of its blend of stealth, smart sensors, advanced displays and internal weaponry. Carrying two tons of precision-guided weapons, plus defensive air-to-air missiles, JSF will still have much greater range than its predecessors. The JSF pilot should be able to detect radar-guided threats long before they see the aircraft, giving the JSF formation the choice of avoiding or attacking them.

JSF's sensors have been designed from the outset in ways that reflect the designers' recognition that high-speed, secure datalinks will be ubiquitous and essential in future conflicts. More than any other fighter, it reflects the concept of 'net-centred' warfare, in which communicating and gathering information and denying your adversary the ability to do the same may be as important as bombs and bullets.

The JSF family is intended to include a STOVL derivative without inflating the cost and degrading the performance of its conventional siblings, a notion that nobody would have taken seriously for a second before 1990. The JSF project takes aim at the idea that cost, in a military programme, cannot be controlled as tightly as it is in the development of an airliner. This is true revolution.

JSF has already changed the way military aircraft are designed and built. It is the first military aircraft designed in an era when military requirements no longer set the

pace of development in computing. (In 1990, when the F-22 was designed, it was possible to report with near-awe that the avionics system was expected to store 200 MB of data.) It is designed with the help of computer systems that were barely dreamed of in the previous decade.

Nevertheless, there is a serious possibility that, by the 2001, JSF could be a footnote in the history books. As this story is written, the Pentagon is engaged in what appears to be a genuine review of its strategy and the force structure that supports it. At the same time, the JSF prototypes are being readied for their most crucial and hazardous flight tests, which should take place in the summer of 2001.

The road to a joint fighter

Most people perceived that the JSF appeared on the scene very quickly in the mid-1990s, under President Clinton's first-term administration. When the new administration took office in early 1993, the USAF and Navy were developing two new fighters – the F-22 and the F/A-18E/F. The two services were jointly planning a heavy attack aircraft (A/F-X), and the USAF was looking at an F-16 replacement. Both these projects were cancelled in 1993. Within less than three years, the Pentagon was firmly

Boeing's novel JSF design came about as a result of several conflicting requirements. The direct lift approach to the STOVL requirement dictated that the engine was positioned in the forward fuselage, with a long duct to the 'up-and-away' propulsion nozzle. The need to keep within the US Navy's carrier dimension restraints in turn dictated a very short nose with an unusual inlet. The high thickness:chord ratio of the wing allows for an enormous fuel fraction, but in turn causes problems with the low-speed approach. Boeing had to redesign the aircraft with conventional tailplanes, but the forward fuselage and wing leading edges remain essentially unchanged.

Right: This artist's impression shows Northrop Grumman's original CALF design, with canards mounted on long LERXes and a two-dimensional vectoring nozzle. The STOVL version would have had a lift engine in the forward fuselage. In conjunction with McDonnell Douglas, Northrop Grumman offered a different design for the JSF competition, based on the YF-23 ATF design. It, too, had fins splayed outwards at 45°. The design was rejected in November 1996, leaving Boeing and Lockheed Martin to fight it out for the EMD contract.

planning a single new fighter which would replace thousands of Navy and USAF aircraft and, in addition, would be built in a version that could replace the Marine Corps' AV-8B short-take-off, vertical landing (STOVL) fighters.

In fact, serious design work on what became the JSF had started in 1990-91, although the project received little attention even in the trade press and was almost unknown outside the aerospace industry, and it had its roots in technology studies which had started several years earlier.

JSF's predecessors owed their existence to two services – the US Marine Corps and British Royal Navy – which flew Harriers. In the early 1980s, both had started re-equipping with new versions of the Harrier – the Royal Navy's Sea Harrier F/A.2 and the AV-8B – but the services recognised that they would need a replacement aircraft after 2000. Without a STOVL replacement, the Marines would go back to relying on the US Navy's carrier aircraft for air support, and would no longer be able to operate jet aircraft from the Navy's amphibious warfare ships. The Royal Navy's small carriers would not be able to operate conventional carrier-based aircraft at all, and would have to revert to being helicopter carriers.

In January 1986, an international joint agreement, covering technology for a Harrier replacement, was signed at NASA's Ames Research Center in California. The principal parties were NASA and the UK Royal Aeronautical Establishment – which later became part of the Defence Evaluation and Research Agency (DERA) – but they worked in close collaboration with the Marines and RN, and with the US and UK industries. The agreement outlined a programme that would compare several different STOVL

designs against a draft requirement for a supersonic, STOVL fighter. The plan was to select the most promising concepts for more detailed investigation and testing, starting in 1988, and to start development of an operational fighter in 1995.

ASTOVL approaches

Of the four concepts selected for development, one was a derivative of the Harrier concept, using direct lift: to make the aircraft hover, the engine would be installed amidships and its thrust would be deflected downwards by swivelling nozzles. Another was called a 'remote augmented lift system' (RALS), which used an afterburner nozzle, fixed to point downwards, located in the fighter's nose and fed with bleed air from the compressor. A third concept, investigated by General Dynamics and de Havilland Canada, involved building large folding ejector ducts into the fighter's wing. The fourth, explored by Lockheed and Rolls-Royce, was a 'tandem fan' engine. This was like a conventional jet engine with an extra compression stage, mounted well ahead of the rest of the engine on an extension shaft. In straight-and-level flight, the engine worked like a conventional jet. All the air would pass through the inlets, the forward compression stage and the engine. For STOVL, the air through the front stage would be diverted to a pair of swivelling forward exhausts, and an extra set of inlets would open to feed the rest of the engine. In this mode, the engine acted like a high-bypass-ratio airliner engine, producing extra thrust.

By 1987, the Marines had taken a key decision: the Advanced STOVL (ASTOVL) aircraft would replace both its Harriers and its conventional F/A-18s. The service also refined its requirement, calling for an aircraft no larger than the F/A-18 (in terms of empty weight) but with greater

Lockheed's original JAST lift fan design, ironically designated X-32, was tested in 86 percent scale propulsion system mock-up form at NASA Ames (note the famous blimp sheds in the background, above). Tests were initially conducted outside, but subsequently moved into an 80-ft (24.38-m) x 120-ft (36.58-m) wind tunnel, also at the Ames Research Center. Power was provided by a Pratt & Whitney F100-PW-220+. The design eventually metamorphosed into today's X-35, losing the canards in late 1995.

range and stealth – characteristics that have remained part of the specification to the present day. The Marine decision was important because it increased the potential size of the programme to 700-plus aircraft – but it was the only good news around ASTOVL.

All the chosen designs turned out to have major drawbacks. Problems caused by the interaction between the fighter's jet exhaust, the ground and its inlets proved more difficult than expected, ruling out the afterburner-equipped direct-lift system and RALS. (When Russia's Yakovlev brought its STOVL Yak-141 to the Farnborough air show in the UK in September 1992, it hovered but did not land vertically because it would have wrecked any surface except a steel deck.) Control of a heavy, powerful aircraft in jet-borne flight was difficult, and would extract a lot of power from the engine. Control during transition from wing-borne to jet-borne flight was particularly complex for the tandem fan and the ejector system. Some of the configurations were less compatible than others with stealth – but that problem could not be discussed in detail because of security concerns.

By 1989, the ASTOVL programme was dead in the water, because none of the concepts under study showed any promise of solving the many detail problems at an acceptable level of risk.

DARPA intervention

It was it this inauspicious point in the programme that the Defense Advanced Research Projects Agency (DARPA) started to look at STOVL. It had been DARPA, 15 years earlier, which had been the catalyst for the development of stealth technology. DARPA had been involved in the UK-US STOVL project and its managers saw, by the late 1980s, that it was in deep trouble. Convinced that, like stealth, ASTOVL could be made feasible with a more focused, more aggressive demonstration programme, DARPA set a new set of goals for the project.

DARPA's leaders eliminated most hard requirements except for a 24,000-lb (10900-kg) maximum empty weight (a surrogate for cost); based the project on the powerful engines developed for the YF-22 and YF-23 Advanced Tactical Fighters; and laid out a programme which started with the construction of a large-scale powered model (LSPM) – a non-flying vehicle with a complete propulsion system, to be used for ground tests – and then proceeded directly into the construction and testing of a manned prototype. The programme was set up to ensure that no company would propose a solution unless they were confident that they could make it fly; and the testing of the LSPM would eliminate any approach which turned out to be a total dud. (The memory of the Rockwell XFV-12A, a 1970s supersonic STOVL prototype that could not lift its own weight, was still fresh.)

Another principle – reflecting the agency's name and charter – was that preference would be given to new solutions that had not been tested before. The effects of this decision would ripple throughout the programme and are still felt today.

Between 1989 and 1991, DARPA funded aircraft design studies by McDonnell Douglas, General Dynamics and Lockheed Advanced Development Company (the Skunk Works), together with propulsion studies at General Electric (which had produced the YF120 engine for the YF-22 and YF-23) and Pratt & Whitney (YF119).

The studies concentrated on two basic problems with the earlier STOVL concepts. The first was that the hot, high-velocity exhaust gas was no longer just a nuisance, but was now a menace, because of the greater size and power of the supersonic aircraft. The jet blast threatened to blow people and equipment off the deck like confetti, while creating a cloud of superheated air that would suck power out of the engine. Even if the challenge of hot-gas ingestion could be solved, operations on ship would be made impractical by the need to clear a large safety zone around a landing aircraft. The second problem was that stealth

appeared to mandate a single, rear-mounted exhaust nozzle in up-and-away flight.

Both these problems could be solved if there was a way to move some of the engine's total energy forwards, to balance the rear-mounted nozzle, while increasing the system's mass flow and reducing its jet velocity.

Lockheed Skunk Works engineer Paul Bevilaqua devised such a method, which was patented in 1993. The new system evolved from the tandem fan, but with three principal differences: the forward fan stream was separate from the core airflow at all times; the fan was shut down in cruising flight; and the fan was rotated so that its axis was vertical. It was a less complex system than the tandem fan and had a more easily controlled transition.

With its airframe essentially complete, the X-32A is towed from the Palmdale workshop for structural tests on 20 August 1999.

Both Lockheed Martin Model 220s (X-35A and X-35C) take shape in the Skunk Works at Palmdale. The X-35A is in the foreground, distinguished by the open doors for the lift fan/STOVL intake assembly.

Above: Boeing's Concept Demonstrator Aircraft was based on the Model 370 design. While construction was under way the design altered considerably, gaining conventional tailplanes and a new wing from Configuration 372.4. The two outwardly-complete X-32s were simultaneously revealed to the world on 14 December 1999 in the old Rockwell facility at Palmdale. A satellite broadcast and webcast enabled around 5,500 employees at Boeing 'One Team'-related facilities to witness the unveiling.

Right: At first glance one of the most obvious features of the X-32 is the extraordinary 'cleanliness' of the upper surface. A single skin forms the entire top surface of the wing, broken only by a few antennas and a cooling intake.

At the same time, General Electric dusted off the data on lift fan systems that it had built for the US Army in the 1960s. The GE fans had been driven by turbines, fed by engine exhaust gas. Coincidentally, GE had developed a variable-cycle engine, the F120, as a candidate powerplant for the Advanced Tactical Fighter: one attribute of this engine was that it could supply a great deal of high-pressure bleed air and continue to operate properly. By 1991, the Lockheed and GE fan-boosted systems emerged – in the view of the DARPA programme managers – as the best hope for a practical system.

During 1991, DARPA persuaded the Navy to issue a draft requirement for a STOVL strike fighter, giving the agency the formal justification for a development programme.

DARPA called for proposals, announcing that it would pick two companies to build near-full-scale models in 1993. In 1995, the most promising candidate would be selected for a flight demonstration programme.

As DARPA refined its requirements, another light bulb went on. Unlike the Harrier, the fan-lift STOVL designs had a conventional internal layout with the engine in the back. If the fan and its hardware were removed, the area behind the cockpit would accommodate a large fuel tank, and the result would be a fighter with an unusually large internal fuel fraction and hence an excellent range. For the USAF, one of the lessons of Desert Storm was that it needed more range in its fighters if it was not going to fight in Central Europe. The DARPA planners started to see the ASTOVL aircraft as a potential replacement for the F-16.

By the time DARPA issued contracts to Lockheed and McDonnell Douglas in March 1993, the project was not only ASTOVL but also the Common Affordable Lightweight Fighter (CALF), and the aircraft was to be designed and demonstrated in both STOVL and conventional take-off and landing (CTOL) forms.

Boeing enters the fray

Two other companies joined the CALF effort in the subsequent 12 months, using independent research and development funds. Boeing had started looking at future fighters as soon as the Advanced Tactical Fighter award went to Lockheed – with Boeing as a major team member – in April 1991. Having placed fourth in the ATF demonstration/validation contest in 1986, Boeing was determined to establish itself as a prime contractor for fighters. Certain that future budgets would be tight, Boeing focused on low cost. The company concluded that what was needed was a multi-service, multi-purpose fighter with an empty weight close to that of an F-16, a price far lower than the F-22, STOVL capability to replace the Harrier, and a better range than in-service fighters.

Boeing's concentration on cost and simplicity defined the AVX-70 design that emerged from a study of 30 configurations. It was a direct-lift design with no separate lift fan, but would be small and light enough to land vertically without lift augmentation. To minimise weight and accommodate a large fuel load, Boeing selected a delta wing. Although it did not win either of the DARPA contracts, the company

The JSF CDAs (Concept Demonstrator Aircraft) were based on the requirements set out in JIRD I. In Lockheed Martin's case the X-35 CDAs emerged similar to the Model 220-2 design. Here the X-35A undertakes high-speed taxi trials at Palmdale, successfully clearing the final hurdle before the first flight could be made.

had enough faith in its concept to take part in the ground-test programme with its funds. Like McDonnell Douglas and Lockheed, the company would build a large-scale powered model and test it on a large outdoor rig.

Northrop Grumman announced its intention to bid on CALF in the summer of 1994. The company selected a lift-plus-lift/cruise design. It had an F119 fitted with a vectoring nozzle, and a separate lift-fan engine in the forward fuselage. Rolls-Royce joined the team to work on the lift engine. The design featured an unusual 'hammerhead' wing planform, with a small canard attached to a large fixed leading-edge extension. Northrop did not intend to build a powered model, arguing that the risks of the lift-plus-lift/cruise configuration were small.

CALF becomes JAST

In September 1993, the incoming Clinton administration axed the individual services' future fighter programmes: the USAF/Navy A/F-X long-range attack aircraft and the USAF's Multi-Role Fighter (MRF), which was intended as the replacement for the F-16. As a meagre consolation prize, the Pentagon established a new programme called Joint Advanced Strike Technology (JAST), intended to look at weapons, avionics and other technologies for new-generation strike aircraft. Within a few months, a tidy-minded Congress had discovered CALF and transferred it from DARPA to the newly formed JAST office.

The new administration's defence policy, it turned out, was defined by several factors. One was the desire to reduce or at least stabilise the budget. On the other hand, the Clinton team also wanted to use the military to support an inconsistently interventionist foreign policy, resulting in a series of expensive overseas deployments. The defence budget was also under pressure from a booming civilian economy; the services had to increase pay to retain key people. The net result was that procurement and research and development funds became very tight. Tactical aircraft procurement almost ceased. Consequently, the USAF and Navy realised that they would need to buy aircraft at much higher rates in the 2000s in order to fill their fighter wings – and with projected budgets, they would have to be relatively inexpensive.

Many people thought that JAST would be an undisciplined collection of technology demonstrations and studies, but what happened in the first few months of the office's existence was dramatic and unexpected. Under the leadership of Major General George Muellner, a fighter pilot who had once commanded the 6513th Test Wing at Area 51 (Groom Lake), the JAST office assembled a massive programme. Muellner's vision was of a 'universal fighter' which could cover all the services' different needs in a largely common airframe. It would be made possible by precision weapons – like the F-117, it would put two bombs in the right place and would not need a multi-bomb internal load like the A-12 – and advanced avionics. New manufacturing and design techniques would make it

affordable – and it would be based on the CALF designs.

Using the latest computer mission-modelling and campaign-level simulation techniques, the JAST office coordinated a tough session of trading among the three services. The Navy was persuaded to accept a single-engined, single-seat aircraft, after extensive studies which showed that combat and accidental loss rates would be comparable. The Air Force agreed to accept an aircraft that would be slower and less agile than the F-22 – in fact, not much faster or more manoeuvrable than the F-16. The result was an aircraft that accomplished the critical elements of the services' missions but was still small enough to form the basis of a practical STOVL aircraft.

In an interview in April 1995, Muellner said that the customers had converged on a family of closely similar designs, different mainly in the way that they landed and took off. The industrial implications were enormous. The Marines wanted to replace 600 older aircraft, the Navy needed 300 aircraft, and the USAF could replace almost 2,000 F-16s. Never had such a massive programme been created so fast. Moreover, JAST looked like the only US tactical aircraft programme that would start before 2010 – and was also being billed as the worldwide replacement for 2,000-plus F-16s and F/A-18s.

Industrial realignment

In 1986, seven companies had submitted proposals for the ATF Dem/Val phase. By late 1994, four companies were ready to compete in JAST – Grumman had been

With Tom Morgenfeld at the controls, the X-35A flew for the first time from Palmdale at 9:06 am, Pacific Daylight Time, on 24 October 2000, landing at Edwards AFB to inaugurate the CTOL flight test programme. Morgenfeld flew the first four envelope-expansion flights, being joined in the test team by the USAF's Lieutenant Colonel Paul Smith on the fifth flight on 3 November.

acquired by Northrop, General Dynamics had been absorbed by Lockheed (which was itself in the process of merging with Martin-Marietta), and Rockwell had virtually left the military aircraft business. The two companies to be eliminated in 1996 would be out of the picture as combat aircraft primes.

As the JAST decision date loomed up, the contractors changed their designs and engaged in a mating dance. Lockheed and McDonnell Douglas had both proposed stealthy canard designs for the DARPA programme. Under the area-rule principle, which holds that transonic and supersonic drag are lowest if the designer avoids a sharp increase in cross-sectional area towards the front of the aircraft, the canard was attractive because it moved the wing aft, away from the inevitable bulge where the inlet ducts wrapped around the fan bay.

Unlike CALF, though, JAST had to land on a carrier. A carrier-based aircraft must be able to fly slowly in a flat attitude – which implies a generous wing span and effective flaps – and must feature responsive and precise control at low speeds. As Lockheed Martin adapted the canard design to these requirements, the canard became awkwardly big. Also, Lockheed had relocated the JAST programme to Fort Worth, where F-16 designer Harry Hillaker had long taught that "the optimum location for a canard is on somebody else's aircraft." In 1995, the canard Eurofighter Typhoon was sitting on the ground while its designers wrestled with flight-control problems, and the Saab Gripen's developers were dealing with a rash of handling gremlins. All in all, the Lockheed Martin team felt that there was enough risk in the JAST programme without adding a canard to the mix.

Lockheed Martin looked at a pure delta wing – at one point, the company was looking at a delta for the USMC, USAF and RN and a tailed configuration for the US Navy –

but the final design echoed the F-22, with four tails and a cropped delta wing. One huge advantage of this design was that it drew on the extensive and flight-validated database from the F-22 programme. Data from the large-scale powered model, unveiled in April 1995 and tested at NASA Ames, was still applicable.

McDonnell Douglas went through even larger changes. Late in 1994, Northrop Grumman agreed to collaborate with McDonnell Douglas and British Aerospace on JAST. The three companies formed a 'dream team' that encompassed all the Western world's STOVL experience, both the surviving groups with carrier-based fighter skills, Northrop's stealth technology and Grumman's expertise in all-weather strike systems.

Two-engined fighter

By mid-1995, however, all was clearly not well with the McDonnell Douglas team. McDonnell Douglas announced in June – only a year before the planned down-select date – that its JAST design would use Northrop Grumman's lift-plus-lift/cruise (LPLC) concept. The nearly completed large-scale powered model of the gas-driven lift-fan design was mothballed.

LPLC eliminated the coupling between the engine and the fan, and many studies showed that it was the lowest-weight solution. McDonnell Douglas could argue that its design would enter service with a thoroughly proven lift/cruise engine (a standard F119) and that the lift engine was little more complex than Lockheed Martin's lift fan. But it had one substantial drawback: USMC's logistics community hated the idea of a fighter with two different engines. "The logistics people start climbing the walls, and rightly," DARPA programme manager Bill Scheuren had commented in 1991.

In 1996, McDonnell Douglas unveiled a previously secret, unmanned experimental aircraft called the X-36. It was clearly a cousin of the CALF design, but while the latter had small vertical fins and a delta wing, the X-36 had a swept wing with a kinked trailing edge and no vertical surfaces at all, and used yaw-axis thrust vectoring instead. Its technology was incorporated into the company's final JAST design.

Boeing and Lockheed Martin had talked about teaming, but neither wanted to give up its own design, so they competed with McDonnell Douglas's team. Boeing's JAST design was bigger than its original AVX-70, but apart from relocated vertical surfaces – on the afterbody rather than the wingtips – it changed relatively little.

From JAST to JSF

In March 1996, the JAST office released a request for proposals (RFP) for the JAST prototypes, with a deadline in early June. Shortly afterwards, the project's name changed from JAST to the Joint Strike Fighter (JSF), reflecting the fact that it was backed by an operational requirement.

Most people expected that Lockheed Martin and the McDonnell Douglas team would win. McDonnell Douglas had massive experience of STOVL and Navy fighters on its side, together with Northrop Grumman's stealth expertise. Add up the total of manned supersonic aircraft, jet fighters and stealth aircraft built by Boeing – and the number was zero. But it had taken McDonnell Douglas several months to organise its 'dream team', spread as it was across the UK, St. Louis and California. Lockheed Martin's design, with its close relationship to the F-22, looked like a low-risk solution; the McDonnell Douglas design was quite similar, but the Boeing proposal was different and definitely riskier. In previous two-track flight demonstration programmes, the rival winners had conformed to a pattern: they would be different, and one would be low-risk and the other adventurous. This logic prevailed, and the Lockheed Martin and Boeing were selected for the next phase of JSF in November 1996.

McDonnell Douglas's erstwhile teammates, BAe and Northrop Grumman, joined the Lockheed Martin team. McDonnell Douglas, facing the near-extinction of its commercial aircraft business and stunned by its defeat in JSF, negotiated a takeover by Boeing and its fighter resources – including the ingenious innovators of the Phantom Works – were added to the latter's effort.

The first phase of JSF was planned as a four-year effort, starting with the issue of formal contracts in early 1997 and ending with the selection of one team to perform engineering and manufacturing development (EMD), planned for March 2001.

There were three main strands of activity within this programme. In the most visible part of the project, Lockheed Martin and Boeing each built two Concept Demonstration Aircraft (CDAs). The CDAs had three principal tasks: to prove the design's 'up-and-away' perfor-

In US Navy service the JSF is intended to replace the F/A-18C/D Hornet on carrier decks, offering a dramatic increase in combat radius. The Marine Corps, too, is seeking to replace its Hornets with JSFs, along with its AV-8B STOVL fleet. Current US Navy requirements stand at 480 CV aircraft, while the Marine Corps want 609, all of the STOVL variety.

Down-select for the JSF EMD contract was expected in mid-2001, leading to a contract covering an expected 10 pre-production aircraft of which the first should fly in 2005. The first 13 LRIP (Low-Rate Initial Production) Block 1 aircraft are scheduled for delivery to the USAF and USMC in 2008 with AIM-120/JDAM capability only. Block 2 will cover 30 aircraft with expanded capabilities. Block 3 will be fully JORD-compliant and should be delivered in late 2010.

mance characteristics (stealth characteristics were validated by model tests); to demonstrate the low-speed performance required for carrier landings; and to prove that the STOVL concept worked. It was clear that the STOVL tests were the most critical and risky area of flight-testing. As a result, teams were required to build two sets of STOVL hardware and to design both their CDAs so that they could be modified into STOVL aircraft.

The CDAs were designated in the X-series, in alphabetical order, so that Boeing's JSF was the X-32 (re-using the CALF designation) and the Lockheed Martin aircraft was the X-35. The JSF office deliberately avoided using 'YF' designations to emphasise that there was no 'fly-off'. There is no commitment to select the better-performing CDA. Ideally, the CDAs will demonstrate that either team's definitive JSF design would work; the Pentagon can then select a winner based on a balance of operational utility and cost. Both

team's CDA prototypes are powered by Pratt & Whitney F119 engines – a selection made by default, because the F119 is the only flight-rated engine with enough power to do the job – with different, substantial modifications by Pratt & Whitney.

The second sector of JSF comprised a variety of technology programmes. Some elements of this work pre-dated JAST: for instance, the Joint Integrated Subsystems Technology (J/IST) demonstration had its roots in USAF research into electrical actuation for flight controls. Others, including much of the avionics activity, were launched in the early days of JAST when it was realised that their effect on cost was decisive.

The third major part of the JSF definition phase was an iterative process in which the customer refined the requirements and the contractors designed their Preferred Weapon System Concept (PWSC). The PWSC includes the design of an operational JSF, detailed proposals for production and support, and a plan for EMD.

In earlier programmes, the customer set the requirement, the contractor tried to meet it, and the cost was a by-product of this process. JSF inverted this process. The cost could and would be controlled independently, and the contractor and customer would agree on what could be designed and built for the money. A cardinal rule was that the cost impact of any change to the requirements had to be fully evaluated. If any change resulted in a cost increase, an equal saving had to be found somewhere else.

This trading process took place through a series of Joint Interim Requirements Documents (JIRDs). JIRD I was produced in 1995 and focused on size, speed and stealth – the factors that determine the aircraft's shape. JIRD II, issued in June 1997, looked at major trades between performance, cost and supportability. JIRD III, released in the autumn of 1998, addressed a range of issues including supportable stealth technology, adverse weather and night capability, and mission planning. As each JIRD was issued, and as design studies yielded new technical answers, the contractors would respond with a revised PWSC approach. Finally, a Joint Operational Requirements Document (JORD) was released in early 2000 and formed the basis for the EMD request for proposals (RFP) issued later in the year. Boeing and Lockheed Martin submitted their proposals in early February 2001.

The programme office used campaign-level simulation to evaluate how changes to the aircraft would affect the outcome of military operations. The Virtual Strike Warfare Environment (VSWE), a joint-service simulation, was extremely important in managing the trade-offs made through JIRD.

Some of the key trades made using this process have included resolution of the differences between the US Navy and USAF desire to carry a 2,000-lb (907-kg) bomb and the Marines' unwillingness to pay for that capability in other areas. The issue of whether and how the JSF should carry a gun has been settled in the same way.

JSF requirements

However, these trades have not affected the three key concepts that have underpinned the JSF requirement from the beginning. The first is the assumption that other aircraft will take care of the most severe air-to-air threats. The USAF and US Navy do not require JSF to be their primary air-to-air fighter, do not need to pay for such a capability and do not want JSF to be perceived as an alternative to the F-22 or Super Hornet.

Although the F stands for 'fighter', the initial requirement was 70 per cent weighted towards air-to-ground missions. The Lockheed Martin X-35, for instance, has a lower thrust/weight ratio and higher wing loading than the F-22 and does not use vectored thrust in flight. It will therefore be less agile, will accelerate more slowly and will have less ability (if any) to supercruise. The JSF's standard AAM is not the AIM-9X Sidewinder, but the AIM-120 Advanced Medium Range Air-to-Air Missile (AMRAAM) – better for self-defence than for dogfighting. In Lockheed Martin's basic design, the AAM locations are not even suitable for an AIM-9X, because the airframe blocks much of the seeker's field of view, although external wingtip AIM-9 stations are an option.

The second principle of the requirement is first-day stealth, which allows the aircraft to perform its first missions as a stealth aircraft, with a limited weapon load, and then carry more ordnance as the campaign continues and the defences are beaten down. In this way, JSF can be stealthy and yet can deliver enough weapons to handle the expected number of targets. Both designs incorporate four large-capacity external hardpoints for extra fuel and weapons.

The third key concept is that the Pentagon expects to have retired its dumb bombs by the time JSF enters service.

JSF's least accurate weapons will be standard Boeing GBU-31/32 Joint Direct Attack Munitions (JDAMs) with an accuracy of 33 ft (10 m). By the time the aircraft enters service, a low-cost precision seeker (such as DAMASK, being developed at the Navy's China Lake centre and based on the same IR sensor now being fitted to Cadillacs) should also be available. The result is that a small weapon load on JSF should be as effective in terms of destruction caused as a much larger load of unguided weapons.

Weapon requirements

The Boeing X-32 and Lockheed Martin X-35 are very different from each other, but are designed to meet the same basic set of requirements. All three services require an internal load of two JDAMs and two AMRAAMs. The Navy and USAF want to carry the 2,000-lb (907-kg) GBU-31 and the USMC is content with the 1,000-lb (454-kg) GBU-32. In 1998, the three services resolved the vexed question of a gun: the USAF version will have an internal gun, while the USMC and Navy aircraft can be fitted with a gun pack which will fit into the weapon bay, displacing one of the JDAMs.

Range requirements vary: the USAF now requires a range of at least 590 nm (1093 km; 679 miles) and has an 'objective' or desired range of 690 nm (1278 km; 794 miles); the USMC will settle for a lesser range but the Navy will require equal or greater range than the USAF. Maximum level flight speed must be at least Mach 1.5, and manoeuvrability must be comparable to that of current aircraft.

The US Navy was initially the most demanding customer in terms of stealth, because the Navy JSFs will be the service's only stealthy aircraft and will have to penetrate the toughest defences with minimal support. The USAF expects

Martin-Baker delivered three of its Mk 16B seats (including a spare) to Boeing for the X-32 programme in November 1999. The seat was tested at up to 450 kt (833 km/h; 518 mph) on Martin-Baker's sled track at Langford Lodge in Northern Ireland. The X-35 uses the Mk 16E seat.

Boeing's X-32A became the first JSF CDA to fly, taking off from Palmdale at 7.53 PDT on 18 September 2000 with Fred Knox at the controls. Terminating at Edwards, the flight was cut short to 20 minutes when a chase aircraft spotted a hydraulic leak.

Right and below: Final engine tests for the X-35A were performed at Palmdale by Tom Morgenfeld, and included dynamic accelerations and decelerations. The aircraft was restrained by a cable holdback system. This first flight-rated F119-611C engine (YF001) was fitted into the X-35A on 9 December 1999.

to have B-2s, F-117s and strike-configured F-22s for this mission. However, as the requirements have evolved, the USAF and Navy requirements have become more closely aligned. The USMC's primary mission is visual close air support with external weapons, so stealth is less important. However, primary features of the design which make stealth attainable – such as shape and internal stores – are inherent to the basic structure of the aircraft, and will be included on all versions.

Internal sensors

The JSF is expected to be able to perform precision attacks at night, under the weather and, to some extent, against targets that are obscured by fog, rain or cloud. Because one of the most serious emerging threats to tactical aircraft are new surface-to-air missiles, JSF is also expected to provide its pilot with much better awareness of

radar-guided threats and missile launches than the systems on current aircraft can support. Stealth rules out external pods, so the necessary electronic and optical sensors must be carried internally.

The most basic conflict in the JSF design has always been typified by the Marine/RN STOVL requirement, and the Navy's weapon load and mission radius. The STOVL version needs to land vertically at the end of its mission, with reserve fuel and unused weapons. This limits its empty weight to a proportion of vertical thrust, which in turn is limited by the power of a derivative F119, and drives the designer to the smallest, lightest possible aircraft. But the Navy aircraft needs to carry a heavy load of weapons and fuel, and a big wing for carrier approaches, together with the extra structural strength required to withstand the shock of catapult launches and arrested landings. The larger the difference between the three service versions, the more the project will cost, both in development and production; but the versions must be different to some extent, because the requirements are different. The challenge in the basic design is to decide what should be different and what should be common.

X-35: the low-risk approach

Lockheed Martin's design flies the low-risk banner. Six months after the CDA source selection, Lockheed Martin had picked up both of the major partners in the defeated McDonnell Douglas team, as Northrop Grumman (with its carrier experience) and British Aerospace (and its STOVL knowledge) joined the X-35 programme. The project is still being run by Lockheed Martin Tactical Aircraft Systems (LMTAS) at Fort Worth, but the prototypes were built by the

Comprehensive engine runs were also performed in the X-32A prior to its first flight. Noticeable in this view are the rudders, which can operate in unison (as here) to give a measure of pitch control or air braking.

Skunk Works at Palmdale. The X-35A CTOL prototype was the first to fly, on 24 October 2000; it completed its first series of flights in late November, and then returned to Palmdale, where it was to be modified into the STOVL X-35B. The carrier-based X-35C is structurally identical apart from a 'picture-frame' structure that increases its wing area, and larger tail surfaces.

The X-35 is clearly a cousin to the F-22: the basic aerodynamics are similar, and the two aircraft take the same approach to stealth, with a combination of flat and curved surfaces and a sharp chine around the perimeter of the airframe. The main differences between the two aircraft (apart from size and the single engine) are the X-35's new 'diverterless' inlet, with a bump on the inner wall rather than a splitter plate, and the axisymmetrical nozzle. The inlet was developed under a USAF programme and tested in 1996 on an F-16. The bump works in conjunction with a swept-forward inlet lip: it creates a local pressure rise which deflects the turbulent boundary layer upwards and downwards, so that it spills past the inlet lips. The USAF and USN versions feature a low-observable axisymmetrical nozzle, with a serrated aft edge, which is lighter and less expensive than the two-dimensional exhaust on the F-22. Unlike the F-22, the X-35 does not use thrust vectoring in up-and-away flight.

The JSF also lacks the larger F-22's 'cheek' missile bays. Instead, it has two bays to the left and right of the keel, each with two doors. The inner door in each bay carries a launch rail for an AIM-120 AMRAAM. The outer door is slightly bulged on the Navy and USAF versions to accommodate a 2,000-lb (907-kg) weapon. The wing includes four hardpoints, rated at 5,000 lb (2268 kg) inboard and 2,500 lb (1134 kg) outboard.

The STOVL version is externally identifiable by a slight bulge in the spine, and a shorter canopy. (Both X-35s have these features, because the X-35C can be converted into a STOVL aircraft if necessary.) The lift fan, developed by Allison Advanced Development Company (AADC), is located behind the cockpit, in a bay with upper and lower clamshell doors. It is driven by a composite driveshaft, connected to the compressor face of the engine by a computer-controlled clutch which uses the same technology as carbon brakes. The shaft ends in a single gear which engages a facing pair of horizontal ring gears, each of which drives one of the two counter-rotating fan stages. The CDA system has a retractable D-section nozzle which deflects its thrust aft for transition and short take-off; the production aircraft will have an array of cascades, which weigh less. The lift fan supports almost half the aircraft's weight in hovering flight, producing 18,000 lb thrust (80.1 kN). The lift fan doubles the mass flow of the propulsion system, and boosts its thrust by 44 percent.

Yakovlev inspiration

Air from the engine fan feeds two roll-control ducts that extend out to the wing fold line. The core exhaust flows through a 'three-bearing' nozzle, developed by Rolls-Royce along the pattern of the Yak-141 exhaust. It has three oblique rotary joints that revolve in opposite directions to deflect the nozzle from the fully aft position to 15° ahead of the vertical. Another distinguishing feature of the STOVL version is an auxiliary inlet for the main engine, above the fuselage aft of the lift fan.

This STOVL system has some inherently useful features. The driveshaft literally extracts energy from the rear of the aircraft and converts it into vertical thrust at the front, balancing the aircraft in hovering flight. Another advantage of this system, compared to a direct-lift system such as employed by the Harrier or Boeing X-32, is that pitch and roll control can be accomplished by modulating the thrust of the four lift 'posts', rather than by bleeding air (and power) from the engine to a dedicated control system. Valves in the roll ducts open and close differentially for roll control. In the pitch axis, energy can be switched between the engine exhaust nozzle and the fan by adjusting the main engine's exhaust nozzle and the inlet guide vanes on the fan. Total thrust and efficiency remain unchanged.

Both STOVL systems have an impressive list of moving parts which must operate successfully in order to recover the aircraft in a vertical landing. However, Lockheed Martin takes the lead with a mechanical transmission, four lift nozzles – two of which vector in hovering flight to provide control – and two large auxiliary inlets. All these apertures are covered by doors, most of which operate in a hot, noisy, high-vibration environment. All the doors must close with a near-perfect fit in order not to compromise the

The main accent of JSF development has been placed on stealthiness, range/load performance, affordability and high-tech systems. That is not to say that out-and-out performance and manoeuvrability have been ignored, both designs offering some advances over current designs. Top-end speed is around Mach 1.7, and the JSFs will not 'supercruise' with the same ease as the F-22. Transonic acceleration is respectable, thanks to the enormous thrust bestowed by the F119. The Lockheed Martin design achieves Mach 0.8 to Mach 1.2 in around 40 seconds at altitude.

From this angle the CV X-35C (left) looks very similar to the CTOL X-35A, but the two versions share less commonality in structure than the CTOL and STOVL variants. In the production versions the differences become greater, as the CV aircraft would have a much stronger undercarriage with twin nosewheels. Handling is also different due to the X-35C's larger wings and tail surfaces, although Lockheed Martin engineers are 'tweaking' the control surfaces of the different versions to achieve near-universal handling qualities. On the X-35A's 24th flight Tom Morgenfeld paved the way for the X-35C's carrier approach trials by performing a series of six FCLP (Field Carrier Landing Practice) approaches.

For its test programme the X-35A wore the standard USAF tactical two-tone grey scheme. The fin stripes were red on the starboard side and blue on the port.

Glossary of important terms

AESA: Active Electronically-Scanned Array
ASTOVL: Advanced STOVL (a USMC programme of the late 1980s to replace AV-8s)
ATF: Advanced Tactical Fighter (programme resulting in Lockheed Martin F-22)
CALF: Common Affordable Lightweight Fighter (programme based on ASTOVL but also including CTOL version for USAF)
CDA: Concept Demonstrator Aircraft
CTOL: Conventional Take-off and Landing
CV: aircraft-carrier (version)
DARPA: Defense Advanced Research Projects Agency
Dem/Val: Demonstration/Validation (of concept by two winning designs, of which one chosen to progress to EMD)
DIRS: Distributed Infra-Red System
EMD: Engineering and Manufacturing Development (pre-production development phase of final winning design)
HMD: Helmet-Mounted Display
JAST: Joint Advanced Strike Technology (programme combining CALF and MRF with US Navy F/A-18 replacement)
JIRD: Joint Interim Requirements Document
J/IST: Joint Integrated Subsystems Technology
JORD: Joint Operational Requirements Document (basis upon which EMD proposals are made)
JSF: Joint Strike Fighter (JAST programme renamed in 1996)
LO: Low Observables
LPLC: Lift Plus Lift/Cruise
LSPM: Large-Scale Powered Model
MIRFS: Multi-Function Integrated Radio-Frequency System (radar/EW system for Boeing JSF)
MRF: Multi-Role Fighter (USAF programme to replace F-16)
PWSC: Preferred Weapon System Concept (final design submission)
RALS: Remote Augmented Lift System
RAM: Radar Absorbent Material
RCS: Radar Cross-Section
SETA: Supportable Electromagnetics Test Aircraft (Boeing stealthy test vehicle)
SigMA: Signature Measurement Aircraft (Lockheed stealth test vehicle)
STOVL: Short Take-Off, Vertical Landing
TFLIR: Targeting Forward-Looking Infra-Red

fighter's stealth characteristics; and if those characteristics are compromised, the pilot will not be aware of it.

Problems with Lockheed Martin's clutch system, encountered early in 2000 and apparently solved by mid-summer, were hardly unexpected. "There are some things that analytical tools won't predict," says a Lockheed Martin engineer. The company has changed its control system to allow for smoother clutch engagements.

Accentuated differences

As the Lockheed Martin design has evolved, the differences between the three variants have been accentuated. In the original concept, the different service variants were to be externally identical, out to the edges of the fixed wing structure: the Navy version would have larger leading-edge and trailing-edge flaps, longer outer wings and larger horizontal stabilisers. However, the CV version now has a different wing structure: its wing is larger than that of an F-15 and 34 per cent bigger than the CTOL/STOVL wing.

Lockheed Martin now feels that its choice of a tail-aft design has been vindicated, because the designers have been able to provide the CV version with a much larger wing, while maintaining the same wing-body geometry. On a delta wing (or the Boeing design's highly tapered trapezoidal shape) any attempt to increase span will tend to lengthen or thicken the root, or drives the designer to a lower sweep angle – which changes the wing's lift characteristics and may not match the centre of gravity of the body.

There is a cost for this. Lockheed Martin figures show that the STOVL version of its JSF design has an internal fuel capacity of 13,316 lb (6040 kg) – a not-very-exciting internal fuel fraction of 0.30. This is on the low side for a supersonic fighter with an augmented low-bypass turbofan. Most aircraft with fuel fractions on that scale routinely operate with external fuel tanks. In a sense, this is of limited importance: the USMC, the dominant customer for the STOVL aircraft, is primarily interested in close support and battlefield interdiction missions where LO is less important. The CTOL and CV versions, with a large fuel tank replacing the lift fan, have much higher fuel fractions.

X-32: Boeing's baby

The X-32 design with which Boeing entered the JSF contest was the direct result of studies, which had started in 1992. The company's goal from the outset was a low-cost, tri-service fighter with the highest possible degree of commonality. Its solution was a daring, revolutionary if not exactly beautiful aircraft that looked unlike any other fighter, above or beneath the skin.

Both cost and commonality persuaded Boeing to choose a direct-lift configuration, with no lift-augmenting devices such as a lift fan. Without a fan behind the cockpit, the main lift nozzles would have to be located on the centre of gravity. Consequently, Boeing's designers put the engine in

the front of the aircraft, with vectoring nozzles behind it. The nozzles were used for take-off, transition and landing, and were retracted in cruising flight. A duct from the engine led to the augmentor and a pitch-axis vectoring nozzle in the tail.

The vertical landing weight was limited by the non-reheated thrust of the largest possible derivative engine – an F119 fitted with a larger fan which gave it an increased bypass ratio and more thrust, particularly at low speeds. This meant that it was crucial to minimise the empty weight, while providing enough internal fuel capacity and wing area to meet payload and range requirements. Boeing consequently selected a thick, structurally efficient, large-volume wing, with enough fuel capacity to make external fuel tanks almost superfluous.

The designers selected a delta wing with a 55° leading-edge sweep angle. This was important for two reasons. First, the high sweep angle made it possible to use a very thick section without excessive transonic drag – with the result that the one-piece wing, spanning only 30 ft (9.15 m) on the STOVL aircraft, accommodates 20,062 lb (9100 kg) of fuel (as much internal fuel as an F-15E with conformal tanks.) Second, the sweep angle and leading-edge volume are favourable for installing communications and electronic warfare antennas that have a good field of regard but which do not cause RCS problems.

Folding a delta wing is difficult, because the fold joint will be long and deep. The delta could fit in the same deck spot as an F-18 without folding the wings, as long as the overall length was kept small. But with the engine in the front, bifurcated inlets would add several feet to the overall length, so Boeing selected a radical forward-swept chin inlet.

The wing was set high on the body, to minimise 'suck-down' effects: the jet exhausts tend to induce high-speed airflows under the wing, creating a low-pressure zone that tends to glue the aircraft to the ground. To reduce costs, the upper and lower skins of the wing would be made in one piece, from a carbon-fibre composite material in a thermoplastic matrix.

The result was an aircraft in three main sections: the one-piece wing, which carried most of the flight loads and the main landing gear; the forebody, containing the cockpit and avionics; and the underwing nacelle, which accommodates the engine, powered-lift system and weapon bays. Most of the components which are unique to the STOVL version are in the nacelle.

Boeing was highly confident of the merits of its design. Compared with the shaft-driven or gas-driven lift-fan approaches, it seemed simple and was likely to cost less to build and operate. The company's approach to commonality, confining differences to the smallest possible number of parts, made sense. The more that the JAST office stressed affordability, the more Boeing believed in its delta-wing design – and, unlike Lockheed Martin or McDonnell Douglas, Boeing did not fundamentally change its CALF design as it approached the CDA downselect, although it did grow compared with the original, relatively small AVX-70 design. The company also had to abandon its pet thermoplastic composites for several reasons (including

The very short nose of the X-32 affords the pilot an excellent view forwards, although visibility downwards and to the side of the X-35 cockpit is considered to be better due to the lack of side chines.

battle damage resistance), switching to a titanium structure with composite skins.

Boeing spread the JSF task across a newly expanded company. The X-32s were assembled, checked out and tested at a former Rockwell facility at Palmdale, California, next door to the Lockheed Martin Skunk Works. The forward fuselage assemblies, including the cockpit, were designed and built at the Phantom Works in St. Louis. St. Louis was responsible for the STOVL portion of the flight control laws.

The integration of the new company was not entirely free from friction, but the JSF team proved able to respond to difficulties. It had always been recognised that landing Boeing's design aboard a carrier was going to present challenges, mainly because the short trailing-edge surfaces would have to provide pitch and roll control and lift augmentation without the aid of a separate tail. Boeing did its best, fitting the CV version with 'apex flaps' which had been invented during the company's supersonic transport studies; mounted above and behind the inner leading edges and hinged at the rear, they opened upwards to trap a vortex above the front of the wing. The result was an upward trim moment which could be countered by deflecting the elevons downwards, increasing lift.

Gaining a tail

Late in 1997, the second revision of the JIRD increased the bring-back weight for the CV version of the JSF – the total load of fuel and weapons which the aircraft was expected to bring back to the carrier. During 1998, Boeing continued to work on the delta design, but also studied a modified version with a separate horizontal tail. This version was adopted late in the year and unveiled early in 1999, complete with a revised and lighter inlet design.

Boeing argued strongly that the differences between the CDA and the PWSC design would not invalidate the data from the former aircraft. The wing design, apart from the trailing edge, is not dissimilar, and like any sharply swept wing it develops much of its lift and drag on its leading edge. More philosophically, Boeing argued that what was being demonstrated was not the fighter design itself – since the JSF requirement was evolving, the design was naturally evolving with it – but the technology behind it. Specifically, Boeing could use the CDA to demonstrate that its computer-aided aerodynamic modelling and its wind-tunnel data would accurately predict the performance of the real aircraft. The differences between the CDA and PWSC designs were relatively minor from the viewpoint of basic aerodynamic science, so the CDA would indeed build confidence in the PWSC design.

Boeing's Configuration 374, unveiled in the form of a full-scale mock-up at Farnborough in July 2000, was 'two tenths of a point' away from the company's definitive PWSC, according to the company. It was the first time that the design had been seen in full scale, and the effect was dramatic. It was hard to avoid the impression that the outer wings had been removed to fit the exhibit location, but that was not the case. Indeed, the STOVL version's wing extends less than 10 ft (3 m) on each side of the body, because the STOVL version's span has been reduced to 30 ft (9.15 m) to save weight: Boeing says that the single most difficult requirement in JSF is the vertical-landing bring-back load, and claims that it beats that by 8 per cent.

The US Air Force's conventional take-off and landing (CTOL) version and the Navy's carrier-based (CV) aircraft have 2 ft 11.5 in (90 cm) more wing on each side, with cambered leading edges and leading-edge flaps on the outer wing sections.

Only the United Kingdom has full partner status in the JSF programme, and is fully involved in the 'down-select' process. Indeed, it was UK insistence that the JSF was kept to within the limits of the 'Invincible'-class deck lift that the overall design was shortened by 12 in (30 cm). Stated British requirements stand at 150 STOVL aircraft, to replace the Sea Harrier FA.Mk 2 from 2012 and the Harrier GR.Mk 7/9 from 2015. However, a final decision as to what aircraft will be procured for the Sea Harrier replacement (FCBA – Future Carrierborne Aircraft) requirement will depend also on the outcome of what nature the UK's new aircraft-carriers will take (small STOVL carriers or large CVs). UK participation in the JSF programme includes the provision of test pilots. Lieutenant Commander Paul Stone, RN, became the fifth pilot to fly the X-32A and, as an experienced Harrier pilot, will be heavily involved in the X-32B STOVL tests. The RAF's Squadron Leader Justin Paines is part of the X-35 test team, as is BAE Systems' Simon Hargreaves, a Falklands War Sea Harrier veteran who is involved in X-35B STOVL testing.

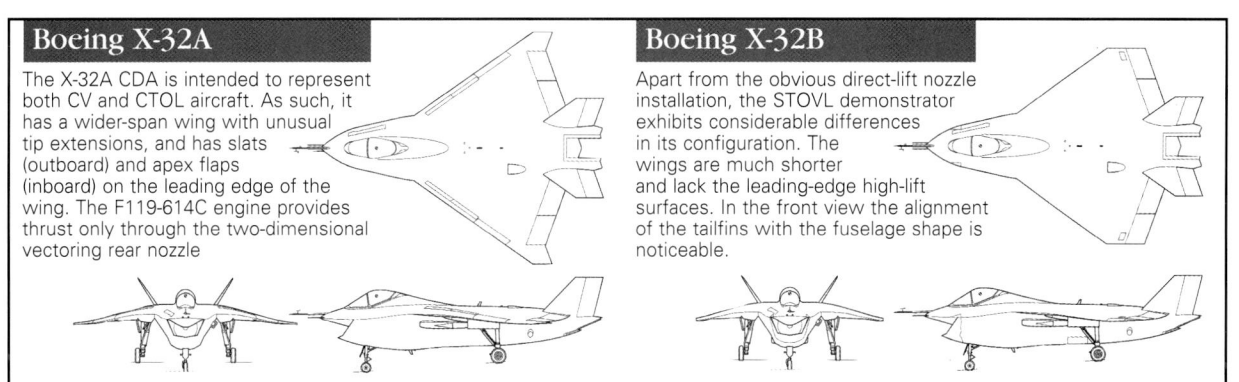

Boeing X-32A

The X-32A CDA is intended to represent both CV and CTOL aircraft. As such, it has a wider-span wing with unusual tip extensions, and has slats (outboard) and apex flaps (inboard) on the leading edge of the wing. The F119-614C engine provides thrust only through the two-dimensional vectoring rear nozzle

Boeing X-32B

Apart from the obvious direct-lift nozzle installation, the STOVL demonstrator exhibits considerable differences in its configuration. The wings are much shorter and lack the leading-edge high-lift surfaces. In the front view the alignment of the tailfins with the fuselage shape is noticeable.

Prior to full FCLP dummy deck landings, the X-32A performed a series of approaches during the 15th flight to test 'wave-off' (i.e. go-around) characteristics. Deployed are the unique apex flaps (vortex fences) located above and behind the leading edges, as well as the more traditional leading-edge flaps.

Boeing engineers prepare to fit the flight-rated F119-614S engine into the X-32B. Note the two nozzles through which thrust is diverted for hovering flight. The engine is designed to be easily and quickly removeable for rapid engine changes 'in the field'.

The Boeing JSF may not look like a classic supersonic fighter design. However, it has enormous engine thrust. Its engine, the Pratt & Whitney JSF 119-PW-614, is the most powerful fighter engine ever designed, believed to produce a thrust in excess of 34,000 lb (151.3 kN) without augmentation, equivalent to the maximum augmented thrust of an F/A-18. It combines the modified F119 core with a scaled-up F119 fan and a new, two-stage low-pressure turbine. On the other side of the speed equation, the fighter's empty weight is low. It carries so much internal fuel that external tanks are superfluous, and has a respectable internal weapon load. The basic airframe may not be a classic example of aerodynamic efficiency – but in clean condition it will have much lower drag than a conventional fighter carrying an equivalent load of fuel and weapons. Another feature of the Boeing propulsion system, with its relatively high bypass ratio and long duct, is that its infra-red signature is relatively low in cruising flight.

The weapon bays are located on each side of the spool duct that connects the engine with the combined augmentor and up-and-away nozzle. One advantage of the side-mounted bays is that the JSF can release weapons from the bay that faces away from the closest threat radar, avoiding a tell-tale RCS spike. Each bay includes two stores stations: one for an AIM-120C AMRAAM air-to-air missile and one for a 2,000-lb (907-kg) air-to-surface weapon carried on a set of swing arms, with the larger-diameter bomb carried above the missile, at the widest point of the nacelle. The arms swing down and out for weapon loading and to release air-to-surface weapons. The AIM-120s can be launched through the lower weapon bay doors, without extending the arms.

The STOVL version of the Boeing design features two retractable vectoring exhaust nozzles, designed by Rolls-Royce. Simple butterfly valves seal the nozzles off in up-and-away flight; in powered-lift mode, the rear nozzle closes down and the valves open. The nozzles vector to 90° aft during transition and continue to rotate after they are shut off, stowing themselves behind flush-fitting doors in the lower fuselage.

Air for control in hovering flight is extracted from two places: the fan stream and the blocked exhaust. A plenum chamber fed by fan air is linked by ducts to two pitch trim and control nozzles, aft of the inlet and either side of the nose landing gear bay, and to a 'jet screen' nozzle behind the nose gear. The latter produces a fan-shaped stream at right angles to the aircraft's long axis, and is specifically designed to inhibit the 'recalculation' of hot exhaust gas into the inlet. Ports in the exhaust nozzle open to admit gas to pitch and yaw control nozzles in the tail and roll control nozzles in the wing.

Stealthy intake

Perhaps the most interesting detail is how the designers have masked the radar return from the engine face. The inlet duct itself does not provide line-of-sight blockage (as the longer ducts on the F-22 and X-35 do), leaving around half 'visible'. An axial-flow RAM-coated baffle is used, perhaps an improved version of the device used on the F/A-18E/F Super Hornet. Such devices are acknowledged to cause a performance loss – which no STOVL aircraft can afford – and are generally not considered to match the low-observable characteristics of a serpentine duct. ("A key feature of a stealth aircraft is a serpentine inlet," charged a Lockheed executive at Farnborough. "Look at aircraft that claim to be LO and see if they have that or not.")

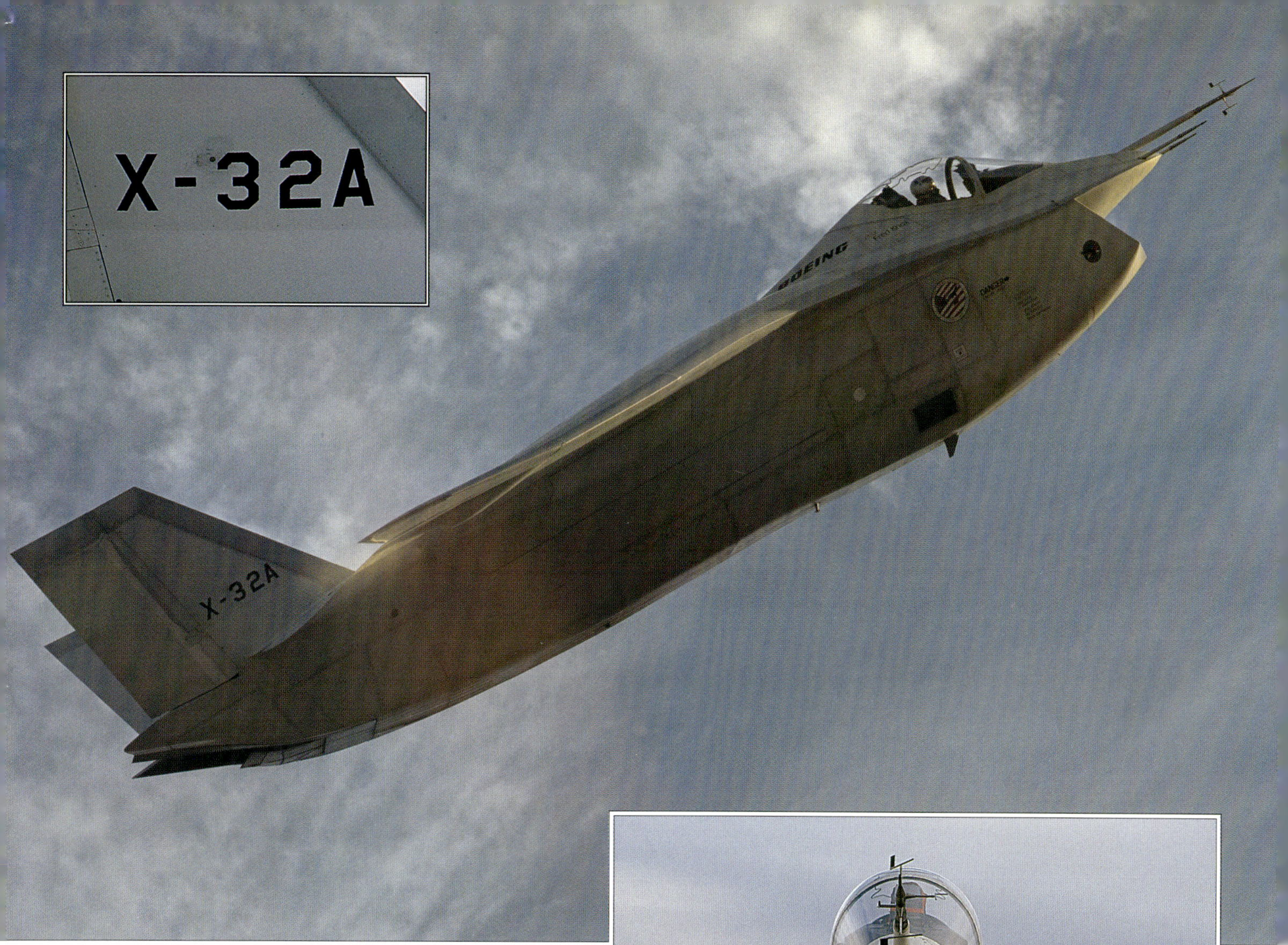

X-32A

Above: This is how Boeing expects the cockpit of its production fighter to look. Although the primary screen area is similar to that in the Lockheed cockpit, it is divided into two side-by-side main displays. The displays are provided by Harris and measure 20 x 25 cm (7.87 x 9.84 in). There are two smaller displays above them. As can be seen in this simulator, the main screens can be sub-divided into windows, so that in this instance four separate displays are presented on one screen. The production cockpit is intended to be HUD-less, relying instead on a BAE Systems helmet-mounted display.

Above: From a stealth point of view the X-32 intake is not an ideal design, leaving some of the engine compressor face 'visible' from certain angles. To overcome this, the engine has a radar blocker in front, in the form of variable inlet guide vanes. The production configuration has a simpler raked back intake lip which performs better at high angles of attack. The STOVL version has a translating intake cowl – the lower portion of the nose moves forward to reveal a blunt-edged lip in the underside which improves airflow capture.

Left: All versions of the Boeing JSF employ a two-dimensional thrust-vectoring nozzle for wing-borne flight. In jet-borne flight the nozzle is closed off, all lift coming from the swivelling direct-lift nozzles which deploy from the centre of the aircraft. The long jetpipe from the forward-mounted engine reduces exhaust temperature, and therefore infra-red signature, considerably.

Lockheed Martin Model 235

Joint Strike Fighter production configurations

Lockheed Martin's PWSC design, submitted to answer the final JORD requirement, closely resembles the X-35 CDAs, although there are some notable differences. The most obvious new feature is the revised shape of the cut-back intake, adopted from Model 230-3 onwards. Weight-saving in areas such as the lift fan installation, weapon-bay and undercarriage bay doors, has allowed Lockheed Martin to add wing area to both CTOL/STOVL and CV versions.

STOVL version – cutaway (left)
The STOVL aircraft is marked by having the large lift fan assembly immediately behind the cockpit, and the 'roll post' ducts leading from either side of the engine to provide stability in the hover. During jetborne flight, air is drawn into the engine through auxiliary intakes positioned aft of the lift fan. In the CV and CTOL versions, the area occupied by the lift fan accommodates extra fuel.

CTOL version – front (above)
The USAF's CTOL version is considered the baseline model. Like the STOVL aircraft, it has a wing span of 35 ft 1 in (10.7 m). The canopy of the production-standard aircraft can resist a 5-lb (2.27-kg) birdstrike.

STOVL version – top (right)
In airframe terms the STOVL aircraft enjoys 81 percent commonality with the baseline CTOL design. The wing is essentially the same. The main external features are the two sets of doors aft of the cockpit, the forward set covering the lift fan and the rear set covering the auxiliary hovering intake. The STOVL version employs a different nozzle to the CV and CTOL aircraft

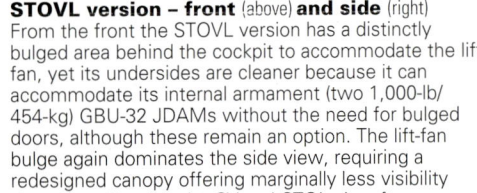

STOVL version – front (above) **and side** (right)
From the front the STOVL version has a distinctly bulged area behind the cockpit to accommodate the lift fan, yet its undersides are cleaner because it can accommodate its internal armament (two 1,000-lb/454-kg) GBU-32 JDAMs without the need for bulged doors, although these remain an option. The lift-fan bulge again dominates the side view, requiring a redesigned canopy offering marginally less visibility than those fitted to the CV and CTOL aircraft.

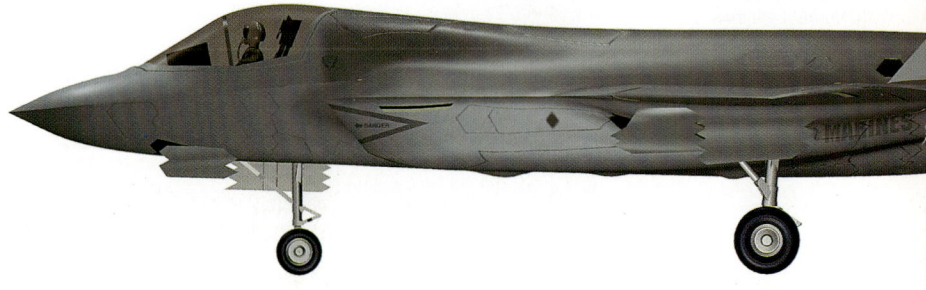

CTOL version – side (above)
Weighing in empty at 26,477 lb (12010 kg), the CTOL model is the only one with an internal 27-mm cannon, mounted in the port wingroot, although it is an option for the other two. The aircraft has bulged weapon bay doors to accommodate a 2,000-lb (907-kg) weapon in each bay (as well as an AIM-120 AMRAAM) and has a low-observable axisymmetric nozzle. A boom receptacle for refuelling is located behind the cockpit. The airframe is designed to withstand 9 *g*.

CTOL version – top (left)
The CTOL aircraft has a wing area of 459.6 sq ft (42.7 m²), which compares to 412.3 sq ft (38.3 m²) for the X-35A/B. Noteworthy in the top view is the Mauser BK 27 cannon installation and the refuelling receptacle.

CV version – top (left)
From the top the differences between the CV model and the other two are obvious: the aircraft has much larger wings and tailplanes, necessary to keep approach speed within the Navy's requirements. This area increase is achieved by 'picture-framing' the existing wing structure The wing area of the CV JSF is 620 sq ft (57.6 m²), compared with 600 sq ft (55.7 m²) for the X-35C. The lack of refuelling receptacle is apparent, although the aircraft has a retractable probe on the upper starboard side of the nose. The extra weight and wing area means that the CV version is normally restricted to 7.5-*g* manoeuvres, although there is an override function which allows limited manoeuvring up to 9 *g* for dogfighting.

CV version – front (below)
From the front the wider span (43 ft/13.1 m) of the CV aircraft is immediately apparent, as are the bulges under the wings used to house the wing-fold actuators. Folded span for the design is 30 ft (9.13 m). Like the CTOL aircraft, it has bulged weapon bays for 2,000-lb (907-kg) class weapons such as the GBU-31 JDAM.

CV version – side (below)
Owing to its larger wings and tail surfaces, and to the strengthened undercarriage, arrester hook and other naval features, the CV is appreciably heavier than the CTOL aircraft, at 29,841 lb (13536 kg) empty. In airframe terms it is only 62 percent common with the CTOL aircraft, but in overall terms (including avionics and powerplant) it is around 70-80 percent common.

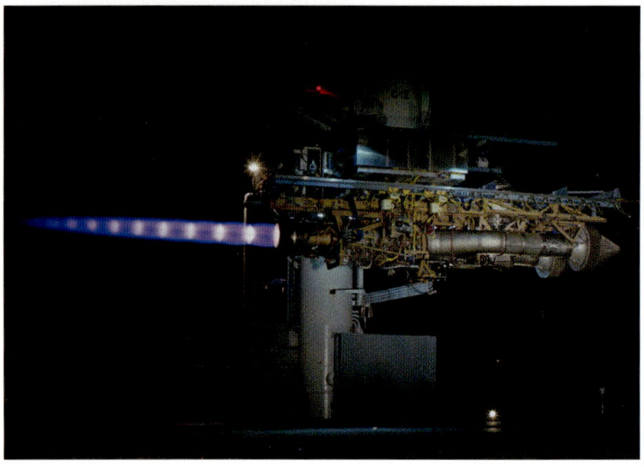

The JSF demonstration phase has required Pratt & Whitney to produce four different flight-rated models of the F119 engine. The Boeing X-32 engines are designated F119-614C for the CTOL/CV X-32A and -614S for the STOVL X-32B, while the X-35 engines are the F119-611C and -611S. The first test runs were accomplished at Pratt & Whitney's West Palm Beach facility in Florida on 11 June 1998, where most of the testing has taken place. Shown here are an F119-611 in full afterburner (left) and the F119-614S STOVL engine (far left).

However, Boeing has devised a variable-geometry radar blocker which can provide optimum LO characteristics for ingress and attack, and high performance for air combat (when the aircraft has by definition been detected) and vertical landing. Unlike the F/A-18E/F's fixed baffle, the X-32's blocker has variable inlet guide vanes which twist to allow maximum airflow for hovering and high-thrust manoeuvring, but close up in the cruise to deliver minimum radar returns. If it works from both the aerodynamic and RCS standpoints, it is an important accomplishment.

Power for the JSF

JSF is much more than the design of a versatile airframe. An array of supporting programmes is working on technologies for other systems that will be needed for the new aircraft.

Both Pratt & Whitney and General Electric are working on designs for production engines. If the Pentagon thinks that commonality is so important for JSF, why are there two engines? One reason is that memories of the P&W F100 engine, which was developed for the F-15 and F-16, are fresh enough to hurt. The F100 suffered from nagging problems, which were not fixed until the USAF commissioned the GE F110 as an alternative engine. Many people still believe that it was the threat of losing future business that spurred Pratt & Whitney to respond to the customer's pleas for reliability. The JSF is also uniquely vulnerable to engine problems. Reliability and performance cannot be traded against one another: a shortfall in performance or handling could render the STOVL version unworkable, while a reliability problem would be unacceptable to the US Navy.

Until a JSF winner is announced, both engine teams are working on two distinctly different engines. The Boeing design has a larger fan and mass flow, and a two-dimensional nozzle which will be integrated into the fighter's afterbody structure. The Lockheed engine has a smaller fan, but its turbine must be sized to drive the forward lift fan, and it has to be integrated with two different final nozzles: a stealth nozzle for the CV and CTOL variants and a vectoring nozzle for the STOVL aircraft. Within each engine team, the groups working with each manufacturer work within security firewalls so that the airframe teams' confidential data is protected.

With its X-32A, Boeing demonstrated both CV and CTOL qualities, as production aircraft of both versions are relatively similar (unlike the Lockheed Martin approach, in which STOVL and CTOL are similar). One of the toughest requirements for both JSF teams to meet is the USMC's need for a STOVL aircraft which can bring back 5,000 lb (2268 kg) of weapons with sufficient fuel for a 5-minute hover and 5-minute taxi.

X-35

301

Above: The X-35's intakes are optimised for stealth, incorporating the familiar trapezoidal cross-section but with a noticeable 'bump'. The bulge, which was tested on an F-16, serves two purposes. Firstly, it turns the intake trunk into a serpentine shape, shielding the engine compressor face from prying radars, and secondly it causes the sluggish boundary layer to spill around the intake, thereby removing the need for a standard splitter plate, or diverter. In the production standard Model 235, the intakes are three- rather than four-sided, and cut back compared to those on the X-35.

Right: The nozzles of the CTOL and CV production versions would have a serrated edge instead of the standard jetpipe fitted to the X-35. In the STOVL version the panels under the jetpipe form doors, which drop down to allow the nozzle to swivel freely to provide jet-borne lift.

Above: This is the actual cockpit of the X-35A and, although it looks modern enough, is completely unrepresentative of the futuristic cockpit planned for the production machine. The latter has a single contiguous 20 x 50-cm (7.87 x 19.68-in) projected display stretching across the whole dashboard and, as with the Boeing design, the HUD has been eliminated in favour of an HMD (in this case made by VSI). A small data entry panel is mounted below the main display, although all key inputs can be made via the throttle or sidestick. Boeing's X-32 demonstrators are also flying with a HUD and different instrumentation.

Boeing X-32A Concept Demonstrator Aircraft

Boeing JSF Test Team
Edwards AFB, California

Whereas Lockheed Martin's X-35 CDA is remarkably close in most respects to its final PWSC design, Boeing's X-32 CDA is somewhat different to the Model 375 which forms the basis of the company's PWSC submission. Production aircraft would have redesigned tail surfaces, including conventional tailplanes, while the wings become swept back. The aircraft also differ more between the various models than is the case with the X-32A/B. The CTOL and CV versions have extended wings (span 36 ft/11 m, area 565 sq ft/52.48 m²) compared to the STOVL aircraft (span 30 ft/9.15 m, area 504 sq ft/46.82 m²), and the CV version has enlarged tailplanes and vertical fins compared to the CV/STOVL aircraft. The STOVL design has its fuselage shortened by 1 ft 3.4 in (0.39 m) by taking out a slice aft of the wing to save weight, although if selected for EMD Boeing hopes to restore all three versions to the same length. Additional differences include heavy-duty undercarriage with twin nosewheel unit, and ailerons to improve low-speed roll control for the CV version. Nevertheless, Boeing claims to retain around 85-90 percent commonality between the three variants.

Accommodation
The X-32 pilot sits under a two-section canopy, although the production standard has a single-piece, rearward-hinging canopy. Lockheed Martin's PWSC design has a two-section forward-hinging canopy. The ejection seat is the Martin-Baker Mk 16 lightweight unit – considered as the state-of-the-art in modern fighter seats. the X-32s have MDC (Miniature Detonating Cord) inlaid in the canopy to shatter the glass prior to ejection. At present there is no stated requirement for a two-seater.

Vertical tails
In its original designs, Boeing placed the vertical fins at the ends of the wings, but a more conventional location was found to be lighter. The fins are canted outwards by 28°, not only for low observability, but also to provide stability and control during high-Alpha carrier approaches should the nozzle vectoring fail. The two-dimensional vectoring nozzle is integrated into the flight control system and provides most of the pitch control.

Control surfaces
The X-32A has two sections of control surfaces on the rear of the wing, operating differentially to provide roll control, or simultaneously to provide pitch control. They also act as flaps. In the production version, the wing has flaperons only in the STOVL/CTOL versions, while the CV version adds ailerons on the outer (folding) section to improve roll authority at low speeds. It also has larger tailplanes and vertical fins. Both CTOL and CV versions have leading-edge surfaces, known as apex flaps, which open upwards into the airflow. The result is a pitch-up moment, countered by a corresponding drooping of the flaperons, which increases lift significantly. The production STOVL aircraft does not have these surfaces.

en approaching the
ears, up to and
elta wing
nd 20° sweep-
ured as it offers
JSF's wing holds
e JSF requirements
lifficulties with
he biggest problem
nce. In late 1998 the
t-back wing (with
conventional
alter the CDA
its upper skin being
posite piece. The
e unusual tip

Powerplant
The Pratt & Whitney F119-614 which powers the X-32 is the most powerful fighter engine ever built, and has produced around 50,000 lb (222.5 kN) in full afterburner during tests, although it would normally be rated at 42,000 lb (186.9 kN). Based on the F-22's engine, the Boeing JSF powerplant has a large (3-ft 9-in/1.14-m) fan to generate a high bypass ratio for STOVL operation. The X-32B STOVL demonstrator has two nozzles which deploy through doors in the aircraft's underside. Around 36,000 lb (160.2 kN) of thrust can be deflected through these doors (the remainder being diverted to hover control outlets and the 'jet screen'), and the nozzles can vector from 45° aft to 15° forward. In hover mode the main jetpipe is completely closed off. When operating normally, the nozzle can vector through 20° above or below the horizontal.

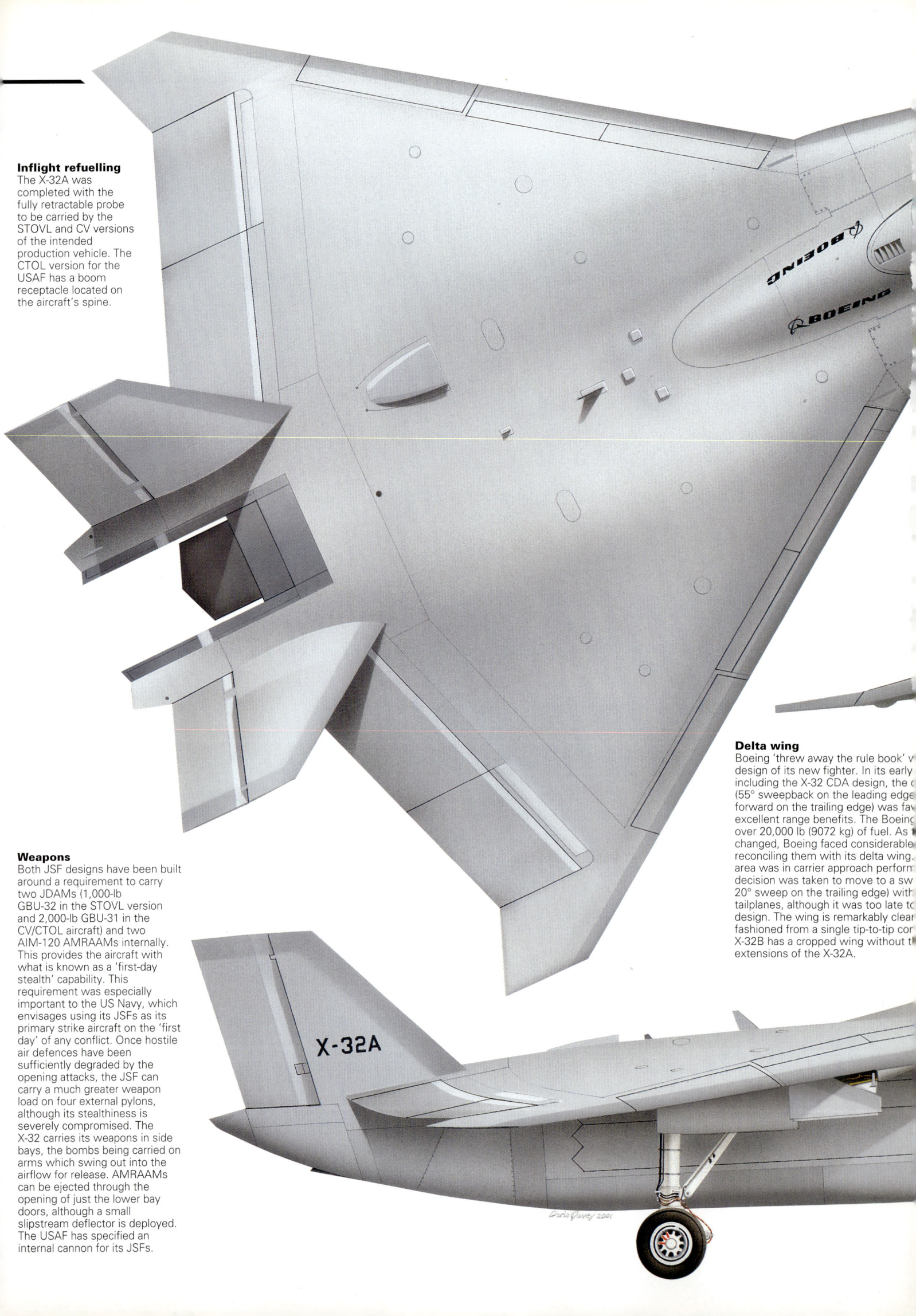

Inflight refuelling
The X-32A was completed with the fully retractable probe to be carried by the STOVL and CV versions of the intended production vehicle. The CTOL version for the USAF has a boom receptacle located on the aircraft's spine.

Delta wing
Boeing 'threw away the rule book' v
design of its new fighter. In its early
including the X-32 CDA design, the d
(55° sweepback on the leading edge
forward on the trailing edge) was fav
excellent range benefits. The Boeing
over 20,000 lb (9072 kg) of fuel. As
changed, Boeing faced considerable
reconciling them with its delta wing.
area was in carrier approach perform
decision was taken to move to a sw
20° sweep on the trailing edge) with
tailplanes, although it was too late to
design. The wing is remarkably clear
fashioned from a single tip-to-tip cor
X-32B has a cropped wing without t
extensions of the X-32A.

Weapons
Both JSF designs have been built around a requirement to carry two JDAMs (1,000-lb GBU-32 in the STOVL version and 2,000-lb GBU-31 in the CV/CTOL aircraft) and two AIM-120 AMRAAMs internally. This provides the aircraft with what is known as a 'first-day stealth' capability. This requirement was especially important to the US Navy, which envisages using its JSFs as its primary strike aircraft on the 'first day' of any conflict. Once hostile air defences have been sufficiently degraded by the opening attacks, the JSF can carry a much greater weapon load on four external pylons, although its stealthiness is severely compromised. The X-32 carries its weapons in side bays, the bombs being carried on arms which swing out into the airflow for release. AMRAAMs can be ejected through the opening of just the lower bay doors, although a small slipstream deflector is deployed. The USAF has specified an internal cannon for its JSFs.

X-32A

replace some of the composites in the F119-PW-100 with heavier but less costly metal, and to use solid fan blades in place of hollow titanium components.

Another new feature of the JSF engine will be a prognostic feature built into its control system, intended to predict failures before they damage the engine or imperil the aircraft. This will comprise sensors that monitor pressures, temperatures, vibration and stresses in the engine and sample the exhaust stream for metal particles. Combined with a computer model of the engine and with a detailed history of its use, this should allow the prognostic system to identify signs of incipient failures.

One respect in which the F119 will foreshadow the JSF engine is in its attention to maintainability. The F119, for example, is designed so that no small items – filler caps, fasteners or clamps – separate from the engine during routine maintenance. Push-open ports are used to replenish and inspect fluids, and clamps are designed so that they stay on the engine. Safety wires (which prevent threaded connectors from rotating) are banished in favour of spider-shaped spring clips that do the same job.

GE has been heading the design of the alternate engine, the JSF120-FX, since 1996, but has not been allowed to say very much about it. The JSF120-FX core was tested in August 2000, and a full-scale prototype engine for the winning design will be complete and should be ground-tested in 2003. EMD should start in the same year and the alternate engine should be available in the fourth production lot of JSFs, for delivery in 2010. However, it appears that the new engine will be only loosely based on the original F120 (which was developed to power the F-22, but beaten by the F119) and will use the same core as an advanced version of the best-selling CFM56 commercial engine.

In 1998, GE and its French partner, SNECMA, announced that they were starting a programme called TECH56, aimed at renewing the technology of the CFM56. This would include a new core (the hot section of the engine, comprising the compressor, combustor and high-pressure turbine) with fewer stages and blades. The GE-developed core uses some of the technology developed by GE and Allison Advanced Development Company (AADC) under the Pentagon's Integrated High-Performance Turbine Engine Technology (IHPTET) programme. GE is also looking at a development roadmap under which more advanced IHPTET technology – including advanced variable-cycle engines requiring no afterburning – could be used for later JSF variants.

Pratt & Whitney's JSF engine will be the only engine available on the first 100 or so aircraft; after that, the Pentagon's JSF engine buy will be split each year, with the size of each supplier's share determined by an annual competition. New export customers will be able to choose either engine.

Flying controls

A key difference between the two JSFs and the Harrier is the use of fly-by-wire control for the airframe and the propulsion system. The Harrier's controls are separately and mechanically connected to the flight controls, the 'puffer' nozzles, the engine control unit and the vectoring nozzles – the control integration takes place in the pilot's head. Harrier operations are both demanding and hazardous. On the JSF, the entire powered lift and propulsion system are controlled by computers.

This should make the aircraft easier to fly. Both contractors have adopted a similar control scheme: as the aircraft transitions from wing-borne to jet-borne flight, the throttle and stick functions change. The stick controls longitudinal and lateral acceleration; the throttle becomes a vertical speed commander. The transition is largely automated; the pilot places a helmet-mounted display cursor over the intended hover point and the aircraft flies to that point.

Propulsion tests have been exhaustive, because of the potential for catastrophe if the control software so much as

The X-35A demonstrated its inflight refuelling capability during its 10th flight, on 7 November 2000. Flown by Lieutenant Colonel Paul Smith, the first USAF pilot to fly the type, the X-35A refuelled four times during the sortie, enabling the test sortie to reach 2 hours 50 minutes duration. Tanking was accomplished at 23,000 ft (7010 m) and employed a Boeing NKC-135E from the Edwards-based 412th Test Wing. The X-35C later confirmed its refuelling compatibility with the KC-10 Extender.

P&W's production engine will resemble the F119 in many respects, but will be very different in one characteristic: cost. The target cost for the JSF engine, one engineer remarks, is "not even close" to the F119 for the F-22. On the production JSF engine, P&W has already decided to

sneezes. Both propulsion systems have been assembled in open-air rigs at Pratt & Whitney's West Palm Beach facility, and operated extensively with pilots in the loop, 'flying' the systems from simulators.

Low-cost stealth

While the JSF will not set any new records in weapon load, speed, agility and range, it will, in many respects, be very unusual under the skin. Structures, subsystems and avionics have all been re-invented. The common factor in all these areas is to save money. Although joint production will help reduce costs, the battle to meet the cost targets will be won or lost on the details.

One of the biggest such challenges will be achieving low-cost stealth. Although details are veiled by national and competitive security concerns, the JSF is likely to follow the approach taken by the F-22's designers, who have attempted to reduce the very high maintenance costs associated with stealth on earlier aircraft.

Gaps and openings in the skin are the biggest cause of high costs in stealth maintenance. Unless a gap is properly sealed, it will interrupt the flow of electromagnetic energy over the skin and cause unwanted and unpredictable radar reflections. Although there are ways to make it cheaper to test and repair breaks in the skin, the first key to affordable stealth is to minimise the number of openings and gaps.

For example, one important thrust in the JSF avionics system is to use shared electronic and optical sensor apertures. In the radio-frequency (RF) band, a total of just over 20 antennas should replace almost 60 antennas on the F-22, covering communications, navigation and identification functions with passive and active surveillance. A common set of IR sensors performs targeting, navigation and threat warning functions. This eliminates 40 specially designed and treated antenna mountings.

Structurally, the use of large, integrated composite parts eliminates skin gaps and fasteners, and the JSF will make the greatest possible use of the weapon bays and landing gear bay doors to provide access to the most frequently maintained systems.

Another basic way to reduce stealth maintenance costs is to minimise maintenance for internal parts. On the YF-22 prototype, Lockheed engineers made a point of measuring the heat and vibration levels inside the structure. Internal components – from pipes to pumps to computers – are designed to withstand the real environment rather than to a standard military specification. Another important tool for LO support is diagnostics – knowing exactly what broke, so the maintainer knows which panel to take off.

Where an access panel is needed, a stealth designer has a choice between two types of access panel. A conventional panel is light and inexpensive, but has to be sealed with tape, caulk or putty after it is removed. Engineers call

this "breaking the LO bubble": after the panel is re-installed, the seal has to be checked to make sure that the aircraft is still stealthy. The alternative is a 'frequent access panel', which can be opened and closed easily. However, it must be rigid and fitted with a secure latching system and a special gasket, so that it will not cause a physical or electromagnetic discontinuity in the surface when it is closed.

Like the F-22, JSF will use fewer different kinds of LO material than the B-2 and F-117, where LO goals were paramount and designers tended to select the material which was best suited to the requirements in any particular location – with the result that different types of material proliferated.

However, both JSF teams have taken the same new approach to LO development. In earlier programmes, pre-EMD signature models were usually simple; apertures and antennas, if they were present at all, were represented generically. But the JSF models – Lockheed Martin's Signature Measurement Aircraft (SigMA) and Boeing's Supportable Electromagnetics Test Aircraft (SETA) – have been constructed to a standard of detail and fidelity which is unprecedented this early in a programme, before EMD. SigMA and SETA are more accurate and detailed, including flight-quality components, than the models in earlier programmes.

Both models were tested at sophisticated facilities which can gather and analyse complex RCS information, includ-

Right: Lockheed Martin engineers apply the special adhesive film to a test F-16 to demonstrate the appliqué covering intended for the JSF in place of paint. The skin was tested at Mach 1.8. As well as the estimated $3 billion saving in JSF life-cycle costs (based on a 3,000-aircraft run), the appliqué also stops the aircraft slowly gaining weight as successive coats of paint are applied, and is far more environmentally-friendly than traditional sprayed-on paints.

1990s. The adhesive-backed polymer sheets – which can be coloured with pigments or treated with infra-red or radar-absorbent material – are pre-cut to fit the aircraft and can be removed and replaced easily.

The stealth export question

A large – and so far undefined – challenge with JSF's stealth requirements is the fact that the aircraft is intended to be exported. Stealth technology was developed under the utmost secrecy in the US and is still subject to tight and specific export restrictions. A secretive committee – the Low Observables/Counter Low Observables Executive Committee (Excom) – rules on the export of stealth-related technologies and ensures that no Pentagon agency accidentally permits the export of technology that could compromise another agency's secret programme.

There are in theory three ways to deal with the LO export problem. One is to deliver the same configuration to all customers; the second is to develop an export configuration with a lower, but known level of LO; and the third is simply to delete sensitive materials from export versions.

In fact, the third option is not acceptable. One of the earliest lessons of stealth was that stealth which cannot be measured and maintained in fine detail cannot be exploited tactically. A sanitised JSF would be a non-stealthy aircraft and would have to operate with the same protection – such as onboard countermeasures and escort jammers – as today's aircraft.

Early in the JSF programme, JSF programme managers talked about modular stealth technology. Export JSFs could be delivered without the most sensitive materials, but would still be stealthy. However, there are problems with this approach. First, developing a JSF variant with higher, fully modelled radar cross-section levels than the standard US aircraft would be expensive. It would involve a complete testing programme and might mean that many components (such as antennas) would be different. Moreover, it would require different software in the onboard systems which compute the detection range of radar threats against the JSF and display that information to the pilot, and that software would have to be separately supported throughout the fighter's service life. Would the export version need an active electronic jammer (unlike the standard model)? Was it worth giving up manoeuvrability and AIM-9 capability for a reduced level of stealth?

By late 1998, according to some JSF programme officials, the commanders-in-chief (CINCs) in charge of US forces around the world had weighed into the debate. Coalition operations, they argued, would be extremely complicated if different partners in the force had JSFs with different stealth characteristics. (This would not only complicate tactical planning; the fact that an ally's JSFs were more vulnerable than those belonging to US forces would be politically sensitive.) In early 1999, there were indications that the single-configuration option had been chosen.

But this raises serious security issues. LO treatments require maintenance at the flight-line level and will be physically accessible to a large number of people. Even more importantly, the threat-warning software in every JSF relies on a database that models the fighter's detectability to all known threat radars: an adversary who obtained that software would be able to optimise his defences against the fighter.

Currently, however, no decision has been taken. The JSF programme office says that it does not have the authority to take a decision, and the LO/CLO Excom has not ruled on the issue, with one exception: the UK has full access to JSF stealth technology, but with tight firewall restrictions which restrict the UK's ability to participate in European LO programmes.

The true 'Electric Jet'

Internally, JSF will pioneer another major change in technology – which stems indirectly from work under the Star Wars programme in the 1980s. Looking at the need to put

All-aspect stealth is an important factor in the JSF designs. Lockheed Martin tested the RCS of its design using its 98-ft (30-m) pole at the Helendale, California, signature test facility. The JSF model can be rotated in azimuth and elevation, and in this view is mounted inverted so that the underside of the aircraft can be tested.

ing detailed modelling of small components and accurate assessments of the RCS-reduction performance of different types of RAM. Lockheed Martin tested SigMA at its outdoor RCS range at Helendale, California, which was comprehensively upgraded in the mid-1980s; Boeing has used its indoor range at Boeing Field in Seattle.

The companies will also be using LO materials that are durable and easy to repair. Lockheed Martin has aimed at LO systems which are damage-tolerant, and tested the SigMA model with significant LO-related damage: tests showed that it was combat-ready, and the damage was repaired in a single shift. The company says the that visitors and technicians "routinely walk on the model wearing street shoes and work boots. No discernible RCS degradation has been detected as a result of months of such handling."

Some of these materials are likely to take the form of appliqué sheets rather than paints. Lockheed Martin and 3M have been working on this technology since the mid-

powerful electrical systems on spacecraft, Star Wars researchers developed new ways of converting and controlling electrical power in lightweight, solid-state packages. This technology now makes it practical to use electrical power to replace hydraulic systems. Electrical wiring requires less maintenance than hydraulic lines and is less vulnerable to combat damage.

The USAF was working on this technology before JSF started, and had concluded that the logical extension was to develop an integrated system that would replace all the mechanical accessories which are normally connected to the fighter's engine. This effort was absorbed by JSF, and is now known as JSF Integrated Subsystems Technology (J/IST).

Lockheed Martin led the inflight demonstration of electric technology, and modified the hard-worked Advanced Fighter Technology Integration (AFTI) F-16 prototype as the first fighter to fly with all its primary flight controls both signalled and powered by electricity, and with no mechanical backup. These tests were completed in early 2001.

A team led by Lockheed Martin, including Honeywell, Northrop Grumman, Hamilton Sundstrand and Pratt & Whitney has demonstrated the Thermal/Energy Management Module (T/EMM), the core of J/IST. The Honeywell T/EMM is an integrated turbine system, on a common shaft, which provides auxiliary and emergency electrical power, air for pressurisation, and cooling for cockpit and avionics.

Its unique feature is that it can operate in three modes. To start the aircraft or provide power on the ground, it operates as a gas turbine APU using outside air. In flight, the T/EMM is driven by engine bypass air and provides electrical power and cool air. In the event of an engine flame-out or stall, the T/EMM is driven by compressed air stored in an onboard reservoir, maintaining essential power to the aircraft's controls until the pilot can get the JSF pointed downhill and perform an air-start. The T/EMM replaces the air-conditioning system, auxiliary generator, APU and emergency power unit (on the F-16, the last-named uses hydrazine and is a logistical nuisance) with a single system.

Potentially, the T/EMM and the more-electric systems can simplify the propulsion system. A modern fighter engine has a 'tower shaft' which links the engine shaft to an airframe-mounted accessory drive (AMAD). The AMAD is a compact package of gears, clutches and constant-speed drives that, in turn, drives the hydraulic pumps, electrical generators and the environmental control system (ECS) compressor. In the JSF, the only system mechanically connected to the engine may be the primary starter-generator.

Advanced construction techniques

JSF will use new structural technology to reduce both weight and cost – a radical change from earlier advanced composite materials, which saved some weight but cost the earth to produce. For example, Lockheed Martin uses fibre-placement technology to build the JSF inlet duct, building the complex component directly from carbon-fibre tape, wound around a mandrel and simultaneously impregnated with epoxy matrix material by a robotic tool. In both designs, components which would usually have been made from many sheet metal parts and innumerable fasteners are produced by high-speed machining.

The tools and materials that are used to build an aircraft are only half the cost battle, though. The cost of building and assembling an aircraft is built into every part, and the way in which it is designed. Lockheed Martin has worked with IBM and Dassault to expand Dassault's CATIA computer-aided design system into a 'virtual development environment'. The goal is 100 percent digital prototyping: as the designer works on a component, the effects of a design decision on part manufacture, assembly and support

On 5 January 2001 Boeing demonstrated the inflight cycling of the weapon bay doors (above), followed later in the flight test programme by similar tests with an instrumented AIM-120 AMRAAM and an inert JDAM inside (top). The bay doors were opened and closed several times to check vibration and acoustic levels. The side-mounted bays of the Boeing design have the advantage of being more stealthy, as the pilot can open the doors on the side opposite to any threat radar. The bays also allow armourers to work at eye level. The AIM-120, in 'compressed carriage' (cropped-fin) form, is so far the only air-to-air weapon envisioned for the JSF.

In its last task before being retired, the long-serving AFTI/F-16 flew with 'power-by-wire' electric flight control/actuation systems to test components destined for the JSF. As the first all-electric fighter it first flew on 24 October 2000 with Steve Barter at the helm. During 1998 the flight control system had been tested using the NF-16D VISTA aircraft, while in the UK the much-modified VAAC Harrier T.Mk 4 undertook a 36-flight test of a new sidestick control system for the STOVL version. The F-16 LOAN tested the low-observable nozzle for the CV/CTOL JSF.

Right: Seen during its 18th flight, the X-32A is piloted by Commander Phillip 'Rowdy' Yates during dummy-deck carrier landing approaches. Boeing's production configuration JSF requires ailerons to meet US Navy approach roll authority requirements.

Below: On 3 March 2001 the X-32A returned to Palmdale at the conclusion of the CV/CTOL tests. During the course of 66 flights it had amassed 50.4 hours and had been flown by six pilots.

are simulated on the computer before any physical work is done. By simulating all these effects, it is possible to calculate the impact of a design decision on life-cycle cost.

Advanced CAD techniques are key to building three distinct JSF versions on the same production line. The designer's dilemma is that each version encounters different structural loads. If the airframes are identical, and all parts are strong enough to take the load imposed by the heaviest version, the other variants will be too heavy. On the other hand, if the aircraft are different the benefits of commonality are lost.

Boeing has emphasised the fact that its X-32s have done more than show how the aircraft will fly; they show how it will be built. Reflecting almost a decade of Phantom Works studies and demonstrations, the X-32s exploit a number of manufacturing and assembly innovations.

Boeing is credited with developing the concept of 'cousin parts'. These might, for example, be components that carry more load on the Navy version than they do on the USMC and USAF aircraft, but are otherwise unaffected

by the different missions. Cousin parts differ in thickness, weight and strength, but are built on the same tools, with the same materials, and are assembled in the same way. Because there are three JSF versions, every component falls into one of five groups: tri-common (common on three versions); dual-common; tri-cousin, dual-cousin and unique. CAD allows the designer to try a series of different combinations of common, cousin and unique parts, and to evaluate which combination is most economical.

Another principle being demonstrated in the X-32 programme is 'design anywhere, build anywhere'. This means the use of computer-aided design and manufacture to fabricate components so accurately that they will fit precisely without shims or trimming. "In the old days," remarks John Priday, leader of the X-32 assembly team at Palmdale, "you allowed half an inch extra on all sides of a skin panel and prayed you had enough. Now, the skins come to us net-trimmed, with zero excess, and they fit like a glove."

One of the new tools used by the X-32 team was a 'smart router' for fuel, hydraulic and oxygen lines. Given the basic outlines of the fighter's plumbing systems, the router defined all the parts in the system in terms of bend radius, wall thickness, junction fittings and loss factors, working from a deliberately constrained parts library. Such was the confidence in this system that parts arrived at Palmdale with hose brackets already in place.

Every one of the 88 lines in the forward fuselage fit correctly, first time, and there was not a single leak when the X-32A's fuel system was pressure-tested in December – to the open amazement of the Phantom Works deputy leader – former USAF programme director George Muellner.

Palmdale's first venture into laser-guided major assembly took place in April 1999, when the forebody arrived from St. Louis to join the mid-body section. "Six hours after it arrived, we had moved it into the mate position, tracked it in with the laser and drilled the holes," remarks Priday. "Most of that time was disassembling the box it came in – there were lots of bolts in it. We did it on April 1 and everyone thought we were kidding."

'Design anywhere, build anywhere' allows the prime contractor to buy large and critical components from outside suppliers, no matter where they are, in the confidence that parts will fit when they arrive and will not have to be returned for re-work. Also, because the new philosophy of assembly calls for major components to arrive on the line with electrical, fuel and hydraulic components in place, they are more valuable than the traditional bare-bones aircraft parts, and represent more work and income for the supplier.

The prime contractors welcome this trend, because they are trying to build less of their products. This apparently paradoxical strategy is called "moving up the value chain", according to Mike Heinz, Boeing vice-president and JSF deputy programme manager. The primes make their greatest profits from designing and integrating aircraft, and from playing a leading role in upgrade and support programmes after they are in service. The slimmest margins, compared to the investment required, are in fabricating aircraft structures and parts.

JSF avionics

Avionics account for as much as a third of the cost of a fighter, so the JSF cost goals give the contractors no option but to find ways to make electronic systems less costly. Broadly speaking, the JSF goal is to take the capabilities of the F-22, add air-to-surface capability and subtract a lot of weight and a lot of money. Like the F-22, JSF will have a centralised system in which most avionics functions (such as mission management and signal processing) reside in an Integrated Core Processor (ICP), a powerful battery of computers. As on the F-22, the ICP is likely to comprise a backplane providing power, cooling and data connections to easily changed snap-in modules.

The main difference will be an emphasis on an open architecture and the use of commercial standards. The goal is to design the ICP so that the modules can use whatever processors the commercial market can supply, as JSFs are built and upgraded. Not only are these commercial chips likely to be cheaper and higher-performing than a custom chip, but a chip developed today for JSF may not even be available in 2008.

As on the F-22, the JSF sensors are apertures which act as peripherals to the ICP, which will fuse sensor information and off-board data with database information before feeding it to the displays.

One example of this new technology is the JSF sensor and processing suite. Raytheon, which is leading this effort for Boeing, unveiled some of its JSF avionics work in mid-2000, including a previously undisclosed link between the JSF and the F/A-18E/F Super Hornet programme.

Raytheon's work is headquartered in El Segundo, California, and is centred on the former Hughes company. Raytheon produces the Multi-Function Integrated Radio-Frequency System (MIRFS) – the forward-looking active, electronically scanned array (AESA) radar. Raytheon is teamed with BAE Systems (the former Lockheed Sanders) to produce the fighter's electronic warfare systems, and works with Boeing and Harris on its integrated core processor (ICP). Raytheon also supplies the two elements of the IR system: the distributed infra-red system (DIRS) and the targeting FLIR (TFLIR).

MIRFS "is no longer just a radar," according to Raytheon JSF team leader Dr Peter Pao. "It detects and jams enemy radars. It's hard to tell where EW ends and radar begins, and we believe the boundary will disappear in 10 years."

The Raytheon JSF radar is one-quarter as heavy as an AESA using 1995 technology, says Pao, and it uses advanced transmit/receive modules which cover four radar channels. As well as offering radar modes such as synthetic aperture radar (SAR) and ground moving target indication (GMTI), it functions as a sensitive passive receiver and a very powerful jammer.

Looking 'through the floor'

The DIRS comprises six fixed, staring focal plane array (FPA) sensors, each with a 60° x 60° field of view, located around the aircraft behind flush windows and covering a complete spherical field of view. The DIRS has three simultaneous functions. It provides all-round imagery to the pilot's helmet-mounted display (HMD), even providing a 'through the floor' view – very useful in a vertical landing. It acts as a missile-warning system (MWS), detecting missile exhaust plumes, and as an infra-red search and track (IRST) system, detecting and tracking high-contrast IR target such as aircraft.

The TFLIR is a long-range, high-performance mid-wave infra-red staring array with a boresighted laser designator. It is carried in a retractable belly turret and is mechanically steerable throughout the lower hemisphere, so that it can

The X-35A ended Lockheed Martin's CTOL portion of the trial on 22 November 2000, logging 27 flights in 30 days. On 21 November it achieved supersonic flight on its 25th flight, with Tom Morgenfeld at the controls. The aircraft was returned to Palmdale for fitment of the lift fan, a task undertaken during late December. Re-emerging from the facility as the X-35B, it was moved out to the hover pit to begin the STOVL portion of the flight test programme.

The Lockheed Martin X-35C made its first flight on 16 December 2000. Flown by Joe Sweeney, it lifted off from Palmdale at 9.23 PST and landed at Edwards AFB 27 minutes later.

Above: Northrop Grumman provided a BAC 1-11 to act as the Co-operative Avionics Test Bed (CATB) to test the radar, DIRS and helmet-mounted display for the Lockheed Martin bid. The aircraft is based at NG's Baltimore, Maryland, facility and began JSF work in late February 2000.

Above right: Lockheed Martin constructed a 40-ft (12-m) tower at Fort Worth to mount its JSF sensor integration mock-up. The tower allows the mock-up to see 'targets' such as traffic on interstates, boats on nearby lakes and aircraft operating from Dallas-Fort Worth airport 20 miles (32 km) away.

Boeing's JSF avionics are being flight tested on the Avionics Flying Laboratory, a modified Boeing 737 which first flew in its new guise on 26 March 2000 from Wichita. During a live-fire exercise at White Sands, New Mexico, in June 2000, the 737 flying lab used its onboard systems to gather targeting data from offboard sensors, fuse them with data from its own sensors, and direct a successful attack made by an F-15E dropping a GPS-guided JDAM.

be rotated aft for bomb damage assessment. The ICS, which manages sensor, communications/navigation/identification (CNI) and display functions, is based on commercial PowerPC chips and uses a commercial software architecture.

More importantly, says Pao, Raytheon has changed the way in which it develops avionics. Older radars, says Pao, "were obsolete by the time that EMD was completed," because the customer demanded low-risk technology and EMD took seven years. "We used block upgrades to solve problems – there are three radars on the F-15 – but we never solve all of them."

Raytheon's new approach is based on "decoupling technology development from EMD," says Pao. The company intends to establish a continuous stream of technology development. When the customer needs a new or improved product, it can be developed quickly using the latest mature technology. As improvements emerge from the technology stream, they are incorporated into upgraded products. The key to this approach is an open architecture and compatibility, so that a new technology, such as the company's new AESA module, can be used on any radar system in the family, for both new and retrofit applications.

The first programmes in this new family concept are Boeing's JSF and F/A-18E/F. The radar for the JSF and the AESA radar for the Super Hornet (due to be installed in aircraft delivered in 2005-06) are the same apart from the array size, with identical transmit/receive [T/R] and processor modules. "We will continue to improve the product as we go though JSF EMD, and the improvements will flow into the F-18," says Pao. The TFLIR on JSF is a repackaged version of the ATFLIR hardware, under development for the Super Hornet. The EW receiver hardware is designed so that it can be fitted into the Super Hornet's ALR-73(V)3 radar warning receiver.

Northrop Grumman, supplying the MIRFS and EO sensors for the Lockheed Martin team, has been flying its MIRFS demonstrator since late 1998, demonstrating technology for simpler T/R modules that can be assembled

automatically. It is likely that the JSF AESA and EO suite bears a resemblance to the integrated AESA and infra-red system that Northrop Grumman is developing for the F-16 Block 60, just as the Raytheon systems on the Boeing aircraft are related to those of the Super Hornet.

Lockheed Martin has chosen Litton Advanced Systems Division (due to be acquired by Northrop Grumman) to team with BAE Systems on the JSF's passive EW system. The Litton radar warning system uses its long-baseline interferometry processing technology, and is claimed to be comparable in performance to the latest Improved Capability III (ICAP-III) version of the EA-6B Prowler at half the size, weight and cost. Unlike current fighters, JSF will be able to identify emitters and locate them quickly and accurately enough to launch a GPS-guided weapon at them, or pass their location on to another weapon system.

Advanced pilot interface

The JSF cockpit will make use of very large-format flat-panel displays and a binocular, full-colour helmet-mounted display (HMD). The HMD (Boeing is working with BAE Systems, and Lockheed Martin with Vision Systems International) will provide the pilot with all-round night vision – even 'through the floor' using the distributed infra-red system. In an environment with several laser threats, it would even make it possible for the pilot to fly with a blacked-out cockpit.

While Boeing has designed its cockpit displays around ruggedised commercial off-the-shelf (COTS) liquid-crystal direct-view displays, Lockheed Martin has teamed with Rockwell Collins (the former Kaiser Electronics) to use an 8 x 20-in (20 x 50-cm) projection display. These displays use the same technology as current commercial LCD projectors. The image is generated on a small reflective LCD, manufactured on a single chip, rather than being produced on the screen itself. A light source illuminates the LCD and the display image is projected on to the front screen. Projection displays can be built in a wide range of shapes and sizes using a common 'optical engine', and improved technology – such as better LCDs – can be shared across a range of different products.

The Lockheed Martin/Rockwell Collins prototype display, combined with the binocular HMD adopted for the JSF, represents the realisation of the Big Picture concept, envisioned by McDonnell Douglas cockpit-design expert

Gene Adam in the early 1980s. It is a measure of Adam's vision that he predicted, in the mid-1980s, that high-definition TV would drive the development of large-format display technology that could be integrated into a fighter cockpit.

Both companies have used their airborne avionics test-beds to demonstrate the use of both onboard and offboard sensors to acquire and attack targets. In Lockheed Martin's demonstration at Aberdeen Proving Grounds in Maryland, a Northrop Grumman Joint STARS detected a set of simulated targets and transmitted their locations to the BAC One-Eleven Cooperative Avionics Test Bed (CATB). This data was used to cue the CATB's electro-optical system on to the target. In a second test, the CATB used its radar in SAR/GMTI mode to acquire and locate the targets. Boeing tests earlier in the year demonstrated the JSF's ability to cue other aircraft on to targets, using the 737-based testbed and an F-15E.

Industry participation

A market projected at 8,000 aircraft not only represents a vast opportunity for the prime contractors and their US team-mates, but also for non-US companies. The US has consistently used industrial participation (IP) to boost its fighter exports. Lockheed's F-104G was the most widely exported Western fighter of its era and did much to rebuild Germany's aerospace industry. General Dynamics put together a strong IP programme to help sell the F-16 to Belgium, the Netherlands, Norway and Denmark in 1975. F-18 sales were backed by a formidable IP team comprising McDonnell Douglas, General Electric and General Motors (which owned the Hughes radar business).

However, US policy has changed dramatically since the days of the F-16 programme. The US government is asking potential partners to contribute to EMD, arguing that investors will more than recover their money in subcontract work on thousands of aircraft. Moreover, subcontractors will be expected to compete on cost for both new and continuing business.

The aerospace industry, too, has changed its structure since the F-16 was designed. The number of US fighter prime contractors has been slashed. Computer technology has brought about many changes and – perhaps the most important change of all – the industry has become much more focused on cost.

Another major difference between the JSF and previous programmes is that the traditional US requirement to have a second, US-based source for foreign-supplied components does not exist on JSF. Foreign suppliers will be able to bid for every JSF, including those for the US market.

On the avionics side, the switch to an open systems architecture (OSA) should change the way that the system is designed and acquired, and how it is supported and upgraded in service. An OSA is intended to be similar in concept to a Windows-based PC: both hardware and software are defined by unclassified specifications, and any subsystem which meets those specifications should work. This should give avionics developers wide latitude in adding new functions to the JSF system, or in developing new and better substitutes for existing components. One of the main aims of OSA, in fact, is to make it easy to introduce new computer technology into the system, reducing the risk that JSF's avionics will be obsolescent before they enter service.

Non-US companies, therefore, are in a position to win a great deal of business on JSF. The bad news is that they will have to win it on price and quality, and will have to tie their operations tightly to those of the US primes.

This trend is apparent in Boeing's commercial operations. The company is pushing its suppliers to reduce costs and integrate their business more closely with Boeing's. Suppliers are expected to join Boeing's integrated product teams (IPTs), and to adopt internal business tracking systems which are compatible with Boeing's. Those suppliers who cooperate with this change, and reduce their costs, will get more work at the expense of those who do not.

Lockheed Martin's CV demonstrator, the X-35C, was built with the bulge and doors behind the cockpit for fitment of the STOVL lift fan, although it is not intended to have it installed unless problems surface with the X-35B. The CV version of JSF is not planned to be procured until the US Navy has received all of its 548 planned F/A-18E/Fs. CV JSF is scheduled to achieve an initial operating capability in 2012 to begin the process of replacing F/A-18Cs. The future carrier air wing is expected to consist of two squadrons (12 aircraft each) of F/A-18Es for the air supremacy role, two squadrons of JSFs (12 aircraft each) for multi-role taskings with an accent on attack, and a single squadron (14 aircraft) of two-seat F/A-18Fs for specialised precision attack and SEAD roles.

Both teams used a dummy FCLP (Field Carrier Landing Practice) deck at Edwards AFB to prove initial carrier approach qualities. A full Fresnel lens landing system was installed alongside the runway. Shown below is the X-35C during CV trials, which were subsequently transferred to NAS Patuxent River, Maryland. US Navy requirements were in many ways the most harsh: a maximum approach speed of 136-142 kt (252-263 km/h; 156-163 mph) and Level 1 handling on the approach were key parameters. Other Navy requirements were a 600-nm (1111-km; 690-mile) combat radius on internal fuel, at least 5,000-lb (2268-kg) weapon bringback and the ability to service the aircraft, including its LO features, in deck hangars lacking any climate control.

In contrast to earlier IP programmes, where subcontracts to a customer nation's industries were an integral part of the sale, negotiated between governments, JSF contracts will be awarded on merit. Boeing's criteria for overseas JSF partners are the same as for any domestic partner," says Heinz. "They have to be world-class companies in terms of their cost structure and technology, who share our philosophy regarding affordability and best practices." Other attributes that will attract Boeing include "long-term relationships, which help us produce aircraft at the affordability levels we want, and costs that can help us win."

So far, several countries have indicated an interest in taking part in the JSF programme. The UK is a full partner, and has announced its intention to contribute as much as $2 billion to the EMD programme. Denmark, Norway and the Netherlands have joined the project as 'associate partners' and their industries have joined the Boeing and Lockheed Martin teams. Other countries, including Italy, Turkey, Israel and Singapore, have indicated an interested in joining the programme.

Whichever team wins JSF, the project has already done a great deal to focus attention on how to build combat aircraft at lower cost, without sacrificing efficiency. Key technologies such as simpler composite structures, integrated power subsystems and commercial-based avionics are being brought to maturity much faster in the JSF programme than they might be otherwise. 3,000 aircraft are

a juicy carrot; being excluded from the Pentagon market for a generation is a threatening stick. And in fact, there is a good chance that history will remember JSF for that, more than anything else.

JSF at the crossroads

In early 2001, the JSF programme is entering a critical stage. Within the next nine months, according to current plans, one of the two competing teams will be chosen to carry out EMD – and historically, once an EMD contract on this scale has been awarded, it is rare for it to be cancelled.

Both teams have flown their conventional take-off and landing (CTOL) prototypes. These first flights are, in themselves, of moderate technological significance. The crucial tests take place during 2001, when the two teams demonstrate the short take-off and vertical landing (STOVL) features of their designs. In 40 years of design and demonstration, no company has yet demonstrated a practical supersonic STOVL fighter. The closest approach was the Yakovlev Yak-141 fighter demonstrator. It used a STOVL system that the JSF programme rejected in 1996.

JSF is of immense importance to the Pentagon and to US national defence. By the time the EMD aircraft flies in mid-2005, the Pentagon will be committed to JSF. If, after that point, its entry-into-service date slips, the US Marine Corps will run out of fighters and the USAF's fighter force will dwindle, and there will not be much that anyone can do about it.

It is therefore of paramount importance to make sure that the technical risks involved in JSF are under control before EMD starts. STOVL is the most conspicuous risk area, but certainly not the only one. JSF is seeking to invent breakthroughs across the board in the relationship of cost and performance, including dramatic reductions in the cost of avionics and of low-observable (LO) systems. Unlike any previous military aircraft, JSF cannot achieve its performance goals at twice the advertised cost and be considered a success.

Tests on full-scale models and airborne avionics test rigs have gone as far as expected in showing that the JSF will achieve price and performance goals in those areas. STOVL demonstrations have yet to be performed as these words are written, and will not be complete before the late summer – even if there are no further delays. Boeing and Lockheed Martin, naturally, are sure that they will demonstrate STOVL successfully. Pentagon officials have expressed less confidence.

Flying as many as five times a day during late November/early December, Boeing completed carrier approach trials (and the CV portion of the trials) with the X-32A before the aircraft moved on to demonstrating performance capabilities in the CTOL configuration. Design landing weight for the naval JSF is around 40,940 lb (18570 kg), flying an approach at an angle of attack around 11.5°. Full control authority has to be maintained in this low-speed flight regime. An important facet of the approach tests was monitoring how the thrust-vectoring nozzle integrated with the flight control system to provide pitch control inputs.

Left: On 31 January 2001 the X-35C began high-speed envelope expansion flights, with Joe Sweeney at the controls. Flying at 25,000 ft (7620 m), the X-35C went first to Mach 1.05, and then to Mach 1.1. On 23 January it had undertaken tanker trials behind a Boeing KC-10A Extender. Further refuelling trials were due to take place from Patuxent River, although these were delayed due to the non-availability of test flight-rated KC-135 tanker crews, who were heavily tasked in the parallel F-22 flight test programme.

Far left: Lockheed engineers fit the lift fan assembly into the X-35A after its CTOL flying programme had ended. In so doing, they turned the aircraft into the X-35B STOVL demonstrator. The fan is driven by a shaft from the engine and blows a 'carpet' of cold air beneath the aircraft, preventing any hot engine exhaust reaching the intake.

In October 2000, Pentagon procurement chief Dr Jacques Gansler expressed reservations on language in the FY2001 defence authorisation act, which requires that both JSF teams amass 20 flight hours on their STOVL prototypes before source selection. "If one of the contractors were having trouble, and you wanted to make an earlier down-select, you can't do that. You have to let both of them complete their testing." That could cause more slippage, Gansler said. This reflected comments which Gansler made in the summer. The downselect, he said "would be done when we have one or both having demonstrated vertical lift... One could self-eliminate if they don't fly. But as we now expect, they will both fly." (As one commentator noted at the time: "If they don't fly? As we now expect?")

CDA test programme

No such doubts emanate from Seattle or Fort Worth. Boeing's CTOL and carrier-configured (CV) X-32A made its first flight on 28 September 2000 and completed 66 flights by early February 2001, when its initial flight-test programme ended. The X-32A test programme started with simulated carrier landings, using carrier deck markings and an optical landing guidance system installed at Edwards AFB. Once the carrier-landing tests were completed, the X-32A was used for "Boeing strategic objectives" – that is, envelope expansion flights that will be measured against sealed-envelope predictions already submitted to the programme office. They included a supersonic sortie on 21 December. The X-32A also demonstrated that its weapon bays could be opened in flight, allowing Boeing to investigate the aerodynamic and acoustic environment of the open bay.

The X-32B STOVL CDA carried out taxi tests in January 2001. As this article was written, it was expected to fly late in the first quarter of 2001, starting a 50-flight, 85-hour programme that is expected to take four months. Early envelope-expansion flights will take place at Edwards, clearing the aircraft to be ferried to the Navy's flight-test centre at Patuxent River. The Navy base, cooler and at a lower elevation than Edwards, is better for STOVL tests. The aircraft will approach the hover gradually, starting with medium-altitude transitions from wing-borne to partially jet-borne flight and proceeding to lower altitudes and lower speeds. The X-32B may also be tested in a 'hover pit', taking off from a grating above a concrete-lined pit (which simulates out-of-ground-effect conditions) and

translating to a pad for vertical landing. Finally, the X-32B will complete a transition to vertical landing.

Lockheed Martin's X-35A flew on 24 October 2000, flown by Tom Morgenfeld, and completed the type's CTOL tests flights by 22 November, including the fighter's first super-sonic sortie the previous day. In late November, the X-35A returned to Palmdale to be converted into the STOVL X-35B, with the addition of the lift fan and thrust-vectoring nozzle. The fan was installed at the end of December, and STOVL tests above a grated pit at Palmdale started in late February. The CV-configured X-35C made its first flight on

On 10 February 2001 the X-35C arrived at NAS Patuxent River, Maryland, to begin sea level carrier suitability trials. Joe Sweeney flew the aircraft on its first leg from Edwards AFB, California, to the LMTAS plant at Fort Worth, Texas. Marine Corps pilot Major Art Tomassetti then took the aircraft to 'Pax'. Trials ended on 11 March, by which time the X-35C had made 73 flights for 58 hours, flown by eight pilots. During the course of the programme 250 FCLPs had been undertaken, during which the X-35C demonstrated an approach speed of 135 kt (250 km/h; 155 mph). Deliberate approach errors were made to monitor the aircraft's corrective responses.

With Dennis O'Donoghue in the cockpit, Boeing's STOVL demonstrator – the X-32B – completed low-speed (30-kt) and medium-speed (60-kt) taxi tests at Palmdale on 10 January 2001, just two days after Pratt & Whitney completed the test runs of the F119-614S engine in the STOVL configuration. During these tests transition times between vertical and horizontal thrust had been accomplished in as little as a second. Following high-speed trials the X-32B was due to move to Edwards for initial flight validation before STOVL transitions began at altitude. Full STOVL testing, involving landings and hovering near the ground, were due to be performed at Patuxent River.

On 7 March 2001 Dennis O'Donoghue performed the first tests of the X-32B over Boeing's hover pit at Palmdale. The hover pit has a cross-shaped grate through which the thrust from the nozzles, jet screen and control nozzles is drawn off and ducted away to an ejector behind the aircraft, thereby simulating free air hover conditions. The aircraft is restrained during the tests by a series of hold-down cables. The engine was run up to full (dry) power with all thrust being diverted through the direct lift nozzles. The nozzles were vectored during these tests. During this trial, and the taxi trials, the X-32B was operated without the translating supersonic intake, showing details of the vertical-sided, round-edged low-speed intake lip. Note the cut-out in the side chine where the translating cowl would be fitted, and the narrow wing span of the STOVL version.

This mock-up, revealed at the 2000 Farnborough air show, shows the Boeing JSF in intended production form (Model 375). It was parked next to an F/A-18F to show the two types which Boeing hopes will dominate the US Navy's carrier decks in the next decade. Although at first glance the production version differs considerably from the X-32 CDAs, Boeing claims that much of the 'front end' is very similar, and that the conventional tailplanes have been created by taking area from the delta wing and using it for the tail surfaces.

16 December 2000, and was ferried to Patuxent River in early February 2001 for simulated carrier landings.

There is no doubt that STOVL tests carry an element of risk. Unlike traditional flight testing, in which speeds and altitudes gradually increase and envelope expansion takes place at high altitude, STOVL testing involves deceleration – and consequently shrinking aerodynamic control authority – at decreasing altitudes. The aircraft is flying slower and lower as it enters the flight regime where the aerodynamic environment is influenced by the interaction between the ambient air and the exhaust flow – some 400 to 660 lb (180-300 kg) of heated and energised air per second. This is a little-understood area, where computer projections are not definitive. Moreover, as Harrier experience has shown, loss of control at low altitude can rapidly place the aircraft in an attitude where safe ejection is impossible. In jetborne flight at 100 ft (30 m) altitude, the pilot is unwise to wait too long to see whether an anomaly will resolve itself.

Winner takes all

In the summer of 2000, Gansler and Defense Secretary William Cohen raised the stakes in the JSF contest by reaffirming a 'winner-takes-all' programme, with no enforced teaming or partnership arrangement by which the winner and loser would share development and production work.

This is a more important issue than it was when the programme started in 1996. Since then, three developments have suppressed hopes that the loser in a winner-take-all JSF contest might have a long-term future as an integrator of combat aircraft. Orders for the F-22 and F/A-18 Super Hornet were cut back in 1997, the export market has remained flat and the turbulent stock market demands that any company should abandon any business where it cannot see growth and profit.

However, the Gansler/Cohen decision was not irrevocable. Its only solid effect, combined with delays in flight testing, was to move the JSF decision firmly into the lap of the next administration – which, as it turned out, was led by Republican George W. Bush.

Lost in much of the sound and fury around the 2000 presidential election was Bush's clearly declared intention to conduct a much deeper review of defence priorities undertaken by the Clinton administration. Many observers also missed the fact that the Bush inauguration meant a change in the climate of defence politics. Through most of the Reagan years and the administration of the elder George Bush, Democrats controlled Congress, and their leaders dominated the committees that approved defence budgets. Reagan and Bush budget proposals were

On 22 February 2001 Lockheed Martin began hover pit testing of the X-35B at Palmdale, with BAE Systems Sea Harrier veteran Simon Hargreaves at the controls. On 10 March the X-35B's F119-611S was run up to full dry power for the first time in hover configuration. The spine doors serve the lift fan (outward-opening forward doors) and the engine intake (inward-opening aft doors). Note also the drop-down doors under the rear fuselage which allow the engine nozzle to swivel down (to a maximum of 105° from the horizontal).

routinely dismissed as 'dead on arrival' by arrogant Democrats.

The 'Gingrich revolution' of 1994, in which Democrats lost the House and Senate, had less immediate effect than some predicted. However, it did disrupt the long-established power structure in Congress. Slender as Republican margins may be, the new Bush administration has considerably greater power to change the direction of national policy – including defence – than any administration has enjoyed in decades.

Bush has appointed Donald Rumsfeld as Secretary of Defense and Andrew Marshall, former leader of the Pentagon's office of net assessments, as leader of a commission to review defence strategy. Neither Rumsfeld, 68, nor the 70-plus Marshall has much to fear from the Pentagon establishment. A cordite-sharp whiff of real reform is in the air.

In February 2001, weeks after the competitors delivered their EMD proposals, what this means for JSF is anybody's guess. There are indications that in computer wargames simulating operations against China in 2015 – a scenario that features strongly in Marshall's vision of the future – the JSF acquits itself well, because of its stealth, all-weather precision, range and 'net-centric' philosophy. But those JSFs may not necessarily be launched from improvised 1,600-ft (500-m) airstrips or Navy amphibious ships, and a defence review could well conclude that three separate fast-jet air forces may be superfluous, even for the US. If the STOVL version of the JSF falls by the wayside, it will make sense to re-examine the designs of the Navy and USAF aircraft to eliminate operational constraints and extra costs that may have been imposed by the STOVL requirement. In late 2000, Marine commandant General James Jones commented in an interview that the service might be ready to accept a non-STOVL aircraft.

The reviewers may also be looking for money to fund other needs, such as aircraft that can strike over great distances – even a revived, regenerated B-2. Some of that money may come out of the JSF budget. Ultimately, the central assumption that underpins JSF – the need to maintain the existing force structure – is in question.

Answers will emerge in the course of 2001 – as the JSF's crucial and hazardous STOVL tests continue. As the possibly-mock-Chinese curse has it: "May you live in interesting times!"

Bill Sweetman

X-32 and X-35, together with their test pilot teams, came face-to-face in a 'meet the press' facility at Edwards AFB on 20 November 2000. If JSF survives a major review of US defence needs expected from the Bush administration, the winner is assured of a huge market, with many export sales to be added to the 3,002 aircraft already planned for the five customer services. Earlier suggestions that production would be divided between the winning and losing teams have been shelved. The outcome of the JSF competition may well spell the end for one or other of the main contractors as a fighter builder.

Lockheed P-3 Orion Foreign Operators

Since entering service in 1962, the P-3 Orion has established itself as the West's standard maritime patrol aircraft. Although the majority serve with the US Navy, a significant number fly with foreign air arms.

Total production of Orions for the US Navy amounted to 550 aircraft (158 P-3As, 125 P-3Bs, 266 P-3Cs and a single RP-3D). Once chosen as the US Navy's standard shore-based maritime patrol aircraft, the Orion was assured of significant sales overseas, and these have accumulated steadily throughout the type's production life.

New Zealand was the first to sign up, ordering P-3Bs in 1965. Australia followed, as did Norway. The introduction of the 'Charlie' led to further sales to the Netherlands, Iran and Pakistan, with follow-on sales to Australia and Norway. Canada opted for a specialist version with considerably different mission systems. By far the largest overseas customer was Japan, which builds the P-3C (and derivatives) under a licence to Kawasaki Heavy Industries. The most recent new-build customer was Korea, this sale requiring the reopening of the P-3C production line at Marietta, Georgia.

Smaller air arms have benefited from the replacement of the US Navy's P-3A/B fleet by the P-3C, which resulted in earlier aircraft becoming redundant. Argentina, Chile, Greece, Portugal, Spain and Thailand have all acquired ex-US Navy aircraft, most of which were refurbished and, in some cases, upgraded or converted prior to delivery.

Many of the Orion operators have upgraded their aircraft, or are in the process of doing

Among the many improvements being applied to several Orion fleets are self-defence countermeasures. Here a Norwegian UIP aircraft releases a shower of flares from its four AN/ALE-47 dispensers.

so, ranging from modest equipment updates to major programmes such as Norway's UIP or the Netherlands' CUP. Further sales for the P-3 airframe are likely, as it is used as the basis for several proposals for new MPAs, notably Raytheon's Procyon programme (which is pitched as a replacement for German and Italian Atlantics), and Lockheed Martin's own Orion-based studies. Additional nations are also likely to acquire Orions from surplus US Navy P-3A/B stocks through FMS channels.

ARGENTINA

Comando de la Aviación Naval/ Armada de Argentina

From 1959 the main asset of the Argentine Navy for maritime patrol was the Lockheed P2V Neptune. During the early 1970s, Argentine naval aviation planned the purchase of five P-3B Orions to be delivered by 1976, but the United States rejected the idea and offered four late-production SP-2H Neptunes instead, which were accepted as a stop-gap measure.

Having been rebuffed by the US, the Argentine navy turned to France and the Dassault-Breguet Atlantic. The requirement was for a six-strong fleet of second-hand Atlantics and new-build Atlantic Mk 4s, with AM.39 Exocet capability. A Request for Proposal document was signed in 1979, including a detailed delivery schedule from 1980. The South Atlantic War interrupted this project, while wartime events exposed Argentina's lack of true maritime patrol capability. To compound matters, the last two SP-2H Neptunes completed their last operational flights during May 1982. To cover the shortfall, a contingency plan was instigated to use second-hand commercial aircraft, locally modified for maritime surveillance. The Lockheed L-188 Electra was selected against the Boeing 707 due to its lower operational costs. Six L-188s of several versions were used as MarPat aircraft, each fitted with a SMA APS-705 search radar in a ventral radome.

In the early 1990s, following Argentina's participation in Operation Desert Storm, the country regained a prominent position as the most favoured Latin American nation for the US. Many restrictions regarding transfer of military equipment were relaxed or lifted, and under such circumstances the Argentine navy found its way to finally obtain the Orion.

Under a Letter of Offer and Acceptance dated 20 May 1997, the Argentine Navy obtained six Lockheed P-3B Orions from US Navy surplus stocks at a bargain cost of only U$7.3 million. A naval mission selected a group of six airframes, all of which were of the TACNAVMOD/Heavy-Weight sub-type, also known as 'Super Bees'. These were re-conditioned and prepared by the US contractor Logistic Services International. Work on the aircraft started at Tucson in late 1997, while a small number of Argentine navy pilots completed flight training with the US Navy's VP-30 between October and December of that year.

The aircraft were initially ferried by USN crews, and the first Orion, coded 0869/6-P-53, departed from Tucson on

5 December 1997. It landed two days later in Argentina with US Navy Cdr Skinner at the controls. With this aircraft the re-equipment of the Escuadrilla Aeronaval de Exploración (EA6E) began, with Captain D. Marinsalta as squadron CO. EA6E is based at Base Aeronaval Vice Admiral Zar, home of the Escuadra Aeronaval no. 6, which specialises in maritime patrol tasks. The Orions, serialled 0867/6-P-51 to 0872/6-P-56, are technically supported by the Arsenal Aeronaval Trelew, as well by the TACE-Taller Aeronaval Central at Comandante Espora NAS. The squadron received its last aircraft on 11 July 1999 when the Orion 0868/6-P-52 landed with Captain (Argentine navy) Giaquinta at the controls. The Argentine navy also purchased an additional P-3B airframe, but this was scrapped for spare parts at Tucson by LSI, which also provided technical training for ground crew.

Transition to the P-3B Orions for both air and ground crew was eased by long experience with the navalised L-188 Electras. The P-3B Orions were soon involved in operations: between 2 and 5 April 1998 one aircraft was actively engaged in a series of dangerous SAR flights over Antarctic waters. Although officially used for fisheries protection tasks, EA6E is mainly tasked with other roles such as anti-submarine/anti-surface strike, maritime patrol and reconnaissance. Argentine navy Orions have taken part in several exercises with foreign forces, such as SAR 2000 (with the USAF), UNITAS XXXIX (with Brazilian and US Navy ships) and, perhaps the most significant, the Millennium Operation with British forces stationed in the Malvinas/Falklands islands. There are several projects under review regarding the update of mission equipment, as well the adaptation of Argentine navy weapons like the Whitehead A.244S ASW torpedo.

Jorge F. Nuñez Padin

Above and below: Argentine Orions wear the standard COAN colour scheme with slate grey upper surfaces. The rudders and tailplanes carry the national colours. The Southern Cross and fox badge on the fin carries the title 'Exploración', while a more formal unit badge is carried either side of the nose.

Left: The Argentine Orions were delivered in their US Navy colour schemes. Most were in the old grey/white scheme, but this aircraft was in the light grey Tactical Paint Scheme. This was initially retained for service, with Argentine markings applied, although the aircraft will receive the definitive scheme in due course.

Variant	c/n	BuNo.	Serial
P-3B	5158	152718	0867/6-P-51
P-3B	5172	172732	0868/6-P-52
P-3B	5186	152746	0869/6-P-53
P-3B	5205	152761	0870/6-P-54
P-3B	5207	152763	0871/6-P-55
P-3B	5216	153419	0872/6-P-56

AUSTRALIA

Royal Australian Air Force

Australia became an early export customer for the P-3 Orion in November 1964, when an order for 10 P-3A aircraft was announced by the government of the day. This was one component of an ambitious programme to expand Australia's defence capability, and broadly coincided with orders for the C-130E Hercules, UH-1B Iroquois, and Macchi MB326H.

Selected as a replacement for the P2V-5 Neptunes of No. 11 Squadron, RAAF, the order was switched to the P-3B, as this model had supplanted the earlier variant on the production line. No. 11 Squadron relocated from Richmond to Edinburgh in South Australia during 1968, receiving the first aircraft in May of that year, when A9-291 arrived from the USA.

Prior to this, training had been conducted with VP-31 at Moffett Field, and the new aircraft quickly proved itself, with No. 11 Squadron sharing the 1971 Fincastle Trophy with Canada, and winning it outright in 1972.

During this period, No. 11 Squadron's sister unit, No. 10 Squadron, was operating the SP-2H Neptune from Townsville, and it was obvious that this type was nearing the end of its useful career. In response, an announcement was made to the effect that the squadron would relocate to Edinburgh, and re-equip with the P-3C in the latter part of the 1970s. Broadly similar to the US Navy's P-3C Update II, Australia's version differed in that it was equipped with the Anglo/Australian Barra sonobuoy system and Marconi AQS-901 processor.

An order for eight (later increased to 10) aircraft was duly announced in May 1975, and the first aircraft, A9-751, departed Moffett Field on delivery to Edinburgh in May 1978, 10 years after the arrival of the first P-3B. Prior to this, 10 Squadron crews had begun flying their colleagues' P-3Bs at Edinburgh, in order to smooth transition to the new aircraft. Although now co-located, the two squadrons operated autonomously, due to the significant differences between the two models, and it was not until No. 11 Squadron converted to the P-3C in 1981 that some synergies of operation could be enjoyed.

An order for a second batch of 10 P-3Cs was placed in October 1981, equating to the P-3C Update II.5 though retaining the Barra system and the Marconi processor. The final aircraft of the batch (A9-665) arrived in the country in November 1981, with the surviving P-3B aircraft being traded back to Lockheed for further service. Second-batch P-3Cs have been referred to as P-3Ws, although this designation is only used internally for maintenance logistics purposes.

No. 92 Wing had earlier formed at Edinburgh in July 1977, as part of the Maritime Patrol Group (MPG), to oversee the two operational squadrons and a newly formed training unit, the Maritime Analysis Training School (MATS). The arrival of the final Update II.5 aircraft (600 series in RAAF parlance, after the serial number range) meant that the RAAF could boast two squadrons of maritime patrol aircraft of a similar standard. Accordingly, the aircraft were pooled within the wing, though each batch retained the markings of the squadron to which they were delivered ('700' series aircraft 10 Sqn, and '600' series 11 Sqn). Technical ownership of the aircraft was entrusted to the maintenance and support unit, No. 492 Squadron.

This formed the basis of Australia's operation of the aircraft through until 1998, though the MATS was renamed No. 292 Squadron in October 1980. The only significant events until then were the loss of A9-754 in a crash on Cocos Island in April 1991, and the gradual repainting of the fleet in a semi-gloss overall grey scheme, with the serial appearing as the 'last three' on the inside of the nosewheel door.

This change to anonymity has never been fully explained by the RAAF, which merely cites 'operational considerations' as the reason behind the removal of individual markings. However, press reports have

Left: This Harpoon-carrying P-3C wears No. 10 Sqn marks. The radome under the aft fuselage is part of the Elta-installed ESM suite.

Below: Complete with No. 292 Squadron markings, this is one of three TAP-3 'bounce-birds' remaining in service with No. 92 Group.

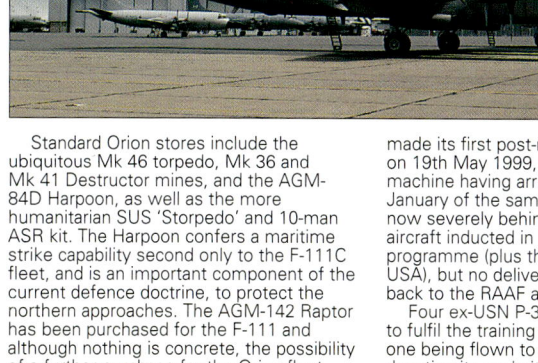

Variant	c/n	BuNo	Serial/notes
P-3B (LW)	5203	152760	spares recovery
TAP-3	5231	153434	A9-434/ex-US Navy P-3B (LW)
TAP-3	5235	153438	A9-438/ex-US Navy P-3B (LW)
TAP-3	5236	153439	A9-439/ex-US Navy P-3B (LW)
P-3B (HW)	5286	154605	A9-605/replacement for A9-296, to Lockheed/USCS as P-3AEW
P-3B (HW)	5401	155291	A9-291/to N. Zealand
P-3B (HW)	5402	155292	A9-292/to Portugal
P-3B (HW)	5403	155293	A9-293/to Portugal
P-3B (HW)	5404	155294	A9-294/to Portugal
P-3B (HW)	5405	155295	A9-295/to Portugal
P-3B (HW)	5406	155296	A9-296/crashed before delivery 14 Apr 1968
P-3B (HW)	5407	155297	A9-297/to Portugal
P-3B (HW)	5408	155298	A9-298/to Portugal
P-3B (HW)	5409	155299	A9-299/to USCS as P-3AEW
P-3B (HW)	5410	155300	A9-300/crashed 27 Oct 1984
P-3C UII	5657	160751	A9-751
P-3C UII	5658	160752	A9-752
P-3C UII	5660	160753	A9-753
P-3C UII	5662	160754	A9-754/crashed 26 Apr 1991
P-3C UII	5664	160755	A9-755
P-3C UII	5666	160756	A9-756
P-3C UII	5668	160757	A9-757
P-3C UII	5672	160758	A9-758
AP-3C	5674	160759	A9-759/built as UII, first Australian AP-3C
AP-3C	5676	160760	A9-760/built as UII, prototype AP-3C
P-3C UII.5	5778	162656	A9-656
P-3C UII.5	5780	162657	A9-657
P-3C UII.5	5782	162658	A9-658
P-3C UII.5	5784	162659	A9-659
P-3C UII.5	5785	162660	A9-660
P-3C UII.5	5787	162661	A9-661
P-3C UII.5	5789	162662	A9-662
P-3C UII.5	5791	162663	A9-663
P-3C UII.5	5793	162664	A9-664
P-3C UII.5	5795	162665	A9-665

speculated that two aircraft were modified by E-Systems in the 1990s, with sophisticated intelligence-gathering equipment for ELINT missions against (primarily) Indonesia. These reports have been denied by both the Government and the RAAF, despite assertions by the Indonesian military that such flights have been flown over East Timor in recent times. It may only be coincidental that the removal of high visibility markings and external serial numbers from the fleet took place shortly before these conversions were reported to have entered service! An upgrade of the aircraft's ESM system did begin in 1989 though, when Elta was awarded a contract to fit its ALR-2001 system to the fleet, with project completion occurring in the mid-1990s.

Standard Orion stores include the ubiquitous Mk 46 torpedo, Mk 36 and Mk 41 Destructor mines, and the AGM-84D Harpoon, as well as the more humanitarian SUS 'Storpedo' and 10-man ASR kit. The Harpoon confers a maritime strike capability second only to the F-111C fleet, and is an important component of the current defence doctrine, to protect the northern approaches. The AGM-142 Raptor has been purchased for the F-111 and although nothing is concrete, the possibility of a further purchase for the Orion fleet exists. Likewise, the AGM-114B Penguin has been purchased for the SH-2G(A), and though an arguably more effective littoral warfare weapon, there are currently no plans to fit the missile to the Orion fleet.

In order to ensure operational viability up to the planned retirement date in 2015, a major upgrade programme, Project Air 5276 (or Sea Sentinel) was commissioned in 1995. Arguably the second-most ambitious upgrade of a Maritime Patrol platform (Britain's Nimrod MRA.4 project possibly winning that honour), the project replaces all major sensors with the exception of the Infra-Red Detection System (IRDS). Other phases of the project include the purchase and modification of three ex-USN P-3Bs as transport and training platforms, and the supply of an Operational Mission Simulator (OMS).

E-Systems, now Raytheon, was awarded the contract in January 1995, and selected equipment includes the Israeli Elta EL/M-2022A(V)3 radar, CDC UYS-503 Acoustic System (an earlier version is fitted to the RAN Seahawk fleet), dual Honeywell H764G embedded GPU/INUs, Comms suite (including UHF MILSATCOM), and a new Data Management System (DDC-060, a derivative of the Lockheed-Martin AN/ASQ-212). The modified aircraft become known as the AP-3C on completion, and all but the first example are being modified by Boeing Australia at Avalon, Victoria.

The first aircraft arrived at Raytheon's Greenville plant in November 1997, and

made its first post-modification test flight on 19th May 1999, with the first Australian machine having arrived at Avalon in January of the same year. The project is now severely behind schedule, with five aircraft inducted in to the upgrade programme (plus the prototype in the USA), but no deliveries have been made back to the RAAF at the time of writing.

Four ex-USN P-3Bs have been acquired to fulfil the training aircraft requirement, one being flown to Edinburgh for spares, donating its cockpit section to the OMS project in the process. The remaining three were stripped and refurbished by the US Navy, becoming TAP-3s on completion, and entering service from 1997. They wear the markings of No. 292 Squadron, but are actually allocated to the two operational squadrons.

Coinciding with the service entry of the TAP-3 was the disbandment of No. 492 Squadron and the distribution of the Orion fleet (and maintenance/support personnel) between the two operational units. This is to enable deployment and operation with a high degree of autonomy.

A new EWSP suite and IR/EO system is under consideration for the fleet later this decade. Once the Sea Sentinel problems are overcome, Australia's Orions will be a potent force in the region for the foreseeable future.

Nigel Pittaway

No. 11 Squadron's badge adorns the fin of this P-3C, which carries destructors and Harpoons on the wings. Note the unusual wingtip antennas, installed by Elta as part of the ESM upgrade undertaken in the early 1990s. The Israeli company provides the EL/M-2022 radar for the AP-3C Sea Sentinel upgrade, which is being conducted by Boeing Australia under contract to systems integrator Raytheon.

BRAZIL

Following the lead of Argentina and Chile, Brazil accepted an offer for surplus US Navy Orions to provide a long-range maritime patrol capability along its long Atlantic coastline, and to provide ASW protection for its fleet. An order was placed in 2000, but by early 2001 had appeared to be either shelved or cancelled entirely. Brazil had expected to receive 12 P-3Bs, of which nine would have been operational and the remainder used for spares recovery and as ground instructional airframes. Initial training would have been undertaken at Montijo in Portugal with the FAP's P-3P fleet.

CANADA

Canadian Armed Forces

Selection of a version of the P-3 by the Canadian government was a very long, drawn-out affair. Plans to replace the Canadair CP-107 Argus were first mentioned in a February 1969 press release, but it was not until 21 August 1971 that the Long Range Patrol Aircraft (LRPA) Committee was first established and the programme was the subject of much political wrangling and delays. On 20 July 1972, the government finally announced that the CP-107 Argus would be replaced and sought proposals from industry.

The original in-service target date was 1977, but this was not to be. A variety of aircraft was proposed to meet the CAF's Air Specification 15-14. These included: Boeing 707, Breguet Atlantic, de Havilland Canada DHC-7 Dash 7, Hawker Siddeley Nimrod, Lockheed C-141 Starlifter, Lockheed P-3 Orion, Lockheed S-3 Viking, McDonnell Douglas DC-9, McDonnell Douglas DC-10, and a Canadair proposal, the aptly-named Phoenix. That was an Argus re-engined with turboprops, a capability designed-in from the beginning.

Both the 707 and P-3 proposals were closely studied and the Canadianised version of the Orion was announced as the winner on 27 November 1975. Eight months later, a budget of Can$1.032 billion was approved to cover the purchase of 18 aircraft, two Data Interpretation and Analysis Centres (DIAC), 30 spare engines, other spares, simulators, initial training, publications, etc. The contract was signed on 21 July 1976. The name Aurora, after the Greek goddess of the dawn who restored Orion's sight, was selected in January 1977 as it had the proper Canadian connotation (aurora borealis being the scientific name for the Northern Lights) and was in the Lockheed tradition of celestial names. The designation CP-140 was also selected and serials from 140101 to 140125 were allocated to allow for future purchases of additional aircraft. The first CP-140, 140101, was rolled out at Lockheed's Burbank facility on 25 January 1979 and made its first flight on 22 March 1979. It finally entered service at CFB Greenwood, having been handed-over in a ceremony there on 29 May 1980. It was preceded there by 140104, which had arrived at the Nova Scotia base on 24 May, two days after being accepted.

The CP-140's interior has six stations in a 'U' arrangement, promoting closer crew co-ordination than is possible in the P-3C which has the stations separated.

Industrial offsets are a key feature of modern military contracts and the LRPA contract was no exception. Major contracts were awarded to Canadair and Fleet, both of which had already been subcontractors to Lockheed on the P-3 Orion, as well as to Canadian Marconi, CAE and Litton Industries. In the case of Canadair, a 1976 contract to produce components for Lockheed-built P-3Cs was expanded to cover the CP-140s. Canadair went on to design new wingtips and storage racks for search stores, to modify the electrical load centre, and to manufacture outer and centre wing boxes, aft body, and radomes for both the CP-140 and the P-3C. Moreover, Canadair designed and produced five Aurora maintenance trainers for the CAF.

CP-140 Aircrew Conversion Course 1 began in March 1980 at Burbank. The members of this course became the CAF's first Aurora instructors. Assigned to 404 (Maritime Patrol and Training) Squadron, these instructors completed training the first three operational crews for 405 (Maritime Patrol) Squadron and a standards crews (standardisation crew in USN parlance) in March 1981. On the 11th of that month, the standards crew flew 405's first operational patrol in a CP-140.

CFB Greenwood was selected as the main East Coast base for the maritime patrol mission. Already home to 404 and 405 Squadrons, it added 415 to its list following the decision to move that unit from CFB Summerside. Also, on 15 August 1978, the Maritime Proving and Experimental Unit (MP&EU), now the Maritime Proving and Evaluation Unit, MPEU) had moved from Summerside to Greenwood.

As mentioned, the first of the new aircraft arrived at CFB Greenwood on 29 May 1980. Thirteen CP-140s were delivered by the end of 1980 and the remaining five were all in Canada by March 1981. 404 (MP) Squadron, which sometimes styles itself VP 404, had taken over the training role from VP 449 on 29 August 1975. It was the first unit to complete the Aurora conversion. It was followed at CFB Greenwood by 405 (MP) Squadron and, upon achieving operational status, Greenwood-based Auroras flew their first NorPat (Northern Patrol) between 1 and 4 September 1980. Just over nine months later, on 11 June 1981, 140109 arrived at CFB Comox, British Columbia, to become the first Aurora to be assigned to 407 (MP) Squadron.

CP-140s were delivered in the CAF's long-standing colour scheme of white upper fuselage and light grey lower fuselage with a red and white 'lightning bolt' as a cheatline. Later, the Auroras began to appear in a dark grey 'tactical paint scheme' (i.e. camouflage), but continued to have a black radome. Eventually, these, too, were painted grey.

Internally, the CP-140 is completely different to the P-3 Orion and should not be considered as just a 'Canadian P-3'. It has been aptly described as being 'two S-3 Vikings in a P-3 airframe'. Externally generally similar to all other ASW Orions, the CP-140 differs visually in having modified wingtips incorporating the specified electronic support measures. The Canadian aircraft retain the MAD boom, fore and aft radomes, and central computer, but has the two AN/APS-115 radar sets of the P-3C – one in the nose radome and one in the aft fuselage forward and under the MAD boom – replaced by a single AN/APS-506 in a nose radome. In addition, its weapons bay has been modified to be able to carry SKAD (Survival Kit Air Droppable) survival gear containers.

The flight deck is broadly similar to that of the P-3C, but the flight instruments have been rearranged in a standard 'T' layout and are illuminated with white, blue-filtered lighting. The layout of the Aurora's tactical compartment is substantially different to other P-3s as a result of the revised equipment installed and is designed to provide the TacNav with a view of the NavCom, ASO and NASO stations in order to optimise crew co-ordination.

Initially, the CP-140 was assigned the following three primary roles:

Sovereignty: surface and undersea surveillance of Canadian territory and ocean areas, and enforcement of Canadian regulatory agencies' acts

Defence of North America: including denial of surprise attack to potential enemies and response to other military threats to North America

NATO: consists of Canada's contribution to the joint defence against attacks on the NATO area, specifically, North America and the North Atlantic Ocean

In addition, the following five secondary roles were assigned:

Under a current review the CAF is set to reduce its CP-140 fleet by five. Three of the casualties are expected to be the CP-140A Arcturus utility aircraft.

Ice reconnaissance
Search and rescue
Fisheries patrols
Ocean pollution monitoring
Maritime intelligence gathering

Later, two further secondary roles were added:

Drug interdiction: broadly similar to maritime intelligence gathering and flown in support of the Royal Canadian Mounted Police (RCMP)

Support to other government agencies

In the mid-1980s, the Canadian government identified a need for greater reconnaissance of the country's vast Arctic territory. Such overflights by CAF aircraft would also assert Canada's sovereignty. The only aircraft capable of carrying out this role in a meaningful way were the 18 CP-140s, but they were already heavily tasked, averaging about twice the flying rate of the US Navy's P-3 Orions. Accordingly, the CAF submitted a requirement for six more CP-140s, but this was cancelled as a result of cutbacks in the April 1989 federal budget.

Although it had cancelled the proposed order of six CP-140s, the Canadian government decided to purchase the last three airframes scheduled to be built on Lockheed's P-3 Burbank production line. At that point, it was intended that the three new aircraft would be used solely as flight crew trainers ('bounce birds'), thereby freeing the fully-equipped Auroras for additional tasking, such as NorPats, and eliminating the risk to the expensive ASW avionics suite incurred when fully-equipped aircraft are flown by student pilots.

The Greenwood Aurora fleet is 'owned' by 14 Wing, and aircraft are drawn by squadrons as required. Consequently, squadron markings are usually only applied for special occasions such as anniversaries or participation in exercises.

A CP-140 overflies its base at Greenwood, Nova Scotia. Visible on the ramp are display examples of its predecessors: Lancaster, Argus and Neptune.

It was intended initially that these trainers be given the CT-140 designation but, after it was suggested that they be used also for non-military surveillance purposes, the CS-140 designation was proposed. However, the Canadian Forces Administrative Order governing designations, names, and serial numbers (CFAO 36-37) made no provision for an 'S for Surveillance' Basic Mission Symbol and the proposal was rejected.

Later, it was decided to install a limited suite of equipment to enable the additional aircraft to carry out Arctic and maritime surveillance. Accordingly, the new designation and name, CP-140A Arcturus, were approved on 24 January 1989. Two days later, the serials 140119, 140120, and 140121 were assigned to the second batch of P-3C derivatives for the Canadian Armed Forces. The contract was signed on 30 June 1989. The three CP-140As were delivered in December 1992, February 1993 and April 1993, in the dark grey scheme in which the CP-140s had already been repainted.

There are few significant external differences between the CP-140 Aurora and the CP-140A Arcturus. The latter has the standard P-3 Orion's sonobuoy launcher tube layout, rather than the modified one of the Aurora, and also lack's the CP-140's wingtip ESM pods. Compared to the standard P-3C, some minor structural changes were made to the cockpit area of the Arcturus's fuselage to increase structural strength and to bring the structure more in line with that of the CP-140. Internally, the Arcturus has selected features of the Aurora, including the cockpit, observer stations, tactical compartment layout and gallery/dinette.

The CP-140A can carry and deploy two SKADs and can also carry the same weapons as the CP-140 in the internal weapons bay, but only for transport purposes. There are no underwing weapons attachment points on the Arcturus and, while it does have the same standard and types of sonobuoy launch tubes, they are not wired and there is no launch capability other than by using the general purpose (free fall) chute. There are limited storage facilities for sonobuoys, marine markers and parachute flares.

The CP-140As have a tail boom extension, but not its associated magnetic anomaly detection equipment. The similarities with the Aurora leave open the possibility that they could be upgraded later to CP-140 standard without a need for structural modifications, such as the fitting of the MAD boom. In the short term, this ensured that the two versions 'feel' the same in the air and simplifies logistics by increasing commonality as much as possible.

Other than the serials, some small antennas, and the lack of underwing hardpoints, the only visible external difference is the lack of wingtip-mounted ESM equipment peculiar to the CP-140 Aurora. Although used most by the training unit, 404 (MP&OT) Squadron, the three CP-140As are pooled in 14 Wing. Some early reports suggested that only two were

Variant	c/n	Serial
CP-140	5682	140101
CP-140	5689	140102
CP-140	5693	140103
CP-140	5697	140104
CP-140	5704	140105
CP-140	5706	140106
CP-140	5708	140107
CP-140	5709	140108
CP-140	5711	140109
CP-140	5712	140110
CP-140	5714	140111
CP-140	5715	140112
CP-140	5717	140113
CP-140	5719	140114
CP-140	5720	140115
CP-140	5722	140116
CP-140	5723	140117
CP-140	5725	140118
CP-140A	5828	140119
CP-140A	5829	140120
CP-140A	5830	140121

to be based at CFB Greenwood with the third going to CFB Comox. In fact, all three Arcturuses are assigned to 14 Wing in Nova Scotia, but one Aurora was transferred to 407 (MP) Squadron at Comox, raising the West Coast complement to five.

The CP-140As have four observer stations with bubble windows and the auxiliary escape hatch behind the pilot's seat has an optical window for handheld photography. Unlike the CP-140s, CP-140As do not have a belly-mounted vertical camera system, and ballast was required to maintain the aircraft's centre of gravity in spite of the reduced equipment fit. This was achieved by constructing the aft galley deck plates from steel.

Detailed below are the primary missions of the CP-140A Arcturus, performed in addition to aircrew training:

Sovereignty: surface surveillance of Canadian territory and ocean areas and enforcement of Canadian regulatory agencies' acts
Arctic and maritime surveillance: search, detection, tracking, and reporting of surface vessels

Its secondary missions are:
Ice reconnaissance
Search and rescue
Fisheries patrols
Protection of the environment

The CP-140As were delivered to IMP in very basic condition and have been fitted out by that company under sub-contract to Lockheed. At one point, they were to have been the last three airframes to come off the Orion assembly line, but it has been reopened following its move from Burbank, California to Marietta, Georgia.

All of the CP-140s and CP-140As based at CFB Greenwood initially belonged to the Greenwood Base Aircraft Engineering Maintenance Organisation (BAMEO) which allocated them to the squadrons on an as-required basis. Those units are 404 (Maritime Patrol and Training) Squadron, 405 (Maritime Patrol) Squadron, 415 (Maritime Patrol) Squadron, and the Maritime Proving and Evaluation Unit (MPEU). 407 (MP) Squadron is located at CFB Comox with its own aircraft and self-contained maintenance organisation under a Squadron Aircraft Maintenance Engineering Officer (SAMEO).

On 1 April 1993, CFB Greenwood's flying and support operations were consolidated as 14 Wing and the BAMEO is now 14 Air Maintenance Squadron.

CFB Comox became 19 Wing, overseeing squadrons from Fighter Group (414 with Dets from 416 and 441), Air Transport Group (442) and Maritime Air Group (407). A further reorganisation of the air force took place on 1 April 1997, with the Groups replaced by a single operational level known, for historical reasons, as

1 Canadian Air Division.

From time to time, aircraft are transferred between Greenwood and Comox. 140101 is used frequently as a trials aircraft by MP&EU, but it is neither permanently nor semi-permanently assigned to that unit, even though it wears that unit's badge on its tail. Similarly, other Auroras occasionally wear squadron badges, usually as a result of their participation in exercises or competitions, but this does not mean those aircraft are assigned to the unit whose badge they wear. Only Comox-based 407 (MP) Squadron 'owns' CP-140s as it provides its own first- and second-line maintenance.

Upgrades for the Aurora fleet have been under discussion almost from the beginning, with numerous proposals offered and rejected, usually for budgetary reasons. The original Aurora Upgrade Project (AUP) was estimated to cost Can$700 million and covered 14 items, including improvements to the EW systems (which are now far from adequate in the CP-140) and the addition of Harpoon anti-ship missiles. That list was then cut by one-third, with only those items having a dual peacetime/wartime application being submitted for approval. (Among the deleted items were a self-protection jamming capability for the ESM, improved overland radar capability, night vision system and colour radar.)

Nineteen sub-projects have been grouped into three major upgrades. One of them involves a Can$58 million contract with BAE Systems Canada (awarded 6 September 2000) to carry out the Navigation and Flight Instruments Modernization Project (NFIMP). This includes replacing the inertial navigation system with a GPS/INS and modern electronic flight instruments. The aircraft will also be upgraded with a digital autopilot and an improved radar altitude warning system. However, only 16 CP-140s will receive NFIMP, which is part

of the Aurora Incremental Modernization Project. AIMP is the umbrella for modifications, upgrades or replacements of the flight and mission avionics of 16 aircraft. It has a potential total value of Can$900 million and is intended to sustain the Aurora for another 20 years. A separate, but parallel, programme will acquire a new CP-140 flight training system and another – at a later date – will add air-to-surface weapons. The goal is to keep the 16 aircraft capable of supporting combined multinational missions as well as independent assignments in both domestic and international, civilian and military situations until at least 2020. Next to be covered by a request for proposals will be a new data management system, which is the core of the aircraft. It has a potential value of more than Can$130 million.

The original plan was to upgrade all 18 CP-140s and three CP-140As, but a force structure exercise completed by the air force in the spring of 2000 determined that the improved capabilities of the upgraded aircraft meant that only 16 were required. It has yet to be decided when the other five aircraft will be withdrawn from their current roles. A new search and rescue study is underway and it will also examine the feasibility of converting the five surplus aircraft to the SAR role so they could replace the CC-130E Hercules of 413 (Transport & Rescue) Squadron at CFB Greenwood and the CC-115 Buffaloes of 442 (T&R) Squadron at CFB Comox. However, it has yet to be determined if the CP-140 and CP-140A could be made into suitable maritime SAR aircraft.

Jeff Rankin-Lowe

Outwardly similar to the fully-equipped Aurora, the CP-140A Arcturus has no ASW equipment fitted. It is used for a wide variety of duties, including pilot training, all of which download the tasks of the operational Aurora fleet.

CHILE

Comando de la Aviación Naval/ Armada de Chile

Variant	c/n	BuNo.	Serial/notes
P-3A	5018	149677	403 (scrapped)
P-3ACH	5033	150507	402 (cvtd. P-3A)
UP-3A	5044	150518	401 (open storage)
UP-3A	5059	150607	406 (open storage)
UP-3A	5067	151354	405 (scrapped)
P-3ACH	5097	151384	407 (cvtd. UP-3A)
UP-3A	5111	152141	408 (pax transport)
P-3ACH	5135	152165	404 (cvtd. UP-3A)

For many years the maritime patrol function was undertaken by the Fuerza Aérea de Chile (Chilean air force), using the Grumman HU-16B Albatross amphibian. When these were retired, responsibility for maritime patrol was transferred to the Comando de Aviación Naval de Chile (Chilean naval aviation). Earlier attempts to acquire four ex-US Navy Lockheed SP-2E Neptunes had failed, but the navy acquired six factory-fresh EMBRAER EMB-111AN Bandeirantes from Brazil, deliveries starting in December 1977. However, due to its limited size, range and mission fit, the Bandeirante was not ideal to patrol Chile's long coastline.

A far better aircraft was found in the shape of the Lockheed P-3 Orion. Thanks to a positive political environment, the US agreed the transfer of a batch of P-3A Orions to Chile. Delivery of the first of eight Orions to the Aviación Naval de Chile began in March 1993. The batch consisted of two standard P-3As and six general-purpose UP-3As, which had mission equipment and weapons systems removed. All were assigned to the Escuadrón de Exploración Aeromarítima VP-1, part of the Fuerza Aeronaval No. 1, home-based at Base Aeronaval Viña del Mar (Concón).

The introduction of the type into the service was made difficult due to the inexperience of the Chilean navy in the operation of heavy multi-engined aircraft, and by the lack of trained crews. The P-3 Orion proved to be an expensive aircraft to operate and maintain. Several specialised items, such as the AN/ASQ-10 MAD

Like its neighbour, Argentina, Chile chose a dark grey scheme for its Orions. This is considered to be more effective over the south Atlantic than a lighter colour.

system, were inoperative in the two P-3As. It was not surprising, therefore, that initially the Orions were used as logistic transports. On 15 July 1995 one aircraft performed the first medevac flight to the Pascua Islands.

In an effort to improve the Orion's effectiveness, the Chilean navy signed a contract with Air New Zealand Engineering Services to perform a complete revision of three airframes, as well the installation of unspecified FLIR and ESM equipment. The first aircraft to be modified to the new P-3ACH standard (aircraft serial 407) departed for Auckland on 25 May 1997.

At the same time, under Project Parina, another aircraft (coded 408) was converted as a passenger transport, under the direction of Aviation Professional Services of Miami. Modification works were performed between March and November 1996 at Viña del Mar, and the aircraft is configured as a 65-passenger transport with a VIP seating section. More recently, the Aviación Naval de Chile has considered placing some maintenance/modification work at the TACE facilities of the Argentine naval air arm at NAS Comandante Espora (Bahia Blanca, Argentina), which conducts work on the Argeninte P-3 fleet.

Currently, VP-1 is operating four aircraft: three for maritime patrol and one for transport. Two others are in storage, while the remaining pair was scrapped. The operational P-3ACHs are mostly engaged on long-range maritime surveillance on behalf of the Chilean navy surface fleet.

Jorge F. Nuñez Padin

Above: This aircraft was the machine converted under the Parina project to act as a passenger transport.

Below: The nosewheel strut compresses as a P-3ACH comes to a rapid halt. The Chilean navy has three of these fully mission-capable aircraft in use to cover the nation's long and rugged coastline.

GREECE

Elliniki Polimiko Aeroporia (Hellenic Air Force)

Like some other smaller Orion operators, the Greek P-3 fleet is under command of the air force, the HAF. The Orions are operated in one squadron as part of the 112 Pterigha Mahis (Combat Wing, PM) at Elefsis Air Base near Athens, which is subordinate to the Dioikissi Aeroporiki Ipostirixis (Air Support Command).

The 353 Mira Naftikis Aeroporikis Sinergasias (Naval Air Co-operation Squadron, MNAS) ceased operations with the Grumman HU-16B Albatross amphibian

The first P-3 to arrive in Greece wore these special navy markings for just two weeks before the air force ordered the removal of the nose markings.

The only outward sign that the Greek P-3s have a navy 'back-end' crew, and operate under naval command, is the small anchor marking on the rear fuselage. The flight crew is provided by the air force, which 'owns' and maintains the six-aircraft fleet.

Variant	c/n	BuNo.	Notes
P-3A	5079	151366	parts
P-3A	5102	151389	parts
P-3A	5151	152181	parts
P-3A	5153	152183	parts
P-3B(LW/TNM)	5184	152744	
P-3B(LW/TNM)	5187	152747	
P-3B(LW/TNM)	5212	153415	
P-3B(LW/TNM)	5221	153424	
P-3B(LW/TNM)	5224	153427	
P-3B(LW/TNM)	5238	153441	

in 1996, although one ECM-dedicated Albatross was kept operational until late 1997. With the Albatross design dating from the 1950s, a successor for the maritime patrol role was badly needed. Since the activation of the 353 MNAS in 1969 it has been the Hellenic Navy which plans the missions and provides the system operators, while the Albatross was flown by air force pilots. The navy has long held the desire to have all-navy crews, but for obvious reasons this has been obstructed by the air force. With the reactivation as an Orion unit, the nickname and callsign of the 353 MNAS was changed from 'Albatross' to 'Triaina' (trident).

Having earlier examined the possibility of acquiring a large number of P-3s, some

of which would have been used for transport and fire-fighting tasks, Greece was initially to have leased four ex-US Navy P-3Bs in a deal signed in February 1994. However, this was soon altered to a sale of six aircraft, the increased number reflecting the rate of unserviceable airframes combined with the large area of the Aegean Sea which needed to be covered. Ahead of the P-3B delivery, four former US Navy P-3A Orions were delivered to Hellenic Aerospace Industries at 114 PM Tanagra Air Base to serve for ground instruction training as well as a source for spare parts, of which the first (BuNo. 151389) arrived in 1995. These Orions never wore the Greek national marking and only had their BuNo. painted on them.

Greek P-3Bs are Lightweight

TACNAVMOD aircraft, and underwent an overhaul at Waco before delivery. A few items of equipment were upgraded, including the powerplants, which are T56-A-14s. The first upgrade (BuNo. 153441) was completed on 22 May 1996 and officially handed over to the HAF on 31 May 1996. On the nose section of this Orion was painted the Hellenic Navy anchor, flanked by the Greek letters P and N for Polimiko Naftikou, or Hellenic Navy. Due to the aforementioned rivalry between the navy and the air force, this logo was short-lived and the HAF had the markings of the P-3B removed two weeks after arrival at Elefsis. Now the P-3Bs are painted in the standard US Navy grey Tactical Paint Scheme, with toned-down Greek roundels and flag, and a small anchor near the BuNo.

During 1996, Greek Orion pilots and crew were trained by former US Navy employees working under civilian contract. Part of the training programme included several visits to the Orion flight simulator at NAS Valkenburg in the Netherlands. The fourth P-3B was delivered to the 353 MNAS by the end of 1996, while the final two arrived the following year. The Greek P-3B fleet is now in need of a modernisation programme to keep up in the field of maritime surveillance. In the Armament Programme of 2001-05, the Hellenic Navy has reserved an unspecified budget for the modernisation of the P-3B Orion fleet.

René van Woezik

IRAN

Islamic Republic of Iran Air Force

In early 1973 the Imperial Iranian Air Force placed an order for six Orions, as part of the massive modernisation and enlargement of the IIAF. The Orions were required to provide modern ASW/MPA coverage of the vital Persian Gulf, and further afield into the Indian Ocean.

US concerns over the transfer of the latest ASW technology (which, as it transpired, were fully justified) led to the creation of the P-3F, an unusual hybrid between the P-3A/B and P-3C. Externally, the airframe was essentially that of the P-3C, with externally-loaded sonobuoy tubes. The aircraft also had the APS-115 radar and undernose surveillance camera from the 'Charlie', as well as ARN-84 TACAN and APN-153 Doppler. However, the basic mission system was that employed by the P-3A/B.

Inside the cabin, the P-3F was also a curious mix of the two generations. The A/B's side-by-side work-stations were retained for three positions, but the navigator was moved forward to the port side in what was the P-3C's Tacco (tactical co-ordinator) station. The radio operator sat opposite this position (nav/com in P-3C).

In February 1975 Lockheed delivered the first P-3Fs to NAS Moffett Field, California, where the US Navy's VP-31 began training Iranian crews. It had been envisaged that the IIAF would provide the flight crews, while the navy provided the mission crew. In the event, P-3F operations remained the province of the IIAF/IRIAF. The aircraft were initially delivered in standard US Navy grey/white, but while at Moffett were

repainted in an unusual three-tone blue scheme. With initial training completed, the first aircraft were flown to Iran in April 1975.

Initially, the P-3Fs were based at Bandar Abbas, strategically located on the shores of the Straits of Hormuz. There Lockheed established a major training and engineering support base, and for many of the early missions Lockheed technicians were aboard. The US Navy also used the base for expanding its P-3 operations in the region. The training phase ended in January 1979. Later that year, the Islamic revolution toppled the Shah, and with it all US aid came to an end. The IIAF was subsequently rechristened as the IRIAF. Shortly before the revolution three P-3Cs had been ordered (with a further nine required) but this order was terminated by the US.

At some point in the early 1980s the P-3Fs moved base to Shiraz, where one crashed on 15 February 1985. This aircraft had been the only one of the six to be equipped with AGM-84 Harpoon anti-ship missile capability, which it had tested in the US in 1978. It returned to Iran with missiles, but it is not known if any were fired in anger during the war with Iraq. The move to Shiraz was primarily as a result of the ongoing war. Shiraz was closer to the main war zone, but was also some way inland, making it less vulnerable to attack.

As spares ran short, the operational P-3 fleet dwindled to just one or two. However, it is believed that among the arms covertly supplied during the Iran/Contra scandal were supplies for the P-3 fleet. After 1988 more aircraft were seen on operations, and at least two were positively identified

Little has been seen of the Iranian P-3F fleet in recent times, although it is believed that at least one remains airworthy.

monitoring operations during the 1990-91 Gulf War. Since then, at least one has remained operational, although without an adequate spares supply it is unlikely to fly for much longer.

David Donald

Variant	c/n	BuNo.	Serial/fate
P-3F	6001	159342	5-8701
P-3F	6002	159343	5-8702 (lost)
P-3F	6003	159344	5-8703
P-3F	6004	159345	5-8704
P-3F	6005	159346	5-8705
P-3F	6006	159347	5-8706

Throughout the Iran-Iraq war Iranian P-3Fs were active in the Gulf, monitoring shipping. They were regularly intercepted by US Navy fighters, such as this VF-213 F-14A in September 1981 (left). In the 1990s they were noted flying near the United Arab Emirates, with whom Iran has an outstanding dispute over sovereignty of certain Gulf islands.

JAPAN
Kaijo Jiei-tai (Japan Maritime Self Defence Force)

On 24 August 1977, the Japan Maritime Self Defence Force (JMSDF) selected the Lockheed P-3C Orion as its next Patrol Aircraft-Land Base (PX-L) to replace its Grumman S2F-1 Trackers and Lockheed P2V-7 Neptunes. Kawasaki Heavy Industries had started its P-2J Study for the PX-L requirement in 1968 and its original design had used four turbofan engines. This was thought to be a strong contender, but Lockheed achieved a notable reversal. While the PX-L outcome was being deliberated, political scandal erupted involving the Japanese Prime Minister and Lockheed. So, when the decision was made by Boei-cho (Japan Defense Agency: JDA) to select the P-3C, extensive documents were issued by the JDA which claimed there was no relation between the political scandal and the P-3 decision.

Under the selection decision, 45 P-3Cs would be purchased as an initial batch, but this figure has been revised four times, and finally stands at 101 aircraft, the final increase being made on 18 December 1992. Also, Kawasaki Heavy Industries (KHI) was named as the prime contractor to manufacture P-3Cs under a license issued in 1978.

In FY 1978's Defence Budget, a purchase of eight P-3Cs was authorised. The first three P-3Cs (5001-5003) were built by Lockheed and purchased directly under the FMS (Foreign Military Sales) contract. The remaining five aircraft were made up from components which were imported from the US and assembled by KHI in Japan (so called 'knock-down' manufacturing). From the ninth P-3C, (5009) full licence production was started by KHI.

Initial P-3Cs for the JMSDF were to the Update II standard. Main mission equipment consisted of AN/AAQ-7 DIFAR, AN/APS-115B search radar, AN/ARS-3 sonobuoy reference system, AN/ALQ-78 or AN/ALR-66(V) ESM, AN/ASQ-81(V) MAD, AN/AAS-36 IRDS and AN/ASQ-114(V) digital central computer. From the 46th aircraft (5046), Phase 1 modernisation was incorporated. This included a change of radar and onboard logistic system to improve the information processing capability. Also, from the 61st (5061)

aircraft, some upgrades of the flight control system were made. This included improvements to the reliability and maintainability of the AFCS, and modification of tabs on the ailerons and rudder.

Phase 2 modernisation began with the 70th aircraft (5070), subsequent Orions being equivalent to the US Navy's Update III. The main alteration was to replace DIFAR with the AN/UYS-1 Proteus single advanced signal processor (SASP). With SASP came improvement in sonobuoy signal detection, increase of the number of sonobuoy channels which could be processed simultaneously, more accurate frequency analysis and improvements in automatic detection, identification and tracking capability. From the 81st aircraft (5081), materials in the engine bleed air ducts were changed.

From the 89th aircraft (5089), SATCOM satellite communication systems were installed. SATCOM aircraft are easily identified by the large black radome mounted above the forward fuselage. From the 97th aircraft (5097), a mainwheel anti-skid system and new missile control system were added. From the 99th aircraft (5099), new functions were added to the SIF, while the 100th aircraft (5100) introduced changes to the passive detection system and tactical information processing system, and had a GPS navigation system installed. The 101st and final KHI-built P-3C (5101) featured environmental improvements in the cabin. This last P-3C was delivered to the JMSDF on 17 September 1997.

In parallel with these upgrades, the JMSDF began to introduce a Phase 3 modernisation to all P-3Cs which will bring them to full Update III standards. After

This VP-6 P-3 flies past Mount Fuji. The Japanese Orion fleet was built in several successively improved models, and many early aircraft have been brought up to the latest standards. The dorsal radome covers a satellite communications antenna.

modification, these Orions feature the following equipment: CP-2004(J)/ASQ-212 Tactical Information Processing System, HLR-109 Passive Detection System, GPS Navigation System, AN/UYS-1(V) Acoustic Processing System, AN/ARS-5 Sonobuoy Reference System, LTN-73(Mod) INS, AN/ARR-78(V)1 Sonobuoy Receive System, SG-1156/A Acoustic Signal Generator, AN/AHQ-4(V)2 Sono-data Recording System, AN/ASA-70(Mod) Tactical Situation Display and AN/ASH-33(Mod) Magnetic Tape Recorder.

A total of 10 JMSDF squadrons (9 VP squadrons and one VT training squadron) was equipped with the Orion, as follows:

Dai 1 Koku-gun (1st Air Wing), Kanoya Air Base

Dai 1 Koku-tai (VP-1): VP-1 formed on 1 July 1954 as the first anti-submarine squadron of the JMSDF, and was equipped with T-34s and SNJs. It started to receive PV-2s during the 1950s. Delivery of the P-3C to VP-1 began on 10 July 1989 and was completed on 8 December, fully replacing the P-2J Neptune. Thus, VP-1 became the fifth JMSDF P-3C squadron. Tail markings of VP-1 are based on the Sakura-jima mountain and the figure '1'. Sakura-jima is one of the largest active volcanoes in Japan, and is the symbolic mountain of Kagoshima Prefecture where Kanoya AB is located. The figure '1' denotes VP-1 rather than the 1st Air Wing.

Dai 7 Koku-tai (VP-7): VP-7 was established on 1 December 1987 as the final JMSDF P-2J squadron. The unit received its first P-3C on 29 July 1991 and became the 7th P-3C VP squadron in early 1992. Although VP-7 had reformed as a P-3C squadron, it continued to operate the P-2J until 22 May 1994, a date which

Left: P-3 training for the JMSDF is handled by VT-203 at Shimofusa. Prospective P-3 pilots graduate from the Beech TC-90s of VT-202 at Tokushima.

Below: VP-3 is at Atsugi, close to Mount Fuji, as reflected in the squadron badge.

marked the final withdrawal of the P-2J from active service. The tail markings of VP-7 show Omega (from the unit's call sign) and seven stars to represent VP-7.

Dai 2 Koku-gun (2nd Air Wing), Hachinohe Air Base

Dai 2 Koku-tai (VP-2): VP-2 is the second oldest anti-submarine squadron of the JMSDF and completed its conversion from the P-2J to P-3C on 31 March 1986 to become JMSDF's third P-3C squadron. VP-2 tail markings consist of a trident, as used by Poseidon, chosen because of the unit's call sign.

Dai 4 Koku-tai (VP-4): Dai 4 Koku-tai was formed on 31 March 1963 as a P2V-7 squadron. Conversion from the P-2J to P-3C was completed on 15 August 1987, the unit becoming the JMSDF's fourth P-3C squadron. Tail markings of VP-4 combine the spread wings of an eagle and the figure '4'. During the 1960s, the JDA allocated original Japanese nicknames to all aircraft, and the P2V-7 was dubbed *Oh-washi* (a kind of eagle), leading to VP-4's choice of tail markings.

Dai 4 Koku-gun (4th Air Wing) at Atsugi Air Base

Dai 3 Koku-tai (VP-3): Dai 3 Koku-tai was formed as a P2V-7 squadron at Kanoya AB and moved to Atsugi AB on 25 December 1973. It started conversion to the P-2J the next year. The unit's first P-3C was delivered on 10 May 1984 and conversion to the Orion was completed on 19 March 1985. VP-3 therefore became the JMSDF's second P-3C squadron. Tail markings of this unit combine Mount Fuji and the letter 't'. Mount Fuji is located close to Atsugi AB, and in shape resembles the letter 'A'. This 'A' and 't' together represents Atsugi.

Dai 6 Koku-tai (VP-6): VP-6 was newly formed at Atsugi AB on 30 March 1983 as the first P-3C unit and to act as the Orion's 'mother' squadron in the JMSDF. Because of the importance of Dai 4 Koku-gun, VP-3 and VP-6 received the latest variants of P-3C as a matter of course. VP-6's tail markings show the hunter (Orion).

Dai 5 Koku-gun (5th Air Wing), Naha Air Base

Dai 5 Koku-tai (VP-5): When Okinawa was returned to Japan, the JMSDF formed Rinji Okinawa Haken-tai (Provisional Okinawa Air Detachment) at Naha AB on 14 July 1972, but initially no aircraft were assigned. On 21 December 1972, P-2Js were delivered to the unit, which changed its name to Okinawa Koku-tai (Okinawa Air Squadron) in 1973. It then became Dai 5 Koku-tai on 15 July 1981. The first P-3C was delivered to this squadron on 11 July 1990 and conversion from the P-2J was completed on 23 January 1991. VP-5 became the JMSDF's sixth P-3C VP unit. The tail marking of VP-5 is a Pegasus, derived from the squadron's callsign.

Dai 9 Koku-tai (VP-9): VP-9 was formed at Naha AB as the ninth and final P-3C VP squadron in the JMSDF on 30 July 1993. The tail marking of VP-9 is the See-Sah (traditional home guards in Okinawa), derived from VP-9's callsign.

Above: The trident insignia identifies VP-2. This SATCOM-equipped aircraft was the last P-3C to be built by Kawasaki Heavy Industries.

Dai 31 Koku-gun (31st Air Wing), Iwakuni Air Base

Dai 8 Koku-tai (VP-8): VP-8 was newly formed as the eighth P-3C VP squadron at Iwakuni AB on 30 July 1992. The tail marking of VP-8 features lightning bolts, derived from the unit's callsign 'Thunder'. Under the current defence plan, the JMSDF has decided to disband one P-3C squadron and VP-8 was selected. Therefore, VP-8 will disappear before 31 March 2001.

Shimofusa Kyoiku Koku-gun (Shimofusa Training Air Group), Shimofusa Air Base

Dai 203 Kyoiku Koku-tai (VT-203): The original training unit for P-3C crew was Dai 206 Kyoiku Koku-tai (VT-206) which was formed on 1 December 1987 at Shimofusa AB. VT-203, which had conducted crew training for the P-2J at Kanoya AB, disbanded on the same day. And a few years later, VT-206 was renamed as VT-203. The tail markings of VT-203 remained unchanged from the days of VT-206, and consist of five triangular arrows. This represents the fact that VT-203 provides the crews for five Koku-gunn (Air Wings).

The JMSDF also developed four derivative types from the original P-3C: EP-3 Elint platform, UP-3C test evaluation aircraft, UP-3D electronic warfare training aircraft and UP-3E image intelligence

Right: The single UP-3C is a dedicated trials vehicle, equipped with a sensitive air data boom. It is operated by the JMSDF's trials unit, VX-51 at Atsugi.

gathering vehicle. All these derivatives are new-build aircraft except for the UP-3Es, which are conversions of existing P-3Cs.

The EP-3 was first ordered in FY 1987. Five have been purchased and the last was delivered to the JMSDF in September 1998. These aircraft are operated by Dai 81 Koku-tai (81st Squadron) under the control of Dai 31 Koku-gun (31st Air Wing) at Iwakuni AB. EP-3s are used to collect, analyse and evaluate the electromagnetic radiations which come from ships. For this mission, the EP-3 is equipped with NH/LR-107 and NH/LR-108 electronic warfare and Elint systems. External features include three large black fairings (two on the spine and one under the forward fuselage) which contain antennas for the mission equipment. The MAD boom was deleted from the tail.

The second P-3C derivative is the UP-3C, of which only one was purchased in FY 1991. This aircraft was delivered to Dai 51 Koku-tai (VX-51) at Atsugi AB on 16 February 1995. The UP-3C is used for test and evaluation of newly developed aircraft equipment, and also for trial support. It is equipped with several measurement and evaluation/recording systems. Externally, the UP-3C is similar to the P-3C but has a long pitot tube which extends from the starboard side of the front fuselage.

Although the UP-3D was developed as an electronic warfare training aircraft for the fleet of JMSDF, it also has operational ECM capabilities. For this reason, details of the UP-3D have not been announced, but it

certainly has a comprehensive electronics warfare suite. Three UP-3Ds were ordered and the final aircraft was delivered in December 2000. UP-3Ds are operated by Dai 81 Koku-tai (81st Squadron) alongside EP-3s and Learjet U-36As from Iwakuni AB.

The UP-3E Imint-gathering aircraft is the fourth P-3C derivative, of which five are to be produced by conversion. The main roles of the UP-3E are to provide surveillance and imagery of surface vessels, to process and edit the image intelligence onboard, to transfer this information to the command structure and friendly ships, and to conduct and support search and rescue activities. For this mission, the UP-3E is equipped with SLAR and data display systems, GPS/SATCOM, ESM and an infra-red search and track device. The first UP-3E will be delivered to the JMSDF before the end of March 2001, and will undergo operational trials with VX-51 from April 2001. After this trial, all UP-3Es will be operated by Dai 81 Koku-tai at Iwakuni AB.

Built by Lockheed			
Variant	c/n	BuNo.	Serial
P-3C UII	7001	161267	5001
P-3C UII	7002	161268	5002
P-3C UII	7003	161269	5003
Assembled by KHI from Lockheed kits			
P-3C UII	5004 to 5008 (5)		
Built by KHI			
P-3C UII	5009 to 5069 (61)		
P-3C UIII	5070 to 5101 (32)		
UP-3C	9151 (1)		
UP-3D	9161 to 9163 (3)		
EP-3	9171 to 9175 (5)		
UP-3E	9181 to 9185 (5 converted from P-3C)		

For the future, the JMSDF has initiated a study of a successor to the P-3C in the ASW role. A four-turbofan aircraft is considered the most likely.

Yoshitomo Aoki

Below: 9161 is the first of three UP-3D ECM aircraft which now fly with the 81st Squadron. Here it is seen undergoing evaluation by the trials unit, VX-51.

Right: Dai 81 Koku-tai operates the five-strong fleet of EP-3s. These have a maritime Elint role, similar to that of the US Navy's EP-3E Aries II fleet.

REPUBLIC OF KOREA

Republic of Korea Naval Aviation

South Korea occupies a strategically important position between the Yellow Sea and Sea of Japan, and commands the vital Tsushima Straits sea lanes. It also experiences a large number of territorial water violations by submarines and small vessels from North Korea, mostly aimed at surveillance and infiltrating agents into the South. Faced with these major maritime commitments, the Republic of Korea Navy has a sizeable need for maritime patrol aircraft (MPA) assets, a requirement admirably filled by the P-3C Orion.

Between 1976 and 1981 the RoKNA received 28 ex-US Navy Grumman S-2E Trackers. These provided good service, but by the 1990s were clearly inadequate. Accordingly, an order was placed in December 1990 for eight P-3C Update IIIs. Production had halted at Palmdale, but the tooling was reinstalled at Marietta, where the eight Korean aircraft were built. The move in production line conveniently

A pre-delivery shot of a Korean P-3C shows the aircraft with its IRDS deployed. The eight-aircraft batch was built at Marietta rather than Palmdale.

allowed the incorporation of more modern manufacturing techniques, alternative materials and greater corrosion protection.

Designated as Update III+s, the Korean aircraft included some non-standard items, and incorporated items which had been retrofitted to Update IIIs while in service. Importantly, these included the ASQ-212 central processing system with Unisys CP-2044 tactical computer and the ALR-66(V)3 ESM system. Korean aircraft were completed with AAS-36 IRDS, APS-134 non-imaging ISAR radar and AGM-84 Harpoon capability.

First flight for a Marietta-built Orion occurred on 12 December 1994, and after initial training of Korean crews had been undertaken by VP-30 at NAS Jacksonville, Florida, the first aircraft was delivered in April 1995. All eight had been ferried to

Korea by the end of the year. In service with 613 ASW Squadron at Pohang, the Orions report to 61 Air Wing.

For the future the RoKNA requires an additional eight aircraft, for which funding had been secured. However, the Asian economic crisis intervened, shelving the placement of an order. Further Orion purchases are once again likely, and may include the acquisition of ex-US Navy aircraft to serve as pilot trainers and utility transports.
David Donald

Variant	c/n	BuNo.	Serial
P-3C UIII+	5831	165098	950901
P-3C UIII+	5832	165099	950902
P-3C UIII+	5833	165100	950903
P-3C UIII+	5834	165101	950905
P-3C UIII+	5835	165102	950906
P-3C UIII+	5836	165103	950907
P-3C UIII+	5837	165104	950908
P-3C UIII+	5838	165105	950909

The RoKNA's capabilities have been greatly enhanced since the arrival of the Orion, especially in the anti-ship role using the AGM-84A Harpoon missile. As of early 2001, the Korean aircraft were the last Orion airframes to be built by Lockheed Martin.

NETHERLANDS

Marine Luchtvaartsdienst

Having earlier selected the Breguet Atlantic to fulfil a maritime patrol aircraft requirement, the MLD ordered 13 P-3C Update IIs in December 1978 to replace its last SP-2H Neptunes. The aircraft were ordered as Update IIs, but received most of the II.5 improvements while in production. AAS-36 was not fitted at the factory, but the SAFIRE FLIR was installed later. The aircraft were not equipped with Harpoon launch capability. In 1981 the first crews

started conversion training at NAS Jacksonville, and the first Dutch Orion was delivered to Jacksonville in November the same year. The first four Orions arrived at Valkenburg Naval Air Station on 21 July 1982 and the last example was delivered in September 1984. Delivery was made to the Groep Maritieme Patrouillevliegtuigen (MARPAT), with 320 Squadron (VSQ-320) flying operational missions and 321 Squadron (VSQ-321) using the aircraft as required for training purposes.

MLD Orions are used in a number of roles. From Valkenburg they fly ASW patrols over the North Sea, and also undertake coastguard work. A single aircraft is detached to Keflavik, Iceland, to work alongside US Navy Orions, and to

provide SAR cover for Dutch F-16s deploying to summer training in Canada or to US exercises. One aircraft (306) was fitted with seats and stretchers for casevac duties during the 1991 Gulf War, while two others were dispatched to the Mediterranean to free US Navy Orions for duties in the war theatre.

Since 1992 two (now three) aircraft have been deployed to Hato, Curaçao, to fly anti-drug patrols in the Caribbean (Operation Fair Trade), and to fly coastguard/fishery/ EEZ patrols around Curaçao and for the government of Surinam. From 1992 MLD P-3s have been involved in operations in the Adriatic, two aircraft being assigned to NAS Sigonella in Italy for Operation Sharp Guard.

In 1998, as operations against Yugoslavia stepped up as a result of events in Kosovo, three P-3Cs were hastily modified for further operations in the Adriatic. These missions were codenamed Eagle Eye. The original SAFIRE FLIR was replaced by the Star SAFIRE, complete with Pioneer relay system which allowed the transfer of imagery to ground stations. The first Star SAFIRE-equipped aircraft (300) flew in November 1998. AAR-47 missile warning systems and ALE-47 chaff/flare dispensers were added, the work being performed by NAWC-AD at NAS Patuxent River, Maryland. The first upgraded aircraft arrived at Sigonella on 13 February 1999, and operations began two days later. When the overall Allied Force operation was launched, Eagle Eye was renamed as Noble Anvil. MLD Orions flew patrols throughout the war, although no significant actions were undertaken, monitoring coastal installations using the Star SAFIRE sensor.

Back in 1995 the Royal Netherlands Navy had launched a requirement for an operational upgrade for the 13 Orions. The MLD arrived at the new requirement because of the changed world security environment. It argued that its maritime units would be engaged more in land or amphibious operations, and that they could well be employed outside NATO territory, in a variety of threat environments, and often operating in Combined Joint Task Forces (CJTF).

Nevertheless, anti-submarine warfare remains an important mission, hence the Orion has to be equipped with appropriate equipment to detect diesel submarines operating closer to shore. Also, the new equipment should be more capable of detecting small naval targets such as patrol boats and coastal anti-ship missile batteries. As noted above, three aircraft received some modifications for the Eagle Eye mission. However, a further reaching programme has been implemented, known as Capability Upkeep Programme (CUP).

Basic systems of the CUP include the AN/ASQ-227 central data management system, AN/APS-137B(V)5 imaging ISAR radar and the AN/AIC-34 internal communcation system. All aircraft will also receive provision for new AN/ALR-66C(V)3 ESM system, AN/USQ-78B acoustic processor and sonobuoy receiver, SATCOM, AN/AAR-47 missile approach warning receiver and AN/ALE-47 chaff/flare dispensers. Lockheed Martin Naval Electronics and Surveillance Systems is the prime contractor and the programme has been funded through Foreign Military Sales channels. It is linked to the AIP improvements being made to the US Navy's Orions. The first aircraft enters the

Due to their overseas commitments in the Netherlands Antilles, Adriatic and Atlantic, it is extremely uncommon to see four MLD P-3s operating together. The occasion here was a commemorative flypast.

Above: When operating from Valkenburg, MLD P-3s undertake patrols over the North Sea and along the Dutch coast.

Right: The chaff/flare dispensers above the nosewheel doors and missile warning receivers identify this aircraft as one of three hastily converted for Eagle Eye operations in the Adriatic.

Variant	c/n	BuNo.	Serial
P-3C UII.5	5733	161368	300
P-3C UII.5	5737	161369	301
P-3C UII.5	5741	161370	302
P-3C UII.5	5745	161371	303
P-3C UII.5	5750	161372	304
P-3C UII.5	5754	161373	305
P-3C UII.5	5758	161374	306
P-3C UII.5	5762	161375	307
P-3C UII.5	5765	161376	308
P-3C UII.5	5769	161377	309
P-3C UII.5	5773	161378	310
P-3C UII.5	5774	161379	311
P-3C UII.5	5776	161380	312

five-month upgrade process in 2002, and the final one will be completed in 2005.

In the autumn of 1999 a new defence white paper called for the retirement and sale of three of the 13 Orions. Seven of the remaining 10 are to receive the full modification, while the remaining three will get provisions for it. In July 2000 one more Orion was added to the coast guard force at Hato, pushing the number there to three. This trio will be the aircraft without full CUP modifications, but may receive additional specialist equipment for their primary anti-smuggling role.

It is almost irreversible that the Orion fleet will move from NAS Valkenburg to NAS De Kooij (home to the Navy's helicopter fleet) in the northwest of the Netherlands. Valkenburg is to be closed in 2010 to make room for large residential areas. Hundreds of millions of Dutch Guilders have to be pumped into De Kooij to make it a major air station, including a runway expansion and large hangars to accommodate Orion operations.

Gert Krombout and David Donald

NEW ZEALAND

Royal New Zealand Air Force

After considering a proposed ASW version of the Lockheed C-130, the New Zealand government ordered five P-3B Orions in 1964 at a cost of £8 million to replace Sunderland MR.5 flying-boats. The aircraft were delivered to No. 5 Squadron, RNZAF at Whenuapai, Auckland in September (the first arrived on the 27th) and December 1966, and have remained with the squadron ever since. No. 5 Sqn's Fijian motto is 'Keitou Kalawaca Na Wasliwa' or 'We Span the Ocean'.

During their service, a number of updates have been undertaken or proposed. The first of these was Rigel I, which was begun in October 1982 and undertaken by Boeing in Seattle. This involved fitting APS-134 radar and a TI AAS-36(NZ) Infrared Detection Set (IRDS) in an undernose turret, as well as Boeing Universal Display and Control System (UDACS). In 1985, a sixth P-3B was purchased from the RAAF for $NZ 19 million, and all aircraft were redesignated P-3K (for Kiwi) in 1986 at the end of the update programme. Rigel II would have seen an upgrade to the weapons system including Harpoon missile capability but was never funded.

The large number of structural repairs and many hours spent at low level compromised the fail-safe design. A 1993 Lockheed/RNZAF study confirmed that the P-3s had fatigue life indexes (FLI) of up to 135. Most USN P-3As and P-3Bs were retired at FLIs around 60 to 80.

The options of replacing the P-3Ks with new-build or second-hand aircraft were discounted in favour of re-winging and structurally upgrading the aircraft under a Structural Life Extension Programme called Project Kestrel.

Under a Phase I contract signed in April 1995, Lockheed Martin Aerial Systems manufactured the hardware and designed the tooling. The outer wings were built at Daewoo Heavy Industries at Changwon, South Korea and tailplanes were rebuilt by BAe Jetstream. Centre section lower panels were fabricated at Lockheed Marietta in Georgia.

Phase II saw these components put together on the P-3s at Richmond, Australia by Hawker Pacific, which added new (ex-RAAF) engine nacelles and refurbished engines. This took place between September 1997 and December 2000 with an estimated cost of NZ$109 million. The

The albatross badge of No. 5 Squadron reflects the unit's task: covering vast tracts of the southern oceans. This aircraft demonstrates the latest gloss grey scheme, similar to that being adopted by the US Navy.

first Kestrel aircraft (NZ4204) flew for the first time on 18 October 1999. Kestrel is due to be completed in mid-2001.

To match the structural upgrade, an avionics upgrade called Project Sirius was approved in March 1998. This would have seen replacement of the data handling system, ESM, infra-red and electro-optics, radar and IFF, acoustic processor, MAD, navigation equipment, communications and the addition of self protection equipment and a datalink. Boeing, Dornier, LM Tactical Defense Systems and Raytheon Systems bid for the tender, which closed in May 1999. Raytheon was the winner of the contract, announced at the end of the year at a value of NZ$240 million. The actual equipment proposed for Sirius was never made public by the NZ MoD, but is thought to have included Elta EL/M-2022 version 3 radar, FLIR Systems Super Star SAFIRE IR/EO system, Elta EL/M-8300 ESM gear, a Computing Devices Canada (CDC) UYS-970 acoustic processor and a CAE Electronics

Having undergone the Rigel update which added, among other items, the AAS-36 IRDS seen here under the nose of this aircraft, the Kiwi Orion fleet was due another major modernisation (Sirius). This was cancelled on cost grounds in 2000.

ASQ-504 MAD system. A separate $9.56 million contract to replace the P-3's autopilot was signed in May 2000 with BAE Systems at Santa Monica in May 1999.

In August 2000, the new Labour/Alliance government cancelled Sirius and called for a review of maritime patrol capability, due in February 2001. Estimated costs of the project had escalated, due in part to the fall in value of the New Zealand dollar until they had reached $NZ 562 million at the time of cancellation. By January 2001, four

of the seven P-3 captains on No. 5 Squadron had resigned. The autopilot project is still going ahead, the first aircraft (NZ4204) flying with it installed in October 2000. A new Data Management System computer is the next small improvement planned for the fleet.

The lack of modern equipment on the P-3s has proved an embarrassment at times. Link 11 Tactical Data Link equipment had to be borrowed from (and returned to) the navy when two Orions were committed to a coalition assembled in February 1998 after the expulsion of UN weapons inspectors from Iraq. This was installed and the crews trained within five days before the aircraft deployed to Diego Garcia. All P-3Ks now have Link 11 receive-only capability, but using a new HF radio and some 'enabling software' can transmit digital imagery to the tasking authority. The acoustic processor has been aided by a locally-designed commercial PC-based

recorder, but otherwise the aircraft are filled with 1966- and 1981-installed technology. Despite this, No. 5 Squadron have won the annual Fincastle competition held between Commonwealth ASW squadrons a number of times.

The RNZAF's P-3s are used for a variety of tasks, including surveillance of the country's Exclusive Economic Zone (EEZ) – which is the fourth largest in the world at 1.2 million square nautical miles, search and rescue, and environmental monitoring for a number of South Pacific nations as well as New Zealand itself. Crew training, ASW training and exercises with allied forces take up the other half of the approximately 2,600 hours flown by the Orions each year. Offensive capability is restricted to Mk 46 torpedoes and Mk 82 'Snakeye' bombs. With few submarines to exercise with locally, the RNZAF trains with the Sippican Mk 39 Expendable Mobile ASW Training Target (EMATT), a powered

simulated submarine dropped by the P-3 which manoeuvres in a programmed pattern for its 3-5 hour battery life.

The colour scheme of the P-3 fleet remained as delivered until June 1994, when NZ4205 began a one-year test with a matt grey finish. This was found to have several maintenance penalties and was replaced by a gloss grey scheme in January 1996. Not all of the aircraft have yet been repainted.

Jim Winchester

Variant	c/n	BuNo.	Serial
P-3K	5190	152886	NZ4201
P-3K	5192	152887	NZ4202
P-3K	5200	152888	NZ4203
P-3K	5202	152889	NZ4204
P-3K	5208	152890	NZ4205
P-3K	5401	155291	NZ4206 (ex-RAAF)

NORWAY
Luftforsvaret (Air Force)

With its long coastline facing the Atlantic Ocean and Barents Sea, and its proximity to the Soviet/Russian Northern Fleet based in the Kola Peninsula, Norway was a front-line state during the Cold War, and remains of strategic significance to NATO today. The acquisition of the P-3 Orion greatly enhanced the Luftforsvaret's ability to detect and track Soviet submarines and

surface vessels as they left their port in the Murmansk area and passed out into their operational areas in the Atlantic.

Initial equipment consisted of five new-build P-3B (Heavyweights), which were delivered from 1968 to replace Grumman HU-16 Albatrosses in service with 333 Skvadron at Andøya. The fleet was bolstered in 1980 by the delivery of two ex-US Navy P-3B(HW)s. The fleet was very active in the 1980s and was involved in many contacts with Soviet forces. In May 1983 a hostile submarine contact in Hardangerfjørd resulted in 333 Skvadron aircraft dropping three depth charges, believed to have been the only occasion

since the end of World War II that live ASW weapons have been used. On 13 September 1987 a P-3B (6602) was involved in a notorious incident when a Soviet Su-27 'Flanker' collided with the Orion's outer propeller, causing damage to the blades and puncturing the fuselage with shrapnel. Both aircraft returned to base safely.

As well as routine ASW work, environmental duties and coastal fishery patrols, Norway's Orions also undertook surveillance missions, for which two of the P-3Bs were given provision for a side-looking airborne radar (SLAR), mounted in the lower rear fuselage. A dedicated

operator station was fitted when the equipment was installed.

In 1989 the hard-worked P-3B fleet was partially replaced. Five of the P-3Bs were sold to Spain to offset the purchase of four P-3C Update IIIs, for which Norway was the first overseas customer. The new aircraft differed slightly from US Navy UIIIs in having an ARC-207 VHF radio and additional electro-optical reconnaissance sensors. The machines also had the ability to carry the SLAR previously fitted to the 'Bravos'.

Norway retained two of its 'Bravos' but these were modified to a new standard, designated P-3N. Work on these aircraft was undertaken at NADEP Jacksonville in 1990-1992. The N conversion entailed removing all ASW equipment, including the sonobuoy chutes, although the APS-80 search radar and AAS-36 Infra-Red Detection System (IRDS) were retained. A single free-fall chute and one pressurised sonobuoy chute was installed in the rear of the cabin to allow the dropping of smoke markers or other stores. The cockpit was raised to Update III standard, and new navigation equipment was installed. The tactical compartment was retained, although modified, while the rear cabin was provided with floor tracks. On these tracks could be fitted airline-style seats for

Norway's P-3s routinely operate in appalling conditions. The UIP modernisation programme makes them among the best-equipped in the world.

Vingtor was the second UIP aircraft. Like the US Navy's AIP aircraft, the UIP birds have comprehensive SATCOM installed, distinguished by the 'batwing' antennas on the spine and rear fuselage sides. Under the fuselage is a large radome containing a spinning antenna for the new ESM suite.

used for pilot training and general transport, and various surveillance duties. Search and rescue is an important role, as is fishery/EEZ surveillance. Ice reconnaissance and environmental duties (pollution monitoring, wildlife migration/census work) are also undertaken. Many of the P-3N's missions are tasked by the Kystvakt (coastguard).

From 1992, the Luftforsvaret has been developing an upgrade for its four P-3Cs, under the Upgrade Improvement Program (UIP). This involves many of the elements of other programmes, such as the US Navy's AIP. Central to UIP is the installation of a Unisys CP-2044 tactical computer, with APS-137 imaging inverse synthetic aperture radar (ISAR), new displays, upgraded ALR-66(V)5 ESM system with dedicated operator station, GPS and Satcoms. Aircraft defences are added, including chaff/flare dispensers and missile

up to 30 passengers, and they provided tie-down points for freight carriage.

Specialised sensors included the AVX-1 Cluster Ranger long-range electro-optical sensor in at least one of the aircraft (located in the port forward window) and the ability to carry the aforementioned SLAR.

So equipped, the two P-3Ns undertake a variety of missions, freeing the four P-3Cs for regular maritime patrol. The Ns can be

Variant	c/n	BuNo.	Serial/notes
P-3N	5257	154576	4576
P-3B (HW)	5264	154583	to Spain
P-3B (HW)	5301	156599	to Spain
P-3B (HW)	5302	156600	to Spain
P-3B (HW)	5303	156601	to Spain
P-3B (HW)	5304	156602	to Spain
P-3N	5305	156603	6603
P-3C UIII	5817	163296	3296 *Vingtor*
P-3C UIII	5818	163297	3297 *Jossing*
P-3C UIII	5819	163298	3298 *Viking*
P-3C UIII	5820	163299	3299 *Ulabrand*

warning receivers. 3299 was the first aircraft to undergo UIP and it was returned to Andøya after refit on 7 July 1999.

Under current plans, Andøya is set to close, and 333 Skvadron is expected to move to Bodø by the end of 2004.

David Donald

PAKISTAN
Pakistan Naval Aviation

Pakistan ordered the P-3C Orion in July 1988 to augment its small maritime patrol force of Fokker F27s and Breguet Atlantics. Three aircraft were required for patrols over the Arabian Sea and Indian Ocean. Although flown by air force crews, the Orions were to be manned by navy operators and tasked by the navy.

Pakistan's Orions are unique in being a hybrid between the Update II.5 and Update III (consequently being unofficially referred to as Update II.75). The basic system is that of the UII.5, but elements of UIII are incorporated, including ARC-182 VHF and ARC-187 UHF radios, APS-134 non-imaging inverse synthetic aperture radar (ISAR) and wiring for the AGM-84 Harpoon missile, although weapons were not supplied.

In November 1990 the first aircraft was delivered to NAS Jacksonville, from where VP-30 began training Pakistani crews in January 1991. However, while training was ongoing, US politicians had been reviewing their stance over arms sales to Pakistan. Concerns over Pakistan's nascent nuclear arms development led to the passing of

the Pressler Amendment in October 1990, which called for potential customer nations to provide a certificate that they did not possess nuclear weapons, and that they were not developing them, before any military equipment could be delivered.

In Pakistan's case no certificate was forthcoming (indeed, Pakistan was already well along the road to possessing a nuclear capability) and a large arms package (including the P-3s and F-16s – all bought and paid for) was embargoed. The three

Orions were flown to AMARC at Davis-Monthan in January 1992.

For the next five years the fate of the Orions was argued between the US and Pakistan, among the options being sale to a third party. Eventually, following a January 1996 bill, the authority was provided for the US to release the aircraft, and they were eventually delivered to Pakistan in 1997.

The trio entered service with No. 29 Squadron of the Pakistan Naval Aviation, based at Mehran (Drigh Road) near Karachi,

and were given some modifications locally, including the addition of chaff/flare dispensers. One aircraft was lost in 1999.

David Donald

Variant	c/n	BuNo.	Serial
P-3C UII.75	5825	164467	81 (prev. 25)
P-3C UII.75	5826	164468	82 (prev. 26)
P-3C UII.75	5827	164469	83 (prev. 27), lost 29 Oct 1999

One of the three embargoed Pakistani P-3Cs is seen shortly after arrival at Davis-Monthan AFB for storage. The trio sat in the Arizona desert for five years while the aircraft's fate was debated in Washington.

PORTUGAL
Força Aérea Portuguesa

With a commanding positon overseeing the Mediterranean approaches, and a large slice of the Atlantic Ocean to patrol (out to Madeira and the Azores), Portugal has a strong maritime patrol requirement. However, between the retirement of the Lockheed P-2 Neptune in 1977 and the arrival of the Orion in 1988 the maritime

surveillance mission was performed by non-specialist types such as the C-130 Hercules and CASA 212. In 1985, the Portuguese air force ordered six Orions to fulfil a renewed ASW commitment to NATO.

Portugal's Orions were P-3B Heavyweight/TACNAVMOD aircraft previously flown by Australia. Ten of these had been traded back to Lockheed in part exchange for the RAAF's new P-3Cs. Originally, eight of the aircraft were due to go to Argentina, but Australia blocked the move following the Falklands conflict. Although owned by Lockheed, the aircraft

remained in Australia until October 1985, when the first two were transferred to Beja in Portugal. In December, two more were delivered, while one was sent to Palmdale in California, where Lockheed began the prototype conversion to Portugal's required standard.

Designated P-3P, the reworked Orions retained much of the P-3B internal configuration, but added several P-3C Update II features, and also several new ones, making the aircraft unique in Orion circles. The radar is a non-imaging APS-134 ISAR unit and the aircraft are fitted with AAS-36 IRDS. An ALR-66(V)3 ESM system

was installed, with a new spinning antenna housed in a radome under the rear fuselage. The P-3P incorporated a dedicated ESM operator's position, and was fitted with paratroop-style webbed seating in the forward cabin to allow the carriage of passengers. AGM-84 Harpoon missile capability was standard.

The Palmdale P-3P was completed and flown to Montijo in Portugal in August 1988, and formed the pattern for the modification of the five other aircraft. This work was undertaken by OGMA, although only after a delay of around a year. During rework the aircraft acquired a unique three-

Portuguese Orions wore the standard grey/white US Navy/RAAF scheme briefly. Until modernisation to P-3P standard, five were used for initial crew training.

Resplendent in its 'Orca' scheme, this is the last of the P-3Ps. Notable external features are the ESM radome under the rear fuselage and the underwing podded searchlight.

tone grey camouflage known as 'Orca'. Training, meanwhile, had begun in November 1986, using the unmodified P-3B aircraft prior to them entering the conversion programme. When the prototype P-3P returned from California it was used for training, while Portuguese personnel also used the Dutch Orion simulator at Valkenburg. The six-aircraft fleet serves with Esquadra 601 at Montijo.

Portugal's P-3Ps have proved to be a valuable asset to NATO, and have taken part in NATO operations against former Yugoslavia, with a single P-3P detached to Sigonella for Adriatic patrols. In keeping with current trends, the FAP is undertaking an update programme to enhance the effectiveness and versatility of the fleet.

There are two elements to the Life Extension and Capabilities Improvment Programme (LECIP), one involving a structural upgrade which will allow the P-3Ps to serve until at least 2025, and the other a comprehensive systems upgrade along similar lines to other current programmes.

David Donald

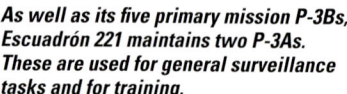

Variant	c/n	BuNo.	Serial
P-3P	4502	155292	4801
P-3P	5403	155293	4802
P-3P	5404	155294	4803
P-3P	5405	155295	4804
P-3P	5407	155297	4805
P-3P	5408	155298	4806

SPAIN

Ejército del Aire

Grupo 22, together with the F/A-18A Hornet-equipped Grupo 11, forms the flying component of Ala 11 based at Morón air base, some 50 kilometres (31 miles) southeast of Seville. The unit was commissioned as 601 Escuadrón de Cooperación Aeronaval (601 Naval Cooperation Squadron) at Jerez Air Base, then forming part of Mando de la Aviación Táctica (Tactical Aviation Command) and in December 1963 received its first three Grumman SA-16B Albatross anti-submarine amphibians (AN.1 in the Spanish military aircraft designation system). The remaining four of the initial batch were received in February, March and April 1964. On 8 May, the designation changed to Grupo 610, while the flying element was designated 611 Escuadrón. Next year, it was again renumbered as 61 Grupo, later becoming 206 Escuadrón. In 1969 another six Albatrosses were acquired, this time from the Royal Norwegian Air Force, which just had re-equipped its maritime patrol squadron with Lockheed P-3B Orions, which ironically would be the next main equipment of 221 Escuadrón. The new batch of Grummans was designated AN.1N due to their more powerful engines. The veteran maritime patrol amphibians were finally phased out of service on 27 July 1978, after logging 27,528 flight hours and three aircraft lost in accidents. Also the Albatross had witnessed the commissioning of Ala 22 (as a follow-up of 206 Escuadrón) on 4 April 1972, with 221 Escuadrón (call-sign CISNE – swan) as its flying unit.

To augment the unit's operational

capability, it was decided to acquire three second-hand US Navy P-3A (Deltic) Orions, which after a period in which the crews trained at NAS Moffett Field, reached Jerez Air Base on 25 July 1973. In 1977 one of these was lost in an accident. In 1978 another four of the same variant were leased for a 10-year period.

In service the Orion proved popular and capable. Despite the desire to have new-build P-3C aircraft, a tight budget precluded this option. However, a programme to acquire updated second-hand aircraft was instigated, and to this end five ex-Royal Norwegian Air Force P-3Bs were acquired (these are also known as Super Bravos as

they are late production machines, incorporating some early C features). They were ferried from Bodø to Jerez by Norwegian crews between November 1988 and September 1989. After receipt, they awaited an upgrade which was delayed at first and then cancelled. However, the five Orions were sent to OGMA (Oficinas Gerais de Material Aeronautico) facilities at Alverca, Portugal, for a general overhaul (SDLM) and at the same time received their two-tone light grey scheme.

Three of the four leased P-3As were returned to the US Navy, while one stayed in Spain for preservation. Meanwhile, two of the original P-3As formed, together with the five P-3Bs, the equipment of 221 Escuadrón.

In order to make good use of the large air bases recently vacated by US Air Force units, the Spanish air force decided to move Ala 22 to Morón air base, starting in October 1992, and its Operations Group became Grupo 22 from Ala 21. Finally, Ala 22 and Jerez Air Base were deactivated by Resolution 10/93 of the Air Staff dated 21 June 1993, the closing ceremonies taking place nine days later.

Left: The Spanish P-3Bs have SAFIRE FLIR installed in the undernose turret.

Below: This 221 Escuadrón aircraft is seen at NAS Sigonella, Italy, during Operation Sharp Guard. Along with other NATO nations, the P-3s enforced a naval blockade against Yugoslavia.

As well as its five primary mission P-3Bs, Escuadrón 221 maintains two P-3As. These are used for general surveillance tasks and for training.

In March 2000, Grupo 22 logged 50,000 flight hours with the P-3 Orion. 221 Escuadrón has five complete and fully operational crews. The Maintenance Squadron performs first- and second-stage checks, while CASA performs the general overhauls, which are scheduled for every four years. The crews, which average some 400/500 flight hours per year, undertake their compulsory simulator time at Valkenburg naval air station, home of the Royal Netherlands Navy Orions.

In the history of Spanish maritime patrol it is worth mentioning that almost a third of its missions have been operational sorties, complementing those for training and exercises. The most important operations break down as follows:

Ejedan O: weapons exercises (rockets, bombs, torpedoes) against naval targets.
Anti-drug patrols: undertaken in collaboration with the Home Affairs Ministry.
Surveillance of maritime traffic: especially over the western Mediterranean, close to Spanish shores.
Surveillance of warships: also includes photographic and electronic reconnaissance of surface warships.
Deb Item: surveillance and control of submarines and surface warships of the former Soviet Union when transiting through/from the Mediterranean, including electronic, acoustic and photographic intelligence.
Pax: airspace surveillance.
Vigilantes MEC (Middle East Crisis): maritime traffic control during the Gulf War. Within the period which ran from 17 January to 20 March 1991, a total of 48 sorties was flown, with an average of six hours over the operations zone, with 314 flight hours recorded, 4,245 reported contacts and 148 photographic reports. All these missions were performed between meridians 006W (Gulf of Cadiz) and 003E (Palma de Mallorca).
SAR: search and rescue.
Sharp Guard: maritime blockade of the republics from the former Yugoslavia, assigned patrols flown over the southern Adriatic, near the Otranto Straits. A P-3B is deployed on a rotational basis to NAS Sigonella, Sicily, under NATO auspices.

For crews newly posted to 221 Escuadrón, the training syllabus is carefully planned until they reach the maximum operational capability as an integrated crew (Combat Ready 3) being capable of

Variant	c/n	BuNo.	Serial
P-3A	5033	150507	P.3-4/ returned to USN
P-3A	5036	150510	P.3-5/ returned to USN
P-3A	5039	150513	P.3-6/ returned to USN
P-3A	5042	150516	P.3-7/ leased from USN, now in EdA museum
P-3A	5115	152145	P.3-3
P-3A	5123	152153	P.3-1
P-3A	5119	152149	P.3-2/ crashed 7 August 1977
P-3B (HW)	5264	154583	P.3-8
P-3B (HW)	5301	156599	P.3-9
P-3B (HW)	5302	156600	P.3-10
P-3B (HW)	5303	156601	P.3-11
P-3B (HW)	5304	156602	P.3-12

Tactical grey paint adorns the Spanish Orion fleet, having earlier worn standard US Navy grey/white or a darker grey. The badge on the nose is that of Grupo 22.

performing any type of mission. Each year, exercises, both on a national or international basis, are numerous, and among the most interesting are the ones denominated Ejedan Q, in which the control of strike aircraft is practised, with Ala 12 F-18 Hornets flying anti-shipping missions armed with AGM-84 Harpoon missiles in Tactical Air Support for Maritime Operations (TASMO). In some circumstances, this same mission can be carried out entirely by the P-3Bs, which can carry up to six Harpoons each.

The P-3B (Super Bravo) is the main operational aircraft of 221 Escuadrón, while the P-3A (Deltic) is the secondary, this variant being employed for photo-recce missions. Its cameras have been supplanted by the high-resolution Vinten sets which were carried by the Spanish RF-5A Freedom Fighters. The P-3As are also used for training missions, having been reengined in 1998 with the higher powered T56-A-14 turboprops used by the P-3Bs. Other upgrades to be incorporated during the next two/three years are FLIR sets and Have Quick secure radios.

The P-3Bs in service with 221 have a basic crew consisting of 13 personnel. The crew comprises two pilots, which are in charge of flying the aircraft and launching the weapons; one navigator; one TACCO (Tactical Coordinator), who is a naval officer in charge of coordinating the crew, selecting the relevant sensors and overseeing the deployment of sonobuoys and weapons; two flight engineers; one radio operator; one radar operator; one ESM (Electronic Support Measures) operator; one electronics technician and, if required, one photographer (unlike in the P-3A, which has a belly-mounted camera, the photographer in the B uses a hand-held camera shooting through the forward port window). During long endurance missions, additional crewmen, in the form of an extra pilot and TACCO, are carried. Independent of their assigned mission task, each crewman has specific roles in case of inflight emergencies – fire, forced landing, ditching, bail-out, etc.

Within the maritime patrol world there are seven main types of different missions, which are: anti-submarine warfare; anti-surface warfare; mine-laying; electronic reconnaissance; photographic reconnaissance; maritime traffic control, and search and rescue. As a weapons platform, the Orion has considerable firepower: besides the bomb bay, it has 10 underwing pylons which can carry an ample variety of weapons (torpedoes, bombs, rockets, mines, depth charges and AGM-84 Harpoon anti-shipping missiles and, in the near future, AGM-65 Mavericks).

The strategic location of Spain, between the Atlantic Ocean and Mediterranean Sea, with island provinces in the Canaries and Balearics, makes it vital to protect its shores and commercial shipping against any type of submarine or surface threat, and although the potential threat of the submarine force from the former Soviet Union has for all purposes vanished, some of its modern diesel attack submarines have been sold to unstable countries relatively near to Spanish shores. Keeping a constant vigil is one of the jobs of Grupo 22. Also, its Orions are tasked more usually in international missions designated by the UN, NATO or UEO, a job they will continue to carry on despite the age of their Orions, until replacement, perhaps late in this new decade by a maritime patrol version of the Airbus A400M.

Meanwhile, on 29 December 2000 the Spanish Government authorised the long awaited upgrade programme for the five P-3Bs to be carried out by CASA. This programme is valued at 18044 M. Ptas, and the first upgraded Orion will be delivered before the end of September 2003.

The upgrade includes the integration of the Mission System (FITS) as well as new equipment, as follows: radar (synthetic aperture), Electronic Support Measures (ESM) system, IFF/SIF, acoustic system, datalink (Link 11), secure comms (V/UHF, HF), navigation (GPS/INS), and ground mission support station (CAM). The upgrade will be carried out by the EADS Military Aircraft Division at CASA's Getafe facilities. *Salvador Mafé Huertas*

THAILAND

Kongbin Tha Han Lur (Royal Thai Naval Air Division)

In the post-Cold War era the Royal Thai Navy has sought to expand its capabilities and move towards blue-water operations. The acquisition of a STOVL aircraft-carrier and a fleet of frigates increased its reach considerably. Such expansion also required a similar increase in the effectiveness of its Air Division, with a need to add a long-range maritime patrol aircraft (MPA) capability to the coastal patrol types.

Thai interest in the Orion dates back to 1988, when the nation was first offered the type to perform the MPA role. However, instability within the government caused the postponement of the programme until late 1993, when Thailand signed a Foreign Military Sales (FMS) deal with the United States. The initial result was the delivery of two unmodified P-3As from US Navy stocks, which arrived in Thailand in early January 1994 to allow Orion operations to commence. Subsequently, these aircraft were retained as spares sources and ground instructional airframes.

Meanwhile, three P-3As were selected to undergo the Thai Orion Mod programme at NADEP Jacksonville. The first of these entered the workshop in late January 1994 and emerged a year later as one of two P-3Ts. The T is based on the P-3A TACNAVMOD, but has some new

Resplendent in its original US Navy paint scheme, this is one two fully mission-equipped P-3Ts flown by 102 Squadron. The aircraft were fully refurbished in the US prior to delivery to Thailand.

systems, including AAS-36 Infra-Red Detection System (IRDS), AWG-19 Harpoon control system (with missiles supplied), new radar monitoring system (although the sensor remained the APS-80B) and new navigation aids such as ARN-118 TACAN and LTN-211 Omega. No acoustic processing system was installed initially, although AQA-7 systems were later supplied and fitted after delivery.

The final aircraft was completed as a UP-3T, with ASW equipment removed. Like Norway's P-3N, the UP-3T has floor tracks for mounting seats or tying down freight, and also has a limited surveillance capability. Installed in the port forward station is the SENTAC operator station, from which control of the APS-80 search radar and IRDS can be undertaken.

Crew training had begun at Jacksonville in the autumn of 1994. Both P-3Ts were flown to Thailand on 16 February 1995, following a formal handover at Jacksonville on 6 February. The UP-3T was delivered in the autumn. All three serve with 102 Squadron alongside Fokker F27-200MEs, part of the RTNAD's Wing 1 at U-Tapao.

This organisation also administers the S-2 Trackers and Dornier Do 228s of 101 Squadron, the inshore patrol unit. Thailand is expected to upgrade all three of its operational Orions with AAQ-22 SAFIRE thermal imaging in place of the AAS-36, and Primus 400 colour weather radar. The UP-3T has been given VIP seating, and its designation changed to VP-3T.
David Donald

Variant	c/n	BuNo.	Serial/notes
P-3T	5112	152142	1204
P-3T	5113	152143	1205
P-3A	5133	152163	parts/ground trainer
P-3A	5147	152177	parts/ground trainer
VP-3T	5154	152184	1206

China

As the People's Republic of China enters a new millennium, its air forces are striving to improve the quality of their equipment through upgrades of existing designs, indigenous production and acquisition of the latest Russian hardware. Until these efforts bear full fruition, the PLAAF, PLA-AAC and PLANAF will still rely heavily on 'dinosaurs' from a bygone age. *David Donald*

People's Liberation Army Air Force

The People's Liberation Army Air Force is subordinate to the Army, and its organisation reflects this to a large degree. The Air Force is divided geographically into seven main Air Force Districts (AFDs), which mirror the Army's Military Regions. Each Military Region (MR) has a headquarters, after which it is named, which includes the AFD staff. As well as liaison with army staff at the MR headquarters, AFD staff also report to PLAAF headquarters in Beijing and the General Staff Department, which is the agency primarily responsible for the day-to-day command of the armed forces. For the Army, each Military Region consists of a number of provinces, each of which is designated as a Military District (MD) for command purposes.

However, the air force arranges itself differently within each MR. Assets near to the headquarters are administered directly by the Military Region Air Force, while those in farther-flung provinces of the Military Region have an intermediate command organisation – either a Command Post or Air Corps. These may control assets in a single Military District, or across two or three. For the most part, the few bomber regiments are controlled by central Air Force Headquarters through the MR Air Force, while fighter/attack divisions are allocated to all three types of command centre.

Moving down the command chain, the next level is the air division, consisting of two or three regiments. Air divisions are assigned specific roles in specific areas – for instance, fighter defence around a certain city. The regiment is arguably the most important command level, for each regiment occupies a single base, operating effectively like a US Air Force wing. Numbers of aircraft vary, but in the fighter/attack regiments it is usually between 70 and 124. Each regiment is further divided into air squadrons (three or four), and these squadrons consist of air sections of four aircraft each. From what little has been discovered about Chinese unit designations, it is believed that the Air Divisions are numbered sequentially from 1 to at least 38, while regiments are numbered from 1 to at least 103.

Logistics and maintenance support is controlled by PLAAF headquarters, but is effected through subordinate Air Armies, which look after specific regions, corresponding to the Military Region Air Force, Command Post or Air Corps. The logistic supply chain is long and cumbersome. Much of the equipment moves by rail, or even by boat along the coast and navigable rivers. Large spares stocks are held at each base, but this hampers the mobility of the regiment. The logistics system is highly inefficient, as there is little commonality between aircraft types, a result of a dispersed manufacturing operation with airframe and powerplant made in the same location. Consequently, parts for similar airframes and engines cannot be exchanged. Furthermore, the older types were largely hand-made, with the result that new parts very often do not fit.

There are a number of first-level maintenance depots controlled by the air force headquarters. Second-level maintenance is performed within each of the Military Regions, while third-level maintenance is undertaken at regiment level. Over 20 airframe/engine repair facilities are located around the country.

Combat aircraft deployment

Traditionally, the PLAAF's role has been to protect centres of industry and population, and key military installations. The fighter force is believed to consist of 43 fighter divisions, of which Lanzhou and Chengdu MRs have eight each. This is not surprising, as these MRs are considerably larger than the other five. In military terms, Shenyang and Nanjing MRs are perhaps the most important – both harbouring a huge population and a large proportion of the country's heavy industry. Shenyang faces north to Russia and Korea, while Nanjing lies across the strait from Taiwan. Accordingly, both

The People's Liberation Army Air Force is a remarkable organisation operating in a remarkable land. Such sights as these elderly Q-5 'Fantan' attack aircraft lined up against a moon-like background, while alien to most in the West, are commonplace throughout the nation.

China – Military Districts and principal cities

RUSSIA

KAZAKHSTAN

MONGOLIA

Hailar

Nei Mongol MD East

Heilongjiang MD

Qiqihar

Harbin

Changchun

Jiling MD

Yining

Ürümqi

KYRGYZSTAN

UZ.

TAJIK.

AFG.

PAKISTAN

Kashi

Nei Mongol MD Central

Nei Mongol MD West

Hohhot

Liaoning MD

Shenyang

NORTH KOREA

Sea of Japan

SOUTH KOREA

Xinjiang North MD

Jiayuguan

Wuhai

Beijing City

Beijing

Tianjin

Tianjin Shih

Dalian

Yinchuan

Hebei MD

Taiyuan

Shijiazhuang

Jinan

Qingdao

Yellow Sea

Xining

Ninxia MD

Lanzhou

Shanxi MD

Shandong MD

Xinjiang South MD

Qinghai MD

Gansu MD

Xian

Shaanxi MD

Zhengzhou

Henan MD

Jiangsu MD

Hefei

Nanjing

Shanghai

Shanghai City

Xizang MD

Lhasa

NEPAL

BHUTAN

Chengdu

Sichuan MD

Chongqing

Hubei MD

Wuhan

Anhui MD

Wuhu

Hangzhou

Zhejiang MD

East China Sea

INDIA

INDIA

Changsha

Hunan MD

Jiangxi MD

Nanchang

Fujian MD

Fuzhou

Xiamen

Taiwan Strait

TAIWAN

BANGLADESH

Guizhou MD

Guiyang

Kunming

Guilin

Guangdong MD

Guangzhou

Yunnan MD

Guangxi MD

Nanning

Hong Kong

Macao

MYANMAR

VIETNAM

LAOS

Gulf of Tongking

Guangdong MD - Hainan-dao

South China Sea

PHILIPPINES

Bay of Bengal

THAILAND

Beijing Military Region airfields

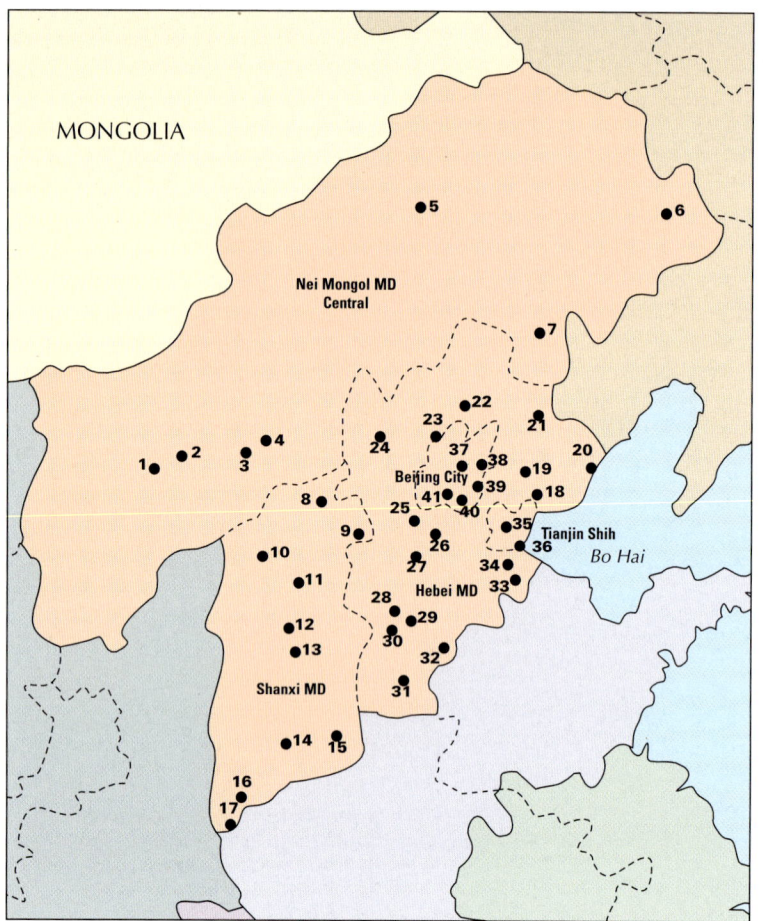

Nei Mongol Military District
1 Umaochieh
2 Baotou
3 Bike Qi
4 Hohhot
5 Xilinhot-Abagner Qi
6 Tongliao
7 Chifeng

Shanxi Military District
8 Datong-Qingshuihe
9 Lingqui
10 Wuzhai
11 Xinxian
12 Tai Yuan-Wu Su
13 Wenshui
14 Linfeng
15 Changzhi Wangzun
16 Yuncheng
17 Yongji

Hebei Military District
18 Tangshan
19 Dongxing Zhuang
20 Shanhaiguan-Qinghuangdao

21 Pingquan
22 Fengning
23 Yongning
24 Zhangjiakou
25 Tonglin Chuan
26 Dingxing
27 Baoding
28 Shijiazhuang
29 Gaocheng
30 Yuanshi
31 Shahe
32 Jiugucheng
33 Canxian-Canzhou
34 Tangguantun

Tianjin Shih
35 Wuqing
36 Tianjin-Zangguizhuang

Beijing City
37 Beijing-Shahezhen/Hsi Chiao
38 Beijing International
39 Beijing East/Tong Xian
40 Beijing-Xiqiao/Nan Yuan
41 Langxianzhen

Beijing MR incorporates three Military Districts and two City Districts (Beijing and Tianjin). Beijing itself is defended by a ring of S-300 SAM batteries, and several fighter regiments of the 38th Fighter Division. Surrounding Beijing/Tianjin as it does, the Hebei MD is home to many fighter regiments (including those of the 7th and 15th Fighter Divisions), and also a regiment of an H-6 bomber division (believed to be the 8th) at Shijiazhuang. Another H-6 regiment is at Datong – another PLAAF power base in Shanxi MD. Elderly H-5s also serve with the bomber division, and a Q-5 attack division is also assigned.

Due to its proximity to the capital, the Beijing MR includes several notable bases, including Beijing East, home to the PLA-AAC centre, and Xiqiao, which is a major PLAAF transport base. Close to the Bo Hai coast are at least two PLANAF bases. To the south of Tianjin is the base of Canzhou, which is the centre for PLAAF flight test and training, and from where the PLAAF operates a dedicated air defence adversary unit, flying J-7s and J-8s.

The sparsely populated Nei Mongol (Inner Mongolia) Central MD has at least three fighter bases with one fighter division.

regions possess seven fighter divisions. Beijing MR has five, primarily for defence of the capital, as does Guangzhou, which looks south to Vietnam and Southeast Asia. Jinan, the smallest MR, weighs in with three fighter divisions.

Bomber assets are spread over six divisions, single divisions being located in Beijing, Shenyang, Nanjing and Guangzhou MRs. Lanzhou MR has two, a reflection, perhaps, of the fact that this huge region encompasses much of China's strategic nuclear forces, and is undoubtedly the most difficult region to attack by virtue of being deep within China's ample territory. Attack regiments are spread around all the MRs, but the short range of the types employed mean that most bases are close to China's borders.

Independent regiments

In addition to the fighter/bomber/attack forces, which are arranged in divisions, a large number of independent regiments fly reconnaissance and transport missions. There are believed to be six Independent Reconnaissance Regiments, equipped with HZ-5s and JZ-6s, which are controlled by Air Force Headquarters. They are strategically located in the more sensitive MRs, that is, Shenyang, Beijing, Nanjing and Guangzhou.

Transport is handled by 17 regiments, of which 10 are independent and are controlled directly by Air Force Headquarters. Beijing also controls two transport divisions, with seven transport regiments. One of these is located in the Beijing area, while another (13th Transport Division) is in Hubei Military District, close to

the main bases of the 15th Airborne Corps. The latter is a dedicated paratroop formation consisting of three divisions, and is administered by the PLAAF rather than the Army. The PLAAF also retains control of a few helicopters, although most were transferred to the PLA-AAC in 1988.

Ground-based defences

Since May 1957 the People's Liberation Army – Air Defence Force (PLA-ADF) has been merged with the PLAAF, and the air- and ground-based elements work side-by-side in the air defence districts. The ground organisation is vast, covering around 100 major SAM batteries and an estimated 16,000 anti-aircraft artillery units. A large array of radars is also maintained, surrounding the borders of the nation. The pride of the air defence network are the Russian-supplied S-300 SAM batteries, which are deployed around Beijing.

Fighters

For the time being, and into the foreseeable future, the PLAAF's inventory is based almost entirely on a series of elderly types put into production in the 1960s. By far the most numerous type in service is the Shenyang J-6 (and the JJ-6 two-seat trainer version). It is questionable how many J-6s remain in everyday use, and many are probably stored or held in reserve. Nevertheless, the type still accounts for the majority of PLAAF fighter assets.

Initial production was based on the Mikoyan-Gurevich MiG-19P radar-equipped fighter, and was started by Shenyang in March 1958, includ-

ing the assembly of Soviet-supplied kits. Soon after, production was started of the MiG-19PM (as the J-6B) at Nanchang. Both factories suffered from inadequate drawings and tooling, and poor quality control. The result was only a handful of aircraft. Production was restarted at Shenyang in 1961, with Soviet-supplied drawings and rebuilt tooling. This time, the standard MiG-19S day-fighter was built, and soon huge numbers were pouring from the line. The first flight of the 'new' J-6 was made on 23 September 1963.

Although this version was by far the most numerous, others were built in significant numbers for the PLAAF and PLANAF. The J-6III first flew in 1969, and featured a shorter but wider wing, a needle-shaped inlet cone and an uprated WP6A engine. The result was a considerable improvement in performance and manoeuvrability, while newly added PL-2 missiles provided an AAM capability. Using the J-6III as a basis, Shenyang developed the J-6IV, which first flew on 24 September 1970. This had a slightly lengthened fuselage with radar mounted in the intake lip and splitter plate. Another radar-equipped version, the J-6A, was subsequently developed by Guizhou, this variant first flying on 21 December 1975. Mikoyan never developed a two-seat version of the MiG-19, but Shenyang proceeded with the JJ-6, which was based on the standard J-6 day-fighter and first took to the air on 6 November 1970. J-6s equip a large number of regiments, spread around the nation, in both PLAAF and PLANAF organisations, while JJ-6s are used for training.

Above and left: Xian's H-6 copy of the Tu-16 'Badger' is the principal strategic bomber, and is assigned both a nuclear and conventional role. The H-6 was supplanted in production by the improved H-6A with YJ-6/HY-4 (C-601) missile capability.

Initially developed as a conventional attack platform, the Nanchang Q-5 (below) was given nuclear capability in its Q-5A version. This had a belly recess to carry the single tactical weapon (left). This version first flew on 1 August 1970.

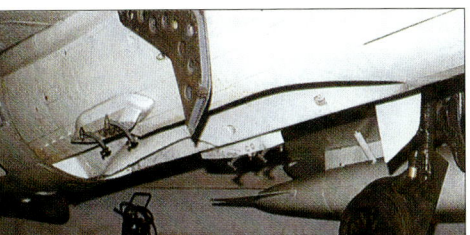

Above and below: The Harbin H-5 (Ilyushin Il-28) partners the H-6 in the bomber divisions, and also has a nuclear role. As well as bomber versions, the HZ-5 is used for reconnaissance, while the HJ-5 is a dual-control conversion trainer.

Left: Arguably the most important aircraft programme in China is the J-10, of which this is believed to be the prototype. A canard-delta fighter with fly-by-wire controls, the J-10 has been developed by Chengdu in association with IAI, using the latter's Lavi technology. It is intended to be an affordable lightweight multi-role fighter to replace the J-6 and J-7. A first flight was reported in 1998, but the programme has suffered numerous problems.

Below: To overcome the technology gap between the PLAAF and its neighbours, the Su-27 was procured as a long-range fighter. The fleet is set to total 276, with 200 assembled by Shenyang as the J-11. To these will be added many more attack-orientated Su-30MKKs (J-13).

Above: An Su-27UBK leads three Su-27SKs. The 'Flankers' allow the PLAAF to provide fighter cover over the Spratly Islands.

Left: Russian weaponry has been supplied in the form of R-40 and R-73 AAMs, plus air-to-ground stores.

Forty Su-27UBK (JJ-11) two-seaters have been supplied by Russia. This high number allowed the PLAAF to begin large-scale training in anticipation of a steady flow of J-11 deliveries from Shenyang.

Lanzhou Military Region airfields

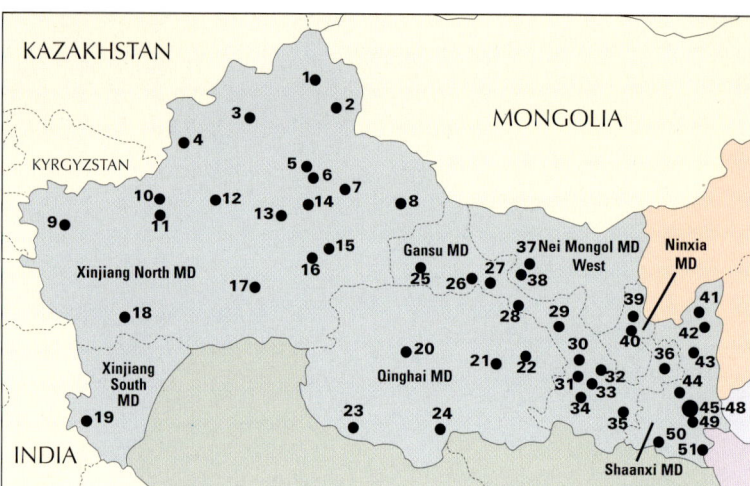

Xinjiang North Military District
1 Altay
2 Fuyun
3 Karamay
4 Yining
5 Urumqi-Diwopu
6 Urumqi South
7 Turfan
8 Hami
9 Kashi
10 Wensu
11 Aqsu
12 Kuqaxian
13 Korla
14 Uxxatal
15 Shanshan
16 Yaerdan
17 Qiemo
18 Hotan

Xinjiang South Military District
19 Fukche South

Qinghai Military District
20 Golmud West
21 Gonghe
22 Xining
23 Buhmangkana Shankou
24 Yushu

Gansu Military District
25 Dun Huang

26 Jiayuguan
27 Qingshui
28 Zhangye
29 Wuwei
30 Lanzhou-Zhonghuan
31 Lanzhou
32 Dalachi/Xingrenbu
33 Xiaguanving
34 Lintao
35 Tianshui
36 Xifeng Zhen

Nei Mongol Military District – West
37 Shuangcheng Tzu North
38 Shuangcheng Tzu

Ninxia Millitary District
39 Yinchuan
40 Hedong-Linhebu

Shaanxi Military District
41 Yulin West
42 Mizhi
43 Yan'an
44 Wugong
45 Xian-Yanliang
46 Xian-Lintong
47 Xian-Giun
48 Xian-Huxian
49 Yuxia
50 Chenggu
51 Angkang

The Lanzhou Military Region is the largest of the seven, and also the most sparsely populated. However, these factors are of great military significance, allowing some of China's most secretive facilities to be located within its confines. The PLAAF within Lanzhou MR is divided into three Air Armies, one covering Shaanxi MD, one covering Xinjiang North and Xinjiang South, and another controlling the remaining MDs. For the most part the regiments are equipped with J-6, J-7 and J-8 fighters in eight divisions, although a single Q-5 attack division serves in the north of the region. H-6 bomber regiments are based at Xian and Wugong in the Shaanxi MD, and another bomber division with regiments at Dalachi (Gansu MD) and Golmud (Qinghai MD).

Important installations in the region are the missile bases in Qinghai MD and Nei Mongol (Inner Mongolia) MD-West, and Lop Nor, the main test and research installation for China's nuclear weapons programme. Other considerations facing the military in the region are the former Soviet Republics along the western flank, and the disputed border areas with India in the southwest.

Fewer in number, but no less important, is the Chengdu J-7 fighter, based on the MiG-21. Development began at Shenyang in 1964, and led to a small number of aircraft being built, almost identical to the MiG-21F-13, of which the first flew on 17 January 1966. Production soon shifted to Chengdu, where the J-7I was built, with minor differences. An uprated WP7B engine and rearward-hinging cockpit canopy were the main features of the J-7II, which became the most numerous model. Many J-7Is were upgraded to the new configuration. Guizhou and Chengdu shared the development of the J-7III, which had a dorsal spine and enlarged radar. Essentially similar to the MiG-21MF, the J-7III has all-weather radar, uprated WP13 engine and a belly-mounted 23-mm cannon. Like the J-7II, it can use a variety of Chinese AAMs, including PL-2s and PL-5s. It first flew on 26 April 1984. Development of a trainer version resulted in the JJ-7, a Guizhou adaptation of the Chengdu J-7II. It is outwardly similar to the MiG-21U, and first flew on 5 July 1985. JJ-7s are used for training pilots destined for J-7 and J-8 regiments.

Further development of the design has resulted in the J-7E (offered for export as the F-7MG), based on the J-7II but with a new double-delta wing. The type is in full PLAAF service, and also equips the 'August 1' national aerobatic team, which was previously equipped with the Shenyang JJ-5 (two-seat MiG-17).

Mighty 'Finback'

Until the Su-27 arrived in service, China's most potent fighter was the large Shenyang J-8, known to NATO as 'Finback'. While the overall configuration and aerodynamics were clearly based on the J-7/MiG-21, the considerably increased size and twin-engine installation represented a major achievement for the

Chinese aviation industry, and the J-8 can be regarded as its first true indigenous jet fighter. However, development obviously proved troublesome: the J-8 first prototype first flew on 5 July 1969 yet it was December 1980 before it entered PLAAF service.

Early J-8s were day-fighters, with limited radar and WP7A engines. Only a few were built, and these may have been used only for test purposes, albeit at unit strength. J-8Is followed, this version first flying on 24 April 1981, introducing all-weather capability and numerous detailed differences. A rearward-hinging canopy was fitted, and the two single 23-mm cannon gave way to two twin-barrelled weapons.

A far more important improvement came with the J-8II. This version had increased-thrust WP13A engines, a large radome in the nose and lateral intakes (not unlike those of the MiG-23). The two fixed ventral fins of the J-8/J-8I were replaced by a single large fin which folded flat for take-off and landing. Limited production followed, as did the Peace Pearl programme under which Grumman in the US devised updated avionics (including APG-66 radar) for the type. However, the Tiananmen Square episode in 1989 brought an end to this programme. Instead, China once again turned to Russia, and especially to Phazotron, which supplied the Zhuk-8 II radar for the new J-8IIM. It is not known if this version is yet in service with the PLAAF, but the Zhuk radar (similar to that fitted in the Su-27) and the ability to use Russian missiles such as the R-27 and (possibly) R-77 make the J-8IIM a potent BVR interceptor. The type's air-to-ground prowess has also been advertised, although only unguided weaponry has been displayed. The first flight was made on 31 March 1996 with increased-thrust WP13B engines.

J-6s, J-7s and J-8s serve with most of the PLAAF's fighter divisions, although the J-8 is assigned in only small numbers. Its longer range and better performance suit it to long-range interceptions, while the J-6 and J-7 are regarded as short-range 'point-defence' fighters.

Chinese 'Flankers'

For many years, China struggled to produce world-class fighters, and its own designs always lagged behind the state of the art. The problem was compounded by the long technical delays which dogged programmes such as the J-8. However, with Taiwan and other nations in the region procuring ever more capable aircraft, and China's own policy of stretching its military might beyond its shores, the acquisition of a long-range, highly-capable fighter became a priority. The answer lay in the Sukhoi Su-27, of which a batch of 24 was ordered in 1991. These comprised Su-27SK single-seaters and Su-27UBK two-seaters, which were delivered in late 1992.

A subsequent batch of 24 was ordered in May 1995, arriving in April 1996. The first two batches covered 36 Su-27SKs and 12 Su-27UBKs. The designation JJ-11 has been reported for the two-seaters. From December 2000 a third batch of 28 (reportedly all Su-27UBKs) began arriving, these being in lieu of repayment for a state debt.

The Su-27s were deployed initially at Wuhu, and were seen taking part in joint exercises near Taiwan. During the course of these exercises, the type's air-to-ground capability was displayed. Subsequently, the aircraft appeared on Hainan island, from where their long range allowed them to fly patrols over the disputed Spratly Islands. The 'Flankers' were supplied with R-40 and R-73 missiles and a variety of air-to-ground stores.

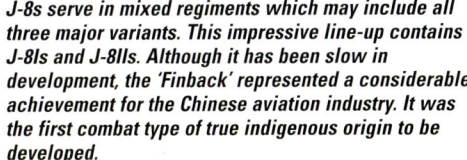

J-8s serve in mixed regiments which may include all three major variants. This impressive line-up contains J-8Is and J-8IIs. Although it has been slow in development, the 'Finback' represented a considerable achievement for the Chinese aviation industry. It was the first combat type of true indigenous origin to be developed.

Above: The first 'Finback' version, designated J-8, was a clear-weather fighter. It had the forward-hinging cockpit inherited from the first J-7 versions.

Below and right: The J-8I had a revised cockpit, all-weather radar and two twin-barrelled 23-mm guns in place of the single-barrelled weapons in the J-8.

PLAAF inventory

TYPE	NUMBER IN SERVICE	REGIMENTS
Fighter		
Sukhoi Su-27SK/J-11	36 (up to 200 to assemble)	3
Chengdu J-10	up to 300 to produce	
Shenyang J-8/J-8II	100+	4
Chengdu J-7	400	18
Shenyang J-6	2,600	104
Bomber		
Xian H-6	100	5
Xian H-6/YJ-6	20	1
Harbin H-5	300	12
Harbin H-5/YJ-1	50	2
Attack		
Sukhoi Su-30MKK/J-13	40-72 to purchase (plus potential licence assembly)	
Nanchang Q-5	500	12
Shenyang J-5	400	20
Reconnaissance/AEW		
Harbin HZ-5	40	2
Shenyang JZ-6	100	4
Beriev/Ilyushin A-50E	6 on order	
Tupolev Tu-154 (Sigint)	2	
Antonov An-30	8	
Transports		
Ilyushin Il-76	10	1
Antonov An-26	12	1
Lisunov Li-2	30	1
Harbin Y-11	15	1
Shaanxi Y-8	25	1
Xian Y-7	30	1
Shijiazhuang Y-5	250	10
Hawker Siddeley Trident	18	1
Canadair CL-601 Challenger	5	
Trainers		
Sukhoi Su-27UBK/JJ-11	40	
Guizhou JJ-7	50	
Shenyang JJ-6	150	
Shenyang JJ-5	100	
Nanchang CJ-5/CJ-6	1,000	

Right: The J-8II marked a considerable improvement over the earlier 'Finbacks', with uprated WP13A engines and a major redesign of the forward fuselage to house the all-weather radar in a large radome. Phantom-style variable inlet ramps were fitted to the intakes, giving good supersonic dash performance.

Left and below: The two ventral strakes of the J-8/J-8I gave way to a single large ventral fin, which folds to the side for landing and take-off. The aircraft can carry the PL-10 missile, based on the Italian Aspide.

Right: Under the designation J-8IIM Shenyang has fitted the Zhuk radar from the Su-27 into the 'Finback'. This gives the type much better target acquisition and tracking capability. The first prototype is seen here with bombs and rocket pods, utilising all seven hardpoints. The variant is not believed to be in PLAAF service yet, and its procurement may be sidelined by further 'Flanker' acquisition.

Chengdu Military Region airfields

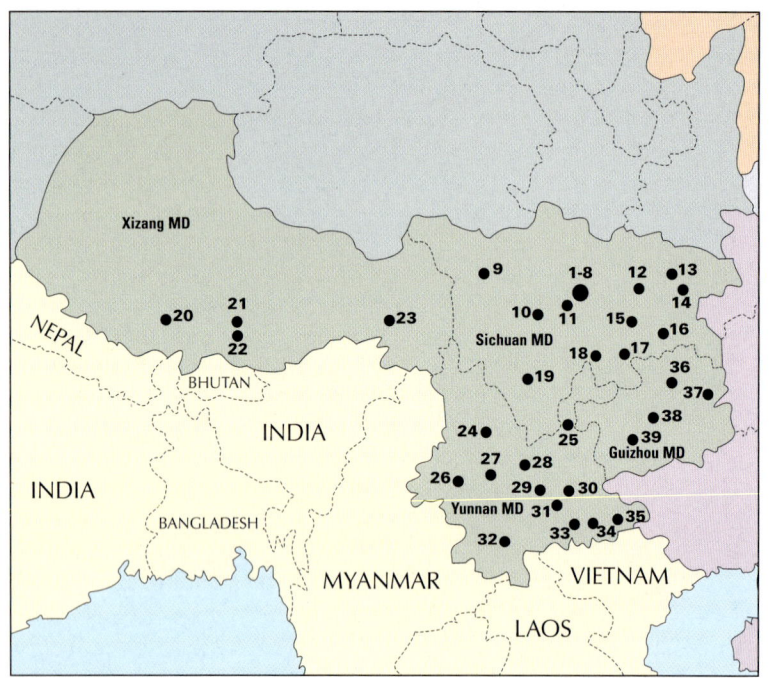

Sichuan Military District
1 Chengdu-Qionlai
2 Chengdu-Pengshan
3 Chengdu-Xinjin
4 Chengdu-Shuangliu
5 Chengdu-Wenjiang
6 Chengdu-Taipingsi
7 Chengdu-Guanghan
8 Chengdu-Feng Huan Shan
9 Ganzi
10 Kangding
11 Jiajiang
12 Nanchong
13 Daxian
14 Liangping
15 Dazu
16 Chongqing-Baishiyi
17 Luzhou
18 Yibin
19 Xichang

Yunnan Military District
20 Xigaze

21 Lhasa
22 Lhasa-Gongar
23 Chudra

Yunnan Military District
24 Lejiang
25 Zhaotong
26 Baoshan
27 Beitun-Yunnanyi
28 Yuanmou
29 Kunming-Wujiaba
30 Zhanyi
31 Luliang
32 Simao
33 Mengzhe
34 Wenshan
35 Pingyanjie

Guizhou Military District
36 Suiyang
37 Tongren
38 Guiyang-Leizhuang
39 Anshun

Chengdu Military Region is a large inland region, the main preoccupation being with India to the south. The region also borders Vietnam, and was important during the 1979 border conflict with that nation. Equipment consists almost entirely of J-6, J-7 and J-8 fighters, with one Q-5 regiment assigned. The MR is divided into a central air force with three fighter divisions and one attack division in Sichuan MD, centred on the Military Region headquarters in Chengdu. Four fighter divisions report to a command post in Kunming, while in the Lhasa region there is another fighter division.

In February 1996, China struck a deal with Moscow covering the licence-production by Shenyang from Sukhoi-supplied components of up to 200 more 'Flankers', designated J-11 by the PLAAF. This programme hit considerable technical difficulties as the Chinese plant could not match the sophisticated manufacturing techniques employed at the Russian plants. The first two J-11s flew in late 1998, but were rejected by the PLAAF, and Sukhoi engineers were dispatched to China to rectify the problems. It is thought that, as of early 2001, deliveries had resumed.

Despite the technical, maintenance and training difficulties posed by bringing the 'Flanker' into service, Beijing was clearly impressed by the Su-27's capabilities, and it represents a powerful counter to the Mirage 2000s and F-16s of Taiwan. Sukhoi development of the type as a true multi-role fighter-bomber led to an August 1999 order for 40 (almost certainly to increase to 72) Su-30MKKs, which the PLAAF designates the J-13. This aircraft has a much expanded air-to-ground repertoire including, it is understood, the ability to carry tactical nuclear weapons. The first 10 aircraft arrived in China in December 2000. Negotiations are under way covering the licence-production of the J-13, a total of 250 of which are required to re-equip the tactical strike/attack force. J-13s will probably also serve with the PLANAF.

Bombers/tankers

China's bomber forces rely exclusively on two elderly types, the Harbin H-5 and Xian H-6. The H-5 is a copy of the Ilyushin Il-28 'Beagle', and the first Chinese-manufactured aircraft flew for the first time on 25 September 1966. Production and service began the following year. Uncomplicated to manufacture and maintain, the H-5 proved a considerable success in Chinese hands, and spawned several variants. The most important of these was a nuclear-capable bomber, which began development in 1967. The first successful live drop was

accomplished on 27 December 1968. The H-5 is arguably the most obsolete type in the PLAAF inventory, and its replacement is something of a priority. Originally, it was thought that the JH-7 was its intended successor, but it now seems as though the JH-7 is a Navy-only project, and that the PLAAF has settled on the J-13 (Su-30MKK) to take over the attack role.

Serving alongside the H-5 in the bomber divisions (but not in mixed regiments) is the Xian H-6, instantly recognisable as a copy of the Tu-16 'Badger'. This type forms the backbone of the PLAAF's strategic bomber force, and is the principal carrier of nuclear weapons, and also possesses a reasonable conventional capability, with a maximum load of 9000 kg (19,840 lb). The first Chinese 'Badger' flew on 24 December 1968, captained by Xu Wenhong. Production followed soon after. In addition to its bombing role, the H-6 was tasked with long-range reconnaissance, equipped with cameras in a bomb-bay installation.

Development of the type led to the H-6A with minor refinements, and the H-6I with improved take-off, climb and range performance. The H-6D, which first flew on 29 August 1981, was a major upgrade with new search radar and systems which allow it to perform the anti-ship attack mission with YJ-6 or HY-4 missiles. As such, the H-6D may serve only with the PLANAF, although some PLAAF 'Badgers' are also believed to be missile-capable. An unknown number of 'Badgers' have been converted to serve as tankers for refuelling J-8s and Q-5s, while reports suggest that some have a Sigint-gathering role.

Attack and reconnaissance

For close air support the PLAAF relies on the few elderly Shenyang J-5s (MiG-17s) which remain operational, and the Nanchang (also referred to as Hongdu) Q-5 'Fantan'. This machine was based on the J-6 (MiG-19), but with a new 'needle' nose and revised intake system.

The Q-5 first flew on 4 June 1965, and several variants were developed. The Q-5I had better all-round performance, while the Q-5A was nuclear-capable. The Q-5 also served as the basis for the A-5M which included Western avionics. Development of this aircraft ceased after the Tiananmen Square crisis.

Reconnaissance is primarily handled by two old veterans: the Harbin HZ-5 and Shenyang JZ-6. These are camera-equipped versions of the H-5 bomber and J-6 fighter, respectively. The HZ-5 carries two large high-altitude cameras in the former weapons bay, and has additional wing fuel tankage. Development of the reconnaissance version started in 1970, and it entered service in 1977. With the development of newer types it is expected that these aircraft will gain a reconnaissance capability, and there have been reports of podded equipment being provided for the navy's JH-7. H-6s have also been used for reconnaissance tasks, including Elint-gathering. This latter role is the province of at least two specially-modified Tupolev Tu-154 airliners.

Transports

The transport fleet is built around copies of Antonov products, of which by far the most numerous is the An-2 'Colt', built as the Shijiazhuang Y-5. This was China's first locally-produced transport, the prototype flying on 7 December 1957. Numerous variants have been produced, including the Y-5B with aerodynamic refinements to improve STOL capability. The An-26 'Curl' is built by Xian as the Y-7 (first flight 25 December 1970), and again China has developed its own variants. The main heavy transport is the Shaanxi Y-8 (first flight 25 December 1974), a copy of the An-12 'Cub' originally developed by Xian. As well as the baseline Y-8, the pressurised Y-8C is in use. Harbin's Y-11 light transport, and its Y-12 turboprop-powered derivative, also serve.

Imported transports include 10 Ilyushin Il-76s procured to provide strategic transport for the

Although many are now retired or in storage, the Shenyang J-6 remains by a considerable margin the most numerous combat aircraft in the PLAAF inventory, assigned an air defence or advanced/weapons training roles. Most are of the basic J-6 standard (above left and left), although a few are J-6IIIs (above), with a shorter, wider wing for better dogfighting agility and a needle cone added to the intake (along with auxiliary intake doors) for increased thrust. The J-6III has better speed performance than the basic J-6, and also a shorter take-off/landing distance.

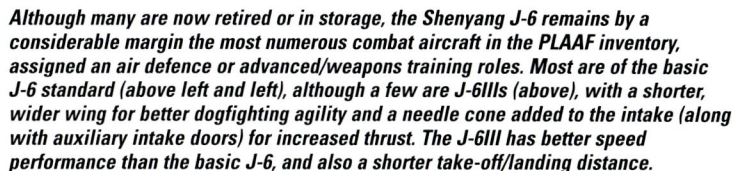

Shenyang JZ-5s serve alongside Harbin HZ-5s in independent reconnaissance regiments. The MiG-19 derivative carries cameras in a fairing under the forward fuselage, necessitating the removal of the nose cannon.

The baseline version of the J-7 in PLAAF/PLANAF service is the J-7II, which introduced the rearward-hinging canopy, uprated engine and other improvements. It remains a day-only fighter, used primarily for point defence of key installations

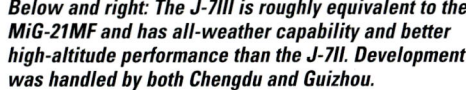

The latest MiG-21 derivative to enter PLAAF service is the J-7E (above), which introduced a double-delta wing (57° sweep on inner section, 42° on outer) to improve low-altitude manoeuvrability and take-off/landing characteristics. The type forms the equipment of the 'August 1' team (left), whose aircraft wear a special scheme and carry smoke dye tanks on the centreline.

Below and right: The J-7III is roughly equivalent to the MiG-21MF and has all-weather capability and better high-altitude performance than the J-7II. Development was handled by both Chengdu and Guizhou.

The vast pilot training effort is based on the Nanchang CJ-6 (above) for primary and basic training, and elderly two-seat JJ-5s and JJ-6s (left) for advanced/weapons instruction. The JJ-6 is used for converting pilots to the Q-5, while the two-seat Guizhou JJ-7 is used for J-7 and J-8 conversion.

PLAAF, and its airborne division in particular. A handful of Hawker Siddeley Tridents remain in use, as do Lisunov Li-2s. The latter is better known as the Soviet-built version of the Douglas C-47. Fast staff/VIP transport is provided by Canadair Challengers.

Trainers

The massive pilot training organisation uses the Nanchang CJ-6 (modified Yak-18) for initial training. This type first flew on 27 August 1958, and is a development of the CJ-5, which was a licence-built Yak-11 and was the first aircraft to be produced in Communist China. A few still serve. Advanced training is performed using the JJ-5 (MiG-17UTI) and JJ-6. The latter is a two-seat MiG-19 derivative developed entirely by Shenyang. It first flew on 6 November 1970. Guizhou was entrusted with the development of a two-seat MiG-21 derivative, the JJ-7, which first flew on 5 July 1985. It is primarily used for converting pilots to both the J-7 and J-8.

Modernisation plans

As the J-13 order is delivered, and plans to put the type into production take shape, China's air forces will undergo a considerable leap in capability. However, the numbers involved are small by Chinese standards, and a new multi-role fighter has been developed to equip the majority of the air force cheaply, as a replacement for the J-6 and J-7. This is the Chengdu J-10, an aircraft which has been in development for many years.

The J-10 was a replacement programme for the J-9 canard fighter, which was cancelled around 1979. In the early 1980s China forged links with Israel, which at the time was developing its Lavi multi-role fighter. When Lavi was cancelled in 1987, much of the effort was transferred to the J-10, which emerged as broadly similar in configuration. The multi-mode radar is almost certainly of Israeli origin, while the powerplant is the Saturn/Lyul'ka AL-31FN, similar to that used in the Su-27. It is also alleged that some F-16 technology has been incorporated, thanks to the loan of an aircraft by Pakistan. A first flight was reported for the J-10 on 24 March 1998, but one of the four prototypes is belived to have crashed during 1999. Chengdu is also involved in developing the FC-1 in collaboration with Pakistan, and it is possible that this aircraft may also be procured by the PLAAF, although it may have been overtaken by further J-7 development.

For some years, rumours have persisted concerning a fifth-generation fighter, known as the XXJ or J-12, allegedly being developed by Shenyang. According to these reports, the J-12 is an air superiority fighter in the class of the F-22 or Mikoyan 1-44, with a two-man crew, two engines and twin fins. It is very likely that a high proportion of Russian technology will be incorporated, and may draw heavily on the 1-44 programme now that fighter is unlikely to proceed beyond single prototype stage. The date for the J-12's service entry has been reported as being 2013 to 2015, although there is no firm evidence to support even the existence of this programme. This aircraft should not be confused with the J-12 light fighter developed by Nanchang in the 1970s, which did not proceed beyond prototype stage.

Even less information has surfaced regarding a next-generation bomber programme to replace the elderly H-5s and H-6s remaining in PLAAF service. Having failed to secure deliveries of Tupolev Tu-22Ms from Russia (in PLAAF service the 'Backfire' would have been designated H-8), development work allegedly began on a new bomber in 1995. It has been reported that this 'H-9' is of a similar size and shape to the Lockheed Martin F-117, but such information is regarded as highly speculative. What is almost certain is that China will have some bomber procurement programme ongoing, for the need to re-equip its bomber regiments is among the most pressing it faces.

A key requirement for many years has been the provision of effective airborne early warning. Trials were conducted using a Tu-4 'Bull' with a dorsally-mounted rotodome, and more recently the Y-8 has been studied as a platform, with at least one being given Searchwater radar. Then, China turned to Israel to provide AEW in the form of the Phalcon-equipped A-50I. This variant of the Beriev/Ilyushin A-50 'Mainstay' looked similar to the standard aircraft, but had a fixed phased-array Phalcon radar in the non-rotating dome. One aircraft was delivered from Russia to Israel for modification, but the sale was eventually blocked by the US. Instead, China turned to Russia, and during a visit by President Putin to Beijing in July 2000, a deal was struck covering six Beriev/Ilyushin A-50Es, based on the Russian Air Force 'Mainstay' with Shmel-M radar. The order was formalised in November.

China is very interested in the Antonov An-70 transport, and in 2000 was offered participation in the programme by Russia.

People's Liberation Army – Army Aviation Corps

For many years China's transport helicopters were operated by the PLAAF, but in 1988 the vast majority were assigned to a new organisation, the PLA – Army Aviation Corps. However, the line between the two is blurred, at least as far as published sources allow, and the PLAAF still operates some of the helicopter force.

Today the PLA-AAC is believed to be organised into five brigades, each with three regiments, assigned to the Group Armies in the cities of Beijing and Shanghai, and in Shenyang, Tianjin and Guangzhou. One regiment of the latter brigade is based in Hong Kong and equipped with Z-9s. An Army Aviation Corps centre is located at Beijing-Tong Xian, from where trials and training of rotary-wing types are undertaken.

For such a huge country, with a massive army, the PLA-AAC operates relatively few helicopters, and for many years they were operated mainly as utility transports with only limited assault roles. Belatedly, the PLA-AAC has embraced the concept of heliborne assault, but it was not until 1996 that any firm evidence of this was provided, when a heliborne assault was observed during a combined forces exercise. However, new equipment obtained in recent times has allowed the PLA-AAC to become more ambitious in widening its tactics and capabilities.

Equipment review

When it was formed in 1988, the PLA-AAC inherited a fleet still dominated by elderly Soviet designs or their derivatives. Although improvements are being made, that position still holds true in 2001. The most numerous type in service is the elderly Harbin Z-5, the locally-produced version of the Mil Mi-4 'Hound'. First flying on 14 December 1958, the Z-5 has been produced in large numbers, and has been adapted to fulfil a wide range of roles, including assault transport, rescue, aerial minelaying and surveillance tasks. Weapons such as rocket pods can be carried on small pylons either side of the cabin. The cabin itself has large clamshell doors at the rear and a ramp to allow it to accommodate light vehicles.

Adapted from the Z-5 is another elderly Harbin product, the Z-6. First flown on 15 December 1969, the Z-6 was China's first turboshaft-powered helicopter, and is still employed in limited numbers for assault transport, resupply and as a platform for paratroops. Production was undertaken by Changhe and Changzhou.

For heavylift purposes the Chinese received around 10 Mil Mi-6 'Hooks', allegedly stolen from Russian rail deliveries destined for Vietnam, and the survivors of these continue to be used. A number of Mil Mi-8s were also acquired in this fashion, and around 30 equip a transport regiment.

Guangzhou Military Region airfields

Hubei Military District
1 Guanghua
2 Enshi
3 Yichang-Tu Men Wu
4 Dangyang
5 Wujia Chi
6 Yingshan
7 Xiaogan
8 Huangbei
9 Wuhan/Hankow-Wang Chia Tun
10 Wuhan-Nanhu
11 Shanpo

Hunan Military District
12 Chansha-Dadou
13 Xupu
14 Shaoyang-Liangshitang
15 Lingling
16 Leiyang

Guangxi Military District
17 Guilin-Qifengling
18 Luizhou
19 Guiping-Mengshu
20 Nanning-Wuxu
21 Bose

22 Tianyang
23 Debao
24 Ningming

Guangdong Military District
25 Kukong-Shaoguan
26 Xingning
27 Shantou
28 Huiyang
29 Guangzhou-Baiyun
30 Guangzhou East
31 Guangzhou-Shadi
32 Kai Tak/Shigang (Hong Kong City)
33 Kowloon (Hong Kong City)
34 Suixi
35 Zhanjiang

Guangdong MD – Hainan-dao
36 Haikou
37 Jialaishi
38 Foluo
39 Lingshui
40 Sanya-Yaxian

Paracel Islands
41 Xisha

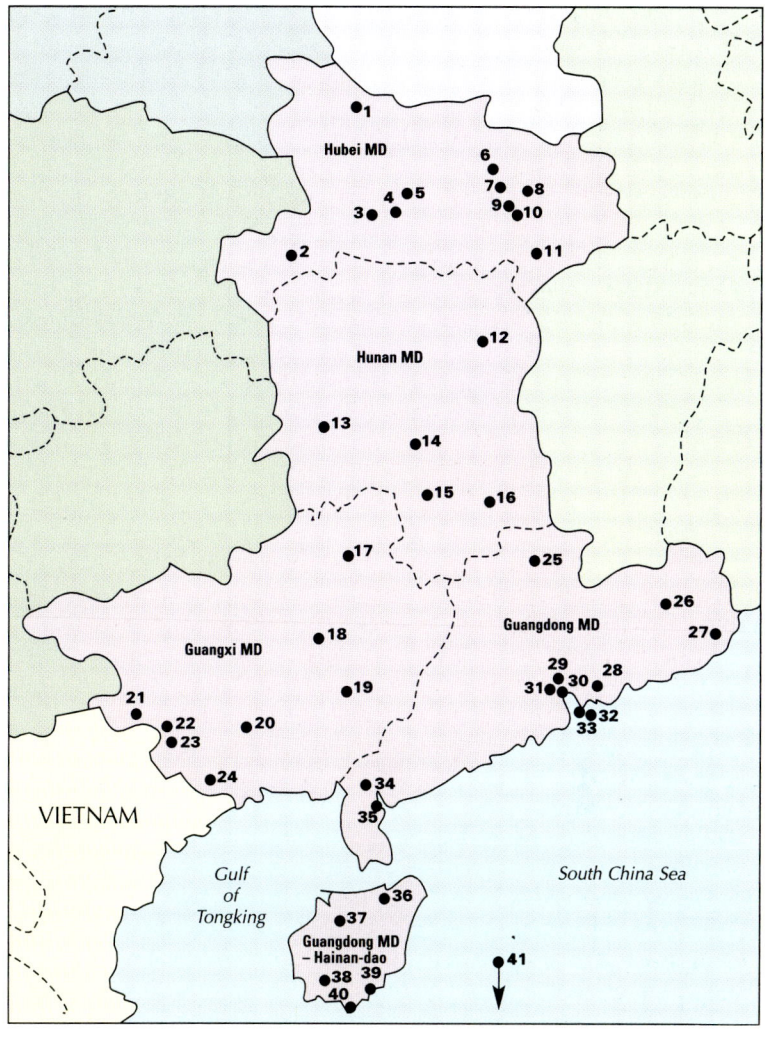

Although the Guangzhou Military Region occupies a large portion of inland China, the main focus of the command is southwards and eastwards from the coast of Guangdong MD and Guangxi MD. The inland districts are administered from a command centre at Wuhan, with only a few assets. The most important of these is the 13th Transport Division, based in the Wuhan area, which operates the PLAAF's Il-76s and most of the An-26s.

Guangxi MD, administered by the 7th Air Corps at Nanning, borders Vietnam, and its air bases were heavily used during the 1979 border conflict, especially Nanning itself. Two fighter divisions remain in the area.

Far more important is Guangdong MD, controlled directly from the Guangzhou MR headquarters. This region has an H-6 bomber division, two fighter divisions, an attack division and a reconnaissance regiment. In its eastern part Guangdong MD is close to Taiwan, while in the centre it incorporates the city district of Hong Kong. A regiment of Z-9 helicopters is now based in the former UK colony, while its defence is handled by a J-8 regiment at Huiyang. In the southern corner of Guangdong is Hainan Dao (island), from where operations are mounted over the disputed Spratly Islands. A new airfield was built in the early 1990 to house Su-27 fighters, the only PLAAF aircraft with sufficient range to reach the Spratlys from Hainan. More recently, an airfield (Xisha) has been built in the Paracel

Islands, cutting the transit time to the Spratly area and allowing other types to be employed in the region.

The PLANAF has a very strong presence in Guangdong MD as part of the Southern Sea Fleet, including a fighter regiment on Hainan Dao. The PLANAF force in the region also includes two anti-ship divisions equipped with H-5s.

Left: China's relatively small transport force employs the Xian Y-7, a local version of the Antonov An-26 'Curl'.

Right: the most capable transports available are the 13th Transport Division's Ilyushin Il-76s. These operate in conjunction with the paratroop division, administered by the PLAAF, and are based nearby.

Right: Although its airliner days are long over, even in China, the Hawker Siddeley Trident remains in limited service with the PLAAF on trooping and staff transport flights.

Two Antonov designs built locally are the An-12 (Shaanxi Y-8, left) and An-2 (Shijiazhuang Y-5, right). The 'Colt' is a Y-5B with aerodynamic refinements.

Nanjing Military Region airfields

Anhui Military District
1 Bengbu
2 Liuan
3 Hefei-Luogang
4 Shih Tang Qiao
5 Wuhu
6 Anqing
7 Tunxi

Jiangsu Military District
8 Xuzhou-Chiuli Shan
9 Xuzhou-Dagouzhang
10 Lianyungang-Baitabu
11 Yancheng
12 Nanjing-Yuxikou
13 Danyang
14 Motou
15 Wuxi-Shonfang
16 Suzhou

Shanghai City
17 Shanghai-Dachang
18 Shanghai-Hongqiao
19 Shanghai-Pudong
20 Shanghai-Longhua
21 Shanghai-Jiangwan

Jiangxi Military District
22 Mahuiling
23 Nanchang-Xiangtang
24 Nanchang North
25 Linjiang

26 Ji'an
27 Taihe
28 Ganzhou
29 Xincheng

Zhejiang Military District
30 Changxing
31 Huzhou
32 Jiaxiang
33 Hangzhou-Jianqiao
34 Hangzhou-Xiaoshan
35 Ningbo
36 Zhujiajian-Zhoushan
37 Dai Shan
38 Jiwu
39 Jinhua
40 Longyou
41 Quxian
42 Luqiao
43 Wenzhou

Fujian Military District
44 Chongan
45 Yixu-Fuzhou
46 Longtian
47 Huian
48 Qingyang-Anhai
49 Shatou-Chinmen
50 Xingling-Xiamen
51 Zhangzhou
52 Liancheng

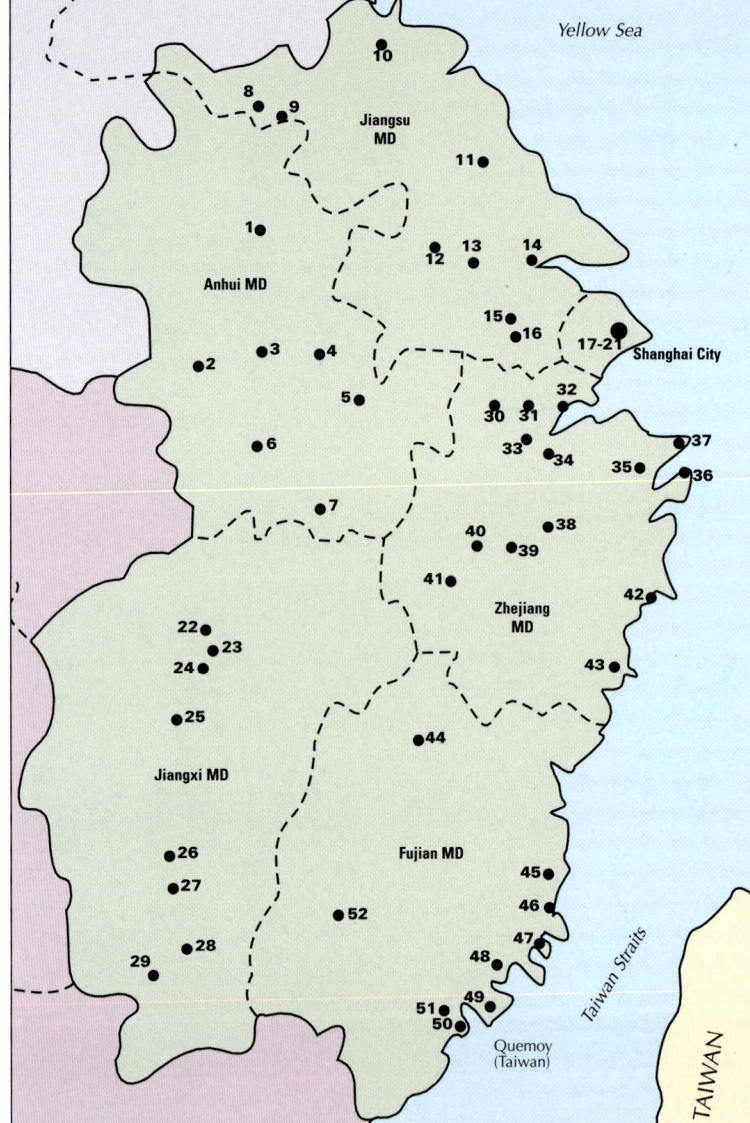

This Military Region is of great significance, for in its southern region it faces Taiwan. As well as numerous well-equipped air bases, it also houses a significant number of intermediate-range ballistic missiles, and contains many important population/industrial centres. The region also surrounds the Taiwanese island outpost of Quemoy, and would be the main jump-off for any assault on Taiwan.

From the headquarters at Nanjing the MR administers the Jiangsu and Anhui MDs, plus the Shanghai City area. These areas support three or four fighter divisions, including the 3rd Fighter Division, which includes a regiment of Su-27s at Wuhu in southern Anhui. The Nanjing MR also administers an H-6 bomber division, one of whose regiments is based at Nanchang.

Headquartered at Fuzhou, the 8th Air Corps controls bases in Fujian, Zhejiang and Jiangxi MDs. This organisation parents four or five fighter divisions, and an independent reconnaissance regiment (with JZ-6s) at Qingyang in Fujian province. Among the 8th Air Corps assets are further Su-27s based at Luqiao and Liancheng. As well as PLAAF units, the region is home to many PLANAF bases, strung out along the coast of Jiangsu, Zhejiang and Fujian.

In the early 1980s China recognised the shortfalls in both number and capability of its helicopters and in its rotary-wing technology. It turned to the West, and Aérospatiale in particular. The French company sold the Chinese 15 SA 321J Super Frelons for the PLANAF, and also licensed the production of the type as the Changhe Z-8. Around 75 are now in service with the PLA-AAC, used for heavylift duties and assault transport. Although considered obsolete by Western standards, the Z-8 provides the Chinese with a useful assault and underslung load lifting capability.

Sikorsky delivered 24 S-70C-II Black Hawks to the AAC in the 1980s, and these are arguably the most capable helicopters in Chinese hands. The high performance of the S-70 suited it to mountain work, and small numbers were dispersed around several bases in central/western China. Following the end of US aid in the aftermath of the 1989 Tiananmen Square massacre, the S-70 fleet has suffered from a lack of spares and only a handful may now be serviceable. In recent years, the PLA-AAC has received at least 24 Mil Mi-17s from Russia, and this type is now the main assault transport.

To provide a modern light helicopter for battlefield duties, China again turned to Aérospatiale (now Eurocopter), with the result

that Harbin now builds the SA 365 Dauphin as the Z-9. The first Chinese-built example flew on 16 January 1992. This excellent machine has also been built for shipboard use by the PLANAF. As well as utility transports, Harbin has produced armed versions, including the Z-9G with roof-mounted sight and the related Z-9W (also reported as Z-9Z or WZ-9) which is armed with HJ-8 anti-tank missiles. The armed Z-9 can also employ the TY-90 anti-aircraft missile for anti-helicopter operations.

First flying on 16 December 1994 was the Changhe Z-11, a Chinese-built version of another Aérospatiale (Eurocopter) design, the AS 350 Ecureuil. This light helicopter is being built to fulfil liaison and training duties, and entered service with the PLA-AAC in 1997. Rounding off the Chinese helicopter fleet are six AS 332M Super Pumas and four Bell 214s, which fly with a VIP transport squadron. These may, in fact, be operated by the PLAAF, which maintains the fixed-wing VIP fleet.

Future plans

Although the armed Z-9 offers the PLA-AAC a guided missile capability it hitherto had not possessed, there exists a requirement for a dedicated attack helicopter. It is possible that China is developing its own helicopter to fill

this need, but it has shown keen interest in an upgraded Mil Mi-24 'Hind' and the Kamov Ka-50 'Hokum'. The South African Denel Rooivalk and Italian Agusta A 129 have been studied also, perhaps with an eye to domestic production. Since the belated adoption of heliborne assault operations, the PLA-AAC is expected to expand its capabilities in that area, with the result that more Mi-17s will probably be acquired.

Helicopter inventory – PLAAF and PLA-AAC

TYPE	NUMBER IN SERVICE	REGIMENTS
Mil Mi-17	24	1
Mil Mi-8	30	1
Mil Mi-6	10	
Harbin Z-9	60	2
Changhe Z-8	75	3
Harbin Z-6	100	4
Harbin Z-5	250	10
Sikorsky S-70C-II	24	1
Eurocopter AS 332M	6 (VIP)	
Bell 214	4 (VIP)	

Developed by Harbin but produced by Changhe and Changzhou, the Z-6 survives in service in small numbers. The type entered service in 1977.

Production of the Super Frelon (as the Changhe Z-8) provided the PLA with a capable medium-lift helicopter, Both radar and non-radar versions are produced.

Harbin's Z-5 (Mil Mi-4 'Hound') is the most numerous Chinese helicopter, and has been adapted to perform many roles. This example is practising water rescue.

For battlefield duties the Z-5 can be armed with rockets or guns, and can also be used to sow minefields, as demonstrated here.

The Z-8's long range and good internal capacity make it an ideal rescue platform. Most of the PLA-AAC's Z-8s are radarless assault transports.

Below and right: Changhe builds a version of the Ecureuil under licence as the Z-11. Its main military roles are training, liaison and scouting.

Considerable advances in modernising the PLA-AAC fleet have been made thanks to the Harbin Z-9, a licence-built Dauphin. Versatile and fast, the type equips several units, including the garrison stationed in Hong Kong (above). Armed versions have been developed (left), featuring a roof-mounted sight and HJ-8 wire-guided missiles. At present these are the PLA's only real attack-capable helicopters, although the purchase of Mi-24s or Ka-50s from Russia is likely in the near future.

People's Liberation Army Navy – Air Force (PLANAF)

By the end of 1953 one PLAAF division – the 6th Air Division – was operating as a naval air arm, and at around that time the People's Liberation Army Navy – Air Force was established formally. Its initial roles were to provide coastal defence, mainly for the naval ports, and to conduct patrols in littoral waters. It appears that PLAAF bases and units situated along or near the coast were handed over to PLANAF control. In recent years the PLANAF's duties have widened to include anti-submarine warfare, while the navy's ambitions have grown considerably, so much so that the PLAN is now a true 'blue-water' service.

PLANAF organisation

For command purposes, the PLAN is split into three divisions: the Northern, Eastern and Southern Sea Fleets. Each controls the activities within a certain geographic region and, like the PLAAF's MR Air Forces, consists of role-specific divisions each with two or three regiments. Each of the three Fleets has a single ASW regiment assigned which provides helicopters for vessels at sea. Like those of the PLAAF, the PLANAF's units are thought to be numbered sequentially from 1 to about 16 for divisions, and 1 to at least 40 for regiments.

The Northern Sea Fleet is headquartered at Qingdao, and has the largest proportion of aviation assets assigned. It controls forces based in Liaoning, Hebei and Shandong Military Districts, and its principal area of concern is the Yellow Sea. It primarily faces the forces of Korea, Russia and Japan, and has four fighter divisions to defend the dense concentration of naval bases, and three attack/anti-ship divisions.

The Eastern Sea Fleet, in Jiangsu and Zhejiang provinces, has two fighter divisions and two attack/anti-ship divisions. Headquartered at Ningbo, its primary concern is Taiwan. Large-scale amphibious exercises are undertaken occasionally to remind Taiwan of the strength of the PLAN in this region. From Fujian and Guangdong Military Districts, the Southern Sea Fleet (HQ: Zhanjiang) operates in the South China Sea, the disputed Spratly Islands being a major preoccupation. Hainan Dao, the large island which represents China's southernmost point, accommodates one of the Southern Sea Fleet's three fighter divisions, although aircraft also use the newly constructed base at Xisha in the Paracel Islands even farther south.

PLANAF fighters and bombers

Most of the types in PLANAF service are similar to those used by the PLAAF. The fighter regiments are primarily equipped with Chengdu J-7 variants, although a number of J-6s survive in use, augmented by JJ-6 two-seat trainers. Around half of China's J-8 'Finback' fleet is under naval control, serving alongside J-7s in mixed regiments. The PLANAF's 'Finbacks' are believed to be mostly of the later J-8II variant, although a reported 24 have been further modified to J-8IID (or J-8D) standard with a bolt-on refuelling probe. These are refuelled by a locally modified version of the Xian H-6 bomber and the capability allows them to provide long-range fighter cover, which is of great use for operations over the Spratly Islands. Only the PLAAF's Su-27s have the range to reach the Spratlys from Chinese territory unrefuelled (apart from forward operations from Xishu in the Paracel Islands).

For attack operations and bombing, the PLANAF relies on the same trio of types as used by the Air Force: Harbin H-5, Xian H-6 and Nanchang Q-5. The elderly H-5 serves in considerable numbers, although these are dwindling rapidly. As well as in standard bomber form, the aircraft is also available in a torpedo-bomber version. A small number of H-6s serve with a single regiment. Around 20 are H-6A free-fall bombers, while around five are believed to have been modified to H-6D standard. This version has a much larger under- nose radome housing a maritime search radar, and is equipped to launch two YJ-1 or YJ-2 anti-ship missiles from underwing pylons. The large radar is used to provide targeting information for the missiles, as well as a maritime search function. The Q-5 is available for short-range attack missions and coastal anti-ship duties, some fitted for the carriage of YJ-1/2 missiles. A radar-equipped Q-5B torpedo-bomber version was developed in the late 1960s, but did not enter service.

New generation attacker

Slowly replacing the H-5 in the PLANAF is the Xian JH-7 (marketed outside China as the FBC-1 Flying Leopard). This large attack fighter created something of a stir when it was first revealed to the West in the mid-1990s, but its development was protracted, and it appears that only a few have been built to date. Furthermore, the PLAAF is believed to have spurned the design in favour of Su-30MKK acquisition, and it is likely that the PLANAF is the sole user.

Power for the JH-7 is provided by two WS-9 turbofans, which are licence-built versions of the Rolls-Royce Spey Mk 202. The first batch of aircraft was produced using UK-supplied engines, and it has been reported that Chinese production of the engine has hit major problems. Recent reports allege that additional Speys have been provided by Rolls-Royce to enable production of the JH-7 to continue.

By any standards, the JH-7 represents a formidable anti-ship weapon in the region. Its primary armament consists of two YJ-1/YJ-2 (C-801/C-802) sea-skimming missiles, similar to the Exocet, carried underwing. The large radar in the nose locates targets for the missiles which, when provided with target co-ordinates, can attack autonomously. Alternatively, the JH-7 can carry the Russian Kh-31 supersonic anti-ship missile, although whether this weapon is in widespread service or not remains unknown. However, photographs have appeared of the Kh-31 suspended from a JH-7 wing pylon.

Jinan Military Region airfields

Covering two provinces – Henan and Shandong – the Jinan Military Region is the smallest in terms of area, but the region is densely populated and highly industrialised. PLAAF assets in the region consist of two fighter divisions in Shandong MD, including one around the headquarters at Jinan itself, and a fighter division and attack division in Henan MD. There are also training and transport assets.

The PLANAF maintains a large number of bases in the region as part of the Northern Sea Fleet, mainly along the peninsular coast and around the ports of Qingdao and Yantai. Qingdao is the base for the navy's flying-boat operations with Harbin SH-5s. Six PLANAF fighter regiments are located in the region in two divisions, along with three regiments of Q-5s for attack duties.

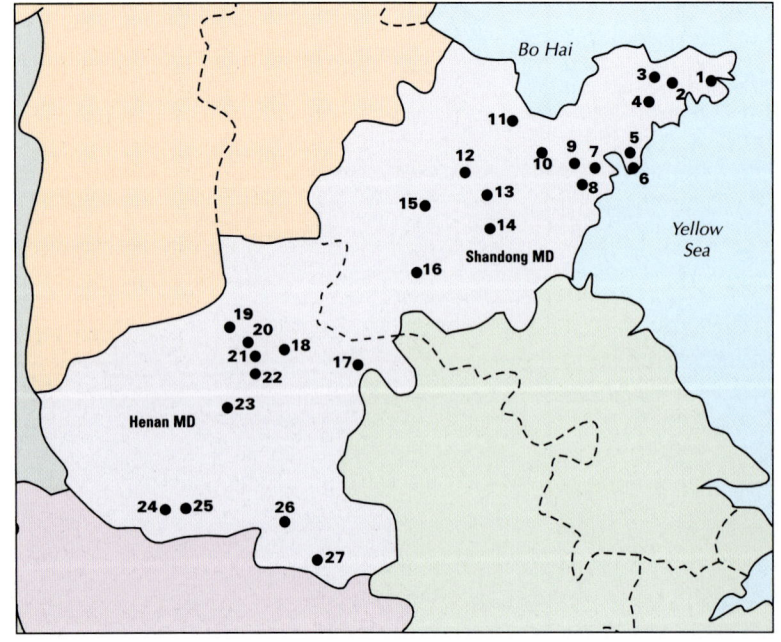

Shandong Military District
1 Wendeng
2 Yantai-South
3 Yantai-Southwest
4 Laiyang
5 Qingdao-Liu Teng
6 Qingdao-Tsang Kou
7 Jiaoxian
8 Zhucheng
9 Gaomi
10 Weixian
11 Dongying
12 Zhoucun
13 Yidu
14 Gouzhuyang
15 Jinan-Tsinan
16 Jining

Henan Military District
17 Zhuji-Guanyintang
18 Kaifeng
19 Jiyuan
20 Xingyang
21 Zhengzhou
22 Changge
23 Ranghe Zhen
24 Neixiang
25 Nan Yang
26 Lixindian
27 Huangchuan

The Xian JH-7 (above) is believed to serve only with the PLANAF, and is the replacement for the H-5 in the anti-ship role. Production has been slow, mainly delayed by problems with the supply of its licence-built Spey engines. The type's principal weapon is the YJ-2 sea-skimming missile, seen on the aircraft at right. Although most have been noted in the standard white scheme, the aircraft below carries a more operational mid-grey scheme, with blue codes.

Above: The Nanchang Q-5 serves with the PLANAF in some numbers, and provides a useful attack function in support of amphibious assault operations and against coastal shipping.

Numerically, the backbone of the PLANAF fighter force is the Chengdu J-7, employed for the defence of coastal installations. This aircraft is a J-7II, with rearward-hinging canopy and relocated brake chute.

The ancient H-5 remains in limited service as both a free-fall bomber (below) and as a torpedo bomber (right). It can also carry the YJ-1 ASM. The replacement of such aircraft is a priority for the PLANAF.

Below: This group of navy 'Finbacks' comprises aircraft from the original J-8 series. These are day-only fighters with rudimentary radar and forward-hinging canopies. The older J-8/J-8I versions serve in mixed regiments with newer J-8IIs.

The most potent fighter available to the PLANAF is the Shenyang J-8, serving mostly in the J-8II radar-equipped version. At least one regiment has the probe-equipped J-8IID, a line-up of which is seen above. Below is a close-up of the fixed refuelling probe used by the J-8IID, while a pair flies overhead in formation with an H-6 tanker.

Air Power Analysis

Shenyang Military Region airfields

Nei Mongol Military District – East
1 Hailar
2 Chaor
3 Yalu

Heilongjiang Military District
4 Nenjiang
5 Yichan
6 Jiamusi
7 Taha Erh
8 Qiqihar-Sanjiazi
9 Harbin-Ping Fang Tien
10 Harbin-Shuang Yu Shu
11 Harbin-Yanjiagang
12 Harbin-Wang Kang
13 Shuangcheng
14 Lalin
15 Shangzi
16 Mudanjiang-Hailang
17 Shih Tou North
18 Ludzigou

Jiling Military District
19 Jilin-Erh Tai Tzu
20 Jiaohe
21 Yanji
22 Changchun-Dafangshen
23 Chachung-Datun
24 Huai De
25 Jichang
26 Shuangliao-Cheng Chia Tun
27 Siping 1

28 Dongfeng
29 Liuhe
30 Sanyaun Pu

Liaoning Military District
31 Kaiyuan
32 Shenyang-Sujiatun
33 Shenyang-Beilin
34 Shenyang-Dongta
35 Shenyang-Yu Hung Tun
36 Shenyang-Hun He
37 Fuxin 2
38 Liaoyang
39 Chaoyang
40 Suizhong
41 Xingcheng
42 Jinxi
43 Jinzhou-Xiaolingzi
44 Jinzhou North
45 An-Shan
46 Kuandian
47 Dapu
48 Dandongi
49 Dandong-Ta Kong Kou

Liaoning MD – Liaodongbandao
50 Fuxian
51 Xinjing
52 Lüda-Choushuitlu
53 Lüda-Sanshilipu
54 Lüda-Cheng Sha Ho
55 Yingchengzi
56 Tuchengzi

The Shenyang Military Region is second in importance only to the Nanjing MR. It protects the approaches to Beijing from the north, and includes the large industrial centres of Harbin and Shenyang, and borders Russia and North Korea. It was the Korean War which saw a large build-up of forces in the region, and Chinese bases were used for combat operations.

Headquarters are in Shenyang, from where the assets in Liaoning MD are controlled. These include a Q-5 attack division and a reconnaissance regiment, equipped with JZ-6s and HZ-5s, as well as fighter divisions. The 1st Air Corps (headquartered at Changchun) is a large organisation assigned to the Shenyang MR, which includes fighter divisions in Nei Mongol MD –

East, Heilongjiang MD and Jilin MD, an attack division and another reconnaissance regiment. The Shenyang MR has a bomber division with H-5s and H-6s assigned, with one of the regiments at Harbin. Another command post is at Lüda on the Liaodong peninsula, controlling a fighter division. Lüda itself is a major naval base, and at least four airfields near the city are PLANAF installations. The navy also has more airfields on the northern shore of Bo Hai.

Other systems associated with the JH-7 include a laser designation pod for use with LGBs, and rumours have surfaced regarding the development of an electronic warfare version. In any case, the JH-7 represents a major improvement in capability over the ancient H-5 it is thought to be replacing.

Maritime patrol and helicopters

Perhaps China's most remarkable military aircraft are its few flying-boats which continue to operate from Qingdao. A single regiment controls the operations of the Harbin SH-5 and the Beriev Be-6. Only a handful of each are in service, but they are widely used on coastal patrols, and are outfitted for a variety of roles, including ASW, SAR and attack. Development of the Be-6 'Madge' dates back to 1945, and it is nothing short of amazing that the type survives in service today.

On the other hand, the much larger SH-5 did not make its maiden flight until 3 April 1976, and is a far more modern flying-boat. Powered by four WJ5A turboprops, the SH-5 is a true flying-boat, although it is equipped with retractable beaching gear. Various weapons can be carried underwing, including free-fall bombs. Among the sensors are a powerful search radar and a MAD (magnetic anomaly detector) boom. The SH-5B is a version intended for fire-fighting.

Land-based maritime patrol is provided by a single regiment of around 20 Shaanxi Y-8Xs,

equipped with a large search radar under the nose and offering a relatively long endurance. There is some confusion surrounding the role of the only Y-8 that so far has been converted with the Racal Searchwater radar. Some commentators suggest that it is an AEW aircraft for the PLAAF, while others contend that it is a PLANAF programme for use in either the AEW role or as a maritime patroller.

In recent years, the helicopter has become increasingly important within the PLANAF. Although sizeable numbers of Harbin Z-5s are in service, the Changhe Z-8 (Aérospatiale SA 321 Super Frelon) and Harbin Z-9 (Eurocopter SA 365) are the most important types, as they routinely deploy aboard the larger vessels of the PLA Navy. Equipped with search radar and able to carry YJ-1/2 missiles, the Z-8 (built under licence but preceded by French-built aircraft) is the largest PLANAF helicopter, and is used in the ASW/ASuW roles, as well as secondary duties such as supply and rescue. The smaller Z-9 is deployed aboard frigates and destroyers as a general-purpose helicopter. Some are armed, and it is likely that the TV-guided C-701 anti-ship missile will be fielded on the Z-9 in the near future. In addition to these types of French origin, the PLANAF has at least eight Kamov Ka-27 'Helix' ASW helicopters for service aboard the ex-Russian 'Sovreminyi'-class destroyers. These can also provide over-the-horizon targeting for the ship's missiles.

Modernisation plans

Like the PLAAF, the PLANAF has big plans for the future, and it is thought that some of the Su-30MKKs are destined for PLANAF service. Highest on the 'wish-list', however, is an aircraft-carrier capability, although funding for this would appear to be unlikely in the immediate future. Nevertheless, studies have been made into the nature of a Chinese carrier air wing. For a small carrier a STOVL approach would be required, in turn necessitating the development of new types. However, if a larger carrier was funded, a conventional air wing could be formed, based either around Sukhoi products, or around the Chengdu J-10. It has been reported that an overwater version of the J-10 powered by two RD-33 engines has been studied for PLANAF service, and it is conceivable that such an aircraft could form the basis of a carrier air wing.

In the meantime, the PLANAF is studying various maritime patrol options. A maritime version of the Xian Y-7 has been under development, although possibly only for export, while development of the Y-8 in the sea search role continues. The PLANAF has been seriously studying the Beriev Be-200 amphibian, presumably as a Be-6 replacement, and it is likely that China will become the first customer for this type. Shipborne airborne early warning is another area interesting the PLANAF, for which the Ka-31 with a rotating underfuselage antenna has been ordered.

The Harbin Z-9 is used by the PLANAF for a variety of duties, including ASW. This aircraft is a standard liaison model, which is used for some ship-to-shore duties.

PLANAF inventory

TYPE	NUMBER IN SERVICE	REGIMENTS
Fighters		
Shenyang J-8II	100	4
Shenyang J-8IID	24	1
Chengdu J-7	240	10
Shenyang J-6/JJ-6	74/24	4
Shenyang J-5/JJ-5	100/36	5
Bomber/attack		
Xian H-6A/D	20/5	1
Harbin H-5	150	6
Xian JH-7	c.30	1
Nanchang Q-5	100	4
Maritime patrol		
Harbin SH-5	5	1
Beriev Be-6	15	
Shaanxi Y-8	20	1
Helicopters		
Kamov Ka-27	8+ (ASW)	
Harbin Z-9	10 (ASW)	
Changhe Z-8/Aérospatiale SA 321	6/15 (ASW)	
Harbin Z-5	40	1

Taxiing out from the Xian flight test facility (note the Y-7 in primer in the background) is an H-6D, carrying two YJ-6 anti-ship missiles under the wings. The H-6D was China's first missile carrier, and is still in use in the anti-shipping role, although it has been superseded by the JH-7/YJ-2 combination. Compared to the bomber version of the H-6, the much larger size of the undernose radome is readily apparent.

Below: This 'Badger' is described as an export version of the H-6D, which explains the unusual camouflage. Iraq received four B-6Ds, with C-601 (export designation of YJ-6) missiles, in the late 1980s, but they were destroyed during the Gulf War.

Harbin SH-5s serve in small numbers on long-range patrol/SAR duties. This large flying-boat has an attack capability, as demonstrated above. The few SH-5s are operated by a single regiment at Qingdao (below).

Above: The radar-equipped Changhe Z-8 (license-built Super Frelon) is the main shipboard helicopter, augmented by French-built SA 321s.

Below: The Y-8X is the maritime patrol version of the Shaanxi-produced An-12 copy. The aircraft has search radar in an enlarged undernose radome.

Alaskan Air Power

Part 1: US Air Force

The US military is a long-standing and powerful economic and political partner in Alaska, and much of the infrastructure of the state would not exist if not for the Herculean efforts of the military during World War II and the Cold War. While the Coast Guard, Army and National Guard play crucial roles, the US Air Force is by far the largest player.

From his headquarters at Elmendorf AFB, Air Force Lt Gen. Norton Schwartz commands Alaskan Command (ALCOM), the 11th Air Force and the Alaska NORAD Region (ANR). ALCOM has no full-time subordinate units – forces are assigned as necessary with ALCOM serving as a deployable Joint Task Force. The three-star billet is an excellent opportunity for a promising general to receive both joint-service and multinational experience, and the job is seen as a grooming position for soon-to-be major command officers.

The ANR is run from the Regional Air Operations Center (RAOC) located beneath ALCOM HQ. It has 15 AN/FPS-117 area surveillance radars at Cold Bay, King Salmon, Cape Newenham, Cape Romanzof, Tin City,

Kotzebue, Lisburne, Wainwright, Point Barrow, Point Lonely, Oliktok, Barter Island, Point Bullen, Sparrevohn and Tatalina. Three AN/FPS-124 cruise missile detection radars are located at Indian Mountain, Fort Yukon and Murphy Dome. Information from the ground radars and datalinked from E-3 AWACS is fused and displayed at the RAOC. The facility averages over 30,000 radar tracks a month, most of them being commercial airliners and bush planes. The elderly AN/FPS-50 3,000-mile (4830-km) detection range BMEWS radar at Clear AFS in central Alaska was recently replaced by a new phased-array radar. Another radar worthy of mention is the AN/FPS-108 Cobra Dane space surveillance radar, situated at the shadowy Eareckson AFS on the western

Aleutian island of Shemya. Cobra Dane is said to be capable of detecting a 1-sq ft (0.09-m²) target at ranges exceeding 25,000 miles (40,230 km). Should the US proceed to field a national missile defence system, Eareckson would be the site for the system's X-band targeting and acquisition radar.

Elmendorf AFB

Elmendorf AFB is located on the northern edge of Anchorage, the state's largest city. The base has one main 10,000-ft (3048-m) runway oriented 05/23, and a 7,500-ft (2286-m) secondary runway oriented 15/33. Being located midway between East and West, the base has had its share of unusual visitors, including Soviet/Russian MiG-29s, Su-27s, Il-38, An-225 and a PLAAF 737-400. In July 2000 a Russian Tu-154M Open Skies reconnaissance aircraft surveyed military points of interest.

In July 1999 the 3rd Wing at Elmendorf celebrated its 80th anniversary with this formation comprising an aircraft from each of the five constituent squadrons. Here the formation passes Denali (formerly Mount McKinley), the highest point in the United States.

The most potent aircraft permanently based in Alaska are the F-15Es of the 90th Fighter Squadron 'Pair-O-Dice'. The Alaskan terrain provides ample opportunity for training in a low-level environment, while large tracts of uninhabited land can be used for exercises on a scale far exceeding of those undertaken in the Southwest Range Complex which includes Nellis.

Alaskan air defence responsibilities are shared by the 12th FS and 19th FS, with two F-15Cs and pilots kept on 30-minute alert at all times – down from the 5-minute Cold War alert response time. The Russian Far East Military District, suffering from a lack of financial and material resources, low readiness and no strong political direction, has mounted few probing forays in the past decade – though the September 1999 approach of two Tu-95 'Bear-H' bombers was mildly surprising but quickly responded to by two Eagles from the now-disbanded 54th FS, along with a KC-135R from the AK ANG 168th ARS at Eielson.

Recent 3rd Wing fighter deployments include a Northern Watch assignment to Turkey, involving both F-15C units. The 54th FS flew in Allied Force in 1999 (and was the first F-15C unit to use NVGs in combat) and Southern Watch in 1998. The 90th FS finds itself often deployed to the Pacific's hottest spot: the Korean Peninsula, most recently in 1999.

AESA fighters

Eighteen F-15Cs of the 12th and 19th FS (nine from each squadron) had received by December 2000 the formerly top secret AN/APG-63(V)2 Active Electronically Scanned Array (AESA) radar, and in doing so became the world's first fighters to be so equipped. The 19th FS took delivery of the first AESA-equipped F-15C in April 2000. The radar contains most of the previous version's black boxes, but replaces the antenna power supply and the mechanically-scanned antenna with a non-moving, solid-state transmit/receive antenna array with highly effective radiated power levels and tightly-focused transmissions with great beam agility. The updated radar is thought to represent a great leap forward in combating low-flying, stealthy cruise missiles and is capable of tracking more targets at further range (100+ miles/160+ km) in an intense ECM/ECCM environment. Officials are tight-lipped about the 'V2', as it is called by Eagle 'drivers', though it is thought to be

The base is home to the 3rd Wing, which parents the 12th (formerly the 54th), 19th and 90th Fighter Squadrons, 517th Airlift Squadron and the 962nd Airborne Air Control Squadron. The 3rd Wing is commanded by Brig. Gen. Douglas M. Fraser, and celebrated its 80th anniversary in July 1999. It is the oldest wing in the USAF having served continuously since 1 July 1919. The 19th and 90th FS date back to World War II. The 12th FS was activated in April 2000 and kept the F-15C/Ds formerly assigned to the 54th FS. The 19th FS 'Gamecocks' (F-15C/D) was activated in June 1917 and, like the rest of the wing, has served in Alaska since

December 1991 after relocation from Clark AB. The 90th FS 'Pair-O-Dice' is equipped with the F-15E Strike Eagle and is the 3rd Wing's long-range strike muscle. The 517th AS 'Firebirds' won the 1998 Airlifter Rodeo and is the largest C-130 Hercules unit in the USAF, with 18 C-130H-1s. The 'Firebirds' have served in Alaska since June 1964, and got their name from Alaskan natives due to their use of RATO assisted takeoffs. Det. 1 of the 517th has two C-12Fs and one C-12J for light transport flights all over the state. Rounding out the 3rd Wing is the 962nd AACS 'Eye of the Eagle' which has two E-3B Block 30/35s.

Elmendorf's two fighter Eagle squadrons are the 12th FS (above, renumbered from the 54th FS) and the 19th FS (right, which took over from the 43rd FS). Each has two F-15D two-seaters assigned along with 18 F-15Cs. As well as the defence of Alaskan airspace, the F-15s are also deployed on global peacekeeping operations, and have been involved in policing the 'No-fly' zones over northern Iraq (Operation Northern Watch). At least 18 of the 3rd Wing's F-15Cs are equipped with the APG-63(V)2 AESA radar – the first US fighters to have this new technology which dispenses with the traditional mechanically-scanned antenna in favour of an electronically scanned fixed antenna array.

capable of being used in an offensive jamming role using highly-focused and agile beams.

F-15E Strike Eagles of the 90th have F100-PW-229 engines and AN/APG-70 radar, along with the same RWR, ECM and chaff/flare dispensers as their air-to-air cousins. All three squadrons' standard AAM 'go to war' kit is a mix of late-model AIM-9M Sidewinders and AIM-120A/C 'Slammers' with the increasingly elderly AIM-7 Sparrow seen less often. The standard 940 rounds of 20-mm ammunition is carried as well. The Strike Eagles are certified to carry nearly every guided and unguided air-to-ground munition in the US inventory, including B61 series and B83 nuclear gravity bombs (no nuclear weapons are based in Alaska). Rumours of dual IR/radar seeker AIM-7s and ramjet-powered AMRAAMs equipping Alaskan F-15s remain anecdotal and unsubstantiated. 12/19th FS F-15Cs do, however, exhibit small bump antennas of unknown purpose – one just forward of the windscreen and one below the cockpit. All C-model Eagles are due to receive the Fighter Datalink (FDL) system though it is unknown how many aircraft can communicate with each other. It is rumoured but uncon-firmed that some 3rd Wing Eagles have been fitted with AIFF.

While not talking much about capabilities, 3rd Wing officials are downright jubilant about operating the system. "We are extremely pleased with the performance of our [V2-equipped] aircraft." According to 3rd Wing Operations Group Commander Col Harold 'Punch' Moulton II. "The reliability and main-tainability of these new systems have exceeded our expectations. Furthermore, the combina-tion of APG-63(V)2 radar and Fighter Datalink (FDL) provides a unique air-to-air weapon system with awesome capabilities to protect our nation – bridging to the next generation of air dominance: the F-22."

Pivotal position

The 3rd Wing is very aware of its pivotal role in the defence of Alaska and the United States and the part it plays in the new AEF force struc-ture. Moulton goes on to put this in perspec-tive, "Alaska may not be regarded as the 'final frontier', but it certainly is a 'great frontier', with worldwide strategic value. The 3rd Wing's abil-ity to exploit Alaska's strategic location is enhanced by the strong military-civilian rela-tionship we enjoy with our local community and also because one in five Alaskans have ties to the military. From this great frontier, Alaska is used as a springboard to quickly reach anywhere in the northern hemisphere. Since a majority of the world's land mass, and therefore population, resides in the northern hemisphere, this is an important capability. Our 54th Fighter Squadron [now 12th FS] demonstrated this capability by joining the war in Kosovo by flying non-stop over the North Pole.

"So, when we think of advantages and chal-lenges, they really are two sides of the same coin. The harsh weather means our personnel (such as aviators, maintainers and security forces) must always be ready to survive. Our proximity to most theatres means our folks are routinely called, as our C-130s have been to East Timor and our F-15Es to Korea, and our low-density, high-demand E-3s have been to every theatre. [3rd Wing F-15Cs also take their part in manning the rotational air defence detachment at Keflavik, Iceland].

The Chugach mountains form an impressive backdrop to operations at Elmendorf. Here a 90th FS F-15E takes off past the active line of 19th FS F-15C/Ds. Elmendorf is situated on the outskirts of Anchorage, and is the main airhead for Alaska-based Army units. Fort Richardson, home of the 6th Infantry Division (Light) adjoins the air force base.

PACAF has two assigned AWACS units, one flying with the 18th Wing at Kadena and the 962nd AACS at Elmendorf. The 962nd has recently upgraded to operating two E-3s in the Block 30/35 configuration with ESM equipment in cheek fairings.

"As a great frontier, Alaska offers 1.5 million acres (607050 hectares) of range space – that's double the space of the largest ranges in the lower 48. This area is vital to our aviators' ability to train without artificial restrictions due to proximity to non-military citizens. It also affords us the opportunity to more easily train in the joint arena, with the army.

Superlative equipment

"The wing's unique qualities come from the varied aircraft we have stationed here and the capabilities they bring to our aerospace force. We have the world's best air superiority fighter, the world's best precision engagement fighter, the world's best airlift squadron, the world's best command and control squadron. Despite the harsh weather, this wing has had a very impressive list of superlatives, and they have been earned by our people, who give their all. Alaska offers several significant training opportunities. Our ability to train over varied and different geography combined with varying weather conditions provides a unique challenge for our aircrews. They learn to adapt their tactics and plans to meet the changing situations they confront in daily training. And, as I said earlier, they train on some of the best ranges and airspace in the world. However, during the winter, the weather provides a

Airlift assets are concentrated in the 517th Airlift Squadron at Elmendorf. As well as its Hercules fleet, the squadron operates two C-12Fs (right) and a single C-12J (above), allocated for staff/liaison work. The small fleet shuttles between Elmendorf and Eielson, the state capital Juneau and outlying airfields. The work entails flying over (and, on occasion, through) some of the most spectacular scenery in the world.

significant challenge to us for maintaining ready forces. All our squadrons (not just the fighters) need to minimise their exposure to the long cold and dark winter so they can maximise their ability to fight the nation's wars at any time. The shortened daylight exacerbates the situation. Reduced flying means reduced training, not only for the aircrew, but for all of the support. That crew chief doesn't get much training on her aircraft if it doesn't fly!

"As the Air Force implements its Expeditionary Air Force concept, we will deploy to existing contingency operations, like supporting Operation Southern Watch, on a scheduled basis. As part of an Air Expeditionary Force (AEF), units and personnel from the 3rd Wing will deploy on a 15-month rotational schedule, which will eventually put our units at home station during the winter, and deployed

(for AEF) during the summer. We are looking into this situation and working to determine how best to deal with this future challenge."

Eielson AFB

Eielson AFB is located to the east of Fairbanks in the central interior. The 18th and 355th Fighter Squadrons comprise the sharp edge of the 354th Fighter Wing, which is commanded by Brig. Gen. Mike DeCurr (being replaced in April by Brig. Gen. Bob. D. Dulaney).

Eielson has a 14,507-ft (4422-m) main runway oriented 31/13. The 150-ft (46-m) wide runway was originally sized for B-36 operations. The runway was resurfaced in 2000, with all Eielson jets being transferred to nearby Ladd Army Airfield at Ft Wainwright. Approximately 2,700 active-duty personnel are stationed at

The A/OA-10A Warthog close air support/ attack aircraft of the 355th FS are standard issue and, like all A-10s, are loved by their pilots. The Eielson 'Hogs' work closely with the 1st Brigade, 6th Infantry (Light) at Fort Wainwright near Fairbanks. The 355th FS was the top scoring team in Gunsmoke 95, as well as winning Sabre Spirit 96. They have also served in Bosnia and, in late 1998, the 355th FS took its turn in Southern Watch and fought in Desert Fox (credited with a 100 percent target hit rate). The 355th FS does not expect to be equipped with the Litening combined IR/radar attack and navigation pod.

The AN/AAQ-13 and AN/AAQ-14 LANTIRN pods used for navigation, low-level flight and combat by both the Strike Eagles of the 90th FS and the 'Vipers' of the 18th FS are not negatively affected by the cold weather (there are times when thermal cross-over prevents the pods from achieving optimal performance) nor evidently are any other systems. This is due to the exceptional efforts of the maintenance troops and the additional intense training that pilots need in order to survive the challenges presented by the demanding Alaskan operating

Above: Only one way in .....a C-130 from the 517th Airlift Squadron approaches a strip near the remote Sparrevohn radar station, the ridge at the far end preventing an approach from the opposite direction and rendering a go-round impossible.

Right: .....and one way out. Having turned round at the far end of the runway the C-130 climbs out at a pace to clear the terrain. After 10 landings at 'one-way' strips crews receive air commendation medals.

Eielson, representing PACAF, AETC and AIA. The base has a POL storage of approximately 20 million gallons and there are two separate ammunition storage areas with multiple igloos and magazines (it is unknown if any are nuclear certified). There are 20 climate-controlled hangars at Eielson of varying sizes that total 576,000 sq ft (53510 m²) in area – including the massive wooden 'Thunderdome' which in its day could hold two B-36s.

Night/All-weather 'Viper'

Eielson-based 18th FS F-16CG/DG 'Vipers' are tasked with all-weather and night attack/ interdiction and offensive and defensive counter-air missions. They are equipped with wide-field-of-view holographic HUDs, F100-PW-220 powerplants, AN/APG-68(V) radar and are thought to be equipped with the AN/ALE-50 towed decoy system. They are armed primarily with late-model AIM-120Cs and late-model AIM-9s, and can carry the full spectrum of US precision-guided munitions and 'dumb' gravity bombs. The 18th was the first PACAF unit to fly against MiG-29s (Malaysian 'Fulcrums' in Cope Taufan in 1997) and served a tour of duty in late 1998 on Operation Southern Watch. Most recently, the 18th FS returned home from Commando Sling held in Singapore during the summer of 2000 where they flew with and against the RSAF's top-notch F-16C/D Block 52s. In September 2000 and as part of AEF 10, several 18th FS Vipers, their crews and support personnel deployed to Incirlik AB, Turkey to train and to fly CSAR Northern Watch missions – the first time the 'Electric Jet' has been used in the role, which is normally an A-10 mission.

environment. Visiting fighter units often have to let their jets warm up for 15 to 20 minutes before deflecting control surfaces, while Alaska-based fighters are acclimatised and require much less warm-up time. Weather cancels a small portion of training flights in the late fall and winter, mostly due to high winds, low visibility and slick runways, though in time of conflict the impact of such conditions would be significantly reduced.

During winter however, the diminished daylight and extreme low temperatures do reduce the number of sorties at Eielson. To ensure mission readiness, both the 18th and 355th FS participate in Cope Thaw, which sends aircraft, pilots and maintainers south to warmer climes to pick up the operations tempo and give crews a much deserved break from the sometimes debilitating cold.

Remote airfields

Two remote fighter alert sites currently in warm storage are located in the rural western village of Galena and the southwest village of King Salmon. King Salmon's main runway is 8,500 ft (2591 m) long and is oriented 11/29. It has three arresting cables. Galena's runway is nearly 7,500 ft (2286 m) in length and is

Eighteen C-130H-1s are the main equipment of the 517th Airlift Squadron. It was the first C-130 unit to adopt the mid-grey colour scheme.

oriented 07/25. During the recent Operation Northern Denial, AESA radar-equipped F-15Cs from both the 12th and 19th FS were deployed to the reactivated fields from 1 December until 14 December 2000. Northern Denial was a

Flying from Eielson, the 354th Fighter Wing is orientated towards close air support, the wing (343rd Wing until 1 August 1993) having pioneered the use of F-16s and OA-10s in the night CAS role. The single F-16 squadron is the 18th FS 'Arctic Foxes'.

F-16CG Block 40s are the workhroses of the 18th FS, equipped with LANTIRN for the night CAS role. The squadron works closely with the co-located OA-10s, which provide a forward air control function.

response to the Russian Air Force deployment of Tu-95 'Bear-H' bombers to the Russian Far East – three to Tiksi AB and two to Anadyr AB. The 3rd Wing's 517th AS and 962nd AACS, along with visiting E-3s from Tinker AFB and Kadena AB and the AK ANG's 210th RQS and 168th ARS provided support during the operation. Frank and open discussions between the US and Russia military leaders led to the mutual understanding that the Russians were simply trying to get some rare training time for their 'Bear' pilots and no attempts were made to provoke US interceptions.

Eareckson AFS (formerly Shemya AFB) is operated by the 611th Air Support Squadron of the 3rd Wing and has a 10,000-ft (3048-m) runway oriented 10/28. The base, also known as 'The Rock', was the home of many classified missions during the Cold War – many of them flown by various EC/RC-135 variants and USN EP-3s. Unconfirmed reports have hinted that early stealth aircraft prototypes may have flown from Shemya against Soviet Far Eastern Military District air defences without detection. The base is currently in a semi-operational status manned by contractors and the remainder of the installation could be rapidly reactivated if needed. Other secret programs based at Shemya included the Navy's Queen Match programme, which launched missile-borne cameras to image Soviet ballistic missile re-entry vehicles and decoys as they flew to western Pacific impact areas.

Ranges and MOAs

Alaskan Ranges and Military Operating Areas (MOAs) are vast and nearly unparalleled – totalling over 66,000 square miles (170927 km²). What Alaska offers is, "Awesome training areas and targets. We have some of the largest training airspace in the world allowing us to train the way we fight. We can vary our targets and type of tactics to simulate any Area of Responsibility (AOR)", said Moulton. By comparison, the highly instrumented and capable Nellis Range Complex is a little over 5,000 square miles (12950 km²) in area. PACAF's top training operation Cope Thunder is directed from Eielson and is run by the 353rd Combat Training Squadron from its state-of-the-art complex.

The A-10 is no stranger to Alaska, having first been deployed with the 343rd Composite Wing in late 1981. The squadron was originally the 18th TFS, before renumbering as the 11th TASS. Today it is designated the 355th Fighter Squadron.

Not only does Alaska have the largest supersonic fly zone in the US, it has over 62,000 square miles (160568 km²) of restricted airspace overlaying a similar amount of real estate which the Army uses for 360° free-fire wargames. There are 90,000 acres (36423 hectares) of impact areas, split between three zones allowing the live-fire of any non-nuclear munition in the inventory. Alaskan impact/drop areas are designated as follows:

- **R-2202:** located west of Fort Greely and contains 894 square miles (2315 km²) including the Army urban warfare training area called Simpsonville.
- **R-2203:** located a few miles north of Elmendorf is not used as a weapons drop range but the 40-square mile (104-km²) area contains the Malamute Drop Zone which is used for C-130 drops of soldiers and heavy equipment. A small gravel strip is also used for assault and short field training.
- **R-2205:** located 12 miles (19 km) east of Eielson AFB and is 180 square miles (466 km²) in area. Targets include a large target airfield which was the location of the final B-2A test drops in 1998 of the B61-11 earth penetrating nuclear bomb.
- **R-2211:** located southwest of Eielson and has 126 square miles (326 km²) of restricted Class A and B ranges which the USAF and Army jointly use.

The Pacific-Alaska Range Complex, as it is now known, is endowed with nearly every possible threat country landform, and is rich with hundreds of targets ranging from fully-equipped enemy airfields and urban areas to submarine pens. The threat emitters are located throughout the ranges and the entire complex is instrumented. All target arrays are covered by remotely operated TV cameras with high-power optics. Almost all participating aircraft carry ACMI pods, enabling the battle to be viewed, dissected and scored in near real-time

by the fourth-generation Yukon Measurement and Debriefing System installed at both Eielson and Elmendorf.

There are currently 27 threats under the PARC contract. However, there are typically around 24/25 on range at a given time, given depot maintenance schedules etc. Threats that can be replicated are four different AAA (S-60, 100-mm, ZSU-23-4, ZPU-4) and six different SAMs (CSA-2, SA-2, SA-3, SA-6, SA-8, SA-15). In conjunction with the above threats, there are eight SAM/AAA visual cueing systems (Smokey SAM and Smokey AAA). Future planned threats include the SA-10 and others. On the conventional range (R-2211) there are three separate 'centre-point' targets consisting of gravel-filled large metal drums, and also a four-pit strafing area. The 'centre-point' targets can be 'scored' via three Television Ordnance Scoring Systems (TOSS), which consist of 2 video cameras. The strafe pits are scored via an acoustic shock-wave measuring system called Acousti-score.

Target arrays

On the two tactical ranges (R-2205, R-2202), targets/arrays include tanks, armoured personnel carriers, small tank formations, SAM and AAA sites, truck/vehicle convoys, aircraft, revetted aircraft, helicopters, train and tracks, special vehicles, general vehicles and facilities such as a power plant, control towers, aircraft hangars, POL facilities, maintenance buildings, headquarters buildings, command post, communications facilities, factory, guard shacks and warehouses.

Only a small percentage of the vehicles are actual 'stripped down' (of hazardous materials etc.) vehicles. These vehicles are used almost exclusively in the live munitions areas. The vast majority of all other tanks, vehicles, artillery pieces, aircraft, helicopters, etc are made of wooden and/or some plastic materials. Buildings are constructed with 40-ft (12.2-m) shipping containers stacked and/or arranged in various configurations.

The Yukon Measurement and Debriefing System is an Air Combat Maneuvering Instrumentation (ACMI) system, based on a four-master, 21-remote set-up (25 ground stations). The system can currently accommodate 36 aircraft as 'high-activity aircraft' (full tracking through YMDS) and up to 100 'low-activity aircraft' (with location information being gained by mode 3 transponder via radar feeds to the system). Through the Alaska ACMI Upgrade (AAU) programme which became

Eielson AFB is located outside Fairbanks in the centre of Alaska, near to the Blair Lakes range complex. Until 1992 the base was home to the 6th Strategic Wing and its RC-135S/X telemetry intelligence specialists. As well as the active-duty 354th Fighter Wing, the base houses the KC-135s of the Alaska ANG.

operational in autumn 2000, the numbers have not changed in live-viewing mode, but through the addition of GPS and a data recorder in the aircraft's ACMI pods, up to 99 'high-activity' aircraft can be followed during post-mission debriefs. Debriefs can be viewed simultaneously in theatres at both Elmendorf (PARC-South) and Eielson (PARC-North).

Running the Range Complex is the job of the 611th Air Operations Group, which is part of the 3rd Wing. Upcoming improvements to the ranges include the addition of simulated WMD manufacturing and storage facilities and hardened C² targets. Another effort underway is to

A 355th FS pilot reefs his A-10 into a high-g evasive turn, releasing flares simultaneously. The 354th FW is one of the main units earmarked for rapid deployment to Korea in a crisis, the attack-dedicated 354th FW being assigned to augment the Osan-based 51st FW in the CAS/BAI role.

work out a solution to deconflict JDAM/JSOW/JASSM use – a problem which similarly faces both the Nellis Range Complex and White Sands Missile Range. Long-range cruise missiles could be fired for training in Alaska but it would require special airspace use permits and would use small windows of time for the test.

Since Alaska has the highest per capita number of aircraft and pilots of any state, work-

ing with civil aviators is of paramount importance. As Lt Col Jim Gentemann who is Chief of Airspace and Range Operations, 611th AOG, puts it, "We work hard with civilians to let them know what we are up to and they have lots of opportunity to be involved in the process of airspace use. We are very proud of the relationship we have with the civilian population."

Mark Farmer

Sukhoi Su-15 'Flagon'

Little known outside its mother country, the Su-15 was a logical development of the Sukhoi's big tailed-delta series, which had already produced the Su-9/11 interceptors. Thanks to its better radar and performance, the Su-15 was assured of a much longer career.

O n 20 May 1953, a few months after Stalin's death, the Sukhoi design team was tasked with the construction of the Mach-2 swept-wing S-1 tactical fighter and the delta-winged T-3 interceptor. This marked the return to favour of the bureau after four years of disgrace; it was known as OKB-1 until 15 February 1954 and then as OKB-51 (OKB, *opytno-konstruktorskoye byuro* = test design bureau). Andrey Kochetkov tested the prototype of the S-1 'Fitter' in flight on 8 September 1955. This aircraft was later developed into the Su-7 series fighter, and then into a family of variable-geometry aircraft known as Su-17, Su-20 and Su-22. Through a series of gradual transformations, the prototype T-3 became the intercept fighters Su-9, Su-11 and Su-15. The leading designer of the delta-winged interceptor family was Nikolay Polenov, closely assisted by his associate Aleksandr Vishnevskiy.

Sukhoi's delta-wing interceptors – the Su-9, Su-11 and Su-15 – were always overshadowed by other Soviet aircraft and were used only in the USSR by the Air Defence Forces, a service shrouded in utmost secrecy.

First delta

At noon on 26 May 1956, Vladimir Makhalin took off for the first time in the prototype T-3 intercept fighter. After its first public presentation at Tushino airfield, near Moscow, on 24 June 1956, the aircraft obtained the NATO reporting name of 'Fishpot-A'. The T-3 had a cylindrical fuselage with front air intake and single Lyul'ka AL-7F turbojet engine. With delta wing and classic swept empennage, its maximum speed was 2100 km/h (1,305 mph) and its service ceiling was 18000 m (59,055 ft). According to its function, the aircraft was fitted with Almaz-3 radar and two K-7L or K-6V air-to-air missiles. The installed radar opened a

Right: This view of an Su-15 'Flagon-A' (with two R-8MT missiles) highlights the tiny wing area of the original versions. Landing speed was exceptionally high, and was reduced in later aircraft by the adoption of a double-delta wing.

Below: The underfuselage hardpoints of late-production Su-15TMs were used for gun pods or, as here, drop tanks. 'Flagon-Fs' theoretically had an air-to-ground capability using these hardpoints and the underwing pylons, but in reality their assignment to the PVO and lack of suitable fire control systems restricted them to pure fighter interceptor missions.

Pandora's box of problems, and making the supersonic adjustable air intake compatible with ever-bigger radar units took several years. The second prototype PT-7 was equipped with the improved Almaz-7 radar and had reshaped radomes.

Demand for the new intercept fighter was so great that series production was launched at Novosibirsk's Factory No. 153, named after V. Chkalov, as early as 1956. This decision led to a number of stumbling blocks, since the

aircraft design had not been properly prepared for production, and feverish changes began at once. In autumn 1957 the Novosibirsk factory built four series aircraft designated PT-8 (the factory designation was *izdeliye* 27; *izdeliye* = item), but production was soon halted following a 4 June 1958 resolution of the government and the Central Committee of the Communist Party that stopped all experiments with Almaz radar and K-7 missiles. The resolution ordered that aircraft be equipped with simpler arma-

Of the 1,290 'Flagons' manufactured, the Su-15TM was the most numerous model. It was also the last fighter version, employing the Taifun-M radar – a slightly smaller version of the MiG-25's Smerch-A unit. As with the 'Foxbat' radar, what Taifun-M (NATO 'Twin Scan') lacked in sophistication it compensated for in terms of sheer emitting power.

What eventually matured as the variable-geometry Su-24 'Fencer' began based on the Su-15's wings and tail, but with lift engines in the fuselage. These were tested in the prototype Su-15, which became the T-58VD. In this view the engine intake doors and louvred exhaust doors can be seen, as can the downward-vectored jet efflux.

ment systems having TsD-30T radar and four short-range K-5MS missiles.

In this form, the Su-9 'Fishpot-B' was good enough to begin mass production at Novosibirsk's Factory No. 153 (as *izdeliye* 34) and at Moscow's Factory No. 30 (as *izdeliye* 10). Production continued until 1962, resulting in 1,014 aircraft. In 1961-1962 the Moscow factory also built 50 Su-9U two-seat combat trainers (designated U-43 by the design bureau and *izdeliye* 11 by the factory).

The Su-9 was a successful aircraft and, after overcoming initial difficulties, it was liked by its pilots. The limited range of the aircraft's weapon system was a drawback, though, and led to the Su-11 aircraft with new Oryol (eagle) radar and K-8M missiles; this made its maiden flight on 6 January 1958 with Yevgeniy Kukushev at the controls, and was officially commissioned on 12 January 1962. However, the Su-11's handling in flight was very poor due its heavy nose disrupting the aircraft's balance. Production of Su-11s in Novosibirsk (where it was called *izdeliye* 36) was soon stopped, after a mere 112 aircraft.

In the late 1950s, several experimental aircraft were derived from the main line of Sukhoi intercept fighters and promised great significance for the future, particularly the Su-15. The first of Sukhoi's designs, the two-seat intercept fighter P-1, flown on 12 July 1957 by Nikolay Korovushkin, had crescent-shaped lateral air intakes. Engine troubles prompted the end of P-1 tests (the last flight was made in

Although handling was regarded as good by Soviet standards, the Su-15 was quite a 'hot ship' and the provision of a two-seat trainer for conversion was necessary. The first-generation Su-15UT (of which this is the prototype) carried no armament or combat systems, although dummy missiles were often fitted.

February 1958) and the programme eventually ended on 22 September 1958.

As the result of incessant troubles with the new Lyul'ka AL-9 turbojet engine, as well as the fact that further development of the AL-7 engine was no longer possible, the designers – on the order of the air forces – tried another propulsion system. The experimental T-5 was a modification of the first T-3 prototype equipped with two Tumanskii R-11F-300 engines installed side-by-side in the rear fuselage. The T-5 took off for the first time on 18 July 1958 with Vladimir Ilyushin at the controls and made 26 flights before the tests came to an end on 1 June 1959. The tests proved difficult as two R-11 engines were heavier than the single AL-7, resulting in the aircraft's centre of gravity moving aft considerably. A serious reconstruction would have been necessary to obtain satisfactory results. The rear section of the T-5 fuselage was used in construction of the T-58D prototype.

The next step towards the Su-15 was the experimental aircraft T-49, which was similar to the Su-11 except for the front fuselage, in which the radar protruded forward while the air intakes were arranged at the sides. The T-49 took off for the first time on 10 January 1960 with Anatoliy Koznov at the controls, but after a few flights in April the tests were stopped following an accident. The aircraft was repaired, but flights were not resumed.

Delayed beginning

The early 1960s in the Soviet Union was not a good time for new aircraft. Under Krushchev's doctrine of general 'missilisation', no new aircraft were necessary. Many air programmes were cancelled and some design teams (such as Lavochkin and Myasishchev) were switched to designing missiles and space-craft. However, these restrictions had only a small effect on intercept fighter aircraft, which were developed intensively by Sukhoi, Yakovlev (with its Yak-27 'Flashlight' and

The Sukhoi P-1 was a two-seat interceptor study. The basic configuration was mirrored in the Su-15.

The T-5 tested the side-by-side R-11F-300 engine installation employed in the Su-15.

The T-49 was based on the Su-11 but had an unusual radar/intake arrangement.

Yak-28 'Firebar'), Tupolev Tu-128 'Fiddler') and Mikoyan with its leading MiG-25 'Foxbat'. Such a situation was possible because an intercept fighter was not considered to be an independent item, rather part of an 'aircraft-missile intercepting system', a platform for air-to-air missiles.

Work on the Su-15 progressed without attracting comment in USSR governmental resolutions. The name Su-15 appeared for the first time in documents in the second quarter of 1960 when Sukhoi proposed an Su-15-40 interception system featuring Su-15 aircraft, Vikhr-P

'Flagon' radar

Radars for the Su-15 were developed by two groups of designers, both employed at OKB-339 in Moscow (now NIIR-Phazotron). Gedaliy Kunyavskiy designed a 'bird' series – the Sokol (falcon), Oryol (eagle) and Korshun (vulture) – whereas Fyodor Volkov produced a 'wind' series – the Smerch (whirlwind), Vikhr (gale), Taifun (typhoon) and Tsiklon (cyclone). Still other designs were prepared by different teams: the TsD-30T radar for the Su-9 and MiG-21 came from design bureau KB-1 of Nikolay Nenartovich; the Almaz (diamond) radar used by the first Su-9 proto-types belonged to a series of 'jewels' designed by Viktor Tikhomirov of OKB-15; and a Pantera (panther) system designed by Andrey Slepushkin of OKB-339 was installed in the intercept fighter P-1.

Oryol-D58 (RP-15, *izdeliye* 303D-58; NATO 'Skip Spin'): The Oryol radar installed in Su-11 fighters was developed from the Sokol radar used in Yak-25 and Yak-27 'Flashlight' aircraft from 1954. Oryol-D58 (*dorabotannyi*, improved for T-58 aircraft, or Oryol-2), seen in the first Su-15, differed from Oryol mainly by having a larger antenna (950 mm/37.4 in diameter), which was possible because of the side air intakes. This antenna increased the detection range of a Tu-16 bomber-type target from 29 km (18 miles) to 40 km (25 miles). Oryol-D radar had a single parabolic antenna driven by a hydraulic system, combining functions of target detection and tracking (unlike such radars as the Izumrud (emerald) and Almaz which had two separate antennas). Series production of Oryol-D radar was undertaken in Factory No. 463 at Ryazan.
Oryol-D58M (RP-15M, *izdeliye* 303D-58M; NATO 'Skip Spin'): Oryol-D58M had better resistance to jamming than its predecessor.
Korshun-58: This radar, successively developed from Oryol, was intended for the

Su-15U designed in 1967 as a 'rival' to the Su-15T with Taifun radar. Korshun-58 was undergoing laboratory tests when its development was halted at the end of 1967.
Taifun (*izdeliye* 250): This reduced-size version of the Smerch-A radar in the MiG-25P intercept fighter was adapted to the size and electric system of the Su-15. Taifun, installed in about 10 Su-15T aircraft, was later replaced by the Taifun-M version.
Taifun-M (RP-26, N004, *izdeliye* 250M; NATO 'Twin Scan'): This improved version of Taifun was installed in the most advanced and most popular 'Flagon' version, the Su-15TM. Taifun-M brought to an end the first generation of Russian fighter radars – those made with electronic valves and using a pulse-type mode in which the signal was processed as a function of time.
Tsiklon: The Tsiklon radar, designed by Fyodor Volkov as a developed version of Taifun, was not implemented because of the cessation of Su-15 production.

Above left: The Oryol-D radar of the Su-15 represented a considerable advance for the Soviet avionics industry, as it employed a single parabolic antenna instead of separate detection/tracking modules.

The cockpit of the Su-15 (above) was dominated by the hooded display for the radar (left).

Maximum ranges of Taifun-M radar

	Bomber-sized target	Fighter-sized target
Search range at high altitude	60-70 km (37-44 miles)	45-55 km (28-34 miles)
Tracking range at high altitude	40-45 km (25-28 miles)	35-45 km (22-28 miles)
Search range at low altitude	10-12 km (6-7.5 miles)	6-10 km (3.8-6 miles)
Tracking range at low altitude	7-10 km (4-6 miles)	5-10 km (3-6 miles)

radar and K-40 missiles. The resolution on building the Su-15 (T-58) was not passed until 5 February 1962, by which time the first proto-types of the aircraft were already under construction. This resolution, however, changed the interception system's composition and required the Su-15 to be a modernised version of the existing Su-11, cured of its imperfections. The resolution was based on the report of a state commission which incorporated the results of state acceptance tests of the Su-11 (T-47) that indicated worse performance and flight handling than the Su-9, and recommended modification. According to the resolution, the 'first stage' Su-15 was to be equipped with an only slightly modernised armament

system of the Su-11, comprising Oryol-D58 radar (D for *dorabotannyi* = improved, for T-58 aircraft) and K-8M1 missiles. The new Smerch-AS radar and K-8M2 missiles were slated for the 'second stage'.

Pavel Sukhoi had an important reason for wanting the Su-15 to be largely a modernisation of the Su-11: he cared deeply about keeping his place in the work schedule at the Novosibirsk factory. In the USSR, production of a good aircraft sometimes was not launched because of a lack of a free assembly plant. Such a situation had happened to Sukhoi during World War II, when his *shturmovik* Su-6 – which was superior to the Il-2 – was not successful because all the factories were already occupied with other

production. There was often strong competition between general designers (design bureau leaders) for the access to production plants.

Sukhoi failed this time, too. Another general designer, Aleksandr Yakovlev, used the Su-11's imperfections to have it removed from the production line at Novosibirsk in favour of his Yak-28P 'Firebar'. The latter interceptor used the same weapons system as the Su-15, including Oryol radar and K-8M1 missiles, and the same R-11F2-300 turbojets. Test flights began in July 1962, even later than Su-15 tests. The total number of Yak-28Ps built in Novosibirsk from 1962 to 1967 amounted to 443 aircraft.

Sukhoi could only 'crowd' into the Novosibirsk factory if his Su-15 proved much better than its Yakovlev rival. It was clearly superior to the Yak-28P as far as parameters essential for intercept were concerned: the Su-15's maximum speed was 2230 km/h (1,385 mph) (compared to 1840 km/h; 1,143 mph for the Yak-28P), and service ceiling was 18500 m (60,695 ft) (16000 m/52,493 ft for the Yak-28P); on the other hand, the Su-15's range was only 55-60 per cent of the Yak-28P's. The Su-15 featured a compact arrangement of the two engines in the fuselage, whereas the Yak-28 had its engines installed in underwing nacelles. Seeing that the performance and flight

Designed as a pure interceptor, the Su-15 gained a measure of close combat capability through the addition of R-60 missiles and, as here, two 23-mm cannon pods carried under the belly. The pods were self-contained and aimed by a simple collimator sight

Above: Developed in an era when high-altitude supersonic bombers were the primary foe, the Su-15 fared badly when the quarry moved to low level. The radar could not discriminate targets from ground clutter.

Left: An Su-15UM 'Flagon-G' lands at a PVO base – note the raised periscope for the instructor in the rear cockpit. Later Su-15s switched to a cruciform brake chute instead of the earlier circular design. The Su-27, seen here in the background, was the principal replacement for the 'Flagon'.

handling of his Yak-28P was not as good as the new Su-15, in 1964 Yakovlev hurriedly prepared a new Yak-28-64 with an aerodynamic configuration similar to that of his opponent. The new aircraft was tested in flight, but without success, because the lateral adjustable air intakes designed by Yakovlev's OKB-115 could not compete with those developed by Sukhoi after almost 10 years of experience.

State acceptance tests of the T-58-8M1 interception complex began in August 1963. It included T-58D aircraft with Oryol-D58 radar and K-8M1 (later K-8M2) missiles in semi-active radar and passive infra-red versions. The commander of the air forces of Air Defence, Marshall Yevgeniy Savitskiy, took part in the tests and made a few familiarisation flights. The aircraft appealed to him and, mainly due to his efforts, the interception complex was officially commissioned on 3 April 1965, a year before the start of series production. Upon commissioning, the interception complex T-58-8M2 was officially redesignated Su-15-98, the T-58D aircraft – Su-15, the Oryol-D58 radar – RP-15 (RP, *radio pritsel* = radio sight) and the K-8M2 missile – R-98 (such dualisms exist for all Soviet air-to-air missiles: a name with 'K' is a designation of the design bureau, whereas 'R' is the designation of the Air Force). The military operational tests were undertaken from September 1967 to July 1969 with 10 series aircraft by the 611th IAP (Istrebitelnyi Aviatsionnyi Polk = Fighter Air Regiment) of the Air Defence Troops at Dorokhovo.

The superiority of the Su-15 was obvious, and so was the decision of the armed forces: the production line was cleared of Yak-28Ps and switched again to manufacturing Sukhoi intercept fighters. Nevertheless, the entanglement with the Yak-28P delayed production of

the Su-15 by several years. The first pre-series Su-15 took off at Novosibirsk on 6 March 1966.

Production of Sukhoi delta-wing interceptors

Su-9 'Fishpot-B'	888	Novosibirsk	1957-1962
	126	Moscow	1959-1961
Su-9U 'Maiden'	50	Moscow	1961-1962
Su-11 'Fishpot-C'	112	Novosibirsk	1962-1963
Su-15 'Flagon'	1,290	Novosibirsk	1966-1979

In 1967 Su-15 aircraft entered service with the Soviet Air Defence Troops (PVO, Protivo-Vozdushnaya Oborona) and gradually replaced Su-9s and Su-11s, as well as Yak-25Ms and Yak-28Ps. The first Su-15 landed at the 148th PVO Pilot Combat Training Centre at Savasleyka (150 km/93 miles southeast of Gorky, Nizhniy Novgorod). The first operational unit equipped with Su-15s was the 611th Fighter Regiment of the Air Defence Forces at Dorokhovo, 70 km (43 miles) west of Moscow. Ten series aircraft from Dorokhovo made a flypast over Domodedovo on 9 July 1967: nine were in a group formation and the 10th, painted black with yellow side number 47, flew alone, taking the place of a T-6-1 prototype damaged a few days earlier.

The Su-15 was used only by Soviet (CIS) Air Defence and did not serve with the Air Force (VVS, Voyenno-Vozdushniye Sily). It was never exported. The only known instance of foreign service of the Su-15 was a small group used for the air defence of Egypt in the early 1970s (with Soviet crews only). Series production came to an end in 1979 after 1,290 aircraft of all versions had been produced.

Pilots liked the aircraft for its safety, resulting from the use of two engines and an automatic landing approach system, and also for its light, agreeable handling. Statistical data regarding the first 10 years of Su-15 service were

published by the monthly review of Russian air forces *Aviatsiya i Kosmonavtika*, issue 5-6 of 1992. The aircraft spent 547,055 hours in the air from 1967 to 1976 (in the peak year, 1976, the flying time was 98,700 hours). Some 37 aircraft were lost during this time, giving a loss index of 6.76 per 100,000 hours, although the failure rate was very high and amounted to 45 during the first dozen or so months of service (a figure which is typical for all aircraft). During the whole of Su-15 service, until 1992, the loss index amounted to 6.2 (this may be compared with about 10 for the MiG-25, 11.5 for the MiG-31, 6 for the Boeing F-15 and 10 for the Lockheed Martin F-16).

Su-15 operational procedures

The tactics of the Su-15 were typical of Soviet intercept fighters of that time, all of which operated within the Vozdukh-1 (air) ground-controlled intercept (GCI) system. After ground-based early warning radars detected an aerial target, the computers calculated the optimum flight trajectory for the interceptor so that it took up an appropriate position with respect to the target. In the manual mode of operation, the generated commands were transmitted by voice to the intercept fighter by the ground-based operator. In semi-automatic mode (typical), commands were transmitted to the aircraft via coded datalink, received by the onboard Lazur-S (azure) system, decoded and transmitted to the pilot in the form of messages on the instrument panel (additional pointers on course, speed and altitude indicators showed values computed by the ground-based system). The pilot just had to match the flight parameters to the system's indications. Additional single messages were also transmitted, such as "afterburner on", "radar on", etc. In such a way, the pilot was guided until the target was engaged by the onboard radar, and then he took the initiative (possibly with hints from the ground).

Su-15 'Flagon-D': Most Su-15s were delivered in natural metal, as was usual with interceptors assigned to the Aviatsiya PVO (air defence organisation). However, a few were given camouflage, including this Su-15 which was painted in brown, green and dark green, with grey-blue undersides.

The Su-15TM 'Flagon-E/F' could operate not only in manual and semi-automatic mode, but also in fully automatic mode (with the modernised Vozdukh-1M GCI system). With the SAU-58 (*sistema avtomaticheskogo upravleniya* = automatic control system) of the Su-15TM, commands from a ground-based control station could be transmitted directly to the aircraft's controls without any intervention by the pilot, including the target indication commands for the Taifun-M (typhoon) onboard radar. The automatic system undertook interceptor guidance to the target, exit from the attack after launching the missiles, return to base and landing approach to an altitude of 50-60 m (164-197 ft). It may be said – with only a little exaggeration – that an Su-15TM's pilot was needed only for take-off and landing manoeuvres. The SAU-58 system was developed by the OKB-118 of Oleg Uspenskiy (now Avionika).

This operational organisation was the optimum solution for intercepting aircraft operating within Soviet territory, particularly during combat against a single bomber or reconnaissance aircraft. The tactics made full use of the fact that the intercept fighter operated over friendly territory and extended its 'field of view' considerably over the range of the onboard radar.

Su-15 production came to an abrupt end in 1975 due to the introduction of transistors, and for several years until 1979 only Su-15UM trainers were made. The Taifun-M radar of the Su-15TM concluded the first generation of Russian fighter radars, which employed electron valves. In the early 1970s a new radar, Sapfir-23 (sapphire), designed by Gedaliy Kunyavskiy and later by Victor Grishin, entered service with the MiG-23 'Flogger'. It was the first Soviet fighter radar to be made with transistors and was capable – thanks to the Doppler effect – of distinguishing targets against the ground flying at low altitude, which was impossible for the Su-15TM. Sukhoi attempted to solve this problem by upgrading the SAU-58

Air-to-air missiles

Basic armament of the Su-15 consisted of two air-to-air missiles of the K-8 (AA-3 'Anab') family, intended for destroying heavy (bomber) aircraft and carried on underwing PU-1-8 launchers (later PU-2-8), each 3.125 m (10.25 ft) from the aircraft centre line. Design work on the medium-range K-8 missile ('medium' by the standards of the time; the range was 7-8 km/4.3-4.9 miles) began at Matus Bisnovat's OKB-4 on 30 December 1954. Work on rival missiles began the same day at Pyotr Grishin's OKB-2 (the K-6 missile) and at Ivan Toropov's OKB-134 (the K-7 missile). The first K-8 was launched initially on 29 December 1956. This missile was the only success of the three ordered, and work on the K-6 and K-7 stopped in June 1958.

R-8M (K-8M, *izdeliye* 24M): The first version of the missile to enter series production was the improved K-8M. In 1958 the first batch of 92 missiles left Factory No. 455 at Kaliningrad near Moscow. In 1960-1961 three other factories joined the Kaliningrad factory, including No. 485 at Kiev (now Artem, it was the main manufacturer of the K-8 family with a

R-60 (AA-8 'Aphid') on inboard pylon

R-98MR semi-active radar homing missile

R-98MT infra-red homing missile

Swedish fighters intercepted this Su-15TM low over the Baltic. The R-60 was added to the 'Flagon' to give it dogfight capability. The AA-3 visible is an R-98MT IR-guided version.

production rate of about 500 missiles per year), No. 575 at Kovrov and No. 622 in Izhevsk. Upon official commissioning of the K-8M missile on 12 January 1962 (together with the Su-11-8M interception system), it was redesignated R-8M. Two versions of this missile were in use: the semi-active radar R-8MR and infra-red R-8MT. The missile's weight was 275 kg (606 lb) including 40 kg (88 lb) of high-explosive warhead, its diameter was 275 mm (10.83 in), its length was 4.0 m (13 ft) (R-8MR) and its wingspan was 1.3 m (4.27 ft). The R-8MR could attack air targets at distances of 2-12 km (1.2-7.5 miles).
R-8M1 (K-8M1, *izdeliye* 24M1): The most important improvement to the R-8M1R missiles manufactured after 1963 was their ability to attack targets flying 300 m (984 ft) above ground level rather than at least 5000 m (16,404 ft), as was the case for the R-8M (the minimum altitude for the IR-homing version remained 5000 m). Resistance to passive jamming was improved and the firing distance range was slightly increased, from a minimum 1.8 km (1.1 miles) to a maximum 14 km (8.69 miles).
R-98 (K-8M2): The missile was manufactured from 1965 to 1973 as radar version R-98R (*izdeliye* 54) and infra-red version R-98T (*izdeliye* 55). The missile weighed 292 kg (644 lb), including a 40-kg (88-lb) warhead, and had a length of 3.93 m (12.89 ft) (R-98R). Missile parameters when launched from the tail-on position remained unchanged (minimum distance 1.8 km/1.1 miles, maximum 14 km/ 8.69 miles), but the R-98R was the first Soviet air-to-air missile that could also be launched from the head-on position (minimum distance 4 km/2.5 miles, maximum 18 km/11 miles).
R-98M (K-98M, K-8M3): In 1973, the R-98 missile was replaced on production lines by the R-98M which featured improved resistance to jamming and an increased launch zone (particularly for the infra-red version). As with all previous versions, the R-98M was made with a semi-active radar seeker (R-98MR, *izdeliye* 56) or an infra-red seeker (R-98MT, *izdeliye* 57). The semi-active radar R-98MR missile, when launched tail-on, could attack targets flying at 500 to 1600 km/h (310 to 994 mph) at altitudes of 300 to 24000 m (984 to 78,740 ft), at a distance up to 18 km (11 miles). When launched head-on, it could attack

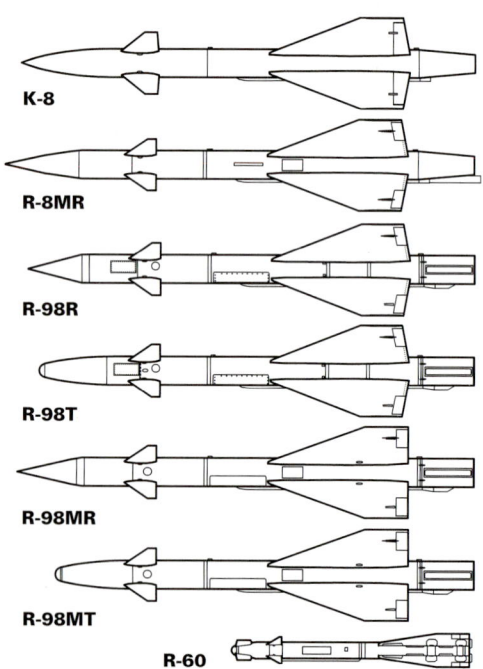

K-8
R-8MR
R-98R
R-98T
R-98MR
R-98MT
R-60

targets flying at 500 to 2500 km/h (310 to 1,553 mph) at altitudes of 5000 to 21000 m (16,404 to 68,897 ft), at distances up to 24 km (15 miles). The minimum altitude of a target for the R-98MT infra-red missile was 2000 m (6,561 ft).
UR-8M (UK-8M): The UR-8M training variant was manufactured from 1966.
R-60 (K-60, *izdeliye* 62; NATO AA-8 'Aphid'): In 1973/74, Su-15s were fitted with two small PD-62 pylons some 1.65 m (5.41 ft) from the aircraft centre line for underwing carriage of R-60 close-air combat missiles. The IR-guided R-60 AAM developed by the design team Molniya (lightning; formerly OKB-4) is the world's smallest air-to-air missile. Its weight is only 43.5 kg (95.9 lb) including a 3.5-kg (7.7-lb) warhead, its length is 2.095 m (6.873 ft) and body diameter is 120 mm (4.7 in). The R-60 has a maximum range of 7.5 km (5.7 miles) and a minimum firing distance of 300 m (984 ft).

Left: Of all the Western air arms, Sweden's Flygvapen became the best acquainted with the Su-15. Several intercepts were made of camouflaged aircraft, like this Su-15TM.

Su-15TM 'Flagon-F': *Another camouflaged 'Flagon', this Su-15TM has a four-tone upper surface camouflage with grey-blue undersides. The aircraft served with an Aviatsiya PVO unit at Bezrechnaya air base in the Trans-Baikal Military District.*

flight control system to -58-2 standard, enabling very low-level flight, but this move was unsuccessful. Moreover, the MiG-23ML 'Flogger-G', that entered production in 1976, had much better performance and manoeuvring than the Su-15TM.

In order to create the MiG-23P (*perekhvatchik* = interceptor) dedicated version for Air Defence, it was necessary to install in the MiG-23ML equipment that could co-operate with the Vozdukh-1M GCI system and to adapt the SAU-23 control system to the needs of remote homing. Thus, the development of the Su-15 came to end.

Early Su-15s and Su-15UTs began to be withdrawn from service in the early 1980s – the same time that the new intercept fighters MiG-31 'Foxhound' and Su-27 'Flanker' entered production -- and had disappeared before the end of the decade. The newer Su-15TMs and Su-15UMs did not die of natural causes: they were abruptly scrapped in the early 1990s even though their service lives had not expired.

As a result of the CFE treaty signed on 19 November 1990 in Paris, the Soviet Union had to reduce the number of its combat aircraft in Europe to 5,150, i.e., 1,461 aircraft had to be withdrawn, comprising 733 from the VVS and 728 from the PVO. Of course, the oldest aircraft were chosen, including all Su-15s. According to official CFE data, in 1990 some 230 Su-15s were based in the European part of the Soviet Union and 90 more in the Asian part. Initially, four Su-15s were scrapped on 17 March 1993 at Samara air base in the presence of representatives from France, Germany, the UK, the US, the Netherlands and Italy. Soon, there were no more operational Su-15s in Russia. After the disintegration of the USSR, two Su-15 regiments

remained on Ukrainian territory and survived a little longer. Su-15s wearing Ukrainian tridents could be seen in the air until a few years ago.

In combat

Su-15s were key participants in some tragic incidents.

On 20 April 1978, a Boeing 707 of Korean Air Lines, flying from Paris to Canada, deviated from its route (as a matter of fact, it did not 'deviate', but turned back) and entered USSR territory near Murmansk. An Su-15TM piloted by Captain A. Bosov took off from the airfield of the 431st IAP of Air Defence in Afrikanda (located north of the Arctic Circle) and made his way towards the airliner, followed by another Su-15 piloted by Captain Gromov; another pair of fighters was sent to patrol the border with Finland. Alert aircraft were then launched from three other regiments in this region (the air defence of the Kola Peninsula is very strong because it houses the naval bases of the Northern Fleet where ballistic missile submarines are stationed). Bosov approached the Boeing signalling "Follow me", but the airliner did not take notice.

Su-15 units in European part of Soviet Union, 1990		
Unit	**Location**	**Number of aircraft**
62nd IAP	Belbek, Ukraine	31
153rd IAP	Morshansk, Russia	4
	Regiment re-equipped with MiG-31s	
166th IAP	Sandar, Georgia	41
	Regiment moved to Russia and dissolved	
265th IAP	Poduzhemye, Russia	38
431st IAP	Afrikanda, Russia	39
	Regiment re-equipped with Su-27s	
611th IAP	Dorokhovo, Russia	38
	Regiment re-equipped with Su-27s	
636th IAP	Kramatorsk, Ukraine	39

The fighter pilot was then ordered to shoot down the intruder, although fully aware of it being a passenger aircraft. At 21:42, Bosov fired an R-60 missile at the airliner (it was too close for him to use an R-98 missile). The missile destroyed the left outer engine and 4 m (13 ft) of the wingtip. Bosov was then ordered to return, while Captain Gromov assumed observation of the airliner, which reduced its altitude from 9000 to 2000 m (29,527 to 6,562 ft) and continued its flight. This time, the Korean pilot answered the signals and followed the Su-15TM to Afrikanda airfield. Gromov was ordered to return and the airliner was taken over by two more Su-15TMs belonging to the 265th IAP at Poduzhemye. The damaged Boeing 707 could not reach Poduzhemye and landed on frozen Lake Korpiyarvi, 30 km (18 miles) from the border with Finland. Among 110 passengers and crew members, two had been killed.

On 18 July 1981 over Georgia, Captain Valentin Kuliapin in an Su-15TM belonging to the 166th IAP at Sandar intercepted an Argentinian Canadair CL-44 transport flying from Iran. Kuliapin rammed the target and both the aircraft crashed, but Kuliapin ejected and survived.

On the night of 31 August/1 September 1983, a Boeing 747-200 of Korean Air Lines (flight KAL-007) en route from Canada to Korea strayed from its route by several hundred kilometres and entered Soviet airspace, where it remained for some 2.5 hours. The airliner was shot down with two R-98 missiles by an Su-15TM piloted by Major Gennadiy Osipovich, in circumstances which are still the subject of debate. All 269 passengers and crew of the 747 were killed.

Su-15s often shot down reconnaissance balloons entering the USSR from the west. The last known case took place on 2 September 1990, when Captain I. Zdatchenko piloting an Su-15TM downed a balloon at 12000 m (39,370 ft) over the Kola Peninsula.

Piotr Butowski

Left: The Su-15 was designed for speed and altitude, and it was not noted for its manoeuvrability. However, during Baltic encounters 'Flagons' occasionally turned aggressively with their Western counterparts. The four-petal airbrake was useful during intercepts of slow-moving aircraft.

Su-15TM 'Flagon-F': *'Red 17' is the most infamous of 'Flagons', for it was the aircraft used by Major Gennadiy Osipovich to shoot down the Korean Air Lines Boeing 747. The Su-15 was launched from its PVO base at Sakhalin in the Far East Military District.*

Su-15 Technical description

The Su-15 is an all-metal mid-wing monoplane of classic layout with delta-shaped wing. The structure is made of D16, D19 and V95 aluminium alloys, with 30KhGSA and 30KhGSNA high alloy steels used for heavily loaded parts.

The **fuselage**, of semi-monocoque structure, is in two parts: front (to frame No. 34) and rear (the last 11 frames). Fuselage length is 19.145 m (62.81 ft) and maximum width is 2.724 m (8.937 ft). The front portion of the fuselage contains the radar, front landing gear compartment, pilot's cockpit (the movable part of the cockpit canopy travels aft) and fuel tanks. The lateral air intakes are adjustable via the UVD-58M system. The rear fuselage contains two engines arranged side-by-side, and four aerodynamic brakes deflected by 50° are installed.

The KS-4 **ejection seat** of Sukhoi's own design (KS stands for *kreslo* Sukhovo = Sukhoi's seat) enables safe ejection of the pilot in flight up to 20000 m (65,617 ft) altitude at an instrument speed up to 1200 km/h (745 mph), as well as ejection from ground level at speeds of at least 140 km/h (87 mph). Prior to ejection, the cockpit canopy is released by means of an explosive charge.

The **wings** have a delta shape, span of 8.616 m (28.268 ft), surface area of 34.56 m² (372 sq ft), sweep angle of 60° along the leading edge, angle of incidence 0° and anhedral of -2°. From the 11th production series, the wing had an attachment at the end (beyond the aerodynamic fence, some 2.625 m/8.612 ft from the aircraft's centre line) that reduced the angle of sweep to 45° and increased the span to 9.34 m (30.64 ft) and the surface area to 36.6 m² (394 sq ft). Aerodynamic twist was introduced by lowering the profile nose by 7°. Incidence and anhedral remained unchanged. Ailerons and externally blown flaps were installed at the trailing edge; the former deflected vertically by 18°, and the flaps extended by 20° (or by 45° with the UPS system). Inside the wings are fuel tanks, compartments for the main landing gear, PRF-4 landing floodlights, and radio aerials, for example for the SRZO-2 IFF system.

The **tailplane** is all-moving with a sweep angle of 55° at quarter chord, anhedral of -6° and 6 per cent thickness. Tailplane span is 5.464 m (17.926 ft) and deflection is +8°/-20°.

The classic **tailfin** with rudder is fastened to fuselage frames 35 and 43. A dielectric housing for the radio set aerial is installed in the upper part of the tailfin and the braking parachute container is enclosed in the tailfin root. The rudder is mass balanced. The tailfin sweep angle is 55° at quarter chord, thickness is 7 per cent and rudder deflection is 25° each side.

The **landing gear** is of tricycle type. The front leg, retractable into the fuselage, has a single KT81/3 self-adjusting 600 x 155-mm (23.62 x 6.1-in) wheel (later a KT-51 wheel, 660 x 200 mm/25.98 x 7.87 in). The Su-15TM version has twin controllable non-braked KN-9 front wheels, measuring 620 x 180 mm (24.41 x 7.09 in). The main undercarriage has single KT117 braking wheels, 880 x 230 mm (34.65 x 9.05 in), which retract toward the fuselage into compartments inside the wing. A braking parachute container with a surface area of 25 m² (269 sq ft) is installed in the tailfin root. The wheelbase is 4.79 m (15.7 ft) and the track of the mainwheels is 5.94 m (19.49 ft).

Above: The Su-15 is powered by two of the engines which are installed in the MiG-21. The Su-15TM had the more powerful R-13 engines, which improved performance at all levels.

Below: The tall nosewheel was introduced following trials with the T-58L. It reduced the danger of debris entering the intakes, and improved takeoff performance by increasing wing incidence.

The **flight control system** is of the mechanical type with BU-49 non-return hydraulic servo units for the control of ailerons, elevator and rudder. The Su-15TM has more powerful BU-220 and BU-250 servos.

The aircraft has four independent **hydraulic systems** with a working pressure of 210-215 kg/cm² (2,986-3,058 PSI) and AMG-10 hydraulic fluid. Two of these systems are used for the port and starboard control system servo units, and the two remaining ones for the retractable landing gear, flaps, aerodynamic brakes, air intake adjustment, radar antennas, etc. The Su-15TM has only three hydraulic systems because the antenna of the Taifun radar is driven by an electric motor rather than hydraulics.

The aircraft has three independent **pneumatic systems** with a working pressure of 200 kg/cm² (2,844 PSI), used for braking the wheels as well as for emergency lowering of landing gear and flaps. AC voltages of 27V DC and 115V/400Hz are used for the electric power system.

The pilot cockpit and avionics compartment are **air conditioned** to provide constant pressure and temperature. There are also ventilation systems for the cockpit and pilot suit, as well as a device preventing condensation inside the canopy.

The **powerplant** consists of two R-11F2S-300 (*izdeliye* 37F2) or later R-11F2SU-300 turbojet engines with maximum dry thrust of 38.25 kN (8,595 lb) and maximum thrust with afterburning of 60.79 kN (13,661 lb). The Su-15TM was equipped with two R-13F-300 (*izdeliye* 95) engines with maximum dry thrust increased to 40.2 kN (9,034 lb) and maximum thrust with afterburning to 64.71 kN (14,542 lb). The **fuel** is carried in three fuselage tanks and two wing tanks, giving a total internal volume of 6860 litres (1,509 Imp gal). Two additional tanks of 600 litres (132 Imp gal) each can be suspended under the fuselage for a maximum fuel volume of 8060 litres (1,773 Imp gal). T-1, TS-1, T-2 or RT type is standard jet fuel used by all Soviet aircraft.

Communication equipment encompasses an RSIU-5V (R-802V) UHF radio set. **Navigation equipment** includes an MRP-56P beacon receiver, RV-UM (later RV-4) radio altimeter, ARK-10 radio compass (its aerial enclosed in the cockpit canopy), KSI-5 course system and AGD-1 artificial horizon. Other **avionics** include the SOD-57M transponder, SRZO-2M Khrom-Nikel IFF unit and Sirena-2 RWR. The onboard component of the GCI system includes the ARL-S (Lazur-S) command datalink. The avionics of the Su-15TM were updated by installing an R-832M (Evkalipt-SM) radio instead of R-802V, RSBN-5S (later RSBN-6S Iskra-K) short-range navigation system, Sirena-3 (SPO-10) RWR, RV-5 radio altimeter and ARL-SM (Lazur-SM) datalink. The Su-15TM also has the SAU-58 automatic control system which, combined with the Vozdukh-1M ground-based homing system and Lazur datalink, enables fully automatic homing of the aircraft.

Su-15 'Flagon' production versions

	Su-15 'Flagon-A'	Su-15UT 'Flagon-C'	Su-15 'Flagon-D'	Su-15TM 'Flagon-F'	Su-15UM 'Flagon-G'
Engines	2 x R-11F2S-300	2 x R-11F2S-300	2 x R-11F2SU-300	2 x R-13-300	2 x R-13-300
Engine rating, dry	38.25 kN (8,595 lb)	38.25 kN (8,595 lb)	38.25 kN (8,595 lb)	40.20 kN (9,034 lb)	40.20 kN (9,034 lb)
afterburning	60.79 kN (13,661 lb)	60.79 kN (13,661 lb)	60.79 kN (13,661 lb)	64.71 kN (14,542 lb)	64.71 kN (14,542 lb)
Length overall	21.44 m (70.34 ft)		21.44 m (70.34 ft)		
Length excl. probe	20.54 m (67.39 ft)	20.99 m (68.86 ft)	20.54 m (67.39 ft)	19.56 m (64.17 ft)	19.56 m (64.17 ft)
Span	8.616 m (28.27 ft)	8.616 m (28.27 ft)	9.340 m (30.643 ft)	9.340 m (30.643 ft)	9.340 m (30.643 ft)
Height	5.00 m (16.40 ft)	5.00 m (16.40 ft)	5.00 m (16.40 ft)	4.843 m (15.889 ft)	4.843 m (15.889 ft)
Wing area	34.56 m² (372.01 sq ft)	34.56 m² (372.01 sq ft)	36.60 m² (393.97 sq ft)	36.60 m² (393.97 sq ft)	36.60 m² (393.97 sq ft)
Empty weight	10220 kg (22,531 lb)	10740 (kg (23,678 lb)	10350 kg (22,818 lb)	10874 kg (23,973 lb)	10635 kg (23,446 lb)
Internal fuel	5600 kg (12,345 lb)	5010 kg (11,045 lb)	5600 kg (12,345 lb)	5550 kg (12,236 lb)	5550 kg (12,236 lb)
Normal TOW*	16520 kg (36,420 lb)	16690 kg (36,795 lb)	16650 kg (36,707 lb)	17200 kg (37,920 lb)	17200 kg (37,920 lb)
Maximum TOW	17350 kg (38,250 lb)	17200 kg (37,920 lb)		17900 kg (39,463 lb)	17900 kg (39,463 lb)
Max. speed at altitude	2230 km/h (1,386 mph)	1850 km/h (1,150 mph)	2230 km/h (1,386 mph)	2230 km/h (1,386 mph)	1875 km/h (1,165 mph)
Max. speed at sea level	1200 km/h (745 mph)	1200 km/h (745 mph)	1200 km/h (745 mph)	1300 km/h (808 mph)	1250 km/h (777 mph)
Maximum cruise speed	1550 km/h (963 mph)	1290 km/h (802 mph)		1700 km/h (1,056 mph)	1700 km/h (1,056 mph)
Service ceiling	18500 m (60,695 ft)	16700 m (54,790 ft)	18500 m (60,695 ft)	18100 m (59,383 ft) **	15500 m (50,853 ft)
Range w/o aux. tanks	1260 km (783 miles)		1305 km (810 miles)	1380 km (857 miles)	
Maximum range	1540 km (957 miles)	1700 km (1,056 miles)	1600 km (995 miles)	1780 km (1,106 miles)	1150 km (715 miles)
Intercept radius	560 km (348 miles)	–	560 km (348 miles)	590 km (367 miles)	–
Take-off speed	395 km/h			370 km/h	340-350 km/h
Approach speed	315-320 km/h (196-199 mph)	330-340 km/h (205-2111 mph)	285 km/h (177 mph)	285-290 km/h (177-180 mph)	260-280 km/h (162-174 mph)
Take-off distance	1150-1200 m (3,773-3,937 ft)	1200 m (3,937 ft)	1100-1150 m (3,609-3,773 ft)	1000-1100 m (3,281-3,609 ft)	1160 m (3,806 ft)
Landing distance	1000-1100 m (3,281-3,609 ft)	1150-1200 m (3,773-3,937 ft)		850-950 m (2,789-3,117 ft)	1120 m (3,675 ft)
g-limit, with missiles	5.0	5.0	5.0	5.0	5.0

* With two R-98/R-98M AAMs and without auxiliary tanks.
** Service ceiling of the early production Su-15TM 'Flagon-E' (with conical nose) was 18500 m (60,695 m)

Early development

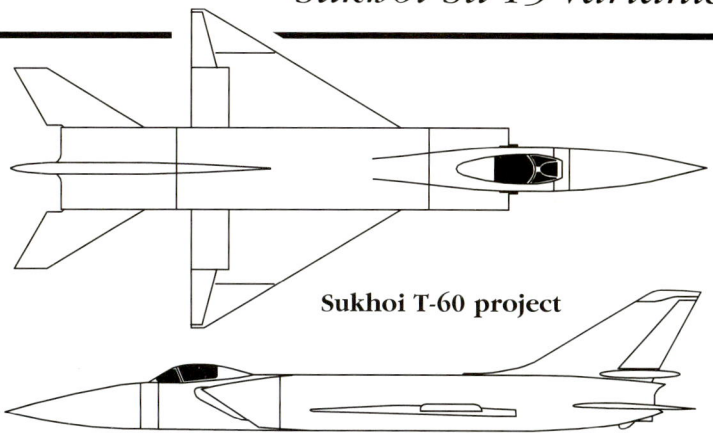

Sukhoi T-60 project

In the second quarter of 1960 Sukhoi began designing the Su-15-40 interception complex. The complex was to contain the following items:

■ Su-15 aircraft (design bureau designation T-58)
■ two K-40 missiles with radar seekers (later introduced on the MiG-25P and known as AA-6 'Acrid' to NATO)
■ Vikhr-P fire-control system with eponymous radar and an infra-red search-and-track device that worked with the K-40 missiles as well as with the aircraft's autopilot, providing automatic control when intercepting an air target. The Vikhr radar, designed by Fyodor Volkov, was to be a reduced version of the Smerch radar in the Tu-128 'Fiddler'
■ joint automatic control, navigation and instrument landing system.

The most important feature of the Su-15-40 system was its ability to attack air targets from any direction, not only from tail-on as in the case of the Su-9 (system Su-9-51) and Su-11 (system Su-11-8M). The range of the Vikhr radar was to be 40-50 km (25-31 miles) instead of the 30 km (18 miles) of the Su-11's Oryol radar, and maximum distance at which to launch a missile was to be 25 km (15 miles) instead of 10-12 km (6-7.5 miles). Being able to launch a missile from the head-on position, the intercept fighter did not need to lose time and distance in approaching

the enemy from behind. As a result, the Su-15-40 could attack targets located 600-700 km (373-435 miles) from its airfield (this distance for an Su-11 was 350 km/217 miles). More powerful radar and greater power let the Su-15-40 attack targets flying at altitudes of 25-26 km (15.5-16 miles) (with a single AL-7F2) or 27-29 km (16.7-18 miles) (with two R-21F-300 engines) and not at 22-23 km (13.7-14.3 miles), as in the case of the Su-11-8M.

Su-15 (T-58) project with single Lyul'ka AL-7F2 turbojet engine: The Su-15 aircraft for the Su-15-40 system was designed as a single-engined variant, having a Lyul'ka AL-7F2 turbojet rated at 99.02 kN (22,266 lb) thrust, the same as the Su-11. It differed from the Su-11 only in having two lateral air intakes in place of a single front intake. These were necessary because of the large Oryol radar, which created problems with adjusting the Su-11's front air intake. It was intended to make the Su-11's intake cone stationary and to have air bleed flaps at the intake sides that controlled the air inflow, but this caused frequent surging of the compressor. In project T-58, rectangular side air intakes were designed, drawing on experience with the experimental P-1 and T-49.

Performance aspects of the Su-15 (T-58) with a single AL-7F2 engine were: maximum speed 2650 km/h (1,646 mph), service ceiling 19-20 km (11.8-12.4 miles) and maximum range 1900 km (1,180

miles). Five T-58 aircraft were to be made for testing (including the static tests). Construction of the prototype began in mid-1960 and by year's end was 31.1 per cent complete. The unfinished aircraft were later used for construction of T-58D prototypes.

Su-15 (T-58) project with two Metskhvarishvili R-21F-300 turbojet engines: At the end of 1960, Sukhoi designers were also working on the Su-15 (T-58) with two R-21F-300 engines of 70.59 kN (15,873 lb) thrust each. The design performances of this variant included a maximum speed of 2800 km/h (1,740 mph), ceiling of 22-23 km (13.67-14.29 miles) and maximum range of 2200 km (1,367 miles). The R-21F-300 turbojet engine developed by Nikolay Metskhvarishvili of OKB-500 was an

uprated modification of the Tumanskiy R-11F-300 engine used by the MiG-21.

T-59 project: A series of alternative intercept fighter configuration projects paralleled the T-58, but did not progress beyond a very early stage. The T-59 was conceived as a development of the high-speed T-37 with TsP radar (used also for Mikoyan's E-150 and E-152 interceptors) and K-9-51 missiles of Sukhoi design. The lateral air intakes were similar to those of the T-49, i.e., in the shape of ring sectors.

T-60 project: The T-60 project was very similar to the twin-engined T-58 with R21F-300 engines, but had oblique rectangular air intakes, similar to those later installed in the MiG-25. An original technical drawing of the T-60 project can be seen in the museum of the Moscow Institute of Aviation.

T-58D prototypes

T-58D-1: Prototypes of the single-engined T-58 variant were already under construction when a twin-engine approach was chosen. The rating of the AL-7F2 engine turned out to be insufficient for the heavier aircraft and there was no possibility of further development of the engine, plus it was expected that twin-engined aircraft would be more reliable and safer. The new R-21 engines were not yet ready so less powerful R-11F2S-300 turbojets (where S stands for Sukhoi), each rated at 60.79 kN (13,668 lb) with afterburning, were substituted, having already been tested in the experimental T-5. The first prototype adapted for two R-11s was designated T-58D-1 (D for *dvigateli* = engines).

When the two R-11F2S-300s were installed, the rear portion of the fuselage was replaced by a part from the T-5 aircraft. At the same time, the air intakes had to be increased to accommodate the greater airflow of two R-11 engines, resulting in an unnaturally slim 'waist'. This was not only aerodynamically

disadvantageous but also limited the capacity of the fuselage to carry fuel. This slim waist occasionally is explained as an application of the 'area rule', but this is not so. The aircraft design had many features in common with Su-9s and Su-11s: the same wing and empennage, cockpit canopy and main landing gear, as well as many elements of the aircraft systems. The prototype did not yet have radar, and its nose was shorter than subsequent aircraft.

The aircraft took off for its maiden flight on 30 May 1962 from the test airfield at Zhukovskiy with Vladimir Ilyushin at the controls. Minor changes introduced in the T-58D-1 during the tests included moving the braking parachute to a container installed at the tailfin root, increasing the tailfin area in order to improve the longitudinal stability, changing the landing gear wheels and lengthening the fuselage nose. Successive corrections were implemented on the aircraft during state acceptance tests in 1963-64, such as a new fuel system with capacity increased to 6860 litres (1,509 Imp gal) (after the slim waist was straightened), ailerons with

The third prototype exhibits the broadened central fuselage which allowed significantly increased fuel capacity in production aircraft.

deflection increased from 15° to 18° 30', and improved air intake control gear. Later, in January 1965, the T-58D-1 obtained new 'cranked' wings and, eventually, the aircraft was transformed into the T-58VD STOL flying testbed (see below).

T-58D-2: The next prototype, the T-58D-2 tested in flight on 4 May 1963 by Vladimir Ilyushin, was already equipped with Oryol-D58 radar and its nose was longer and broader than that of the first prototype. In June 1963, the T-58D-2 flew to NII VVS (Nauchno-Issledovatelskiy Institut Voenno-Vozdushnikh Sil = Scientific-Research Institute of the Air Force) in Akhtubinsk, where state acceptance tests ran until June 1964. The T-58D-2 prototype was later used for landing skid testing as the T-58L (see below). Since 22 January 1974 it has been in the Monino museum.

T-58D-3: The third prototype, T-58D-3, flew on 2 October 1963 and differed from its two predecessors in fuselage shape. The earlier prototypes had a broad rear fuselage connected to a narrow central part designed for a single engine. The fuselage lines of the T-58D-3 were straightened by adding an external layer of plating. The additional inner space was to be used for fuel tanks but, since the fuel system of the third prototype was still

almost unchanged, the fuel capacity was increased by only 180 litres (40 Imp gal). The inner structure of the fuselage was radically improved in series aircraft, increasing fuel tank capacity by one-third from 5120 to 6860 litres (1,126 to 1,509 Imp gal). Later, in 1965-1967, the T-58D-3 prototype was used for testing modernised Oryol-D58M radar and the SAU-58 flight control system for successive versions of the Su-15.

T-58D-2 introduced the long conical radome employed by all variants until the final Su-15TM production series.

Su-15 (T-58D, *izdeliye* 37) 'Flagon-A'

When it was commissioned into Air Force service in April 1965, the T-58D was officially designated Su-15. The first pre-series Su-15 (factory number 0015301, in which 00 stands for zero series, 153 is the code number of Novosibirsk factory and 01 is the aircraft number) was tested in flight by I. Sorokin at Novosibirsk on 6 March 1966. Full-scale manufacturing began in the second half of 1966 and continued until the end of 1970. At the Novosibirsk factory, the Su-15 was known as *izdeliye* 37.

Although the Su-15-98 interception complex was officially commissioned with K-8M2 (R-98) missiles, the aircraft initially operated with older R-8M1 missiles. Additional tests of the armament system

were carried out from 1965 to 1967 with the T-58D-3, and then series aircraft were

Sukhoi Su-15 (Series 6) 'Flagon-A'

equipped with modernised RP-15M (Oryol-D58M) radar featuring improved jamming resistance, as well as with R-98 missiles. A particularly prized advantage of the Su-15's armament system, when

compared with the Su-11's, was its increased ability to attack targets flying at low and medium altitude, and also from the head-on position.

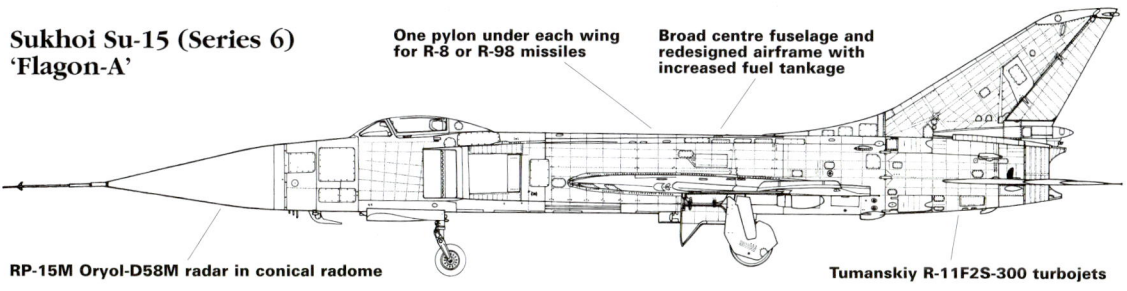

One pylon under each wing for R-8 or R-98 missiles

Broad centre fuselage and redesigned airframe with increased fuel tankage

RP-15M Oryol-D58M radar in conical radome

Tumanskiy R-11F2S-300 turbojets

Typical of early Su-15s is this 'Flagon-A' on display at the Khodinka museum. The delta wing was inherited from earlier Sukhoi interceptor designs.

A trio of Su-15s takes part in a flypast, each armed with one K-8 missile under each wing. Radar-guided missiles are carried to starboard, with IR-guided to port.

T-58M/T-58VD 'Flagon-B'/T-58R

T-58M: The Su-24 'Fencer' tactical bomber began life as the T-58M, a modification of the Su-15. The first project had an Su-15 wing and empennage, and the fuselage was altered extensively to fit four RD36-35 lift engines, having air intakes at the top and outlets at the bottom. This configuration of the propulsion system was tested with the T-58VD which follows.

T-58VD 'Flagon-B': In 1966 the T-58D-1 prototype was converted into the T-58VD

(*vertikalniye dvigateli* = vertical engines) testbed for use in the T-58M (Su-24) programme. Three small RD36-35 engines designed by Pyotr Kolesov's OKB-36 at Rybinsk were arranged vertically in tandem inside the fuselage, for use in short take-off and landing. The first flight of the T-58VD occurred on 6 June 1966 with Yevgeniy Solovyov at the controls. Tests were completed in June 1967. The take-off speed of the T-58VD aircraft was reduced from 390 to 290 km/h (242 to 180 mph)

and the touch-down speed from 315 to 240 km/h (196 to 149 mph). Take-off and landing distances were 500-600 m (1,640-1,968 ft), which was half that of series Su-15s. At the same time, problems with the aircraft's stability meant that the rear vertical engine had to be switched off during the landing approach. Additional engines inside the fuselage occupied the place of fuel tanks, reducing range to an unacceptable level.

T-58D take-offs and landings were shown to the public by Yevgeniy Solovyov on 9 July 1967 during the air show at Domodedovo airport near Moscow. Upon completion of its tests, the T-58VD landed at the Moscow Institute of Aviation, where it was kept for many years as a teaching aid. Later, when the Su-27 began its

teaching service, the old T-58VD was scrapped.

T-58R: The experimental T-58R, which first flew in May 1972, was a derivative of the series Su-15 with Relyef (relief) terrain-following radar installed under a dielectric nose cover in place of fighter radar. Relyef was destined for the Su-24 'Fencer'.

The T-58VD's three RD36 lift engines were aspirated through intakes in the aircraft's spine, which were covered by doors. The T-58VD (originally the first prototype) had earlier tested the cranked wings.

This view of the T-58VD landing shows the three lift engine exhausts in the lower fuselage. The installation dramatically decreased field length and approach speed, even though only two of the three engines could be used for landing.

Su-15 flying testbeds

T-58L: Under a recommendation of a state committee, an adaptation of the Su-15 with an allowed tyre pressure of more than 8 kg/cm² (113.48 PSI) (which was the norm in the USSR at the time) was prepared for use from unpaved airfields. In 1965 a lubricated skid landing gear was installed on the T-58D-2, and in this form the aircraft was designated T-58L (*lyzhnyi* = skid). In order to make the take-off run shorter and to protect the air intakes from dust, the front undercarriage leg was made steerable and was extended by 35 cm (13.78 in). The aircraft took off for the first time on 6 September 1965 piloted by Vladimir Ilyushin, and then continued tests on various runway surfaces until 1973. The landing skids eventually were abandoned, but the longer front leg entered series production from 1969's Su-15T. The T-58L (T-58D-2) is displayed in the Monino museum with wheel-type landing gear.

LLSu-15: An aircraft with side number 16 was used by the Flight Research Institute at Zhukovskiy for testing all Soviet chaff and flare dispensers for the self-defence of aircraft of various classes. It was later used for testing various electronic warfare devices. In 1981-82, the LLSu-15 tested changeable inflight stability and steerability, and a side control stick in the pilot's cockpit.

Su-15 inflight refuelling: The first pre-series aircraft (c/n 0015301) was used in 1974 for testing an inflight refuelling system for tactical aircraft within the

An early-series Su-15TM was used as the receiver during refuelling trials for the Su-24's UPAZ pod (carried by an early Su-15). The bolt-on refuelling probe was not adopted for service.

Sakhalin-6A programme carried out for the Su-24 (T-6). A unified refuelling UPAZ pod was suspended under the fuselage of c/n 0015301 and Su-15TM c/n 0215306 was equipped with a fixed refuelling probe on the right-hand side of the nose. After intensive testing, the Sakhalin system is now commonly employed by Russian air force aircraft (although was not used by the Su-15).

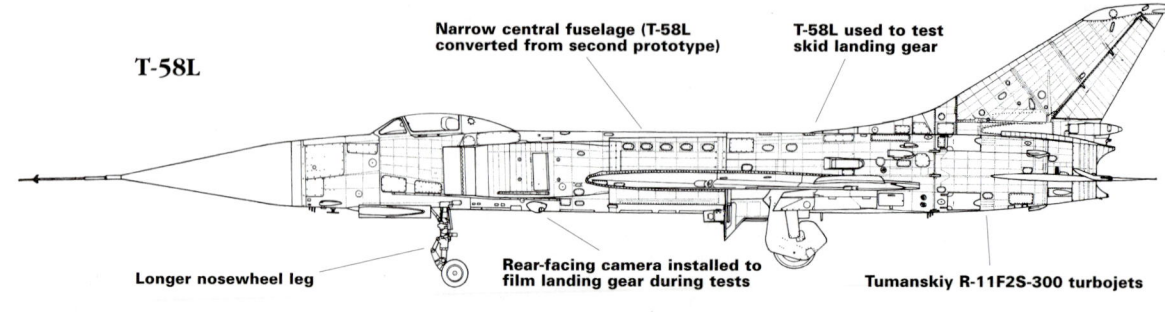

T-58L

Narrow central fuselage (T-58L converted from second prototype)

T-58L used to test skid landing gear

Longer nosewheel leg

Rear-facing camera installed to film landing gear during tests

Tumanskiy R-11F2S-300 turbojets

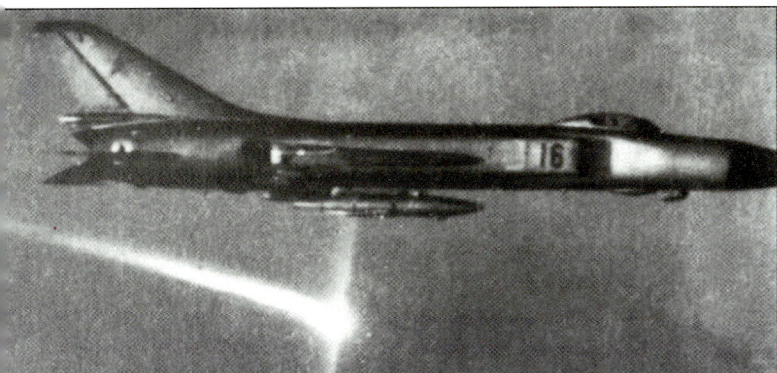

The LLSu-15 played an important part in the development of Soviet expendable countermeasures. Here it releases an infra-red decoy flare.

Having been used for EW equipment trials, the LLSu-15 was given a variable-stability flight control system, for which a sidestick controller was added.

Su-15UT (U-58T, *izdeliye* 42) 'Flagon-C'

Design work on a two-seat training version began in 1965, just after the decision was made to begin series production of Su-15 single-seat combat aircraft. In October 1965 the air force committee approved a mock-up front part of a U-58 fuselage, which differed from combat Su-15s only by having a two-seat cockpit. It was stressed that the armament system – including radar and missiles – was to be the same. The U-58 prototype was to be built in the second quarter of 1967, but disputes connected with the choice of radar delayed the construction work. As in the single-seat version, there was competition between the Korshun-58 and the Taifun

radars. The original project U-58 was designed with the Korshun-58 but, in the event, the 1967 decision was in favour of the Taifun. At this stage the project was divided into two versions: a simple U-58T without radar and a 'full' U-58B with radar.

To hasten the introduction of the two-seat trainer, it was decided to make a simple variant – U-58T (*trenirovochnyi* = training) – without radar and with a reduced avionics set. Yevgeniy Kukushev flew the prototype for the first time on 26 August 1968. Upon completion of state acceptance tests on 3 July 1970, the aircraft, by decree of the Minister of Defence, entered the operational inventory

under the name of Su-15UT (*uchebno-trenirovochnyi*). Series production began in Novosibirsk in 1970 and continued until 1972, with the factory designation of *izdeliye* 42.

To accommodate an instructor cockpit, the fuselage was lengthened by 45 cm (17.7 in) and some avionics devices were removed, including radar, Lazur-M datalink and Sirena-2 (siren) radar warning receiver (RWR). The capacity of the front fuel tank was reduced by 900 litres (198 Imp gal) and, with an additional 190-litre (42-Imp gal) fuel tank installed in the rear fuselage, total fuel capacity was 6110 litres (1,344 Imp gal). The cockpits of pupil (front) and instructor (rear) had a common canopy with separate rear-hinged panels, and

communication was via an SPU-9 intercom system. KS-4 ejection seats were installed.

Deprived of radar and weapons, the Su-15UT was suitable only for pilot training and its performance was not as good as that of the single-seat Su-15. Two R-98 missile mock-ups were generally carried under the wings.

U-58B

The prototype U-58B combat trainer, piloted by A. Gribachev, took off for the first time on 24 June 1970. Tests were soon stopped due to an unacceptable forward shift in the centre of gravity, caused by the Taifun.

An officer examines the rear cockpit of a Su-15UT at Slupsk in Poland as a Su-15TM lands in the background. UTs were distributed among the interceptor regiments to provide a vehicle for continuation training and check rides. They were unarmed.

The Su-15UT instructor sat in the back. A retractable periscope was provided to give forward vision during the approach.

Sukhoi Su-15UT 'Flagon-C'

Second cockpit for instructor in lengthened fuselage

Internal rearrangement of fuel tankage

Standard radome but no radar fitted

Underwing pylons usually carried dummy missiles

Tumanskiy R-11F2S-300 turbojets

Su-15 late production series 'Flagon-D'

Take-off and landing properties of the Su-15 were very poor initially, and proved troublesome for pilots. As a remedy, wing area was increased and flaps were used in the boundary layer control system. From the 11th production series, of 1969, series Su-15s gained a new wing with greater surface area and with an aerodynamic twist (the outer sweep angle was decreased to 45°). This change was introduced in order to reduce take-off and landing speeds, and to reduce induced drag in flight. The new wing was tested in 1966 with the T-58D-1 first prototype and with pre-series aircraft c/n 0015301. The NATO designation for the rewinged aircraft was 'Flagon-D', although the Soviet name

remained unchanged.

At the same time, the aircraft obtained a UPS (*upravleniye pogranichnym sloyem*) boundary layer control system at the wing flaps. Applying blown air from the engine compressor to the upper surface of the flaps, the UPS system was intended to prevent flow separation at high flap deflection angles: the flaps could be deflected by 45° for landing and 20° for take-off. The engines adapted for the UPS system were designated R-11F2SU-300. However, insufficient delivery by the compressors rendered this system unusable. Flap deflection was limited to 25° for landing and 15° for take-off, with full deflection only possible in later aircraft

A cranked wing was introduced to the Su-15 from series 11 onwards. This 'Flagon-D' has the extra inboard pylon for the R-60 missile fitted.

with R-13-300 engines.

When the Su-9, Su-11 and Su-15 were coming into being, their sole task was to attack single bombers or reconnaissance aircraft. It was expected that any combat would be won in a surprise attack that used medium-range missiles. The 1970s brought a renaissance in manoeuvring air combat, and it was judged that intercept fighters also needed short-range weapons. In 1973/74 Su-15 aircraft, both new-build and existing ones, were equipped with small inner-wing pylons for R-60 air-to-air missiles. A gun armament was also considered and, as early as 1968, a fixed GP-9 gun pod and GSh-23 cannon had been installed on the left-hand side under the fuselage of a single aircraft. This solution was not accepted, however, and in 1975 series Su-15s were adapted for two UPK-23-250 gun containers carried under the fuselage. A simple K-10T collimator sight was installed for aiming R-60 missiles and cannon.

Su-15 projects

Su-15Sh (T-58Sh): In 1969-70, under the influence of the Vietnam War and recent Sino-Soviet conflict, Sukhoi prepared an initial design of the T-58Sh supersonic ground-attack aircraft. It faced competition from Yakovlev's Yak-28Sh and Mikoyan's MiG-21Sh and MiG-27. The latter MiG eventually was chosen and entered service in the mid-1970s.

Su-15-30: In 1966-67, along with an Su-15T equipped with Taifun radar and an Su-15U with Korshun-58 radar, project Su-15-30 was considered. It consisted of applying the armament system of the MiG-25P 'Foxbat-A', i.e., Smerch-A radar and two K-40 missiles. The aircraft was to be powered by two D-30 turbofan engines, hence the '30' in the project designation.

Su-15U (T-58U): In 1965-1967 Gedaliy Kunavskiy proposed a derivative of the Oryol radar, named Korshun-58, for a 'second stage' Su-15 interceptor. Sukhoi's OKB worked on the Su-15U (T-58U) project with this radar, but at the end of 1967 work was stopped when the government commission decided that the parallel project incorporating the Taifun radar in an Su-15T (see below) was more advanced. (At the same time, Kunavskiy was dismissed from OKB-339 because of failures of the MiG-23's Sapfir-23 radar.)

Su-15T (T-58T, *izdeliye* 37M)

The government resolution launching the Su-15 programme in February 1962 provided for modern Smerch-AS radar to be used for 'second stage' aircraft. The new radar was not ready until 1968, by when it was known as Taifun (typhoon). It was a variant of the RP-25 Smerch-A radar installed in the Mach-3 MiG-25P 'Foxbat-A' interceptor, adapted for the reduced space and electric power supply system of the smaller Su-15.

After a brief delay caused by consideration of the Korshun-58 radar (see the T-58U entry), the Taifun radar was eventually fitted to the Su-15, and on 31 January 1969 pilot Vladimir Krechetov began tests of a modernised T-58T (for Taifun) interceptor. Series production started even before tests were finished, which was a common practice in the USSR at that time. However, after about 10 Su-15T (*izdeliye* 37M at the factory) aircraft had been built in 1970-71, production was stopped when defects were revealed in the Taifun radar. Production did not resume until modernisation of the radar to Taifun-M standard (see Su-15TM below).

In addition to the new radar, other modifications included new R-13-300 engines, a longer front undercarriage leg and advanced avionics, all of which formerly had been trialled on testbed aircraft. Installing more powerful R-13-300 turbojet engines – developed for the MiG-21SM 'Fishbed-J' and rated at 40.20 kN (9,039 lb) thrust dry and 64.71 kN (14,550 lb) with afterburner – gave a slight improvement in acceleration and range. It also meant that the boundary layer control system, installed on the wing flaps from the very beginning, could at last be applied fully to improve take-off and landing characteristics. The air intake section area had to be increased slightly to accommodate the greater airflow. First tests of the R-13-300 engines were carried out between 1967 and 1970 with several series Su-15 aircraft. Initially only one engine (starboard) was replaced, leaving the other R-11FS-300 unchanged, and then both R-13-300s were installed. The adjusted air intakes were tested in 1970/71.

The most important non-radar change to the avionics was the implementation of the SAU-58 automatic flight control system to several of the first Su-15Ts, which had not yet been fitted with it. Other modifications included a new RSBN-5S short-range navigation system (a TACAN analogue),

Only 10 Su-15Ts were built before production was halted owing to problems with the radar. The new Taifun set was housed in the original radome.

R-832M communication radio replacing the previous R-802V unit, upgraded Lazur-SM datalink, Sirena-3 RWR in place of Sirena-2, and more. The second primary hydraulic sub-system was deleted because the new radar did not employ hydraulic drives.

Su-15TM (T-58TM, *izdeliye* 37M) 'Flagon-E/F'

Production of the Su-15T continued from December 1971 in the form of the Su-15TM with modernised Taifun-M radar (the factory numbering was a continuation of version T, so the first TM had factory number 03-01, indicating the first aircraft of the third series). Tests of Taifun-M began as early as 1969 and state acceptance tests ran from 18 August 1970 to 5 April 1973. Initially, tests involved only one Su-15, then another joined in February 1971 followed by two first series Su-15TMs in December 1971. A government resolution regarding commissioning the interception complex Su-15-98M was not passed until 21 January 1975, after many amendments

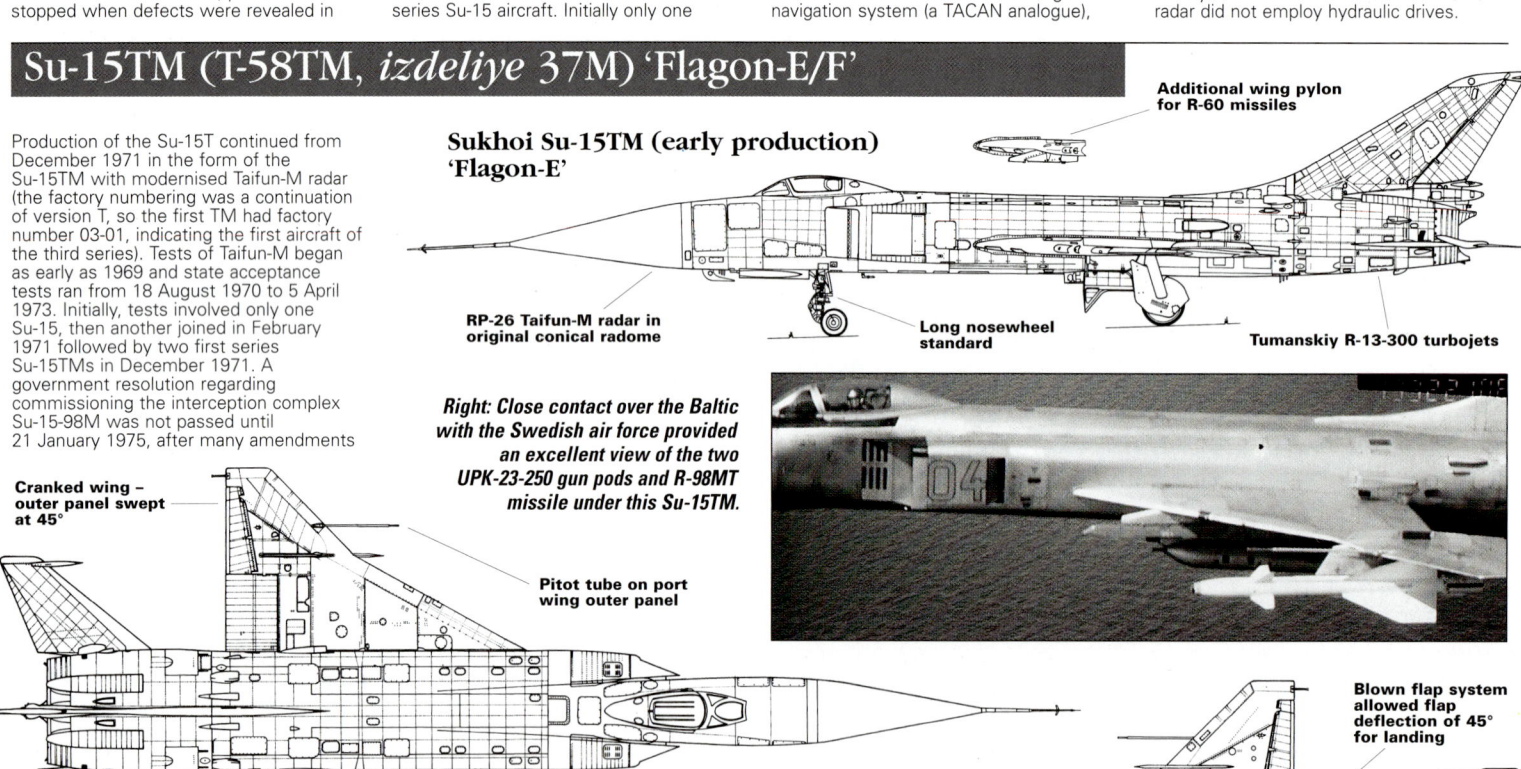

Sukhoi Su-15TM (early production) 'Flagon-E'

Additional wing pylon for R-60 missiles

RP-26 Taifun-M radar in original conical radome

Long nosewheel standard

Tumanskiy R-13-300 turbojets

Right: Close contact over the Baltic with the Swedish air force provided an excellent view of the two UPK-23-250 gun pods and R-98MT missile under this Su-15TM.

Cranked wing – outer panel swept at 45°

Pitot tube on port wing outer panel

Anti-flutter weights in tailplane bullet fairings

Small fence on upper wing above weapons pylon

Su-15TM (early production)

Blown flap system allowed flap deflection of 45° for landing

Provision for two gun pods under belly

Underwing pylons for R-98 missiles

In the West the ogival radome of the later production Su-15TM was initially thought to signify a new radar. However, it was only the radome which had changed to improve signal propagation.

(note that series production of the aircraft was by then nearing its end). As usual, after being commissioned the T-58M aircraft were officially redesignated Su-15TM, the Taifun-M radar became the RP-26 and the K-98M missiles were known as R-98M. Military tests of 10 Su-15TM interceptors with the 148th PVO Pilot Combat Training Centre at Savasleyka were made from 15 February 1975 until 20 July 1978. Production of the Su-15TM continued until 1975; this was the last series Su-15 combat variant.

The longer range of the Taifun-M radar, compared to the Oryol, was obtained by increasing relay power. This had the unwelcome side effect of generating inner reflections of the radar pulse under the cover in the aircraft nose. In all former

versions of the Su-15, the radar antenna had been covered with a cone but this design, which was most appropriate from aerodynamic and manufacturing considerations, was not suited to the operation of the powerful Taifun-M. (The best shape of a cover would have been hemispheric, as seen on the Yak-25 interceptor, but such a solution would be impossible for supersonic aircraft.) From the eighth production series, the nose of

the Su-15TM was ogive-shaped, a compromise between the demands of electronics and aerodynamics.

When adapting Su-15TMs to carry the UPK-23-250 gun containers, the underfuselage pylons were replaced by the BD3-59FK type that could carry not only fuel tanks and gun containers, but also bombs up to 500 kg (1,102 lb), UB-32 (UB-16) rocket launchers, heavy S-24 unguided rockets or ZB-350 incendiary tanks. PU-1-8 underwing launchers were replaced by PU-2-8s suitable for the same types of armament. However, the use of this armament by the Su-15 should be considered as theoretically possible only, due to a lack of the fire control devices that are necessary for effective attacks against ground targets.

The need to attack very low flying targets, resulting from new tactics in strike aviation, was a challenge for the Su-15TM. The Taifun radar could not trace targets flying against a background of the earth's surface, so another method had to been found. The SAU-58-2 flight control system installed on late production series Su-15TMs was modified to read low-altitude radio altimeter data. Using the SAU-58-2 system, an Su-15TM intercepting a low-altitude target was guided automatically by the Vozdukh-1M system to an altitude of 200 m (656 ft) so that the target was before it or even a little higher. Pilots, however, did not accept these extreme low-level attacks with the Su-15TM fighter. Very soon after this, production of the Su-15TM was stopped.

Su-15TM (late production) 'Flagon-F'

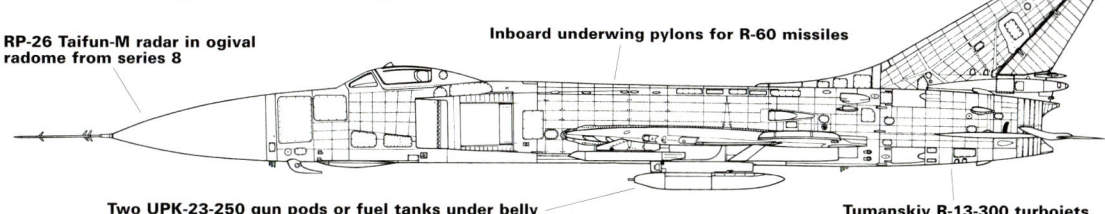

RP-26 Taifun-M radar in ogival radome from series 8

Inboard underwing pylons for R-60 missiles

Two UPK-23-250 gun pods or fuel tanks under belly

Tumanskiy R-13-300 turbojets

Su-15UM (U-58TM, *izdeliye* 43) 'Flagon-G'

On 23 April 1976 at Novosibirsk, pilots Vladimir Vylomov and V. Belanin took off for the first time with the prototype U-58TM combat trainer. The aircraft then was ferried to Zhukovskiy for further testing, and by 25 November 1976 the state acceptance tests had been completed at Akhtubinsk. The U-58TM – with military designation Su-15UM and factory designation *izdeliye* 43 – was a two-seat combat trainer developed from the late production Su-15TM. Unlike the former Su-15UT trainer, in which the

fuselage was extended to fit a second cockpit, the length of the Su-15UM fuselage remained unchanged. Inner fuel tank capacity was also the same, and only

An ogival radome was the main distinguishing feature of the Su-15UM, although this variant had a limited combat capability – unlike the earlier trainers. Although the type had a normal fighter radome, there was no radar.

some equipment was sacrificed to accommodate the second cockpit. The Su-15UM had no radar, but it could carry R-98MT and R-60 IR-guided missiles as

well as gun containers. It also lacked the SAU-58 control system, Lazur-M datalink, Sirena RWR and RSBN-5S short-range navigation system. A small number of Su-15UM trainers were made from 1976 to 1979, and it was the last Su-15 production series.

Su-15bis (T-58bis)

From 3 July until 20 December 1972, pilots Vladimir Ilyushin, Aleksandr Isakov and Vladimir Krechetov undertook tests at Novosibirsk of the prototype Su-15bis (T-58bis), a converted series Su-15TM with R-25-300 engines. The purpose of this modification was to improve air combat

characteristics at altitudes up to 4000 m (13,123 ft). The R-25-300 engine is a version of the R-13F-300 with an additional 'extraordinary' working range. As the result of the short (up to 3 minutes) increase of compressor speed to 106 per cent, engine thrust increased to 69.9 kN (15,652 lb) with afterburning; this in turn reduced aircraft acceleration time (one of the most important combat parameters for intercept

fighters) and increased low-altitude speed. Ceiling and interception range were slightly increased, too. The Su-15bis passed the full tests but its series production could not begin due to a lack of engines. R-25-300 engines were being installed in the MiG-21bis 'Fishbed-L' at the same time as

the Su-15bis and the rate of production by Factory No. 26 in Ufa, manufacturer of the R-25-300, was insufficient to supply both aircraft types; unfortunately for Sukhoi, modernisation of the MiG-21 – and its resultant enhanced export potential – was considered to have priority.

Two views show the single Su-15bis, complete with R-98M missiles. The aircraft had engines optimised for extra thrust at low-altitude. Otherwise, the aircraft was similar to the late production Su-15TM 'Flagon-F'.

Su-19 and Su-19M

A programme was developed in the late 1960s/early 1970s to modernise the Su-15TM with a new wing, from which better performance was expected. In the first stage, the Su-19 was to be powered

by two available R-25-300 turbojet engines, as in the Su-15bis. For the later Su-19M, two advanced Tumanskiy R-67-300 turbofans, each of 78.44 kN (17,637 lb), were planned (at that time, these engines were intended for further MiG-29s). The new Su-19 wing was to be of ogival shape, the wing's surface area was to be increased and four

a development which was then being studied intensively in the USSR. Sukhoi tested the ogival wing with flying testbed *izdeliye* 100L from 1967 to 1969, mainly for the T-4 strike aircraft (*izdeliye* 100), but also for other projects. The wing's surface area was to be increased and four

armament pylons were proposed instead of two. The fire control system was to remain unchanged. It was expected that the new wing and additional fuel would considerably increase aircraft range and endurance, and the more powerful engines would improve the acceleration.

The A-7 came to Desert Storm very much as an also-ran to the F/A-18 Hornet. In fact, but for the whims of Saddam Hussein and his timely invasion of Kuwait, it would not have been there at all. Nevertheless, history records that VA-46 and VA-72 flew the Corsair II on its final, combat missions from the deck of USS *John F. Kennedy.*

Vought's Corsair II is often compared to a squashed F-8 Crusader, but it was really a new design when it flew for the first time in September 1966, the result of a competition to replace the Douglas A-4 Skyhawk. Vought's chief test pilot, John Konrad, who had made the first flight in the XF8U-1 11 years earlier, also took the Corsair for its maiden flight. After joining the fleet, the A-7 flew its first combat missions in Vietnam with VA-147 in USS *Ranger* (CV-61) in December 1967.

Corsairs continued to fly combat over Vietnam, in both Navy grey and later in Air Force green-and-brown. They carried the war to the North Vietnamese during Operation Linebacker in 1972, and patrolled the oceans and trouble-spots of the world thereafter. Corsairs were ready to rattle windows in Iran during the aborted rescue of the hostages in 1980, and three years later, VA-15 and VA-87 flew strikes in Grenada and Lebanon.

The Middle East became the Corsair's most common area of operations. In March and April 1986, it showed Ghadaffi's navy what the 'Line of Death' was all about. VA-46 and VA-72 provided suppression of enemy air defences

(SEAD) for USAF F-111s attacking Tripoli and Benghazi. When Iran flexed its muscles in the Persian Gulf in April 1988, A-7s of the 'Mighty Shrikes' of VA-94 and the 'Fighting Redcocks' of VA-22 tangled with the Ayatollah's forces.

By early 1990, several A-7 light attack squadrons had either decommissioned or transitioned to the capable McDonnell Douglas F/A-18 Hornet. Things seemed generally quiet around the world (the result of the 'Peace Dividend' that followed the fragmentation of the former USSR), and it seemed to be time to say goodbye to the faithful Corsair.

Desert Storm reprise

However, Iraq's President Saddam Hussein changed matters with the invasion of Kuwait in 1990. Suddenly, everything was put on hold, and as US President George Bush and his planners asked the old question – "Where are the carriers?" – the A-7 was called into action one more time. Halfway through VA-46's and VA-72's pre-transition to the F/A-18 (they had sent away half their people and aircraft), the

Six Mk 7 dispensers prepare to depart Kennedy *aboard their VA-72 carrier aircraft. These weapons, when deployed, dispersed submunitions over a wide area. VA-72, along with VA-46, was a second choice A-7 unit for deployment to the Gulf. Original plans had called for VA-37 and VA-105 to perform the Corsair's swansong.*

'SLUF' swansong

A-7 Corsair II in the Gulf, 1990-1991

units rushed out to meet USS *John F. Kennedy* (CV-67) as the huge carrier left Norfolk, Virginia on 15 August, and headed east. The *Kennedy's* flight deck had not yet been modified to operate Hornets, and the big ship's requirement for light-attack squadrons resulted in the Navy's last two A-7 Corsair II units being recalled for one more combat cruise with the ageing attacker.

Operation Desert Storm was to be the Corsair's finest hour and, together with newer, more technologically advanced aircraft, the two light-attack squadrons of 'JFK' frequently put up nearly their entire complement – 20 aircraft (of 24 assigned) – to fly strikes with 'iron' bombs or to defend other strikers in SEAD missions with high-speed, anti-radiation missiles (HARMs). Each squadron shot 78 HARMs and dropped 1,000,000 lb (454000 kg) of ordnance. Along with the more modern F/A-18 and its older veteran brother, the A-6, the A-7 was part of the first missions on the night of 16-17 January 1991.

Captain John Warren, *Kennedy's* Air Boss and himself a former Corsair pilot, commented on the success of VA-46 and VA-72. "I really enjoyed watching the A-7s get out there and participate in their last war. It was a pleasure having them on the deck because they were so agile and so consistently up. They were always ready and easier to get to the catapults than larger aircraft. We launched 18 loaded A-7s in

"…I used to bull's-eye womprats in my T-16 back home…". While Luke Skywalker relied on 'The Force' in the Star Wars *epic, US Navy Corsair pilots relied on their low-level flying skills – honed in a number of valleys nicknamed 'Star Wars Canyon' – for their survival. These valleys were typically bounded by sandstone cliffs between 1,500 and 2,000 ft (460 and 610 m) high and this fact, allied with the close proximity of the aircraft to the valley floor, demonstrates just how hard this 'SLUF' driver was trying. This particular valley was in northern Saudi Arabia.*

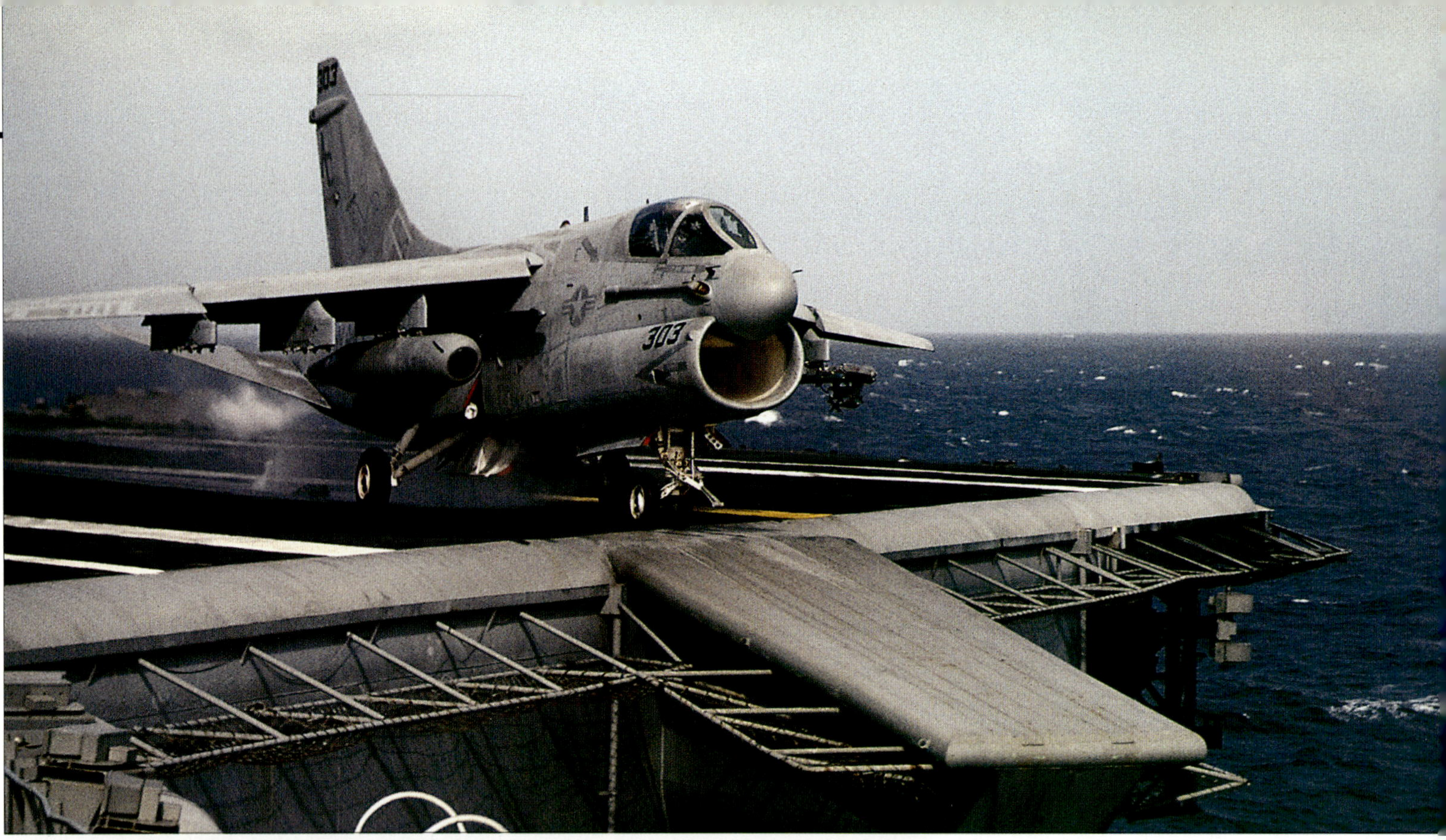

Above: An unarmed 'AC/303' launches from Kennedy*'s waist cat for a training hop. The Forward-Looking Infra-Red pod beneath the starboard wing was fully integrated with the aircraft's systems, allowing flawless low-level navigation and accurate attacks to be carried out at night.*

Left: On 16 January 1991, the opening night of Desert Storm, aircraft of both squadrons prepare for night-time cat shots to set them off on their first sorties. Note that drop tanks are a standard fit among these aircraft, while both AGM-88 missiles and Rockeyes are being carried.

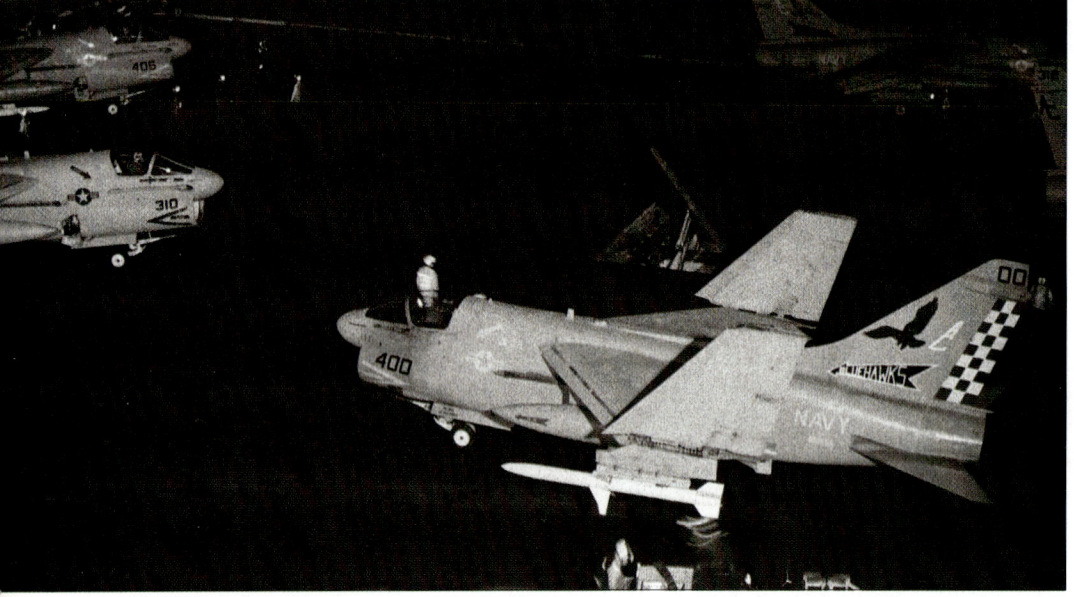

one cycle, nine per squadron. It was incredible! Two major strikes per day on the average."

Commander John Leenhouts, one of the primary exponents of the A-7 – he had accumulated more than 1,000 traps as a lieutenant commander and was occasionally billed as the 'Corsair Kid' – was the executive officer (XO) of VA-72 during the 1991 cruise. "Probably the most important facet of training we used was precision flying, tight formations, specific timing, being where you're supposed to be in time and space, absolutely without error, on the dime. The number of aircraft in the same area at the same time was horrendous. If you weren't where you were supposed to be, the potential for mid-air collisions was extremely high."

Although the Corsair II was equipped to defend itself and had, since its introduction in Vietnam, carried one or two Sidewinder air-to-air missiles on cheek racks, along with its internal 20-mm cannon, its main mission has always been ground-attack. A later addition was SEAD, and the A-7Es of *Kennedy*'s squadrons toted HARMs along with their Mk 83 and Mk 84 iron bombs. (The first night's A-7 missions were almost all SEAD using HARMs.) The second wave, on 17 January, included A-7s with HARMs, which together with EA-6Bs, US Air Force F-4Gs and EF-111s formed a protective ECM/SEAD package.

VA-72 pilot Lieutenant J. T. Young described a SEAD mission during the Gulf War. "We were part of an A-7 strike package. I was with another pilot from VA-72 and we set up a racetrack pattern. This was later in the war, and we had decided not to use so many pre-briefed shots because the Iraqis were blinking their radars; their radars weren't on solid. We wanted to wait and do a killer mission, like a Wild Weasel, and catch them with their radars up with our guys in the target area.

"We had an interesting problem. Instead of using a specific run into the target, shooting off the HARM, covering the strike group during a specific window, we covered them by loitering close to the target. We found that our planning, while it was pretty accurate, was made a little more difficult by the winds, which were slightly different than forecast. We had decided to hold off 25 to 30 miles [40 to 48 km] from the target, but we found ourselves going in much farther, closer to the target, to give our buddies the support they needed. We saw plenty of SA-2 and SA-3 radars blinking that were underneath us, [and we were] well within their envelopes. Now, besides protecting the strike package, we two SEAD players had to give mutual support.

"We set up a racetrack pattern and waited until the last aircraft was clear of the target before we bugged out. We fired three HARMs that mission, two pre-briefed and one against an SA-3 radar."

Air Force tankers

Without a doubt, however, after going through all the enemy flak and SAMs, what seemed to most concern the A-7 pilots was refuelling in a sky crowded with other aircraft, clustering around the Air Force KC-135 tankers, whose short-coupled basket-hose arrangements were, at best, *ad hoc* affairs to accommodate the various naval aircraft they now had to service. The diverging philosophies of the Navy and Air Force had allowed the design of the refuelling equipment to develop into a receiver-driven process in the Navy, while it was the boom operator in the Air Force tanker that guides the refuelling cycle.

Thus, the make-do, unstable basket wobbling behind the large Stratotanker has never inspired confidence in Navy and Marine Corps crews. However, when down to the last 1,000 lb (454 kg) of fuel, the availability of the tanker is infinitely more important than its size or system.

The 'Bluehawks' of VA-72

If for nothing else, VA-72 holds a unique place in naval aviation history as the first fleet squadron to fly the A4D-1 Skyhawk. Commissioned in April 1956, and originally using the nickname 'Skyhawks', the squadron changed to the 'Bluehawks' to avoid confusion with its new aircraft.

The squadron moved from NAS Quonset Point, Rhode Island, to NAS Oceana, Virginia Beach, in July 1957 before sailing in USS *Randolph* (CVA-15) for its first Mediterranean cruise. During the next 12 years, VA-72 travelled around the world, including a combat cruise in 1966 aboard the *Franklin D. Roosevelt* (CVA-42), that ship's only Southeast Asia deployment. By that time, the 'Bluehawks' had moved again, this time to NAS Cecil Field, near Jacksonville, Florida.

In September 1969, the squadron began transitioning to the A-7B, eventually sailing in the carrier *John F. Kennedy* (CV-67) to the troubled Middle East, in December 1971. During that cruise, VA-72 became the first fleet jet squadron to

'Bluehawks' A-7Es – including the 'CAG bird' with its coloured rudder checks and more flamboyant fin markings – take on fuel from a USAF KC-135E Stratotanker and a US Navy KA-6D Intruder.

accumulate 15,000 mishap-free flight hours. The next cruise found the squadron and its carrier in the eastern Mediterranean as a result of the 1973 Yom Kippur War between Israel and its Arab neighbours.

In 1978, VA-72 swapped its veteran A-7Bs for A-7Es. In 1982, it also changed ships, going aboard USS *America* (CV-66) to help support UN peacekeeping efforts in Lebanon. In 1986, the squadron participated in combat operations against Libya. The late 1980s brought several deployments and exercises. Although chosen to transition to its third major type, the F/A-18 Hornet, VA-72 was reassembled in August 1990 in a hurried recall to deploy with *Kennedy's* Air Wing 3 as part of the Desert Shield build-up and subsequent six-week war of Desert Storm.

John Leenhouts explains. "The night tanker rendezvous were, without a doubt, petrifying. During the day, they were fine. It was almost like an ACM engagement where everyone was going for the same piece of sky at the same time. We avoided each other, although some of the 'belly checks' could surprise you. At night, there was no doubt that if you erred, you put not only your own life in jeopardy but those of dozens of others.

"Once you were on the tanker, just staying there, in some cases, going through difficult weather, demanded that you just suck it up, tighten up until you couldn't see anyone behind you, and focused on the guy in front of you and maybe the two in front of him. If you relaxed and got out of line, the 'snake' would start whipping and the tail-end guy would take a beating.

"The way the planes were stacked up, you couldn't vary your altitude. When you ran in-

country, if you got off your altitude over Iraq, you had the potential of running into someone else, since we were all running around lights out, 200-300 airplanes all within 45-50 minutes. You just couldn't violate good airmanship in this arena."

Lieutenant Commander 'Bud' Warfield, also of VA-72, adds his impressions of aerial

Empty bomb racks and Sidewinder rails indicate that these VA-46 aircraft are on a training mission during Desert Shield. Their relatively clean appearance shows that the pace of operations has yet to truly speed up. Kennedy sailed for the Gulf region and Desert Shield operations on 15 August 1990, its crew having been given just five days to prepare the ship for combat.

Left: A HARM streaks away from a VA-72 A-7. The Corsair was no stranger to the lethal SEAD (suppression of enemy air defences) role, the type having flown the Iron Hand SEAD mission with the US Navy over Vietnam. The high altitude of this HARM launch, along with its attitude, suggests that this missile is being 'lobbed' ahead of a friendly strike package.

Below left: A posse of CVW-3's Corsairs lines Kennedy's foredeck ready for the next strike. The aircraft are mostly armed with Mk 7 dispensers, which could contain anti-armour or anti-personnel submunitions, anti-personnel mines or Gator anti-tank mines. In practice however, the Mk 7 was used almost exclusively in anti-armour Rockeye II form.

refuelling during the war. "I think one of the most important training issues was that we hadn't worked with the Air Force during the work-ups. We saw this big flail coming, we were working some pretty intense fuel figures, working on how we could get in-country using organic tanking.

"As soon as we got situated, we started seeing the Air Force tasking order telling us to meet Air Force tankers. Probably the most significant thing we did to ensure success during the first few days was to fly the 'mirror image' strikes. We'd load up 45 airplanes with iron bombs, meet the -135 tankers and do the real, live tanking.

"The first day of the war we joined up our strike with 8th Air Force KC-135s, 60 airplanes all joined up. We flew to Iraq without one word on the radio. We had had a chance to get to know the [USAF] people from Jeddah when they came out to the ship. It was like a big vacation for them."

Commander John Sanders, VA-72's 'boss' for the duration of Desert Storm, remarked that the A-7 could carry almost every weapon in the US Navy inventory. Commander John Leenhouts, Executive Officer with VA-72, noted that in addition to this versatility, the aircraft's long-range, high cruising speed and heavy weapon load placed it among the few types able to fly the long transits to the target areas with relative ease.

Top: Almost a decade after the conflict finished, the full extent of Saddam Hussein's involvement in the 1991 Gulf War has still not been realised. It seems he flew at least one Desert Shield training op from USS John F. Kennedy, in this VA-72 A-7E.

Above: Desert Storm was truly a most public operation. Viewers worldwide had graphic images of the war beamed into their homes, often in near-real time. This VA-46 pilot became the subject of a CNN news team as he prepared for a mission on 20 January 1991.

Top right: This view of a VA-72 aircraft clearly shows the two ventral ECM blisters. A fairing to starboard and level with the aft end of the rear-most blister housed a strike camera.

Like other American pilots, Lieutenant Young also sampled refuelling from British aircraft. "Tanking went smoothly, because we had practised tanking from different types of airplanes. One night, we had a mission that wasn't as large as a regular strike; it was a SEAD escort for a British strike group. We showed up on the tanker and it was a VC10, something I had never tanked off before. It was another interesting experience. They had the same drogue-and-hose system we used, but with a little more outboard station with more wing vortices messing with your airplane. I found it very easy to work with the RAF as well as our own crews."

Corsair's final barricade

For the most part, the hardy little attack bomber – which had acquired another nickname, 'Harley', in its later years, referring to the powerful American motorcycle – enjoyed impressive mission-ready availability, and none was lost to Iraqi defensive fire. However, A-7E BuNo. 158830/AC 403 achieved the dubious distinction of taking the last Corsair barricade on 24 January 1991. The aircraft's nosegear was damaged during the catapult launch at the beginning of a mission at 12.41, and its pilot, Lieutenant Tom Dostie, a 26-year-old native of Lewiston, Maine, had to decide whether to

abort the mission and return to the *Kennedy*. The VA-72 A-7 carried four 1,000-lb Mk 83 bombs on stations 1, 2, 6 and 8, 20-mm ammunition, and two Sidewinders. The target was a lightly defended facility in western Iraq.

'AC/403' and its pilot shot down the track, but Dostie felt his aircraft wobble – something wasn't right. Once airborne, he checked things. An observer on the flight deck called that the A-7 seemed to have blown a tyre. Checking his instruments, Lieutenant Dostie saw his No. 2 hydraulic pressure rapidly declining, but the jet's engine sounded OK. Nevertheless, he kept his landing gear down and locked.

As the spare A-7 launched to take his place, Dostie had another pilot look him over. "Looks like the nosegear is trailing," he reported.

Once in the area designated for such activity, Dostie punched the salvo jettison button. Everything dropped except for the Mk 83 on station 6, right above the AIM-9. With the gear down, an interlock prevented ordnance from jettisoning from the inboard weapons stations.

Maintaining 200 kt (368 km/h), the VA-72 pilot prepared for a low approach so the people on the ship could examine the aircraft. After two passes, the people on the deck sent another A-7 toward the crippled Corsair; not a good sign, as far as Tom Dostie was concerned.

Mission markings

CVW-3's Corsairs – here represented by VA-72 aircraft – rapidly built up impressive mission logs. These were recorded on the port side beneath the cockpit. All of the A-7s were nominally assigned to a single pilot, but in practice pilots flew whichever aircraft were mission ready. The inscription '20 COMBAT MISSIONS' beneath the pilot's name on AC 410 for example, demonstrates the

method of recording the number of sorties flown by the named pilot. For each combat mission flown by the aircraft a camel was applied. In addition, the mission log was further broken down with the application of weapon symbols. GP bombs, Rockeye IIs (Mk 7 dispensers loaded with Mk 118 anti-armour submunitions and represented by a Rockeye symbol), HARMs and Walleye were all employed, with each weapon represented by a symbol. A number beneath the weapon type indicated how many rounds of each had been expended by the individual aircraft.

Above: Eight 1,000-lb Mk 83 bombs head towards an Iraqi target under the wings of a 'Clansmen' aircraft. Between them, VA-46 and VA-72 delivered in excess of 2,000,000 lb (907180 kg) of ordnance in 745 Desert Storm combat missions.

Below: Even taking into account the Corsair's long legs, especially by comparison with the F/A-18, air-to-air refuelling was still an integral part of A-7 operations. Here a VA-46 A-7 tops off its tanks before continuing on its sortie.

As the second A-7 approached, its pilot wasted no time. "Oh, man, there's no way you're gonna trap this one."

On a discrete frequency, the two pilots had a confidential chat.

"The good news is your strut is down and locked," the check pilot said. "The bad news is there aren't any wheels on the end of it. The axle beam is broken, one wheel is gone, and the other is barely hanging on."

"Beauty," was all the unfortunate Lieutenant Dostie could reply.

Then the ship's tower called. "We've talked it over and decided it would be best to barricade you."

After each senior officer on the ship took his turn offering words of encouragement, it remained for Lieutenant Dostie to do his best. At least the weather was good, the *Kennedy* had a huge flight deck, and the wind was steady. He'd take the 4° glide slope to the 1-wire.

Setting up for a 6-mile (9.60-km) straight-in, he began his approach. At 4 miles (6.40 km), the low-fuel master-caution light lit up. For the next 2 miles (3.20 km), Dostie was a little below glide slope but otherwise in a good position. He realised the glide-slope setting was off by 0.5°, and corrected. Making minor adjustments close-in, the hard-pressed pilot concentrated on getting his aircraft over the deck.

At 14:36, his tailhook snagged the targeted 1-wire and slipped past the remaining three cables to push through the nylon barricade.

Ordinarily, the aircraft would have been repaired, but as this was its last cruise, 158830 was struck below, its flying days over. Two days after it had been stripped of any valuable parts that could be used to keep other A-7s flying, 158830 was buried at sea with full military honours. However, although it eventually

The obligatory pair of Sidewinders, plus two 300-US gal (1136-litre) Aero 1-D drop tanks and a brace of HARMs weigh down this VA-46 aircraft; just visible on the VA-72 machine in the foreground are Rockeyes.

The 'Clansmen' of VA-46

Commissioned in July 1955 as the Navy's first jet attack squadron, this VA-46 quickly adopted its Scottish nickname because of the heritage of its first commanding officer, Commander C. A. McDougal. He provided the McDougal Clan tartan for use as the squadron's insignia.

Originally flying the Grumman F9F-8 Cougar, the squadron soon transitioned to the A4D-2 (A-4B), cruising in several carriers including *Randolph, Intrepid, Roosevelt, Shangri-La,* and *Saratoga.* Its combat cruise aboard USS *Forrestal* in 1967 was cut short by a devastating flight-deck fire. Post-Vietnam deployments included service in *Kennedy, Eisenhower* and *America,* the deployment in the last ship becoming a combat cruise with the squadron's participation in retaliatory strikes against Libya in 1986.

Deploying with the A-7E in the late 1980s, the squadron joined VA-72 as the last fleet A-7 squadron as it deployed aboard *Kennedy* as part of Operation Desert Shield.

Left: A VA-46 aircraft departs for another combat sortie. The green helmet just visible in the lower right hand corner of the photograph belongs to the catapult officer.

Below left and right: With the shooting over, 'AC/301' was repainted in the old Light Gull Gray over Insignia White scheme. Its mission scoreboard was reapplied and a fin marking showing the unit's service dates was added.

slid from *Kennedy*'s elevator 4, 158830 held on, refusing to sink beneath the waves, floating on the surface until strafed by air wing jets, which administered the *coup de grâce* befitting the tough old bird's heritage.

Aside from the rare operational problem, the Corsair was usually ready for whatever mission it drew; SEAD became the most common. Lieutenant Commander Warfield described such a mission. "The SEAD missions were very precise missions. You had to have your A-7 in the exact point in the sky, and distance from the target. You had to fire at the exact time. We flew some very precise missions, especially with 90-kt [166-km/h] winds at altitude, jinking, and the SAMs and AAA. The AAA was just mesmerising.

"A week into the war, we were flying a night SEAD mission for an A-6 strike. I was about 30 miles [48 km] away from the Al Qaim super-

The AGM-62 Walleye proved to be a useful weapon against bridges and other hard targets. Some 131 of these glide bombs were expended, the majority of them being Walleye II ER/DL weapons. Guidance was by IR seeker, with a two-way datalink between the missile and aircraft (not necessarily the launch aircraft).

was. By that time we had beaten down their defences to the point where they never shot a missile or a gun until the first bomb hit. Typically, they didn't know we were there. They were too chicken to turn on the tracking radars of their SAMs and most of their GCI radars were jammed up pretty good.

"On this mission, when the first bomb went off, the AAA was pretty heavy. I came off target, and it was my first chance to see flak bursts actually going off above me. I was weaving in and out of the flak bursts, which was probably a dumb thing to do. You should always fly right through the burst of a shell that just went off.

"We were jinking around and everyone was yelling on the radio. I looked back over my shoulder and saw my Dash 3 and Dash 4 were weaving. Dash 3 was actually bracketed. You could see the flak bursts following behind his airplane as he went through the sky. They had him in their sights. He was actually Dash 15 coming off target, and they were mad as hornets down there. No one from our air wing was hit, and it was total elation to see the target go away like that.

"AAA has never got the press that SAMs have; everyone thinks that SAMs are magic weapons. The fact is that of all the SAMs we saw, none hit us, including the non-tactical SAMs – like the SA-14 and SA-16, which they shot at us – but there were also no hits on CVW-3 aircraft by SA-2s, -3s, -6s, or -8s. All the SAMs were fired unguided because the Iraqis were afraid of HARMs. I think they had the picture after the first night when we took out the SA-6 sites at H-3 airfield."

H-2 airfield was another Iraqi base that was

phosphate plant which was being hit at the same time by two SLAMs [stand-off land-attack missiles, AGM-84Es]. Al Qaim was surrounded by something in the order of 175 AAA guns, three SA-3 sites and two SA-2 sites. They also had 300-ft [91-m] towers with cable strung between them.

"I saw a SLAM go off and the place turned into a fusillade of AAA. I looked at it from 30 miles and thought, 'Boy, I'm glad I'm not down there.'"

Three days later, he was on a mission with 16 A-7s all loaded with Mk 83 bombs. "I didn't know if anyone else had the same feeling for the amount of defences the target had. We briefed with a little trepidation; there would be some lead in the air. And sure enough, there

LTV A-7E Corsair II

VA-72, CVW-3
USS *John F. Kennedy* (CV-67)
February 1991

A-7E BuNo. 158842 ('AC/402'), was assigned to Commander John Leenhouts. VA-72's executive officer and a leading exponent of naval Corsair operations. Leenhouts also produced the finest A-7 photography of the 1991 Gulf War.

Insatiable appetite
With its low-slung, gaping engine air intake, the A-7 presented particular problems on the carrier deck. Even with the engine running at low power, considerable suction was generated and with no barrier between the outside world and the engine's front fan, anything sucked in was inevitably shredded. During almost 25 years of front-line service, the Corsair's menu included at least one mop, various items of clothing and one unfortunate Aviation Structural Mechanic.

TF41 turbofan
Carrier operations with the Pratt & Whitney TF30-powered A-7A/B were occasionally marred by problems with the engine ingesting steam from the ship's catapult. From the 68th A-7E onwards this problem was solved by the installation of the 15,000-lb st (66.70-kN) Allison TF41-A-2 turbofan. The latter, a licence-built Rolls-Royce RB.168-62 Spey 25 engine, provided more thrust and greater reliability than the P&W unit.

Ejection seat
Should any A-7 pilot have been forced to eject during Desert Shield/Storm, his escape would have been courtesy of the McDonnell Douglas ESCAPAC Model 1G2 ejection seat. Miniature detonating chord would shatter the canopy with the initiation of the ejection sequence, although pop-up canopy breakers on the seat allowed egress through the glazing.

AIM-9 Sidewinder
Mounted on LAU-7/A launch-rails, the A-7E's pair of AIM-9Ls gave the aircraft a respectable self-defence capability. In fact, in low-level manouevering combat, a well-flown 'clean' A-7 could out-fight the majority of interceptors thanks to its 7-*g* manoeuvre limit and 140° per second roll rate.

Corsair colours
For both the Desert Shield and Desert Storm operations, the A-7Es wore an overall coat of Dark Gull Gray (FS36320). The blue-grey staining along the aircraft's panel lines shows were an anti-corrosive solution has been applied and then subsequently weathered.

Wing fold
Having created a warplane of relatively compact dimensions, the only provision Vought made towards carrier stowage was to provide the A-7 with folding wings. The outer panel on each side could be folded vertically along a prominent hinge line.

Avionics
While it did not have the technology levels of the F/A-18, the A-7E was still an accurate attack platform, thanks to its comprehensive navigation/attack avionics suite. Primary systems included the CP-953A/AJQ air data computer, ALQ-126(V) radar, AN/APN-190(V) Doppler radar, AN/ASN-91(V) tactical computer, AN/ASN-90(V) inertial measurement set and an AN/AVQ-7(V) HUD.

AGM-88B HARM
Expended in huge numbers by a wide range of warplane types, the high-speed anti-radiation missile gave the A-7E a formidable lethal SEAD capability. An interesting tactic developed during the war was to 'lob' a number of missiles ahead of an advancing strike package, the presence of such a threat being more than enough to force the Iraqi air SAM/AAA search radar operators to shut their systems down.

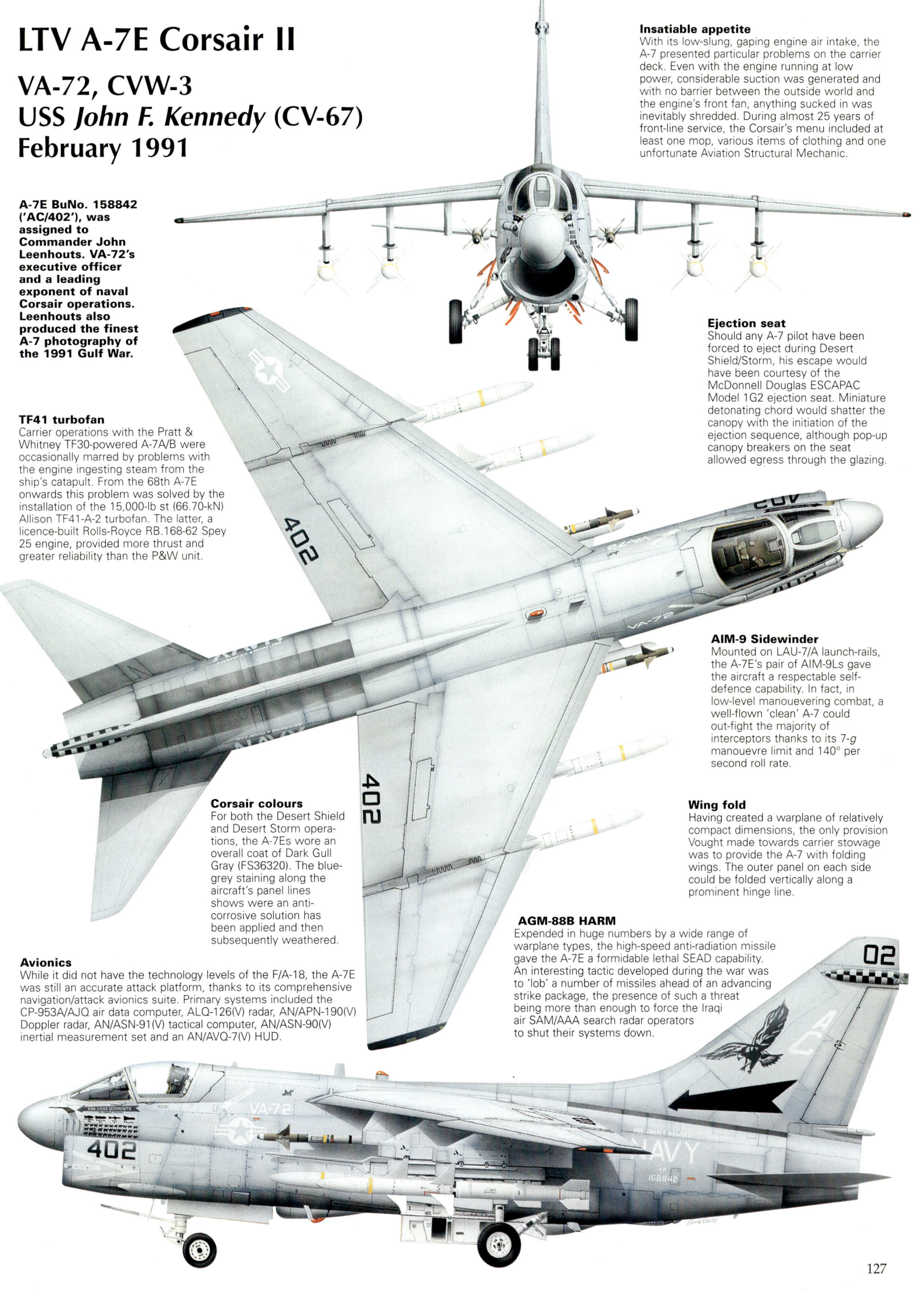

USS John F. Kennedy, CV-67, carrying air wing CVW-3, sailed in the Red Sea for the duration of its Desert Shield/Storm deployment, along with USS America (CV-66) and USS Saratoga (CV-60). Kennedy posed for this picture during the cease-fire in the immediate post-war period. Its deck is filled with A-6 and A-7 attack aircraft, E-2 Hawkeyes, EA-6B Prowlers, F-14 Tomcats, S-3 Vikings and a single SH-3 Sea King. 'JFK' was the only carrier to deploy without an F/A-18 Hornet unit embarked.

A pair of VA-46 A-7Es approaches a KC-135. On the first night of the war the 'Clansmen' visited Baghdad and subsequently joined VA-72 in going everywhere that the F/A-18 went – often at the same speed, because 'we had the gas to do it'.

the object of coalition attention. On one such mission, the weather forecast for the primary target area in Kuwait was not good. H-2 was selected as a secondary target. It was also closer to the tanker tracks over Saudi Arabia.

Lethal 'popcorn'

Commander Leenhouts, conducted the strike brief for his force of six aircraft from both VA-46 and VA-72. Each Corsair was loaded with seven Mk 20 Rockeye cluster weapons, and the two A-6 Intruders from Kennedy's VA-75 accompanying the A-7s each carried 12 Mk 82 general-purpose 500-lb bombs. The strike force

launched into a clear night sky with a full moon.

The plan was to hit the airfield, destroying as many Iraqi aircraft in their protective revetments as possible. The AWACS called 'picture clear' and all the warning devices in the Navy aircraft were quiet as they approached their target. Commander Leenhouts spotted the Iraqi airfield, and called, "Target is 11 o'clock at 5 miles [8 km]."

Each pilot picked his aim point, helped by the brilliant moonlight, but even with the natural illumination, the strikers found it necessary to release flares to help light the MiGs on

Above: On the way back to the US in March 1991, VA-72 applied this special camouflage to its CAG bird. During the war at least one VA-65 A-6E Intruder had flown bombing missions from USS Theodore Roosevelt in a similar scheme. Both camouflage and low-level flying soon became irrelevant during the air war as the superiority of the Allied air forces became apparent.

Right: BuNo. 160552 shows off its two-tone brown colour scheme in contrast to three standard VA-72 'SLUFs'. The special camouflage was also similar to that applied to USAF special ops/CSAR helicopters. Note that all the machines boast impressive mission tallies.

the ground. Eight LUU-2 flares, each with 2 million candlepower, began their four-minute decent, lighting up the Iraqi field. Lieutenant Commander Warfield and his wingman rolled in and dropped 14 Rockeyes, each filled with 247 armour-piercing bomblets. The resulting hits looked like popcorn exploding.

Commander Leenhouts and his wingman rolled in next, just in time to be bracketed by more popcorn. The XO now realised that a lot of the 'popcorn' was actually intense enemy AAA. Flak traps were everywhere. Twenty SAMs also came rocketing toward the American strikers. Fortunately, the missiles flew past the *Kennedy* group and eventually fizzled out several thousand feet above them as they emptied their chaff buckets.

Later, Commander Leenhouts wrote, "It was like being suspended in the middle of a Fourth of July fireworks display's grand finale!" All the A-7s and A-6s made it off target and back up to 20,000 ft (6096 m), safe from the intense AAA.

Retirement

Some 40 US Navy squadrons flew the A-7 during its quarter-century career. At the end, the tough little bomber went out with the two last fleet squadrons in a manner befitting a highly decorated warrior. The day-long affair was a fitting farewell to the last CV Corsair squadrons and their pugnacious bomber. On 16 May 1991, the 'Clansmen' of VA-46 and the 'Bluehawks' of VA-72 said goodbye to the A-7s they had flown since 1970, turned out their own lights, and closed their own doors.

Peter B. Mersky

During the victory celebrations of 10 June 1991, this aircraft was towed through the streets of New York in honour of the A-7 and its crews. Ironically, the machine was from VA-105, Kennedy's aircraft having returned straight into storage. VA-105 had been slated for decommissioning, but when VA-45 and -72 went to war, -105 was one of the units that filled their Hornet conversion slots.

No. 51 Squadron Canberras
Wyton's Cold War spyplanes

Throughout the Cold War the RAF's shadowy No. 51 Squadron gathered signals intelligence from around the periphery of the Soviet Union and its allies. At the heart of the operation was the high-altitude Canberra.

Above: Photographed from a Canberra PR.Mk 9, one of No. 51 Squadron's B.Mk 6 (Mod) aircraft cruises near its Wyton base. Unusually for Canberras based in the UK, the aircraft has a sun shield fitted in the canopy glazing. This gave some indication of the amount of time 51's aircraft spent in the Mediterranean and Middle East.

Below: This No. 51 Squadron line-up at RAF Watton is headed by WH698, which carries the unit's goose emblem on the tip tank. Next to it is the unit's first T.Mk 4 (WJ873) while at the far end is WJ640, with the badge on the fin. The latter had arrived with the unit shortly before it renumbered from No. 192 Squadron.

No. 51 Squadron's existence has never been officially secret, though details of the squadron's exact role and its operations have always been shrouded in mystery. No. 51 Squadron's presence on the front line was never advertised and the squadron was usually omitted from orders of battles and descriptions published in official and semi-official documents. The squadron eschewed the limelight, and its aircraft were never displayed unnecessarily. For the Queen's Silver Jubilee Review of the RAF at Finningley in 1977, for example, No. 51 Squadron was the only UK-based front-line unit which did not have an example aircraft in the otherwise comprehensive static display. When referred to at all, the unit's role was usually described as 'calibration' or 'special duties', or even 'telecommunications research'.

The RAF began collecting and analysing enemy radio and radar signals during World War II, initially with small specialised units like the Blind Approach Training Development Unit and the Wireless Investigation Development Unit, and subsequently with 'B' Flight of No. 109 Squadron at Gransden Lodge. This became No. 1474 Flight on 10 July 1942, and No. 192 Squadron on 4 January 1943. The latter unit was responsible for many of the electronic and signals intelligence breakthroughs of the war, and developed the tactics, techniques and equipment used in the Elint and Sigint roles for years afterwards. The squadron disbanded on 22 August 1945, but its aircrew and support staff formed the basis of the new Central Signals Establishment at Watton. Operational Elint missions were flown by *ad hoc* detachments of CSE Lancasters and Lincolns from Habbaniyah in Iraq and from other bases around the peripheries of the Soviet Union and, as the Cold War intensified, pressure mounted

for the formation of a dedicated front-line Elint-gathering unit.

No. 192 Squadron was reformed on 15 July 1951, the numberplate being applied to one of the squadrons of the CSE's Flying Wing. Equipped with Avro Lincolns (and, from March 1952, also with three Boeing Washingtons), the unit undertook a range of tasks, including ECM training, operator training, and operational Elint and electronic reconnaissance flying. The 'B' Flight Lincolns were replaced by two Canberra B.Mk 2s in March 1953, while de Havilland Comets eventually replaced a trio of Boeing Washingtons with 'A' Flight from February 1958.

The Canberra, at the time, was the RAF's most capable high-performance jet bomber, with a high-altitude performance that rendered it all but immune to interception. Canberras had already been used in the conventional photo-reconnaissance role – such as in Operation Robin, a series of dangerous overflight missions conducted during 1953-55 that

included a mission to photograph the Soviet missile test facility at Kasputin Yar, for which the aircraft took off from Germany and landed (with considerable flak damage) in Iran.

Elint Canberras

The Canberra's unique combination of high altitude performance and capacious bomb bay made it equally useful in the Elint role, and No. 192 received two B.Mk 2s (WH670 and WH698) in February 1953, and two B.Mk 6s (WJ775 and WT301) in December 1954. One of the B.Mk 2s ('698) and both B.Mk 6s soon had new equipment fitted in the nose, and thus had their transparent nosecones replaced by similarly-shaped dielectric radomes. These probably carried a passive Elint receiver, while the bomb bay housed electronic black boxes and a primitive, breakage-prone single-channel wire recorder, later replaced by a 14-channel tape recorder using modern ferric oxide tape.

The second B.Mk 2, WH670, seems not to

The first two Elint Canberras were B.Mk 2s WH670 (above, possibly the only available photo of a Canberra in No. 192 Sqn service) and WH698 (right, seen at Nicosia in 1959). Along with two B.Mk 6s they formed the operational equipment of No. 192 Squadron's 'B' Flight. WH670 did not receive any nose modification, retaining the glazed bomb aiming position during its three-year career with No. 192. Note the two-tone grey and PRU blue camouflage worn by both aircraft.

have been modified in the same way, and externally remained identical to a standard B.Mk 2. This aircraft was transferred to No. 527 Squadron in April 1956, but was replaced on 4 March 1958 by WJ640, another 'standard' B.Mk 2, while a third B.Mk 6, WT305, was taken on charge on 6 May 1957.

The Washingtons carried a crew which included six to 10 special operators, and the Comets carried 12 including three interpreters (crews later increased), but the Canberras were crewed by a pilot, a navigator/plotter and a single special operator, who might be an Elint specialist or a linguist. This limited the scope of inflight analysis and emitter location, and meant that Elint and Comint missions were quite separate, requiring the aircraft (or at least the special operator's station) to be reroled. This made the aircraft effectively similar in capability to the USAF's RB-47s, which carried only two special operators and seldom carried linguists; at the time, the USAF preferred to separate the Elint and Comint roles, whereas the Comets could simultaneously monitor, record and analyse many different radar and radio channels.

Despite this relatively limited capability, the Canberra soon formed the backbone of No. 192 Squadron, with four on charge from December 1954, and five after February 1958. They were augmented by three 'missionised' Washingtons, a standard Washington bomber used as a flight-crew trainer, and a Varsity used for training new special operators. The four Washingtons gave way to three Comets in early 1958. The squadron lost its Varsity and the CSE Development Squadron assumed the responsibility for operator training.

No. 192 Squadron was renumbered as No. 51 Squadron on 21 August 1958, as part of an RAF-wide reorganisation aimed at resurrecting some of the RAF's oldest and most historic units. Reports that the redesignation was a security precaution are believed to be entirely erroneous. The squadron stationery, flying suit badges and signboards changed, but the redesignation otherwise made little difference. Some aircraft also received small representations of No. 51 Squadron's 'goose' badge on their fins or wingtip tanks.

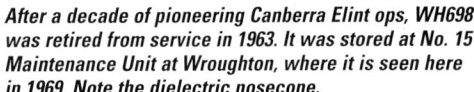

After a decade of pioneering Canberra Elint ops, WH698 was retired from service in 1963. It was stored at No. 15 Maintenance Unit at Wroughton, where it is seen here in 1969. Note the dielectric nosecone.

No. 51 Squadron initially may have retained No. 192's 'A' Flight (Comet)/'B' Flight (Canberra) organisation, although by the late 1960s (and perhaps earlier) 'A' Flight was responsible for front-end aircrew, 'B' Flight for ground crew, and 'C' Flight for rear crew operators. The squadron transferred to the control of the new Signals Command when it formed on 3 November 1958. Royal Air Force Signals Command titles were applied to the Comets (which also briefly gained a black-edged yellow cheatline), and to at least one Canberra B.Mk 2 (WJ640).

Canberra trainer

No. 51 Squadron, like No. 192, generally had five converted Canberra bombers on charge, and from 4 September 1959, also had a T.Mk 4 dual-control trainer on strength. The first T.Mk 4, WJ873, served until 29 June 1962, its replacement, WH845, having been received two weeks earlier, on 14 June. This, in turn, gave way to WJ877, which arrived on 14 June 1963 and remained with the unit (apart from a few brief loans to other Wyton units) until February 1975.

The third B.Mk 2, WJ640, left the unit on 6 April 1962, but No. 51 Squadron had already gained another (third) B.Mk 6 (WT206) on 12 March 1962. The latter aircraft had previously served with No. 76 Squadron, and had been fitted for atomic cloud sampling. Some reports suggest that it had also been equipped with an auxiliary Napier rocket engine in the

bomb bay, though there is no suggestion that this would have been required for its brief stay with No. 51 Squadron. The aircraft later served with No. 58 Squadron. As a relatively low-houred airframe, it may have been used simply for training, or it may have been intended as an operational aircraft. However, WT206 was returned to No. 15 MU on 30 November, and No. 51 Squadron found another B.Mk 6 already equipped with Blue Shadow SLAR (side-looking airborne radar), which had come to be a vital part of No. 51 Squadron's Canberra equipment fit. This was WJ768, which had served as a bomber with Nos 109 and 139 Squadrons, and which had gone to Boulton Paul for modifications in August 1962, prior to joining No. 51 Squadron.

No. 51 Squadron moved from Watton to Wyton (transferring from Signals Command to No. 3 Group, Bomber Command) on 1 April 1963, becoming part of the Central Reconnaissance Establishment alongside No. 543 Squadron's Valiants and No. 58 Squadron's photo-reconnaissance Canberras.

The arrival of WJ768 at Wyton in September 1963 was followed by the departure of the one remaining ex-No. 192 Squadron B.Mk 2, WH698. This brought the strength of the Canberra Flight to four B.Mk 6s and a single T.Mk 4. At Wyton these were augmented by three de Havilland Comet 2Rs, a single Comet trainer/trial installation aircraft, a Handley Page Hastings transport (for supporting overseas detachments) and an occasional Vickers Varsity for operator training and for missions in the Berlin corridor.

WJ640 flew with No. 51 for four years, and was possibly used for trials and training work, rather than for operations. Here it is seen during a very rare public appearance at a Battle of Britain air show at Waterbeach in September 1960, wearing the title of its parent command.

With its uprated Avon engines the B.Mk 6 offered better altitude, range and load-carrying performance than the B.Mk 2. WT301, first assigned to No. 192 Sqn in 1954, had the Blue Shadow SLAR and small dielectric nose radome fitted .

When it left the unit, WH698 still had a small dielectric radome, identical in outline to the standard B.Mk 2 nosecone. The B.Mk 6s, by contrast, had changed. Simply replacing the standard bomber glazed nosecone with a similar-shaped dielectric nose gave relatively little space for a receiver antenna, and at a relatively early stage in its career, WJ775 had a new dielectric nose radome added from frame 1, just in front of the pilot's instrument panel – the same point at which the T.Mk 4's solid nose was attached. The new nose followed the external contours of the existing bomber nose, but was black, with a prominent metal band running horizontally forward to the tip. Some other Watton-based aircraft flew in the same configuration, although they were not assigned to No. 192 or No. 51 Squadron. They may have been used by the unit, or may have been used for development work by other elements of the Central Signals Establishment. One such aircraft was WJ984.

This new nose shape seems to have been relatively short-lived, and by the time WJ768 joined No. 51 Squadron, the other three B.Mk 6s had been modified even more extensively, gaining T.Mk 11-type nose sections. The Canberra T.Mk 11 was a highly specialised trainer, designed for training Javelin all-weather fighter aircrew, fitted with AI.17 radar in an extended nose, with a sharply pointed conical tip. The appearance of a T.Mk 11 nose on No. 51 Squadron's Canberras led some to assume that AI.17 radar was also fitted, but this was not the case. The new nose, with its radome, was already flight-cleared and offered massive internal volume for a large receiver antenna, together with favourable non-refraction characteristics.

Aircraft designations

The installation of the new radome led to a change of designation, to B.Mk 6 (Mod) – unofficially, at least, since the No. 51 Squadron Canberras remained resolutely plain B.Mk 6s on their aircraft record cards. The aircraft were known by a number of designations during their lives, including B.Mk 6(RC) (RC for Radio Countermeasures) and, according to some sources, even PR.Mk 16. Since they were fitted with Blue Shadow the Canberras were actually B.Mk 6(BS) aircraft, though even this designation, official as it was, was little used.

The No. 51 Squadron Canberras were seldom photographed, so it is difficult to ascertain when major configuration changes took place. WJ775 gained Blue Shadow SLAR fairings only after being fitted with the AI.17-type pointed nose, whereas WT301 (equipped with Blue Shadow when it joined No. 192 Squadron) was photographed without them when it had the longer nose in 1962, though these characteristic strakes had been refitted by 1964.

Soon after the installation of the AI.17-type nose, the conventional 'blunt' Canberra tailcone was replaced by a new dielectric tail fairing with flattened sides, which tapered in plan view but had a flat, sharp trailing edge. This is thought to have accommodated a J/K/Ku-band horn antenna for a new passive tail warning system, which had an 'audio select' in the cockpit. Soon after this new tailcone was fitted, a new fairing was added below the tailplane trailing edge, on the fuselage centreline. The fairing had an aft-facing dielectric radome and is believed to have accommodated the Orange Putter active tail warning radar displaced from the original tailcone, though some sources suggest that the No. 51 Squadron aircraft never carried an active tail warning system, and that the under-tail antenna served another passive warning system.

The next major change to the No. 51 Squadron Canberras' appearance came in late 1965, when the pointed, conical radome of the T.Mk 11 was replaced by a similarly lengthened, but more rounded and blunt, nose radome. It was similar in shape to the nose radomes fitted to some Radar Research Establishment (RRE) trials aircraft, and was interpreted by some as marking a change of radar. In fact, the No. 51 Squadron Canberras never carried radar, and the new nose was adopted only because it gave better performance for the antennas carried in the nose, consisting of a steerable, spinning AN/APA-6 direction finder.

The next change to the aircraft's external configuration came in 1966, when the slab-sided squared-off tailcone was replaced by a more conventional tailcone. This was probably fitted for aerodynamic reasons, and may not have indicated any further change in equipment. The new under-tail fairing remained. By this time, all four B.Mk 6s had been fitted with Blue Shadow, which was retained until the end of their careers.

Published histories of Cold War reconnaissance missions suggest that the No. 51 Squadron Canberras used Blue Shadow as a means of obtaining precise navigational 'fixes'. A primitive SLAR, Blue Shadow was particularly useful for mapping coastlines, and produced a paper print-out (on special thermally sensitive paper) at the same scale as the navigator's standard plotting chart, which enabled him to compare the aircraft's position with his own calculated position. The print-outs were rolled up continuously throughout the flight and stowed alongside the Nav against the aircraft sidewall. Some aircrew recall that print-outs were only made when an updating fix was taken to avoid them drowning in paper!

A 'vis recorder' was eventually installed to record the Blue Shadow picture for post-flight analysis. When operating in the Baltic, for example, they crossed the Danish peninsula before descending to surveillance altitude (using the islands of Bornholm or Gotland as cover). The aircraft would then fly a circuit of the Baltic, using Blue Shadow and Green Satin Doppler to remain in international airspace, but

Above: WJ775 was one of two original Elint B.Mk 6s, although it was not initially fitted with Blue Shadow SLAR. However, it was the first aircraft to adopt a new, larger dielectric nose radome with a metal strip, as illustrated here.

Right: From about 1961 to 1965 the B.Mk 6s were given the pointed and much larger radome of the T.Mk 11, modelled here by WT301 (which, unusually, has had its Blue Shadow SLAR removed). The new nose provided greater internal volume for larger antennas.

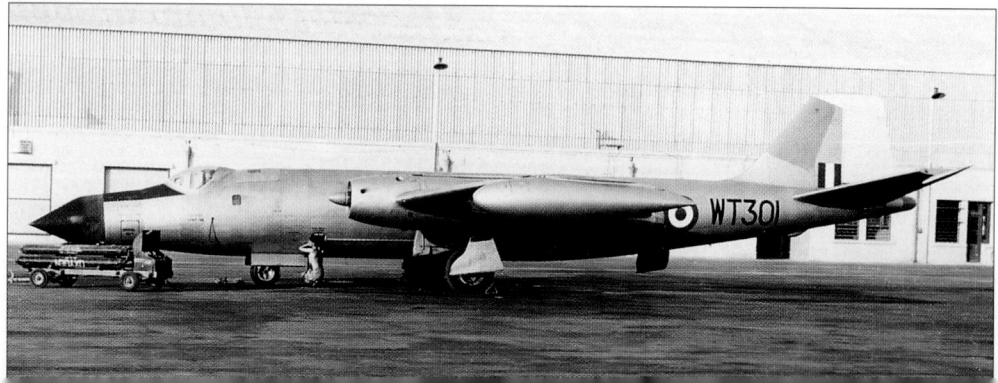

Below: As well as its operational Canberra fleet, No. 51 Squadron operated a T.Mk 4 trainer. WJ877 was the third such aircraft to be assigned, but was also the longest-serving. It outlived all but one of the B.Mk 6s in service with the unit.

flying from the Gulf of Finland along the coast of the Baltic states and Poland before climbing back to altitude for the transit home. Blue Shadow and Green Satin were the only two radiating systems carried by the Canberras (at least in the later years) and were only used because they could provide accurate updates for the Canberra's otherwise basic, wartime-era navigation equipment. The penalty of breaking radio silence had to be accepted in order to guarantee the accuracy of navigation which was paramount on all routes flown, to avoid the embarrassment and danger of any border incursions

The Canberra's external antennas were fixed, but black boxes in the bomb bay, aft equipment bay and Special Operator's equipment racks were changed according to mission requirements. Elint equipment carried by the Canberras included a Radio Research Laboratory AN/APR-4 superheterodyne radar interceptor receiver with TN180 and TN181 tuning heads, and an AN/ALR-8 communications band receiver. In the Comint role, the Canberra's main radio system was the R216 manually tuned tank receiver, a radio normally used in Army tanks. Also in the Canberra's voice suite was the so-called 'Auto-voice box', a 20-channel VHF system 'borrowed' from the Chipmunk (other RAF types used the same system in the 1960s). It was only in the late 1960s that the Special Operator was able to monitor these additional 20 channels directly – until then the system was switched on and it was simply hoped that the radio and recorders were working properly!

High-altitude operations

A hi-lo-hi mission profile may have been atypical, since the Canberra's principal advantage over the Comet lay in its ability to fly at very high altitude. This may have given the Canberras the ability to detect emissions (and perhaps to listen to radio signals) emanating from farther over the border, since the radar/radio horizon was effectively 'pushed back' with increased altitude. That the No. 51 Squadron Canberras were routinely used for high altitude work can perhaps be gauged from the fact that sunscreens were attached to the

WT301 sits on a rain-soaked Luqa ramp. The Malta base was one of several regularly used by 51's Canberras in the Mediterranean/Middle East. Egypt and Syria were watched closely for much of the Canberra era. Further afield, the Canberras used Iranian bases to fly along the southern Soviet borders.

inside of the goldfish bowl canopy, above the pilot's head. By contrast, the first three No. 192 Squadron Comets were converted from undelivered early-model Comet Mk 2s, and as such had the original square windows which had caused the run of accidents to BOAC's Mk 1s. In consequence, the aircraft were unable to be fully pressurised, and had a cabin altitude of 25,000 ft (7620 m) (requiring oxygen masks to be worn) at maximum altitude, and therefore were usually flown at lower heights. It is believed that No. 51 Squadron's fourth Comet (which replaced XK663, which burned out in a 1959 hangar fire) was subject to the same limitations, despite its oval windows. The Comets reportedly could achieve about 41,000 ft (12500 m) as fuel burned off, giving them a line-of-sight range of about 300 miles (482 km) 'beyond the enemy border'. The Canberras could operate routinely at 50,000 ft (15240 m), and far higher than that if pressure jerkins and helmets were worn.

The Canberras usually operated autonomously, but sometimes in close co-operation with the squadron's Comets. The Comets had a comprehensive analysis capability which the Canberra lacked, and a real emitter location capability, which the Canberra (with only one special operator and a limited antenna suite) could not match. The Canberra's principal role was detecting signals, which could be located broadly for further examination by the Comets. It has sometimes been suggested that the Canberras would fly feints towards enemy airspace, turning away at 'the latest safe distance' while high-flying Comets stood-off and monitored enemy radars and communications for any reactions.

Although there have been fanciful stories of No. 51 Squadron Canberras and Comets limping back to Wyton with battle damage, the truth is that the squadron's aircraft never conducted the kind of shallow-penetration 'ferret' missions flown by the USAF, and its aircraft were never

fired upon. The Comets usually maintained a 'respectable and respectful' distance of 50 miles (80 km) from Warsaw Pact borders, which might reduce to 20 miles (32 km) from an occasional irregular protrusion on the map. The Canberras are assumed to have used the same separation distances. Some aircrew remember a 20-mile separation distance, which may have been the figure used at the end of the Canberra/Comet era.

Regular intercepts

Simply avoiding an overflight was no guarantee of safety: the Cold War was full of examples of Warsaw Pact and Chinese fighters firing on aircraft in international airspace. No. 51 Squadron's aircraft were regularly intercepted over the Baltic and elsewhere by fighters from Sweden, plus the USSR and other Warsaw Pact countries, and crews frequently picked up enemy fighter radar transmissions. The types most frequently encountered were the MiG-19 'Farmer', MiG-21 'Fishbed', Sukhoi Su-9 'Fishpot' and Yak-28 'Firebar'. Sometimes enemy fighters locked on, indicating that they were potentially ready to fire their missiles, and there were reports of No. 51's linguists hearing enemy fighter controllers ordering their charges to make ready to fire. Although this could doubtless make things fairly tense, no enemy fighter pilot ever opened fire on a No. 51 Squadron aircraft, and the only time the aircraft came under fire, the 'attackers' were Turkish fighters firing warning shots after the No. 51 Squadron aircraft was confused for an unidentified intruder.

Although surrounded by great secrecy and security, No. 51 Squadron's operations were described by one former squadron member as being "fairly routine and relaxed, although the operators monitoring busy frequencies could certainly have periods of hectic and quite stressful activity". There was great melodrama, for crews were not allowed to tell wives or families the dates or times of missions or detachments, and operations usually were scheduled for a 10-day window around the new moon, when radio propagation characteristics were at their best. Some aircrew expressed disbelief that operations were planned around lunar cycles, believing that such an arrangement would have required

No. 51 Squadron Canberras

The final nose configuration for the B.Mk 6 (Mod) was this rounded radome, which distorted incoming signals less and allowed for more accurate intelligence-gathering. WJ768 (left) is seen with the new radome (but original tail antenna group) at Luqa in February 1966, while above WT305 is seen landing at the same base in 1969 with revised tail configuration.

more 'foresight', than circumstances usually permitted. It may be that this kind of timing was common in the early days, but was then abandoned, perhaps as equipment improved. Front and rear crew were briefed separately and the flight crew did not know what frequencies were being monitored by their special operator. In the air, even in the Comets, flight crew and operators were not separated, contrary to popular rumour, and reports of a frangible bulkhead between compartments were erroneous. Besides, such separation would have been impossible in the Canberra's cramped confines. In the B.Mk 6 (Mod)s at least, the special operator's equipment rack formed the roof of a tunnel between the cockpit side and the pilot's bulkhead, and the navigator and special operator had to clamber through this (usually 'limbo-dancing' backwards underneath it) to reach their seats.

Overseas detachments

Most operations were mounted from overseas bases, depending on the area of interest. Most Canberra sorties were flown from bases in the Mediterranean and Middle East, or from Wyton and Watton. Akrotiri was used for missions listening to signals from Egypt and Syria (especially before and during the Suez operation in 1956), and for some flights over the Black Sea. No. 51 Squadron's Canberras were also seen frequently at Luqa, Malta, and at Sharjah in what is now the United Arab Emirates. Before the revolution in Iran, Tehran-Mehrabad was also a regular destination for the squadron, allowing easy access to the border between the USSR and Iran, and the Caspian Sea.

Canberras also flew regular missions in northern and central Europe. Flights along Russia's northern coast off Murmansk and in the Barents Sea were flown from Watton or Wyton, with a refuelling stop at Bodø or Andøya in Norway. Flights along the inner German border and along the Berlin corridors (and some Baltic missions) were flown from a variety of airfields in RAF Germany, especially Wunstorf, which for many years was the nearest RAF airfield to the East German frontier. Operations were later moved to the 'Clutch' airfields at Wildenrath and Laarbruch (but not, apparently, Brüggen) when it was suspected that Russian agents were watching operations at Wunstorf. The Canberras also flew regular operations from Karup in Denmark, and even from Ballykelly in Northern Ireland. Less regular destinations included El Adem (Libya), Habbaniyah (Iraq, before 1956), Khormaksar (Aden, before 1967), Salisbury (Rhodesia, before 1965), Changi (Singapore), and Labuan (Borneo).

Great care was taken not to give any warning of No. 51 Squadron's missions, in order to make sure that interesting radars were not deliberately shut down, and to ensure that Soviet fighter controllers were not too tight-lipped. It was common for missions to be launched in complete radio silence (with ATC instructions being given by Aldis lamp and Verey light), or for the squadron's Canberras to shadow other aircraft operating from the detachment airfield as they taxied out and took off, breaking away as their 'host' climbed out. There have even been reports of No. 51 Squadron's Canberras starting up inside hangars and taxiing out under their own power, and of taxiing back into their hangars after landing, but this cannot be confirmed.

Operators plotted their intercepts on real world maps and charts, and thus knew exactly where they were operating. They were given their assigned frequencies on rice paper (which was then eaten!) and recordings and plots were rushed away (under armed guard) for analysis (perhaps by GCHQ?) as soon as aircraft landed.

Hawker Siddeley Nimrods were ordered to replace the ageing Comets and the first of these (XW664) was delivered to Wyton on 8 July 1971. Equipment installation was a drawn out process, and Nimrod training missions did not begin until late 1973, the first operation being flown on 3 May 1974. This finally allowed the retirement of the four Canberras, and two of the three Comets, on 1 July 1974. One of the Canberras, WJ775, flew four times after 1 July and made its final flight on 4 September 1974, before being assigned to the Central Servicing

Left: The Wyton reconnaissance Wing put up this formation in June 1969. It comprised a Sigint-gathering Comet (lead) and Canberra B.Mk 6 (Mod) (port wing position) of No. 51 Squadron, a Canberra PR.Mk 7 of No. 58 Squadron (starboard wing) and a Victor SR.Mk 2 of No. 543 Squadron (in the slot).

Below: A rare air-to-air photograph of WJ775 after adoption of low-level camouflage (although the aircraft did not routinely operate at low altitudes) shows detail of the antennas. The revised tail group returned to the standard bullet-shaped tailcone but was painted black and white.

Development Unit at Swanton Morley for use as a ground instructional airframe. WJ768 went to Akrotiri for firefighting training on 9 July, while WT301 went to the Defence Explosives Ordnance School at Chattenden on 12 July.

Even after the squadron lost its B.Mk 6s, some Canberra expertise was retained (many pilots having been dual-rated on Comet and Canberra), and the unit's T.Mk 4 was retained until February 1975. Even this did not prevent No. 51 Squadron from maintaining some Canberra aircrew, since Wyton's Station Flight operated a handful of T.Mk 4s to support No. 39 Squadron's PR.Mk 9s and, from August 1975, No. 360 Squadron's T.Mk 17s.

Special project

Thus, perhaps it was not entirely surprising when one of the last Canberra B.Mk 6 (Mod)s returned to No. 51 Squadron in January 1976 for what was described as a special project, possibly designated Operation Zabra. The aircraft (WT305) previously had been loaned to the Procurement Executive, and had been flown at the RRE (Pershore) and RAE (Farnborough). While the aircraft was at Pershore an American 'radiometer' had been installed in a turret fitted to the hatch above the navigator's and special operator's ejection seats. The hatch was normally jettisoned using explosive bolts, but the additional weight of the sensor turret made this impossible, so the explosive bolts were supplemented by a rocket motor on the forward edge of the hatch, designed to lift the edge into the slipstream and let it be blown back. To prevent the rear of the hatch from settling back into the aperture, two aft outrigger hinges were fitted, having forks which allowed the hatch to separate as it swung up and back.

The turret was still fitted when the aircraft returned to Wyton, resembling an inverted flower pot with a prominent window of extremely expensive, optically perfect glass on one side. Its base was protected at the front by a slipstream deflector. The turret is understood to have accommodated a US-supplied infra-red surveillance system, though it has also been described as a 'stand-off reconnaissance radar'. The use of the term 'radar' is believed to have been technically correct, but misleading. Radar can be used to describe any device which measures the range and bearing (direction) of a target – and is not actually restricted to equipment operating in particular wavelengths. Thus the Zabra device could be described as an infra-red radar. It is understood to have been

The B.Mk 6 (Mod)s were busy right to the end – here WT301 taxis in at Luqa in June 1974, its last full month of operations. The missions were handed over to the Nimrod R.Mk 1, which also assumed the taskings of 51's Comet fleet.

From 1963 to 1974 the No. 51 Squadron Canberra fleet settled down at four regular aircraft (WJ768, WJ775, WT301 and WT305). They were assigned individual code-letters, worn only on the nosewheel doors. WJ768 was 'Y', and was seen at Akrotiri (above) at the time of its retirement. All four are seen in a flypast (right).

used to obtain accurate IR emission signature characteristics of the newly deployed Su-15 and MiG-25, although the latter rarely ever ventured into the Baltic from the nearest IA-PVO base at Baranovichi. The Zabra aircraft probably also collected the IR signatures of other Soviet aircraft operating in the Baltic, especially those exercising in the Baltic water range complex, and the range at Tartu. Interestingly, the aircraft's dielectric nose- and tailcones had been overpainted in camouflage colours, perhaps indicating that the old DF receivers and J/K/Ku-band tail warning system were no longer in use. The Zabra project (which was probably intended to test the newly fitted equipment) began with a sortie from RAF Laarbruch in Germany on 16 February 1976, and concluded on 14 October. The number of sorties flown remains unknown, though most are believed to have been flown from Laarbruch. The aircraft was allocated to Wyton as a gate-guard on 15 November 1976.

In the late 1970s, things had become rather more relaxed and No. 51 Squadron's existence became more openly acknowledged. This was perhaps inevitable after the retirement of the RAF's Comet C.Mk 2 transports, which had left four Mk 2s very obviously operating, yet without an obvious owner! When the last of the Comets was retired the Ministry of Defence even issued a brief press release, although it stressed the age and sortie total of the aircraft and some of its crew, and ignored the subject of the squadron's role. The withdrawal of the Canberras went without official recognition. Moreover, the degree of secrecy surrounding the unit was such that details of its equipment

did not even filter through to publications like the *Royal Air Force Yearbook*, which was still listing the squadron as a Canberra operator in 1979 – five years after routine Canberra operations had ended, and a full three years after the final retirement of WT305. Even today, more than quarter of a century later, details of the squadron's Canberra era remain shadowy, and much of the narrative above must remain a matter for conjecture and guesswork.

Useful in retirement

Despite the secrecy surrounding the No. 51 Squadron Canberras, all of the aircraft survived for some time following their final groundings. In Cyprus, WJ768 was used for crash-rescue training before finally succumbing to the flames. WJ775 was used for servicing development and for training in NDT (Non Destructive Testing) for 18 years before being replaced by a Harrier in early 1992. The aircraft was dismantled in April 1996, moved to St Athan, and then moved to the Army's STANTA (Stanford Training Area, now Bodney Camp, Army Training Estate, East), for use as a target in the FIBUA (Fighting in Built Up Areas) training ground. As far as can be ascertained, the aircraft is a passive target (i.e., is not shot at)

Above: WT305 was the aircraft chosen to be resurrected for the 1976 special project called Zabra, which is thought to have collected IR signatures of Soviet interceptors. Both the tailcone and nose radome were painted over, suggesting that the previous equipment had been removed.

WT305's special project IR turret was mounted on the escape hatch for the navigator and systems operator. A mock-up is seen (left) on an RRE Canberra at Pershore (with Viscount in the background), which differed slightly from the operational installation (right) on WT305, which had a slipstream deflector.

and thus remains substantially complete. One day, perhaps it could be saved for restoration and preservation. WT301 served as an instructional airframe for MoD bomb disposal experts at Chattenden until January 1993, when it was replaced by a Phantom. The aircraft went to Hanningfield Metals at Stock, Essex in October 1993. This company had an enviable record for saving historic aircraft which passed through their hands, or sometimes just their nose sections, but WT301 slipped through the net and had been scrapped and processed by May 1995.

WT305 looked set to be preserved for posterity when it was placed on RAF Wyton's main gate on 5 July 1977, following a long period of preparation (e.g., the removal of classified equipment, including the dorsal turret). It was joined later by a Canberra PR.Mk 7 and a PR.Mk 9. Unfortunately, the aircraft fell victim

to a short-sighted policy under which stations were limited to one gate-guard only, and the aircraft was dismantled and scrapped in October 1989. Some reports suggest that the aircraft's nose was subsequently saved and preserved, but this cannot be confirmed.

Since the end of the Cold War, No. 51 Squadron has become slightly less reclusive and it is now widely acknowledged as being a reconnaissance unit, specialising in the collection of electronic intelligence. During 1996, the RAF Waddington station magazine, *The Sentry*, carried a brief piece by the squadron's CO which stated that:

"Many of you will be aware of the aura of secrecy which surrounds 51 Squadron's operations. However, in broad outline, we are a reconnaissance squadron and our official role is 'routine communications and radar research'. We do fulfil a high priority operational role, and the majority of our current operational tasks are carried out on overseas deployments."

In broad terms, then, it seems that little has changed since the days of the Canberra and Comet. It seems a pity that the squadron's vital importance during the Cold War has not been properly acknowledged or recognised.

Jon Lake

Final resting places

Right: WJ768 was scrapped on-site at RAF Akrotiri, having been used as a fire/crash rescue trainer.

Below: WT305 was displayed on the main gate at RAF Wyton until scrapped under a gate-guard rationalisation programme.

WJ775 spent many years after retirement in the hangar at Swanton Morley (illustrated) until it was moved to Stanford Training Area (STANTA), where it remains.

WT301 was dispatched to the Defence Explosive Ordnance Disposal School (DEODS) at Chattenden. It was subsequently scrapped.

Canberra colours

No. 192 Squadron's first two Canberra B.Mk 2s were delivered to the unit in the early Bomber Command colour scheme of PRU blue undersides with medium sea grey and light slate grey camouflaged topsides. Otherwise, the unit's early aircraft all wore the high-speed silver finish used by most Bomber Command Canberras after about 1953. Squadron markings were carried briefly during the late 1950s, consisting of a small red goose on the tip tanks of camouflaged aircraft, and a slightly larger red goose on the tail of silver aircraft.

No. 51 Squadron was not the only Canberra operator at Wyton. When the PR.Mk 7s of co-located No. 58 Squadron were repainted with dark green and dark sea grey topsides (the first being repainted in August 1966, the rest following in 1967 and 1968), the No. 51 Squadron B.Mk 6 (Mod)s followed suit, though WT305, at least, was still silver overall in April 1969. Some interpreted the repainting as an effort by the squadron to make its aircraft look more like the new T.Mk 17s then entering service with No. 360 Squadron. The T.Mk 17 had a broadly similar nose profile to the B.Mk 6 (Mod), but this still seems unlikely. Nor was the new camouflage colour scheme indicative of any switch to low-level operations, though this has also been suggested. A further change in colour scheme (again applied across the Canberra force) saw camouflaged aircraft receiving toned-down red/blue roundels and fin flashes in 1972-73.

Radar warning

For most of their careers, 51's Canberras had a passive warning receiver in the tailcone, and another rear-facing sensor (possibly Orange Putter) in a fairing mounted under the tailcone.

EE Canberra B.Mk 6 (Mod)
No. 51 Squadron, RAF Wyton, 1976

Visually at least, the most radically modified of the No. 51 Squadron aircraft was WT305, which appeared in this configuration during 1976 for a classified programme code-named Zabra. As well as its fuselage fairings, distended nose and RWR, the aircraft featured a prominent turret aft the canopy, which housed an infra-red sensor. The turret had been removed by the time WT305 went on display at RAF Wyton's main gate in July 1977.

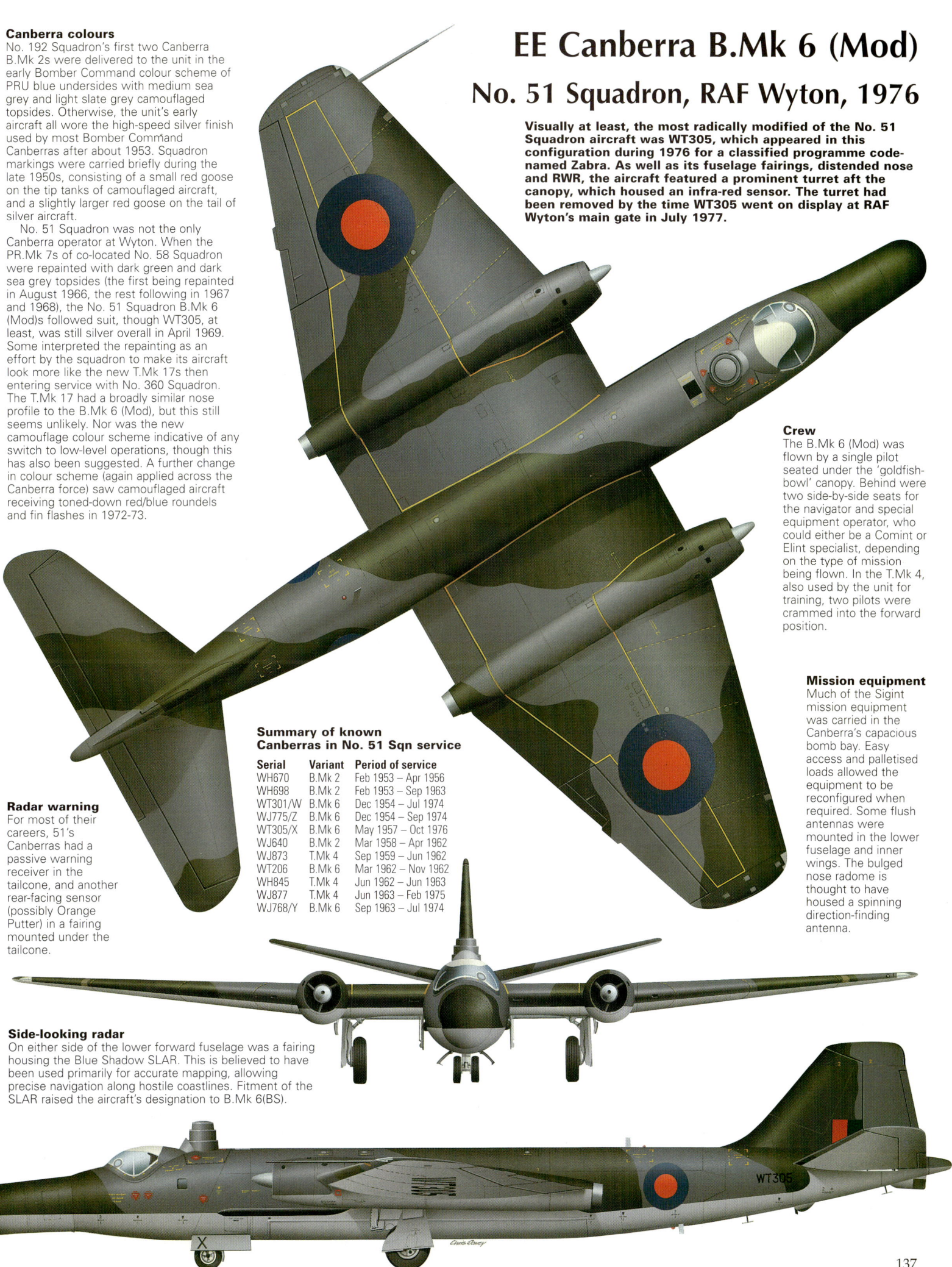

Crew

The B.Mk 6 (Mod) was flown by a single pilot seated under the 'goldfish-bowl' canopy. Behind were two side-by-side seats for the navigator and special equipment operator, who could either be a Comint or Elint specialist, depending on the type of mission being flown. In the T.Mk 4, also used by the unit for training, two pilots were crammed into the forward position.

Mission equipment

Much of the Sigint mission equipment was carried in the Canberra's capacious bomb bay. Easy access and palletised loads allowed the equipment to be reconfigured when required. Some flush antennas were mounted in the lower fuselage and inner wings. The bulged nose radome is thought to have housed a spinning direction-finding antenna.

Summary of known Canberras in No. 51 Sqn service

Serial	Variant	Period of service
WH670	B.Mk 2	Feb 1953 – Apr 1956
WH698	B.Mk 2	Feb 1953 – Sep 1963
WT301/W	B.Mk 6	Dec 1954 – Jul 1974
WJ775/Z	B.Mk 6	Dec 1954 – Sep 1974
WT305/X	B.Mk 6	May 1957 – Oct 1976
WJ640	B.Mk 2	Mar 1958 – Apr 1962
WJ873	T.Mk 4	Sep 1959 – Jun 1962
WT206	B.Mk 6	Mar 1962 – Nov 1962
WH845	T.Mk 4	Jun 1962 – Jun 1963
WJ877	T.Mk 4	Jun 1963 – Feb 1975
WJ768/Y	B.Mk 6	Sep 1963 – Jul 1974

Side-looking radar

On either side of the lower forward fuselage was a fairing housing the Blue Shadow SLAR. This is believed to have been used primarily for accurate mapping, allowing precise navigation along hostile coastlines. Fitment of the SLAR raised the aircraft's designation to B.Mk 6(BS).

P-47 Thunderbolt

Part 1: Early development and combat in the ETO

Carrying bombs under the wing pylons and a drop tank under its belly, a P-47D-22-RE of the 410th Fighter Squadron, 373rd Fighter Group, cruises along the Normandy coast with Mont St Michel in the background. The date was September 1944 and the 9th Air Force's P-47 force (which numbered 15 fighter groups) had been in France for some time, supporting the Allied breakout from the Normandy beachhead. As well as providing close support for the advancing ground forces, 9th AF P-47s ranged across France, the Low Countries and into Germany itself, seeking out airfields and cutting German lines of communication, often encountering fierce flak defences. In September the 373rd distinguished itself with a series of successful attacks against barges and tugs on the Rhine. Although most air-to-air fighting was by then being performed at high level by Mustangs and RAF Spitfires, 9th AF P-47s still tangled regularly with the Luftwaffe, particularly at low altitude where the P-47's speed and power made it a formidable foe. Several Messerschmitt Me 262 jets fell to the Thunderbolt's guns.

While other US fighter designers turned to the slim liquid-cooled Allison V-1710 engine to produce small, sleek fighters, Republic's Alexander Kartveli persisted with ever more powerful air-cooled radial engines. The culmination of this development was the mighty P-47 Thunderbolt, a warplane which dwarfed its rivals but which was to become one of the most influential aircraft of World War II, and the most widely built US fighter. Its first combat assignment was in England, where what was to become the 'Mighty Eighth' was building a massive force of daylight bombers. With the arrival of the P-47, the US fliers at last had a fighter with which they could provide a measure of escort protection for their charges. As longer-ranged P-51s became available for the bomber escort role, the P-47 turned to fighter-bomber duties. In doing so, it found its true niche, and did as much as any type to pulverise the Third Reich into final submission.

Today it is the P-51 which is best remembered for its part in the air war over western Europe, yet it was not until January 1944 that P-51s crossed into German airspace on a bomber escort mission, and it was to be April before the force became a truly effective one. For the year previous, the P-47 had held the line, and despite the transition of 8th AF Thunderbolts units to the Mustang, the P-47 continued to be highly successful in air combat to the last day of the war. Typical of the 'Jugs' which, as far as their fuel would allow, braved flak and fighters daily to protect the bombers is this P-47D-23-RA of the 82nd Fighter Squadron, 78th Fighter Group.

Until the arrival of the P-47 the fledgling USAAF fighter community in England had flown Spitfires. While a delight to fly, the Spitfire was inadequate for the bomber escort role. The P-47, too, had range deficiencies until drop tanks were developed. One of the earliest successful types is carried by this VIII Fighter Command P-47D: a 108-US gal (409-litre) tank made from paper and painted with silver dope.

During its operational career, the P-47 was always overshadowed by the sleeker, more glamorous P-51 Mustang – and still is. When it is remembered at all, the P-47 is assumed to have been a second-rate 'also-ran', in much the same way that history has tended to remember the Spitfire while writing off the Hurricane, or the way in which posterity has remembered the Lancaster while consigning the Halifax to the footnotes. The truth is more complex and, in some key respects, the Thunderbolt was a better aircraft than the Mustang, and was preferred by some pilots. Some fighter groups even preferred to retain the Thunderbolt rather than to convert to the Mustang.

Many of the most famous and popular aircraft in aviation history have been characterised by their compact dimensions and graceful lines. No one suggests that fame and popularity rest on beauty alone, though it may be the case that ugly aircraft have an uphill struggle when it comes to gaining recognition, especially if they are fighters. The Thunderbolt's huge size and ungainly lines thus may have counted against it receiving popular acclaim and recognition. And the Thunderbolt was a leviathan among fighters, longer than any of its rivals and with a deeper, wider fuselage and curiously stubby wings. The P-47's empty weight was nearly twice as great as a fully laden Spitfire Mk IX, Bf 109G-6 or A6M5 Zero, and one-third more than the weight of a loaded P-51D.

The extent to which the Thunderbolt has failed to grab popular attention is reflected in many ways. Of thousands built, only about half a dozen remain airworthy, and the type is often referred to by an unflattering nickname – one seldom used by its pilots, and of post-war origin. Everyone knows that the P-47 was the 'Jug' – supposedly a contraction of the term Juggernaut, or, according to some contemporary publicists, a result of the aircraft's resemblance to a milk jug. But the nickname beloved by post-war historians was not widely used by wartime aircrew, who inevitably knew their fighter as the 'Bolt' or 'T-Bolt', or simply as the P-47. For the record, it should perhaps be pointed out that

it is now believed that when post-war fliers first coined the term 'Jug' they were abbreviating the term 'Thunder-Jug' (US military slang for a chamber pot), rather than the word Juggernaut.

However, the P-47's actions spoke for themselves. The P-47-equipped 56th Fighter Group was the top-scoring group in the entire Eighth Air Force, and two of its pilots (Francis Gabreski and Robert Johnson, with 28 and 27 kills, respectively) were the top-scoring USAAF aces in Europe. This single group destroyed 674 aircraft in air combat, including a number of Me 262 jet fighters.

Russian revolution

Remarkably, the large and rather stout Thunderbolt was derived from a family of small, lightweight aircraft. These were the products of the Seversky Aircraft Corporation, a small company founded in 1931 by Major Alexander Prokoviev de Seversky, a leading 13-victory Imperial Russian ace during World War I who became Russia's Air Attaché to Washington, and who decided not to return home when the revolution came. After working as a test pilot and as a scientific advisor to General 'Billy' Mitchell, Seversky sold a bombsight patent to the USAAC for $50,000, and in 1931 formed his own company, the Seversky Aero Corporation. A native of Tiflis, Georgia, Seversky was proud to be a naturalised American citizen (since 1927) and a major in the USAAC reserve. Despite his pro-America sentiments, he employed Alexander Kartveli (another Georgian-Russian émigré) as his chief designer.

Kartveli had been an artillery officer, and was studying in Paris when revolution overwhelmed Russia. He decided to stay, teaching mathematics and working as a circus trapeze artist while studying the then-unusual combination of electrical and aeronautical engineering. Kartveli then worked for a succession of French aviation companies, including Bleriot and Wibault, before working for Charles Levine, owner of the Columbia Aircraft Corporation, who made the first passenger flight across the Atlantic in 1927. Kartveli moved to the USA, and later moved to Fokker's Atlantic Aircraft Corporation in New Jersey.

Seversky and Kartveli set up shop in a Long Island hangar leased from float manufacturers Edo, while their own plant was being built at Farmingdale. The first Seversky aircraft was the SEV-3, first flown in June 1933 as an amphibious three-seat floatplane, with retractable wheels in underfuselage floats. Six were built for Colombia, and the prototype was re-engined and set a new world speed record for amphibians. Seversky had always planned to use his design as the basis of a family of aircraft, and the SEV-3 went on to form the basis of the BT-8 trainer for the USAAC, the SEV-2XP two-seat fighter, the single-seat SEV-1XP fighter, and the X-BT (in single-seat SEV-2PA Convoy fighter, AT-12 gunnery trainer and two-seat bomber forms).

The SEV-1XP formed the basis of the P-35 fighter for the USAAC, 77 of which were ordered for the Army Air Corps after the design won an official evaluation against the

Curtiss P-36 and the Consolidated P-30. The SEV-1XP also formed the basis of the XNF-1 fighter prototype for the Navy (evaluated against the Brewster F2A Buffalo), and the EP-1-106 for Sweden, known locally as the J-9. Sixty Swedish aircraft were not delivered, instead being pressed into US service as P-35As.

The P-35 marked a very real improvement over the biplanes which it succeeded, and over the fixed-gear, open-cockpit Boeing P-26 'Peashooter', but the margin of improvement was relatively small, and the P-35 was virtually obsolete by the time it entered service in 1937. The landing gear, for example, was only semi-retractable, raising into streamlined fairings but remaining partly exposed. The aircraft was also inadequately armed, having single 0.50-in (12.7-mm) and 0.30-in (7.62-mm) machine-guns in the top of the nose. The Swedish J-9s and the P-35As had twin 0.50-in machine-guns in the top of the nose, and twin 0.30-in guns in the wingroots.

Civil P-35 derivatives proved extremely successful in the air racing world, underlining the high-speed/long-endurance capabilities which radial-engined monoplanes could possess. This had some influence in legitimising the configuration.

The P-35 bore only a passing resemblance to the later P-47, and to compare the two designs is largely futile, despite the common use of (very different) radial engines, a related undercarriage design and layout, a commonality in wing and tailplane planforms, and a vague similarity in tailfin and rudder outline. The two types were fundamentally different, not least in being products of their respective eras, separated by five years which marked the most rapid development in aviation. The P-47 was 50 per cent longer than the P-35, and more than twice as heavy, and although both aircraft were fighters, they were designed to meet very different requirements.

Improving the P-35

The last series-built P-35 was completed (on the instructions of the Army Air Corps) as the XP-41, which was better streamlined, with a lowered canopy, fully retractable undercarriage and a 1,200-hp (895-kW) Pratt & Whitney R-1830-19 engine with a two-stage, two-speed supercharger, in place of the P-35's 850-hp (634-kW) R-1830-9. While the XP-41 was built to fulfil a USAAC contract, the Seversky firm simultaneously built a similar aircraft as the private venture AP.4. It was fitted with an exhaust-driven turbo-supercharger, and showed such promise when evaluated that, in March 1939, 13 more were ordered for service test as the YP-43.

The Seversky company became the Republic Aviation Company on 13 October 1939, after other stockholders bought out Seversky's holdings in the company. Kartveli remained at the head of the design department, however, and later created the F-84 Thunderjet and Thunderstreak and the F-105 Thunderchief. The Army had just placed an order for 80 more powerful production derivatives of the AP.4 as R-2180-1-engined P-44 Rockets, and this order almost immediately was augmented by orders for 225 (and eventually, on 9 September 1940, for 827) even more powerful P-44-2s, with 2,000-hp (1492-kW) R-2800-7 engines. These aircraft were cancelled on 13 September 1940, and 54 more-modest derivatives of the type were ordered as P-43 Lancers. The P-43 eventually was built in several versions, and production reached 272, although some went directly for export, being supplied to Australia and China.

Similarities between the P-43 and the P-47 were more marked than the resemblance between the P-35 and the Thunderbolt, although, again, the similarities were confined to appearance and the types were entirely dissimilar. Republic, as the company by then had become, never built a P-44, but artists' impressions showed an aircraft which looked even more similar to the later Thunderbolt.

During the summer of 1939, Kartveli began work on a new design, reluctantly turning his back on what had been

With its wing heavily tufted for airflow observation, the first YP-43 undertakes a test sortie. With its R-1830-35 Twin Wasp developing 1,200 hp (895 kW), the YP-43 could reach a speed of 350 mph (563 km/h) and an altitude of 38,000 ft (11582 m). The armament (not fitted here) was two 0.5-in (12.7-mm) guns in the wings and two 0.3-in (7.62-mm) guns in the nose.

P-43 Lancer – pre-war pursuit

The performance increase shown by the company-funded AP.4, especially at high altitude, was dramatic, and resulted in an order for the P-43 Lancer. Thirteen YP-43s were built (the AP.4 acting as the XP-43) and were followed by 54 P-43s and 80 P-43As for the USAAC, and 125 P-43A-1s intended for service in China. Many of the aircraft were converted for reconnaissance duties, becoming P-43Bs in the process. A few saw action in Chinese hands against the Japanese.

a succession of increasingly large and increasingly powerful radial-engined aircraft to produce a tiny fighter design powered by one of the fashionable new inline, liquid-cooled Allison engines. The AP.10, as it was known, followed European design practice (as demonstrated in aircraft like the Supermarine Spitfire, the Messerschmitt Bf 109E and the Dewoitine D.520), having the smallest possible airframe wrapped around a powerful, liquid-cooled inline engine. The AP.10 design remained unbuilt, but was submitted for evaluation in August 1939.

41-31449 was the second of the P-43A-1 batch for China (although only 108 were delivered). Notable improvements were the fitting of 0.5-in (12.7-mm) guns in the nose, self-sealing tanks and the provision to carry bombs or a drop tank.

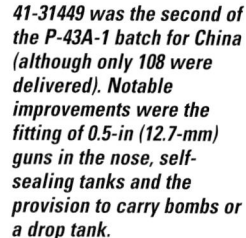

By the XP-44 Rocket design, shown in this contemporary artist's impression, the portly lines of the Thunderbolt are clearly beginning to emerge.

XP-44 Rocket – last stepping-stone to the Thunderbolt

While the YP-43s were under construction, Alex 'Sasha' Kartveli was working on an even better version (company designation AP.4J), with lowered canopy, streamlined forward fuselage and an R-2800 Double Wasp engine. The results looked promising, and 80 were ordered off the drawing board as the XP-44. However, events in Europe during 1940 had shown that even the new XP-44 would be markedly inferior to the Spitfire and Bf 109, and the P-44 order was converted to P-43s as a means of keeping Republic's factory busy while the design office came up with another, better design. Kartveli's team immediately set to work on the AP.10.

The design showed great promise, and in November 1940 the Army ordered two Allison V-1710-39-engined prototype AP.10s as the XP-47 and the XP-47A. The contract was not approved, however, since (in the light of reports from Europe, where the air war was raging) Washington felt that the aircraft would be inadequately armed, while offering no improvement in performance over the rival Curtiss XP-46. Although the XP-47 and XP-47A were destined to remain unbuilt, a full-scale wind tunnel model was completed (and sent to NACA for Allison engine cooling trials), and by the time the programme was cancelled, $60,000 worth of work had been completed.

The rejection of the XP-47 and XP-47A led to further discussions between the Army Air Corps and Kartveli and his design staff, who were encouraged to increase armament, weight and performance; at the same time, worries about the development of the Allison engine led to increasing pressure on designers to explore the use of alternative powerplants. Kartveli happily killed off his XP-47 and XP-47A and turned his attention to an enlarged aircraft powered by a 2,000-hp (1492-kW) Pratt & Whitney XR-2800 Double Wasp, a derivative of the engine originally proposed for the P-44 Rocket. While the Army Air Corps had concentrated on the Allison-engined XP-40, the French

placed massive orders for Pratt & Whitney-engined Curtiss Hawks, which revitalised Pratt & Whitney's fortunes, allowing that company to complete development of turbocharged Twin Wasp and Double Wasp engines – engines which Kartveli saw as suitable powerplants for a big, high-performance fighter design.

The new Kartveli fighter aircraft design was the eight-gun XP-47B, a radial-engined monster which would be more than twice as heavy as the original XP-47A, but which would still be capable of 400 mph (643 km/h) at 25,000 ft (7620 m), while packing a punch consisting of at least six 0.50-in machine-guns. This design marked the birth of the Thunderbolt as we know it today.

Kartveli began sketching the XP-47 design (literally on the back of an envelope) on the train taking him and C. Hart Miller (Republic's chief of military contracts) back to Farmingdale after a meeting in Ohio. It may have been on this same railway journey that Miller dreamed up the 'Thunderbolt' name. This had been the meeting at which the XP-47 and P-44 had been flagged for cancellation, and followed the release of the Emmons report, which criticised the AAC's reliance on Allison-powered fighters, and outlined some objections to the lightweight fighter concept as practised in Europe. At this meeting, Republic had been asked to develop a new heavyweight high-performance fighter, with the clear intent that this would be a redesign of the P-44 with a 2,000-hp (1492-kW) Pratt & Whitney Double Wasp R-2800-11 engine. This turbocharged engine was a masterpiece of engineering, and years later, when Blohm und Voss's chief designer, Dr Richard Vogt, examined a captured example, his response was full of admiration. "How could our leaders ever have dreamed of going to war against a nation which could afford to build so beautiful an engine for a fighter?"

Supercharged performance

In order to achieve the required performance at high altitude, supercharging was required. A piston engine operating at higher altitudes loses power because the thinner, less-oxygenated air does not burn as well. The best solution to this problem is to compress the thin high-altitude air to the same density as sea level air, feed it to the carburettor to be mixed with the fuel, then pass the resulting fuel/air mixture to the cylinders for combustion. The most effective superchargers in the early 1940s were driven by exhaust gases from combustion, and were known as turbo-superchargers.

In drawing up the XP-47B, Kartveli began by sketching the supercharging system, laying two side-by-side oil coolers under the engine, ducting ambient air back along the lower fuselage in a flattened box-section duct. This arrangement gave the Thunderbolt its distinctive 'inverted

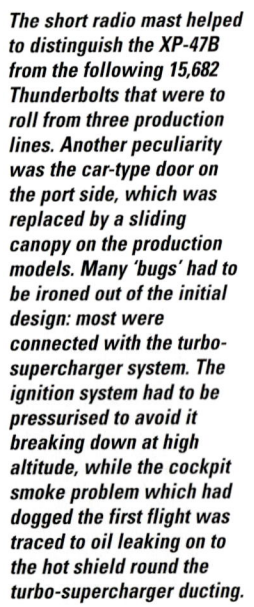

The forward-raked radio mast served as an excellent identification feature of the P-47B. Production totalled 170, and they were assigned to the 56th and 78th Fighter Groups only. The 56th bore the brunt of the development process – a long haul to turn the new design into a combat-worthy fighter.

egg' oval cross-section cowling. The duct for ambient air was adjacent to the pipes which took engine exhaust gases back to drive the supercharger, buried in the belly behind the wingroot. Supercharged ('compressed') ambient air was then piped back along the upper 'corners' of the fuselage (on each side of the cockpit) to the carburettor.

Having sorted out the engine and supercharger, Kartveli wrapped a stretched version of the P-44 design around his 'core', and added stretched roots to a P-43-type wing, using the same S-3 aerofoil section and a similar planform. This stretched airframe design was produced by Costas E. 'Gus' Pappas. In order to maximise power from the massive engine, Kartveli selected a four-bladed, variable-pitch propeller of massive size. The propeller's huge 12-ft 2-in (3.71-m) diameter dictated very long undercarriage legs to provide adequate prop clearance which, in turn, influenced the design of the landing gear. Kartveli came up with a neat telescoping oleo, which shortened (by about 9 in/23 cm) as it retracted, thereby allowing the undercarriage suspension points to be closer inboard than would otherwise have been possible. This, in turn, left sufficient wingspan for the XP-47B's six-gun armament.

An increased emphasis on range led to an AAC requirement for an internal fuel tankage of 315 US gal (1192 litres) but, in the event, Republic failed to achieve this, the two self-sealing bladder tanks in the fuselage accommodating only 298 US gal (1127 litres). This was close enough, but nevertheless caused some sleepless nights among company executives. Republic's Farmingdale plant was rapidly running out of work, and the company faced a difficult and uncertain future. Much was riding on the success of the new fighter, the construction of which allowed the company to hire or re-hire 2,000 workers.

Into the air

The prototype (40-3051) made its maiden flight on 6 May 1941, chief test pilot Lowry Brabham accessing the cockpit via a sideways-opening car-type 'door' like that fitted to the Bell P-39 or the British Hawker Typhoon. Shortly after this first take-off, the cockpit began to fill with smoke, but Brabham completed his planned sortie and landed safely at Mitchell Field at the pre-arranged time – the sortie having been planned to allow senior staff at Republic to witness the take-off and then drive to Mitchell Field to watch the landing. The smoke had been caused by oil burning on the stainless steel heat shields which took hot exhaust gases to the turbo-supercharger. Brabham had also encountered some flutter in the tail unit, and vibration in the wing, but nevertheless gave an enthusiastic thumbs up and pronounced that in the XP-47B, "We've got a winner here."

The XP-47B stayed at Mitchell Field for official evaluation, swapping its polished Alclad finish for olive drab camouflage. Performance was not officially measured, although unofficially it became clear that the aircraft was overweight by nearly 1,000 lb (454 kg), with a commensurate effect on rate of climb (taking 30 per cent longer to reach 15,000 ft/4572 m). It was also discovered that the aircraft reached a speed of 412 mph (663 km/h), 12 mph (19 km/h) faster than was required. Whatever its shortcomings, the XP-47B showed sufficient promise for the Army Air Force to order 773 Thunderbolts, at a cost of

P-47B – the Thunderbolt enters service

The first of 170 'production' P-47Bs, 41-5895, was actually a hand-built prototype completed in December 1941. Full production aircraft were completed from 4 March 1942, and the first was accepted by the USAAF on 26 May 1942. Service with the 56th Fighter Group began in June, but there were numerous aircraft losses in the early weeks. Many of these were connected with the fabric-covered ailerons and rudder, which were replaced by larger metal units.

One element which the P-47 designers got right from the outset was the armament: the eight '50-cals' served the type excellently throughout World War II, in both air-to-air and ground attack roles. The weapons were harmonised to converge on a point approximately 500 ft (152 m) ahead of the aircraft.

$56,499,923. To keep the Farmingdale plant active while it tooled up for P-47 production, the newly redesignated USAAF (which had been the USAAC until 20 June 1941) placed orders for P-43s and P-43As.

The first two production Thunderbolts (41-5895 and 41-5896) were officially designated as YP-47Bs, and were followed by three more aircraft (41-5897 to 41-5899) built to the same standard as the XP-47B, with car-type entry doors, fabric-covered control surfaces and rounded quarterlights behind the cockpit, but with armament fitted and a distinctive forward-sloping antenna mast on the spine. At least one of these first five aircraft was powered by a lightened R-2800-21, with twin carburettors.

The early aircraft suffered their share of problems. 41-5899 was lost on 26 March 1942, with pilot George Burrell, after losing part of its tail unit in flight. By the time it was realised that the fabric-covered elevators had ballooned and ruptured, another aircraft (the first true production aircraft, 41-5900) had been abandoned by its pilot after losing elevator control.

The elliptical wing design had been retained throughout the Seversky/Kartveli fighter series, but was enlarged for the P-47. The scalloping on the 'razorback' (a term not used until after the war) is noticeable. The stripes on the wings were associated with sighting the guns.

143

The first XP-47B was lost on 8 August 1942, when the pilot interrupted his landing gear retraction sequence. The tailwheel tyre, left dangling in the stream of exhaust gases from the turbosupercharger, burst into flames, followed by the magnesium wheel. When the burning wheel was then retracted, it set fire to control rods in the tail, and the pilot (a former naval aviator) was forced to 'abandon ship' before the aircraft fell out of control into the sea.

Production of the P-47B (including the YP-47s, but not the XP-47) eventually totalled 171 aircraft (41-5895 to 41-6065), although the initial order was for 773 aircraft (most of which were delivered as later models). To facilitate this, a second production line was established at Evansville, Indiana. All but the first few P-47Bs (probably up to and including 15900) had the original car-type entry hatch replaced by a more conventional sliding canopy, together with metal-covered control surfaces.

USAAF service

The first Thunderbolt was handed over to the USAAF on 26 May 1942, and deliveries to the 56th Fighter Group at Bridgeport Municipal Airport, Connecticut, began in June. The runways at Bridgeport were insufficient for the Thunderbolt, and the 56th trained at nearby Mitchell Field, New York, and at Bradley Field at Windsor Locks, Connecticut. Following the Japanese attack on Pearl Harbor, the US had been gripped by fear of additional 'surprise attacks' (especially by the inventive and resourceful Germans), and the air defence of major cities was accorded a high priority, however unreal or improbable the danger of attack.

The 56th Pursuit Group had been transferred to the East Coast as part of the response to this perceived German bomber threat, equipped mainly with Curtiss P-40s, Bell P-39 Airacobras and some obsolete P-36s. The unit redesignated as a fighter group in May 1942, shortly after it moved north from the Carolinas to Teaneck Armoury, New Jersey. This, at least, was the group's headquarters, the flying squadrons being based at Bridgeport Municipal Airport (the 61st Fighter Squadron), Bendix, New Jersey (the 62nd Fighter Squadron) and the factory airfield at Farmingdale (the 63rd Fighter Squadron). The latter aerodrome also received the newly arrived 80th Fighter Group, forcing the relocation of the 63rd to Bridgeport, while the 62nd moved to Bradley Field, Windsor Locks. At much the same time, the USAAF disbanded headquarters squadrons, and the unit's presence at Teaneck ended.

It soon became clear that the best and most rapid way of sorting out the P-47's teething troubles would be to put it in the hands of a front-line USAAF fighter group, and the 56th, now on Republic's doorstep, was the obvious choice for the task. The first group personnel to be familiarised with the Thunderbolt were the engineers and mechanics, who went to the Republic Mechanics' School to learn the engineering and maintenance tasks and procedures. They were pleasantly surprised by the accessibility and maintainability of the big Double Wasp engine, especially after the complexities of the P-39's liquid-cooled Allison engine. Several aircraft were allocated for engineer training, and soon won many converts.

The pilots received one aircraft for familiarisation, operating it from Mitchell Field's long runways. They proved less easy to win over than the ground crews: the cockpit was unfamiliar, with a mass of hydraulic lines, electrical

cables and strange controls for the turbo-supercharger and other new systems. There was, of course, no two-seat Thunderbolt, and few of the early pilots had flown even the company's earlier products, such as the P-35. To this unfamiliarity was added an unimpressive climb performance, so that the first few minutes of a pilot's first flight would tend to reinforce any preconceptions and prejudices he might have against the aircraft. And there were many prejudices and preconceptions, not least because the bulky, flat-fronted P-47 didn't look like other fighters, with their sleek lines and 'needle noses'. The sheer size and 6-ton (5.4-tonne) weight of the P-47 made no sense to pursuit pilots used to the P-39 and P-40, while the 0.5-mile (805-m) take-off run came as an unpleasant surprise.

At higher altitudes, though, the Thunderbolt was transformed, becoming nimble and eager. The ASI would dash towards the 400-mph (644-km/h) mark without much provocation, and few young fighter pilots could resist the temptation of hurling their new steeds into high-speed dives.

High-speed problems

As more P-47s were allocated to the 56th Fighter Group, the new fighter suffered a correspondingly alarming accident rate, and by the end of June, the 56th had written off half of the P-47Bs it had received. For the record, service testing of the Thunderbolt cost the lives of 13 pilots, and wrecked 41 aircraft. Many accidents occurred in high-speed dives, and several aircraft returned to base with badly buckled rudders following such manoeuvres.

Remarkably, morale was not severely dented, and affection for the Thunderbolt began to grow. The aircraft offered a wild ride at height, and pilots who experienced the need to belly land the big fighter found that the deep fuselage and supercharger ducting combined to offer superb protection to the pilot. The Thunderbolt's ability to absorb battle damage was not tested, but people did begin to realise that the aircraft was extremely rugged and dependable, and this engendered a degree of confidence in the machine.

Morale was further boosted in September by the arrival of a new group commander, Major Hubert Zemke from the 80th Fighter Group. Already a highly skilled exponent of the P-40, Zemke had been sent to Britain in early 1941 to advise the RAF on the operation of its new Kittyhawks. When the RAF sent a number of Tomahawks to Russia in the wake of the German attack, Zemke was one of the Americans who accompanied the RAF advisory group to Russia, where he acted as a test pilot.

In mid-November 1942, operational limitations were imposed, including an airspeed limit of 300 mph (483 km/h), an embargo on aerobatics and 'violent manoeuvres', and limitations on fuel balance. This led to the allocation of an 'R-for-restricted' designation prefix, and ensured that the B model never flew in combat overseas, though the variant was used for training by Stateside units. Fortunately, the first examples of the new C model had already started to arrive with the first front-line units.

On 13 November 1942, two 63rd Fighter Squadron pilots were tasked with a number of level speed runs in their new P-47Cs. After the first run, the two pilots entered a dive so

P-47C – the first combat model

During the summer of 1942 Republic and the 56th FG endeavoured to overcome the problems with the P-47B. The result was the P-47C, of which an eventual total of 602 was built. The first P-47Cs differed little from the P-47B, but the P-47C-1-RE introduced an 8-in (20.3-cm) plug at the engine firewall. The C-2 and C-5 which followed had provision for ferry tanks, and it was these two sub-variants which were sent to England to open the Thunderbolt's combat career.

that they could fly the next run at lower altitude. Encountering compressibility almost immediately, they were astonished to see their ASIs reading 725 mph (1167 km/h) – well beyond the speed of sound. This figure was seized upon with relish by Republic's publicists, although the speed indicated was mainly due to instrument error, of course. The aircraft actually reached only 500 mph (805 km/h) or less, but the two pilots still had great difficulty recovering to level flight.

The last P-47B built (41-6065) was delivered with a pressurised cockpit and a more powerful 2,300-hp (1716-kW) R-2800-59 engine. As the XP-47E, the aircraft was used to support the development of later, high-altitude Thunderbolt versions.

The first 57 C-model Thunderbolts (41-6067 to 41-6123) were hard to distinguish from the P-47Bs which preceded them. Designated P-47C-RE (the -RE suffix indicated that they were built at Farmingdale; Evansville machines used an -RA suffix), the aircraft had a strengthened rear fuselage and empennage, and were delivered with metal-covered control surfaces. They also had a new tachometer, ciné gun camera and radio control box, and the dorsal aerial mast was changed to an upright position. The single oxygen

Demand for the Thunderbolt required a new Republic factory to be built at Evansville, Indiana. The first product was the P-47D. A few were delivered to the 56th Fighter Group, being used for training before the unit embarked for England. At the time the 56th denoted squadron assignment by cowling colour (here yellow for the 62nd Fighter Squadron).

Newly arrived from the US, a P-47C taxis past a B-17 at a base in England. The Thunderbolt was dispatched to the VIII Bomber Command (8th Air Force from 22 February 1944) to provide fighter escort for the B-17 daylight raids, but initially lacked the necessary range. Accordingly, the first missions were cross-Channel fighter sweeps.

tank of the B model gave way to three separate D-2 bottles in the fuselage, with another in the port wing leading edge, while the Morse downward identification light and flap indicators were removed. When Farmingdale and Evansville were finally joined by a third Thunderbolt production line (Curtiss Aircraft at Buffalo), that source initially produced 20 aircraft similar to the original P-47C-RE, though they were designated P-47G-CU (42-24920 to 24939).

Fuselage stretch

The P-47C-RE gave way in October 1942 to the P-47C-1-RE, 55 of which were built at Farmingdale (41-6066 to 41-6124). Curtiss built 40 similar aircraft (42-24940 to 24979) under the designation P-47G-1-CU. The new sub-type introduced new engine-bearers and an improved fire-wall, designed to make engine removal and installation more rapid, that was known as the QEC (Quick Engine Change) Modification. This modification required an 8-in (20-cm) stretch to the forward fuselage, and a wedge-shaped deflector was added between the oil-cooler control flap and the waste-gate valves, under the nose. The new version had a new, stainless steel dome under the rear fuselage, which directed turbo-supercharger exhaust gases back along the rear fuselage, and had a lockable castoring tailwheel, hydraulic flap equalisation, and throttle, super-charger and airscrew control improvements. Bobweights were added within the elevator control circuit, to counter the tendency towards elevator reversal during high-speed dives. Some limitations remained in force – a 259-mph (417 km/h) IAS limit above 30,000 ft (9144 m), for example – and the P-47C-1-RE was not sent overseas.

A P-47C-1-RE was evaluated extensively at Eglin, Florida, where Air Corps test pilots found, to their surprise, that the barrel-like Thunderbolt was actually faster than the slender and streamlined inline-engined P-38F, P-39D-1, P-40F and P-51A. The aircraft's rate of climb was less remarkable, but the roll-rate (and especially the roll-reversal time) was extremely impressive. Despite this agility, the po-faced test pilots recommended that the P-47C-1-RE should "avoid combat with enemy fighters", and reserved particular criti-cism for the huge engine cowling, which impinged on the pilot's view and made deflection shooting more difficult.

Interestingly, the RAF also evaluated the P-47C-1-RE, exploring its potential as a night intruder. Flames from the waste-gate and the glow from the super-heated turbocharger dome were adjudged to be unacceptable, and the British pressed on with Hurricanes, Defiants and a range of twin-engined types. The RAF had first expressed an interest in the P-47B during 1941, seeing the aircraft as a potential alternative to the Hawker Typhoon and request-ing 100 aircraft instead of some of the Kittyhawks on order. Fortunately, USAAF requirements meant that insufficient aircraft were available to make RAF deliveries practical, and the plan was quietly dropped. It was only later in the war that the RAF's Air HQ India requested the allocation of P-47Ds as long-range ground attack aircraft.

The first true combat-ready Thunderbolt was the P-47C-2-RE, 128 of which were built at Farmingdale (41-6178 to 41-6305). These aircraft had a range of externally invisible modifications which together addressed the controllability problems experienced in high-speed dives, and incorpo-rated fuel system modifications to allow the carriage of a 200-US gal (757-litre) ferry tank. The tanks were housed in dome-like fairings which scabbed directly onto the belly, and were nicknamed 'babies' or 'udders'. Some were later modified for combat use. The C-2 was followed on the Farmingdale line by 362 P-47C-5-REs (41-6306 to 41-6667) which introduced minor modifications to the radio and instruments, as well as cockpit heating, and which were externally distinguished by the substitution of a whip antenna in place of the solid antenna mast. P-47C-2s and C-5s were destined to be the first Thunderbolt variants despatched overseas for combat.

Escort fighter

The P-47 originally had been designed as a home-defence interceptor fighter, heavily armed and fast, and optimised for intercepting enemy bombers, with a secondary role of defending friendly ground forces. But when the Thunderbolt went to war, it was to fulfil the very different role of fighter escort, shepherding friendly

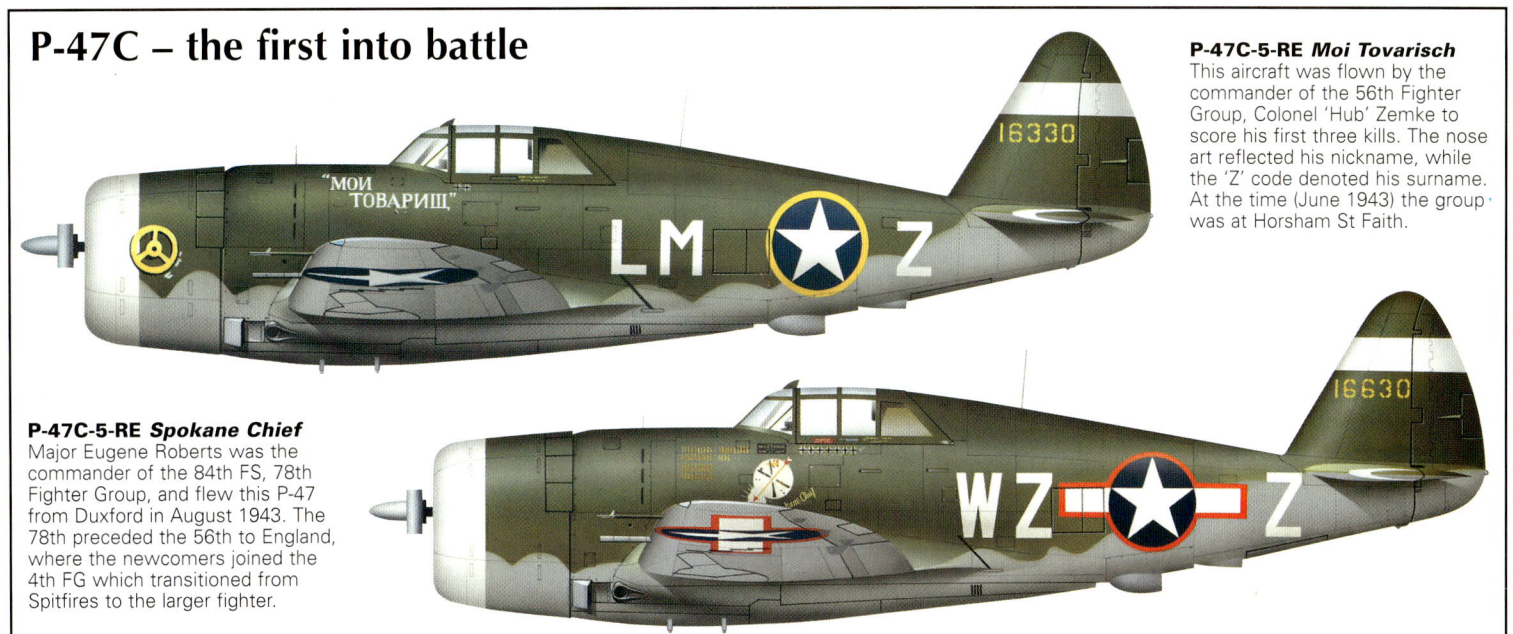

P-47C – the first into battle

P-47C-5-RE *Moi Tovarisch*
This aircraft was flown by the commander of the 56th Fighter Group, Colonel 'Hub' Zemke to score his first three kills. The nose art reflected his nickname, while the 'Z' code denoted his surname. At the time (June 1943) the group was at Horsham St Faith.

P-47C-5-RE *Spokane Chief*
Major Eugene Roberts was the commander of the 84th FS, 78th Fighter Group, and flew this P-47 from Duxford in August 1943. The 78th preceded the 56th to England, where the newcomers joined the 4th FG which transitioned from Spitfires to the larger fighter.

bombers to their distant targets and engaging enemy fighters over their own territory.

When America entered the war after the Pearl Harbor attack, the Allies agreed on a 'Germany First' policy; prior to the eventual invasion (or liberation) of mainland Europe, the USAAF joined the RAF's strategic bombing offensive. While the RAF relied primarily on unescorted night bombers, the USAAF pinned its hopes on day-bombing. Thus the US Eighth Air Force (then known as VIII Bomber Command) came into being as a high-altitude, daylight precision-bombing organisation. It also parented a small fighter arm (the VIII Fighter Command), including three P-38 groups and the former American-manned RAF Eagle Squadrons, which transferred, with their Spitfires, to form the 4th Fighter Group.

Thunderbolts for Europe

The USAAF established two P-47-equipped fighter groups in the UK to support its bomber operations, and decided that the 56th Fighter Group would be one of them, and that the 4th, already in the UK, would be the other. In the event, a third group (the 78th) was also re-equipped, giving the 'Mighty Eighth' a three-group Thunderbolt wing.

The Eighth Air Force had lost most of its fighters in October 1942, when they deployed with the new 12th Air Force to North Africa. Only the 4th Fighter Group remained, clinging to its links with the RAF with a stubborn tenacity and a degree of arrogance. Many of its pilots had been fighting since before America even entered the war, and they were inclined to view some of their colleagues as newcomers. The pilots of the 4th were especially attached to their Spitfires, and news that they were to be equipped with a new American fighter was not greeted with the greatest of enthusiasm.

The first P-47C-2 for the Eighth Air Force arrived in Britain as deck cargo on 20 December 1942, and subsequently was delivered to the 'Eagle's Nest' at Debden in early January. The aircraft was one of an initial batch of 88 P-47Cs for the Eighth Air Force – a batch which soon was augmented by additional deliveries. The reaction of the Eagle Squadron pilots to the new fighter ranged from amusement to disbelief to anger. The 6-ton P-47 was no Spitfire, and was likened by some wags to a dive bomber and by others to a milk bottle. The more open-minded welcomed the Thunderbolt's remarkable armament – eight 0.50-in machine-guns in place of the Spitfire's rifle-calibre 0.303-in Brownings – while others believed that its long-range potential would free them from the routine grind of convoy patrols and relatively short-range raids by the RAF's light bombers.

The stream of P-47Cs arriving in Britain was delivered to three fighter groups, which converted to the new aircraft type in parallel. The 4th Fighter Group and the 78th Fighter Group were already in Britain. The 78th at Goxhill passed its new P-38s (and most of its 'line pilots') to the 12th Air Force as attrition replacements, and received P-47s in their stead. The remaining pilots of the 78th included the group CO, the squadron commanders, operations officers and flight commanders, who had to train a new group of pilots

In-theatre training

In August 1942 the 6th Fighter Wing was sent to England to join the VIII Fighter Command to continue its task of providing combat training for newly-arrived pilots. After a brief period as the 2906th Observation Training Group, it became the 495th Fighter Training Group in December 1943. From its Atcham base (Cheddington from February 1945), the 495th FTG trained P-47 pilots for both the 8th and 9th Air Forces. Although the pupils had already converted to the Thunderbolt, they were given further instruction in combat tactics for both air-to-air and air-to-ground roles. The 495th had two units assigned – the 551st and 552nd Fighter Training Squadrons.

The first Thunderbolts to arrive in England were P-47C-2s and C-5s. They were initially marked with individual three-digit numbers, as worn by this 62nd FS C-2. From February 1943 white ID bands were added.

Flying from Atcham, the 495th FTG used 'hand-me-down' aircraft cascaded from the front line as newer models were introduced. An example was this P-47C-2 wearing the 'VM' codes of the 552nd FTS. A natural metal P-47C was something of a rarity.

Above: Although the 4th Fighter Group – already in England flying Spitfires – was the first to get the Thunderbolt, it was the 78th Fighter Group which was the first to deploy from the US. Initially settling at Goxhill, it moved to Duxford on 3 April 1943, and remained there for much of the war. This 84th FS P-47C is shown carrying the 85-US gal (322-litre) drop tank, which was the Thunderbolt's first practical means of carrying extra fuel.

Above right: P-47Cs and Ds served side-by-side during the early period in England, as this 62nd FS, 56th FG formation testifies. The lead aircraft is a D-1, No. 2 is a C-2 while No. 3 is a C-5. The third aircraft, assigned to Captain Gene O'Neill, carries the Al Capp 'Lil' Abner' character on the nose.

P-47s took off to attempt their first combat mission on 10 March (10 days after the group was supposed to have been operational). During this fighter sweep off Walcheren, radio interference was so severe it made communications impossible but, fortunately, the sweep was ignored by the Luftwaffe. The radio problem was grave enough to prevent further operations until a technical fix could be found, and the three groups continued training, or, in the case of the 4th, flying operations in their beloved Spitfires. The aircraft also experienced some minor engine problems, mainly due to the higher humidity and lower temperatures experienced in northern Europe, which necessitated damp-proofing of spark plugs and their leads, and the lagging of engine push-rod covers. Just over a week later, on 17 March, a group of 56th Fighter Group pilots returned to base after an air-to-air firing exercise at Llanbedr, uneasy that something had gone awry. Their Lysander target tug failed to return.

The 78th Fighter Group moved to Duxford on 3 April 1943, while the 56th Fighter Group moved to Horsham St Faith two days later, ready to begin operations with the new fighter. By then, the Thunderbolts had received white rings around their cowlings, and encircling tailplanes and vertical fins, these distinctive markings being intended to prevent confusion with the Fw 190. By this time, the original batch of P-47C-2-REs sent to England had been joined by a number of C-5-REs, and the first D models began arriving in April.

'Bolts from Indiana

The second production plant to begin producing Thunderbolts was the new Evansville plant, whose first aircraft were broadly equivalent to the P-47C-2-REs. The first four (42-2250 to 42-2253) used Farmingdale-built P-47C fuselages, with wings supplied by a sub-contractor and tail units from the Budd Company, and were designated P-47D-RE (Evansville's assigned suffix of -RA remained unused). The P-47D-RE was almost indistinguishable from the P-47C-2, but the D model was destined to become the most important, near-definitive Thunderbolt, even though the succession of 'block improvements' which accompanied every new production batch meant that the last D model differed hugely from the first. The earliest P-47D differed from the C-2 only in having extra cooling flaps around the trailing edge of the cowling, together with minor refinements and enhancements to the exhaust pipes, the vacuum distribution system, the pilot's armour protection and the fuel and oxygen systems. Farmingdale built 105 similar aircraft (42-7853 to 7957) as P-47D-1-REs and 445 more (42-7958 to 42-8402) as P-47D-2-REs, differing only in having no turbo-supercharger cover.

in-theatre procedures. They were less than ecstatic about switching their P-38s for the heavyweight P-47s.

"It was like changing from thoroughbreds to plough horses," recalled one of the 78th's senior pilots afterwards.

Fortunately, one of the Eighth Air Force's three P-47 units was already used to the Thunderbolt, and its pilots were thus more enthusiastic about the aircraft. This was the 56th Fighter Group, led by Colonel 'Hub' Zemke, which had been the first P-47 unit in the USA. The personnel of the 56th Fighter Group arrived in Britain aboard the SS *Queen Elizabeth* on 11 January, moving to Kings Cliffe for theatre familiarisation.

The reservations of other pilots were partly addressed by HQ Eighth Air Force (or VIII Bomber Command as it was then still known). A test pilot attached to the Air Technical Section, Major Cass Hough, was given every opportunity to fly one of the new Thunderbolts (42-7921) at Bovingdon aerodrome, during which he dived the aircraft to terminal velocity. The aircraft was also flown against a captured Fw 190, allowing suitable tactics to be developed.

Pilot conversion was undertaken at Atcham, and also at the groups' own three airfields at Debden, Goxhill and Kings Cliffe. The work-up of the three groups was not without incident, not least when 14 4th Fighter Group

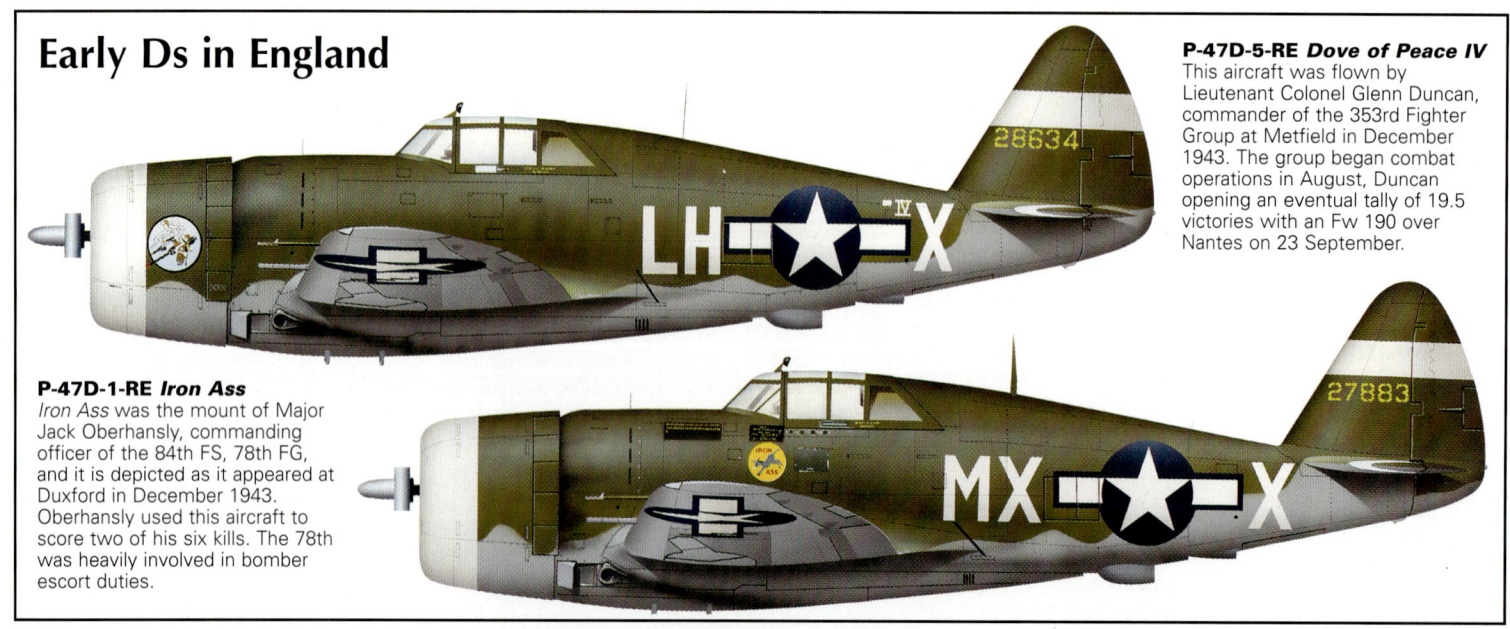

Early Ds in England

P-47D-5-RE *Dove of Peace IV*
This aircraft was flown by Lieutenant Colonel Glenn Duncan, commander of the 353rd Fighter Group at Metfield in December 1943. The group began combat operations in August, Duncan opening an eventual tally of 19.5 victories with an Fw 190 over Nantes on 23 September.

P-47D-1-RE *Iron Ass*
Iron Ass was the mount of Major Jack Oberhansly, commanding officer of the 84th FS, 78th FG, and it is depicted as it appeared at Duxford in December 1943. Oberhansly used this aircraft to score two of his six kills. The 78th was heavily involved in bomber escort duties.

This pastoral scene was recorded at Halesworth in 1943, and shows a P-47D of the 56th Fighter Group – a unit which became the propagandists' favourite as 'Zemke's Wolfpack'. The attention was merited, for by the end of January 1944 it had racked up 200 air-to-air kills, and ended the conflict with 677, the highest of any USAAF unit in the ETO.

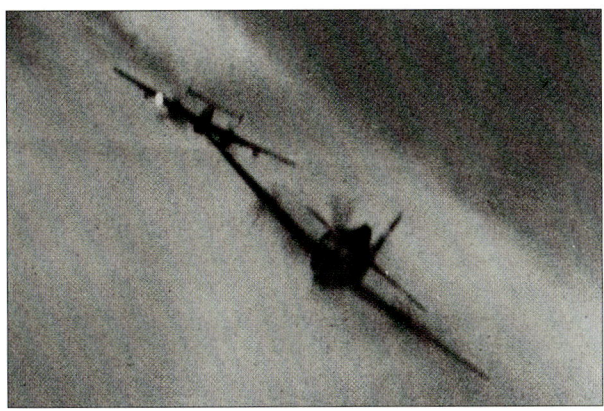

Far left: Major Everett Stewart (whose gun camera recorded this image) and Lieutenant John Coleman (flying the visible aircraft), were both credited with the victory of this Messerschmitt Bf 110. The 'broadside' from the eight guns of the P-47 was sufficient to bring down most aircraft with a short burst, while packing a heavy punch in the ground attack role. At least one German warship succumbed to the guns of the Thunderbolt.

In the event, it was the 4th Fighter Group which launched the P-47's combat career, leading 24 aircraft of different sub-types (including some from the other two groups) on a sweep named Circus 280 over the Pas de Calais on 8 April. The 4th's RAF heritage made it inevitable that RAF terminology and tactics would be retained wherever they were proved to be effective. A Circus, for example, was a fighter sweep by a large number of fighters, with a small number of bombers whose primary purpose was to draw the enemy into the air. A Rodeo, by contrast, was a simple fighter sweep, without bombers, while a Ramrod was a straightforward escort mission for bombers whose primary purpose was to bomb the enemy rather than act as decoys for enemy fighters.

The Thunderbolts did not engage the enemy at all during their first week of operations, and suffered their first loss on 13 April when Lieutenant Colonel Dickman, the 78th Group's executive officer, had to bale out of his aircraft when its engine failed over the Channel. Fortunately, Dickman was retrieved by the RAF's Air Sea Rescue service, to fly and fight again. Later that day another pilot (this time from the 56th Group's 63rd Fighter Squadron) suffered an engine failure near Dunkirk, but turned back for England, gliding across the Channel to belly-land near Deal, where a local AA battery claimed him as an "Fw 190 shot down". Fortunately, they were less accurate than they thought, and Captain Dyar (one of the 'supersonic pilots' of the previous November) was soon back in action.

First kills

Two days later, on 15 April 1943, the 4th Fighter Group finally drew first blood for the P-47, during a sweep by 60 aircraft, comprising 12 from the 4th and 24 each from the 56th and 78th Fighter Groups. During this mission – Rodeo 204 – Major Don Blakeslee, commander of the 335th Fighter Squadron, shot down one Fw 190 near Ostend, his fourth kill of the war. Other pilots claimed two more. One P-47 was shot down, and two more failed to return after suffering engine failures. One of the latter was flown by operations officer Lieutenant Colonel Chelsey Peterson, who had shot down one of the two Fw 190s to gain his seventh combat victory.

The Thunderbolt's propensity for engine failures following combat was becoming extremely worrying, and an investigation was put in hand. It soon became clear that, during combat, pilots failed to make the correct throttle, rpm and turbo-supercharger settings, so that the engine

would become over-pressurised or over-boosted, raising cylinder head temperatures to a dangerous level. The initial solution was to educate pilots in better throttle/rpm and supercharger handling techniques, while Republic worked hard to devise automatic safeguards which would prevent over-boosting.

The Germans seldom responded to the USAAF's fighter sweeps, except when they could be sure of gaining an advantage. On 29 April, for example, Fw 190s ambushed the 56th Fighter Group and shot down two P-47s without loss – a poor result for the senior Thunderbolt group during its first contact with the enemy. On other occasions, the German fighters stayed on their airfields, preferring to wait for the unescorted formations of B-17s.

The P-47 groups, meanwhile, grew in size and by the end of April the individual groups were routinely able to despatch 36 P-47s at once, and were working towards being able to send out 48 aircraft.

The first bomber escort mission was flown on 4 May 1943. The 4th Group's experienced pilots shot down an Fw 190 during the mission, adding to their steadily growing tally. The 56th Fighter Group was still having some trouble 'finding its feet' and escorted the bombers as they withdrew. Its pilots enthusiastically attacked and shot down

P-47G – Curtiss production

Following Farmingdale and Evansville, a third production line was established at Curtiss-Wright's Buffalo plant in New York state. The products were known as P-47Gs, and were built in five blocks. Production totals, and their equivalent Republic models, were as follows: 20 P-47G-CU (P-47C-RE), 40 P-47G-1-CU (P-47C-1-RE), 60 P-47G-5-CU (P-47D-1-RE), 80 P-47G-10-CU (P-47D-5-RE) and 154 P-47G-15-CU (P-47D-10-RE). There were numerous production delays at the Curtiss plant, with the result that its output was usually at least one block behind the 'state-of-the-art' at the other two factories. For this reason most P-47Gs were assigned to second-line training duties, while Curtiss ceased making Thunderbolts in March 1944.

Due to production problems, Curtiss-built aircraft were few and far between, with just 354 emerging from the Buffalo plant. Shown below is a P-47G-1 (similar to the C-1), while the battered P-47G-15 shown right was used as a ground trainer. The fuselage placard reads 'This airplane is for taxiing instruction only'.

Right: Captain Walker 'Bud' Mahurin of the 63rd FS, 56th FG, was credited with 19.75 kills, and all but three were scored using this War Bond P-47D-5-RE seen at Halesworth. Mahurin was shot down by a Do 217 gunner on 27 March 1944, but later commanded the 4th FIG in Korea, scoring 3.5 kills.

Above: Eighth Air Force P-47 units worked up in the US before being thrown into combat in England. This aircraft is from the 375th FS, 361st FG, seen at Langley Field, Virginia in July 1943. The group was sent to Bottisham in England on 29 November to become the last of the 8th AF Thunderbolt units.

Right: Diablo was assigned to the 56th Fighter Group. It is seen here setting out for France in early 1944 as part of the pre-invasion softening-up effort.

The P-47 groups flew 2,279 sorties during April and May, and were credited with the destruction of 10 enemy aircraft, with seven more assessed as 'probables' and 18 more as 'damaged'. This was probably an over-generous assessment, unless all Luftwaffe combat losses in the period were caused by P-47s! Against this, 18 P-47s had quite definitely failed to return, though it was believed that at least five of these had been lost due to engine failures.

The 56th Fighter Group, with more P-47 experience than any other unit, had failed to score a single confirmed victory, while the Thunderbolt 'new boys' of the 4th and 78th Groups had gained several air combat successes, underlining the value of real air combat experience in-theatre. New pilots tended to lack gunnery aptitude and had poor recognition skills, and had the same problem as all pilots new to the air combat game – underestimating the range at which they opened fire and consequently firing too early. There was also an element of luck involved, since the enemy was only encountered on every fifth mission, on average, and the 56th had fewer opportunities to engage.

Fighter leaders

The 56th had potential, though, and once the over-exuberance of some pilots was curbed and channelled by the strict Zemke, the unit became frighteningly proficient in the deadly art of fighter combat. Zemke was one of the great 'fighter leaders' of the war, and was lucky in having a succession of superb squadron COs serving under him. The most famous of these was Major Dave Schilling, CO of the 62nd FS, who rose to lead the 56th FG and ended the war with 23 kills and a logbook which recorded 132 combat sorties and 360 combat flying hours. The 61st and 63rd Fighter Squadrons were commanded by the equally proficient (if less colourful) Loren McCollom and Phillip Tukey. McCollom was rated highly by Zemke, who selected him to be group flying executive officer and Zemke's deputy. Captain Francis Gabreski was appointed to lead the 61st Fighter Squadron in McCollom's place.

an aircraft they thought was a Bf 109 — but which was, in fact, an RAF Spitfire. More successful was a bomber escort mission on 14 May 1943, in which some 118 P-47s drawn from all three groups escorted B-17s to Antwerp. This was within the P-47's radius of action on internal fuel, meaning that the Thunderbolts could escort the bombers all the way. The Luftwaffe chose to engage, and shot down three P-47s, although the Thunderbolt pilots claimed four victories.

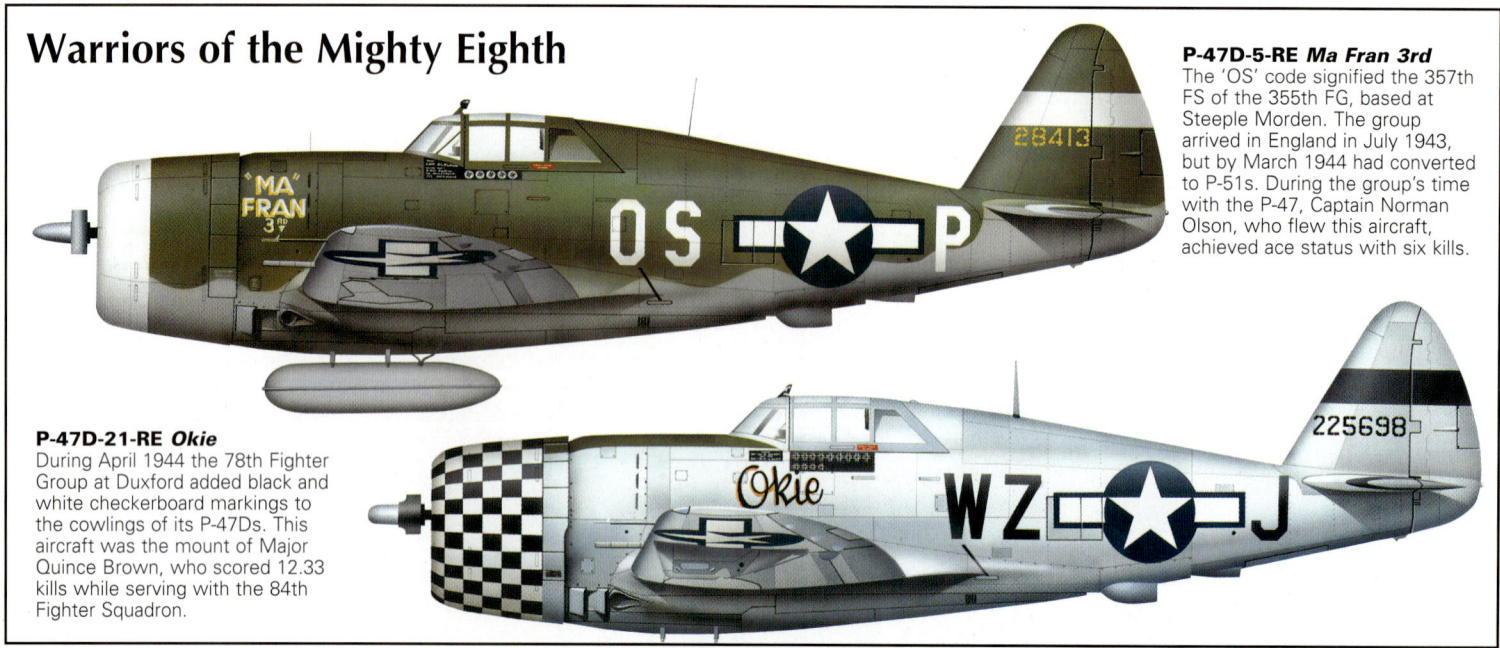

Warriors of the Mighty Eighth

P-47D-5-RE *Ma Fran 3rd*
The 'OS' code signified the 357th FS of the 355th FG, based at Steeple Morden. The group arrived in England in July 1943, but by March 1944 had converted to P-51s. During the group's time with the P-47, Captain Norman Olson, who flew this aircraft, achieved ace status with six kills.

P-47D-21-RE *Okie*
During April 1944 the 78th Fighter Group at Duxford added black and white checkerboard markings to the cowlings of its P-47Ds. This aircraft was the mount of Major Quince Brown, who scored 12.33 kills while serving with the 84th Fighter Squadron.

Gabreski was a Polish-American who had flown in combat over Pearl Harbor before joining the 56th Fighter Group. Upon arrival in Britain, Gabreski had been detached to fly 13 operational missions with the Pole-manned No. 315 Squadron at Northolt, building up friendships which later resulted in several of the RAF's Poles flying with the 61st Fighter Squadron as 'lodgers'.

The group's fortunes finally began to change in June. Captain Walter Cook of the 62nd Fighter Squadron opened the group's score on 12 June, downing an Fw 190 during a sweep. Three more fell to the group the next day: Zemke himself shot down one and scored strikes on another, while Second Lieutenant Robert S. Johnson broke formation to destroy another.

On 26 June the Luftwaffe fighter pilots again demonstrated their superior training and experience. Zemke led an escort mission, his P-47s landing at Manston in Kent to top up their tanks before continuing with the bombers. The P-47s and their charges were intercepted by 40 to 50 enemy fighters near Forges. The US fighters broke up the enemy attacks, but lost four of their number; other aircraft limped home, only to be written off as unfit for further service. Lieutenant Gerald W. Johnson scored the only American victory of the day.

The Thunderbolt's war continued with both successes and failures, victories and losses. On 1 July 1943, for example, the 78th Fighter Group downed four enemy aircraft, but in doing so lost one of the pillars of its great success, Colonel Arman Peterson, CO of the 78th Fighter Group. Some sources give the date of Peterson's death as 14 May, but this is believed to be incorrect.

Extending the P-47's range

The P-47 carried a massive 305 US gal (1154 litres) of internal fuel, but burned it at an an average rate of 100 US gal (378 litres) per hour. The Spitfire, by contrast, carried only 100 Imp gal (120 US gal/454 litres) but used less than 45 Imp gal (54 US gal/204 litres) per hour. Without external fuel, the P-47 had a reach of 175 to 190 miles (282 to 306 km) – insufficient to escort the Eighth's bombers beyond all but their nearest targets. Extending the range of the P-47

was therefore accorded a high priority. The CO of the Eighth's Air Technical Section at Bovingdon, Colonel Ben Kelsey, tasked his deputy, Major Cass Hough, with investigating the use of auxiliary tanks.

The first use of external tanks came at the end of July 1943, with the emergency use of what had hitherto been viewed as ferry tanks. These bulbous, belly-hugging domes looked like an inverted steel helmet, and were suspended from four points. Initially they could not be jettisoned, but were modified to be dropped. Simple wooden wedges on the leading edge forced the tanks down and away when jettisoned. Although the tanks could contain 200 US gal (757 litres) of fuel, they were unpressurised and so could not be used above 18,000 ft (5486 m), giving them an effective capacity of only about 100 US gal (378 litres).

Nonetheless, it was a start, and proved an unpleasant blow to the Luftwaffe. On the 28 July mission, the B-17s were attacked by about 45 enemy fighters as they returned from targets in northwest Germany. The German pilots evidently were surprised to encounter Thunderbolts so far from the UK, and nine were claimed as shot down (for one Thunderbolt lost).

Eighth Air Force engineers planned to modify the tanks, pressurising them using exhaust air from the vacuum pump. However, the impregnated, compressed-paper tanks were leaky and imposed a considerable drag penalty, and often failed to release, so other tanks were soon being commissioned, evaluated and used. From the end of September, civilian engineers from the US began a programme of fitting centreline B-7 bomb shackles under the bellies of the P-47s, one squadron at a time, while service mechanics had already started piecemeal modifications. The teardrop-shaped metal tanks used by the P-39 and P-40 were tried first, from the end of August. These tanks contained only 85 US gal (322 litres) (though they were officially known as 85 [Imperial] gal tanks), and were too small, as was a locally-produced cylindrical metal tank which held 108 US gal (409 litres). Cass Hough supervised the design and emergency production of impregnated paper tanks based on those originally designed for the Hurricane. These silver-doped tanks contained 108 US gal

Above: Throughout the first half of 1944 9th Air Force built up its P-47 force at bases in southern England, with an aim to getting as many pilots combat-ready as possible for the forthcoming invasion. As well as ground attack sorties, bomber escorts were undertaken, especially for the 9th AF 'mediums' which were systematically cutting off German lines of communication into the invasion area. This aircraft, named Lil' Sunshine, served with the 379th FS, 362nd FG based at Wormingford.

Above left: 'Little friends' was what the bomber crews affectionately dubbed their escorts, be they P-47s or P-51s, and the only sight more pleasing to the bomber crew was the home field on their safe return. Here, Lieutenant Charles Reed provides a close escort for a B-24 Liberator in his 63rd FS aircraft Princess Pat.

The 'starter' flags away a pair of 390th FS, 366th FG 'Jugs' right on time as they head for France from Thruxton on 26 April 1944. The bomb legend reads: 'With love from Butch. This'll kill ya!'. In May, the 366th began experimenting with skip-bombing with 1,000-pounders as a means of destroying bridges, for which the unit became known as 'Bennett's Bridge Busters'. The name was adopted to honour the new CO, Lt Col Donald Bennett, who had taken command of the group on 30 April, but was lost after a mission on 21 May. Another nickname was the 'Varga Boys', as many of the aircraft carried 'Varga Girl' pin-ups.

Ground crew prepare to replace the cowls of a 78th Fighter Group P-47D. The aircraft in the background wears the black and yellow diagonal checkerboard cowls of the 353rd Fighter Group.

The 356th Fighter Group flew from Martlesham Heath from October 1943 until the end of the war, although it converted to P-51s in November 1944. This P-47D-22-RE, Angel Eyes, was from the 361st Fighter Squadron. At around this period at least one of the squadron's aircraft wore a sharkmouth marking on the cowling. The 356th's aircraft had mostly been delivered in natural metal, but a dark green upper surface camouflage had been applied at group level.

(later, 150 US gal/568 litres) and, despite problems with leaks, proved useful until they could be replaced by new grey-painted sheet steel tanks of 200-US gal (757-litre) capacity in January 1944.

Phased improvements

In parallel with the makeshift innovations, production aircraft continued to incorporate ever more modifications and improvements. From an early stage, D models began to integrate provision for fuel tanks, at least on the centre-line. Evansville got into its stride and produced 200 P-47D-2-RAs (42-22364 to 22563) without any such provision, and then 100 aircraft with minor fuel system modifications known as P-47D-3-RAs (42-22564 to 42-22663) and finally 200 aircraft with a water injection system and a new C-21 supercharger. These latter (42-22664 to 42-22863) were designated P-47D-4-RA.

The new water injection system and supercharger had already made their debut on the Farmingdale-built P-47D-5-RE, which also introduced a centreline pylon capable of carrying either bombs or jettisonable fuel tanks. The new pylon was not a reliable recognition feature, however, as a shortage of pylons meant that some D-5s were delivered without them, and the pylons were subsequently retrofitted 'in the field' to earlier P-47Cs and P-47Ds. Production of the P-47D-5-RE totalled 300 aircraft (42-8403 to 42-8702), with an additional 350 (42-74615 to 42-74964) delivered as

P-47D-6-REs with minor modifications. P-47D-5-REs were the first Thunderbolts to be flown to Britain via the North Atlantic Ferry route, arriving in the UK during the summer of 1943.

As the P-47 units gained combat experience, tactics were developed and honed, while the aircraft's strengths began to be appreciated. The weight of fire delivered in a short burst by the eight 0.50-in machine-guns (viewed by many as being the next best thing to 20-mm cannon) was usually deadly (at 800 rounds per minute per gun), and with 425 rounds of tracer, incendiary and armour-piercing ammunition per gun, the aircraft had enough firepower for several short engagements. The Thunderbolt itself proved remarkably resilient. Time and time again, Thunderbolts returned to base after sustaining battle damage which would have destroyed lesser fighters.

As experience built up, and as the P-47's strengths and weaknesses came to be more clearly understood, the Thunderbolt units became progressively more successful.

Captain Charles London of the 78th Fighter Group became the first Thunderbolt 'ace' on 30 July 1943, with the destruction of two Bf 109s. The German aircraft made the fatal mistake of diving away to escape – a manoeuvre which would have let them escape from a Spitfire, but this was no way of evading a P-47. During the same mission, Major Eugene Roberts became the first Thunderbolt pilot to down three enemy aircraft in a day. These pilots' successes formed only part of a major milestone for the 78th Fighter Group, which kept most of the 80-100 attacking German fighters off the bombers, inflicting heavy losses on the enemy for the loss of only three pilots, though these included the group commander, Lieutenant Colonel Melvin McNickle, who became a PoW. The day's score eventually reached 25 confirmed kills, plus four probables and eight damaged, for the loss of seven Thunderbolts. Sixteen of the victories were claimed by the 78th, five by the 4th and four by the 56th. Another victory of sorts was scored by Lieutenant Quince Brown, who shot up a German railway locomotive as he hedge-hopped home.

Rising stars

An increasing number of pilots began to enjoy air combat success, and many became aces. Interestingly, the two top-scorers in the Eighth Air Force both flew P-47s and not the more glamorous P-51. Colonel Francis S. Gabreski of the 56th Fighter Group scored his first victory on 24 August 1943 while flying with the 56th Fighter Group's 61st Fighter Squadron. He made ace three months later, scoring two kills on 26 November. He scored his 28th and final victory on 5 July 1944, then was downed during a strafing run 15 days later and went 'into the cage' for the rest of the war.

Robert S. Johnson opened his score before Gabreski, downing his first victim on 13 June 1943. He was almost shot down on 26 June, but limped home to pull off a successful forced landing at Manston, after being attacked again and again by Oberst Egon Meyer of JG 2 until the latter ran out of ammunition. His tally had reached 27 (exceeding Rickenbacker's 1918 tally of 26 kills) by the time he was rotated home in late May 1944.

Below: P-47Ds from the 63rd Fighter Squadron, 56th Fighter Group depart on a mission from Boxted in the summer of 1944, around the time of the Normandy landings. Carrying a drop tank under each wing allowed the P-47 a healthy time on station for the kind of air superiority missions that were conducted over the beachhead. At least one 'bubbletop' is in the gaggle.

'Zemke's Wolfpack' – 1944

P-47D-15-RE *Little Chief*
This aircraft was the mount of Lieutenant Frank Kibble, and is depicted as it appeared in March 1944. Kibble was assigned to the 61st Fighter Squadron of the 56th Fighter Group, then stationed at Halesworth. This aircraft was used to gain four of Kibble's seven confirmed kills. During this period the 56th was employed on long-range escorts for bombers, having received drop tanks in February.

P-47D-6-RE *Lady Jane*
Lady Jane was the personal aircraft of Lieutenant John Truluck, who scored seven kills (five in this aircraft). This aircraft carries the 63rd Fighter Squadron's colours (blue) on the cowling: later this was applied to the rudder while the cowling was painted red to signify the 56th FG.

P-47D-22-RE
Despite the delivery of newer aircraft, war-weary 'razorbacks' continued in service into 1945. This aircraft was flown by Captain Cameron Hart of the 63rd FS from Boxted in December 1944. The nose motif was inspired by a Wehrmacht Panzer unit badge. Hart scored six kills, one of 42 pilots to achieve ace status with the 56th FG.

P-47D-25-RE *Happy Warrior/Oregon's Britannia*
The single 'Z' code signified to both friend and foe that this Thunderbolt was flown by no ordinary pilot – at the helm was Colonel Hubert 'Hub' Zemke, leader of the 56th 'Wolfpack' and responsible for 18 confirmed kills. This War Bond aircraft had RAF-style upper-surface camouflage. The aircraft was later flown by Harold Comstock.

P-47D-26-RA *Ole Cock III*
The squadrons of the 56th adopted various non-standard camouflages for their P-47s – this aircraft was flown by the CO of the 61st FS, Captain Donovan Smith. It is shown how it appeared in June 1944, at the time of the D-day invasions, complete with identification stripes. During this period the 56th flew close support missions.

P-47D-25-RE
With *Hairless Joe* – a 'Dogpatch' character – emblazoned on the nose, this 'Jug' was flown by Colonel David Schilling, CO of the 56th in the latter part of the war. On 23 December 1944 he flew this aircraft to score five kills in a single sortie over Germany, during the last mass dogfight to be fought by the 56th Fighter Group. Schilling ended the war with 22.5 kills.

Republic P-47D-25-RE Thunderbolt

Commanding Officer
56th Fighter Group, 8th Air Force
Boxted, England, December 1944

This aircraft was the mount of Colonel David Schilling, commanding officer of the 56th Fighter Group. Schilling had been a long-time member of the group, and had been deputy CO until 12 August 1944, when the famous Colonel 'Hub' Zemke had left to oversee the transition of the 479th FG from the P-38 to the P-51. Schilling stepped up to take command and was an admirable replacement, steering the group through the final year of the war and to its position of pre-eminence among 8th AF fighter groups. Schilling himself was credited with 22.5 air-to-air kills, and including ground kills his score rose to 34.5, making him the leading 8th AF ace in terms of aircraft destruction (although others had higher air-to-air tallies). The group itself was credited with 677 air-to-air victories and it produced 42 individual aces.

The group had been established in California on 20 November 1940 as the 56th Pursuit Group (Interceptor), and was activated on 15 January 1941. Training was initially conducted on Bell P-39s and Curtiss P-40s, before the operational equipment of P-47B Thunderbolts arrived in May 1942. The three squadrons of the group were stationed at Bridgeport, Connecticut, Bendix, New Jersey, and at Farmingdale on Long Island, the latter sharing the airfield with the Republic factory. Owing to this location, and the fact that the 56th was the first unit to get the Thunderbolt, the group was heavily involved in preparing the type for its combat debut. By September 1942 P-47Cs were being delivered, and it was this model that the group took to England. The aircraft began to arrive in-theatre in December 1942, and in mid-January 56th personnel arrived to begin local training. The first base was King's Cliffe, but the group soon moved to Halesworth. The first mission was flown on 13 April 1943 although initially the P-47s performed only cross-Channel fighter sweeps. The first kill was achieved by Captain Walter Cook on 12 June. By August, under the aggressive tutelage of Zemke which had revised the group's formation tactics to make the most of the P-47's speed and firepower and to closely follow those of the Luftwaffe *experten* facing them across the Channel, the 56th began to achieve significant successes. These were to continue to the war's end, by which time the group was the only VIII Fighter Command unit still equipped with the Thunderbolt (flying the 'sprint' P-47M).

In the post-war era the 56th operated P-80s, F-86s, F-94s and F-101s as its main equipment. It was reactivated as a special operations wing in Southeast Asia, and then became a training unit for the F-4 Phantom at MacDill AFB, Florida. Today the numberplate is assigned to the massive F-16C/D training organisation (56th Fighter Wing) at Luke AFB, Arizona.

Propeller
Throughout its career the Thunderbol[t]
four main types of propeller. The first
Electric C542S four-bladed unit, of 12
diameter. This was applied to the P-4[7]
many P-47Ds up to and including the
was the first fully controllable-pitch p[ropeller on a]
US fighter. The P-47D-22-RE, howeve[r]
Standard 24E50-65 paddle-blade prop[eller]
13 ft 1.875 in (4.01 m) in diameter. Th[ese were]
built at Farmingdale while those cons[tructed]
concurrently at Evansville (P-47D-23-[RE) used the]
Curtiss Electric propeller. This was al[so a paddle-]
blade type but differed by having not[ches in]
the Type 836 blades. Diameter was 1[3 ft.]
Farmingdale went on to produce the [P-47D-27,]
Block 27 with the HamStan propeller, [but Evansville]
continued to use the Curtiss paddle-b[lade on Blocks 27]
and 28. Farmingdale also built Block 2[8, joining the]
Evansville plant in using Curtiss props [thereafter. All]
P-47s were completed with Hamilton [Standard or]
P-47M and P-47N used a Curtiss Elec[tric]
propeller, which retained the 13-ft dia[meter but had]
internal changes to allow its operation [in conjunction]
with the control of boost and engine
operation. The HamStan props used a [more]
pointed boss than the Curtiss units, r[educing the]
overall length of the aircraft by aroun[d]

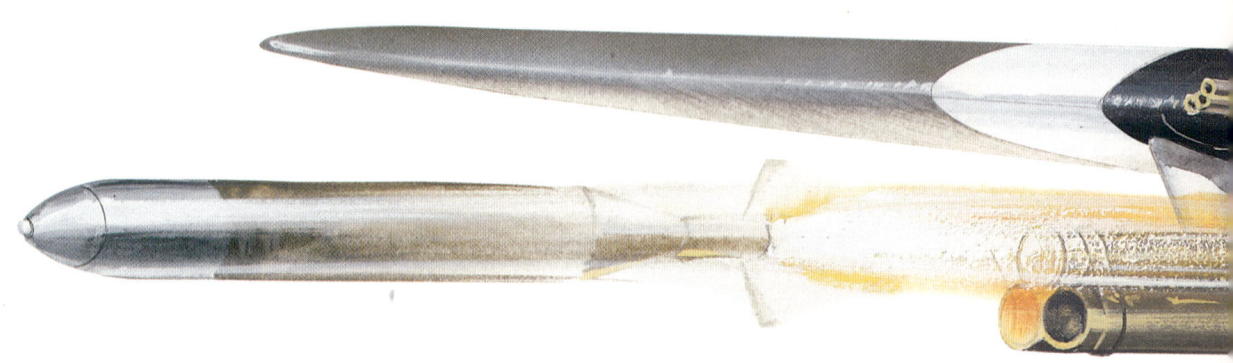

External stores
For the fighter-bomber role the P-47 could carry a variety of weapons, including bombs of up to 1,000 lb (454 kg). The maximum load was 2,500 lb (1134 kg) but in practice a 1,000-pounder under each wing was the normal maximum. Bombs could be carried on either the centreline shackles or the wing pylons added from P-47D-15s onwards (retrofitted to some earlier aircraft). The initial design was replaced by a less draggy pylon from Block 20. Anti-personnel fragmentation bombs were carried in clusters.

Rockets were frequently employed. The standard weapon was the M8 4.5-in (11.43-cm) rocket, carried in M10 triple launcher tubes just inboard of the wing pylon (as illustrated here). The tubes were fabricated from a plastic/paper material, and each cluster weighed around 225 lb (102 kg), complete with projectiles. The British 5-in rocket, launched from a rail, was also tested, and despite being more efficient and accurate, was not adopted. The M8 rockets were not popular, although were effective against armour if they could be aimed accurately enough. Problems with the M8 and its launcher led to the adoption of the 5-in (12.7-cm) High-Velocity Aircraft Rocket (HVAR), for which the last P-47D model, the Block 40, introduced zero-length launch stubs (also retrofitted to some Block 30s). Five could be carried under each wing, two below the gun barrels and three outboard of the wing pylon. From 1945, smoke-laying equipment could be carried from the wing pylons

The specialist air-sea rescue P-47s of the 5th Emergency Rescue Squadron were adapted to carry marker flares either under the rear fuselage or under the wings behind the main wheel wells. They could also carry air-droppable rubber liferafts on the centreline or wing pylons.

was fitted with
was a Curtiss
ft 2-in (3.71-m)
7B, P-47C and
P-47D-21, and
opeller fitted to a
r, had a Hamilton
eller, measuring
ese aircraft were
ructed
A) had a new
o of the paddle-
ceable 'cuffs' on
3 ft 0 in (3.96 m).
Block 25 and
while Evansville
ade in Blocks 26
8s, but joined the
. No further
units. The later
ric C642S-B40
neter but had
to be linked in
om in a single
shorter and less
ducing the
3 in (10 cm).

'Bubbletop' Thunderbolt

One concern commonly voiced by P-47 pilots was the lack of rearward-visibility – of vital importance to one's well being if being pursued by an enemy fighter. The high spine (the term 'razorback' was not used until after World War II) of the early P-47s created a blind spot of around 20°. A rear-view mirror was installed as standard at the top of the cockpit, although individual pilots and units introduced several variations, including the addition of 'wing' mirrors either side, or the use of round mirrors raided from Spitfire stocks. Other attempts to improve rearward visibility involved using bubbled Plexiglas observation windows (designed for the B-26 Marauder) in place of the standard flat side panels, which allowed the pilot to get his head further out to the side, while a lucky few Thunderbolts gained the excellent blown Perspex Malcolm hood. To fully answer the pilots' wishes, Republic produced the 'bubbletop' P-47D-25, with a cut-down rear fuselage and 360° vision canopy. The canopy was developed from that produced for the Hawker Tempest, and was electrically driven. The redesign of the fuselage allowed additional oxygen and fuel to be installed, while the cockpit required a layout alteration. The windscreen was changed to a single flat panel instead of the earlier two-panel screen with a central dividing strut. With the 'bubbletop' and new windscreen, the view was dramatically enhanced but speed was reduced slightly and directional stability suffered. The latter factor led eventually to the installation of a dorsal fin in Block 40 aircraft (and retrofitted to many earlier aircraft).

By early August, the 56th Fighter Group was performing no worse than the other two groups, and so was chosen to assist the Eighth's newest Thunderbolt group, the 353rd Fighter Group. The 353rd had arrived in England in June, but a shortage of aircraft led to an extended period of training and acclimatisation at Goxhill before the unit finally moved to Metfield on 3 August. The 56th Fighter Group at nearby Halesworth shepherded the new group on many of its early operations.

The reversal in fortunes of the 56th Fighter Group was further demonstrated on 17 August, when the group set out to escort B-17s returning from Schweinfurt. Some 51 P-47s fell upon about 50 Bf 109s and Fw 190s (plus about six Bf 110s) which were attacking the bombers. The group took responsibility for 15 of the 19 enemy aircraft claimed as destroyed by P-47s, plus three probables and four damaged, losing three pilots in the process. The successful pilots included Walker Mahurin (who claimed two), Captain Gerald Johnson (three) and Lieutenant Glen Schiltz (three). Among the victims were Major Wilhelm Galland, brother of Adolf and victor in 55 previous engagements.

Red silk jacket

On 19 August, the 56th enjoyed more success, and Captain Gerald Johnson shot down a Bf 109E to become his group's first Thunderbolt ace, and only the second P-47 ace in England. Zemke authorised Johnson to have his flight jacket lined in red silk – a distinction allowed only to the group's aces. Even as the 56th Group finally was becoming an effective team, Major General William Kepner (newly appointed commander of the Eighth Fighter Command) had bad news for Zemke, ordering him to post his deputy, Loren McCollom, away to become the new CO of the 353rd Fighter Group. Schilling was promoted to replace McCollom, and was himself replaced by Horace Craig. Fortunately, the 56th now had such a pool of talent that even officers of McCollom's calibre were replaceable. Later in August, Zemke lost another of his original squadron COs, Phillip Tukey, who was posted to HQ as an operations officer.

Two more P-47 units flew their first missions in September. The 352nd Fighter Group at Bodney began operations on 9 September, and the 355th Fighter Group at Steeple Morden on 14 September. Both units had reached England in July 1943.

September witnessed the first occasion on which B-17s were escorted all the way to a German target by P-47s. On 27 September, the 4th and 353rd Groups met the bombers off the Frisians and escorted them to the target (Emden), while the 56th and 78th Groups shepherded a second force in the same way. The 352nd and 355th Groups flew covering fighter sweeps over the Low Countries. The P-47s scored 21 victories, and lost only one of their number.

Although the introduction of auxiliary tanks allowed Thunderbolts to penetrate ever farther into enemy airspace, the Luftwaffe eventually reacted by making real attempts to intercept the P-47s as they crossed the coast. This forced the P-47s to engage and jettison their tanks, thereby reducing their remaining endurance, and leaving the bombers unprotected over the target.

Zemke himself became an ace on 4 October, as did Walker Mahurin, who was finally making amends for the P-47 he destroyed by colliding with a B-24 some weeks before. During October, a host of pilots joined the roster of aces, including Major Dave Schilling and Lieutenant Robert Johnson of the 56th Fighter Group, Eugene Roberts of the 78th and Captain Walter Beckham of the 353rd, who downed six enemy aircraft in the space of only six missions.

The first six Thunderbolt groups were reinforced by the 356th Fighter Group in September 1943, while the 358th Fighter Group arrived in October 1943 and the 359th Fighter Group in November. The 56th Fighter Group (by then fully into its stride) set a shining example to the new groups, not least on 26 November, one of its best days, when it claimed 26 of the 36 enemy aircraft shot down by Eighth Air Force Thunderbolts as they escorted B-17s to and from a raid against Bremen. Earlier in the month, the 56th had become the first fighter group to achieve 100

Above: Category "E" was one of a small number of War Weary (note serial prefix) P-47Ds converted at unit level to two-seat 'Doublebolt' configuration. This aircraft served with the 63rd FS as a training hack.

Above left: The first P-47 groups to convert trained initially on Lockheed P-38s, Bell P-39s or Curtiss P-40s, but as P-47s became available in greater numbers, and were superseded at the front line by later variants, aircraft became available for training units in the US. Training yellow was liberally applied to these aircraft for greater conspicuity in the often crowded skies around the instructional bases.

Captured by the Luftwaffe

The Luftwaffe flew at least three captured P-47s, which were extensively tested, and also used for other purposes, such as propaganda films and type affiliation with the Beute-Zirkus Rosarius. The latter, headed by Flugkapitän Ted Rosarius and more officially known as 2. Staffel, Versuchsverband Oberbefehlshaber der Luftwaffe, was a unit which travelled round front-line Luftwaffe fighter bases to allow pilots to become acquainted with Allied types.

The first Thunderbolt to be captured was *Beetle*, a P-47D-2 of the 354th FS, 353rd FG which was landed by mistake at Caen on 7 November 1943. The unlucky pilot was Second Lieutenant William Roach. The 'Jug' was tested at Rechlin in Luftwaffe marks (coded 7+9), before being returned to USAAF marks for a role in a film. It then joined the 2. Staffel Zirkus. This unit also operated two more P-47s, coded T9+FK and T9+LK, the first of which had been captured when it landed at Rome-Littoria in May 1944.

When the Beute-Zirkus Rosarius retreated to Bad Worishofen from Göttingen in late 1944, it left behind this P-47D, coded T9+LK, which was discovered in this state (left) by the US Army. The aircraft may have been the one used for a number of clandestine reconnaissance flights over England in the run-up to D-day in June 1944.

176 Auxiliary (No. 3) wing spar outboard section (aileron mounting)
177 Multi-cellular wing construction
178 Wing outboard ribs
179 Wingtip structure
180 Starboard navigation light
181 Leading-edge rib sections
182 Bomb shackles
183 500-lb (227-kg) M-43 demolition bomb
184 Undercarriage leg fairing (overlapping upper section)
185 Mainwheel fairing (lower section)
186 Wheel fork
187 Starboard mainwheel
188 Brake lines
189 Landing gear air-oil shock strut
190 Machine-gun barrel blast tubes
191 Staggered gun barrels
192 Rocket launcher slide bar
193 Centre strap
194 Front mount (attached below front spar between inboard pair of guns)
195 Deflector arms
196 Triple-tube 4.5-in (11.4-cm) M10 rocket launcher
197 Front retaining band
198 4.5-in (11.4-cm) M8 rocket projectile

This P-47D forward fuselage shows the complete installation of the Pratt & Whitney two-row 18-cylinder R-2800 Double Wasp engine. Of course, the turbo-supercharger was situated in the rear fuselage, connected to the engine and nose intake by several yards of ducting which passed underneath and to either side of the cockpit. Air from the main intake and exhaust gases from the engine were fed separately under the cockpit to the supercharger, although some of the intake air was diverted to either side of the rear fuselage for the intercoolers. Exhaust gases drove the turbine which in turn pressurised the intake air. The side ducting, which fed pressurised air back to the carburettor intercooler, is clearly visible here. As well as Pratt & Whitney production, R-2800s were also made by Chevrolet.

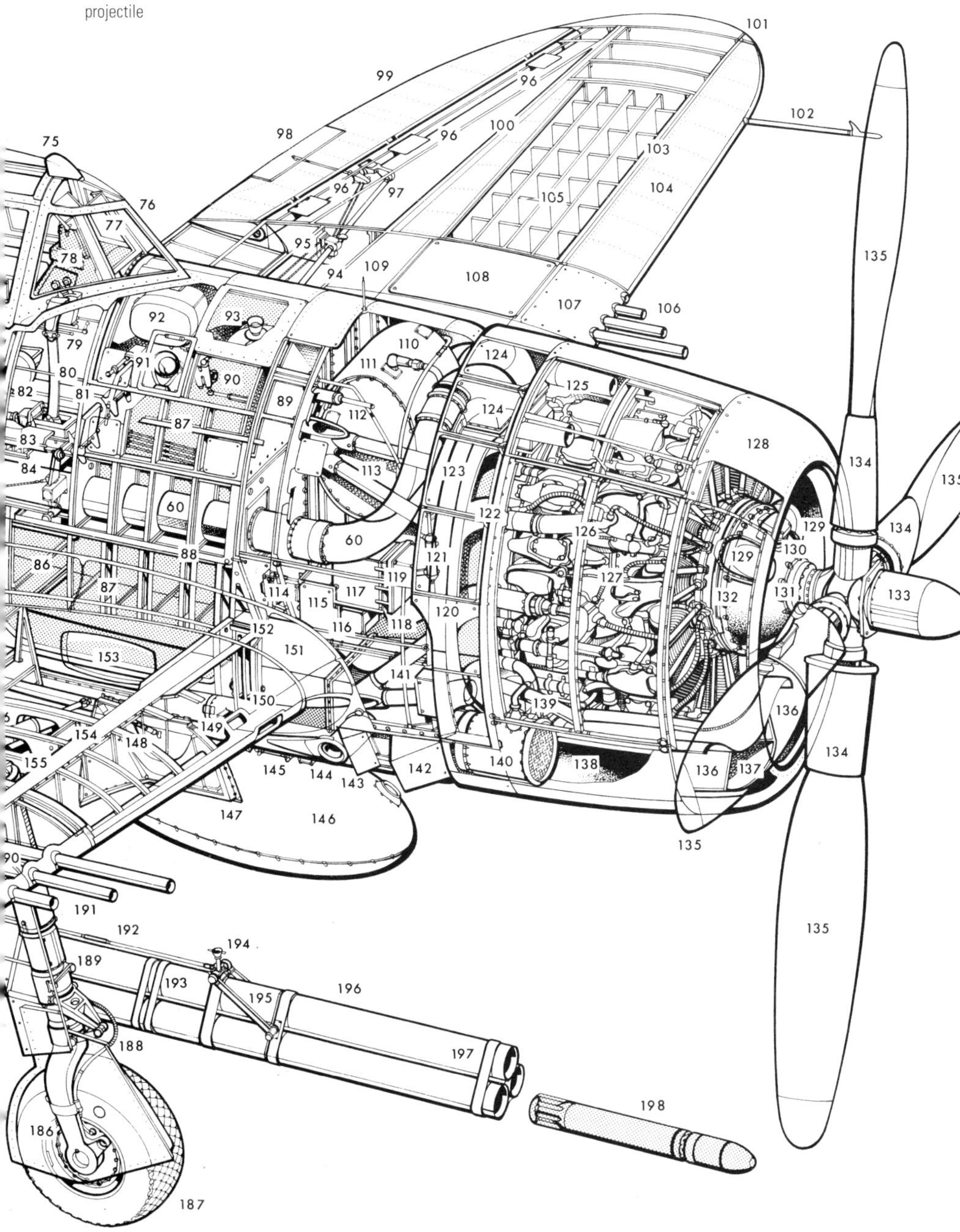

P-47D development

P-47D-1: the first P-47Ds (P-47D and P-47D-RE) were simply P-47Cs built at the new Evansville factory. However, the first major production block, the P-47D-1-RE, introduced various improvements. Externally the most notable was additional cooling gills at the rear of the engine cowling.

P-47D-6: from the P-47D-5-RE a two-point bomb shackle was introduced on the centreline, as was the provision for water injection, operated by a switch on the throttle. The D-6 was similar, with a few minor electrical system changes.

P-47D-11: water injection was fitted as standard from the P-47D-10-RE along with other modifications. The D-11 (standardised at both Evansville and Farmingdale plants) had the injection control operated automatically by the throttle lever, rather than a separate switch.

P-47D-22: wing pylons were introduced by the P-47D-15, along with greater fuel capacity, while the D-20 switched to the R-2800-59 engine. The D-22 had a Hamilton Standard propeller.

P-47D-27: the most notable P-47 improvement, the 'bubble' canopy, was introduced by the P-47D-25, which also featured a revised cockpit, fuel and water systems. The D-26, -27 and -28 were very similar, with detailed changes.

P-47D-30: the Block 30 had blunt-nosed ailerons for better control at high speed, and divebrakes. Many had zero-length rocket launchers fitted (as on this aircraft).

Camouflage and markings

Early P-47s were finished in a standard scheme of olive drab upper surfaces and neutral gray undersides. For service in England identification markings were added in the form of white cowlings and white bar across the tail and tailplanes, principally to distinguish the P-47 from the Focke-Wulf Fw 190. In October 1943 camouflage was officially dropped from production aircraft, so natural metal aircraft began to appear in-theatre from early 1944. In these instances, the identification bands were in black. For a short time in 1943 the fuselage national insignia had a yellow ring around it, although this changed to blue in September 1943. Underwing insignia were usually large to help avoid friendly groundfire. Two-letter RAF-style squadron codes were added for commonality with the host nation at an early stage, together with an individual aircraft letter. These codes were applied to both 8th and 9th Air Force aircraft. Nose art was rife from an early stage. In June 1944 black and white invasion stripes were added – mostly to the undersides only but on occasion, as with this aircraft, wrapped round the entire rear fuselage and wings.

Inevitably, markings began to diversify as the war neared its end, and the 56th Fighter Group's aircraft became more 'non-standard' than most, playing on the group's considerable reputation. From late 1943 the red nose band appeared while the identification bands were removed. In 1944 aircraft began to receive unusual camouflage patterns. Several were based on the RAF's green/grey disruptive scheme (prevalent in the 62nd FS), while others employed midnight blue upper surfaces (mainly 61st FS) or two-tone blue (mainly 63rd FS). This scheme, applied to Schilling's aircraft, used RAF dark green and medium sea grey but in an unusual pattern. Fuselage codes began to be presented in the squadron colours which were also applied to the rudders. Other groups, such as the 78th, 353rd and 356th, also applied non-standard camouflage in the form of RAF dark green.

From an early point, the 56th FG, and 62nd FS in particular, had revealed a penchant for using the 'Lil Abner' characters from the Al Capp *Dogpatch* cartoons as nose arts. Schilling's aircraft featured 'Hairless Joe'.

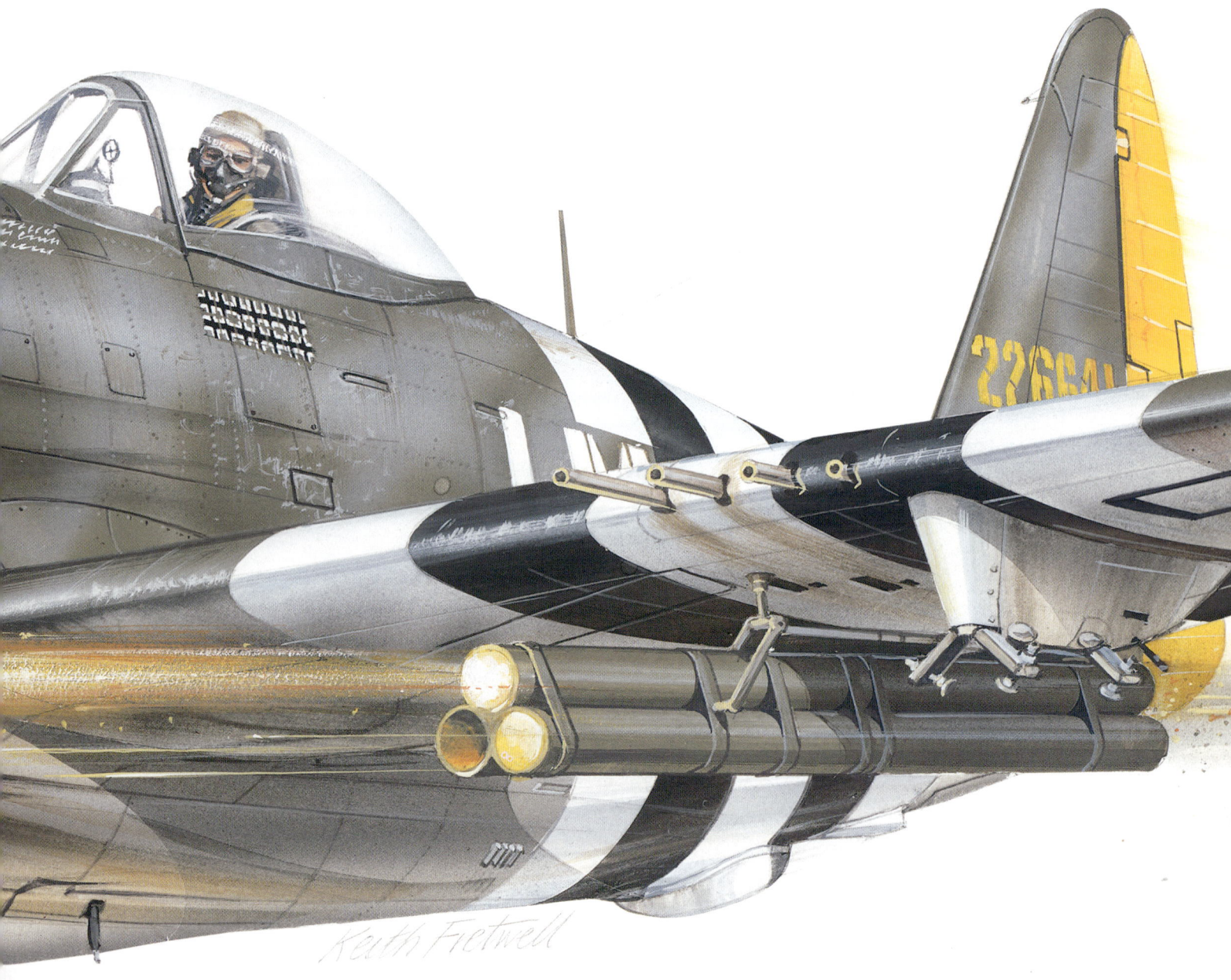

Gun armament

The standard internal armament of the P-47 was eight 0.5-in (12.7-mm) machine-guns, a fit considered to be more than adequate throughout the conflict. However, some units removed two of the guns to enhance manoeuvrability and to save weight, while aircraft flying in low-threat environments often had six removed. The guns were located side-by-side, but staggered chordwise so that the ammunition belts could be laid side-by-side in the outer wings between the two main spars. A study to fit four 20-mm cannon was undertaken, and a trial installation with a packaged 20-mm cannon was tested on a wing pylon for ground strafing. Neither was adopted. In P-47Cs and early P-47Ds the guns were aimed using a 70-mm Mk VIII reflector sight, backed up by a simple ring-and-bead sight. From late 1944 the K-14 gyroscopic gunsight became standard for new production aircraft, although many aircraft had these fitted earlier in-theatre. One unit, the 406th FG, employed a British 100-mm reflector sight in place of the Mk VIII. When fitted, the M10 rocket tubes were aligned with the guns so that the pilot could use the standard sight to launch them.

Squadron codes and colours

The following table presents the two-letter RAF-style squadron codes applied to P-47s in the ETO. Many squadrons within each group were assigned colours, usually applied to the engine cowlings or rudders. Where appropriate these are given.

8th Air Force fighter groups

Group	Squadron	Code	Colour
4th FG	334th FS	QP	
	335th FS	WD	
	336th FS	VF	
56th FG	61st FS	HV	red
	62nd FS	LM	yellow
	63rd FS	UN	blue
78th FG	82nd FS	MX	red
	83rd FS	HL	white
	84th FS	WZ	black
352nd FG	328th FS	PE	
	486th FS	PZ	
	487th FS	HO	
353rd FG	350th FS	LH	
	351st FS	YJ	
	352nd FS	SX	
355th FG	354th FS	WR	
	357th FS	OS	
	358th FS	YF	
356th FG	359th FS	OC	
	360th FS	PI	
	361st FS	QI	

Group	Squadron	Code	Colour
358th FG	365th FS	CH	yellow
	366th FS	IA	white
	367th FS	CP	red
359th FG	368th FS	CV	
	369th FS	IV	
	370th FS	CR	
361st FG	374th FS	B7	
	375th FS	E2	
	376th FS	E9	
495th FTG	551st FTS	DQ	
	552nd FTS	VM	
(no assignment)	5th ERS	5F	

9th Air Force fighter groups

Group	Squadron	Code	Colour
36th FG	22nd FS	3T	red
	23rd FS	7U	yellow
	53rd FS	6V	blue
48th FG	492nd FS	F4	red
	493rd FS	I7	blue
	494th FS	6M	yellow
50th FG	10th FS	5T	
	81st FS	2N	
	313th FS	W3	
354th FG	353rd FS	FT	
	355th FS	GQ	
	356th FS	AJ	
358th FG	365th FS	CH	white
	366th FS	IA	yellow
	367th FS	CP	red

Group	Squadron	Code	Colour
362nd FG	377th FS	E4	red
	378th FS	G8	green
	379th FS	B8	yellow
365th FG	386th FS	D5	red
	387th FS	B4	yellow
	388th FS	C4	white
366th FG	389th FS	A6	
	390th FS	B2	
	398th FS	A8	
367th FG	392nd FS	H5	red
	393rd FS	8L	blue
	394th FS	4N	yellow
368th FG	395th FS	A7	red
	396th FS	8L/C2	yellow
	397th FS	D3	blue
371st FG	404th FS	9Q	red
	405th FS	8N	blue
	406th FS	4W	yellow
373rd FG	410th FS	R3	
	411th FS	U9	
	412th FS	V5	
404th FG	506th FS	4K	
	507th FS	Y8	
	508th FS	7J	
405th FG	509th FS	G9	red
	510th FS	2Z	blue
	511th FS	K4	yellow
406th FG	512th FS	L3	yellow
	513th FS	4P	red
	514th FS	O7	blue

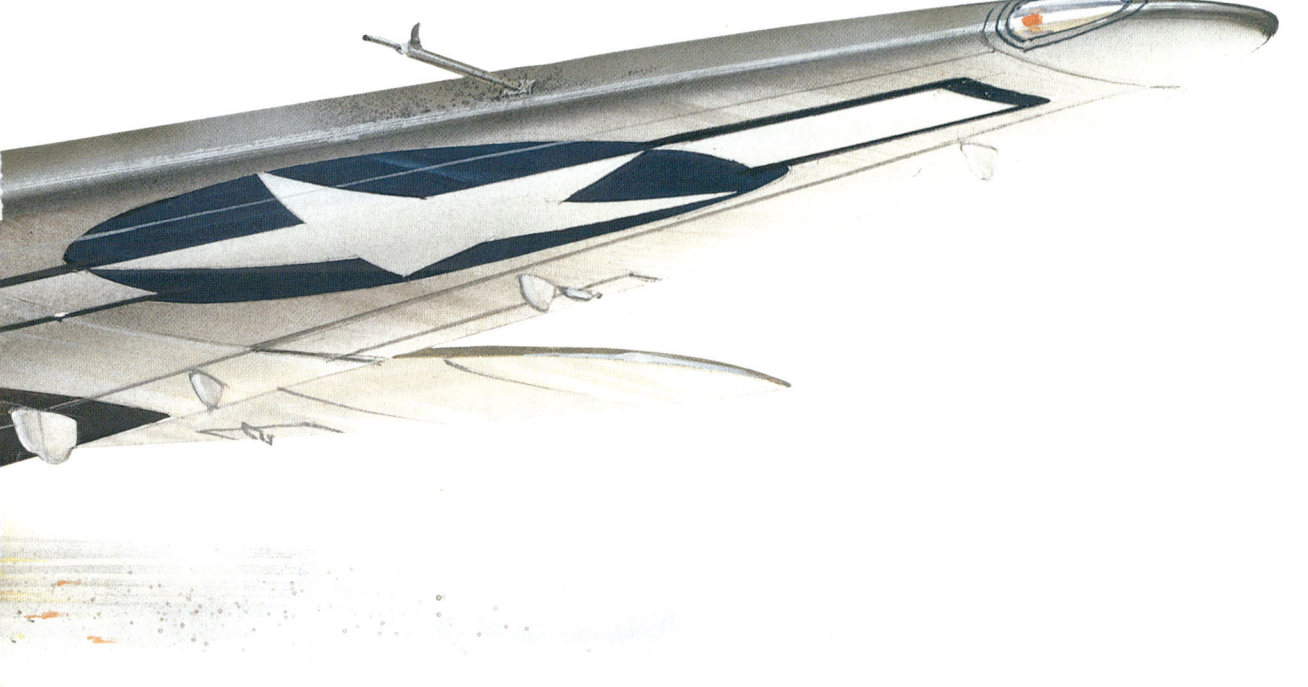

Fuel

In the early 'razorback' variants (P-47B to P-47D-23) internal fuel was held in a main tank of 205-US gal (776-litre) capacity and an auxiliary tank of 100-US gal (379-litre) capacity, both situated in the central fuselage below the cockpit. When the 'bubbletop' P-47D-25 was introduced, the main tank was increased to 270 US gal (1022 litres), giving 370 US gal (1400 litres) in total. This remained standard for all remaining P-47Ds and the P-47M. The long-range P-47N used in the Pacific had internal fuel raised to 556 US gal (2105 litres).

In its first intended role as a fighter escort for the 8th Air Force's day bombers, the P-47 lacked sufficient range to even reach the German border. Additional tankage was urgently needed, and many of the answers were found in-theatre by resourceful engineers. The first auxiliary tank to be tried in combat was a 200-US gal (757-litre) ferry tank, which was carried on the centreline and was faired into the lower fuselage. These were nicknamed 'Babies', and had a wooden fairing fitted to the front to ensure a clean separation from the aircraft when jettisoned. Made in the US from impregnated paper, the tanks could not be used above 20,000 ft (6096 m) and could not be fully filled. However, their first employment in July 1943 allowed the P-47s to reach the Dutch/German border. The first effective tank was the 75-US gal (284-litre) unit, as carried by this aircraft. Originally designed for the Bell P-39, this metal tank could be used in conjunction with a pressurisation system developed by 8th AF engineers and could deliver its entire capacity at any altitude. It was first fielded by the 78th FG on 30 July 1943. Further range could be gained by using a 108-US gal (409-litre) paper tank originally developed for the Hawker Hurricane and made in Britain. A similar capacity metal tank was also used. To confuse, the paper tanks were painted in silver dope, while the metal tanks were grey. These tanks allowed the P-47s to escort the bombers into northern Germany, but it was not until the P-51 arrived that the bombers could be covered to more distant targets. As development progressed and wing pylons were added to the P-47, larger tanks became available. A 'flat belly' tank holding 165 US gal (625 litres) was used in Europe, while in the Pacific tanks of 110-US gal (416-litre), 150-US gal (568-litre), 200-US gal (757-litre) and even 300-US gal (1136-litre) capacity were employed. Some tanks were given bomb fins to decrease the chance of them hitting the aircraft when jettisoned.

Republic P-47D-10 Thunderbolt

1 Rudder upper hinge
2 Aerial attachment
3 Fin flanged ribs
4 Rudder post/aft spar
5 Fin front spar
6 Rudder trim tab worm and screw actuating mechanism (chain driven)
7 Rudder centre hinge
8 Rudder trim tab
9 Rudder structure
10 Tail navigation light
11 Elevator fixed tab
12 Elevator trim tab
13 Starboard elevator structure
14 Elevator outboard hinge
15 Elevator torque tube
16 Elevator trim tab worm and screw actuating mechanism
17 Chain drive
18 Starboard tailplane
19 Tail jacking point
20 Rudder control cables
21 Elevator control rod and linkage
22 Fin spar/fuselage attachment point

46 Outlet louvres
47 Intercooler exhaust doors (port and starboard)
48 Exhaust pipes
49 Cooling air ducts
50 Intercooler unit (cooling and supercharged air)
51 Radio transmitter and receiver packs (Detrola)
52 Canopy track
53 Elevator rod linkage
54 Aerial mast
55 Formation light
56 Rear-vision frame cut-out and glazing
57 Oxygen bottles
58 Supercharged and cooling air pipe (supercharger to carburettor) port

84 Rudder cable linkage
85 Wing rear spar/fuselage attachment (tapered bolts/bushings)
86 Wing supporting lower bulkhead section
87 Main fuel tank (205 US gal/776 litres)
88 Fuselage forward structure
89 Stainless steel/Alclad firewall bulkhead
90 Cowl flap valve
91 Main fuel filler point
92 Anti-freeze fluid tank
93 Hydraulic reservoir
94 Aileron control rod
95 Aileron trim tab control cables
96 Aileron hinge access panels
97 Aileron and tab control linkage
98 Aileron trim tab (port wing only)
99 Frise-type aileron
100 Wing rear (No. 2) spar
101 Port navigation light

119 Storage battery
120 Exhaust collector ring
121 Cowl flap actuating cylinder
122 Exhaust outlets to collector ring
123 Cowl flaps
124 Supercharged and cooling air ducts to carburettor (port and starboard)
125 Exhaust upper outlets
126 Cowling frame
127 Pratt & Whitney R-2800-59 18-cylinder two-row radial engine
128 Cowling nose panel
129 Magnetos
130 Propeller governor
131 Propeller hub
132 Reduction gear casing
133 Spinner
134 Propeller cuffs
135 Four-bladed Curtiss constant-speed electric propeller
136 Oil cooler intakes (port and starboard)

142 Oil cooler exhaust variable shutter
143 Fixed deflector
144 Excess exhaust gas gate
145 Belly stores/weapons shackles
146 Metal auxiliary drop tank (75 US gal/284 litres)
147 Inboard mainwheel well door
148 Mainwheel well door actuating cylinder
149 Camera gun port
150 Cabin air conditioning intake (starboard wing only)
151 Wingroot fairing
152 Wing front spar/fuselage attachment (tapered bolts/bushings)
153 Wing inboard rib mainwheel well access
154 Wing front (No. 1) spar
155 Undercarriage pivot point
156 Hydraulic retraction cylinder
157 Auxiliary (undercarriage mounting) wing spar
158 Gun bay warm air flexible duct

159 Wing rear (No. 2) spar
160 Landing flap inboard hinge
161 Auxiliary (No. 3) wing spar inboard section (flap mounting)
162 NACA slotted trailing-edge landing flaps
163 Landing flap centre hinge
164 Landing flap hydraulic cylinder
165 Four 0.5-in (12.7-mm) Browning machine-guns
166 Inter-spar gun bay inboard rib
167 Ammunition feed chutes
168 Individual ammunition troughs
169 Underwing stores/weapons pylon
170 Landing flap outboard hinge
171 Flap door
172 Landing flap profile
173 Aileron fixed tab (starboard wing only)
174 Frise-type aileron structure
175 Aileron hinge/steel forging spar attachments

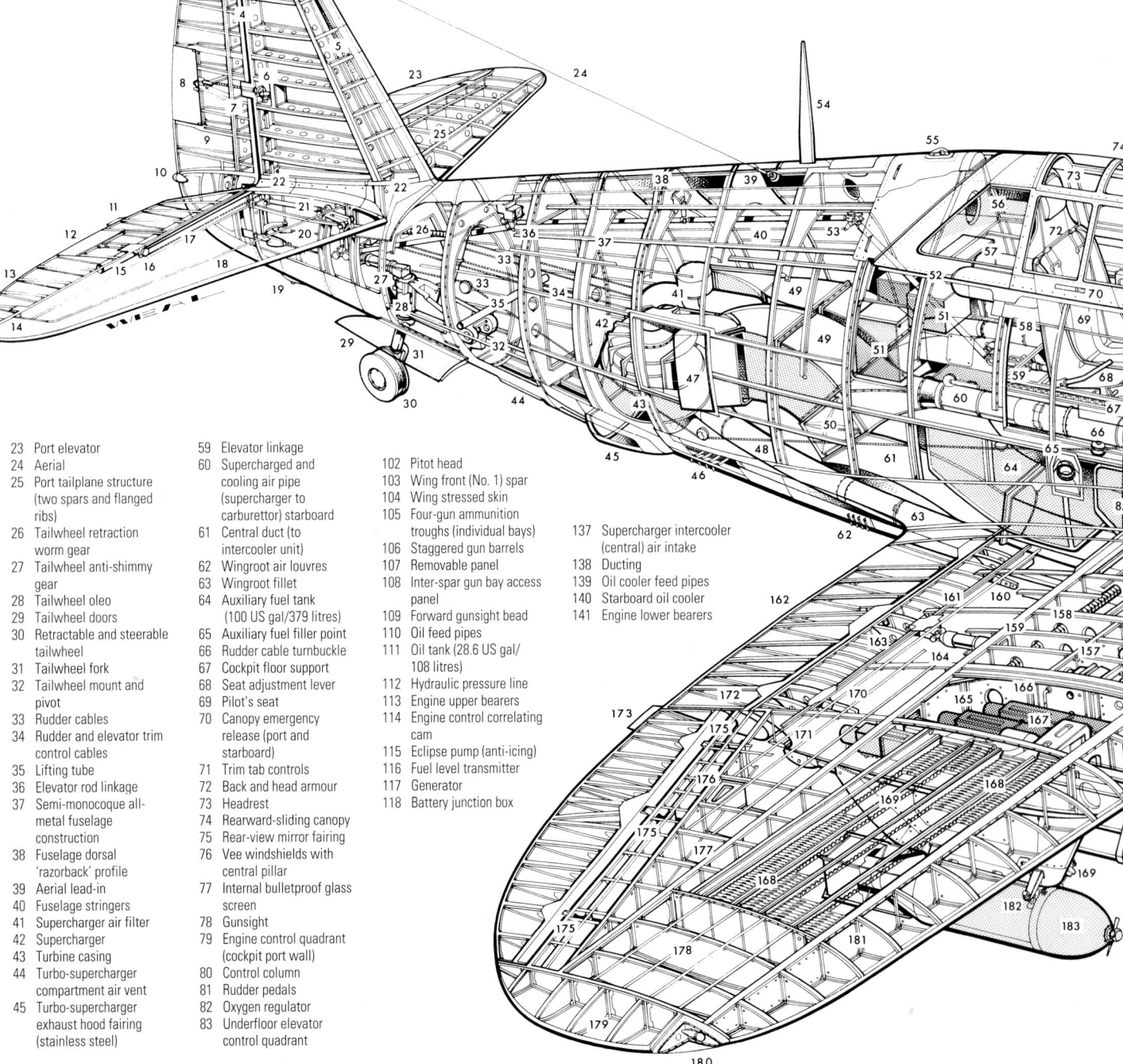

23 Port elevator
24 Aerial
25 Port tailplane structure (two spars and flanged ribs)
26 Tailwheel retraction worm gear
27 Tailwheel anti-shimmy gear
28 Tailwheel oleo
29 Tailwheel doors
30 Retractable and steerable tailwheel
31 Tailwheel fork
32 Tailwheel mount and pivot
33 Rudder cables
34 Rudder and elevator trim control cables
35 Lifting tube
36 Elevator rod linkage
37 Semi-monocoque all-metal fuselage construction
38 Fuselage dorsal 'razorback' profile
39 Aerial lead-in
40 Fuselage stringers
41 Supercharger air filter
42 Supercharger
43 Turbine casing
44 Turbo-supercharger compartment air vent
45 Turbo-supercharger exhaust hood fairing (stainless steel)

59 Elevator linkage
60 Supercharged and cooling air pipe (supercharger to carburettor) starboard
61 Central duct (to intercooler unit)
62 Wingroot air louvres
63 Wingroot fillet
64 Auxiliary fuel tank (100 US gal/379 litres)
65 Auxiliary fuel filler point
66 Rudder cable turnbuckle
67 Cockpit floor support
68 Seat adjustment lever
69 Pilot's seat
70 Canopy emergency release (port and starboard)
71 Trim tab controls
72 Back and head armour
73 Headrest
74 Rearward-sliding canopy
75 Rear-view mirror fairing
76 Vee windshields with central pillar
77 Internal bulletproof glass screen
78 Gunsight
79 Engine control quadrant (cockpit port wall)
80 Control column
81 Rudder pedals
82 Oxygen regulator
83 Underfloor elevator control quadrant

102 Pitot head
103 Wing front (No. 1) spar
104 Wing stressed skin
105 Four-gun ammunition troughs (individual bays)
106 Staggered gun barrels
107 Removable panel
108 Inter-spar gun bay access panel
109 Forward gunsight bead
110 Oil feed pipes
111 Oil tank (28.6 US gal/108 litres)
112 Hydraulic pressure line
113 Engine upper bearers
114 Engine control correlating cam
115 Eclipse pump (anti-icing)
116 Fuel level transmitter
117 Generator
118 Battery junction box

137 Supercharger intercooler (central) air intake
138 Ducting
139 Oil cooler feed pipes
140 Starboard oil cooler
141 Engine lower bearers

Storming the Reich – 9th Air Force 1944/45

P-47D-30-RE
One of the best-known 9th AF 'Jugs', this aircraft was flown by Major Glenn Eagleston, CO of the 353rd Fighter Squadron, 354th Fighter Group. At the time (December 1944) the unit was operating from Rosières-en-Haye in France, and involved in heavy fighting in the Ardennes region. Eagleston was the 9th AF's highest-scoring ace, with 18.5 kills, although they were all scored on P-51s.

P-47D-30-RE *Wee Speck*
The crack 354th Fighter Group had achieved considerable fame on P-51s, but its Mustangs were replaced by P-47s between November 1944 and February 1945. Few of the group's aces, like Captain Lowell Brueland whose aircraft this is, scored during the Thunderbolt period, although the kills returned when the group got its Mustangs back. However, the P-47s were instrumental in halting the Wehrmacht counter-offensive in the Battle of the Bulge.

P-47D-30-RA *Ole Trapper IV*
Lieutenant Robert Ward of the 367th FS, 358th FG flew this Thunderbolt from Toul in March 1945. Most of his recorded kills were against aircraft on the ground, although he was credited with four in the air. The 358th had earlier been an 8th AF group, but had been reassigned on 1 January 1944. It moved to France the day after D-day, and advanced eastwards. By March 1945 its P-47s were hitting the Wehrmacht hard as it attempted to flee across the Rhine.

P-47D-27-RE *Shirley Jane III*
A meticulously recorded sortie and victory tally adorned the Thunderbolt of Captain Edwin Fisher of the 377th FS, 362nd FG at Lignerolles in August 1944. The tally included seven air-to-air victories (plus three V-1 flying-bombs). The 362nd followed the US Army to France, and was involved in the Battle of the Bulge. It saw heavy action during March 1945 against German resistance in the hilly Moselle-Rhine region.

P-47D-30-RA *Five by Five*
Colonel Joseph Laughlin, who flew this aircraft, was the CO of the 362nd Fighter Group. It is shown as it appeared in May 1945, when the unit was based in Germany at Straubing. Last in a succession of P-47s with this name, this aircraft had a cowling and fin adorned with the colours of the three squadrons under Laughlin's command. Although he was not credited with any air-to-air victories, Laughlin did sink a warship and destroyed three aircraft on the ground.

P-47D-30-RE *Just Bess*
Lt Arnold Abel was the pilot of this Thunderbolt, while serving with the 392nd FS, 367th FG at Eschborn, Germany in May 1945. In the final months of the war the 367th performed a large-scale attack against the Wehrmacht's western headquarters, and was heavily involved in the campaign to destroy aircraft on Luftwaffe airfields.

Air-sea rescue with the 5th ERS

War-weary P-47s were used for air-sea rescue patrols, carrying flares to mark the positions of downed aircrew, and air-droppable dinghies. Established as a detachment of the 65th Fighter Wing, the rescue unit was redesignated 5th Emergency Rescue Squadron (5th Air Sea Rescue Squadron from 26 January 1945). Using war-weary P-47D-5s and -21s, the squadron flew its first mission on 10 May 1944. The aircraft were armed, although they scored no air-to-air kills. However, the unit was responsible for the 8th AF's first V-1 kill, achieved by Lt J. Tucker on 30 June 1944. The Thunderbolts usually carried a 150-US gal (568-litre) belly tank, with a dinghy under each wing and markers below the rear fuselage.

Above and below: P-47Ds of the 5th ERS (also known as 65th FW Det B) are seen between missions. The 'WW' on the fin signified 'War Weary'. Yellow bands were worn by the rescue machines to denote their special status, while the squadron applied a red/white/blue cowl marking.

Right: Visible on this 5th ERS P-47D are the racks for carrying smoke markers. These were located under the fuselage behind the centreline bomb shackles and could carry four markers. The aircraft has had four of its guns removed to save weight. Some of the 5th ERS aircraft had Malcolm hoods fitted for better visibility.

victories, while one of the group's pilots, Walker Mahurin, had become the first Eighth Air Force pilot to gain a two-figure kill tally. The 56th had overhauled the 4th during September and now had nearly twice as many victories as its Debden-based rival, and was responsible for more than one-third of the entire Thunderbolt force's tally.

By this time, the older P-47 groups had become massive organisations, with large numbers of aircraft and pilots. On 5 November, for example, the 78th Fighter Group was able to fly two separate formations simultaneously, each consisting of three 12-aircraft squadrons; such deployments became routine by early 1944.

The 358th and 359th Groups commenced operations in December. The 10th and final Eighth Air Force P-47 unit, the 361st Fighter Group, arrived in December 1943 and began operations in January 1944. Meanwhile, the first Mustangs began operations in December 1943, and would soon supplant all but one of the P-47 groups.

By the time the new Thunderbolt groups began flying operational missions, a new clutch of sub-variants was in service. The first of these was the P-47D-10-RE, which introduced a further improved turbo-supercharger, the GE C-23, which could operate continuously at 20,000 rpm and had a 15-minute emergency overspeed setting of 22,000 rpm. This was accompanied by modifications to the

2,300-hp (1716-kW) R-2800-63 engine, with improved water injection for enhanced cooling in this War Emergency Power setting, which gave an increase in power of about 15 per cent, or 200-300 hp (150-224 kW). The redundant flap equaliser was finally ditched on the D-10-RE, while the electric gun firing wires were replaced by simpler and more reliable Bowden cables. Farmington built 250 P-47D-10-REs (42-74965 to 75214).

From the P-47D-11, the same numerical sub-variant designations were used by both Farmingdale and Evansville, though the factories retained their -RE and -RA suffixes. The new version introduced the R-2800-63 engine, which featured an electrically driven water pump, which was automatically actuated in the last 0.5 in (1.27 cm) of throttle travel, providing automatic water injection. Farmingdale built 400 D-11s (42-75215 to 75614) while Evansville built 250 (42-22864 to 23113), the last 30 with a pilot-actuated switch for the gun camera. Kits were produced to bring earlier R-2800-21 engines to the same standard, with automatic water injection, which thus rapidly became the norm on front-line Thunderbolts. Most of the aircraft used by the older Eighth Army Air Force Thunderbolt units had been modified by the end of 1943.

More fuel, more range

Underwing pylons were added to the P-47D-15, allowing the carriage of bombs or drop tanks. The ability to carry underwing fuel tanks made a dramatic difference to the Thunderbolt's range, and allowed the aircraft to escort bombers to more distant targets. Internal tankage was increased to 375 US gal (1419 litres). Some earlier P-47Cs and Ds were fitted retrospectively with the same wing racks. Farmingdale built 496 -15s (42-75615 to 75864 and 76119 to 76364) and Evansville built another 157 (42-23143 to 23299). The -16 had modifications to allow the use of 100/150 grade high-octane petrol, of which Farmingdale built 254 (42-75865 to 76118) and Evansville built 29 more (42-23114 to 23142).

The introduction of a plumbed centreline pylon revolutionised the P-47 as an escort fighter, but the underwing hardpoints introduced on the P-47D-15, and retrofitted to earlier variants, opened up a new world of opportunities for the Thunderbolt. Tentative steps towards the fighter-bomber role were taken relatively early in the Thunderbolt's career, when pilots escaping at low altitude began to strafe targets of opportunity with their eight 0.50-in calibre machine-guns – a surprisingly effective ground attack weapon.

What had been an unauthorised sport for individual pilots soon became a part of the Thunderbolt groups' official role. The Eighth Air Force issued orders that permitted P-47 pilots to strafe enemy airfields, countering Luftwaffe efforts to conserve its fighters by keeping them on the ground, and allowing the USAAF to go on the offensive even when unfavourable weather kept the high-flying bombers on the ground. The first recorded strafing victory was achieved on 21 January 1944, when Glenn Duncan and two other 353rd Fighter Group pilots shot up a Do 217 on an airfield north of Amiens, though the kill was not officially recognised. The first credited air-to-ground kills came on 11 February when 'Hub' Zemke led two squadrons on a single-pass strafing attack against a fighter airfield as they transited home.

Airfield strafing was dangerous work, and became progressively more dangerous as the Luftwaffe strengthened its airfield defences. The only route to success was via careful planning, and by making a single ultra-low-level pass to ensure maximum surprise. Even then, losses were always high, and many Thunderbolt aces were shot down during ground strafing attacks. Walter Becker (then the leading Eighth Air Force ace, with 18 kills) was shot down on 22 February, when he led his formation in an attack on the Ju 88 base at Ostheim near Bonn, whose defences had just been alerted by a strafing attack by Glenn Duncan's formation. Becker's aircraft, *Little Demon*, was hit in the engine, and he pulled up and bailed out into captivity, after calling his wingman on the radio. "Stay down, take the boys home, George, I can't make it!" he said coolly. Becker's great rival, Walker Mahurin, then added to his score before he, too, was shot down (with 21 kills) in March 1944. Gerald Johnson (also downed in March) had 18 kills to his credit when he fell to ground fire during a ground strafing run.

Ground attack specialists

A special strafing flight (manned by some of the best pilots from the Eighth and Ninth Air Forces) was formed in March 1944, operating as an operational and tactical evaluation unit, developing the best possible tactics and techniques for ground attack missions. This flight was hosted by the 353rd Fighter Group at Metfield, which pioneered the use of the Thunderbolt in the dive-bomber role, carrying 500-lb (227-kg) fragmentation bombs underwing.

The group flew its first dive-bombing mission on 25 November 1943, against a Luftwaffe fighter airfield in France. The Thunderbolts dived from 15,000 ft (4572 m), releasing their bombs at 10,000 ft (3048 m). This allowed sufficient altitude to pull out, but accuracy was relatively poor. Despite the high altitude, group CO Colonel McCollom was hit by flak and had to bale out. On subsequent attacks, the group experimented with dive angles and bomb release heights, and even tried level bombing with a B-24 Liberator 'lead ship', following work carried out by Zemke's 56th Fighter Group, which had also experimented in level bombing using various 'lead ships'.

Even as the Thunderbolt began to embrace an additional new role, its pilots continued to battle for air supremacy.

The first 'bubbletop' P-47D-25s reached England in late May, being first assigned to the 56th FG. Prudence was flown by Major William Tanner, a 5.5-kill ace with the 350th FS, 353rd FG. This 8th AF group transitioned to Mustangs in October 1944.

The 56th Fighter Group, by now widely known as 'Zemke's Wolfpack', had achieved a score of 250 victories, and one of its squadrons, the 61st Fighter Squadron, had claimed 100 victories – almost as many victories as the entire 78th Fighter Group, and not far short of the elite 4th Fighter Group's total. Such results were the result of some exceptionally successful missions. On the first Big Week mission (six days of strikes against Germany in February 1944), the 56th shot down 18 of 24 Bf 110Gs caught over Minden, then a dozen Bf 109s and Fw 190s the next day, and 17 the following day.

Use of the Thunderbolt at low level had been hamstrung by the perception that it was at a disadvantage if it met enemy fighters at altitudes below 15,000 ft (4572 m). This was something of a hindrance to tactical flexibility, and Republic made major efforts to improve the Thunderbolt's performance, not least by adding more engine power.

Below: Betty flew with the 353rd FG. The aircraft is fitted with the round, Spitfire-style rear view mirror, one of a number of attempts to improve the rearward visibility in the deep-spined versions.

Photographed at Boxted in July 1944 is Lieutenant Colonel Francis 'Gabby' Gabreski. Since June 1943 he had been commanding officer of the 61st Fighter Squadron (the aircraft's codes were 'HV-A'), and on 5 July 1944 had scored his 28th kill to pass Robert Johnson's score of 27 to become the leading USAAF ace in Europe. It was to be his last kill of World War II, as he force-landed after hitting the ground during a strafing run on Bassinheim airfield on 20 July. After five days on the run, he was captured and held as a prisoner-of-war. Later, Gabreski added 6.5 kills flying Sabres as CO of the 51st FIW in Korea.

This scene at Duxford in November 1944 shows the red-ruddered aircraft of the 82nd FS, 78th FG, which on 18 September had been heavily involved in providing air cover for Operation Market Garden, the Allied operation to take Arnhem. Market Garden was a disaster for all concerned: the P-47s suffered disproportionately large losses to heavy flak, including at least one to friendly fire. The 56th FG at Boxted was also involved, losing 16 of the 39 P-47s it dispatched. By this time the 78th had adopted a non-standard dark green upper surface camouflage. In December the group gave up its 'Jugs' in favour of P-51 Mustangs.

Below right: This P-47D-28-RA wears an unusual two-tone light grey camouflage, one of several non-standard schemes applied by the 56th Fighter Group. The cowling was red (for the 56th FG) and the rudder blue (for the 63rd FS).

Below: Cylindrical tanks for the wing pylons and 'flat-belly' tanks for the centreline litter this corner of Boxted in the summer of 1944. The aircraft are from the 56th Fighter Group's 62nd FS, as indicated by the yellow rudders. During June the 8th AF P-47s had helped to provide air superiority over the Allied beachhead, and from then on were increasingly involved in tactical ground attack missions, leaving the bomber escort mission to the P-51 Mustang.

The R-2800-59 engine, with GE high-tension ignition cables, made its debut on the P-47D-20, which also featured a longer tailwheel oleo, modified underwing pylons and ducted air heating in the gun bays, together with other minor improvements and refinements. The parent company built 300 aircraft (42-76365 to 76614 and 42-25274 to 25322) at Farmingdale.

The 250th D-20-RE (42-76614) was delivered in natural metal finish, all previous Thunderbolts having been delivered in camouflage. Evansville built 187 D-20s (43-25254 to

25440), delivering all in the old camouflage colour scheme.

The gradual transition to overall natural metal finish was paralleled by the increasing use of colourful group and squadron markings. The 56th Fighter Group, delighted with its performance and status as the Eighth's leading unit, led the rush towards colourful unit markings, mimicking the Luftwaffe's bright yellow-nosed Fw 190s and Bf 109s by painting the noses of its P-47s in squadron colours.

A new manual water injection button was fitted to the throttle lever on the P-47D-21. Farmingdale built 216 (42-25323 to 25538) and Evansville produced 224 (43-25441 to 25664). Water injection in the intake manifold alone was not enough, and it was soon decided that a broader-chord propeller blade would be required to take the fullest advantage of the increased power. The parent factory then built 850 aircraft (42-25539 to 26388) similar to the P-47D-21, but fitted with a new Hamilton Standard Hydromatic paddle-blade airscrew and an A-23 turbo regulator, under the designation P-47D-22-RE. Broad-chord airscrews were also retrofitted to some earlier versions.

There was no direct equivalent to the D-22RE at Evansville, which instead added a Curtiss Electric C542S paddle-blade propeller with Type 836 blades and an A-23 turbo regulator to produce 889 P-47D-23-RAs (43-25665 to 25753 and 42-27389 to 28188).

Apart from the 56th Fighter Group, which expressed a preference for the Thunderbolt and requested permission to continue with the big Republic fighter, the other P-47 groups within the Eighth Air Force converted to Mustangs between November 1943 and November 1944, and two transferred to the 9th Air Force. The timetable was rapid, and the disappearance of the P-47 from the Eighth began with two of the first three groups. The 78th Fighter Group transferred to the Ninth Air Force in November 1943, later equipping with the Mustang. The 4th Fighter Group, never comfortable with its P-47s, was the next to go, transitioning to the Mustang in February 1944, while the 358th Fighter Group transferred to the Ninth Air Force the same month.

Even after the loss of these units, the Thunderbolt remained the USAAF's most numerous escort fighter. During Operation Argument (or Big Week, as it became known), P-47s from the Eighth and Ninth Air Forces outnumbered all other escort fighters. On the initial raid against Leipzig and other targets, the bombers were accompanied by 668 P-47s, as well as 94 P-38s and 73 P-51s. On the mission to Augsburg on 25 February, 755 bombers were escorted by 687 Thunderbolts, and by only 73 P-38s and 139 P-51 Mustangs. During the whole of Big Week, the P-47s accounted for 140 of the 218 enemy aircraft claimed, for only 21 losses, many of which fell to flak.

The remaining Eighth Air Force Thunderbolt units all transitioned to the Mustang during the remainder of 1944: the 355th Fighter Group in March 1944, the 352nd Fighter Group in April 1944, the 359th and 361st Fighter Groups in May 1944, and the 353rd and 356th Fighter Groups in November 1944.

Building up the Ninth

Conversion of Eighth Air Force P-47 groups to the P-51 was paralleled by the arrival of new P-47-equipped fighter groups with the Ninth Air Force. The P-47 remained in the ETO, rapidly becoming the backbone of the Ninth Air Force, operating mainly in the fighter-bomber role. The Ninth Air Force had formed as a tactical air arm, and increased in size and importance as the invasion of western Europe drew closer. Once the invasion began, the force provided the backbone of American ground attack and air support capability. The Ninth would eventually

This photograph from 1945 shows a P-47 from the 405th FG 'Thunder Monsters'. At the time the group painted the canopy frames in the squadron colours, these aircraft wearing the red of the 509th FS. The 405th undertook a series of notable actions, culminating in two big airfield raids against Gutersloh (30 March 1945) and Altengrabow (16 April) during which 97 aircraft were completely destroyed and many others badly damaged.

Into France

By 8 June 1944, two days after the D-day landings, USAAF engineers had laid a landing strip on Utah Beach, which could be used as a forward strip by P-47s engaged on close support. At the end of each day's action they returned to their bases in England. However, it was not long before the Ninth Air Force began to transfer its Thunderbolt groups to France permanently. The 368th FG was probably the first, an initial cadre landing at Strip No. 3 at Cardenville on 13 June. The remainder of the group arrived on 19 June. The 366th FG was in place at St Pierre-du-Mont on the following day, and on 25 June the 50th FG moved across the Channel from Lymington to Carentan. The rest of the P-47 groups had been transferred to France by the end of July. Initially, while RAF fighter-bombers largely handled targets close to the beachhead, the P-47s supported the Allied breakout, and also ranged inland to interdict supplies intended for the German defences.

'Razorbacks' and 'bubbletops' served side-by-side until the end of the war in Europe, as evidenced by these views of 373rd FG P-47Ds operating in France in August 1944. The 200-US gal (757-litre) 'flat-belly' tank was fairly standard issue by this stage of the war in Europe, providing the 'Jug' with a good range but keeping the wing pylons free for the carriage of bombs.

Ninth AF fighter-bombers

P-47D-20-RE *Peg O'My Heart*
Lieutenant Floyd Hass of the 391st FS, 366th FG flew this old 'razorback' from Asch in Belgium in January 1945. This field was one of those hit by the Luftwaffe during Operation Bodenplatte on New Year's Day. A flight of 366th FG P-47s managed to shoot down 12 of the attacking aircraft.

276464

A8 O

P-47D-22-RE *Kansas Tornado II*
The 405th Fighter Group moved to France on 30 June 1944, and this aircraft is seen as it appeared at St Dizier in September. The group framed the canopy in the individual squadron colour, in this instance the blue of the 510th FS. The pilot was Captain Howard Curran, officially credited with three kills although the pilot claimed four.

Kansas Tornado II

226742

2Z D

One of the many perils of low-level strafing is graphically illustrated by the results of Captain Raymond Walsh strafing what turned out to be an ammunition truck. Amazingly, the P-47 and its lucky pilot emerged unscathed, if a little startled.

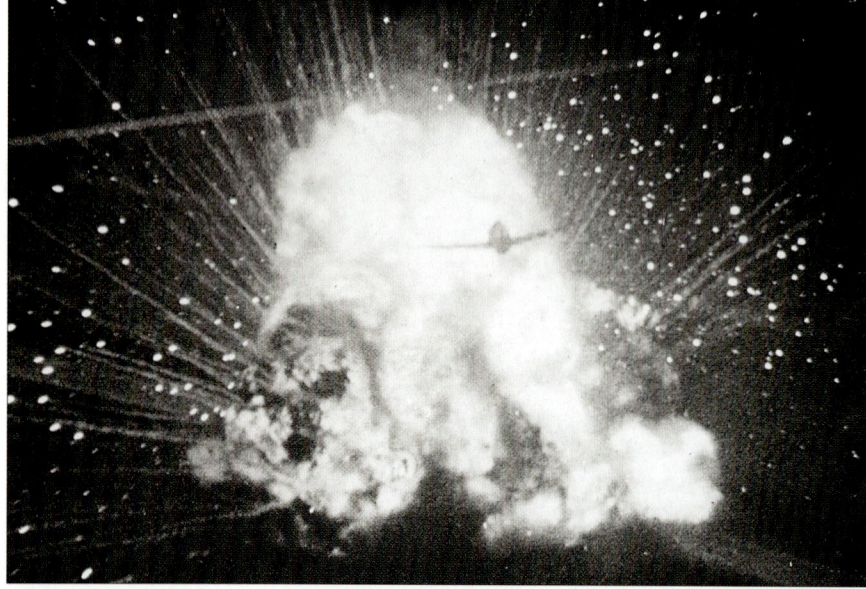

Right: A flight of 9th AF P-47s prepares to take off from a French airfield in the winter of 1944/45, each carrying a 500-lb (227-kg) bomb on the wing racks and an anti-personnel bomb on the centreline. In many respects the Battle of the Bulge in January – the last German counter-offensive of the war – was the Thunderbolt's finest hour. P-47s kept up a continuous assault on German armour and the supply chains. The eventual Allied victory laid Germany itself open.

become the most important Thunderbolt operator, with an eventual 16 front-line fighter groups.

By May 1944, despite the draw-down in the Eighth Air Force, there were 20 P-47 groups operational in England. The first Ninth Air Force Thunderbolt unit was atypical – transferring in from the Eighth Air Force (while the Mustang-equipped 357th transferred in the opposite direction) on 31 January 1944, already (albeit recently) fully operational and already flying missions. Most Ninth Air Force Thunderbolt groups were new to combat, having

activated and trained in the USA during 1943, before 'shipping out' to the ETO. Although several groups arrived in England before Christmas 1943, further training and familiarisation followed, and it was not until 8 February 1944 that the 362nd Fighter Group flew its first operational mission. Led by Lt Col Lance Call, a former enlisted US Navy pilot, who had then flown Sunderlands with the RAF, the 365th Fighter Group (soon to become known as the 'Hellhawks') was next to make its operational debut, doing so on 22 February. The 366th and 368th Fighter Groups joined the fray next, on 14 March 1944. The groups were still primarily flying bomber escort missions, although the 'Hellhawks' had already stood down (on 8 March) to begin dive-bomber training.

Fighter-bomber sorties

By April 1944, the Ninth Air Force P-47s were increasingly flying ground attack missions, with the 368th Fighter Group ('Thunder-Bums') taking an early lead. The group flew its first dive-bombing mission on 24 March, and on 13 April launched the USAAF's campaign against the V-1 launch sites. The next day, by contrast, the group went train-busting, killing nine locomotives in one mission. On 12 May, the group destroyed the railway bridge at Namur – the first of 33 bridges which would eventually be destroyed by the unit.

On 20 May, the Ninth Air Force launched a major two-week interdiction effort against the French railway network, which supplied German forces in the invasion area. Units including the 365th and 371st Fighter Groups participated in Operation Chattanooga Choo Choo, and accounted for 475 locomotives, while cutting railway lines in 150 places. By this time, eight more Ninth Air Force

Groups had flown their first missions – the 405th Fighter Group on 11 April, the 371st Fighter Group the following day, the 48th Fighter Group on the 20 April, the 50th and 404th Fighter Groups on 1 May, the 36th and 373rd Fighter Groups on 8 May, and the 406th Fighter Group on 9 May.

In May 1944 combat units started receiving P-47Ds featuring the cut-down 'bubble' hood more often associated with later variants. These aircraft were originally to have been given a new designation (the prototype being known as the XP-47L), but were instead designated P-47D-25-REs (385 aircraft, 42-26389 to 42-26773) when produced by Farmingdale, or as P-47D-26-RAs (250 aircraft, 42-28189 to 42-28438, with Curtiss propellers) when built at Evansville. Both types had increased internal fuel tankage and increased oxygen. The P-47D-27-RE was similar, but with a new starter unit and improved drop tank release system. A total of 615 was built (42-26774 to 42-27388), and from 42-27074 the engine had an extra 130 hp (97 kW) in War Emergency Power, and 64 hp (48 kW) otherwise.

The use of different propellers by Farmington and Evansville ended with the P-47D-28, which adopted the Curtiss Electric C-542S-A-114 airscrew as standard. There were 750 P-47D-28-REs (44-19558 to 44-20307) and 1,028 P-47D-28-RAs (42-28439 to 42-29466). The 'Dash 30' was similarly built by both factories, but introduced new rear-view mirrors, blunt-edged ailerons and slab airbrakes, while eliminating the old 'ring-and-bead' sight. Farmingdale built 800 (44-20308 to -21107) while Evansville produced 1,800 (44-32668 to -33867, and 44-86984 to -90283). They were followed by 665 Evansville-built P-47D-40-RAs (44-90284 to 90483 and 44-49090 to 49554), with rocket pylons and a dorsal fin, and with a new K-14 gyro gunsight. While the most skilled and highly experienced pilots found the new sight's complexity irritating, the sight allowed less experienced pilots to engage in 'deflection shooting' with much greater accuracy. The sight soon became known as the 'Ace-maker'.

'Superbolt'

In the Eighth Air Force, the remaining Thunderbolt units were determined not to be second-best to the growing force of Mustang groups. Accordingly, in May 1944, the 356th Fighter Group had converted an initial four of its P-47D-22-REs to 'Superbolt' standards, with the camouflaged paint waxed to a low-drag high gloss, and with weight-saving measures including the removal of four of the eight 0.50-in calibre machine-guns and of windscreen armour. Ammunition was restricted to 200 rounds per gun, and the engines were modified to use higher octane fuel.

The beautifully polished finish of the 'Superbolts' was soon marred, however. In early June the various 8th and 9th Air Force bases were effectively sealed off, with visits

to local pubs and villages banned, and with telephone services suspended. Groundcrew were ordered to paint alternating black and white bands around wings and fuselages – signifying that the invasion of occupied Europe was imminent.

On D-Day itself, the Thunderbolts were heavily committed to ground attack duties, and were credited with preventing the complete annihilation of the troops who landed on Omaha Beach. In the immediate aftermath of the invasion, the role of the P-47s was two-fold – preventing the Luftwaffe from attacking the beachhead, and cutting off opposing ground forces from their sources of ammunition,

Above: Along with the RAF's Hawker Typhoon, the P-47 became the nemesis of German lines of communication. The rail network was particularly hard hit, as this presented the Wehrmacht with its primary means of moving its forces and supplies. Here P-47s set about a supply train while it was waiting in a siding.

Above: Bombed-up P-47s of the 365th Fighter Group 'Hellhawks' taxi across the steel matting at an airfield in France in the late summer of 1944. Many of the 9th AF missions, especially those made in support of the advancing Allied armies, were of short range, and the P-47 could dispense with any form of drop tank. The pierced steel planking (PSP) was not the ideal surface from which to operate heavily-laden fighter-bombers, and pilots treated the taxi to the runway accordingly.

Left: By early 1945 the 365th was at Chièvres in Belgium, where Captain George King of the 386th FS is seen taxiing his P-47D-30.

Complete with kicking mules on the cowling flaps, That's Uras's was a P-47D-28 assigned to the 367th FS, 358th FG. The 'Orange Tails' group was reassigned from the 9th AF to the 1st TACAF in November 1944, flying alongside Free French P-47 units on the southern front.

Far right: Airfield strafing was a hazardous pastime, as the targets were well defended, but one at which the P-47 excelled. Here a 'razorback' is caught in the gun camera of a squadron-mate as the pair strafes a French Lioré-et-Olivier LeO 451 bomber.

Below: Major Glenn Eagleston taxis 'his' P-47D-30 over steel matting laid at a French airfield in the winter of 1944. A troop lies across the wing to give steering instructions to the pilot. The skull-and-crossbones was a 353rd FS marking, presented on a bright yellow cowling. The eagle was Eagleston's personal marking.

supplies, reinforcements and replacements. This placed a particularly heavy emphasis on the destruction and disruption of railways and bridges.

In the air-to-air role, both the Eighth and Ninth Air Forces performed well. Gabreski shot down his 28th enemy aircraft on 4 July (a feat which remained unsurpassed in the ETO), while the 371st had shot down five Fw 190s in a single mission on 8 June.

Several of the Ninth Air Force P-47 fighter groups moved to France during the three months following D-Day. The 368th led the movement, although some sources suggest the 358th was in France on 7 June. Some 13 groups were in France by the middle of August – most operating as veritable 'Flying Circuses', moving between forward airstrips with the Army units they were supporting, living under canvas and operating from grass or PSP runways.

Close support for the army

As Allied forces broke out from their beachheads, the P-47s flew close air support missions, often 'talked in' by US tank commanders to attack opposing armour. Many people believed that 0.50-in machine-guns would be inadequate to destroy heavily armoured tanks, but this proved to be without foundation. The P-47's eight guns poured out sufficient firepower to destroy even the mighty Tiger, particularly when rounds ricocheted into the tank's belly off a hard surface. An early anti-tank success was scored by the 366th Fighter Group, which destroyed 20 tanks before having to return to base to refuel and re-arm. Returning to the scene, the group's aircraft destroyed 15 more, preventing an enemy breakthrough and winning the group a Distinguished Unit Citation. A larger scale anti-armour

operation began on 24 July, as Operation Cobra, supporting an armoured assault by General Omar Bradley near St Lô. Heavy bombers attacked defences on 24 July, while the P-47s joined the fray on 25 July.

August saw the introduction of new weapons to the Thunderbolt, the first of these being triple-clusters of unguided tube-launched rockets. These proved erratic and inaccurate and were soon abandoned. The 'Spike Bombs' introduced the same month proved more successful. These were forerunners of later 'Daisy Cutters' and had their fuses at the end of an 18-in (46-cm) nose spike, this causing the weapons to explode above the ground rather than in it, maximising blast and fragmentation damage. Another weapon introduced to the ETO in August was the napalm bomb – a devastatingly effective weapon against enemy troops and soft-skinned vehicles.

The P-47s of the Eighth and Ninth Air Forces supported the Allied Armies as they drove through France, the Low Countries and Germany itself. Opposition from enemy fighters became progressively weaker, as fuel became harder for the Luftwaffe to find, and as the ranks of the *Experten* were progressively replaced by hastily-trained and inexperienced youngsters, who were no match for the USAAF's fighter pilots. The destruction of enemy aircraft as they sat on their airfields became increasingly important, if only to prevent the chance of some desparate 'final fling' using the last of what fuel remained.

For the rest of the war in Europe, the P-47s continued to fly bomber escort, close air support and battlefield air interdiction sorties. Targets included enemy troop and armour concentrations, railway locomotives and rolling stock, road transport, military headquarters, bunkers, bridges and even inland and coastal shipping.

Highlights in August included an attack by the 358th FG on a convoy of hay wagons (in which were concealed heavy AA guns) on 1 August, and a successful day's train-busting by the 405th FG on 13 August, during which the group destroyed 11 locomotives and 130 railway cars. The next day, 405th Fighter Group Thunderbolt pilots were astonished to see German truck crews abandon their vehicles and wave white flags. The P-47s buzzed them to encourage them to march towards the waiting 7th Armoured Division as PoWs. Between 12 and 17 August P-47s tore into German armour trapped in the Falaise pocket, causing huge destruction.

Also in August, 'Hub' Zemke finally handed over the reigns of the 56th Fighter Group to Dave Schilling. Zemke avoided a staff tour by taking over the newest Fighter Group in the 8th, the 479th Fighter Group, but his Mustang was shot down soon afterwards, and Zemke spent the rest of the war as a prisoner-of-war.

September followed much the same pattern, though heavy losses were suffered during Operation Market Garden, when the Thunderbolts were committed to support the Allied airborne operation at Arnhem. November saw the introduction of a Microwave Early Warning station on Dutch soil, and this allowed P-47s operating over western Germany to be 'vectored' onto targets by fighter controllers. The air-to-air kill ratio climbed steeply.

Thunderbolts helped blunt the German advance during the German offensive in the Ardennes in December, shooting down large numbers of enemy fighters and tearing into enemy armour. P-47s were also involved in combating the Luftwaffe's last desperate throw, Operation Bodenplatte. The 366th FG shot down 12 enemy aircraft, while 352nd FG downed 23 more.

The 'sprint' Thunderbolt

The field-modified 'Superbolts', which had appeared just before D-Day, were outshone by the final 'basic' factory-built Thunderbolt – the P-47M. The M-model was basically a P-47D-30, fitted with a new 'C' series R-2800 engine. This was an R-2800-57 fitted with a new CH-5 turbo-supercharger, and drove a 13-ft Curtiss Electric C642S-B40 airscrew. A P-47C-5RE (41-6601) was converted to serve as the 'XP-47M', an unofficial designation for what was effectively the proof-of-concept aircraft and demonstrator. Three YP-47M-REs were converted from P-47D-27-REs (42-27385, -27386 and -27388) to serve as prototypes, and these proved capable of speeds of up to 473 mph (761 km/h) at 32,000 ft (9754 m), and 130 were built at Farmingdale as

Conquerors of the Reich

The final statistics for the P-47 in Europe in the ETO record 423,435 sorties, during the course of which over 7,000 enemy aircraft were destroyed. Of these, 3,752 were claimed in air combat for the loss of 846 P-47s. On the ground over 3,000 aircraft, 9,000 trains, 86,000 rolling stock, 6,000 tanks and 68,000 vehicles succumbed to the bombs, rockets and guns of the 'T-bolt'. 113,939 tons of bombs were delivered, a figure nearly three times greater than that for all the other US fighters put together. The loss rate per sortie of 0.7 per cent was commendably low for the period.

Impressive those these figures are, they still cannot fully convey the enormous contribution made by the Thunderbolt, especially in the last year of the war when it turned to fighter-bomber activities.

the P-47M-1-RE (44-21108 to 21237). The aircraft proved unstable at high speeds, however, and a dorsal fin was added 'in-theatre'. Minor engine problems (many directly equivalent to those which had plagued the first P-47Cs) and corrosion damage also had to be addressed before the type could begin operations.

Only the 56th Fighter Group used the variant during the war, and then for a brief period. The group's 61st Fighter Squadron began to re-equip in mid-January 1945, but was forced to revert to D-Models after about one week. The 61st FS became operational with P-47Ms on 14 February, but only briefly, and it was not until mid-March that the group was truly operational with the new variant. It was worth the wait, however, the new P-47M enjoying better performance than the latest Mustangs, and finally allowing the 56th's pilots to forget that they were flying the heaviest single-engined fighter of the war. The Luftwaffe was seldom seen due to a chronic shortage of fuel, but the 56th still managed to shoot down five Me 262s and a pair of low-flying Arado Ar 234 jet bombers.

The last months of the war were marked by an intensification of the campaign against enemy airfields, and on a number of occasions P-47 groups returned from missions with claims of more than 50 enemy aircraft destroyed.

Jon Lake

Thunderbolt operations continued until the last days of the war, many 9th AF units having moved into Germany itself. This scene shows P-47s of the 9th AF's 404th FG parked at Fritzlar, recently vacated by the retreating Luftwaffe. In the background are a group of German aircraft – mostly Ju 88 night-fighters but also including a Bf 109, Bf 110 and a Ju 87.

No fewer than 159 P-47s have been herded into this corner of Speke airfield, near Liverpool, the main port by which aircraft were ferried into and out of Britain. Having arrived in the ETO, they had not yet been assigned to a front-line unit when the war in Europe came to an end. Here they await processing for shipment back to the US, and onward travel to the Pacific theatre. Few made the whole journey, most ending up in a Stateside scrapyard with just a few hours on the clock.

Part 2 of this report will be featured in a forthcoming volume, and will cover the later development of the P-47, its service in the MTO, CBI and Far East, and its post-war career

Breguet Br.1001 Taon

Designed to meet a NATO lightweight fighter requirement, the Breguet Br.1001 Taon was, in many respects, an outstanding prospect. But for its inferior take-off performance, the Taon may well have defeated the victorious Fiat G91 and entered production in significant numbers. As it is, the aircraft will be best remembered for twice breaking the world 1000-km closed-circuit speed record.

The Breguet 1001 programme began in the early 1950s, with the company commencing design work on a twin-engined fighter-bomber for the Armée de l'Air designated Br.1001. This aircraft spawned a single-engined derivative, then known as the Breguet 1001B in 1953, before the two types were re-designated in 1955. The original twin-engined aircraft became the Breguet 1100, while the single-engined version took over the plain Breguet 1001 designation. Originally intended only as an interim type, the Breguet 1001 was offered to meet NATO's light fighter-bomber requirement.

The seeds for a European aircraft for use by NATO were sown at the Lisbon Conference of

Above: A total of six initial configurations was investigated for the twin-engined Br.1001 and the Br.1001B (as they were then designated). This model represents an early configuration of the Taon before extensive wind tunnel work resulted in a redesign of the fuselage to incorporate area ruling, in accordance with Whitcomb's law.

Right: The first prototype Br.1001 is seen at Melun-Villaroche shortly before its first flight in July 1957. A number of modifications from the original design were incorporated, including a redesigned upper fuselage aft of the cockpit, a lengthened nose section and the area-ruling of the fuselage. At this stage a taon (gadfly) symbol was carried below the cockpit on the starboard side.

1952. Here, the concept of mutual assistance between NATO nations was underlined and the first NATO aircraft specification (NBMR-1) for a lightweight tactical attack aircraft was issued. The requirement called for a lightweight, low-cost, high-performance battlefield ground-attack aircraft. Increasing concern as to the danger of a pre-emptive Soviet atomic attack, and the production of 'more than 2,000 MiG-15s' led to a perceived need for the new NATO fighter-bomber to have the necessary performance characteristics to be able to operate from dispersed sites, and to be cheap enough to be purchased in very large numbers. The requirement thus demanded that the new aircraft should be able to take-off from grass with a full warload and clear a 50-ft obstacle within 1,000 yards, and that it should be able to be re-armed and refuelled rapidly. The new aircraft would also have to be rugged and reliable with simple maintenance procedures.

Performance requirements were no less demanding. The new fighter-bomber was expected to be able to loiter over the battlefield for up to 8-10 minutes some 175 miles (282 km) from its base – which in turn could be a semi-prepared airstrip or suitable length of *autobahn*. Its maximum speed of Mach 0.95 was to be attainable for 30 percent of the

The first Br.1001 Taon prototype is seen here in the winter of 1957-58. The aircraft has newly acquired engine intake bleed doors, but lacks the aerodynamic bulges (carènes) at the wing roots, which not only enhanced the 'area-ruling' of the fuselage, but were also used to house additional fuel. Note the nose-high attitude and deployment of the slats, indicating low-speed flight.

mission, with a cruising speed of 350 kts (later re-stated as 400 mph) for the rest of the mission profile. The aircraft would also have to be agile, and a roll rate of 100° per second at Mach 0.9 was specified. However, the aircraft also had to be small, light and cheap to produce, with an empty weight of no more than 5,000 lb (2268 kg). NATO placed a secondary emphasis on the air-to-air role, so that a gyro gunsight was specified. The aircraft was expected to operate primarily at low-level, and therefore did not require a fully-pressurised cockpit.

This austere lightweight was expected to pack an impressive punch and the requirement called for an internal armament of four 0.5-in (12.7-mm) Browning machine-guns with 300 rpg, or two ADEN 20-mm cannon with 200 rpg, or two 30-mm cannon with 120 rpg. These would be augmented by two 220-kg (485-lb) bombs underwing, or napalm tanks, or up to 36 unguided rocket projectiles.

Above: Groundcrew check over the Br.1001-01 prior to its first flight. By this time the taon (gadfly) symbol had been replaced by a silhouette of the aircraft with the inscription TAO(N)ATO running along the silhouette's wings in reference to the all-important NATO contract on which the development of the aircraft depended.

Right: Breguet's chief test pilot Bernard Witt was at the controls for the Taon's first flight. He subsequently flew the majority of the development flights, and piloted the aircraft during its successful 1000-km closed-circuit world speed record-breaking attempts in April and July 1958.

Above: Br.1001-01 returns to Melun-Villaroche on completion of its maiden flight on 25 July 1957. At this stage the aircraft lacked armament, and clearly visible is the ventral nose fillet (which was later relocated to underneath the rear fuselage). To reduce the approach speed both leading-edge slats and trailing-edge flaps are fully deployed. It was however, the aircraft's take-off and landing performance that was to prove to be the design's Achilles heel.

Supreme Headquarters Allied Powers in Europe (SHAPE) estimated a total requirement for between 600 and 1,000 aircraft, equipping between 25 and 50 NATO squadrons. These would be partly nationally funded, but would also be supported by the Mutual Weapon Development Programme (MWDP). With such a potentially lucrative contract on offer, Breguet, along with a host of other manufacturers, especially on the continent, began immediate design work on the single-engined Br.1001.

The Taon name means Gadfly in French, but more importantly was a useful anagram of NATO (or OTAN in French terms). By comparison with the twin-engined Breguet 1100 (of which construction of the prototype was well advanced), the Taon featured a lengthened nose and an aerodynamic area-ruled fuselage, but retained the same undernose strake and bulges below each intake. These improved airflow to the engines at high Mach numbers, and also reduced the risk of FOD ingestion, while also providing an ideal location for the aircraft's internal armament.

The first Taon (F-ZWUX) made its maiden flight at Melun-Villaroche in the hands of Bernard Witt on 25 July 1957. This aircraft had French instruments and equipment, while the second (flown in 1958) had British equipment.

The aircraft itself was remarkably light, despite its rather 'chunky' appearance, thanks to extensive use of honeycomb sandwich panels. Other advanced features included twin-section leading-edge slats, servo-assisted ailerons and spoilers and flexible bag-type fuel tanks.

The ailerons, elevator and rudder were all power-operated using hydraulic servo actuators with artificial 'feel' devices. The hydraulic system itself had two pumps and emergency accumulators. Spoiler panels on each wing were linked to the ailerons to provide increased rate of role and lateral stability without the problems of aero-elasticity encountered at higher speeds. This arrangement gave a quoted rate of roll of some 200° per second.

The fuselage consisted of three main parts. The nose section housed the radio equipment, the centre section carried the cockpit, internal armament, air ducts, fuel tanks and engine mounts and the rear section, which was easily removable, covered the engine, its accessories, tail pipe and carried the empennage.

The fuel system itself consisted of a sump tank and four flexible cells, having a total capacity of 1703 litres (450 US gal) which was supplied to the engine through a high-pressure pump.

Passing through the centre of the fuselage, the wing structure consisted of two variable thickness skins bonded to an aluminium honeycomb 'core'.

Rough-field operations

Stability for rough field and crosswind operations was granted by the 2.70-m (8-ft 8-in) wide track tricycle undercarriage designed and built by Messier and consisting of two main gears which retracted inwards into the lower surface of the wing and a single nose wheel which retracted rearwards to lay in a fuselage bay. For rough-field operations the tyre pressure could be set at a low level of 3.5 kg/cm² (54 psi) and each wheel was linked to the strut by a cantilever leg acting as an external shock absorber which damped both horizontal and vertical movement.

Breguet Br.1100

Originally designated Br.1001, (the single-engined Taon, based on the Br.1100 design, was briefly designated Br.1001B), the Br.1100 project began in 1951 and from 1953 its development ran in parallel to the Taon. Designed as a twin-engined fighter-bomber the Br.1100 was aimed at potential orders from both the Armée de l'Air and the Aéronavale.

The aircraft featured a shorter nose, however, the design had advanced too far to incorporate the area-ruled fuselage of the Taon. Power was provided by two Turboméca Gabizo afterburning turbojets mounted side-by-side in the centre of the fuselage, with paired jet pipes terminating aft of the tail unit. Like the Br.1001, extensive use of honeycomb sandwich construction techniques was employed. The Br.1100 had larger span wings of greater area with large-span narrow-chord trailing-edge flaps and wide-chord short-span ailerons. Three prototypes were ordered for construction including one (designated Br.1100M) for the French navy. The first prototype made its maiden flight on 31 March 1957, exceeding Mach 1 during the duration of the flight. The Armée de l'Air order was eventually given to the Super Mystère with the navy order going also to Dassault in the shape of the Etendard IV.

Above: One of the NATO evaluation pilots returns to Bretigny in Br.1001-01 after one of the 31 evaluation flights flown by the Taon during the three-week NATO trials. The aircraft had by then been fitted with four Browning 0.5-in (12.7-mm) machine-guns in the forward fuselage and two weapons pylons beneath each wing.

Left: Parked on the apron at Bretigny, the Taon is inspected by members of the press on 13 September 1957. The lateral instability encountered during the early test flights had been partially cured by moving the ventral strake from its nose position to beneath the rear fuselage. Parked alongside is Fiat's competing design – the G91.

Layout of the cockpit was in accordance with full A.B.C standards to a specification outlined by the NATO technical committee. Visibility from the cockpit was good forwards and to the sides, although rear visibility was fairly restricted. The cockpit itself was fully pressurised and the pilot was protected by both armour plating and a reinforced windshield. The pilot sat on a Martin-Baker Mk 4 fully-automatic ejection seat equipped with a survival pack.

Standard internal armament on the prototypes was four Colt-Browning 0.5-in (12.7-mm) machine-guns, although this was designed to be interchangeable with either two DEFA 30-mm cannon each with 240 rounds or two MATRA rocket launchers with 15 rockets each. Breguet claimed that the armament change

could be effected using the field equipment of an operational unit. Externally, the Taon was to be fitted with two weapons hardpoints beneath each wing capable of carrying an assortment of stores including two 500-lb (227-kg) napalm tanks, rockets, HVAR rockets and Nord 5103 guided missiles.

Powerplant

The two Taon prototypes were powered by a single Bristol Orpheus BOr.3 turbojet. With low weight, simplicity and ease of maintenance prime considerations, the Orpheus was the natural choice and both the competing Fiat G91 and Etendard VI also both adopted various forms of the engine. In its Mk 3 form the Orpheus consisted of a seven-stage single-spool compressor and single-stage turbine and deliv-

ered static thrust of 4,850 lb (21.58 kN) at a unit weight of only 810 lb (367 kg). The engine relied on a cartridge start mechanism which was mounted on the upper starboard side of the engine, the corresponding port side held the oil tank. It was proposed that production versions of the Taon would have been fitted with the Orpheus BOr.12 which incorporated an additional compressor stage with a corresponding increase in engine length of 3.5 in (8.9 cm) which raised static dry thrust to 6,730 lb (29.95 kN). The engine was also fitted with reheat raising thrust to 8,170 lb (36.36 kN), making the engine some 70 per cent more powerful than the Orpheus 3. Production versions of the Taon fitted with this engine had been allocated the advance designation Br.1003.

Breguet Br.1001-01 Taon

1 Instrumentation boom
2 Nose electronics equipment bay
3 Ventral strake
4 VHF antenna
5 Aft retracting nose undercarriage
6 Nosewheel leg door with landing/taxiing light
7 Hydraulic retraction jack
8 Rudder pedals
9 Control column
10 Instrument panel shroud
11 Gunsight
12 Frameless windscreen panel
13 Upward-hinging cockpit canopy
14 Pilot's Martin-Baker Mk 4 ejection seat
15 Port side console panel with engine throttle lever
16 Port engine air intake
17 Machine-gun muzzle apertures
18 Nosewheel door-mounted standby UHF antenna

23 Airbrake hydraulic jack
24 Forward fuselage bag-type fuel tanks
25 Intake ducting
26 Cockpit air system
27 ADF antenna
28 Two-segment automatic leading-edge slat
29 Pitot head
30 Starboard navigation light
31 Starboard aileron
32 Aileron and spoiler operating linkage
33 Two-segment double-slotted flap
34 Spoiler panels, linked to aileron
35 Rear fuselage bag-type fuel tanks

36 Engine oil tank
37 Bristol Orpheus B.Or.3 turbojet engine
38 Rudder trim actuator
39 Rudder hydraulic booster
40 UHF antenna
41 Tail navigation light

49 Central hydraulic flap actuator
50 Mainwheel, stowed position
51 Hydraulic retraction jack

54 Flap operating linkage
55 Port two-segment double-slotted flap
56 Port spoiler panels
57 Aileron hydraulic booster
58 Aileron/spoiler inter-connecting spring link
59 Port aileron
60 Port navigation light

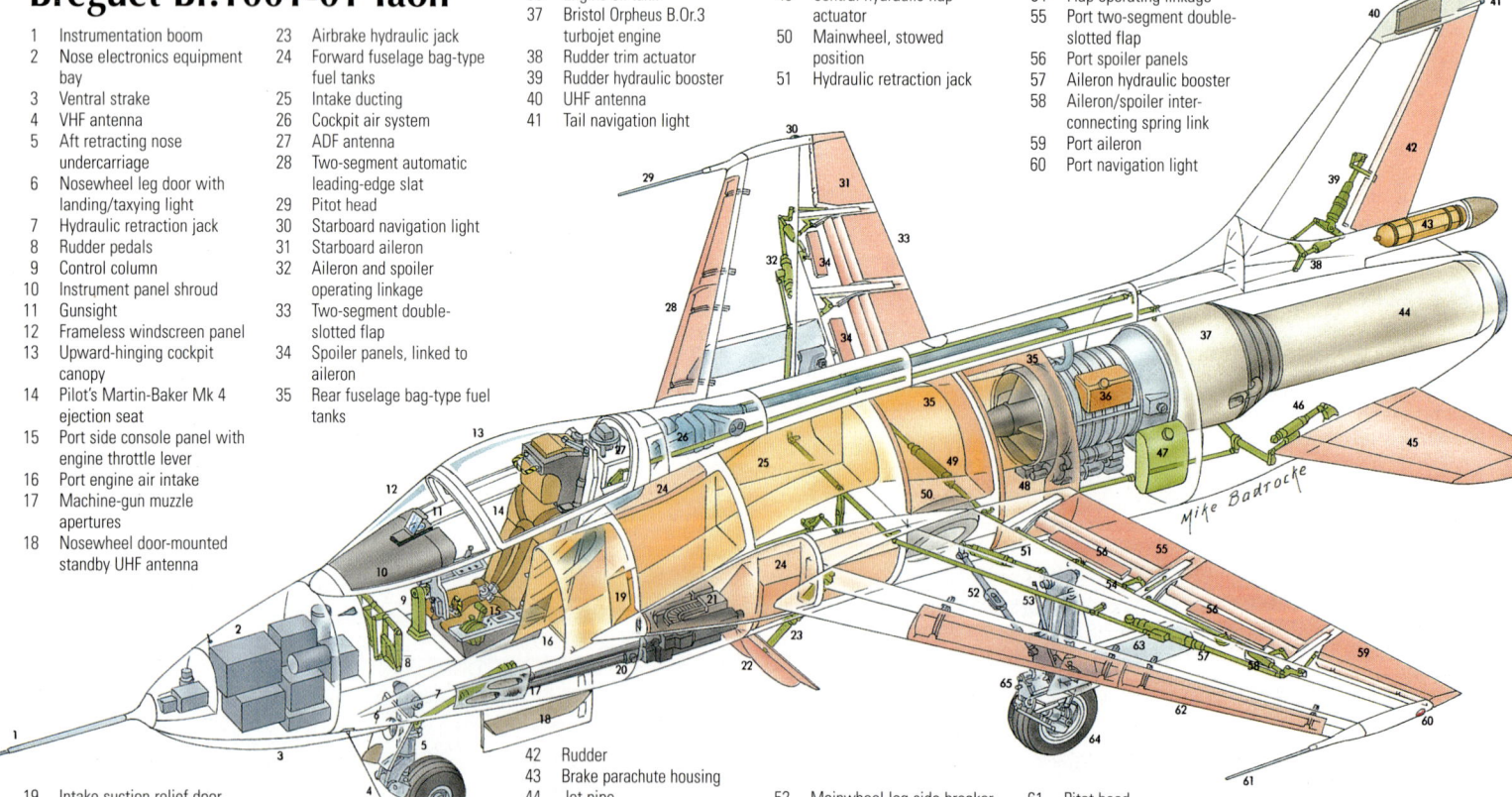

Mike Badrocke

19 Intake suction relief door
20 Browning 0.5-in (12.7-mm) machine-guns, two per side
21 Ammunition magazines
22 Ventral airbrake

42 Rudder
43 Brake parachute housing
44 Jet pipe
45 Port all-moving tailplane
46 Tailplane hydraulic actuator
47 Hydraulic reservoir
48 Engine accessory equipment

52 Mainwheel leg side breaker strut
53 Levered suspension main undercarriage leg strut and shock absorber

61 Pitot head
62 Automatic leading-edge slat
63 Stores pylon
64 Port mainwheel
65 Pivoted axle mounting

The nose section could hold a variety of radio and navigation equipment. Standard fit for the Taon was envisaged to consist of a single ARC-34 UHF radio, an APX-6 IFF, an MSQ 1 set, a Bezu NR.AN.8B radio-compass, a Bezu type 30 gyromagnetic compass and a telebriefing set. The radio-compass could be exchanged for a similar Marconi unit, an ARN-21 TACAN and a GTA 122 position marker.

For a maximum speed turnaround 10 groundcrew could work simultaneously to complete ammunition reloading, refuelling, hydraulic landing gear check, replacement of engine starter cartridges, fuel system check, cockpit check, oxygen replenishment, radio and navigation equipment check and external stores reloading. More in-depth servicing could also be completed under operational conditions thanks to the quick disassembly and replacement of many of the essential components. The aircraft was also fitted with numerous access doors and panels for rapid and frequent inspection.

With production of the winning design likely to incorporate a degree of sub-contracting under a European co-operation scheme, the Taon was designed to be broken down into several main and sub-assemblies. Most of these components were constructed of light alloy honeycomb sandwich panels bonded to sheet metal. Honeycomb sandwich was selected because it combined minimum structural weight with excellent strength and rigidity and could also be relatively simply mass-produced. The forming, assembling and bonding tool designs would have been based on mouldings made from master models allowing high production rates by duplication of the toolings.

Evaluation

Like the other short-listed candidates (the Fiat G91 and Dassault Etendard VI), the first prototype Taon participated in the NATO evaluation held at Bretigny between 16 September and 5 October 1957. By this time a number of improvements and modifications had been made to the aircraft, including the undernose strake being replaced by a similar surface below the rear fuselage, and engine intake modifications.

The Taon completed 31 flights during the 20-day evaluation period, and won great admiration for its general handling qualities and manoeuvrability. The aircraft also excelled in gunnery trials, proving both stability and accuracy. Routine maintenance and aircraft turnaround times were also a major consideration and again the Taon outperformed its rivals, achieving a full rearm/refuel in 6 minutes 40 seconds and an engine change (with a full rearm and refuel) in only 47 minutes from landing to take-off. Servicing was further aided by the provision of quick-release access panels for vital components and the aircraft had a US-style removable rear fuselage/tail unit for engine access and some eight refuelling points. Breguet introduced the concept of daily servicing, and took care to allow the largest possible team to work on the aircraft simultaneously without getting in each other's way.

The Bristol Orpheus engine combined with the aerodynamically clean fuselage and low-drag wing gifted the Taon exceptional performance, with the aircraft able to reach Mach 1. On 25 April 1958 the first prototype set a new speed record for a 1000-km closed circuit at an average speed of 650.36 mph (1046.62 km/h). Three months later, on 23 July, the record was raised further to 667.98 mph (1074.98 km/h.

The manufacturer placed great emphasis on the Taon's superb Messier all-terrain undercarriage with low-pressure tyres which allowed operations from semi-prepared or damaged runways. However, ironically it was the aircraft's take-off performance that proved the Taon's undoing. The high level of performance granted by the small wings of thin aerofoil section were to the detriment of lift at lower speeds, and the aircraft's take-off run was judged by NATO to be longer than acceptable, a problem with which the manufacturers had insufficient time to rectify.

In the end the competition was destined to be almost pointless. None of the competing nations was actually prepared to abide by the decision of the evaluators. Some accused NATO of pre-judging the competitors, pointing to its order for 27 G91As before the competition began – an order none of the other competitors received. However, the fact that the G91 was declared the winner of the competition can have come as no surprise. It was the only one of the three contenders that met the tight short-field take-off requirements, and also impressed the evaluation pilots with its pleasant handling characteristics, agility and performance.

The Taon was highly commended for its handling, fast turnaround times and maintain-

Top and centre: The take-off, landing and low-speed performance of the Taon was always the greatest concern for Breguet's design team. Between the first flight in July and the start of the NATO competition in September 1957 a large hydraulically-operated ventral airbrake was added to the centre of the lower fuselage to improve the aircraft's approach characteristics. A number of configurations for the airbrake was investigated before the final design was selected. It featured a rounded cut-out centre-section ensuring that the aircraft's lateral stability was not unduly affected when deployed.

Above: In addition to the new airbrake, the efficiency of the spoilers was enhanced which increased the aircraft's rate of roll and provided a further degree of stability at lower speeds. The Taon's trailing-edge flaps (seen here fully deployed) were also modified to increase lift. However, this measure could not improve the Taon's take-off performance within the parameters set by the NATO committee.

ability, but could not match the G91 in meeting all the criteria. In the end the evaluation pilots unanimously preferred the G91, and even the French test pilot shared this opinion, although he proposed the development of a second-phase aircraft and a second competition for this order.

The final selection of the Fiat G91 spurred Breguet into further developments for this possible second-generation competition. But none of these was destined to enter production.

After the potential for orders evaporated, the two Breguet 1001s were used in support of the company's twin-engined Br.1100 and Br.1100M projects which were being considered for service with the Armée de l'Air and Aéronavale, respectively. However, like their single-engined brother, these developments were to also miss out to competing designs in the shape of the Dassault's Super Mystère and Etendard IV.

Photo-reconnaissance variant

Breguet envisaged several other variants of the Taon if the initial ground-attack version was selected for production. These included a photographic reconnaissance variant which retained the Br.1001s general layout but would incorporate a redesigned nose section to accommodate four cameras. The proposed camera layout consisted of five Omera T31 cameras (one oblique forward in the centre of

Right: The eventual winner of the NATO lightweight fighter competition was the Italian Fiat G91, but as predicted only two countries initially ordered the type – Germany and Italy. Three G91 prototypes were ordered on 3 June 1955, followed by 27 G91A production examples, for evaluation, on 30 July 1955.

Below: Originally designated Mystère XXVI, the Dassault Etendard VI was developed from the earlier Mystère XXII (Etendard II). Like its competitors, the aircraft was powered by the Bristol Orpheus turbojet and made its maiden flight on 15 March 1957.

Breguet Br.1001-01 Taon

Melun-Villaroche, France
March 1958

Construction
The Taon was a beautifully engineered aircraft, making extensive use of honeycomb panels and designed for easy servicing and rapid turnarounds.

Armament
The first prototype was fitted, for the majority of its test programme, with four Browning 0.5-in (12.7-mm) machine-guns in the forward fuselage with 1,200 rounds of ammunition. The guns and ammunition were mounted on an easily interchangeable chassis.

Cockpit
Br.1001-01 was fitted with French instrumentation and equipment. However, the second prototype was more representative of production models with a NATO-approved layout.

Powerplant
The two prototype Br.1001s were powered by a single Bristol Siddeley Orpheus B.Or.3 turbojet, rated at 4,850 lb (21.58 kN) thrust. This engine also powered the two competing designs, so whichever aircraft entered production Bristol would also win.

Carènes
Conical wing fairings were added to Br.1001-01 after the NATO competition to improve the aircraft's area-ruling. This allowed the maximum speed of the aircraft to be increased to Mach 1 at high altitude.

Badge
The Breguet 1001 was named Taon to suggest aggressiveness, while using an anagram of the word NATO. The two names were combined in a small badge on the intake.

the nose cone, one port and one starboard on the lower portion of the nosecone and one vertical just forward of the nosewheel door). The radio and navigation equipment would be situated in the port armament bay, with the starboard armament bay retaining two 0.5-in (12.7-mm) Browning machine-guns or one 30-mm DEFA cannon or an additional internal fuel tank.

Two-seat trainer

Design work was also instigated on a two-seat version of the Taon for primary or advanced training duties. The drawing board layout demonstrated the main modifications that, naturally enough, centred on the cockpit, which was extended both forward and rearwards to incorporate a tandem layout with two Martin-Baker ejection seats. Radio equipment would have been more basic and the armament would have been removed for the primary/basic training role. However, for advanced training additional armament could be installed to meet the customer's demands. The engine selected was a derated version of the Orpheus 3, designated Orpheus 4, which countered its lower thrust rating with improved fuel consumption and therefore aircraft endurance. A twin-seat version of the Orpheus 12-powered Taon was also proposed but neither version made it off the drawing board.

Final developments

In 1957 Breguet began work on a variant powered by the afterburning Orpheus 12 engine. Designated Br.1003 or 'Taon 3', the aircraft would have been supersonic at high altitude and was offered to NATO as a 'second-generation' aircraft in March 1958. Offered in ground-attack and photo-reconnaissance versions, the 'Taon 3' attracted little interest from NATO, which deemed the aircraft's increased performance as unnecessary in the ground-attack role. Breguet later proposed a navalised variant (Br.1003M) for the Aéronavale with catapult attachments, a reinforced structure and strengthened undercarriage.

Aiming to improve the design, Breguet abandoned Br.1003 development at the end of 1958 in favour of the Br.1005 'Taon 5'. Taking account of previous failures to meet NATO's exacting specifications, the Br.1005 was aimed squarely at the second-generation competition.

A larger wing (similar to that fitted to the Br.1100) was to be incorporated and power was initially to be the Orpheus 12SR, later to be replaced by the even more powerful Orpheus 14SR. Numerous other improvements were to include four underwing and one underfuselage hardpoints, more internal fuel, Doppler radar and a computerised bomb-aiming system. With much of the flight testing already having been conducted by the two Br.1001 prototypes, Breguet claimed that the aircraft would be ready for entry into squadron service by 1962. However, in 1959 NATO simply abandoned the second-generation fighter-bomber competition on which the Br.1005 depended, thus bringing to a close any further development of what might have been, with more luck and less politics, one of the most important European combat aircraft of the 1960s. *Daniel J. March*

Above and right: Coded 'E', the second prototype Taon made its first flight on 18 January 1958. It differed from Br.1001-01 in having a slightly lengthened fuselage, British instruments and avionics, and lacked the wing root 'carènes'. More representative of an operational aircraft, Br.1001-02 was used for weapons trials and had similar performance figures to Br.1001-01, being slightly slower at high altitude, but slightly quicker below 25,000 ft (7620 m).

Specification

Br.1001-01 Taon (October 1957)
Powerplant: One 4,850-lb (21.58-kN) Bristol Orpheus B.Or 3 single-stage turbine turbojet
Span: 22 ft 4 in (6.80 m)
Length: 36 ft 10.5 in (11.24 m)
Height: 12 ft 3.5 in (3.75 m)
Wing area: 156 sq ft (14.50 m²)
Fuel: 450 US gal (1167 litres)
Armament: Four Colt-Browning 0.5-in (12.7-mm) machine-guns with 300 rounds per gun, production versions to incorporate two underwing hardpoints for a wide range of stores
Operational empty weight: 7,551 lb (3425 kg)
Normal take-off weight: 11,464 lb (5200 kg)
Maximum take-off weight: 12,258 lb (5560 kg)
Velocity, never exceed: Mach 1.27
Maximum speed at sea level: Mach 0.95
Maximum speed at 30,000 ft (9144 m): Mach 0.98
Minimum speed: 95 kt (109 mph; 176 km/h)
Landing speed: 120 kt (138 mph; 222 km/h)
Rate of roll: 150° per second
Take-off distance to 15 m (50 ft): 4265 ft (1300 m)
Ferry range: 1,000 nm (1150 miles; 1850 km)
Combat radius with full warload: 150 nm (173 miles; 278 km)

Br.1001-01 incorporated a number of modifications for the world 1000-km closed circuit record attempts in 1958. In addition to the 'carènes' fitted to the wing roots, the internal armament was replaced by fuel and the gun ports were faired-over. The changes raised the aircraft's maximum speed at altitude from Mach 0.98 to Mach 1.

Avro Lincoln

Slightly too late to see service in World War II, the Avro Lincoln has always been overshadowed by its illustrious forebear, the Lancaster. The Lincoln had a long and distinguished career post-war, seeing active service on a number of occasions and serving into the 1960s, but it was never regarded as very glamourous, though it proved far more durable and versatile than the Lancaster from which the type was derived. The Lincoln was overshadowed first by the mighty Boeing Washington, and later by the Royal Air Force's first jet bombers. Nonetheless, the Lincoln was effective, reliable and popular with its crews, and quickly gained an enviable reputation.

Resplendent in the medium sea grey and black gloss finish with blue spinners worn by aircraft belonging to the Bomber Command Bombing School, Lincoln B.Mk II RF570 is captured off Spurn Point, Humberside by the camera of Avro's chief photographer Paul Cullerne in February 1960. By this time the Lincoln was very much in the twilight of its career with Bomber Command, BCBS withdrawing the final aircraft from service in October of that year. RF570 did, however, subsequently serve briefly with electronic warfare specialists No. 151 Squadron.

Despite the popularity and success of the Lancaster in Bomber Command service, it was always clear that there was plenty of scope for improvement of the type. The Halifax, plainly inferior in its Merlin-engined form, was soon fitted with Hercules radials, and matured into a more versatile, more survivable aircraft. As it became apparent that the war against Germany would soon come to an end, attention increasingly switched to what threatened to be a long and bloody campaign in the Far East, where the Lancaster's existing weaknesses would have posed a danger. Avro therefore designed a much-improved Lancaster Mk IV; production was planned to begin in March 1945 at 66 aircraft per month, rising to 200 per month by August. Lancaster production, meanwhile, would be phased out, from a monthly total of

284 in November 1944 to a full stop one year later.

The Lincoln prototype (PW925) made its maiden flight from Ringway on 9 June 1944, in the capable hands of Captain H.A. Brown. It initially flew unarmed, with nose and tail turrets faired over, and with an empty mid-upper turret. The aircraft later gained a Glenn Martin mid-upper gun turret.

The Lincoln was designed as a Lancaster replacement for RAF Bomber Command, to meet Specification B.14/43, and was originally to be designated Lancaster B.Mk IV and B.Mk V. The Lincoln shared the same configuration as the Lancaster, but with detail differences. These included a fuselage stretched to 78 ft 3 in (23.85 m) (except on the prototype) with an 8-ft 11.5-in (2.73-m) plug aft of the trailing edge, and with wingspan increased to

120 ft (36.58 m) with a higher aspect ratio planform. Being optimised for very-long-range missions with Tiger Force, the aircraft had an increased fuel capacity of 2,850 Imp gal (12956 litres), and could carry two 400-Imp gal (1514-litre) overload tanks in the bomb bay, if required. The Lincoln also introduced more powerful two-stage Merlin engines, installed as 'power eggs' in low-drag armoured cowlings, with neat semi-annular radiators. The Lincoln's maximum take-off weight was set at a relatively modest 75,000 lb (34020 kg), only 10 per cent heavier than the Lancaster, though it was subsequently increased to 82,000 lb (37195 kg).

Most obviously, the Lincoln had a redesigned bomb-aimer's position, with a 'greenhouse' of optically flat panels replacing the blown Perspex dome of the Lancaster. Because the Lincoln used the basic Lancaster centre fuselage, it had the same-sized bomb bay. This limited the aircraft to the same 14,000-lb (6350-kg) internal bombload, although it could carry its load higher, and faster.

The Lincoln also introduced a more modern and effective defensive armament, with pairs of 0.5-in (12.7-mm) machine-guns in the powered nose, tail and dorsal turrets. The nose guns were housed in a remotely controlled Boulton-Paul Type F turret above the bomb-aimer's position, the others in conventional turrets. The new weapons marked a real improvement over the inadequate rifle-calibre 0.303-in (7.69-mm) guns fitted to all but the last Lancasters.

The Lincoln's obvious derivation from the Lancaster led many to view it as old-fashioned. Although it lacked the pressurisation and 'all electric' services of the Boeing B-29, in many respects it was a better-performing and more effective aircraft, with more modern armament. In the early stages of the project, the RAF and Avro had expected the aircraft to feature inflight-refuelling capability (against American opposition to the concept) and two of the Lincoln squadrons to be used in Tiger Force were expected to carry the massive 12,000-lb (5443-kg) Tallboy bombs. There was some talk that the aircraft could have an FN.88 or Redwing ventral gun turret fitted in place of the H2S, if required.

The changes to the Lancaster Mk IV prompted the issue of a new Avro type number (Type 694) and the new name of Lincoln. This was resisted by the Air Ministry, but was pushed through by the Ministry of Aircraft Production, which feared confusion and more difficult logistics support if the very different new aircraft retained the Lancaster name. With the rapid advance on Berlin and the imminent collapse of Nazi Germany, the programme was not accorded the once-planned degree of priority, and only 529 Lincolns were delivered to the RAF between 1945 and March 1951, of 2,791 ordered by VE-Day. Avro set up production lines for the Lincoln at Chadderton (which built 162 aircraft for the RAF and 18 for Argentina), Yeadon (which built only six!), Baginton and Bitteswell (both Armstrong Whitworth factories, accounting for 281 aircraft), and Trafford Park (where Metropolitan Vickers built 80 Lincolns); deliveries began in February 1945.

Into production

The second and third prototypes were followed by 82 similar production aircraft, known as B.Mk Is. They were fitted with Rotol four-bladed electric constant-speed propellers or, after December 1946, de Havilland airscrews which were fitted to cure vibration problems experienced by the prototypes. The production aircraft were fitted with interim Martin mid-upper and Fraser-Nash FN.121 tail turrets (the latter with four 0.303-in/7.7-mm machine-guns), pending the availability of the planned Bristol Type 17 mid-upper turret (not fitted to the B.Mk I) and the FN.82 tail turret.

A handful of Lincoln B.Mk Is were delivered to the Bomber Development Unit at Feltwell and a number of test and trials units, and although some sources suggest that small numbers entered front-line service, others insist that none was issued to operational units. Most aircraft were delivered directly to RAF MUs, Woodford or Langar for storage.

In addition, a production contract for six Lincoln Mk XVs to be built in Canada by Victory Aircraft Ltd commenced, however, only a single Mk XV (FM300) was completed before

the contract was cancelled. The aircraft served with the RCAF from 17 August 1946 to 4 March 1947 and was joined for a short period by one Mk I and one Mk II delivered from RAF stocks.

The second main production version for the RAF was the Lincoln B.Mk II (originally known as the Lancaster B.Mk V) with Packard-built Merlin 68 or Merlin 300 engines and 15-ft (4.57-m) diameter Hamilton A5/148 or de Havilland Hydromatic propellers. Most B.Mk IIs were delivered with a Boulton Paul Type F nose turret, and a Boulton Paul Type D rear turret with automatic gun-laying radar, each with two 0.50-in (12.7-mm) machine-guns. A Bristol Type 17 mid-upper turret was usually installed, fitted with two Hispano No. 4 Mk 5 20-mm cannon.

A few of the new Lincoln B.Mk IIs entered front-line service with No. 57 Squadron at East Kirkby for operational trials from 22 August 1945, and with No. 75 Squadron at Spilsby on 27 August. These early Lincolns were about to be dispatched to the Far East as part of Tiger Force, when the war was brought to a close by the dropping of the atomic bombs on Hiroshima and Nagasaki.

Defensive armament was a matter of much debate during the Lincoln's development. The Air Ministry's insistence that the rifle-calibre machine-guns fitted to the Lancaster were unsuitable for modern combat resulted in the design of new nose, dorsal and rear turrets. The nose section (left) was redesigned so the bomb aimer no longer had to lie prone to operate his sight, which then precluded him from manning the gun turret during the bomb run. He was repositioned to a forward-facing seat where he could man the forward guns using a suspended gunsight. All-round vision was also markedly improved with extended flat windows surrounding his position. Situated above the gunner's position, the turret itself was a Boulton Paul Type F with twin 0.5-in Browning machine-guns. The Bristol Type 17 Mk II dorsal turret (below centre) mounted a pair of 20-mm Hispano cannon, as shown on this No. XV Squadron Lincoln Mk II. However, due to lack of availability, early examples were equipped with a Martin turret with twin 0.5-in machine-guns. The rear turret (below right) was initially intended to be of Rose or Fraser-Nash design, ultimately the decision was made to fit the Boulton Paul Type D with twin 0.5-in Brownings. It was important to ensure that the rear turret was centralised on take-off as the drag imposed could cause the aircraft to swing.

The type then began equipping No. 44 Squadron at Mildenhall, during October 1945, following the disbandment of No. 75, which returned to RNZAF control. No. 57 Squadron disbanded on 25 November, although its Lincoln flight moved to Scampton becoming the Lincoln Service Trials Flight, while a new No. 57 stood up the following day through the renumbering of No. 103 Squadron at Elsham Wolds. No. 103 Squadron had already formed a Lincoln flight, but had not yet started to receive the new aircraft.

The first Lincolns were delivered in standard wartime-type colours, with black undersides, fins and fuselage sides and with disruptive green and dark earth camouflage on the topsides. Others wore the Tiger Force scheme of black undersides with white upper surfaces and fuselage sides (with a low demarcation line). Later aircraft had medium sea grey topsides rather than disruptive camouflage, and usually had D-type roundels with equal-diameter white and blue rings, rather than the previous C1 roundels that had a narrow white ring and a narrow yellow outline.

Squadron structure

No. 1 Group (formed from the wartime Nos 1 and 5 Groups) was the first to begin re-equipping with the Lincoln, followed by No. 3 Group, and by February 1950, 22 front-line Bomber Command squadrons had converted to the Lincoln. They were (initially, at least) smaller than wartime bomber units, usually with only eight aircraft, and were commanded by a squadron leader (making them about equivalent to a wartime flight). Conversion was informal and leisurely, and performed at squadron level, with a gradual phasing from Lancaster to Lincoln. Between 1946 and 1948, No. 1 Group's squadrons shared (on a rotational basis) the task of flying meteorological sorties, carrying an extra eighth crew member with an M-brevet. The Hemswell Wing was responsible for pathfinding and target-marking using flares (Nos 83 and 97 Squadrons) and for ECM/RCM training (No. 199 Squadron).

The Lincoln B.Mk 2s (as they were known after 1948) served in two distinct sub-variants, the original aircraft (retrospectively redesig-

Top: Shortly after delivery to Boscombe Down for handling trials in March 1945, the second production Lincoln B.Mk I was attached to Rolls-Royce at Hucknell for engine trials. The Mk I was fitted with Merlin 85s driving three-bladed propellers, a combination which was so markedly inferior to the Mk II's Merlin 68 with four-bladed propellers that many Mk Is were delivered straight to Maintenance Units and were destined never to fly again.

Right and above: From the outset the Lincoln was designed to carry H_2S radar in a ventral radome. Two versions of the radar were carried RE218 (right) is fitted with H_2S Mk IIIG while RA664 (above) carries the more bulbous H_2S Mk IVA, seen here in a transparent radome. These two sub variants received individual designations B.Mk II/IIIG and B.Mk II/IVA in February 1947 (later revised to B.Mk 2/3G and B.Mk 2/4A when arabic numerals were introduced in 1949). All early operators were issued with the B.Mk II/IIIG before No. IX Squadron received the first B.Mk II/IVA in June 1949.

nated B.Mk 2/3G) with H_2S Mk IIIG, Rebecca Mk II and Gee Mk II, and the B.Mk 2/4A with H_2S Mk IVA, Rebecca Mk II or IV and G-H Mk II. The later B.Mk 2/4A lacked the usual tandem whip aerials on the spine, and had a much larger ventral H_2S radome.

Tallboy specialists

No. XV Squadron was uniquely equipped with a number of aircraft specially modified to carry 12,000-lb Tallboy bombs, which required the fitting of bulged bomb-bay doors. They were used for trials during 1948. Some aircraft were also used for trials associated with

Britain's earliest nuclear weapon programme, including air-testing various prospective weapon shapes.

The 1,500-lb (680-kg) mid-upper turret was soon deleted in service, and was rarely seen after about 1954. Many of these supposedly redundant turrets found their way into Coastal Command Shackletons. A number of aircraft even had their nose guns removed, and a few Signals Command aircraft had their tail turrets removed and replaced by a streamlined fairing, leaving them entirely unarmed.

Even when turrets were fitted, Lincolns often flew without ammunition. This proved critical

Seen in the night and white colour scheme applied to aircraft destined for service with Tiger Force in the Far East, RF385 was the first B.Mk II to be delivered to active squadron service. Based at East Kirkby, No. 57 Squadron received three examples in late-August 1945 which benefited from 'tropicalisation' resulting from trials undertaken by RF370 at Khartoum. The white upper surfaces were intended to reflect heat, particularly from the wing fuel tanks, but in the event the dropping of the atomic bombs ended the war and Tiger Force was subsequently disbanded.

on 12 March 1953, when two Lincolns from the Central Gunnery School set off on a routine flight to Germany, for fighter affiliation with a variety of NATO fighters. Two Soviet MiG-15s menaced the first aircraft as it neared the inner German border, but the MiGs did not open fire during their mock attacks. The second aircraft (RF531) was attacked by two pairs of MiG-15s in the corridor between Hamburg and Berlin: these aircraft did open fire, following the Lincoln down as it frantically dived to escape. The MiGs set fire to the starboard wing and the aircraft broke up, only three of the crew getting out. One parachute failed to open, and the other two crew were strafed in their parachutes and died of their injuries soon after landing. The Russians claimed that the aircraft was outside the zone (some wreckage and one of the crew who bailed out landed in the Russian sector) and that it had opened fire. The mid-

upper and nose turrets had no belt mechanisms, however, while the rear turret carried no ammunition, so the Lincoln could not have fired.

There were lighter moments, too. One Lincoln on a navigational exercise, night-stopping at Gibraltar, returned to Waddington minus two of its crew, who had been arrested and jailed after relieving themselves in the local bull ring! Lincolns were also used as set-dressing in a number of films, bulking out smaller numbers of Lancasters. The sharp-eyed viewer would notice Lincolns in movies like *Appointment in London* and the classic *The Dam Busters*, for example. An RAE Lincoln was used to provide aircraft noise for a much later film, *The Guns of Navarone*.

The rundown of the Lincoln force began in 1951, spurred by two factors. The first of these was the perception that the aircraft would not

be suitable for the coming era of atomic warfare (having inadequate altitude and speed to escape the blast of a bomb), and this in turn led to the acquisition of the US-supplied B-29, known to the RAF as the Boeing Washington. The second factor was the introduction of the Canberra B.Mk 2, the RAF's first jet bomber.

Lincoln replaced

The RAF received 88 B-29s, and these equipped eight front-line bomber squadrons from March 1950. Although they were fast, long-ranging, high-flying, warm, comfortable and well-appointed, the Washingtons also proved difficult and costly to support and operate, and were no more suitable for modern warfare than the Lincoln. The Washingtons were just as vulnerable to interception (perhaps more so than those Lincolns which had 20-mm cannon), yet were much less suitable for the kind of expeditionary and colonial policing role carried out with such success by the Lincolns. They were also considerably less

No. XV Squadron – 'Tallboy' carriers

One of the major driving forces behind the Lincoln's development was to produce an aircraft capable of operating against the Japanese over the vast distances of south-east Asia. Part of the plan was to establish two squadrons of Lincolns specially modified to carry the 12,000-lb 'Tallboy' deep penetration bomb. The aircraft would be refuelled in flight en-route to the target and, for extra protection against Japanese day and night fighters, the H₂S radar would be replaced by a Fraser-Nash FN.88 or a Redwing ventral turret. VJ-Day brought a halt to such ambi-

tious plans, however, development of a variant capable of carrying the 'Tallboy' continued. No. XV Squadron, based at RAF Wyton, had already carried out trials during 1945-47 with both 'Tallboys' and 22,000-lb 'Grand Slam' bombs using the Lancaster B.Mk I (Special). These aircraft were retained as the squadron began re-equipping with the Lincoln in February 1947, and in 1948 at least five Lincolns, suitably modified by Avro with a deeper bomb bay, were added to the trials section. No. XV Squadron was destined to be the only RAF squadron equipped with the 'Tallboy' Lincoln and operated the variant between 1948-50.

Above: RF514 (LS-B) was one of at least five Lincolns converted with more bulbous bomb bay doors for the carriage of the 12,000-lb 'Tallboy' bomb. Other known conversions were RF370 (LS-A), RF532 (LS-D), RF395 (LS-E) and RF503 (LS-F).

Above: The 'Tallboy' Lincolns retained their H₂S/IIIG radar and never received inflight-refuelling capability, as was once proposed. The aircraft could, however, have been deployed operationally if the need had arisen. Note that the aircraft lacked nose turret armament.

Right: A 12,000-lb 'Tallboy' bomb lies on its trolley in No. XV Squadron's hangar at RAF Wyton in 1948, prior to being loaded aboard one of the converted aircraft for one of the many trials flights conducted in that year.

Far right: The Lincoln was undoubtedly used in trials associated with the UK's early atomic weapon programme. This strangely-shaped object (possibly a fusing device), being loaded aboard a No. XV Sqn Lincoln, may be associated with these experiments.

Below: Seen here releasing a stick of 500-lb (227-kg) bombs from its capacious bomb-bay on the Wainfleet range is RF523 Thor II, which served as the flagship of the Empire Air Armament School, Manby from July 1946 until June 1950. In addition to its weapons testing role, the aircraft also made many goodwill and liaison visits overseas, and for this purpose was modified to carry passenger seats, a rest bed and windows in the rear fuselage.

Seen prior to departure on their 20,000-mile 10-day 'flag-waving' deployment to Santiago, Chile, are three Lincoln B.Mk IIs drawn from Nos 100, 83 and 97 Squadrons. The aircraft bore the special codes 'AS' allocated to the detachment, however, hours before their final departure from RAF St Mawgan on 27 October 1946, the Foreign Office ordered the codes to be changed to 'GB', presumably signifying 'Great Britain'. Wing Commander Jim Bell of No. 100 Squadron led the detachment flying RF463 (AS-A).

accurate in the bombing role. A Lincoln crew dispatched to the 1952 SAC Bombing Competition scored highest in radar bombing, and dropped to fifth overall only because it was operating with an uncalibrated visual bombsight. The Washingtons therefore were retired early, from March 1953, while the Lincolns (whose units should have re-equipped with Canberras first) soldiered on.

Combat operations

From a relatively early point in its career, the Lincoln's principal contribution was made overseas, rather than as part of home-based Bomber Command. Although they were never permanently based overseas, Bomber Command's home-based Lincoln squadrons made regular overseas detachments and deployments on exercises, on 'flag-waving' goodwill visits and even on operations. The Lincoln was ideally suited to such use, having good 'hot-and-high' performance, adequate engine cooling, and the ability to operate from primitive, semi-prepared airstrips with limited engineering support. This made them far better equipped to support overseas detachments than Bomber Command's new jets and, accordingly, they were heavily used on such duties.

The first long-range overseas visit by RAF Lincolns was made by three Lincolns and crews from Nos 83, 97 and 100 Squadrons (wearing special 'GB-' code prefixes), which visited Chile in October 1946. This 40,000-mile (64372-km) round trip was followed by a tour of North America by 16 Lincolns of No. 617 Squadron between July and September 1947, during which they visited New York, Los Angeles and Canada. In 1948 No. 44 Squadron visited Southern Rhodesia and No. 97 deployed to Singapore, and in 1949 No. IX Squadron dispatched six aircraft to Egypt to participate in Operation Sunrise, these aircraft then flying on to visit Pakistan. Even after the Lincolns were replaced as Bomber Command's newest and most glamourous aircraft by the Canberra, the Lincolns tended to be sent on overseas 'flag-waving' tours as support aircraft.

Such peaceful overseas visits were quickly overshadowed by the Lincoln's war-fighting prowess, which it was called upon to demonstrate more than any other RAF aircraft at the time. Between March 1950 and July 1955, Bomber Command's Lincoln squadrons supported permanent rotational operational deployments, either in Malaya (for operations against the Chinese-backed Communist terrorists) and/or in Kenya, for operations against the Mau Mau. Small numbers of Lincolns remained in use with Nos 7, 83 and 97 Squadrons until the end of 1955, when they were finally replaced in the front-line home-based bomber role by the first of the V-Bombers.

Operation 'Firedog'

A total of six RAF Lincoln B.Mk 2 squadrons flew combat operations in Malaya, these consisting of Nos 57, 100 and 61 Squadrons for Operation Musgrave (March 1950-April 1951) and Nos 83, 7 and 148 Squadrons for Operation Bold (August 1953-April 1955). During the Lincoln's involvement in Firedog 18,137 flying hours were completed in 5,576 sorties without a single loss due to enemy action or accident – a truly remarkable achievement.

Below: A No. 57 Squadron crew pose in front of 'DX-L' at Tengah in June 1950. As the first unit to be deployed, No. 57 had to devise its own bombing techniques over the featureless jungle using grid references and 'Mark I eyeballs'.

Above: During their five months at Tengah, between August 1953-January 1954, No. 83 Squadron made regular detachments to Hong Kong. RF358 and RA677 visited RAF Kai Tak in November 1953 to provide fighter affiliation for the resident No. 80 Squadron Hornets and Vampires from No. 28 Squadron based at Sek Kong. As part of Bomber Command's Flare Force all No. 83 Squadron Lincolns were fitted with H₂S /4A radar.

Armament
No. 100 Squadron aircraft deployed to RAF Tengah had their front turrets removed but retained the twin 20-mm Bristol Type 17 mid-upper turret and the Boulton Paul Type D rear turret with two 0.5-in Browning machine-guns. The turrets were used to great effect on low-level strafing runs which followed daylight bombing raids.

Avro Lincoln B.Mk 2/3G

No. 100 Squadron, Royal Air Force
RAF Tengah, Singapore
June-December 1950

No. 100 Squadron deployed to RAF Tengah, Singapore from its home base of RAF Waddington in June 1950 for participation in Operation Musgrave against Malayan guerrillas. The unit continued the bombing and strafing attacks against well hidden enemy positions in the thick jungle initiated by No. 57 Squadron. No. 100 was itself replaced by No. 61 Squadron in December 1950.

Radar
The No. 100 Squadron Lincolns deployed to RAF Tengah were fitted with $H_2S/3G$ bombing radar housed in a prominent radome beneath the rear fuselage. The radar proved of little use over the featureless jungle terrain and bombing raids, both by day and night, were completed visually.

Bombing techniques
Although later in the conflict day and night raids were flown in equal measure, No. 100 Squadron's operations were mainly conducted during daylight. The targets were approximately 1,000 square yards and loads consisted of 14 1,000-lb (454-kg) or 18 500-lb (227-kg) bombs usually dropped in sticks at one-second intervals. At this time, RAF Dakotas and Sunderlands dropped flares for target marking, a task later taken over by Army Air Corps Austers.

Powerplant
The Rolls-Royce Merlin 85s fitted to the Lincoln Mk I were replaced in the Mk II by Packard-built Merlin 68s. Initially, the Mk II was plagued with airframe vibration and engine overheating problems, which were cured by replacing the three-bladed propeller with a de Havilland four-bladed unit and fitting an automatic charge temperature control as the Merlin 68A.

Markings
RF476 carries the pennant of No. 100 Squadron's commanding officer, Squadron Leader Danny O'Brien. Along with the squadron's skull and crossbones crest and mission markings, the aircraft also carries the nose inscription *The Burra Hornet* (literally, 'The Head Hornet') in reference to the unit's motto 'Never stir up a hornet's nest'. By 1950, Bomber Command had replaced the dark green and dark earth upper camouflage with medium sea grey, however, the three-letter squadron codes were still applied (until replaced by large white serial numbers in 1952).

Above: No. 1 Squadron Lincoln B.Mk 30s of the Royal Australian Air Force unleash their load of 1,000-lb bombs on the southern command headquarters of the Malayan communists, near Kluang, Johore State in January 1956.

Above: The longest serving of any Lincoln unit during the Malayan emergency was No. 1 Squadron, RAAF. The standard bombing raid involved five-seven aircraft attacking a designated area in loose formation. Other operations included large scale raids with RAF Lincolns, single-aircraft night nuisance raids, and the dropping of 4,000-lb (1814-kg) bombs to clear landing areas for helicopters. After daylight raids the formations would often return to base at ultra low-level passing over towns in villages, in what became known as 'the flag wag'.

Left: Bomb symbol mission marks were routinely applied to RAAF Lincolns. A black symbol was used for a daylight operation and red for night. Some RAAF machines chalked up in excess of 200 operational sorties.

Even after the disbandment of the last Lincoln bomber units, a flight of Lincolns (No. 1426 Flight) was based in Aden until January 1957, flying combat missions against dissident tribesmen and Yemeni insurgents.

In the Middle East, aircraft on Sunray and Lone Ranger deployments to Shallufa, Egypt were sometimes called upon to bomb dissident tribesmen in Aden. No. 101 Squadron forward-deployed to Khormaksar in October 1947 and dropped loads of 14 500-lb (227-kg) bombs on rebel positions after locally-based Ansons dropped warning leaflets. No. 138 Squadron continued the task two weeks later. The first full-scale operational deployment of Lincolns began in January 1952, when No. 148 Squadron deployed to Shallufa in the wake of the coup by Colonels Nasser and Neguib against King Farouk. The squadron did not see much action, and was replaced by No. 100 Squadron in June 1952. In the same month that No. 148 Squadron detached to Egypt, a No. 7 Squadron detachment in Aden was redesignated as No. 1426 Flight. The unit's six (later five) Lincolns were used for colonial policing, under the command of HQ British Forces, Aden Protectorate, conducting transport, reconnaissance, supply-dropping and occasional bomber missions. The Flight flew its final sortie on 16 January 1957, and the unit's last two aircraft left Khormaksar on 21 and 28 January.

As if in a bid to maintain a degree of 'company continuity', the ageing Lincolns were themselves replaced by Avro Shackletons. The Shackleton, of course, was another Lancaster derivative, once known as the Lincoln Mk III.

The first operational deployment for the RAF Lincoln was prefaced in April 1948, when a 'show of force' deployment to Malaya by the Lancasters of No. 7 Squadron was continued by the Lincolns of No. 97 Squadron, under Operation Red Lion II. In Malaya, resistance to the Japanese had been dominated by the ethnic Chinese minority, and the Communist party (which was also predominantly Chinese) and the same guerrillas formed the backbone of the

movement that materialised after the war to resist and counter the re-imposition of British colonial rule. The campaign of violence began in June 1948, with the murder of three unarmed British planters, and soon began to spiral out of control.

Operation Firedog

From an early stage, it became clear that air power would be of incalculable value in attacking the terrorists in their hide-outs in the impenetrable jungle, and that the Lincoln (with its 'hot-and-high' performance, rugged dependability and heavy bombload) would play a vital role. No. 57 Squadron deployed to Tengah in March 1950 under Operation Musgrave, and pioneered the visual bombing techniques which came to be used throughout the campaign. H_2S was of little use over the featureless jungle, and there was no Gee chain. It was found that 18 500-lb bombs (or 14 1,000-lb/454-kg) were the best loads, and that dummy runs over the target offered the terrorists too much warning, giving them the chance to evacuate their camps. It could sometimes take up to 14 days to obtain political clearance to attack a target, a process that was gradually streamlined.

No. 57 Squadron was relieved by No. 100 in June 1950, while No. 61 Squadron took over in December 1950, staying at Tengah until April 1951. RAF Lincolns were sent back to Malaya in August 1953, under Operation Bold, with the deployment of No. 83 Squadron. No. 7 Squadron took over in January 1954, and No. 148 in October 1954. When No. 101 Squadron assumed the commitment in April 1955, it was equipped with Canberras, and the

A No. 61 Squadron Lincoln B.Mk 2 cruises sedately above the impressive backdrop of Mount Kenya during the squadron's tour to Africa in the spring of 1954. By this time, Bomber Command's Lincolns had lost their mid-upper turrets and were painted in medium sea grey and black with large white serials. Squadron codes were generally not applied.

RAF Lincolns' role in Malaya was over, though the Royal Australian Air Force Lincolns remained. These aircraft operated principally from Tengah in Singapore, but mounted deployments to other RAF stations in the area, from Sek Kong and Kai Tak in Hong Kong to Kuala Lumpur and Butterworth in Malaya.

The RAF's rotational deployments of Lincoln bomber squadrons were augmented by No. 1 Squadron, RAAF, whose Lincolns were permanently based at Tengah, Singapore from 26 July 1950 until July 1958. The RAF stationed Beaufighters, Brigands, Hornets, Vampires, Venoms and Canberras at Tengah during the Malayan emergency, but the Lincolns were never permanently based there.

The other operational theatre for the RAF's Lincolns was East Africa, where the aircraft were used against the Kikuyu tribal secret

Most of the Lincoln Mk Is and a large proportion of the early Mk IIs were placed straight into open storage at the various Maintenance Units (MUs) around the UK. It was soon discovered that the aircraft rapidly developed corrosion problems and many were scrapped with only a handful of flying hours. Another more expensive solution was to cocoon each aircraft in a protective plastic coating, as shown on these Lincolns and Tempests in January 1952.

Below: Bomber Command's Lincoln squadrons made a substantial contribution to the Queen's Coronation Review at RAF Odiham on 15 July 1953. A total of 45 took part in the flypast, arranged in five groups of nine. The timing and accuracy of the formations were a testament to three months of intensive formation practices and rehersals for the big day.

society known as the Mau Mau. The first Lincoln deployment to Kenya began in November 1953, when three aircraft from No. 49 Squadron arrived at Eastleigh airport from Shallufa in Egypt. Eastleigh was 5,500 ft (1675 m) above sea level, and Mount Kenya rose to 17,000 ft (5180 m), so the Lincoln's 'hot-and-high' performance and ceiling made it well suited to operations in the area. A radar was situated atop Mount Alsop and was used as a beacon, allowing the Lincoln crews to bomb accurately from altitudes in excess of 20,000 ft (6096 m). The aircraft bombed from low altitude, too, when circumstances dictated, and later in the campaign one aircraft was lost when it hit a ridge. These first three No. 49 Squadron Lincolns were then joined by the rest of the squadron, which began mounting four-aircraft strikes against Mau Mau hide-outs and other targets on the slopes of Mount Kenya, in the Aberdare mountains, and in the thick forests north of Nairobi.

In January 1954 No. 49 Squadron was replaced by No. 100, which itself returned to the UK to disband in March, being replaced by No. 61 Squadron. No. 61 was replaced by No. 214 in June 1954, and No. 49 took over again in December 1954, remaining at Eastleigh until its last operation on 16 July 1955. By then the Mau Mau rebellion was under control, the rebel tribesmen's resolve having been broken by the robust British response, and particularly by the intensive bombing. The Security Forces in Kenya contained the Mau Mau in a relatively confined area, and then inflicted heavy casualties. The terrorists lost popular support and were effectively defeated. In recent, more politically correct, times, some observers have criticised the heavy death toll among the rebels (sometimes painted as 'ordinary' freedom fighters) and contrasted it to the relatively light losses suffered by government forces, but this ignores the savagery and inhuman nature of the atrocities committed by the Mau Mau against their victims.

ECM/Elint role

The RAF's last Lincoln bombers in use were those of No. 1426 Flight in Aden. Even after the type's withdrawal from the bomber role, the Lincoln remained in use in the electronic countermeasures and electronic warfare roles. At Hemswell, the 'Flare Force' units – Nos 83 and 97 Squadrons – disbanded on 1 January 1956, freeing up their numberplates for the V-Force. The units remained in existence, known respectively as Antler and Arrow Squadrons, and were tasked primarily with training navigators for the V-Force.

No. 199 Squadron finally converted to Canberras in 1957, and on 1 October its Lincolns merged with those of Antler and Arrow Squadrons to form No. 1321 Flight. The Lincoln Conversion Flight moved to Lindholme in April 1958 to join the Bomber Command Bombing School, whose 'B' Squadron still operated 14 Lincolns. Plans to purchase six Viscounts to replace these aircraft fell through, and the Lincolns lingered until 6 October 1960, when the last Bomber Command Lincoln was finally replaced by modified Hastings transports.

The last and longest-serving RAF operator of the Lincoln was the RAF's Central Signals Establishment at Watton, several of whose units relied on the big Avro bombers. Both parts of Calibration Squadron (N for navaids and R for radar) used Lincolns, as did other elements of the establishment. These functional squadrons gained 'proper' numberplates in 1951 and 1952, forming No. 192 Squadron (for Elint duties), No. 199 Squadron (for ECM/RCM), No. 116 Squadron (for navaid calibration) and No. 527 Squadron (for radar calibration). By 1956 most Lincolns had been grouped within Research and Development Squadron, and were used mainly for jamming. It was said that four aircraft could neutralise the whole West European radar chain, and that a single aircraft flying at 15,000 ft (4572 m) could shut down the UK east coast radar stations. The unit became No. 151 Squadron on 1 January 1962, operating a mix of Lincolns, Varsities and Hastings.

Another 'oddball' Lincoln unit was the Radar Reconnaissance Flight, which formed on 2 October 1951 from a flight of No. 58 Squadron. The Lincolns were used to prove the usefulness of using H_2S radar photo overlays to enable bomber navigators to identify and pinpoint their targets on their own radar sets. The Radar Reconnaissance Flight flew intensive sorties while building up a library of target overlays, and developing H_2S into a dedicated side-looking reconnaissance tool. The Lincolns continued until August 1957, when the Valiants of No. 543 Squadron assumed the task.

Aircraft used by Signals Command were extensively modified, and are sometimes referred to as Lincoln B.Mk IVs. This designation was little-known in service, and was officially applied to the 60 bomber-roled B.Mk 2s re-engined with Merlin 85s so that their original Packard-built Merlins could be used as spares for other B.Mk 2s.

In addition to its extensive front-line career, the Lincoln was also widely used as a testbed and trials aircraft. A significant number of aircraft were converted for use as engine testbeds, flying for different engine manufacturers, while others were used by service and ministry trials units for an array of purposes, including the dropping of various new weapons. One of the most impressive performing Lincolns was the

Left: 'B' Squadron of the Bomber Command Bombing School based at RAF Lindholme, was the last Bomber Command unit to operate the Lincoln. After a brief ceremony on 6 October 1960 WD143 made the final take-off from Lindholme heading for 23 MU at Aldergrove, Northern Ireland.

Below: Part of RAF Signals Command, the Central Signals Establishment was the longest serving operator of the Lincoln. Many of the aircraft received additional equipment, including this example from radio and electronics countermeasures specialists No. 151 Squadron which features an additional radome under the nose for ECM/jamming and a special 'window' dispenser. The squadron finally retired its Lincolns in March 1963, thus ending the Lincoln's days in RAF service.

Below: WD148 served out its time with the CSE's B Flight Development Squadron. Along with ECM and RCM work, the aircraft was used on long-range detachments to test operational flying in North African, East African and Middle Eastern conditions

RAE's specially stripped and lightened SX974, which had a cutaway bomb bay and four Mosquito NF-type two-speed, two-stage Merlin 113s. The aircraft proved capable of reaching heights exceeding 42,500 ft (12954 m), and the crew (wearing pressure waistcoats) always included a wing commander doctor from the Institute of Aviation Medicine. Concern over 'the bends' prompted the RAE to assign taller, thinner aircrew (believed to be less susceptible) to the aircraft's crews! The aircraft was used principally for high-altitude camera, film and photo-flash development.

Australian service

The Lincolns that saw most active service were the B.Mk 30s of No. 1 Squadron, Royal Australian Air Force. They were based at RAF Tengah in Singapore for some 7.5 years and flew more than 4,000 combat sorties over

Malaya, dropping some 33 million lb (15 million kg) of bombs. This represented an astonishing 85 per cent of the total bomb tonnage expended during Operation Firedog (the Malayan Emergency). The Squadron remained in action after the RAF's Lincolns were replaced by light-weight Canberras, and between April 1955 and July 1958 were the only heavy bombers permanently based in-theatre. The Squadron notched up some astonishing feats, including one-day record bomb total of 196,000 lb (88905 kg), and its crews won six DFCs (and two Bars), one DFM, one OBE, four BEMs and 15 'Mentions in Dispatches'.

The Lincoln proved to be a surprisingly effective anti-terrorist weapon, causing great destruction when bombing suspected jungle hideouts. The use of bombing enabled the RAF and RAAF to deny large areas of jungle to the enemy, and was even used to drive the

enemy towards friendly troops on the ground. The Lincolns demonstrated an unexpected degree of precision, especially when used in conjunction with airborne forward air controllers. The main success of the bombing campaign was in keeping the enemy on the move and preventing them from establishing fixed bases or building links with villages. The terrorists were resourceful, and bomb-aimers had to count bomb flashes to ensure that all had exploded. If they hadn't, the aircraft would go round again and strafe, if possible, to prevent insurgents recovering an unex-ploded bomb and re-using its explosive. The relentless and accurate bombing sapped the morale of the enemy, and laid the groundwork for eventual victory.

Australia ordered the Lincoln directly off the drawing board in 1943, with war raging, even before a prototype had flown. The order was

Right: Along with regular bombing and SAR duties, Royal Australian Air Force Lincoln B.Mk 30s were called on for more unusual duties. In January 1947 a single example was modified to carry fire-fighting 'bombs' as part of an extensive test programme to combat large scale bush fires. The 'bombs' contained a mixture of water and ammonium sulphate and were dropped from altitudes as low as 300 ft (91 m).

Below: A No. 1 Squadron B.Mk 30 passes Royal Navy units and RAF Sunderland flying boats off the coast of Singapore during the squadron's operations against Malayan insurgents. This aircraft later went on to serve with the ARDU as a 'rainmaker' carrying a generator which could deliver a 500,000-volt charge through 'Betsy' – a 4-ft long bomb-shaped drogue which was lowered through the bomb bay doors on high-tension electric cables.

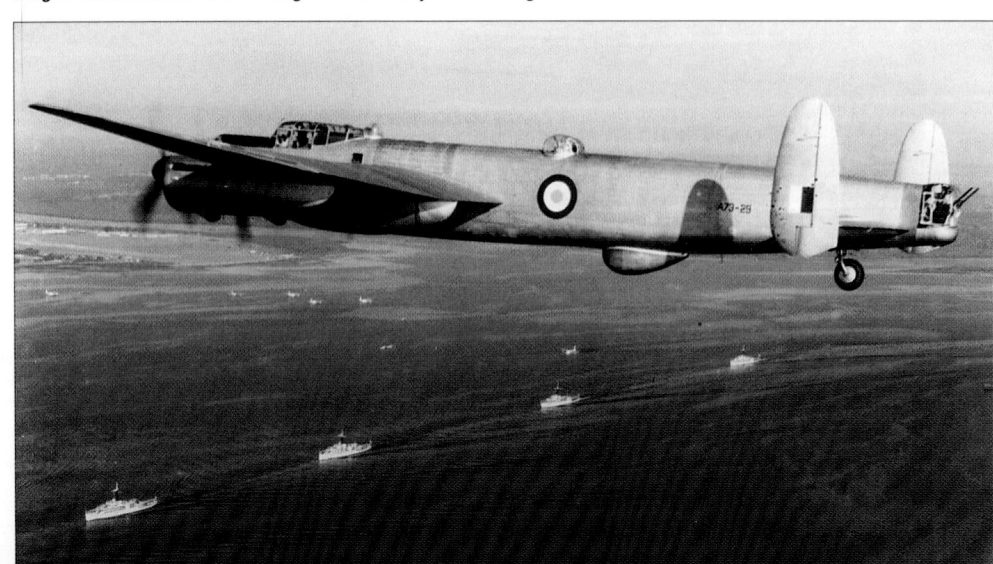

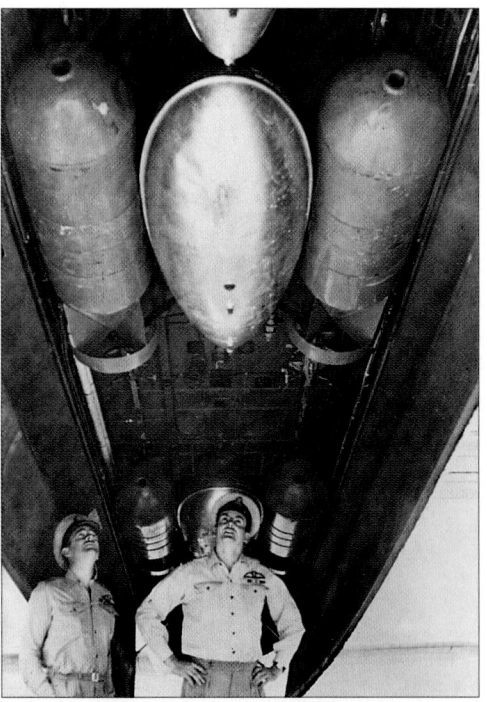

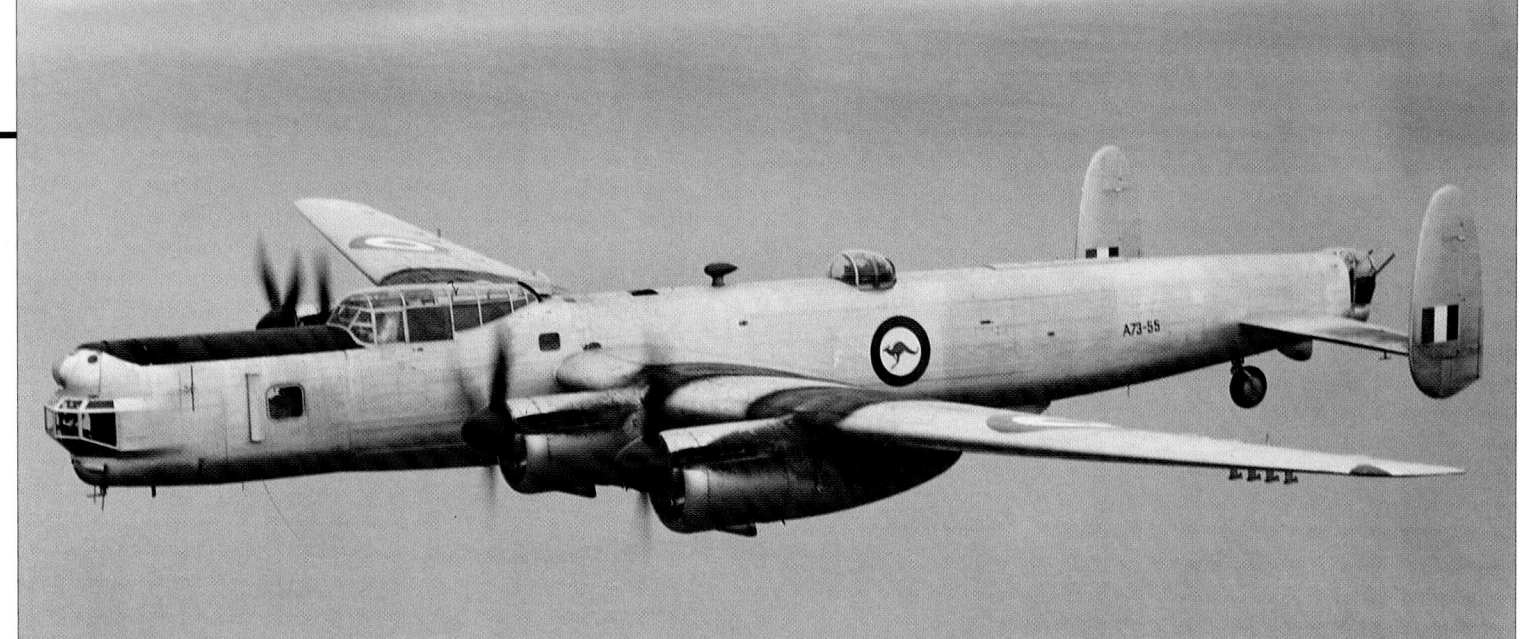

A total of 20 long-nosed Lincoln Mk 31s was produced for service with No. 10 Squadron, RAAF at Townsville, Queensland, serving between 1953 and 1961. With no air conditioning, temperatures in the cabin during summer long-range patrols could reach over 100°F, making such patrols a true test of stamina.

placed on the basis that it was the latest and most capable version of the Lancaster bomber, already in use by a number of RAAF squadrons based in England. Avro's own factories (and those of other UK aircraft companies) were already working at full stretch producing Lancasters, so Australia's intention to build its own aircraft was extremely welcome. As it became increasingly clear that World War II was drawing to a close, the size of the Australian order dwindled, but the aircraft remained the preferred choice to replace the RAAF's Liberators, and the programme was not cancelled. Australian officers noted, with some surprise, that the aircraft "equalled and in some respects surpassed in performance and capacity the Super Fortress." By July 1945, the Australian order stood at 61 Lincoln bombers and 12 of the related Tudor transports, all to be built at the Government Aircraft Factory at Fisherman's Bend. It originally had been envisaged that Australian industry would build much larger numbers of Lincolns, and that all but the first 100 would be powered by the same Pratt & Whitney R-2800 Double Wasp radial engines that powered the country's much-loved Liberators. The Tudors were dropped from the order in July 1948, replaced by 12 more Lincolns.

The first five Lincolns of the 73 produced were built from Avro-supplied kits, but the remaining 68 were built from locally-made components. Australian production plans were further cut back at the end of the war, and only 61 of the planned 73 aircraft were completed initially, the remainder being stored incomplete.

The RAAF Lincoln bombers served with Nos 1, 2 and 6 Squadrons of No. 82 Wing at Amberley, Qld, and were regarded in some circles as being a virtual Southern Hemisphere extension of the RAF's Lincoln bomber force, arrayed against a common Cold War foe. Co-operation between the RAF and the RAAF was certainly routine, as was demonstrated in the joint Exercise Cumulative in 1949, in which

B-008 (previously RE355) was one of 12 Avro-built Lincoln Mk IIs intended for RAF service but placed straight into open storage at Langar in the autumn of 1945. In June 1947 the aircraft were sold back to Avro for resale to Argentina. Before delivery, the aircraft were stripped of certain equipment such as the H₂S radar and Rebecca homing gear, but retained the full three-turret armament. In 1948 a further batch of 18 new-build Lincolns, from Armstrong Whitworth's Baginton factory, was delivered and all examples initially served with Grupo 1 de Bombardeo, V Brigada Aérea, Fuerza Aérea Argentine.

Lincolns flew long-range strikes across the breadth of Australia, simulating taking off from bases in 'England' to bomb 'Moscow'. Missions were flown twice per week for five months, routing through any unfavourable weather, with crew performance monitored very closely.

Australia and Britain also co-operated closely in the development of weapons, including Britain's early nuclear bombs, and Lincolns were heavily involved in these trials. At least nine RAF Lincolns found their way to Woomera, including two aircraft with Theseus turboprops outboard, and one with Pythons. During Operations Hurricane and Totem (at Monte Bello and Emu, during October 1952 and October 1953, respectively), RAAF Lincolns flew range patrol and atomic cloud sampling missions, and carried atomic samples back to Canberra for analysis. Nine of the 12 RAAF Lincolns used in Totem were heavily contaminated, four so seriously that they had to be withdrawn from use and scrapped, their remains reportedly being buried in an unmarked pit!

No. 1 Squadron finally relinquished its Lincolns in 1958, after returning from Singapore, and re-equipped with Canberras. This left the Lincoln operating only in the maritime role.

Maritime Lincolns

The final 12 Australian Lincolns (which had been stored incomplete following the delivery of the 61st B.Mk 30) were finally completed as

maritime reconnaissance GR.Mk 31s. These aircraft had a lengthened nose, housing a tactical navigator and three sonics operators, with pyrotechnic flare dispensers aft of the existing bomb bay, which was modified to carry sonobuoys and torpedoes. To allow the equipment of two squadrons, seven B.Mk 30s were withdrawn from the bomber role and converted to the same standard. Ten GR.Mk 31s were subsequently upgraded to MR.Mk 31 standards, with further improvements. The maritime Lincolns served with Nos 10 and 11 Squadrons at Townsville, Qld: although No. 11 used them for only a year (1950-1951), No. 10 soldiered on until the discovery of corrosion in the wing spars forced the type's retirement in 1961.

Argentina

The only other overseas operator of the Lincoln was Argentina. The Fuerza Aérea Argentina received 30 Lincolns (18 of which were newly built, and followed 12 ex-RAF machines) from September 1947, augmenting a batch of 15 ex-RAF Lancasters and two Lancastrian transports delivered at the same time. The Lincolns and Lancasters entered service with Grupo I de Bombardeo of V Brigada Aérea in 1947.

Inspired by the wartime raid on the dams of Germany, the Fuerza Aérea Argentina even formed a special unit, the Brigada Apicella, tasked with attacking dams, bridges and dykes. This unit operated six Lincolns from July 1953, and worked up in the high-speed, low-altitude role, though the planned special weapons were

Delivered to the Empire Air Navigation School (EANS) at Shawbury in February 1947, Aries II replaced its famous predecessor, a converted Lancaster named Aries I. In its short career the aircraft conducted advanced navigation training and made numerous long-range overseas flights, each recorded below the cockpit on the starboard side. A route-finding trip to Tengah in Singapore (below) was made in October 1947 prior to Bomber Command Lincoln deployment to the base. In addition, the aircraft visited a host of other countries including the USA, Canada, Iraq, Kenya, Ceylon and Burma. The aircraft's 'high-speed' natural metal finish is well illustrated (left) in this view of Aries II at Luqa, Malta, only one month before it was extensively damaged in a hangar fire.

never procured and the aircraft returned to the 'straight' bomber role. The Argentine Lincolns saw active service in the 'Freedom Revolution' in which General Perón was ousted from power.

By 1957, the operational fleet consisted of 16 aircraft, with four more in reserve, and these gradually adopted an ASW role, initially using their H_2S Mk III radar, and later a modern American ASV radar (possibly Ekco ASV 19b) housed in a retractable ventral 'dustbin' radome. Plans for Avro to refurbish and convert 12 aircraft with this radar and depth charges, markers and directional sonobuoys came to nothing, and Neptunes were acquired instead. The type hitherto had served mainly in the bomber role, but had also undertaken Antarctic support duties and various transport and tanker tasks. One Argentine Lincoln had been converted to tanker configuration in-country, and another was sent back to the UK for conversion to Lincolnian standards. The latter aircraft was then used mainly used for supply dropping in the Antarctic, and gained a temporary civil registration.

The Lincolnian transport

The first Lincolnian was *Aries II* (RE367), delivered to the Empire Air Navigation School at Shawbury on 20 February 1947. The aircraft was specially fitted with extra fuel tanks, bringing total capacity to 4,600 Imp gal (17413 litres), and rest bunks and seats were installed in the sound-proofed fuselage. Gun turrets were removed and replaced by streamlined fairings. The aircraft was eventually written off in a hangar fire and was replaced by the similarly modified *Aries III* (RE369), itself subsequently transferred to the new RAF Flying College at Manby. Six long-range Lincolns were delivered to the RAFFC in October 1952, one remaining in service until March 1961.

Paraguay ordered three even more radically modified Lincolnian freighters, which were converted to Type 595 standards by Field Aircraft Services from B.Mk IIs RE376, RF417 and RF458. The aircraft were equipped with a huge ventral freight pannier for carrying meat, and this faired into a new, deeper nose fairing. They were completed and fully painted in Paraguayan civil colours, but the deal fell through at the last minute and the aircraft were scrapped.

Another ex-RAF B.Mk II, RE290, was similarly converted by Airflight Ltd and was used by Surrey Flying Services Ltd on the Berlin

Airlift. The aircraft made 45 flights carrying fuel oil into the beleaguered city before the Russian blockade was lifted, and the aircraft was retired and scrapped.

Retirement

The RAF's last five Lincolns (RA685, RF398, RF461, RF505 and RF570) were withdrawn from service with No. 151 Squadron in March 1963, following a final formation flight on 12 March. One aircraft (RF398) went to Henlow for the planned RAF Museum's store on 30 April, finally going to the RAF Museum's out-station at Cosford in 1975. The aircraft remains on display there to this day – and is reputedly haunted. But that, as they say, is another story!

RF398 is not the only surviving Lincoln. Napier's icing research aircraft (RF342) went to the College of Aeronautics at Cranfield in 1962, and to the museum at Southend in 1967. The aircraft was sold in 1983, and dismantled. It remains extant (but incomplete) at Sandtoft.

In Argentina, the type served in diminishing numbers until early 1965, when 11 remained in use. Six aircraft were withdrawn from service at the beginning of 1965, but the type was not officially declared obsolete until 1 August 1967, when three remained active; the last of the Lincolns (B-016) was finally retired in January 1968. Two Argentinian Lincolns survive, one (B-004, marked as B-010) on display in the country's Museo Nacional de Aeronáutica at Buenos Aires, the other (B-016, marked as B-017) at Villa Reynolds.

Jon Lake

Seen on its first post-preservation appearance at the Royal review at RAF Abingdon in 1968, RF398 now resides at the RAF Museum Cosford. The aircraft is allegedly haunted by the ghost of an airman killed in an RAF Whitley in 1943 from which an engine was recovered and placed next to the Lincoln in the 1980s.

Specification

Lincoln B.Mk 2
Powerplant: Four 1,750-hp (1305-kW) 27-litre Packard Merlin 68 12-cylinder liquid-cooled piston engines with two-speed superchargers Rated at 1,725 hp (1285 kW) for take-off, 1,775 hp (1325 kW) at 4,000 ft (1220 m) and 1,655 hp (1235 kW) at 16,500 ft (5030 m)
Propellers: Four four-bladed constant speed Hamilton A/5 or de Havilland D.20/445 Hydromatic propellers
Span: 120 ft 0 in (36.57 m)
Length: 78 ft 3.5 in (23.86 m)
Height: 17 ft 3.5 in (5.27 m)
Wing area: 1,421 sq ft (132 m²)
Fuel: 2,850 Imp gal (12955 litres) in six integral wing tanks, provision for two 400-Imp gal (1820-litre) tanks in bomb bay. Oil capacity 150 Imp gal (680 litres)
Bombload: Normal maximum 14,000 lb (6350 kg)
Defensive armament: Boulton Paul Type F.Mk 1 remotely controlled hydraulically operated nose turret with 2 x 0.50-in Browning machine guns and 460 rounds; Bristol Type 17 electrically operated mid-upper turret with 2 x 20-mm Hispano Mk.V cannon and 722 rounds; Boulton Paul Type D.Mk 1 electro-hydraulically operated tail turret with 2 x 0.50-in Browning machine guns and 3,040 rounds.
Crew: Seven (standard bomber) comprising pilot, flight engineer, navigator, wireless operator, bomb-aimer/gunner, two air gunners.
Maximum speed: 310 mph (499 km/h)
Best cruising speed: 260 mph (418 km/h) at 20,000 ft (6095 m)
Initial rate of climb: 800 ft (245 m) per minute
Service ceiling: 28,000 ft (8535 m)
Range: with 14,000-lb bombload 2,800 miles

Lincoln testbeds

Above: *After serving with Telecommunications Flying Unit on highly secret radar trials, RF342 was acquired by the Napier Icing Research Unit and allocated the civil identity G-APRJ. This aircraft, along with RF402 (G-APRP), were modified with the Spraymat system consisting of a multi-nozzle 'washboard' mounted on top of the fuselage spraying water from two 60-Imp gal (273-litre) tanks in the bomb bay onto aerofoil test sections. G-APRJ is seen here carrying a Sud Caravelle wingtip section.*

Left: *The second Napier 'Ice Wagon', RF402, is seen here carrying a full-size Blackburn Beverley wingtip. The intake behind the section was for the combustion heater which supplied hot gas for de-icing the section as required.*

Above: *Seen at Stansted in 1961, RF533 was modified with a stepped canopy by Portsmouth Aviation Co. Ltd for RAE Farnborough, initially for high-altitude meteorological research. The aircraft was later used for observing rain erosion on a Gloster Javelin radome fitted on the nose of the aircraft and subsequently served with the RAE as a flight laboratory. The aircraft was to end its days on the fire dump at Stansted.*

Above: *In the immediate post-war period Flight Refuelling Ltd was in the process of developing its 'probe and drogue' inflight refuelling system. RA657 was loaned to the company from the RAF in 1949 and converted to carry the new system. The aircraft is seen here refuelling one of two USAF F-84 Thunderjets during the record-breaking first non-stop east-west jet crossing of the Atlantic on 22 September 1950. The aircraft later went on to complete refuelling trials with the prototype DH.106 Comet and with RAF Meteors from No. 245 Squadron. RA657 was subsequently re-converted to B.Mk 2 standard and served with No. 199 Squadron based at Hemswell.*

Airframe testbeds

Airframe	Operator	Purpose
RA284	Bristol Aeroplane Co.	Undercarriage testbed for Brabazon
RA637	C Flight, RAE	GPI calibration
RA657	Flight Refuelling Ltd	Tanker
RE293	Flight Refuelling Ltd	Tanker
RE364	Empire Air Navigation School	*Aries II* Lincolnian navigation trainer
RE367	Empire Air Navigation School	*Aries III* Lincolnian navigation trainer
RE414	Empire Radio School	*Mercury II* radio navigation trainer
RF322	Eagle Aviation Services	Camera aircraft
RF342	Telecommunications Flying Unit	Radar trials
RF342	Napier Icing Research Unit	Icing rig for aerofoil sections (G-APRJ)
RF368	C Flight, RAE	Various trials
RF402	Napier Icing Research Unit	Icing rig for aerofoil sections (G-APRP)
RF498	Central Bomber Establishment	*Crusader*
RF523	Empire Air Armament School	*Thor II* for advanced bomber training
RF533	RAE	Met. research with test boom
RF533	RAE	Radome erosion testbed (for Javelin)
RF561	Telecommunications Flying Unit	Radar testbed with extended nose
SX716	C Flight, RAE	H₂S Mk IVA radar development
SX974	C Flight, RAE	High altitude research
SX993	Flight Refuelling Ltd	Tanker
WD125	C Flight, RAE	Weapons trials
A73-2	RAAF School of Air Navigation	'Brenool', long-range navigation/survey
A73-29	RAAF ARDU	Electrical 'cloud seeding' trials
A73-34	RAAF ARDU	Cosmic ray measurement platform

Engine testbeds

Airframe	Operator	Engine under test
RA643	Bristol, Filton	Phoebus turbojet in bomb bay
RA716/G	Bristol, Filton	Theseus 11 turboprops in outboard nacelles
RA716/G	Rolls Royce, Hucknall	Avon turbojets in outboard nacelles
RE339/G	Bristol Filton	Theseus 21 turboprops in outboard nacelles
RE339/G	Armstrong Siddeley	Python turboprops in outboard nacelles
RE418	Bristol, Filton	Theseus 21 turboprops in outboard nacelles
RF368	Bristol, Filton	Proteus turboprops in outboard nacelles
RF402	Napier, Luton	Dummy Naiad in nose for icing trials
RF403	Armstrong Siddeley	Python turboprops in outboard nacelles
RF530	Napier, Luton	Naiad turboprop in nose
RF533	Rolls Royce, Hucknall	Tyne turboprop in extended nose (G-37-1)
SX971	NGTE	Reheated Derwent in ventral pod
SX972	Bristol, Filton	Proteus turboprops in outboard nacelles
SX973	Napier, Luton	Nomad 1 turboprop in nose

Left: This atmospheric image depicts the 'Proteus Lincoln' SX972 landing in front of the Bristol Brabazon at Filton in 1951. Two Bristol Proteus turboprops were mounted outboard with the standard Merlin 68As retained inboard. First flying in this configuration on 12 December 1950, it went on to complete 958 hours of development flying.

Below: The Bristol Theseus turboprop was first tested on Lincoln RA716/G in February 1947. The aircraft later conducted flight trials of the Rolls-Royce Avon turbojet.

Left: Delivered to the National Gas Turbine Establishment Flight in May 1951, SX971 was converted by Air Service Training Ltd to carry a ventrally-mounted reheated Rolls-Royce Derwent turbojet. To prevent damage from the heat of the afterburner, the rear under fuselage was covered in stainless steel and twin retractable tail wheels were fitted.

Below: Two further Lincolns, RE339 and RE418 (seen here) were converted with Bristol Theseus turboprops in the outer nacelles. This pair flew regular services to the Canal Zone, operated by the Theseus Lincoln Flight, RAF Transport Command, based at RAF Lyneham.

Lincoln variants

Type 694 prototypes: Three prototypes built by Avro. PW925, 929 and 932 (3). Painted in standard disruptive dark green dark earth camouflage, with yellow undersides.

Type 694 Lincoln B.Mk I: Initial production version (Lancaster IV), with Merlin 85 engines, four-bladed propellers, Boulton Paul F Type nose turret (2 x Browning 0.50-in), Martin mid-upper turret (2 x Browning 0.50-in) and FN.121 (4 x 0.303-in Brownings) or FN.82 tail turret. 82 built, comprising RA628-655 (28), RE227-268 (42), RE281-288 (8), and RF333-334 (2). SS713-714 (2). Not issued to front-line squadrons. Conversion with Merlin 85A engines ordered, but not carried out.

Type 694 Lincoln B.Mk II: Second production version (Lancaster V) with Packard Merlin engines. Known as B.Mk 2 after 1948. Merlin 68, 68A or 300 engines, Boulton Paul F Type nose turret, Bristol Type 17 mid-upper turret (with 20-mm cannon) and Boulton Paul Type D tail turret initially with 'Village Inn' AGLT. Early aircraft with H2S Mk IIIG known as B.Mk 2/IIIG, later aircraft with H2S Mk IVA known as B.Mk 2/IVA. 447 built, comprising RA656-658 (3), RA661-693 (33), RA709-724 (16), RE289-325 (37), RE338-380 (43), RE393-424 (32), RF329-332 (4), RF335-370 (36), RF383-427 (45), RF440-485 (46), RF498-539 (42), RF553-577 (25), SS715-718 (4), SX923-958 (36), SX970-993 (24), WD122-133 (12), and WD141-149 (9).

Type 696 Lincoln GR.Mk III: Designation reserved for maritime reconnaissance version which eventually emerged (considerably changed) as the Shackleton.

Type 694 Lincoln B.Mk 4: 60 B.Mk 2s were re-engined with Merlin 85As after delivery (to compensate for a shortage of Packard Merlins) and issued to some squadrons. SX923-958, SX970-993.

Type 694 Lincoln U.Mk 5: Two B.Mk 2s converted as prototypes for a series of unmanned target drones. RF395 flown as a drone (with safety pilot) on 29 February 1956, after RF358 had flown initial trials. Programme abandoned as work began on 20 Lincolns stored at Langar. Planned second prototype (RF366) remained unflown. Other aircraft awaiting conversion included RE376, RF417, RF458 and RF564.

'Lincoln C.Mk 6': The Bristol Aero Engine Company's second Theseus 21 testbed, RE418, with the new turboprops in its outboard nacelles, was loaned to Transport Command and used for regular services between Lyneham and Middle East destinations under the unofficial designation Lincoln C.Mk 6.

Type 694 Lincoln B.Mk XV: Six aircraft of planned initial Canadian production batch were started, but only one, FM300, completed by Victory Aircraft of Malton. This first flew on 25 October 1945. Merlin 68A engines and Martin Type 23A dorsal turret. Aircraft then used as GI airframe, and may not have flown again.

Type 694 Lincoln B.Mk 30(B): Lincoln B.Mk II equivalents (with British Merlin 85B engines like the B.Mk I and 4) for the RAAF (who used the simple B.Mk 30 designation). 25 built by the Government Aircraft Factory (the first five using British-supplied kits of parts). Serialled A73-1 to A73-25. First 10 with 70,000-lb max AUW, rest with 75,000-lb limit. H2S Mk III bombing radar in small ventral radome, Boulton Paul Type F nose turret, Bristol Type 17 mid-upper and Boulton Paul Type D tail turret, (first aircraft initially fitted with Martin mid-upper and Frazer Nash rear turrets, but re-fitted with standard units).

Type 694 Lincoln LRC: Two Mk 30s (A73-14 and -18) converted for Long Range Communications (LRC) duties with turrets removed and faired over, extra windows, a galley in place of the mid-upper turret and eight passenger seats.

Type 694 Lincoln B.Mk 30A(B): 36 Government Aircraft Factory-built Lincolns for the RAAF (who used the simple B.Mk 30A designation) serialled A73-26 to A73-61. Structural modifications to allow 82,000-lb max AUW. A73-26 to A73-50

powered by Merlin 85B engines, rest (plus A73-41 as testbed) with Commonwealth Aircraft Corporation-built Merlin 102s. Some aircraft received ex-Spitfire VIII Merlin 66s in outboard nacelles as an interim measure. Otherwise identical to B.Mk 30(B).

Type 694 Lincoln LRN: 14 Mk 30As modified with Long Range Navigation (LRN) equipment for participation in 1949 joint RAF/RAAF exercise 'Cumulative'. Aircraft had electric Mk 9 autopilot (instead of pneumatic Mk 8), long range fuel tanks and a new distance reading compass. A73-31, -32, -33, -34, -36, -37, -38, -39, -40, -42, -43, -44, -45, -46.

Type 694 Lincoln GR.Mk 31: Final 12 Australian-built Lincolns ordered as Tudor transports, until Tudor dropped from Australian production plan in July 1948. These final 12 aircraft (A73-62 to A73-73) completed to revised maritime recce/ASW configuration, following evaluation of prototype (converted from Mk 30A A73-48). Seven more produced by conversion of Mk 30As A73-28, -55, -56, -57, -59, -60 and -61. All fitted with Mk 9 autopilot, Bendix radio compass and radio altimeter. New 6 ft 6-in D1A section added in front of cockpit, accommodating a tactical navigator and three sonobuoy operators, with openable direct observation windows incorporating adjustable slipstream deflectors. Bomb bay modified to carry two homing torpedoes, two racks of active sonobuoys, and two jettisonable 188-Imp gal (855-litre) fuel tanks. H2S radar converted to ASV.Mk 7 standard. Multi-barrel pyrotechnic flare dispenser added in rear fuselage, plus increased stowage for marine markers and sonobuoys. Rear facing camera to record attacks.

Type 694 Lincoln MR.Mk 31: 10 GR.Mk 31s converted with enhanced ASW capabilities from 8 March 1955. One sonobuoy operator's position deleted, radar upgraded to ASV.Mk 7A standard, fitted with improved low-level bombsight. Powered by Merlin 102 engines. A73-28, -55, -57, -60 (prototype), -61, -62, -65, -66, -67, -68. Most converted by GAF, -28 and -67 by the RAAF.

Type 694 Lincoln MR.Mk 32: Tentative designation for further upgrade with P2V Neptune radar and radio equipment. One MR.Mk 31 aircraft used as mock-up with new radome and MAD tailboom, but not flown.

Type 694 Argentine Lincoln: 12 (B-001 to B-012, ex RE343, 349, 350, 351, 352, 353, 354, 355, 356, 408, 409 and 410, respectively) converted from ex-RAF aircraft refurbished and converted by Short Brothers and Harland. 18 new-build B.Mk IIs (known as Lincoln As) from Armstrong Whitworth as B-013 to B-030. Similar to B.Mk 2, but without H2S, Rebecca and Gee, but with H2S radomes installed. B-022 converted locally to serve as a tanker (transporting fuel to refuel fighters on the ground during deployments), B-003 returned to Avro for conversion as a Lincolnian transport, as LV-ZEI.

Type 694 'Lincolnian': Two RAF Lincolns (RE367 and RE369) used by the Empire Air Navigation School for very long-range flights were fitted with enhanced navigation equipment, including G.3 compass, API Mk.II, and GPI Mk.II. Aircraft also gained passenger accommodation with oxygen and intercom to all seats and crew positions. Externally distinguished by extra windows, and streamlined nose and tail fairings. Fuel load increased to 4,615 Imp gal (20980 litres) by the addition of new tanks in the nose, and H2S replaced by ground mapping radar. Lincolnian name unofficial for these aircraft.

Type 695 Lincolnian Freighter: More radically modified freighter conversion, with similar tail fairing, and deeper nose fairing leading back to deep ventral pannier. Three B.Mk IIs acquired by Field at Tollerton for Paraguayan use as meat freighters (RE376, RF417 and RF458 becoming ZP-CBP-96, ZP-CBR-97, and ZP-CBS-98). One fully converted (ZP-CBR-97) but not granted a C of A, after Avro objections, and eventually sold for scrap. Another aircraft similarly converted by Airflight for Surrey Flying services for carrying fuel oil on the Berlin airlift (RE290 becoming G-ALPF).

Type 717: Provisional designation for proposed Met. reconnaissance Lincoln variant.

Type 717: Provisional designation for proposed Lincoln version with Napier Nomad turboprops in the outer nacelles.

Lincoln operators

Royal Air Force

No. 7 Squadron: Converted from Lancasters to Lincolns at Upwood in September 1949 and retained these until January 1956, when it disbanded. Known as No. 7/76 Sqn (to keep No. 76's numberplate 'alive') between February 1949 and December 1953. One Flight continued as No. 1426 Flight, in Aden. Codes MG-.

No. IX Squadron: Operated Lincolns from Binbrook as part of 1 Group between July 1946 and May 1952, when it converted to the Canberra. Codes WS-.

No. 12 Squadron: Partnered No. IX and No. 101 within the Binbrook Wing from August 1946 until March 1952. Codes PH-.

No. XV Squadron: Converted to Lincolns at Wyton in February 1947, relinquishing them and moving to Marham in March 1950. Known as No. XV/21 Sqn between February 1949 and September 1953. Codes LS-.

No. XV Sqn Lincoln Mk IIs deployed during a 'Sunray' at RAF Shallufah, Egypt in 1948.

No. 35 (Madras Presidency) Squadron: Converted to Lincolns at Mildenhall in September 1949, as part of 3 Group. Disbanded in February 1950, later converting to the Boeing Washington. Codes TL-.

No. 44 (Rhodesia) Squadron: Operated Lincolns on a trial basis, from October 1945 to May 1946, participating in Operation Sinkum, dumping surplus incendiaries in Cardigan Bay. Reverted to Lancasters in March 1946. Re-equipped with Lincolns in December 1946, at Wyton, becoming the first 3 Group Lincoln squadron. Known as No. 44/55 Sqn between February 1949 and July 1957. Converted to the Boeing Washington in January 1951. Codes KM-.

A trio of No. 44 Sqn Lincolns conducts a training flight from its base at RAF Wyton.

No. 49 Squadron: Re-equipped with Lincolns at Upwood in October 1949, subsequently moving to Waddington in June 1952, to Wittering in August 1953 and back to Upwood in February 1954, disbanding there in August 1955. Known as No. 49/102 Sqn between February 1949 and October 1954. Codes EA-.

No. 50 Squadron: Converted to Lincolns at Waddington in July 1946 and disbanded there at the end of July 1951. Known as No. 50/103 Sqn between February 1949 and January 1951. Codes VN-.

No. 57 Squadron: Operated a flight of Lincolns from East Kirkby between August and November 1945. Re-formed at Elsham Wolds in November 1945 through re-numbering No. 103 Sqn. Moved to Scampton in December 1945, Lindholme in May 1946 and Waddington in October 1946 and relinquished the Lincoln in April 1951. Known as No. 57/104 Sqn from 1949. Codes DX-.

No. 58 Squadron: Operated a Lincoln flight between November 1950 and September 1951, from Benson.

No. 61 Squadron: Operated Lincolns from Waddington between May 1946 and August 1953, moving to Wittering where it disbanded in August 1954. Known as No. 61/144 Sqn from February 1949. Codes QR-.

No. 75 Squadron: Re-equipped with Lincolns at Spilsby in September 1945 but disbanded, its numberplate transferring to the RNZAF, in October. Codes AA-.

No. 83 Squadron: Converted to Lincolns at Coningsby from July 1946, moving to Hemswell in November. Known as No. 83/150 Sqn from February 1949. Disbanded January 1956, but continued as 'Antler Squadron' until 1 October 1957. Codes OL-.

No. 90 Squadron: Re-equipped with Lincolns at Wyton from April 1947, and disbanded there on 1 September 1950. Codes WP-.

No. 97 Squadron: Converted to Lincolns at Coningsby from July 1946, moving to Hemswell in November. Disbanded January 1956, but continued as 'Arrow Squadron' until October 1957. Codes OF-.

A No. 97 Squadron Mk 2, with H₂S/4A radar, parked at Blackbushe in September 1955.

No. 100 Squadron: Converted to Lincolns at Lindholme from May 1946, moving to Hemswell in October, Waddington in March 1950 and Wittering in August 1953. Converted to Canberras in April 1954. Codes HW-.

No. 101 Squadron: Converted to Lincolns at Binbrook in August 1946 but converted to the Canberra in June 1951. Codes SR-.

No. 103 Squadron: One flight may have converted to Lincolns shortly before the unit re-numbered as No. 57 Sqn in November 1945. Codes PM-.

No. 115 Squadron: Converted to Lincolns in September 1949 at Mildenhall, but disbanded there on 1 March 1950. Known as No. 115/218 Sqn between February 1949 and February 1950. Codes KO-.

No. 116 Squadron: Formed from 'N' Calibration Squadron of the CSE in August 1952, equipped with Ansons and Lincolns. It retained Lincolns until April 1954.

No. 138 Squadron: Re-equipped with Lincolns at Wyton from September 1947, and disbanded there on 1 September 1950. Codes NF-.

In autumn 1947, No. 138 Sqn became the final constituent of the three-sqn 'Wyton Wing'.

No. 148 Squadron: Re-equipped with Lincolns at Upwood in January 1950, disbanding there on 1 July 1955. Codes AU-.

No. 149 Squadron: Converted to Lincolns in October 1949 at Mildenhall, but disbanded there on 1 March 1950. Codes OJ-.

No. 151 Squadron: Re-formed at Watton on 1 January 1962 from the CSE's Signals Development Squadron with Canberras, Varsities, Hastings and Lincolns. The Lincolns were retired in March 1963, two months before the unit re-designated as No. 97 Sqn.

No. 192 Squadron: Re-formed at Watton on 15 July 1951 from an element of the CSE, equipped with Mosquitoes and Lincolns. The Lincolns served in the Elint role until February 1953, when they were replaced by Canberras.

No. 199 Squadron: Re-formed at Watton on 15 July 1951 from an element of the CSE, equipped with Lincolns in the ECM/RCM jamming role. Moved to Hemswell in April 1952, and to Honington (with Valiants) in October 1957. The Lincoln element then remained at Hemswell as No. 1321 Flight.

No. 207 Squadron: Converted to Lincolns in July 1949 at Mildenhall, but disbanded there on 1 March 1950. Codes EM-.

No. 214 Squadron: Re-formed with Lincolns at Upwood in February 1950, disbanding there in December 1954. Codes QN-.

No. 527 Squadron: Re-formed at Watton on 1 August 1952 from the CSE's 'R' Calibration Squadron, equipped with Mosquitoes, Ansons and Lincolns. The Lincolns served in the calibration role until September 1954, when they were replaced by Canberras.

No. 617 Squadron: Converted to Lincolns at Binbrook in September 1946 but then converted to the Canberra in January 1952. Codes KC-.

Famous for its exploits with the Lancaster, No. 617 Sqn flew its successor for six years.

No. 230 OCU: Lincolns supplanted Lancasters with No. 230 OCU at Scampton from February 1949. Moved to Upwood April 1952. Split to form 1 and 3 Group Lincoln Conversion Flights at Waddington and Upwood and disbanded on 15 October 1954. Reformed as No. 230 OCU at Upwood in August 1953. Disbanded into the Lincoln Conversion Flight on 1 February 1955. Codes SN-.

No. 1321 Flight: Formed by the merger of No. 199 Sqn's, Antler and Arrow Squadrons on 1 October 1957.

No. 1426 Flight: Formed June 1952 from a No. 7 Sqn detachment at Khormaksar. Disbanded on 31 December 1956, but final sortie 16 January 1957.

Radar Reconnaissance Flight: Formed 2 October 1951, from a flight of No. 58 Sqn. Replaced by No. 543 Sqn August 1957.

Bomber Command Bombing School: Joined by the Lincoln Conversion Flight from Lindholme in April 1958. 'B' Squadron then operated 14 Lincolns until 6 October 1960, when replaced by modified Hastings.

Lincoln Conversion Flight: Formed in January 1953 from the Waddington Station Flight to take over the role of No. 230 OCU within 1 Group. Disbanded into No. 230 OCU on 1 August 1953. Reformed at Upwood from No. 230 OCU 1 February 1955. Moved to Hemswell 9 January 1956. Disbanded February 1957.

Radar Reconnaissance Flight: Formed on 2 October 1951, from a flight of No. 58 Sqn at Benson. Moved to Upwood, March 1952, then Wyton in October 1955. Replaced by No. 543 Sqn August 1957.

Other units: Aircraft and Armament Experimental Establishment; Armament Division, Technical Training Command; Armament and Instrument Experimental Establishment; Bomb Ballistics Unit; Bombing Trials Unit; Central Bomber Establishment; Central Gunnery School; Central Navigation and Control School; Central Signals Establishment; Empire Air Armament School; Empire Air Navigation School; Empire Radio School; Empire Test Pilots' School; RAE; RAF Flying College; TFU, Defford

Royal Australian Air Force

A No. 1 Sqn Lincoln B.Mk 30 releases its load of 1,000-lb bombs during Operation Firedog.

No. 1 Sqadron: Formed in February 1948 as part of No. 82 Wing at Amberley by re-numbering No. 12 Squadron as it converted to the Lincoln from the B-24. Transferred to No. 90 (Composite) Wing at Tengah in July 1950 for operations in Malaya. Returned to Amberley to re-equip with Canberras July 1958.

No. 2 Squadron: Formed in February 1948 within No. 82 Wing, from No. 21 Squadron. Flew its final Lincoln sortie in December 1953, converting to Canberras.

No. 6 Squadron: No. 6 Squadron followed the same pattern as No. 2, forming at Amberley through the redesignation of No.23 Squadron. The unit functioned as a frontline bomber unit and as the Lincoln OCU, until it finally converted to the Canberra in July 1955.

No. 10 Squadron: Reformed at Townsville in March 1949, with Lincoln B.Mk 30s, in the general and maritime patrol roles. The unit re-equipped with the long-nosed GR.Mk 31 in 1953, and operated these until June 1961.

No. 11 Squadron: Operated Lincoln B.Mk 30s in the maritime role between 1950 and 1951, before re-equipping with Neptunes.

Other units: RAAF Lincolns also served with a Lincoln Conversion Flight (which took over from No. 6 Squadron), and with the School of Air Navigation at East Sale, the Aircraft Research and Development Unit (ARDU) at Laverton, and with No.1 Air Trials Unit, at Woomera and No. 2 Air Trials Unit, at Edinburgh.

Fuerza Aérea Argentina

I Grupo de Bombardeo, V Brigada Aerea: The Argentine Lincolns served at Base Aérea Militar General Pringles at Villa Reynolds from 1947 until 1967.

Based at General Pringles, I Grupo made regular deployments to other bases including Moron, Cordoba, San Luis and Rio Cuarto.

Stukageschwader 2 'Immelmann' – 1935-1941

In 1935 the Luftwaffe formed a new unit dedicated specifically for the dive-bombing role. Named in honour of the famous German World War I ace Max Immelmann, 'Stuka 2' became one of the most feared Luftwaffe units during the German *Blitzkrieg*, before taking its Ju 87s to the Balkans, the Mediterranean and North Africa.

Although the National Socialist regime fostered the myth that it alone had created the new German Luftwaffe after it came to power in January 1933, that is not strictly the case. The foundations for the air arm which played such a decisive role in the early years of World War II had been laid, in part, in the late 1920s under the auspices of the previous Weimar Republic.

The advantage of Adolf Hitler and his military chiefs was to recognise the potential in the basic structure they had inherited, and to initiate a rapid and ambitious series of expansion programmes. These then enabled them to lift the veil of secrecy surrounding Germany's hitherto covert aerial activities and to present the Luftwaffe as a new and threatening factor on the already unstable European political scene.

In order to instil a sense of tradition and continuity into the fledgling force, three of the earliest units to be formed were given the names of World War I fighter aces. The first, a fighter Gruppe, was awarded the honour title 'Richthofen' – after the greatest of them all – on 14 March 1935. Fewer than three weeks later, on 3 April, a bomber Gruppe was named 'Boelcke' and the title 'Immelmann' was conferred upon a third and entirely new type of unit.

The latter was intended specifically for the dive-bombing role. It owed its origins to the above-mentioned fighter Gruppe, which supplied a cadre of pilots to be trained in this then-novel form of aerial warfare. Initial equipment comprised a dozen Heinkel He 50 dive-bombers delivered early in 1935; another 24 followed later.

Early equipment

By October 1935 the unit was established at Schwerin. The He 50 quickly proved itself unsuitable as a dive-bomber, so early in 1936 the Fliegergruppe Schwerin was temporarily re-equipped with He 51s while awaiting acceptance into service of the dedicated Henschel Hs 123.

Due, perhaps, to its being a new and untried branch of the service, the pre-war development of the dive-bomber arm was particularly convoluted, even by Luftwaffe standards of the day.

During the spring of 1936 the generic term 'Fliegergruppe', which had hitherto been applied to all units irrespective of function, began to be replaced by a branch-specific three-figure designation. Under this new system the Fliegergruppe Schwerin became I./StG 162 (with '1' indicating seniority, '6' being the code for dive-bombers, and '2' referring to the command area in which the unit was based: Luftkreiskommando II Berlin).

On 1 April 1936 a Geschwaderstab (StG 162) was established at Schwerin, and a second Gruppe, II./StG 162, activated at Lübeck-Blankensee. Exactly six months later, however, I./StG 162 departed Schwerin for Barth, on the Baltic coast, where it was incorporated into Lehrgeschwader 1, a specialised trials and evaluation unit, as IV.(StG)/LG 1. The following month the Geschwaderstab was disbanded.

Despite this, a third Gruppe, III./StG 162, was

Early in 1936, with the Heinkel He 50 having proved itself to be totally unsuitable for the dive-bombing role, the Fliegergruppe Schwerin reverted temporarily to the Heinkel He 51 – the aircraft on which the Fliegergruppe's pilots had begun their training in 1934. This example wears the quasi-civilian five-letter identification code of this period.

brought into being at Anklam on 1 April 1937. It, too, lasted just six months as such, being redesignated I./StG 163 and transferring to Breslau-Strachwitz on 1 October of that year, taking the 'Immelmann' title with it. By that time, II./StG 162 had also undergone change. Initially remaining at Lübeck, it had become I./StG 167 on 1 May 1937 before moving into newly-annexed Austria as I./StG 168 11 months later.

With the Stab disbanded and all three Gruppen redesignated, the StG 162 slot remained vacant for over a year. It was not until 1 November 1938 that an entirely new I./StG 162 was activated at Jever. It was formed from the Hs 123-equipped Fliegergruppe 30, one of five emergency units that had been set up at the height of the Munich crisis a few weeks earlier.

Finally, on 1 May 1939, the introduction of a new and much simplified block designation system saw the emergence of Stukageschwader 2 – but even this was not without its complications. I./StG 163 at Breslau had been keeping aloft the 'Immelmann' banner in the interim. On 1 November 1938 a second Gruppe had been established at Langensalza and II./StG 163 was formed from one of the Munich emergency units. Fliegergruppe 50. I. and II./StG 163 now became I. and III./StG 2 'Immelmann', respectively, the latter remaining at Langensalza and the former moving from Breslau to Cottbus in the process.

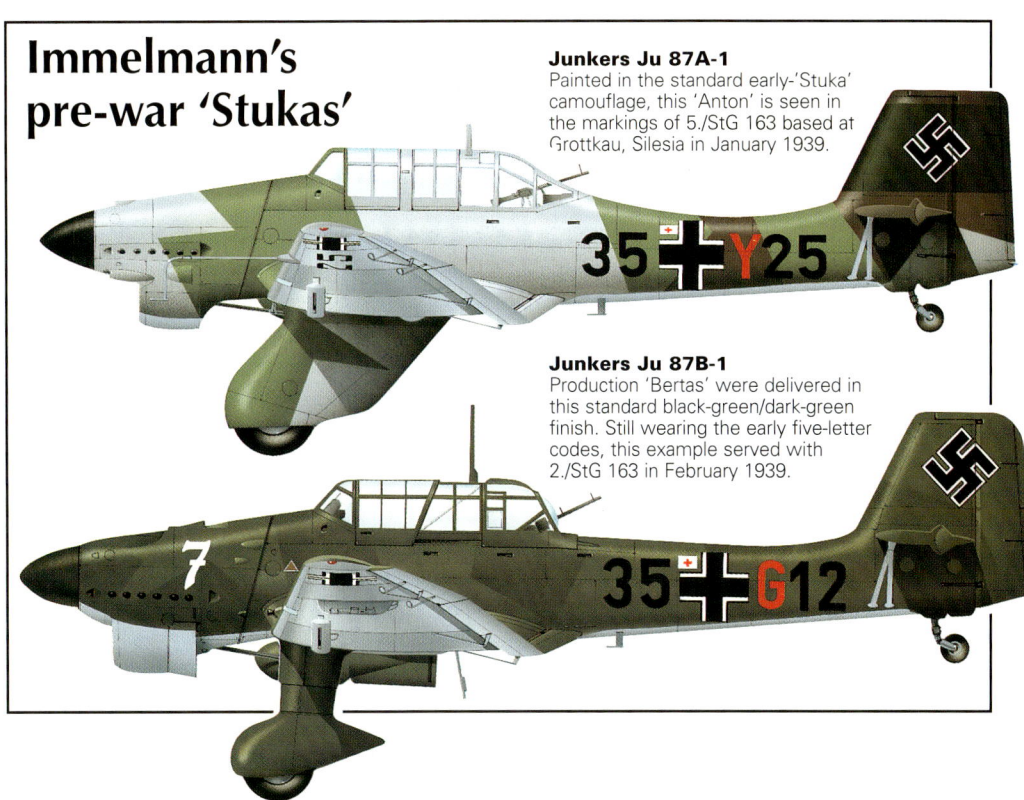

Immelmann's pre-war 'Stukas'

Junkers Ju 87A-1
Painted in the standard early-'Stuka' camouflage, this 'Anton' is seen in the markings of 5./StG 163 based at Grottkau, Silesia in January 1939.

Junkers Ju 87B-1
Production 'Bertas' were delivered in this standard black-green/dark-green finish. Still wearing the early five-letter codes, this example served with 2./StG 163 in February 1939.

The He 51s were replaced by Henschel Hs 123s in the summer of 1936, but these lasted little more than six months before they, in turn, gave way to the Ju 87A. Major external differences of the 'Anton', compared to later variants, included large main gear 'trousers', smoother nose contours with a smaller rectangular radiator intake and a hinged-section cockpit canopy. Here, members of the groundcrew use the specially designed bomb hoist to attach a bomb to the aircraft's launching fork.

By mid-1937 II./StG 162 had been redesignated I./StG 167. This Ju 87A is seen shortly after the transformation, confirmed by the new unit's identification code (71) on the aft fuselage and below the starboard wing. Note the twin aerial mast horns situated above the rear cockpit.

The immediate pre-war years were a period of intense working-up for the Luftwaffe's untried 'Stuka' units. A pair of Ju 87As overflies a column of SdKfz 221 armoured cars advancing along an unpaved dusty country road during military manoeuvres in the summer of 1937.

A strong sense of tradition was fostered in the newly formed Luftwaffe from the very beginning. Well into the war years 'Stuka' units continued to parade their official standard, complete with honour guard, whenever aircraft departed on an operational mission. Here a staffel of bomb-laden III./StG 2 Ju 87Bs receives its traditional farewell in the summer of 1940.

Positioned between the two in the table of organisation, but far removed geographically, I./StG 162 staged from Jever to Stolp-Reitz on the Baltic coast to assume the identity II./StG 2.

The two ex-Fliegergruppen units soon relinquished their Hs 123 biplanes for Junkers Ju 87As. By the late summer of 1939 all three Gruppen of Stukageschwader 2 'Immelmann' were standardised on the Ju 87B.

The outbreak of hostilities found StG 2 fully engaged in the war against Poland. II. and III. Gruppen formed part of Luftflotte 1 on the northern flank, while I./StG 2 operated under Luftflotte 4 in the south.

Paradoxically – despite there being close to 500 Bf 109 fighters actively engaged in the air war over Poland – it fell to a Ju 87 of I./StG 2 to claim the first aerial victory of World War II. Shortly after 04.45 on 1 September 1939 the Gruppe took off from its Nieder-Ellguth base in Upper Silesia to attack the Polish airfield at Cracow. Returning from their objective, the 'Stukas' unwittingly overflew Balice, a small satellite field housing the PZL P.11 fighters of the Polish Air Force's No. 121 Squadron.

The Polish squadron commander scrambled immediately. With his wingman in attendance, and while still clawing for height, the pair attempted to engage one of the passing 'Stukas'. Intent on his prey, Captain Medwecki was unaware of another Ju 87 closing on his tail. Leutnant Frank Neubert, the pilot of aircraft T6+GK, lined up his fixed wing guns on the

Pole's cockpit area and pressed the trigger. The P.11 exploded in mid-air, 'bursting apart like a huge fireball'.

Blitzkrieg

After participating in the opening pre-emptive strikes against the Polish Air Force, the 'Stukas' of I./StG 2 reverted to their intended primary role of 'flying artillery'. The Wehrmacht's carefully rehearsed tactics of *Blitzkrieg* (lightning war) – co-ordinated fire, close air support, and rapid advance – were about to be put to the test for the first time in the crucible of combat.

Meanwhile, in the north, the heavy ground mist shrouding the coastal plains had greatly hampered II. and III./StG 2's early missions. Once the weather cleared, they too began to hit the enemy hard, striking at troop concentrations and smashing open the Polish defences to allow the German armour to pour through.

Within 18 days it was all but over. The remnants of the Polish army in the field had been harried back to Warsaw and beyond. Many Luftwaffe units had been withdrawn before the campaign had run its full course. The 'Stukas', though, remained to the end, blasting the last pockets of defenders holding out in the Polish capital and its surrounding forts into final submission on 29 September.

The month-long air war against Poland cost the dive-bomber arm just 31 aircraft. It also earned the Ju 87 a fearsome reputation.

After a winter of relative inactivity – the

so-called 'Phoney War' – the 'Stukas' were ready to play their part in the invasion of the Low Countries and France. Here in the west, they would repeat the *Blitzkrieg* tactics which had served them so well in Poland: neutralise the enemy's air power, breach the frontier defences, and support their ensuing armoured breakthrough.

The 'Immelmann' Geschwader again found itself divided between two commands. Dispersed on airfields around Cologne, the Stab, I., and III./StG 2 formed part of VIII. Fliegerkorps, a specialised close-support corps subordinated to Luftflotte 2 on the northern flank. Although not far distant, II./StG 2 – based at Siegburg near Bonn – came under the control of Luftflotte 3 to the south.

The key to northern operations was the huge Belgian fort of Eben Emael close to the Dutch border. Completed only five years earlier, this massive defence emplacement, manned by over 1,000 soldiers, was considered impregnable. Yet it was captured at first light on 10 May 1940 by just 78 German troops in a daring, and now historic, glider-borne landing.

While the bulk of I. and III./StG 2 supported this operation by dive-bombing the fort's outer defences and surrounding emplacements, four specially selected crews made a pinpoint attack on an innocuous building some 14 km (8 miles) to the north. This housed the Belgian officer charged with ordering the demolition of three vitally important bridges should they be in danger of capture by the enemy.

The attack succeeded. Although one bridge was blown up in the face of advancing German ground troops, the other two remained intact and Wehrmacht columns were soon flooding across them.

StG 2's casualties on the first day of the war in the west had all been the result of anti-aircraft fire. On 11 May a massed formation of some 60

During the 'Phoney War' of winter 1939-40, the Ju 87Bs of Immelmann's III. Gruppe are seen shrouded in tarpaulins at their Ollesheim base (between Aachen and Cologne). Running alongside the field, the local tram service into town was an added bonus for thirsty off-duty Flieger!

Battle of France

Junkers Ju 87B-1 (Geschwaderstab/StG 2)
Based at Cologne-Ostheim in the spring of 1940, the aircraft wears the Stabskette badge beneath the cockpit and carries the small propellers on the undercarriage leg which produced the 'Stuka's' infamous 'wail'.

Ju 87B-2 (1./StG 2)
All I./StG 2 aircraft were distinguished at this time by the prominent gruppe badge modelled on Major Hitschhold's pet scottie dog 'Molch'. This 'Berta' was based at Cologne-Ostheim in May 1940.

Ju 87B-2 (4./StG 2)
Carrying the individual aircraft letter 'G' under the wing, this Stuka is fully-bombed up with a single 250-kg bomb beneath the fuselage and four 50-kg bombs fitted with 'screamers' beneath the wings. II. Gruppe Staffeln had their own individual badges, such as this 'four-leaf clover' emblem carried by aircraft of 4. Staffel.

Ju 87B-1 (9./StG 2)
III. Gruppe's staffeln also carried individual badges. 9. Staffel was based at Nörvenich in the spring of 1940 and its aircraft were adorned with a 'dancing devil' emblem on a yellow shield. The first two letters of the aircraft's code identify the Gruppe (StG 2), the third letter was the individual aircraft's identity and the final letter signified the unit (9. Staffel).

'Immelmann' 'Stukas' was engaged over Belgium by half a dozen RAF Hurricanes, marking the first time the Ju 87 had encountered determined fighter opposition. And the machine's basic deficiencies – in speed, manoeuvrability, defensive armour and armament – were cruelly exposed. Six of the dive-bombers were chopped down.

The Allies' own growing confusion and disorganisation in the face of the inexorable German pressure meant that the 'Stukas' were able to continue supporting the Panzers as they rampaged across France towards the Channel coast. Moving into occupied territory to keep pace with the daily advances, the crews of StG 2 attacked lines of communication, troops and artillery positions without respite. They broke up penny-packet counter-attacks by Allied armour. The banshee wail of diving 'Stukas' caused terror among the tide of civilian refugees clogging the roads of France.

After raids on the Channel ports of Boulogne, Calais and Dunkirk – and attacks on British evacuation shipping off Dunkirk's beaches – the Ju 87s of StG 2 ended their second *Blitzkrieg* campaign by harrying the French army as it retreated southwards past Paris. Their last sorties were flown in the area around Dijon during the third week of June. Another respite followed the French armistice. It lasted only a matter of days. And it was to prove the lull before a storm of unimaginable proportions.

As the Luftwaffe began gathering along the

Right: Once the rapid advance across France got underway, there were none of the amenities of the home base. A member of III./StG 2 takes the opportunity during a brief lull to get some washing done 'in the field', with a bush serving as a clothes line.

Below: Although Allied air forces were in disarray by the time the Blitzkrieg in the west neared its close, no chances were taken. Ju 87B T6+LS of 8./StG 2 is well camouflaged against discovery from the air, as a bowser refuels it before the next operation.

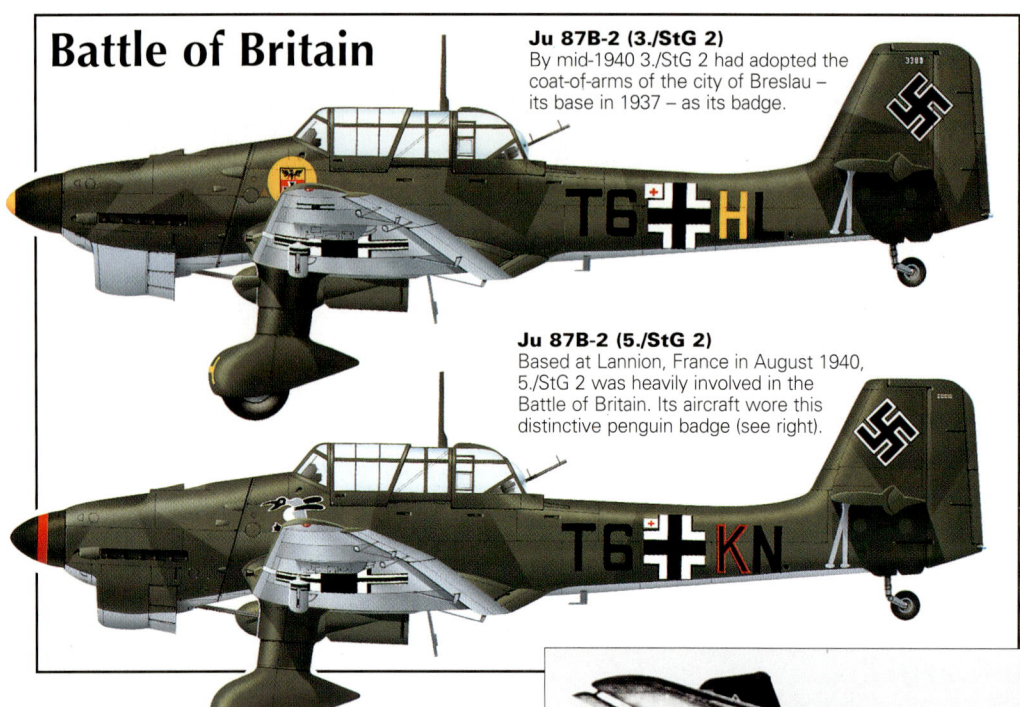

Battle of Britain

Ju 87B-2 (3./StG 2)
By mid-1940 3./StG 2 had adopted the coat-of-arms of the city of Breslau – its base in 1937 – as its badge.

Ju 87B-2 (5./StG 2)
Based at Lannion, France in August 1940, 5./StG 2 was heavily involved in the Battle of Britain. Its aircraft wore this distinctive penguin badge (see right).

Above: Individual gruppe and staffel badges proliferated among the component units of StG 2. They ranged from heraldic symbols to cartoon characters. Why 5. Staffel should choose a flightless penguin – however aggressive its attitude – remains obscure. The triangle beneath the cockpit identifies the type of fuel to be used – Einheitstreibstoff 87 Oktan (Standard 87 Octane Fuel).

Below: The scottie dog badge identifies this machine as belonging to I./StG 2, one of the Gruppen which saw extensive action against merchant convoys in the western Channel during the opening phase of the Battle of Britain.

Channel coast in preparation for the forthcoming assault on southern England, StG 2 – still part of VIII. Fliegerkorps – took up residence on the Brittany peninsula. The principal area of operations was to be the western half of the Channel.

The first phase of the aerial assault was intended to close the Channel to British shipping. The 'Immelmann' 'Stukas' mounted a number of raids along the Dorset coast, III./StG 2 carrying out two such strikes on 11 July for the loss of just one machine. By the month's end the Channel had, to all intents and purposes, been swept clear. Now was to come stage two in the conquest of Great Britain. In yet another replay of the tactics which had proven so successful in Poland and France, the 'Stukas' were ordered to knock out the enemy's fighter airfields in a series of precision attacks. But the myth of the Stuka as an invincible weapon of war was about to be exploded once and for all.

With the long overwater approach from Brittany, the element of surprise was gone. Britain's radar defences picked up the incoming raids. The Spitfires and Hurricanes of RAF Fighter Command were ready and waiting. Within the space of a week, the 'Stuka's' reputation was shattered. Even with a strong fighter

escort of its own, the Ju 87 simply could not survive in a hostile airspace against organised and determined fighter opposition.

Heavy losses

On 13 August (Eagle Day) six of the 27 aircraft of II./StG 2 failed to return from an abortive strike against Middle Wallop. Forty-eight hours later the Gruppe lost three more 'Stukas' in a raid on Portland. The following day it was the turn of I. and III./StG 2, which suffered nine losses between them, plus many more damaged, after attacking Tangmere.

Such a rate of attrition could not be borne indefinitely. It would take just one more bloody reversal to end the 'Stuka's' daylight career in the west, and that reversal was not long in coming.

It was not StG 2, but StG 77, which paid the price with 17 aircraft lost on 18 August; that day's action brought the 'Stuka's' role in the Battle of Britain to an abrupt close.

The 'Stukas' may have been driven from the daylight skies of southern England, but there was another theatre of war where the inherent defects of the Ju 87 would not be of such import, where enemy fighters were thinly spread and mainly obsolescent, and where early-warning radar was non-existent. That theatre was the Mediterranean.

Consequently, in December 1940 when Hitler dispatched a specialist anti-shipping Fliegerkorps from Norway to the aid of his Italian Axis partner Mussolini, two of the Stukagruppen which had been sitting idle in the Pas de Calais since the late summer were added to the force.

One unit of the pair selected for transfer was II./StG 2. On 10 December it began to stage southwards, down the leg of Italy, to Trapani on Sicily. By the beginning of January 1941 a sizeable force of some 80 Ju 87s was established on the island. Their orders upon arrival were explicit: "Locate and sink the *Illustrious*".

This vessel was the Royal Navy's newest aircraft-carrier. It had been in the Mediterranean for only four months and its presence there was perceived as a direct threat to the Italian navy.

Preparing for take-off back to Germany for urgent repair, this StG 2 'Berta' reveals extensive shrapnel damage, either from a close burst of anti-aircraft fire or a near miss from a bomb while on the ground. The landing gear fairings and all other unnecessary weight has been removed, as every fuel tank, bar one, has been punctured.

Above: After its drubbing over southern England, the 'Stuka' was next employed in the Mediterranean. Its first target was the Royal Navy's latest aircraft carrier, HMS Illustrious, pictured here under heavy attack by II./StG 2 and I.StG 1 Ju 87Bs north-west of Malta on 10 January 1941.

Right: The 'Scottie dogs' of I./StG 2 followed II. Gruppe to sunnier climes early in 1941. Lined up at Krainici, awaiting inspection by King Boris of Bulgaria, these aircraft would soon be engaged in the invasions of Yugoslavia and Greece.

The Ju 87, with its ability to place bombs with pinpoint accuracy (enemy opposition permitting!), was the ideal weapon to ensure the ship's destruction.

On 6 January II./StG 2 – accompanied by I./StG 1 – struck at the British fleet, which also included the battleships *Valiant* and *Warspite*. An earlier attack by Italian torpedo-bombers had drawn off *Illustrious*'s defending Fulmar fighters and gave the 'Stukas' a clear run.

It had been estimated that four direct hits would be required to sink the carrier. In the event, hampered only by the fleet's own anti-aircraft defences, the dive-bombers scored six hits on the *Illustrious*, plus three almost equally damaging near misses close alongside. Although the ship was grievously hurt, its engines were untouched and *Illustrious* managed to limp into the dockyard at Malta. There it was subjected to additional attacks, and damage, by II./StG 2 before escaping to Alexandria and thence to the USA, where the carrier spent almost a year undergoing extensive repairs.

During the fortnight the *Illustrious* had been holed up in Malta, the two Stukagruppen had also bombed the island's airfields. They had also attacked another British naval force, damaging the cruisers *Gloucester* and *Southampton*, the latter so badly that it had to be sunk by its destroyer escort.

With the Royal Navy's capital ships retired from the central Mediterranean to recover, the 'Stukas' mounted several more raids on Malta's airfields. Then, in mid-February 1941, II./StG 2 was transferred again – this time to Libya to support the Axis ground forces in North Africa.

At about the same time the bulk of the 'Immelmann' Geschwader, consisting of the Stab, I. and III. Gruppen, was bidding farewell to northern France after close to six months of enforced inactivity. Their destination, however, was not the Mediterranean but Bulgaria, which they reached after leisurely stopovers in both Austria and Rumania.

Combat in the Balkans

Their transfer was also occasioned by Hitler's readiness – or, in this case, need – to help his southern partner. Mussolini was in difficulties after having invaded Greece, and the Führer could not let the tinder-box of the Balkans flare up and threaten the southeastern extremities of his Reich. Plans therefore had been drawn up to invade and occupy both Greece and Yugoslavia. From their bases close to the Bulgarian capital of Sofia, the 'Immelmann' Gruppen were tasked with the support of the German 12. Armee as it drove into southern Yugoslavia.

On 6 April 1941, while attention was largely focused on the advance towards Belgrade in the north, I. and III./StG 2 put their previous experience to good use by smashing open the mountainous frontier defences in the south of the country, thereby enabling German ground forces to thrust simultaneously into both lower Yugoslavia and neighbouring northern Greece.

Once the Greeks' main line of defence had been breached, the 'Stukas' followed the advance southwards. In a repeat of the campaign in France 11 months earlier, they chased the enemy's troops – Greek and the hastily organised British and Imperial expeditionary force alike –

back towards the sea and evacuation. This time, however, the latter's goal was not Dunkirk and the safety of England, but half a dozen improvised evacuation beaches and the more dubious sanctuary of the island of Crete.

Little more than a fortnight after the invasion of Greece had been launched, 'Stukas' of the 'Immelmann' Geschwader were attacking vessels gathered off southern Greece ready to begin the evacuation. On 22 April aircraft of I./StG 2 had sunk a number of Greek merchantmen in the Gulf of Corinth. The following day they struck further afield, raiding the main anchorage at Suda Bay in Crete.

The retreat to Crete, some 100 km (62 miles) from the southernmost tip of the Greek mainland, gained the weary Allied troops little respite. It was quickly decided that the island, too, should be captured – from the air! In the first operation of its kind, the assault was mounted by Luftwaffe paratroop and glider-borne forces on 20 May.

The story of the Cretan campaign is rightly dominated by the exploits of the airborne troops. The 'Stukas' also played an important role as they exacted a heavy toll on the Royal Navy warships which braved the gauntlet of total Luftwaffe air superiority to support yet another evacuation.

One of their first victims was the RN destroyer *Juno*, which broke in half and sank east of Crete after being hit by Ju 87s of III./StG 2 shortly after midday on 21 May. The following morning I. and III./StG 2 machines damaged two cruisers, *Gloucester* (which had survived attack by II. Gruppe off Malta four months earlier) and *Fiji*. Both vessels were later sunk by other units.

Balkan 'Stukas'

Ju 87R-2 (Geschwaderstab StG 2)
Wearing the requisite Operation Marita yellow markings, this is one of four long-range Ju 87Rs, equipped with extra fuel-tanks in the outer wings and underwing drop tanks, operated by Major Oskar Dinort's Stabsschwarm while based at Belica-North, Bulgaria in April 1941.

Ju 87R-2 (Stab III./StG 2)
This machine was the personal mount of Heinrich Brücker, Gruppenkommandeur of III./StG 2 based at Belica-North in April 1941.

Above: A formation of 4./StG 2 'Stukas' sets off to bomb Allied positions in the western desert in spring 1941. A key role at this time was the bombing of British-held ports along the Cyrenaican coast to prevent vital supplies reaching General Wavell's forces.

Right: Having arrived in Libya, 4./StG 2s earlier 'four-leaved clover' badge gave way to a more appropriate motif – the Luftwaffe eagle superimposed on the palm tree and swastika emblem of the Afrika-Korps – applied to the starboard side of the engine cowling.

Twenty-four hours later still, over 20 'Stukas' of I./StG 2 found a trio of British destroyers retiring to the south of Crete after having shelled the island during the hours of darkness. The *Kashmir* and *Kelly* both went down in minutes; the *Kipling* rescued 279 survivors from its two sister ships. The last vessel to succumb was the *Hereward*, another destroyer, struck close inshore by a single bomb from a III. Gruppe aircraft on 29 May, and foundered before it could be beached.

While I. and III./StG 2 were engaged on anti-shipping sorties, II. Gruppe was fighting a very different war in the Western Desert.

Desert 'Immelmanner'

Arriving in Libya in mid-February 1941, II./StG 2 (along with the accompanying I./StG 1) was the sole striking force available to the newly-established Fliegerführer Afrika. This small Luftwaffe command was tasked with supporting the equally new and embryonic Afrika-Korps, a ground force initially comprising just part of the 5. Light Division, which had been despatched by Hitler to help the Italians who had already lost half of their Libyan colony to British troops advancing from Egypt.

Hitler's orders to the commander of the Afrika-Korps, Erwin Rommel, stipulated that he should assist the Italian army in stopping the

Right: Its empty bomb fork swinging in the slipstream, an aircraft of 4./StG 2 races its own shadow back across the desert floor as it returns to base after a sortie. The aircraft has yet to receive the 'Africa-Korps' badge, retaining the original 'four-leaved clover' symbol.

Below: To help cope with the all-pervading dust and desert sand, II./StG 2's aircraft were fitted with engine sand filters and desert survival equipment to Ju 87B-2 trop standard.

British offensive. Rommel, though, had ideas of his own. A thinly disguised 'reconnaissance' of the enemy's positions soon grew into a full-blown counter-offensive which pushed the British back into Egypt.

The two Stukagruppen were heavily involved in this offensive from the onset, not only attacking the enemy's positions on the ground, but also bombing the ports along that part of the Libyan coast held by the British in order to disrupt their seaborne lines of supply. One after another these ports fell to Rommel's troops as they pushed towards the Egyptian border. Soon all were back

in Axis hands except for one: Tobruk. This small Libyan harbour town became the focal point of the desert war for the remainder of the year. Garrisoned mainly by Australians, it continued to hold out as the remainder of the British army withdrew into Egypt.

A thorn in Rommel's side, Tobruk was subjected to near-constant ground and air attack. On 11 April II./StG 2 carpet-bombed Tobruk's outer defences as a prelude to the opening ground assault on the beleaguered defenders. By the end of the month, the last few RAF fighters stationed within its perimeters had been recalled to Egypt. Henceforth, the air battle was a straight fight between dive-bombers and the town's anti-aircraft defences.

On 12 May II./StG 2 sank the gunboat *Ladybird* in Tobruk harbour. Although now

Below: Wearing the distinctive new green and desert tan segmented camouflage scheme, II./StG 2 flies a tight formation high in the Libyan sky sometime in the latter half of 1941. By this time however, the days of the Luftwaffe's dominance were numbered.

StG 2 in North Africa

Ju 87R-2 trop (4./StG 2)
Fitted with the underwing 300-litre (66 Imp gal) external fuel tanks, T6+HM retains the standard European camouflage with which it arrived in Libya in January 1941.

Ju 87B-2 trop (4./StG 2)
This aircraft appears in one of two 'desert' patterns, of brownish-green on tan, adopted by II./StG 2.

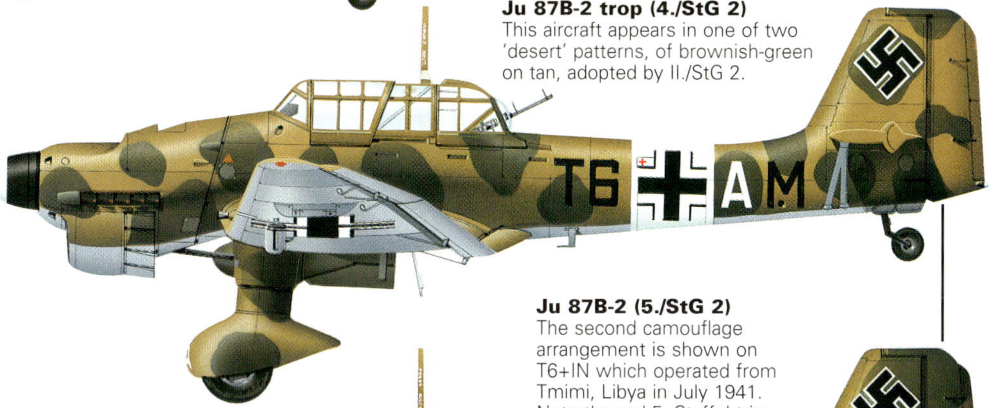

Ju 87B-2 (5./StG 2)
The second camouflage arrangement is shown on T6+IN which operated from Tmimi, Libya in July 1941. Note the red 5. Staffel trim.

Ju 87R-2 trop (6./StG 2)
Negating somewhat the effect of the camouflage, this aircraft was the mount of Hubert Pölz when based at Tmimi, Libya in the summer of 1941.

Ju 87B-2 trop (4./StG 2)
The effect of strong sunlight and sand in fading the camouflage actually produced a more effective scheme, as illustrated by this 4. Staffel 'Berta' based at Gambut, Libya in October 1941.

resting on the bottom, its weapons were clear of the water and the gunboat continued to play a part in the town's immediate defence.

In mid-June the two Stukagruppen helped repulse an attempt by the enemy to relieve Tobruk overland from Egypt. Then it was back to the daily pounding of the ruined town and its outer ring of fortifications. Finally, in mid-November, an all-out offensive – codenamed Crusader – was launched by British and Empire forces. It was backed by growing Allied air power. 'Stuka' casualties were heavy, both in the air and on the ground. On 20 November II./StG 2 lost more than a dozen machines, shot up at their Tmimi base west of Tobruk.

On 7 December 1941 – a day overshadowed by the Japanese attack on Pearl Harbor – the eight-month siege of Tobruk was finally lifted. The war in the desert swung back and forth for 15 months more, but the 'Immelmann' Geschwader's association with North Africa soon came to an end. In January 1942 II./StG 2 was redesignated as III./StG 3.

A new II. Gruppe was immediately formed in the Reich from a miscellany of other units and despatched to the Eastern Front, where I. and III./StG 2 had been in action since June 1941, just days after their anti-shipping successes off Crete.

It was against the Soviets that the 'Immelmanner' were to fight for the remainder of the war. ***John Weal***

Above: The most colourful of all desert 'Stukas' were, without doubt, those flown by 6. Staffel's Leutnant Hubert Pölz (see profile). At least two of his machines featured a spectacular red and white snake marking along the length of their fuselages.

The British Crusader offensive of November 1941 resulted in heavy losses for II./StG 2, both in the air and on the ground. This abandoned 5. Staffel machine is a source of obvious interest to a group of Allied soldiers. Two months later II./StG 2 was redesignated III./StG 3.

Picture acknowledgments

Front cover: Lockheed Martin, Boeing, US Navy, Sergey Skrynnikov. **4:** USAF, Boeing. **5:** USAF (two). **6:** BAE Systems, Matra BAe Dynamics. **7:** Sikorsky (two), Simon Watson (four). **8:** Shlomo Aloni, EMBRAER. **9:** John Battey, Jim Dunn, USAF. **10:** Peter R. March (three). **11:** Simon Watson, Sikorsky. **12:** BAE Systems, Lockheed Martin. **13:** Peter R. March, RAF, USAF. **14:** USAF (three), Shlomo Aloni. **15:** Howard Gethin (four), US Navy. **16:** Boeing, Peter R. March (four). **17:** Simon Watson (two), ADA/NFTC. **18:** Simon Watson (three). **19:** Simon Watson, Piotr Butowski (two). **20:** Frédéric Lert. **21:** Ph. Claude Haller/SIRPA-AIR via Henri-Pierre Grolleau, Frédéric Lert. **22:** Frédéric Lert (two), Henri-Pierre Grolleau, Gert Kromhout. **23:** Frédéric Lert (three), Gert Kromhout. **24:** Gert Kromhout (two), Henri-Pierre Grolleau. **25:** Ph. Claude Haller/SIRPA-AIR via Henri-Pierre Grolleau, Frédéric Lert, Henri-Pierre Grolleau, Gert Kromhout. **26:** Gert Kromhout, Frédéric Lert (two). **27:** Frédéric Lert, Gert Kromhout (two). **28-31:** Marnix Sap. **32:** Boeing (two). **33:** Lockheed Martin (two). **34:** Lockheed Martin. **35:** Boeing. **36:** Northrop Grumman, Lockheed Martin (two). **37:** Boeing, Lockheed Martin. **38:** Boeing (two). **39:** Lockheed Martin (two). **40:** Boeing, Lockheed Martin. **41:** Boeing, Lockheed Martin. **42:** Lockheed Martin, Boeing. **43:** Boeing (two). **44-45:** Lockheed Martin. **46:** Lockheed Martin, Boeing. **47-48:** Boeing. **49:** Boeing (two), Lockheed Martin. **50:** Ted Carlson/Fotodynamics (three), Boeing (two). **55:** Ted Carlson/Fotodynamics (three), Lockheed Martin (two). **56:** Lockheed Martin (two). **57:** Boeing (two). **58:** Lockheed Martin (two). **59:** Boeing. **60:** Lockheed Martin, Boeing. **61:** Lockheed Martin (two). **62:** Lockheed Martin, Boeing. **63:** Lockheed Martin. **64:** Lockheed Martin, Boeing. **65:** Lockheed Martin (three), US Navy. **66:** Boeing (three). **67:** Lockheed Martin, Ted Carlson/Fotodynamics. **68:** US Navy, Juan Carlos Cicalesi, Jorge F. Nuñez Padin, Cees-Jan van der Ende. **69:** David Donald, Nigel Pittaway (two). **70:** P.M. Schenk, Dean Sorochan, Andrew H. Cline. **71:** Simon Watson, Andrew H. Cline. **72:** R. Westerhuis, Claudio Caceres G. via Jorge F. Nuñez Padin, Patrick Laureau, K. Dimitropoulos via René van Woezik, Peter R. Foster. **73:** René van Woezik, Kian-Noush (two), US Navy. **74:** Hajime Ishihara via Yoshitomo Aoki (three). **75:** Hashime Ishihara via Yoshitomo Aoki, Yoshitomo Aoki (three). **76:** Lockheed Martin, Roland van Maarseveen and Cees-Jan van der Ende, Peter R. Foster, Gert Kromhout. **77:** AVDKM via Gert Kromhout, Gert Kromhout, RNZAF. **78:** RNZAF, Terje Nonstad. **79:** US Navy, Robert F. Dorr, Emiel Sloot/STAS (two). **80:** Salvador Mafé Huertas (two), G. Fassari. **81:** Chris Lofting, Simon Watson, Cees-Jan van der Ende and Roland van Maarseveen. **82-97:** NFA Press Agency, René van Woezik. **98-105:** Mark Farmer. **106:** Sergey Skrynnikov, Piotr Butowski (three). **107:** Aerospace (two), Piotr Butowski (three). **108:** Piotr Butowski (three), Aerospace. **109:** Sergey Skrynnikov (two). **110:** Sergey Popsuyevich via Piotr Butowski, Swedish Air Force, Piotr Butowski (two). **111:** Swedish Air Force, Piotr Butowski. **112:** Sergey Skrynnikov, Sergey Popsuyevich via Piotr Butowski. **113:** Piotr Butowski (two). **114:** Piotr Butowski (three), Aerospace (two). **115:** Piotr Butowski (five). **116:** Piotr Butowski, Swedish Coast Guard. **117:** Sergey Skrynnikov, Sergey Popsuyevich via Piotr Butowski, Piotr Butowski (two). **118:** John Leenhouts via Peter B. Mersky. **119:** John D. Klas via Peter B. Mersky, John Leenhouts via Peter B. Mersky. **120:** Peter B. Mersky (two). **121:** Peter B. Mersky, John D. Klas via Peter B. Mersky. **122:** John Leenhouts via Peter B. Mersky (two), Peter B. Mersky. **123:** Peter B. Mersky (two), John Leenhouts via Peter B. Mersky (three). **124:** Peter B. Mersky (two), John D. Klas via Peter B. Mersky. **125:** Peter B. Mersky, US Navy via Peter B. Mersky (two), John D. Klas via Peter B. Mersky. **126:** US Navy, Charles Moore via Peter B. Mersky (two), US Navy via Peter B. Mersky (two). **128:** US Navy via Peter B. Mersky (two). **129:** John Leenhouts via Peter B. Mersky, Peter B. Mersky, US Navy via Peter B. Mersky. **130:** via David Donald, RAF Museum via Jon Lake. **131-133:** via Jon Lake. **134:** Dennis Robinson via Jon Lake, Godfrey Mangion via Jon Lake, RAF Museum via Jon Lake, via David Donald. **135:** via David Donald, RAF Museum via Jon Lake, Godfrey Mangion via Jon Lake. **136:** Peter R. Foster (two), via Jon Lake (two), via David Donald, Paul Jackson, Jon Lake. **138-139:** Charles E. Brown. **140:** Republic, USAF. **141:** Republic (three). **142:** Larry Davis Collection (two), Republic. **143:** Republic (two), USAF. **144:** Republic, USAF. **145:** Republic, USAF (two). **146:** USAF, Charles E. Brown/RAF Museum. **147:** Larry Davis Collection, MoD. **148:** Imperial War Musuem, USAF. **149:** Larry Davis Collection, USAF, Aerospace, Curtiss. **150:** Larry Davis Collection (two), Martin Bowman. **151:** Larry Davis Collection, USAF, Aerospace. **152:** Martin Bowman (three). **153:** USAF (two), Larry Davis Collection. **160:** Aerospace, Republic (five), US Air Force. **162:** Mark Brown/AFA via Warren Thompson (two), Aerospace. **163:** Martin Bowman (two), Larry Davis Collection. **164:** USAF, Larry Davis Collection, Mark Brown/AFA via Warren Thompson. **165:** Jack Woolner via Warren Thompson, Charles E. Brown (two). **166:** USAF (two). **167:** USAF, Martin Bowman (two). **168-169:** USAF. **170-171:** Breguet. **172:** Breguet, US Army. **173:** Breguet (three). **174:** US Army, Dassault. **175:** Breguet (three). **176:** Avro via BAE Systems. **177:** Hawker Siddeley, MoD, Avro, D.H. Newton via R.L. Ward (two). **178:** MoD, Avro (two). **179:** Aerospace, D.H. Newton via R.L. Ward (three). **180:** MoD (two), Aerospace, via R.L. Ward (two). **182:** RAAF (two), via R.L. Ward, MoD. **183:** Aerospace, R.L. Ward. **184:** R.L. Ward, Aerospace (three), RAAF. **185:** RAAF, Aerospace. **186:** Aerospace (two), R.L. Ward. **187:** Napier (two), R.L. Ward, Flight Refuelling. **188:** via Peter R. March (two), Air Service Training Ltd, Bristol Siddeley via Peter R. March. **189:** D.H. Newton via R.L. Ward (three), via R.L. Ward, J.D.R. Rawlings, Aerospace (two). **190:** MacClancy Collection, John Weal. **191-193:** John Weal. **194:** John Weal (two), MacClancy Collection. **195:** John Weal, Aerospace. **196-197:** John Weal.